Investment
Volume 3:
Lifting the Burden

Investment

Volume 3:
Lifting the Burden: Tax Reform, the Cost of Capital, and U.S. Economic Growth

Dale W. Jorgenson and
Kun-Young Yun

The MIT Press
Cambridge, Massachusetts
London, England

This book was printed and bound in the United States of America.

Library of Congress Cataloging-in-Publication Data

Jorgenson, Dale Weldeau, 1933–
Investment / Dale W. Jorgenson.
p. cm.
Includes bibliographical references and index.
Contents: v. 1. Capital theory and investment behavior—v. 2. Tax policy and the cost of capital—v. 3. Lifting the burden: Tax reform, the cost of capital, and U.S. economic growth
ISBN 0-262-10056-8 (v.1: alk. paper) — ISBN 0-262-10057-6 (v. 2: alk. paper) — ISBN 0-262-10091-6 (v.3: alk. paper)
1. Capital investments—United States. 2. Capital costs—United States. 3. Income tax—United States. 4. Corporations—United States—Taxation. I. Title.
HG4028.C4J67 1996 95-45426
332.6—dc20 CIP

Contents

List of Tables

List of Figures

Preface

Dale W. Jorgenson

This book presents the cost of capital approach to tax policy analysis. Jorgenson (1963) introduced the cost of capital almost forty years ago. Chapter 1 shows how this concept became an essential tool for modeling the impact of tax policy on investment behavior. Chapter 2 presents the conceptual framework and applies it to capital income taxation. The widespread success of the cost of capital approach is due to its ability to assimilate virtually unlimited descriptive detail on alternative tax policies, as we demonstrate in our description of the U.S. tax system in Chapter 3.

Auerbach and Jorgenson (1980) introduced the closely related concept of the marginal effective tax rate, the focus of Chapter 4. This emerged from debates over tax reform in the United States, beginning with the Economic Recovery Tax Act of 1981 (ERTA) and culminating in the Tax Reform Act of 1986. The marginal effective tax rate brings out the distorting effects of specific tax provisions in a highly succinct and comprehensible way. Horizontal equity, the equal treatment of taxpayers in similar circumstances under the law, is achieved by equalizing marginal effective tax rates for all types of capital.

Christensen and Jorgenson (1973a) incorporated a complete description of the U.S. tax system into a system of national accounts for the United States. The most important innovation in this system is that production, income and expenditure, and wealth accounts are presented in both current and constant prices. The cost of capital emerges within the system as the price of capital input and a source of income for the owners of capital. This accounting system is used to generate the data required for econometric modeling of the impact of tax policy in Chapters 5 and 6.

Jorgenson and Yun (1990) employed an earlier version of our econometric model in analyzing the impact of the Tax Reform Act of 1986. In Chapter 7 we present the methodology for evaluating the welfare impacts of tax reform. We then show that eliminating distortions resulting from different capital income tax treatment for different sectors and different types of assets would produce large gains in welfare. Eliminating the progressive tax on labor income as well would enhance these welfare gains considerably.

The major thrust of recent tax reform proposals is to shift the base for taxation from income to consumption. Substitution of consumption for income would have the effect of eliminating capital income taxes altogether, thereby equalizing the tax treatment of different sectors and assets. In Chapter 8 we show that the welfare impact of this fundamental tax reform would be comparable in magnitude to eliminating the distortions of capital income taxation considered in Chapter 7. Eliminating the progressive tax on labor income would result in substantial additional gains in welfare.

Jorgenson and Yun (1991b) introduced measures of the efficiency cost of different types of taxes. In Chapter 9 we extend these measures to include the sources of tax revenues, the allocation of these revenues among different categories of spending, and the type of benefits resulting from the spending programs. We use this framework to analyze the welfare impact of cuts in defense spending made possible by the end of the Cold War. This dwarfs the effects of the tax reforms considered in Chapters 7 and 8.

It is a pleasure to acknowledge the contributions of many colleagues and former students at Berkeley, Chicago, and Harvard to the cost of capital approach. The modeling of tax provisions for capital cost recovery presented in this book was a product of collaboration with Robert Hall, then an undergraduate student at Berkeley. The system of national accounts used in generating the cost of capital was developed in collaboration with Laurits Christensen, then a graduate student at Berkeley. Erwin Diewert, Sidney Handel, Charles Hulten, Sung-Woo Kim, Robert Oster, Calvin Siebert, James Stephenson, Tait Ratcliffe, and Frank Wykoff are among the many former Berkeley students who have made important contributions to tax policy and the cost of capital.

The cost of capital was originated in a paper written while Jorgenson was Ford Foundation Research Professor of Economics at the University of Chicago. Stimulating conversations with the late Zvi Griliches, Arnold Harberger, and Robert Lucas, then a graduate student at Chicago, were especially valuable at this stage. Griliches kindly arranged for the paper to be presented at a meeting of the

American Economic Association. The paper was published in the *American Economic Review* for May 1963.

As a consequence of the research and teaching in public finance at Harvard by Martin Feldstein and Lawrence Summers, Harvard has been a center of active research on the cost of capital for the past three decades. The concept of the marginal effective tax rate was developed in collaboration with Alan Auerbach, then Assistant Professor of Economics at Harvard. Our collaboration began when Kun-Young Yun was a graduate student at Harvard. Christophe Chamley, Robert Fry, Roger Gordon, Fumio Hayashi, Taewon Kwack, John Laitner, Peter Merrill, Kevin Stiroh, Eric Stubbs, Martin Sullivan, and Brian Wright are among the many former Harvard students who have made important contributions to tax policy and the cost of capital.

Renate D'Arcangelo of the Editorial Office of the Division of Engineering and Applied Sciences at Harvard edited the manuscript, proofread the final version, and prepared the manuscript for typesetting. Gary Bisbee of Chiron Incorporated typeset the manuscript and provided camera-ready copy for publication. William Richardson and his associates provided the index. The staff of The MIT Press, especially Elizabeth Murry, Jane Macdonald, Mel Goldsipe, Terry Vaughn, and Michael Sims, was helpful at every stage of the project. Financial support for the research was provided by the Program on Technology and Economic Policy of the Kennedy School of Government at Harvard.

1 Introduction

The purpose of this book is to provide a comprehensive treatment of the cost of capital approach for analyzing the economic impact of tax policy. This approach has provided an important intellectual impetus for reforms of capital income taxation in the United States and around the world. When President Ronald Reagan took office in January 1981, there was widespread concern about the slowdown of U.S. economic growth. Tax reform received overwhelming support from Congress with the enactment of the Economic Recovery Tax Act of 1981. The 1981 Tax Act combined substantial reductions in tax rates with sizable enhancements in incentives for saving and investment.

Beginning with the introduction of accelerated depreciation in 1954 and the investment tax credit in 1962, U.S. tax policy had incorporated progressively more elaborate tax preferences for specific forms of capital income. The 1981 Tax Act brought this development to its highest point with adoption of the Accelerated Cost Recovery System and a ten percent investment tax credit. These tax provisions severed the connection between capital cost recovery and the economic concept of income.

The 1981 Tax Act continued the shift from income to consumption as a tax base that had characterized the postwar period. In order to stimulate saving, individuals were allowed to establish tax-favored accounts. In the United States these took the form of pension funds for corporate and noncorporate businesses and Individual Retirement Accounts. Savings were removed from the tax base by excluding contributions to these accounts from income for tax purposes and exempting earnings from taxation until withdrawn for consumption. The tax base could be shifted from income toward consumption by the simple expedient of allowing larger contributions to the tax-favored accounts.

More rapid write-offs of investment outlays through accelerated cost recovery also provided enhanced investment incentives. Subsidies for investment like the investment tax credit reduced tax liabilities. The ultimate investment incentive is to treat investment expenditures symmetrically with outlays on current account, thereby removing investment from the income tax base and shifting the base to consumption. Three landmark reports in Sweden, the United Kingdom, and the United States proposed taking these developments to their logical conclusion by replacing income by consumption as a tax base.[1]

The tax reforms of the early 1980s substantially reduced the burden of taxation on capital income. However, these policies also heightened discrepancies among tax burdens on different types of capital. This gave rise to congressional concerns about tax distortions in the allocation of capital. In the State of the Union Address in January 1984, President Reagan announced that he had requested a plan for further reform from the Treasury, initiating a lengthy debate that eventuated in the Tax Reform Act of 1986.[2]

The 1986 Tax Act abruptly reversed the direction of U.S. tax policy. The income tax base was broadened by wholesale elimination of tax preferences for both individuals and corporations. The investment tax credit was repealed for property placed in service after December 31, 1985. Capital consumption allowances were brought into line with economic depreciation. Revenues generated by base broadening were used to finance sharp reductions in tax rates at corporate and individual levels.[3]

The 1986 Tax Act reflected a new conceptual framework for the analysis of capital income taxation. This framework had its origins in two concepts introduced in the 1960s—the effective tax rate, pioneered by Arnold C. Harberger (1962, 1966, 1969), and the cost of capital, originated by Dale W. Jorgenson (1963, 1965). The concept of the marginal effective tax rate, introduced by Alan J. Auerbach and Jorgenson (1980), combined the cost of capital and the effective tax rate.

Marginal effective tax rates must be carefully distinguished from the average effective tax rates introduced by Harberger (1962, 1966). Marginal and average tax rates differ substantially, since changes in tax laws typically apply only to new assets. In the model of capital as a factor of production introduced by Jorgenson (1963), new and existing assets are perfect substitutes in production, so that marginal rather than average tax rates are relevant for measuring distortions in the allocation of capital.

Jorgenson's testimony before the Committee on Finance of the U.S. Senate on October 22, 1979, and the Committee on Ways and Means of the U.S. House of Representatives on November 14, 1979, provided the initial impetus for the use of marginal effective tax rates in reforming the taxation of income from capital. This testimony employed marginal effective tax rates to quantify differences in the tax treatment of different types of capital. Although the cost of capital approach had no effect on the 1981 Tax Act, this approach was adopted quickly by tax policy analysts, both inside and outside the government.

An important milestone in diffusion of the cost of capital approach was the Conference on Depreciation, Inflation, and the Taxation of Income from Capital, held at the Urban Institute in Washington, D.C., on December 1, 1980. The participants in this conference included tax analysts from universities, research institutions, the U.S. Department of the Treasury, and the staff of the U.S. Congress. Jorgenson and Martin A. Sullivan (1981) presented marginal effective tax rates for all types of assets and all industries.

The publication of the Urban Institute Conference Proceedings in 1981 was followed almost immediately by the first official estimates of marginal effective tax rates by the President's Council of Economic Advisers in early 1982. Subsequently, marginal effective tax rates helped to frame the alternative proposals that led to the Tax Reform Act of 1986. An important objective of this legislation was to "level the playing field" by equalizing marginal effective tax rates on different types of capital income.[4]

The literature on the cost of capital approach developed at an explosive pace during the 1980s, leading to the presentation of the Treasury proposal, requested by President Reagan, in November 1984.[5] This proposal was accompanied by estimates of marginal effective tax rates for different types of assets. An important objective of the proposal was to equalize these rates. A second objective was to insulate the definition of capital income from the impact of inflation. The cost of capital provided the analytical framework for achieving both of these objectives.

The issues in implementing the cost of capital and marginal effective tax rates have been debated for more than three decades, following the introduction of Jorgenson's (1963) cost of capital. Statutory tax rates and the definition of taxable income provide only part of the information required. In addition, estimates of economic depreciation are required in order to assess the adequacy of tax provisions for capital cost recovery. Since the income tax base is not insulated from inflation, rates of inflation must also be taken into account.

The first empirical issue in measuring the cost of capital is the description of capital cost recovery. Jorgenson's cost of capital formula allowed for differences between tax and economic depreciation. Modeling provisions for capital cost recovery as the present value of deductions from income was the crucial innovation in papers by Hall and Jorgenson (1967, 1971). This formulation of capital cost recovery has been adopted in nearly all subsequent studies.

Laurits R. Christensen and Jorgenson (1973a) extended the cost of capital for corporate capital income originated by Hall and Jorgenson (1967) to noncorporate and household capital incomes. This made it possible to include differences in returns due to differences in taxation among corporate, noncorporate, and household sectors into measures of the cost of capital. In chapter 2 we present a complete model of the cost of capital for these three sectors of the U.S. economy.

The initial modeling of tax provisions for capital cost recovery by Jorgenson and his associates was based on the plausible assumption that taxpayers choose among alternative provisions to minimize their tax liabilities.[6] Jorgenson and Sullivan (1981) presented a detailed study of actual practices for capital cost recovery. This description has been employed in many subsequent studies, including our 1991 book, *Tax Reform and the Cost of Capital*, and our description of the U.S. tax system in chapter 3.

The second empirical issue in measuring the cost of capital is inflation in asset prices. A comparison of alternative treatments of inflation in measures of the cost of capital was included in Jorgenson and Calvin D. Siebert (1968a, 1968b). The assumption of perfect foresight or rational expectations of inflation emerged as the most appropriate formulation and has been used in most subsequent studies.

The third empirical issue in implementing the cost of capital is measuring economic depreciation.[7] Charles R. Hulten and Frank C. Wykoff (1981a) developed an econometric methodology for measuring economic depreciation. Hall (1971) had modeled prices of assets as functions of age and asset characteristics. The important innovation by Hulten and Wykoff was to allow for "censoring" asset prices by retirements. They demonstrated that a geometric decline in efficiency of assets with age provides a satisfactory approximation to the actual decline.[8]

The marginal effective tax rates introduced by Auerbach and

Jorgenson (1980) included corporate taxes.[9] The tax base for corporate income depends on provisions for capital cost recovery, while the tax base for personal income depends on the treatment of corporate distributions—dividends, interest, and capital gains. To analyze the impact of tax incentives for investment the corporate income tax is the focus. Incentives to save are reflected in the personal income tax. Of course, both levels of taxation are required in assessing the impact of the corporate income tax.

The incorporation of personal taxes into the corporate cost of capital raised a host of new issues.[10] In the "new" view proposed by King (1977) the corporation retains earnings sufficient to finance the equity portion of investment and dividends are determined by the residual cash flow. The marginal source of equity funds is retained earnings, so that the tax rate on dividends does not affect the price of capital services or the effective tax rate on corporate income.

Under the new view of corporate finance and taxation, the most attractive investment available to the corporation is to liquidate its assets and repurchase its outstanding shares. Each dollar of assets liquidated enhances the value of the remaining shares. Repurchase of the firm's outstanding shares is ruled out by assumption, so that equity is "trapped" in the firm. Accordingly, this view of corporate taxation has been characterized as the "trapped equity" approach.

Our model of the corporate cost of capital in chapter 2 is based on the "traditional" view of corporate finance and taxation.[11] In the traditional view the marginal source of funds for the equity portion of the firm's investments is new share issues, since dividends are fixed by assumption. An additional dollar of new share issues adds precisely one dollar to the value of the firm's assets.

It is important to underline the critical role of the assumption that dividends are a fixed proportion of corporate income. If the firm were to reduce dividends by one dollar to finance an additional dollar of investment, stockholders would avoid personal taxes on the dividends. The addition to investment would produce a capital gain that is taxed at a lower rate and shareholders would experience an increase in wealth. It is always in the interest of shareholders for the firm to finance investment from retained earnings rather than new issues of equity.

As Sinn (1991) has emphasized, both the traditional and the new views of corporate taxation depend crucially on assumptions about financial policy of the firm. The traditional view depends on the assumption that dividends are a fixed proportion of corporate income, so that the marginal source of funds for financing investment is new issues. The new view depends on the assumption that new issues of equity (or repurchases) are fixed, so that the marginal source of funds is retained earnings.

In fact, firms use both sources of equity finance, sometimes simultaneously. King and Fullerton (1984) employed the actual distribution of new equity finance from new issues and retained earnings. Since retained earnings greatly predominate over new issues, this approach turns out to be empirically equivalent to adopting the new view. Sinn (1991) suggests choosing new issues and retained earnings to minimize the cost of equity finance. This is also equivalent empirically to the new view for most countries.

The second set of issues raised by the introduction of personal taxes into the corporate cost of capital relates to the treatment of debt and equity in the corporate tax structure. In chapter 3 we assume that debt-equity ratios are the same for all assets within the corporate sector. This assumption was also employed by King and Fullerton (1984).

The inclusion of personal taxes on corporate distributions to equity holders also raises more specific issues on the impact of inflation in asset prices. A comprehensive treatment of these issues is provided by Feldstein (1983). Since nominal interest expenses are deductible at the corporate level, while nominal interest payments are taxable at the individual level, an important issue is the impact of inflation on nominal interest rates. Feldstein and Summers (1979) assumed that Fisher's Law holds, namely, that a change in inflation is reflected point for point in changes in nominal interest rates, and we retain this assumption.[12]

In chapter 4 we summarize the tax burden on capital income by means of marginal effective tax rates for all assets and all sectors of the U.S. economy. We show that the Tax Reform Act of 1986 significantly reduced differences in tax burdens among corporate, noncorporate, and household sectors. Differences between short-lived and long-lived depreciable assets were almost eliminated by this legislation. However, substantial differences between household and corporate sectors still remain, resulting in large potential losses from the misallocation of capital.

Jorgenson (1993) presented international comparisons of tax reforms for capital income over the period 1980–1990 in the G7 countries—Canada, France, Germany, Italy, Japan, the United Kingdom, and the United States—together with Australia and Sweden. These comparisons were based on marginal effective tax rates for different types of capital income in all nine countries for the years 1980, 1985, and 1990. Nine teams, one from each country, constructed estimates of these tax rates using a common methodology incorporating that of King and Fullerton (1984).

Jorgenson's (1993) international comparison of marginal effective tax rates revealed widespread changes in the taxation of income from capital, similar to those in the U.S. Tax Reform Act of 1986. Base broadening through elimination of investment and saving incentives and reductions in tax rates were nearly universal. This resulted in considerable "leveling of the playing field" among different assets. However, wide gaps among effective tax rates remained in all nine countries, so that important opportunities for tax reform still remain.

The cost of capital has become an indispensable analytical tool for studies of the economic impact of tax policies. These studies have taken two forms. First, the cost of capital has been incorporated into investment functions in macroeconometric models. These models are useful primarily in modeling the short-run dynamics of responses to changes in tax policy. More recently, the cost of capital has been incorporated into applied general equilibrium models that focus on the impact of tax policy on the allocation of capital. These models are essential for capturing the long-run effects of tax reforms.

Hall and Jorgenson (1967) presented the first application of the cost of capital approach to the analysis of tax policy. They modeled the introduction of accelerated depreciation in 1954 and new guidelines for asset lifetimes in 1962. They also considered the impact of the investment tax credit, also introduced in 1962. Finally, they analyzed the impact of a hypothetical tax reform, treating investment expenditures in the same way as expenditures on current account, thereby shifting the tax base from income to consumption.

Hall and Jorgenson (1971) analyzed the adoption of the investment tax credit in 1962. They also analyzed the 1964 repeal of the Long Amendment, which had reduced the base for depreciation by the amount of the credit. Finally, they considered reduction in the corporate income tax rate in 1964 and suspension of the investment tax credit in 1966.

The economic impacts of the tax policy changes analyzed by Hall and Jorgenson (1967, 1971) were limited to simulations of investment expenditures and capital stocks. They modeled the short-run dynamics of investment by holding prices and interest rates as well as the level of economic activity constant. By incorporating investment functions into the DRI quarterly model, Jorgenson (1971b) was able to project impacts on employment and economic activity, prices and interest rates, and government deficits—all determined endogenously by the DRI model.

At the beginning of the debate over the Economic Recovery Tax Act of 1981 the investment equations for all the major forecasting models for the U.S. economy had incorporated the cost of capital.[13] Simulations of alternative tax policies had become the staple fare of debates over the economic impacts of specific tax proposals. Illustrations of this type of simulation study are provided by Jorgenson (1971b) and Gordon and Jorgenson (1976), using modifications of the DRI model.

An important issue in this type of application, emphasized by Robert E. Lucas (1976) in his critique of econometric methods for policy evaluation, is modeling expectations about future prices of investment goods. This is required in measuring the cost of capital and simulating the impact of changes in tax policy. Since Jorgenson and Siebert (1968a, 1968b), future prices have been modeled by means of perfect foresight or rational expectations. However, macroeconometric models, such as the DRI model, did not incorporate rational expectations into simulations of alternative policies.

The model of capital as a factor of production contains two dynamic relationships. The first is an accumulation equation, expressing capital stock as a weighted sum of past investments. The second is a capital asset pricing equation, expressing the price of investment goods as the present value of future rentals of capital services. Both relationships should be incorporated into simulations of the effects of changes in tax policy. Macroeconometric models have incorporated the backward-looking equation for capital stock but have omitted the forward-looking equation for the price of investment goods.

The omission of the capital asset pricing equation from macroeconometric models was due to the lack of simulation techniques appropriate for perfect foresight or rational expectations.[14] To evaluate the economic impact of the 1981 tax reforms, we constructed a dynamic general equilibrium model that incorporated both the backward-looking equation for capital stock and the forward-looking equation for asset pricing. The model presented in our 1986 paper, "The Efficiency of Capital Allocation," overcame the "Lucas critique."

In our 1986 paper on tax reform, "Tax Policy and Capital Allocation," we found that the 1981 Tax Act increased U.S. economic welfare by 3.5 to 4 percent of U.S. private national wealth in 1980. We also considered alternative reforms, including a shift from income to consumption as a base for taxation. We found that the replacement of corporate and personal income taxes by a consumption tax would have produced dramatic gains in welfare, amounting to 26 to 27 percent of national wealth!

We evaluated the economic impact of the 1986 tax reform in our 1990 paper, "Tax Reform and U.S. Economic Growth." We summarized the 1986 reform in terms of changes in tax rates, the treatment of deductions from income, the availability of tax credits, and provisions for indexing. We also summarized reform proposals that figured prominently in the debate leading to the 1986 Tax Act. For this purpose we utilized marginal effective tax rates, defined in terms of differences in tax burdens imposed on different types of capital.

We found that much of the potential gain in welfare from the 1986 tax reform was dissipated through failure to index the income tax base for inflation. At rates of inflation near zero the loss is not substantial. However, at moderate rates of inflation, like those prevailing in the United States in the mid-1980s, the loss is significant. Second, the greatest welfare gains would have resulted from equalizing tax burdens on household and business assets. The potential welfare gains from an income-based tax system would have exceeded those from a consumption-based system.

Shortly after the passage of the Tax Reform Act of 1986, the Department of the Treasury (1987) published a study by Fullerton, Gillette, and Mackie (1987) of the effect of the new legislation on marginal effective tax rates. The results were incorporated into an applied general equilibrium model by Fullerton, Henderson, and Mackie (1987) and used to estimate the economic impact. Fullerton (1987) presented a closely related study of marginal effective tax rates, while Fullerton and Henderson (1989a, 1989b) conducted a parallel simulation study.[15]

The model presented in chapter 5 updates our earlier dynamic general equilibrium models. Equilibrium is characterized by an intertemporal price system that clears markets for labor and capital services and consumption and investment goods. This equilibrium links the past and the future through markets for investment goods and capital services. Assets are accumulated through investments, while asset prices equal the present values of future services. Consumption must satisfy conditions for intertemporal optimality of the household sector under perfect foresight. Similarly, investment must satisfy requirements for asset accumulation.

Christensen and Jorgenson (1973a) embedded the cost of capital into a complete system of U.S. national accounts. They distinguished two approaches to the analysis of economic growth. They used data on inputs and outputs from the production account to allocate the sources of economic growth between investment and productivity. They divided the uses of economic growth between consumption and saving by means of data from the income and expenditure account. The critical innovation in this accounting system was the construction of internally consistent accounts for income, product, and wealth.

In the Christensen-Jorgenson accounting system, saving was linked to the asset side of the wealth account through capital accumulation equations. These equations provided a perpetual inventory of assets of different vintages. Prices for these different vintages were linked to rental prices of capital inputs through a parallel set of capital asset pricing equations. The complete system of vintage accounts contained stocks of assets of each vintage and their prices. Stocks were cumulated to obtain asset quantities, while prices were used to derive the cost of capital for each asset.

Christensen, Jorgenson, and Lawrence J. Lau (1973) constructed an econometric model of producer behavior based on the translog production possibility frontier. In chapter 6 we estimate this model from recent data on inputs and outputs in the production account of our complete accounting system for the U.S. economy. We have incorporated this production model into the model of U.S. economic growth presented in chapter 5.

An important feature of the model of chapter 5 is the representation of costs of adjustment. The production possibility frontier captures the demand for capital services and costs of adjusting this demand through the supply of investment goods. The production of investment goods entails foregoing the opportunity to produce consumption goods. The costs of adjusting capital services through investment are external rather than internal and are reflected in the market price of investment goods.

By contrast Jorgenson (1973) presented a model of investment behavior with internal adjustment costs and irreversibility.[16] Internal adjustment costs are reflected in the loss of capital services that must be devoted to the installation of capital rather than the production of marketable output. The cost of capital in these models is a shadow price that reflects both the market price of investment and the shadow value of installation. The model of external adjustment costs in chapter 5 has the decisive advantage that the cost of capital depends only on the market price of investment.

Christensen, Jorgenson, and Lau (1975) constructed an econometric model of consumer behavior based on the translog indirect utility function. In chapter 6 we estimate this model from recent data in the income and expenditure account of our complete accounting system. We have incorporated this model of consumer behavior into the model presented in chapter 5.

In chapter 7 we employ our econometric model of U.S. economic growth to simulate the economic impact of alternative policies for reforming the taxation of capital income. Estimates of tax wedges, like those presented in chapter 4, are useful in identifying potential sources of inefficiency. However, the welfare costs of taxation depend not only on these differences in tax wedges, but also on the elasticities of substitution along all the relevant margins captured in our model.

We first present a methodology for evaluating the welfare effects of tax reform. For this purpose we design a computational algorithm for determining the time path of the U.S. economy following the reform. This algorithm is composed of two parts. We first solve for the unique steady state of the economy corresponding to the Tax Policy of 1996, our reference tax policy. We then determine the unique transition path for the U.S. economy, consistent with the initial conditions and the steady state. This is the base case for our analysis of changes in tax policy.

The second part of our algorithm is to solve our model for the unique transition path of the U.S. economy following tax reform. We first consider the elimination of tax wedges among different classes of assets and different sectors—ten alternative programs for reforming the taxation of capital income in the United States. We also consider the cost of progressivity in the taxation of labor income by comparing the existing labor income tax with a flat labor income tax. These are the alternative cases for our tax policy analysis.

We compare the level of social welfare associated with each policy with the welfare level in the base case. We translate these welfare comparisons into monetary terms by introducing an intertemporal expenditure function, giving the wealth required to achieve a given level of welfare for the representative consumer in our model of the U.S.

economy. Using this expenditure function, we translate the differences in welfare into differences in wealth.

The most dramatic welfare gain from reform of U.S. capital income taxation is through the elimination of tax wedges among all assets and all sectors. This would produce a gain of $2.02 trillion or nearly one-quarter of the U.S. gross domestic product of $8.11 trillion in 1997, the reference year for our welfare comparisons. Alternatively, this gain is the equivalent of an 8.0% increment to the value of U.S. national wealth of $25.38 trillion at the beginning of 1997. These welfare gains are large in relative terms, compared with our earlier estimates of the gains from the Tax Reform Act of 1986.[17]

Finally, we measure the distortions associated with the progressive tax on labor income. This results in marginal tax rates far in excess of average tax rates. Our point of departure is the elimination of all intersectoral and interasset distortions in capital income taxation. We replace the progressive labor income tax by a proportional labor income tax with identical marginal and average tax rates. This would produce a welfare gain of as much as $4.90 trillion, the largest gain from any tax reform we have considered. This amounts to 60 percent of 1997 U.S. GDP or more than 19 percent of 1997 U.S. national wealth!

Tax wedges do not complete the analysis of distortionary effects of capital income taxes. These effects also depend on substitutability among assets. As an example, consider the allocation of capital between short-lived and long-lived depreciable assets in the corporate sector. Even if the interasset difference in tax treatment is large, the distortion of capital allocation would be small if services of the two types of assets are not substitutable. Similarly, the distortion in resource allocation over time would be small if intertemporal substitutability in consumption is small.

In chapter 7 we introduce the concept of the excess burden of taxation in order to assess efficiency losses due to taxation. We measure this burden by comparing the growth of the U.S. economy under the actual tax system with growth under a purely hypothetical "lump sum" system. Under the alternative system taxes are levied as a lump sum deduction from wealth, rather than as taxes on transactions in outputs and factor services. Taxes on these transactions insert tax wedges between demand and supply prices and result in losses in efficiency.

We summarize our comparisons of alternative tax policies in terms of average and marginal excess burdens per dollar of tax revenue raised. The average excess burden is the cost per dollar if the tax is wholly replaced by a lump sum tax. The marginal excess burden is the cost of replacing only the first dollar of revenue raised by the tax. We find that the marginal excess burden of all taxes under the 1996 Tax Law was 26.6 cents per dollar of tax revenue raised.

Marginal excess burdens are relevant for designing the appropriate direction for tax reform. Under the 1996 Tax Law the marginal excess burden of sales taxes was only 17.5 cents per dollar of revenue raised, while the cost of property taxes was even lower at 13.9 cents per dollar. By contrast the cost of income taxes was 33.4 cents per dollar. The marginal excess burden of corporate income taxes was 27.9 cents per dollar. The burden of labor income taxes was 40.4 cents, while the burden of individual taxes on capital income was 25.7 cents for every dollar of revenue raised. These large discrepancies are an indication of important opportunities for gains in economic efficiency through tax reform.

In the United States proposals to replace income by consumption as a tax base revived during the 1990s.[18] These include the Hall-Rabushka (1983, 1995) Flat Tax proposal, a European-style consumption-based value added tax, and a comprehensive retail sales tax on consumption. In chapter 8 we compare the economic impact of these proposals, taking the 1996 Tax Law as our base case. In particular, we consider the impact of the Hall-Rabushka proposal and the closely related Armey-Shelby proposal. We also consider the economic impact of replacing the existing tax system by a National Retail Sales Tax, levied on personal consumption expenditures at the retail level. We impose the requirement that both proposals are revenue neutral, that is, that they raise the same amount of revenue as the 1996 Tax Law.

The Hall-Rabushka (1995) Flat Tax proposal divides tax collections between firms and households. Firms expense all purchases from other firms, including purchases of investment goods. Firms also expense all forms of labor compensation and this compensation is taxed at the individual level. This permits the introduction of family allowances for low-income taxpayers in order to retain a progressive rate structure. A flat rate is applied to the consumption tax base, excluding the family allowances. Hall and Rabushka (1995) have chosen a federal tax rate of 19 percent.

We show that the Hall-Rabushka (1995) Flat Tax proposal falls considerably short of revenue neutrality. The reason is that the Flat Tax imposes a lump sum tax on "old" capital, accumulated prior to the tax reform, along with a tax on labor income. However, the Flat Tax does not impose any tax burden on "new" capital, accumulated through investment after the reform. The tax base from old capital shrinks dramatically as new capital replaces old, leaving a large revenue shortfall. The Armey-Shelby Flat Tax proposal has a lower Flat Tax rate after the first two years and more generous family allowances, so that the revenue shortfall is even greater.

We have designed versions of the Flat Tax proposal that retain the family allowances of the Hall-Rabushka and Armey-Shelby proposals, but achieve revenue neutrality through a higher tax rate. We assume that state and local income taxes, which now employ a tax base similar to the federal income tax base, will shift to the Flat Tax base after reform. We raise the Flat Tax rate to accommodate the revenue requirements of federal, state, and local governments. The Flat Tax rate ranges from 27.5 to 28.7 percent for the Hall-Rabushka proposal and from 31.2 to 32.4 percent for the Armey-Shelby proposal.

Substitution of the Hall-Rabushka Flat Tax proposal for existing corporate and individual income taxes at federal, state, and local levels would produce a welfare gain of $2.06 trillion. This is slightly greater than the welfare gain from the reform of the capital income tax to equalize tax burdens for all assets and all sectors that we consider in chapter 7. If existing sales taxes, mainly at the state and local level, are also replaced by the Hall-Rabushka Flat Tax, the welfare gain falls to $0.81 trillion. The corresponding welfare gains for the Armey-Shelby Flat Tax are $1.23 trillion for replacement of income taxes and $-0.76 trillion for replacement of sales taxes as well. The reason for the relatively poor performance of the Armey-Shelby proposal is the high marginal rate of tax on labor income due to more generous family allowances.

We next consider replacing the revenues of the government sector by a National Retail Sales Tax, collected on personal consumption expenditures at the retail level. Under certain conditions, a consumption tax can be considered to be a tax on labor income, together with a tax on "old" capital, accumulated prior to the tax reform. We first design prototype sales and labor income taxes with family allowances like those incorporated into the Hall-Rabushka Flat Tax proposal. We find that a sales tax with the same progressivity as the Flat Tax generates welfare gains of $3.32 trillion, exceeding those of the Hall-Rabushka proposal by more than 50 percent! This is due to the fact that a sales tax is less distorting than the Hall-Rabushka Flat Tax. The National Retail Sales Tax is clearly superior to the Flat Tax when both retain an element of progressivity.

The cost of progressivity in terms of lost economic efficiency is substantial. One way to measure this cost is to compare a progressive sales tax with a flat sales tax that raises the same revenue. This produces a welfare gain of $1.37 trillion, added to the welfare gain from a progressive sales tax of $3.32 trillion, for an overall gain of $4.69 trillion—more than double the gain from the Flat Tax! The efficiency gain from the elimination of progressivity is a measure of the cost of the higher marginal tax rates that result from a progressive tax structure. The marginal tax rate for a progressive sales tax is approximately 40 percent, while the corresponding flat sales tax has a rate of 29 percent.

We can also assess the efficiency costs of consumption tax by comparing the marginal excess burdens of taxation with those of the 1996 Tax Law. The marginal excess burden for the Hall-Rabushka and Armey-Shelby Flat Tax proposals is 17.8 and 21.1 cents per dollar, respectively, by comparison with 26.6 cents per dollar under the 1996 Tax Law. These proposals substantially improve economic efficiency. However, the marginal excess burden for a progressive National Retail Sales Tax is 13.1 cents per dollar and for a flat sales tax is only 7.7 cents per dollar! A progressive sales tax improves efficiency relative to the Flat Tax proposals, but progressivity has a substantial efficiency cost. We conclude that the potential gains in economic efficiency from reform of the U.S. tax system are very substantial.

Our final objective is to measure the cost of public spending under the 1996 Tax Law and under alternative tax reform proposals. For this purpose, in chapter 9 we introduce the concept of the marginal cost of public spending, defined as the cost of raising one dollar of tax revenue to finance government spending on a particular category of goods and services. This depends on the tax instrument, the allocation of funds among different categories of public spending, and the type of benefits resulting from the spending. We consider benefits that are separable from the benefits of private spending, such as law enforcement and national defense, as well as benefits that are perfect substitutes for private consumption, such as transfer payments to individuals.

We consider the marginal cost of public spending for ten different tax programs and four categories of public spending—transfer payments to households and to government purchases of consumption goods, investment goods, and labor services. We also consider proportional expansion of government spending on all four categories. We assess costs of public spending under two polar assumptions about the benefits of government purchases, namely, that they are separable from the benefits of private spending and that they are perfect substitutes for private spending. We assume that government spending on transfer payments is a perfect substitute for private consumption, since these payments are simply added to the budget constraint of the household sector. Altogether, we consider ninety different combinations of tax programs, spending categories, and benefit types.

The marginal cost of public spending is highest for transfer payments to individuals and lowest for government purchases of consumption goods. The cost is intermediate between these two for government purchases of investment goods and labor services. The marginal cost of public spending is highest for labor income taxes, second highest for the corporate income tax, and third for the individual capital income tax. This cost is the lowest for property taxes and next lowest for sales taxes. The marginal cost is higher for spending that is a perfect substitute for private spending and lower for spending that is separable from private consumption.

Government programs, other than transfer payments to individuals, involve combinations of spending on different types of goods and services, raise revenue from different types of taxes, and yield different types of benefits. To illustrate the evaluation of the costs of a government program, in chapter 9 we consider the benefits of the "peace dividend" resulting from the end of the Cold War. The end of communism in Eastern Europe and the former Soviet Union, and the dissolution of the Warsaw Pact made possible permanent reductions in U.S. defense expenditures. To evaluate the welfare impact of these cuts in defense spending, we employ the dynamic general equilibrium model of the U.S. economy presented in chapter 5.

The change in welfare from a reduction in defense spending depends on the composition of defense spending and the composition of the accompanying tax reduction. We take defense spending as a proportion of the U.S. gross domestic product in 1990 as a benchmark for Cold War expenditure. We compare spending at this level with the spending that has actually taken place, extrapolated into the future by the Congressional Budget Office. The welfare gains range from $7.38 trillion to $6.42 trillion depending on the taxes that are reduced. By comparison U.S. GDP in 1990 was $5.74 trillion, so that the welfare gain from the end of the Cold War was the equivalent of more than one year's GDP! This is very large, even by comparison with the most substantial potential gains from tax reform.

Our final objective is to evaluate the cost of capital as a practical guide to reform of taxation and government spending. Our primary focus is U.S. tax policy, since the cost of capital has been used much more extensively in the United States than other countries. Auerbach and Jorgenson (1980) introduced the key concept, the marginal effective tax rate, early in the debate over the U.S. Economic Recovery Tax Act of 1981. They showed that the tax policy changes of the early 1980s, especially the 1981 Tax Act, would increase barriers to efficient allocation of capital.

By contrast we showed that the Tax Reform Act of 1986 substantially reduced barriers to efficiency. The erosion of the income tax base to provide incentives for investment and saving was arrested through vigorous and far-reaching reforms. Incentives were sharply curtailed and efforts were made to equalize marginal effective tax rates among assets. The shift toward expenditure and away from income as a tax base was reversed. Jorgenson's international comparisons of 1993 showed that these reforms had important parallels in other industrialized countries.

The cost of capital approach has also proved its usefulness in pointing the direction for future tax reforms. For this purpose information about the cost of capital must be combined with estimates of the substitutability among different types of outputs and inputs by businesses and households. The dynamic general equilibrium model of the U.S. economy we present in chapter 5 provides both types of information. In chapter 7 we show that reform of capital income taxation would generate large welfare gains by equalizing the tax burdens on housing and business capital.

The cost of the progressive tax on labor income is very large due to high marginal tax rates. Equalizing tax burdens among all assets and replacing the progressive tax on labor income by a proportional tax would produce welfare gains amounting to more than three-fifths of the U.S. GDP or almost one-fifth of U.S. private national wealth. These dramatic gains are due to the equalization of tax burdens between business and household assets and the sharp reduction in marginal tax rates on labor income. Although the welfare gains from a proportional income-based tax system would exceed the gains from the proportional consumption-based systems considered in chapter 8, the economic impact of these alternative systems would be very similar.

During the 1990s, tax reformers renewed their interest in replacing income by consumption as the basis for taxation. In chapter 8 we show that the most popular Flat Tax proposals for achieving this objective would generate welfare benefits that are comparable to those from equalizing the tax burdens on different forms of capital discussed in chapter 7. However, a National Retail Sales Tax would produce benefits that are fifty percent higher! The cost of maintaining a progressive rate structure within the framework of the National Retail Sales Tax is very large. The benefits of a National Retail Sales Tax with a flat rate structure are double those of a Flat Tax.

The cost of capital approach has suggested two promising avenues to tax reform. The first would retain the income tax base of the existing U.S. tax system but would equalize tax burdens on all forms of assets and equate average and marginal tax rates on labor income. Either of these components of income tax reform would produce substantial benefits. The second avenue would substitute consumption for income as a tax base while equating average and marginal tax rates on labor income. This could be achieved through a combination of a proportional National Retail Sales Tax and a proportional labor income tax. Either avenue would equalize the tax burden on all forms of assets while minimizing the marginal tax rate on labor income.

Finally, we have extended the conceptual framework employed in our analysis of alternative tax reforms to the evaluation of government spending programs. We show that the "peace dividend" from the end of the Cold War is far greater than the gains from tax reform. This amounts to more than a full year of the U.S. gross domestic product! Our overall conclusion is that the cost of capital and the closely related concept of the marginal effective tax rate have provided an important intellectual impetus for tax reform. Effective tax rates at both corporate and personal levels are now available for many countries around the world. International comparisons of tax reforms have provided extensive illustrations of successful applications of the cost of capital approach.

The new frontier for analysis of tax and spending programs is to combine the cost of capital and the marginal effective tax rate with estimates of substitution possibilities by businesses and households. This combination makes it possible to evaluate alternative tax reforms and spending programs in terms of economic welfare. We have illustrated this approach for a variety of tax reforms, both incremental and fundamental, as well as a variety of spending programs, including the defense cuts following the end of the Cold War. Our hope is that these illustrations will serve as an inspiration and a guide for policy makers who share our goal of making the allocation of capital within a market economy more efficient.

Notes

1. See Sven-Olof Lodin (1976), James E. Meade (1978), and U.S. Treasury (1977).
2. An illuminating account for the tax debate preceding the 1986 Tax Act has been given by Jeffrey H. Birnbaum and Alan S. Murray (1987).
3. Robert E. Hall and Alvin Rabushka (1983) and David F. Bradford (1986) presented detailed proposals for a consumption-based tax system in the United States. These were rejected in favor of an income-based approach by the U.S. Treasury (1984).
4. The objectives of the 1986 tax reform are discussed by Charles E. McLure and George R. Zodrow (1987).
5. See U.S. Treasury (1984).
6. Hall and Jorgenson (1967) and Christensen and Jorgenson (1973a) used this assumption.
7. The theory of economic depreciation was originated by Harold S. Hotelling (1925) and subsequently developed by Kenneth J. Arrow (1964) and Hall (1968).
8. See, especially, Hulten and Wykoff (1981a), p. 387. Jorgenson (1996) surveys the empirical literature.
9. Marginal effective tax rates for corporate source income including both corporate and personal taxes provided the basis for detailed comparisons of taxes in Germany, Sweden, the United Kingdom, and the United States for 1980 by Mervyn A. King and Don Fullerton (1984). Fullerton (1987) and Fullerton, Robert Gillette, and James Mackie (1987) provided comparisons among tax rates for corporate, noncorporate, and housing sectors of the United States.
10. Summaries of the alternative views of taxation and corporate finance are given by Anthony B. Atkinson and Joseph E. Stiglitz (1980), esp. pp. 128–159, Auerbach (1983b), and Hans-Werner Sinn (1991).
11. This view is employed, for example, by Harberger (1966), Martin S. Feldstein and Lawrence H. Summers (1979), and James Poterba and Summers (1983).
12. Summers (1983) provided empirical evidence on Fisher's Law.
13. See, for example, Robert S. Chirinko and Robert Eisner (1983) and Jane G. Gravelle (1984).
14. Techniques for perfect foresight or rational expectations were subsequently introduced by David Lipton, James Poterba, Jeffrey Sachs, and Lawrence Summers (1982) and Ray C. Fair and John B. Taylor (1983).
15. Henderson (1991) surveys six studies of the economic impact of the 1986 Tax Act by means of applied general equilibrium models. Only the Jorgenson-Yun (1990) model included a capital asset pricing equation and is not subject to the "Lucas critique." Feldstein (1995a,b) analyzes the effects of the Tax Reform Act of 1986 on taxable income in a partial equilibrium context. Feldstein and Feenberg (1996) extend the analysis to estimate the efficiency loss due to the increase in personal income tax rates in 1993. Slemrod (1990) contains papers looking at various aspects of the Tax Reform Act. For a survey of the literature on the Tax Reform Act of 1986, see Auerbach and Slemrod (1997).

16. This model combined features of models originated by Arrow (1968) and Lucas (1967).
17. Jorgenson and Yun (1990).
18. See Aaron and Gale (1996), Boskin (1996), Joint Committee on Taxation (1997), Auerbach (1997), Hubbard (1997), and Slemrod (1977).

2 Taxation of Income from Capital

The purpose of this chapter is to present the cost of capital approach to the analysis of tax policy for capital income. Widespread application of the cost of capital is due to the fact that this concept makes it possible to represent the economically relevant features of highly complex tax statutes in a very succinct form. The cost of capital summarizes the information about the future consequences of investment decisions required for current decisions about capital allocation. The marginal effective tax rate characterizes the tax consequences of investment decisions in a way that is useful for comparisons among alternative tax policies.

We begin by showing how the cost of capital arises in the management of capital as a factor of production. We introduce the concept of an effective tax rate within a highly simplified system for taxation of income from capital. We define a tax wedge as the difference between the remuneration of capital before taxes, which corresponds to the marginal product of capital, and the compensation after taxes available to holders of financial claims on the firm. The effective tax rate is the ratio of this tax wedge to the marginal product.

We employ features of the U.S. tax system to illustrate the complexities that arise in practical discussions of tax policy.[1] Corporate capital income is taxed at both corporate and individual levels, noncorporate capital income is taxed only at the individual level, and household capital income is not taxed at either level. We begin with the taxation of household capital income, since the tax treatment of this form of income is the simplest. We then consider the taxation of income from corporate and noncorporate capital.

We distinguish among assets employed in three different legal forms of organization—households and nonprofit institutions, noncorporate businesses, and corporate businesses. Income from capital employed in corporate business is subject to the corporate income tax, while distributions of this income to households are subject to the individual income tax. Income from unincorporated businesses—partnerships and sole proprietorships—is taxed only at the individual level. Income from equity in household assets is not subject to the income tax. Capital utilized in all three forms of organization is subject to property taxation.

Although income from equity in the household sector is not subject to tax, property taxes and interest payments on household debt are deductible from income for tax purposes under the individual income tax. The value of these tax deductions is equivalent to a subsidy to capital employed in the household sector. Interest payments to holders of household debt are taxable to the recipients. Capital gains on household assets are effectively excluded from taxable income at the individual level by generous "roll over" provisions for owner-occupied residential housing. Capital gains on owner-occupied housing are not included in income so long as they are "rolled over" into the same form of investment.

Income from capital employed in noncorporate businesses is taxed at the level of the individual. Income from noncorporate equity is treated as fully distributed to equity holders, whether or not the income is actually paid out. Interest payments to holders of debts on noncorporate businesses are subject to taxation. Property taxes and interest payments are treated as deductions from revenue in defining income from noncorporate businesses for tax purposes. Revenue is also reduced by deductions for capital consumption allowances. Tax liability has been reduced by an investment tax credit that is proportional to investment expenditures. Capital gains on noncorporate assets are subject to favorable treatment as outlined below.

Property taxes and interest payments are treated as deductions from revenue in defining corporate income for tax purposes. Revenue is also reduced by allowances for capital consumption and an investment tax credit has been directly offset against tax liability. At the individual level distributions of corporate income in the form of interest and dividends are subject to taxation as ordinary income. Capital gains realized from the sale of corporate equities are subject to special treatment outlined below. Interest payments to holders of corporate bonds are also taxable.

The special treatment of capital gains arises from three separate features of U.S. tax law. First, capital gains are taxed only when they are realized and not when they are accrued. This feature makes it possible to defer tax liability on capital gains until assets are sold. Second, capital gains have often been given favorable treatment by including only a fraction of these gains in income defined for tax purposes. Finally, capital gains taxes on assets received as part of a bequest are based on their value at the time of the bequest. Capital gains accrued prior to the bequest are not subject to tax.

We conclude by considering alternative approaches to corporate income taxation. The approach presented in this chapter is based on the "traditional" view that dividends are a fixed proportion of corporate income. In this view the marginal source of funds for the equity portion of corporate investments is new issues of equity. An alternative to this approach is provided by the "new" view that the marginal source of funds is retained earnings. In this view new issues of equity are fixed exogenously and dividend payments are determined as a residual.

2.1 Cost of Capital

The simplest form of the cost of capital arises in a model of production with durable capital goods.[2] In this model a producer acquires capital goods through investment and rents or leases them to generate income. The cost of capital plays a natural role in the management of capital, since it transforms the price of acquisition of a capital good into a rental price that generates income. The cost of capital can be avoided by postponing acquisition of a capital good. However, a delay in acquisition results in foregoing the rental value.

The rental price of capital services is the unit cost of using a capital good for a specified period of time. For example, a building can be leased for a number of months or years, an automobile can be rented for a number of days or weeks, and computer time can be purchased by the second or the minute. The cost of capital transforms the acquisition price of an asset into an appropriate rental price. This cost depends on the rate of return and depreciation. The rate of return is the opportunity cost of holding a capital good rather than a financial asset. Depreciation arises from the decline in the price of a capital good with age.

In the simplest model of a firm the production process is financed by issuing equity. The income generated from production is distributed to the shareholders through dividends. The firm's objective is to choose a production plan that maximizes the value of the firm's outstanding shares. This coincides with the interests of the shareholders in maximizing their wealth. The rental price of capital services makes it possible to decompose the maximization of the value of the firm into a sequence of one period problems, each involving the maximization of profit.

The distinguishing feature of capital as a factor of production is that durable goods contribute services to production at different points of time. We describe the technology of this model in terms of *relative efficiencies* of capital goods of different ages. The relative efficiency of a capital good depends on the age of the good and not on the time it is acquired. When a capital good is retired, its relative efficiency drops to zero. For simplicity we assume that the relative efficiencies of durable goods of different ages decline geometrically.[3] The *rate of decline in efficiency* δ is constant, so that the relative efficiencies take the form:

$$1, 1-\delta, (1-\delta)^2 \ldots, \tag{2.1}$$

where we normalize the relative efficiency of a new durable good at unity.

In order to characterize the durable goods model of production in greater detail we require the following notation:

I_t—quantity of capital goods acquired at time t.

K_t—capital stock at time t.

q_t—acquisition price of investment goods at time t.

c_t—rental price of capital input at time t.

We assume that capital input is characterized by perfect substitutability among the services of capital goods of different ages. Under the additional assumption that the services provided by a durable good are proportional to the initial *investment* in this good, we can express *capital stock* as a weighted sum of past investments:

$$K_t = \sum_{\tau=0}^{\infty} (1-\delta)^{\tau} I_{t-\tau} \, . \tag{2.2}$$

The weights are given by the relative efficiencies $(1-\delta)^{\tau}$. The quantity of *capital input* is proportional to capital stock at the beginning of the period K_{t-1}.

Capital goods decline in efficiency at each point of time, giving rise to needs for replacement to maintain productive capacity. The proportion of an investment to be replaced during the τ-th period after its acquisition is equal to the decline in efficiency during that period. Taking the first difference of the expression for capital stock in terms of past investments, we obtain:

$$\begin{aligned} K_t - K_{t-1} &= I_t - \delta \sum_{\tau=1}^{\infty} (1-\delta)^{\tau-1} I_{t-\tau} , \\ &= I_t - \delta K_{t-1} , \end{aligned} \tag{2.3}$$

where *replacement* requirements δK_{t-1} are proportional to capital stock at the beginning of the period with a constant *rate of replacement* δ.

In the durable goods model of production the price counterpart of capital stock is the acquisition price of investment goods. The rental prices of capital goods of different ages are proportional to the rental price of a new capital good. The constants of proportionality are the relative efficiencies $\{(1-\delta)^\tau\}$. The *acquisition price of investment goods* q_t is the sum of future *rental prices of capital services* $\{c_t\}$, weighted by the relative efficiencies of capital goods in each future period:

$$q_t = \sum_{\tau=0}^{\infty} (1-\delta)^\tau \prod_{s=1}^{\tau+1} \frac{1}{1+r_{s+t}} c_{t+\tau+1} , \tag{2.4}$$

where r_{s+t} is the *rate of return* in period $s+t$. The future rental prices are discounted in order to express prices for different time periods in terms of present values at time t. This expression can be compared with the corresponding expression (2.2) giving capital stock as a weighted sum of past investments.

The acquisition price of a durable good declines with age. *Depreciation* reflects both the current decline in efficiency and the present value of future declines in efficiency. Taking the first difference of the expression for the acquisition price of investment goods in terms of future rentals, we obtain:

$$q_t - q_{t-1} = -\frac{1}{1+r_t} c_t + \frac{r_t+\delta}{1+r_t} \sum_{\tau=0}^{\infty} (1-\delta)^\tau \prod_{s=1}^{\tau+1} \frac{1}{1+r_{s+t}} c_{t+\tau+1} , \tag{2.5}$$

so that the rental price of capital services is given by:

$$c_t = q_{t-1} r_t + \delta q_t - (q_t - q_{t-1}) . \tag{2.6}$$

The *cost of capital* is an annualization factor that transforms the acquisition price of investment goods into the price of capital input:

$$\frac{c_t}{q_{t-1}} = (r_t - \pi_t) + (1 + \pi_t)\,\delta\,, \tag{2.7}$$

where π_t is the *rate of inflation* in the price of investment goods:

$$\pi_t = \frac{q_t - q_{t-1}}{q_{t-1}}\,. \tag{2.8}$$

The cost of capital is the sum of two terms. The first term $(r_t - \pi_t)$ is the rate of return, net of inflation. The second term $(1 + \pi_t)\,\delta$ is the *rate of depreciation* δ, corrected for inflation.

The durable goods model of production is characterized by price-quantity duality. In this duality capital stock K_t corresponds to the acquisition price of investment goods q_t and investment I_t corresponds to the rental price of capital services c_t. Capital stock is a weighted sum of past investments, while the acquisition price of investment goods is a weighted sum of future rentals. Capital input is the service flow from the capital stock available at the beginning of the period. The price of capital input is the rental price of capital services.[4]

In the definition of capital stock the weights on past investments correspond to relative efficiencies of capital goods of different ages. These weights are also applied to future rental prices in defining the acquisition price of investment goods. Replacement requirements are generated by the decline in efficiency of a capital good with age. Depreciation results from the decline in the price of acquisition of a capital good with age. A special feature of geometrically declining relative efficiencies is that the rate of replacement and the rate of depreciation are equal to the rate of decline in efficiency δ.

2.2 Capital as a Factor of Production

The second level of complexity in analyzing the cost of capital arises in a model of the firm with capital as a factor of production. The durable goods model of production can be embedded in an elementary model of the firm with the flow of capital services as capital input. Taking the price of capital input as the rental price of capital services, capital is analogous to any other factor of production. In the simplest version of this model production is financed by issuing equity. All revenue generated from production is distributed to the shareholders.

We can regard a firm with capital as a factor of production as composed of two departments. The first department manages capital input, purchasing investment goods and supplying capital services. The second manages production, transforming capital and labor inputs into final output. In this model the cost of capital arises in a natural way. The rental price of capital is an internal transfer price at which capital services are made available to the production process. To represent the technology of a firm with capital as a factor of production we require the following additional notation:

L_t—labor input at time t.

Q_t—output at time t.

w_t—price of labor input at time t.

p_t—price of output at time t.

We represent the technology of the firm by means of a *production function*, say F, where:

$$Q_t = F(K_{t-1}, L_t) . \tag{2.9}$$

In this technology output is a function of capital and labor inputs. For simplicity we assume that production is characterized by constant returns to scale. The specification of technology also includes the relationship between capital stock and past investments (2.2). The management of capital input involves purchasing investment goods and supplying capital services to production.

To complete the specification of our model of the firm we must consider the objectives of the shareholders. For this purpose we require the following notation:

D_t—dividends distributed to equity holders at time t.

S_t—new share issues at time t.

V_t—value of the firm's outstanding shares at time t.

P_t—profit of the firm at time t.

Production is financed through the issue of *equity*, which we represent in the form of new share issues. The income generated from production is distributed to shareholders in the form of dividends. The portfolio equilibrium of the holders of equity requires:

$$D_t + V_t - V_{t-1} - S_t = r_t V_{t-1} \,. \tag{2.10}$$

Dividends D_t and the change in the *value of outstanding shares*, $V_t - V_{t-1}$, less *new share issues* S_t, are equal to the rate of return on equity r_t, multiplied by the value of outstanding shares at the beginning of the period V_{t-1}.

We can treat the condition for portfolio equilibrium of the shareholders as a difference equation in the value of outstanding shares. Using this equation, we can express the share value in the current period V_t as a discounted sum of future dividends less issues of new shares:

$$V_t = \sum_{\tau=0}^{\infty} \prod_{s=1}^{\tau+1} \frac{1}{1+r_{s+t}} (D_{t+\tau+1} - S_{t+\tau+1}) \,. \tag{2.11}$$

The objective of the firm is to maximize the value of the outstanding shares V_t. This objective coincides with the interests of the shareholders in maximizing their wealth.[5]

In each period the firm operates under a constraint on cash flow:

$$D_t - S_t = p_t Q_t - w_t L_t - q_t I_t \,. \tag{2.12}$$

The value of dividends distributed D_t, less the value of new share issues S_t, must be equal to the cash flow generated from production, $p_t Q_t - w_t L_t$, less investment expenditures $q_t I_t$.

Substituting the cash flow generated from production, less investment, into the expression for the share value, we obtain:

$$V_t = \sum_{\tau=0}^{\infty} \prod_{s=1}^{\tau+1} \frac{1}{1+r_{s+t}} (p_{t+\tau+1} Q_{t+\tau+1} - w_{t+\tau+1} L_{t+\tau+1} - q_{t+\tau+1} I_{t+\tau+1}) \,. \tag{2.13}$$

Finally, expressing investment in terms of the change in capital stock and replacement requirements:

$$\begin{aligned} V_t = {} & \sum_{\tau=0}^{\infty} \prod_{s=1}^{\tau+1} \frac{1}{1+r_{s+t}} (p_{t+\tau+1} Q_{t+\tau+1} - w_{t+\tau+1} L_{t+\tau+1} \\ & - q_{t+\tau+1} [K_{t+\tau+1} - (1-\delta) K_{t+\tau}]) \,, \\ = {} & q_t K_t + \sum_{\tau=0}^{\infty} \prod_{s=1}^{\tau+1} \frac{1}{1+r_{s+t}} (p_{t+\tau+1} Q_{t+\tau+1} - w_{t+\tau+1} L_{t+\tau+1} - c_{t+\tau+1} K_{t+\tau}) \,, \end{aligned} \tag{2.14}$$

and

$$\sum_{\tau=0}^{\infty} \prod_{s=1}^{\tau+1} \frac{1}{1+r_{s+t}} \{ q_{t+\tau}(1 + r_{t+\tau+1}) K_{t+\tau} - q_{t+\tau+1} K_{t+\tau+1} \} = q_t K_t$$

where c_t is the rental price of capital services:

$$c_t = q_{t-1} r_t + \delta q_t - (q_t - q_{t-1}) \,. \tag{2.15}$$

We can define the *profit of the firm* P_t as the difference between the value of output and the value of labor and capital inputs:

$$P_t = p_t Q_t - w_t L_t - c_t K_{t-1} \,, \tag{2.16}$$

using the rental price of capital services c_t. The value of outstanding shares V_t is equal to the value of the firm's capital stock $q_t K_t$, plus the discounted sum of future profits:

$$V_t = q_t K_t + \sum_{\tau=0}^{\infty} \prod_{s=1}^{\tau+1} \frac{1}{1 + r_{s+t}} P_{t+\tau+1} \,. \tag{2.17}$$

In order to achieve the objectives of the firm's shareholders, the production plan must maximize the firm's share value. For this purpose it is sufficient to maximize profits in every period. Under constant returns to scale this maximum is zero, so that the share value is equal to the value of the firm's capital stock:

$$V_t = q_t K_t \,. \tag{2.18}$$

We can treat the rental price of capital services as a difference equation in the price of investment goods. The price of investment goods in the current period is a weighted sum of future prices of capital services, as in equation (2.4) above. Rental prices are discounted at the rate of return on equity to express prices in different time periods in terms of present values. The durable goods model can be regarded as a description of one of the two departments of the firm. This department invests in capital goods and generates income from the rental of capital services. A second department transforms labor and capital services into final output. The rental price of capital services is an internal transfer price that links these decisions.

2.3 Rates of Return

We can extend the model of a firm with capital as a factor of production by permitting borrowing and lending. We assume that the firm can borrow or lend at a fixed rate of interest by issuing or purchasing debt in the form of bonds, notes, or mortgages. We assume further that the rate of interest is less than or equal to the rate of return to equity. Finally, we assume that the firm has a maximum debt capacity that is proportional to the value of the firm's capital stock. As before, the objective of the firm is to maximize the share value.

We can think of a firm with borrowing and lending as consisting of departments for managing capital, production, and the liabilities of the firm. The first two departments are present in the simplest model of a firm with capital as a factor of production. The third is a finance department that issues and redeems debt and equity in order to satisfy the cash flow requirements of the firm. The objective of this department is to minimize the cost of financing the firm's investments.

With a fixed rate of interest the cost of capital plays the same role with debt and equity financing as with equity financing alone. However, the rate of return is now a weighted average of rates of return on debt and equity. These rates of return represent the opportunity costs of holding durable goods rather than financial claims. The weights correspond to the relative proportions of debt and equity in the value of the firm's capital. The weighted average rate of return is an internal transfer price at which financial capital is made available to the department that manages capital goods.

The optimal financial strategy for the firm is to finance investment through new share issues and new borrowing in fixed proportions. The proportions of debt and equity reflect the firm's debt capacity. To represent the financial structure of the firm with borrowing and lending we require the following additional notation:

i_t—rate of interest at time t.

ρ_t^e—rate of return on equity at time t.

β—ratio of debt capacity to the value of the firm's capital stock.

Given the portfolio equilibrium condition for shareholders, the value of the firm's equity is equal to the sum of future dividends less issues of new shares, discounted at the *rate of return on equity* ρ_t^e:

$$V_t = \sum_{\tau=0}^{\infty} \prod_{s=1}^{\tau+1} \frac{1}{1+\rho_{s+t}^e} \left(D_{s+\tau+1} - S_{s+\tau+1}\right) . \tag{2.19}$$

However, the cash flow constraint must be modified to permit borrowing or lending.

If β is the ratio of the firm's debt capacity to its capital stock, the cash flow constraint takes the form:

$$D_t - S_t = p_t Q_t - w_t L_t - q_t I_t - \beta[i_t q_{t-1} K_{t-1} - \pi_t q_{t-1} K_{t-1} - q_t(K_t - K_{t-1})] \,. \tag{2.20}$$

The cash flow generated by production, less the value of investment, is reduced by interest payments on outstanding debt $\beta i_t q_{t-1} K_{t-1}$ and augmented by new issues of debt. These new issues are required to finance the increase in the value of capital stock due to inflation in the price of capital goods $\pi_t q_{t-1} K_{t-1}$ and the value of investment net of replacement, $q_t(K_t - K_{t-1})$.

With a fixed ratio of debt to capital stock β the value of the firm's equity can be written in the form:

$$V_t = (1-\beta) q_t K_t + \sum_{\tau=0}^{\infty} \prod_{s=1}^{\tau+1} \frac{1}{1+\rho_{s+t}^e} P_{t+\tau+1} \,, \tag{2.21}$$

where P_t is profit, as in equation (2.16). The rental price of capital services c_t takes the same form as in equation (2.15). Finally, the rate of return r_t is a weighted average of the rate of interest i_t and the rate of return on equity ρ_t^e:

$$r_t = \beta\, i_t + (1-\beta)\, \rho_t^e \,. \tag{2.22}$$

We can treat the rental price of capital services as a difference equation in the price of investment goods, as in equation (2.4) above. This price is a weighted sum of future prices of capital services, discounted at the weighted average rate of return to debt and equity (2.22). We conclude that the availability of debt financing does not alter the role of the price of capital services or the cost of capital. However, the rate of return on equity in a firm without debt financing must be replaced by the weighted average rate of return appropriate to a firm with debt financing.

We can consider a separate department of the firm, the finance department, with responsibility for managing the firm's cash flow by issuing and redeeming debt and equity. The objective of this department is to minimize the cost of financing the firm's investments. The weighted average rate of return is an internal price at which finance is made available to the department that manages capital. As before, the rental price of capital services is an internal price at which capital services are supplied to the production process.

To meet the objectives of the firm's shareholders it is sufficient to maximize profit in every period. Under constant returns to scale this maximum is zero, so that the share value is a constant fraction of capital stock:

$$V_t = (1-\beta)\, q_t K_t \, . \tag{2.23}$$

The remainder of the value of capital is, of course, the outstanding debt.

2.4 Capital Income Taxation

In order to complete the presentation of our elementary model of the firm, we introduce a simplified tax on income from capital. To represent this tax we require the following additional notation:

T_t—tax revenue at time t.

e_t—effective tax rate at time t.

σ_t—social rate of return at time t.

In every period the income from capital is the rental value of capital services. However, this rental value is gross of depreciation on capital goods. We define the tax base for the capital income tax by reducing the rental value of capital services by the value of depreciation. The *tax revenue* generated by taxation of income from capital is equal to the effective tax rate, multiplied by the tax base:

$$T_t = e_t[c_t K_{t-1} - (1+\pi_t)\delta q_{t-1} K_{t-1}] \, . \tag{2.24}$$

To characterize the effective tax rate we find it useful to define the *social rate of return* as the cost of capital before taxes, plus the rate of inflation in the price of capital goods, less depreciation, so that:

$$\sigma_t - \pi_t = \frac{c_t}{q_{t-1}} - (1+\pi_t)\,\delta \, . \tag{2.25}$$

This before tax rate of return, adjusted for inflation, is the cost of capital less the rate of depreciation. The social rate of return corresponds to the marginal product of capital as a factor of production.

Second, we can define the *private rate of return* as the cost of capital after taxes, plus the rate of inflation and less depreciation, so that:

$$\rho_t - \pi_t = \frac{c_t}{q_{t-1}} - (1+\pi_t)\delta - e_t(\sigma_t - \pi_t) \, . \tag{2.26}$$

This after-tax rate of return, adjusted for inflation, represents the rate of compensation of holders of the firm's debt and equity after all taxes have been paid.

Finally, we define the *tax wedge* as the difference between social and private rates of return. The *effective tax rate* is equal to the tax wedge, divided by the social rate of return, net of inflation:

$$e_t = \frac{\sigma_t - \rho_t}{\sigma_t - \pi_t} . \qquad (2.27)$$

The effective tax rate is the proportional difference between the remuneration of capital in production and the compensation available to the holders of financial claims on the firm.

We have described the taxation of income from capital by means of an elementary model of the firm and a simplified tax system. The firm employs capital as a factor of production and transforms capital and labor inputs into output. We measure the income from capital generated in production by means of the cost of capital. The cost of capital is an annualization factor that translates the price of acquisition of investment goods into the rental price of capital services. In the absence of taxation the cost of capital is the sum of the return on capital, adjusted for inflation, and depreciation on investment goods.

The effective tax rate corresponds to the tax wedge between the remuneration of capital before taxes and compensation received by the holders of financial claims on the firm after taxes. These claims take the form of both debt and equity. The effective tax rate is defined in terms of the cost of capital. The social rate of return is the cost of capital before taxes, adjusted for inflation and depreciation. The private rate of return is the cost of capital after taxes. The effective tax rate is equal to the difference between social and private rates of return, divided by the social rate of return, net of inflation.

Actual tax systems for income from capital differ from the simplified tax system we have considered in many respects. First, income from capital may be taxed at the level of the corporate firm and the level of the individual, so that the distribution of the income to holders of the firm's equity in the form of dividends or capital gains may affect tax liabilities. Second, distributions of income to shareholders may be treated differently from interest payments. Third, the definition of income from capital for tax purposes may differ from the compensation of capital in production. Fourth, income from newly acquired assets may be taxed differently from existing assets, giving rise to differences between *marginal tax rates* on new assets and *average tax rates* on all assets.

We next employ features of the U.S. tax system to illustrate the characteristics of tax systems encountered in practical discussions of tax policy. We consider the tax treatment of income from assets held by households, noncorporate businesses, and corporations under U.S. tax law. For assets held in each sector we define an appropriate cost of capital and rate of return. We begin with the household sector, where the taxation of income from capital takes its simplest form. We then consider the taxation of income from noncorporate business under the individual income tax. Finally, we analyze the taxation of corporate income, which requires the integration of provisions of individual and corporate income tax laws.

2.5 Households

Distributions of income from household assets take the form of capital services provided directly to consumption. The value of these services is not included in income for tax purposes. Household assets are subject to taxation as property, but property tax payments and interest on household debt are deductible from income for tax purposes under the individual income tax. We analyze the management of household assets by means of the elementary model of the firm presented in the preceding chapter.

We treat the household as encompassing a "firm" that invests in residential and nonresidential real estate and consumers' and producers' durables and "rents" the services of these capital goods to the household itself. The financial structure of the household includes both debt and equity. We assume that the household can borrow and lend at a fixed rate of interest that is less than or equal to the rate of return to household equity. We also assume that the household has a maximum debt capacity that is proportional to the value of household capital.

The optimal financial strategy for the household is to finance investment through new equity and new debt in fixed proportions. Of course, all new equity is "issued" to the household itself. To represent the portfolio equilibrium of the household sector we require the following notation:

β_h—ratio of debt capacity to the value of the household's capital stock.

t_h^e—marginal tax rate on income from which interest payments and property taxes on household assets are deductible.
t_h^p—property tax rate on household assets.

The portfolio equilibrium of holders of equity in household assets requires:

$$D_t - T_t + V_t - V_{t-1} - S_t = \rho_t^e \, V_{t-1} \, , \tag{2.28}$$

where tax liabilities for ordinary income from capital in the household sector T_t are negative and represent an implicit subsidy to the consumption of household capital services:

$$T_t = - \, t_h^e q_{t-1} K_{t-1} (t_h^p + \beta_h i_t) \, . \tag{2.29}$$

The value of capital services provided to the household for consumption D_t, plus the value of tax deductions for property taxes $t_h^e q_{t-1} K_{t-1} t_h^p$, interest payments on household debt $t_h^e q_{t-1} K_{t-1} \beta_h i_t$, and the change in the value of household equity, $V_t - V_{t-1}$, less new equity S_t, is equal to the rate of return on equity ρ_t^e, multiplied by the value of equity at the beginning of the period V_{t-1}. The value of tax deductions is equal to the reduction in tax liabilities on income taxed at the marginal rate t_h^e. Treating the condition for portfolio equilibrium as a difference equation in the value of equity in household assets in the current period, we obtain:

$$V_t = \sum_{\tau=0}^{\infty} \prod_{s=1}^{\tau+1} \frac{1}{1 + \rho_{s+t}^e} \left[D_{t+\tau+1} - T_{t+\tau+1} - S_{t+\tau+1} \right] . \tag{2.30}$$

Under the assumption that debt is a fixed proportion of the value of household capital stock, the cash flow constraint for the household sector takes the form:

$$D_t - S_t = p_t Q_t - q_t I_t - (t_h^p + \beta_h i_t) \, q_{t-1} K_{t-1} + \beta_h [\pi_t q_{t-1} K_{t-1} + q_t (K_t - K_{t-1})] \, . \tag{2.31}$$

Net benefits provided to the household D_t, less new equity S_t, are equal to the value of household capital services $p_t Q_t$, less the value of investment $q_t I_t$, and less property taxes $t_h^p q_{t-1} K_{t-1}$ and interest payments on debt $\beta_h i_t q_{t-1} K_{t-1}$. This flow is augmented by new issues of debt to finance the increase in the value of household capital due to inflation $\pi_t q_{t-1} K_{t-1}$ and investment net of replacement $q_t (K_t - K_{t-1})$.

Substituting household net benefits D_t, less the equity share of net investment S_t, into the value of equity in household assets, we obtain:

$$V_t = (1 - \beta_h) q_t K_t + \sum_{\tau=0}^{\infty} \prod_{s=1}^{\tau+1} \frac{1}{1+\rho_{s+t}^e} P_{t+\tau+1} , \tag{2.32}$$

where P_t is the "profit" of the household:

$$P_t = p_t Q_t - c_t K_{t-1} , \tag{2.33}$$

c_t is the rental price of household capital services:

$$c_t = q_{t-1}[r_t^h - \pi_t + (1+\pi_t)\delta + (1 - t_h^e)\, t_h^p] , \tag{2.34}$$

and r_t^h is a weighted average rate of return:

$$r_t^h - \pi_t = \beta_h[(1 - t_h^e)\, i_t - \pi_t] + (1 - \beta_h)\,(\rho_t^e - \pi_t) . \tag{2.35}$$

Since the output of the household sector consists entirely of capital services provided to the household itself for consumption, "profit" is zero.

The key provisions of U.S. tax law for income from household assets are represented in the rental price of household capital services and the household rate of return. Property taxes are net of the value of tax deductions under the individual income tax $t_h^e t_h^p$. Similarly, the rate of return on debt financing is net of the value of tax deductions $t_h^e i_t$. Capital gains on household assets are not included in taxable income, since households are permitted to "roll over" investments in owner-occupied residential real estate into new assets of the same type without incurring tax liabilities for realized capital gains.

To characterize the effective tax rate on household assets, we require the following notation:

e_t^h—effective tax rate on income from household assets at time t.

σ_t^h—social rate of return on household assets at time t.

ρ_t^h—private rate of return on household assets at time t.

t_h^d—marginal tax rate on income from interest payments on household debt.

We define the *social rate of return on household assets* σ_t^h as the cost of capital before taxes, plus the rate of inflation and less depreciation, so that:

$$\sigma_t^h - \pi_t = \frac{c_t}{q_{t-1}} - (1+\pi_t)\delta \, . \qquad (2.36)$$

This before tax rate of return represents the rate of remuneration of capital in the production of household capital services. Similarly, we define the *private rate of return on household assets* ρ_t^h as the compensation of the holders of the household's debt and equity after all taxes have been paid:

$$\rho_t^h - \pi_t = \beta_h[(1-t_h^d)i - \pi_t] + (1-\beta_h)(\rho_t^e - \pi_t) \, . \qquad (2.37)$$

Finally, we define the *tax wedge on household assets* as the difference between social and private rates of return. The *effective tax rate on household assets* is equal to the tax wedge divided by the social rate of return, net of inflation:

$$e_t^h = \frac{\sigma_t^h - \rho_t^h}{\sigma_t^h - \pi_t} \, . \qquad (2.38)$$

We can also define tax wedges and effective tax rates separately for equity and debt financing by substituting the rate of return on equity ρ_t^e or the after tax rate of interest on debt $(1-t_h^d)i_t$ for the private rate of return ρ_t^h in the definitions of the tax wedge and the effective tax rate.

2.6 Noncorporate Business

We next consider the tax treatment of income from capital employed in noncorporate businesses under U.S. tax law. Income from noncorporate capital is treated as fully distributed to the owners of a noncorporate business. In defining noncorporate income for tax purposes interest payments and capital consumption allowances are treated as deductions from income. The investment tax credit results in a direct reduction in tax liabilities that is proportional to the level of investment expenditures. Capital gains on noncorporate assets are subject to tax, but the tax rate differs from the rate on ordinary income.

To represent the portfolio equilibrium of the noncorporate sector we require the following notation:

β_m—ratio of debt capacity to the value of noncorporate capital stock.

t_m^e—marginal tax rate on income from noncorporate equity.

t_m^g—marginal tax rate on capital gains on noncorporate capital.

t_m^p—property tax rate on noncorporate assets.

The portfolio equilibrium of holders of equity in noncorporate business implies:

$$D_t - T_t + (1 - t_m^g)(V_t - V_{t-1} - S_t) = \rho_t^e \, V_{t-1} \,. \tag{2.39}$$

The required rate of return on equity ρ_t^e, multiplied by the value of equity at the beginning of the period V_{t-1}, is equal to the value of distributions D_t, less tax liabilities for ordinary income from capital T_t, plus the change in the value of equity, $V_t - V_{t-1}$, and less the equity portion of investment net of replacement S_t, net of capital gains taxes. Treating the condition for portfolio equilibrium as a difference equation in the value of equity in noncorporate assets in the current period, we obtain:

$$V_t = \sum_{\tau=0}^{\infty} \prod_{s=1}^{\tau+1} \frac{1}{1 + \dfrac{\rho_{s+t}^e}{1 - t_m^g}} \left[\frac{1}{1 - t_m^g} (D_{t+\tau+1} - T_{t+\tau+1}) - S_{t+\tau+1} \right]. \tag{2.40}$$

Capital gains taxes are assessed on the change in the value of equity in noncorporate assets, less the equity share of investment net of replacement. The tax rate on noncorporate capital gains t_m^g reflects the deferral of taxes due to taxation of capital gains after they are realized, rather than when they are accrued. This tax rate also reflects the facts that only a fraction of capital gains are taxed and that gains on assets received in the form of a bequest are assessed only on gains in the value of the assets after the bequest is made.

We model provisions for capital consumption allowances and the investment tax credit under U.S. tax law as equivalent reductions in the acquisition price of investment goods.[6] This price is reduced by the investment tax credit and the present value of tax deductions for capital consumption. We assume that the present value of deductions for capital consumption on a new asset is precisely offset by an equal amount of debt. This debt is amortized over the lifetime of the asset as the tax deductions are actually realized.

We employ the following notation in representing provisions for capital consumption allowances under U.S. tax law and the investment tax credit:

A_τ—capital consumption allowances on an asset of age τ.

k_m—rate of the investment tax credit on noncorporate assets.

z_m—present value of capital consumption allowances on a new asset.

The present value of capital consumption allowances is:

$$z_m = \sum_{\tau=0}^{\infty} \prod_{s=1}^{\tau+1} \frac{1}{1+i_{s+t}(1-t_m^e)} A_{\tau+1} . \tag{2.41}$$

In this expression the discount rate is the interest rate i_t after taxes on noncorporate income at the rate t_m^e.[7]

Under the assumption that the firm finances investment net of replacement through new equity and new debt in fixed proportions, new equity is:

$$S_t = (1-\beta_m)(1-k_m-t_m^e z_m)q_t(K_t-K_{t-1}) . \tag{2.42}$$

The acquisition price of investment goods is reduced by the investment tax credit k_m and the present value of tax deductions for capital consumption $t_m^e z_m$. Tax liabilities for ordinary income from capital in the noncorporate sector are given by:

$$T_t = t_m^e \, [p_tQ_t - w_tL_t - (1-k_m-t_m^e z_m)q_{t-1}K_{t-1}\beta_m i_t - t_m^p q_{t-1}K_{t-1}]. \tag{2.43}$$

Property taxes on noncorporate assets and interest payments on the proportion of these assets financed by debt are deductible from income for tax purposes.

Under the assumption that debt is a fixed proportion of the value of noncorporate capital stock, the cash flow constraint for the noncorporate sector takes the form:

$$\begin{aligned} D_t - S_t = {} & p_tQ_t - w_tL_t - (1-k_m-t_m^e z_m)q_tI_t - t_m^p q_{t-1}K_{t-1} \\ & - \beta_m(1-k_m-t_m^e z_m)[(i_t-\pi_t)q_{t-1}K_{t-1} - q_t(K_t-K_{t-1})] . \end{aligned} \tag{2.44}$$

Distributions D_t, less new equity S_t, are equal to the cash flow generated by production, $p_tQ_t - w_tL_t$, less investment $(1-k_m-t_m^e z_m)q_tI_t$, and less deductions for property taxes on noncorporate assets $t_m^p q_{t-1}K_{t-1}$ and interest payments on noncorporate debt $\beta_m(1-k_m - t_m^e z_m)i_t q_{t-1}K_{t-1}$. In addition, a fixed proportion of debt to the value of noncorporate assets β_m is maintained by issuing new debt to finance the increase in the value of noncorporate assets. This increase is due to inflation $\pi_t q_{t-1}K_{t-1}$ and investment net of replacement $q_t(K_t-K_{t-1})$.

Substituting the equity share of investment net of replacement (2.42) and tax liabilities on ordinary income (2.43) into the expression (2.40) for the value of noncorporate equity, we can rewrite this expression in the form:

$$V_t = (1-\beta_m)(1-k_m-t_m^e z_m)q_t K_t + \sum_{\tau=0}^{\infty} \prod_{s=1}^{\tau+1} \frac{1}{1+\dfrac{\rho_{s+t}^e}{1-t_m^g}} \frac{1-t_m^e}{1-t_m^g} P_{t+\tau+1} , \tag{2.45}$$

where P_t is the profit of the firm:

$$P_t = p_t Q_t - w_t L_t - c_t K_{t-1} , \tag{2.46}$$

c_t is the rental price of capital services:

$$c_t = \frac{1-k_m-t_m^e z_m}{1-t_m^e} q_{t-1}[r_t^m - \pi_t + (1+\pi_t)\delta] + t_m^p q_{t-1} , \tag{2.47}$$

and r_t^m is a weighted average rate of return:

$$r_t^m - \pi_t = \beta_m[(1-t_m^e)i_t - \pi_t] + (1-\beta_m)[\rho_t^e - (1-t_m^g)\pi_t] . \tag{2.48}$$

Under constant returns to scale the maximum value of profit is equal to zero.

The key features of U.S. tax law for income from noncorporate assets are represented in the rental price of noncorporate capital services and the noncorporate rate of return. The denominator of the first term in the rental price of capital services represents the after-tax proportion of noncorporate income from capital at the tax rate t_m^e. Second, the price of investment goods is reduced by the investment tax credit k_m and the present value of tax deductions for capital consumption $t_m^e z_m$. Third, the rental price includes the property tax rate t_m^p. Fourth, the rate of return includes the rate of interest, also net of tax deductions $t_m^e i_t$. Fifth, the tax rate on capital gains t_m^g enters the cost of capital through the rate of inflation in the acquisition price of investment goods π_t.

To characterize the effective tax rate on noncorporate assets, we require the following notation:

e_t^m—effective tax rate on income from noncorporate assets at time t.

σ_t^m—social rate of return on noncorporate assets at time t.

ρ_t^m—private rate of return on noncorporate assets at time t.

t_m^d—marginal tax rate on interest payments on noncorporate debt.

We define the *social rate of return on noncorporate assets* σ_t^m as the cost of capital before taxes, plus the rate of inflation and less depreciation, as in (2.36) above. This before tax rate of return represents the rate of remuneration of capital in noncorporate business. Similarly, we define the *private rate of return on noncorporate assets* as:

$$\rho_t^m - \pi_t = \beta_m[(1-t_m^d)i_t - \pi_t] + (1-\beta_m)(\rho_t^e - \pi_t) . \tag{2.49}$$

This after-tax rate of return represents the compensation of the holders of the noncorporate firm's debt and equity after all taxes have been paid.

Finally, we define the *tax wedge on noncorporate assets* as the difference between social and private tax rates of return. The *effective tax rate on noncorporate assets* e_t^m is the tax wedge divided by the social rate of return, net of inflation, as in (2.38) above. As before, we can define tax wedges and effective tax rates for equity or debt financed investments in the noncorporate sector separately by replacing the private rate of return ρ_t^m by the rate of return on equity ρ_t^e or the after-tax rate of interest $(1-t_m^d)i_t$ in the definitions of the tax wedge and the effective tax rate.

2.7 Corporate Business

Finally, we consider the taxation of income from capital employed in corporate businesses. Corporate income, as defined for tax purposes, is taxable at the corporate level. Interest payments and capital consumption allowances are treated as deductions from corporate income. The investment tax credit results in a reduction in corporate tax liabilities that is proportional to investment expenditures. Distributions of corporate income in the form of dividends and capital gains are taxable at the individual level, where the tax rate on dividends differs from the rate on capital gains.

We can introduce personal income taxes on distributions of corporate income through the portfolio equilibrium of holders of equity in corporate business. To represent this equilibrium we require the following notation:

β_q—ratio of debt capacity to the value of corporate capital stock.

t_q—corporate income tax rate.

t_q^e—marginal tax rate on dividends.

t_q^g—marginal tax rate on capital gains on corporate equities.

t_q^p—property tax rate on corporate assets.

The condition for portfolio equilibrium of holders of corporate equity is precisely analogous to the corresponding condition for noncorporate business:

$$D_t - T_t + (1 - t_q^g)(V_t - V_{t-1} - S_t) = \rho_t^e V_{t-1} , \tag{2.50}$$

where D_t is corporate dividends, taxes T_t are proportional to dividends:

$$T_t = t_q^e D_t , \tag{2.51}$$

and t_q^g is the tax rate on capital gains accrued on corporate equity at the personal level. This rate reflects the favorable treatment of capital gains relative to ordinary income. The value of corporate equity in the current period is:

$$V_t = \sum_{\tau=0}^{\infty} \prod_{s=1}^{\tau+1} \frac{1}{1 + \dfrac{\rho_{s+t}^e}{1 - t_q^g}} \left[\frac{1}{1 - t_q^g} (D_{t+\tau+1} - T_{t+\tau+1}) - S_{t+\tau+1} \right] . \tag{2.52}$$

As before, we model provisions for capital consumption allowances and the investment tax credit under the U.S. corporate income tax as equivalent reductions in the acquisition price of investment goods. To represent these provisions of U.S. tax law we require the following notation:

k_q—rate of the investment tax credit on corporate assets.

z_q—present value of capital consumption allowances on a new asset.

The discount rate for capital consumption allowances is the interest rate i_t after deductions from corporate income for tax purposes at the corporate tax rate t_q.

We assume that the corporation maintains a fixed proportion of debt to the value of corporate assets. However, the corporate firm can finance investment through equity by retaining earnings or issuing new shares. We assume that dividends are a fixed proportion α of income after corporate taxes C_t:

$$\begin{aligned} D_t = \alpha[& p_t Q_t - w_t L_t - (1 - k_q - t_q z_q)\delta q_t K_{t-1} - t_q^p q_{t-1} K_{t-1} \\ & - \beta_q (1 - k_q - t_q z_q)(i_t - \pi_t) q_{t-1} K_{t-1} - C_t] . \end{aligned} \tag{2.53}$$

Corporate taxes C_t are proportional to the cash flow generated by production, less deductions for interest payments and property taxes:

$$C_t = t_q[p_t Q_t - w_t L_t - (1-k_q - t_q z_q)q_{t-1}K_{t-1}\beta_q i_t - t_q^p q_{t-1}K_{t-1}] \,. \tag{2.54}$$

Under the assumption that debt is a fixed proportion of the value of corporate capital stock, the cash flow constraint for the corporation takes the form:

$$\begin{aligned} D_t - S_t = {} & p_t Q_t - w_t L_t - (1-k_q - t_q z_q)q_t I_t - t_q^p q_{t-1}K_{t-1} \\ & - \beta_q(1-k_q-t_q z_q)[(i_t - \pi_t)q_{t-1}K_{t-1} - q_t(K_t - K_{t-1})] - C_t \,. \end{aligned} \tag{2.55}$$

Dividends D_t, less new share issues S_t, are equal to the cash flow generated by production, $p_t Q_t - w_t L_t$, less investment $(1-k_q - t_q z_q)q_t I_t$, less deductions for property taxes on corporate assets $t_q^p q_{t-1}K_{t-1}$ and interest payments on corporate debt $\beta_q(1-k_q-t_q z_q)i_t q_{t-1}K_{t-1}$, and less corporate taxes C_t. In addition, a fixed proportion of debt to the value of corporate assets β_q is maintained by issuing new debt to finance the increase in the value of corporate assets. This increase is due to inflation $\pi_t q_{t-1}K_{t-1}$ and investment net of replacement $q_t(K_t - K_{t-1})$.

Substituting dividends and corporate tax liabilities into the expression given above for the value of corporate equity, we can rewrite this expression in the form:

$$\begin{aligned} V_t = {} & (1-\beta_q)(1-k_q-t_q z_q)q_t K_t \\ & + \sum_{\tau=0}^{\infty} \prod_{s=1}^{\tau+1} \frac{1}{1+\dfrac{\rho_{s+t}^e}{1-t_q^g}} \, \frac{(1-t_q^e)\alpha + (1-t_q^g)(1-\alpha)}{1-t_q^g} (1-t_q)P_{t+\tau+1} \,, \end{aligned} \tag{2.56}$$

where P_t is corporate profit, defined in the same way as in (2.46) above, and c_t is the rental price of corporate capital services:

$$c_t = \frac{1-k_q-t_q z_q}{1-t_q} q_{t-1}[r_t^q - \pi_t + (1+\pi_t)\delta] + t_q^p q_{t-1} \,, \tag{2.57}$$

and r_t^q is a weighted average rate of return:

$$r_t^q - \pi_t = \beta_q[(1-t_q)i_t - \pi_t] + (1-\beta_q)\left[\frac{\rho_t^e - \pi_t(1-t_q^g)}{(1-t_q^e)\alpha + (1-t_q^g)(1-\alpha)}\right] . \tag{2.58}$$

Under constant returns to scale the maximum value of corporate profits is zero.

The key features of the U.S. corporate income tax and the taxation of distributions of corporate income through the individual income tax are represented in the rental price of corporate capital services and the corporate rate of return. The denominator of the first term in the rental price of capital services represents the after-tax proportion of income from corporate capital at the corporate tax rate t_q. Second, the price of investment goods is reduced by the investment tax credit k_q and the present value of tax deductions from corporate income for capital consumption $t_q z_q$. Third, the rental price includes the property tax rate t_q^p. Fourth, the rate of return includes the rate of interest, also net of tax deductions at the corporate level $t_q i_t$. Tax rates at the individual level on capital gains on corporate equities t_q^g and corporate dividends t_q^e enter the cost of capital through the rate of return on corporate equity ρ_t^e and the rate of inflation π_t.

To characterize the effective tax rate on corporate assets, we require the following notation:

e_t^q—effective tax rate on income from corporate assets at time t.

σ_t^q—social rate of return on corporate assets at time t.

ρ_t^q—private rate of return on corporate assets at time t.

t_q^d—marginal tax rate on income from interest payments on corporate debt.

We define the *social rate of return on corporate assets* σ_t^q as the cost of capital before taxes, plus the rate of inflation and less depreciation, as in (2.36) above. This before tax rate of return represents the rate of remuneration of capital in corporate business. Similarly, we define the *private rate of return on corporate assets* ρ_t^q as:

$$\rho_t^q - \pi_t = \beta_q[(1 - t_q^d)i_t - \pi_t] + (1 - \beta_q)[\rho_t^e - \pi_t] \,. \tag{2.59}$$

This after-tax rate of return represents the compensation of the holders of the corporate firm's debt and equity after all taxes have been paid.

Finally, we define the *tax wedge on corporate assets* as the difference between social and private rates of return. The *effective tax rate on corporate assets* e_t^q is the tax wedge divided by the social rate of return, net of inflation, as in (2.38), above. As before, we can also define effective tax rates for equity or debt financed investments in the corporate sector separately by replacing the private rate of return ρ_t^q by the rate of return to equity ρ_t^e or the after-tax rate of return to debt $(1 - t_q^d)i_t$ in the definitions of the tax wedge and the effective tax rate.

The tax wedge and the effective tax rate on corporate assets can be divided into two components—a component that can be attributed to taxation at the corporate level and an additional component attributable to taxation at the individual level. This separation is useful in comparing effective tax rates with statutory rates. We first define the *total tax wedge* on corporate assets as the difference between private and social rates of return, as before. We then define the *corporate tax wedge* as the difference between the social rate of return and the after-tax *corporate rate of turn*

$$r^c - \pi = r^q - \pi + \beta_q t_q i_t \; . \tag{2.60}$$

Similarly, we can define the *individual tax wedge* as the difference between the corporate rate of return (2.60) and the private rate of return.

Given corporate and individual tax wedges, we can define the *effective corporate tax rate* as the corporate tax wedge divided by the social rate of return, net of inflation. Similarly, we can define the *effective individual tax rate* as the individual tax wedge divided by the social rate of return, net of inflation. The effective tax rate on corporate assets is the sum of the effective corporate and individual tax rates.

2.8 Alternative Approaches

In this chapter we have described the characteristic features of U.S. tax law in terms of the cost of capital and the rate of return. We have modeled provisions of U.S. tax law on corporate income taxes, individual income taxes, and property taxes. We have also incorporated the effects of the financial structure of the firm on the taxation of capital income. The financial structure determines the form of distributions of capital income to owners of financial claims. We have distinguished between equity, associated with distributions in the form of dividends and capital gains, and debt, associated with distributions in the form of interest payments.

Under U.S. tax law income from corporate businesses is taxed at the level of the corporation. Distributions of this income in the form of dividends and capital gains are taxed at the level of the individual. Income from equity in noncorporate businesses is treated as if it were fully distributed to equity holders, but this income is taxed only at the individual level. Income from equity in household capital is not subject to income taxation at either corporate or individual levels. However, interest payments to holders of household debt, like interest payments to holders of corporate and noncorporate debt, are taxable to the recipients.

Property taxes and interest payments are treated as deductions from revenue in defining corporate and noncorporate income for tax purposes. While income from equity in household assets is not subject to tax, property taxes and interest payments on household debt are deductible from income for tax purposes at the individual level. This is equivalent to a subsidy to capital employed in the household sector. Revenue is reduced by allowances for capital consumption in defining income from corporate and noncorporate assets for tax purposes. Tax liabilities are reduced directly by a tax credit for investment expenditures.

The introduction of the marginal effective tax rate by Auerbach and Jorgenson (1980) was limited to the effective corporate tax rate we have presented in section 2.7. This concept was employed in detailed studies of effective tax rates by type of asset and industry by Jorgenson and Sullivan (1981). The integration of corporate and individual income tax provisions into the marginal effective tax rate for the corporate sector was initiated by Hall (1981). Alternative marginal effective tax rate concepts are compared and analyzed by Bradford and Fullerton (1981).

The marginal effective tax rate for the corporate sector, including both corporate and individual taxes, provided the basis for the detailed studies of taxation of the corporate sector in Canada by Boadway, Bruce, and Mintz (1984), Germany, Sweden, the United Kingdom, and the United States by King and Fullerton (1984), and Australia, Canada, France, Germany, Italy, Japan, Sweden, the United Kingdom, and the United States by Jorgenson (1993). The effect of the individual income tax on the corporate cost of capital depends on the determinants of corporate financial policy. A number of alternative approaches to corporate taxation have been discussed in the literature.[8]

We have presented a model of the cost of capital in the corporate sector based on a fixed ratio of dividends to corporate income in Jorgenson and Yun (1986b). This is the "traditional" view of corporate taxation employed, for example, by McLure (1979), Summers (1981), and Poterba and Summers (1983). In this view the marginal source of funds for the equity portion of the firm's investments is new issues of equity, since dividends are fixed. An important implication of the traditional view is that an additional dollar of new issues adds precisely one dollar to the value of the firm's assets. The value of outstanding financial liabilities of the firm is equal to the value of the firm's assets.

It is important to emphasize the critical role of the assumption that dividends are a fixed proportion of corporate income in the traditional view of corporate taxation. This view does not provide an explanation of the corporate firm's dividend policy. If the firm were to reduce dividend payments by one dollar and retain the earnings in order to finance investment, stockholders would avoid taxes on dividend payments at the rate on corporate equity t_q^e. The addition to retained earnings would result in a capital gain taxed at the rate t_q^g. Since the effective tax rate for capital gains is lower than the rate for dividends under U.S. tax law, shareholders would experience an increase in wealth. Following this line of reasoning, it would always be in the interest of the shareholders for the firm to finance investment from retained earnings rather than new issues of equity.

An alternative approach to corporate taxation proposed by King (1977), Auerbach (1979), and Bradford (1981b) is that new issues of equity rather than dividends are fixed. This view is employed in modeling the cost of capital by Boadway, Bruce, and Mintz (1984) and King and Fullerton (1984). The corporate firm retains earnings sufficient to finance the equity portion of investment. Dividends paid by the firm are determined by the cash-flow constraint (2.55). In this "new" view of corporate taxation the marginal source of equity funds is retained earnings, so that the corporate rate of return (2.58) is replaced by a rate of return with pay-out ratio α equal to zero. In this view the corporate rate of return is independent of the tax rate on dividends at the individual level t_q^e, so that taxation of dividends does not affect the rental price of capital services or the effective tax rate on income from corporate assets.

Under the new view of corporate taxation each dollar of investment financed by decreasing dividend payments and increasing retained earnings raises the value of the firm's outstanding shares by $(1-t_q^e)/(1-t_q^g)$ dollars. Unless the possibility of repurchasing the firm's outstanding shares is ruled out by assumption, the most attractive investment opportunity available to the firm is to liquidate its assets and repurchase its outstanding shares. Each dollar of assets liquidated reduces the value of the firm's outstanding shares by $(1-t_q^e)/(1-t_q^g)$ dollars. Accordingly, this view of corporate taxation has been characterized as the "trapped equity" approach. If repurchase of the firm's outstanding shares is ruled out, equity is "trapped" in the firm and it makes sense for the firm to continue holding assets.

Both the "traditional" or the "new" views of corporate taxation depend critically on assumptions about financial policy of the firm. The traditional view depends on the assumption that dividends are a fixed proportion of corporate income, so that the marginal source of funds for financing investment is new issues of equity. The new view depends on the assumption that new issues of equity (or repurchases) are fixed, so that the marginal source of funds is retained earnings. Neither of these views is completely satisfactory.[9] Empirical support for the traditional view has been presented by Poterba and Summers (1983, 1985), while support for the new view is given by Auerbach (1984).

In chapter 3 we provide a quantitative description of U.S. tax law. We first provide estimates of the rates of income taxation at both corporate and individual levels for the period 1970–1996. We also present property tax rates for household, noncorporate, and corporate sectors. We then discuss provisions for capital cost recovery, including capital consumption allowances and the investment tax credit. We also describe features of the financial structure of corporate and noncorporate businesses and households that affect the taxation of income from capital. Our data can be used to implement either the traditional or the new view of the corporate cost of capital.

Notes

1. The standard reference on U.S. tax policy is Pechman (1987). Jorgenson (1993) compares the taxation of capital income in nine countries—Australia, Canada, France, Germany, Italy, Japan, Sweden, the United Kingdom, and the United States. On capital income taxation, see Bradford (1986), Feldstein (1987), and Gravelle (1994).
2. The durable goods model of production was originated by Walras (1954). Capital as a factor of production has been discussed by Jorgenson (1967a,b), Diewert (1980), and Hulten (1990).
3. While the assumption of geometric decline in relative efficiency of capital goods is a convenient simplification, this assumption is inessential to modeling capital as a factor of production. For a more general treatment, see Jorgenson (1973, 1989) and Biorn (1989).
4. The dual to the durable goods model of production was originated by Hotelling (1925) and Haavelmo (1960). The dual to this model was further developed by Arrow (1964) and Hall (1968).
5. The relationship between the objective of the firm and the interests of the shareholders was introduced by Fisher (1961). This relationship was discussed in detail by Hirshleifer (1970).
6. This approach to modeling investment incentives was introduced by Hall and Jorgenson (1967, 1969, 1971).
7. Discounting capital consumption allowances at the after-tax rate of interest is suggested by Summers (1987).
8. Summaries of the alternative views of corporate income taxation are given by Atkinson and Stiglitz (1980), esp. pp. 128–159, Auerbach (1983b), and Jorgenson (1993).
9. A third view of corporation taxation is presented by Stiglitz (1973). This view drops the assumption we have made that the debt-equity ratio is fixed, so that the cheapest source of source of finance is debt, which is tax deductible at the corporate level.

3 U.S. Tax System

The purpose of this chapter is to provide a quantitative description of the U.S. tax system. We first estimate income and property tax rates at both corporate and individual levels. Our estimates of corporate income tax rates are based on statutory rates at federal and state and local levels. We take into account the fact that state and local tax payments are treated as deductions from revenue in defining corporate income at the federal level. We represent the corporate income tax as a flat rate tax, so that corporate tax liabilities are simply proportional to corporate income.

By contrast with the corporate income tax, liabilities under the individual income tax are a steadily rising proportion of the income of each taxpayer. Accordingly, we can say that the individual income tax is progressive at both federal and state and local levels. State and local personal income tax payments are deducted from revenue in defining individual income for tax purposes at the federal level. We employ the concept of the average marginal tax rate to summarize the progressive rate schedules for the individual income tax. We estimate average marginal tax rates under the individual income tax by assuming that the amounts of income subject to tax at various marginal rates will increase or decrease in the same proportion.

In order to estimate average marginal tax rates on individual income from debt and equity we distinguish among alternative forms of legal ownership by individuals. This makes it possible to incorporate differences in the tax treatment of different types of income such as dividends and interest. We first estimate the average marginal tax rate by type of income and form of ownership in section 3.1. We then determine the distribution of financial claims on assets among ownership categories from the U.S. Flow of Funds Accounts in section 3.2. Finally, we compute average marginal tax rates as a weighted average of the corresponding tax rates for all ownership categories, using the distribution of financial claims as weights.

Capital consumption allowances are permitted as a deduction from revenue in defining taxable income for both corporate and noncorporate businesses. These allowances permit taxpayers to recover capital outlays over the lifetime of an investment good. The investment tax credit can also be viewed as a form of capital cost recovery. The Haig-Simons definition of income requires that tax deductions for capital cost recovery must equal economic depreciation, as defined in chapter 2. Economic depreciation corresponds to the decline in the acquisition price of an investment good with age. In section 3.3 we outline the econometric methodology for analyzing data on prices of assets of different ages. In section 3.4 we describe the measurement of economic rates of depreciation, present values of capital consumption allowances, and the investment tax credit rates.

Property taxes are levied on assets in household, noncorporate, and corporate sectors, primarily by local governments. Property taxes on household and noncorporate assets are deductible from revenue under the individual income tax; similarly, property taxes on corporate assets are deductible from revenue under the corporate income tax. We use the average rate of property taxes in each sector for all assets in that sector. The average property tax rate is computed as the ratio of total property tax liability to the value of capital stock. We describe the estimation of the value of capital stock for each legal form of organization in section 3.5.

There are important interactions between the taxation of income from capital and financial policies of business firms and households. For our purposes the most important characteristics of the financial structure of a firm are the allocation of the value of capital between debt and equity and the dividend policy of a corporate firm. Similarly, the allocation of household wealth between debt and equity is important in determining the impact of tax policies.

The features of tax policy that are most affected by the financial structure are tax deductions for interest expenses, deductions for dividends paid and received, and the differential tax treatment of dividends and retained earnings of corporations at the level of the individual income tax. In section 3.5 we estimate the dividend pay-out ratio of the corporate sector and ratios of debt to the value of capital stock for households and noncorporate and corporate businesses. Of course, the dividend pay-out ratio does not affect the corporate rate of return in the "new" view of the corporate income tax discussed in chapter 2.

In section 3.6 we consider alternative approaches for describing the U.S. tax system. We employ estimates of depreciation based on the decline in the acquisition price of an asset with age. Estimates based on rental prices of capital input and investment for replacement purposes have also been proposed. In this chapter we document changes over time in provisions for capital recovery under U.S. tax law. These provisions have allowed taxpayers the possibility of selecting among alternative methods for calculating capital consumption allowances. Our estimates are based on the choices actually made. An alternative approach is to assume that taxpayers minimize their tax liabilities.

3.1 Tax Rates

We begin with estimation of the corporate income tax rate. Corporate profits are subject to state and local taxes as well as the federal corporate income tax. Corporate income tax rates differ among states and localities. We assume that all corporate firms are subject to the maximum statutory tax rate at the federal level, say t_q^f, since almost all corporate income is taxed at this rate.

In most states and localities the base for the corporate income tax is the same as the federal tax. However, state and local taxes are deductible from corporate income, as defined for federal income tax purposes. If the average tax rate for state and local taxation of corporate income is t_q^s, then the corporate income tax rate t_q, including both federal and state and local taxes is:

$$t_q = t_q^f + t_q^s - t_q^f \, t_q^s \,. \tag{3.1}$$

Table 3.1 and figure 3.1 present the statutory rate of the corporate income tax at the federal level t_q^f and our estimates of the corporate income tax rate t_q and the state and local tax rate t_q^s.

Capital gains received by corporate taxpayers are subject to an alternative tax rate t_q^{gqf} at the federal level whenever this rate is lower than the regular corporate tax rate. This alternative tax rate was 30 percent until 1978 and 28 percent thereafter. Since almost all corporate income is subject to the maximum corporate tax rate, we assume that capital gains on assets held by corporations are taxed at the alternative rate. Taxation of corporate capital gains is based on realization rather

Table 3.1
Corporate income tax rates

Year	Federal, state and local t_q	Federal t_q^f	State and local t_q^s
1970	0.5198	0.4920	0.0546
1971	0.5089	0.4800	0.0555
1972	0.5114	0.4800	0.0604
1973	0.5100	0.4800	0.0576
1974	0.5118	0.4800	0.0612
1975	0.5140	0.4800	0.0654
1976	0.5151	0.4800	0.0675
1977	0.5164	0.4800	0.0701
1978	0.5135	0.4800	0.0645
1979	0.4955	0.4600	0.0657
1980	0.4991	0.4600	0.0724
1981	0.5017	0.4600	0.0773
1982	0.5078	0.4600	0.0885
1983	0.5066	0.4600	0.0863
1984	0.5058	0.4600	0.0847
1985	0.5082	0.4600	0.0892
1986	0.5198	0.4600	0.1108
1987	0.3882	0.3400	0.0730
1988	0.3887	0.3400	0.0738
1989	0.3833	0.3400	0.0657
1990	0.3802	0.3400	0.0609
1991	0.3849	0.3400	0.0681
1992	0.3831	0.3400	0.0654
1993	0.3914	0.3500	0.0637
1994	0.3907	0.3500	0.0626
1995	0.3867	0.3500	0.0564
1996	0.3880	0.3500	0.0585

Note: For derivation of t_q and t_q^s, see text.

than accrual, so that we must adjust the effective tax on accrued capital gains for the effects of tax deferral. We assume that deferral reduces this rate by 50 percent. Thus the effective marginal tax rate on accrued capital gains was 15 percent until 1978 and 14 percent thereafter. This rate is adjusted upward to obtain the overall tax rate at both federal and state and local levels. We multiply the federal rate t_q^{gqf} by the ratio of the corporate income tax rate t_q in equation (3.1) to the federal corporate income tax rate t_q^f.

We next consider the estimation of the average marginal tax rates on income to holders of debt and equity under the individual income

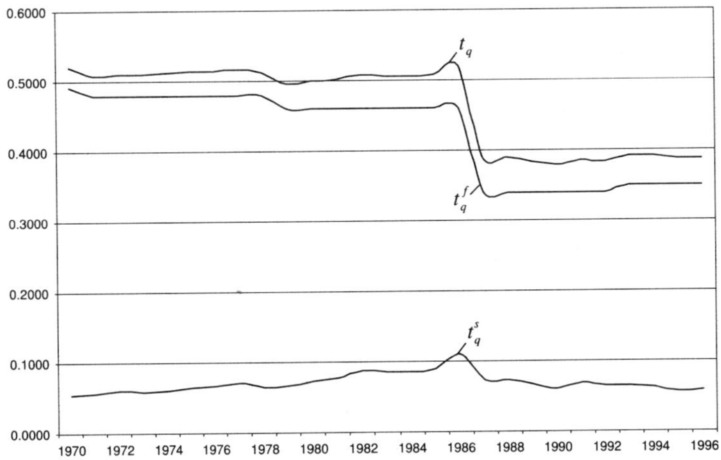

Notes: t_q: Federal, state, and local (estimated); t_q^f: Federal (statutory rate); t_q^s: State and local (estimated)

Figure 3.1
Corporate income tax rates.

tax. We distinguish among three alternative forms of ownership by individuals in estimating average marginal tax rates for different types of income from capital.[1] These are households, tax exempt institutions, and insurance companies. The financial institutions in these ownership categories provide legal channels through which individuals own claims on the assets employed in the private sector of the U.S. economy.

The household ownership category includes individuals and financial institutions. These institutions include commercial banks, savings institutions—such as savings and loan associations, mutual savings banks, and credit unions—mutual funds, mortgage pools, finance companies, and real estate investment trusts. Demand deposits in commercial banks and savings institutions generate nontaxable returns in the form of financial services. The tax exempt ownership category includes private pension funds, the pension business of life insurance companies, nonprofit institutions, and state and local government retirement funds. The final ownership category is insurance companies, which are subject to special provisions for income taxation described in more detail below.

In order to estimate average marginal tax rates for returns to debt and equity, we utilize the distribution of adjusted gross income (AGI)

Table 3.2
Distribution of adjusted gross income (AGI), 1995 (%, millions of dollars)

Marginal tax rate	Adjusted gross income
15.0[1]	1,630,314
28.0	1,434,927
28.0[2]	67,472
31.0	314,728
36.0	213,369
39.6	431,303
39.6[3]	1,797
Total	4,093,910

Notes:
[1]Includes children's interest and dividends reported by parents in Form 8814.
[2]Capital gains.
[3]Children's investment income taxed at the parent's rate if the parents rate is higher than the child's rate (Form 8615).
Source: *Statistics of Income: Individual Income Tax Returns*, 1995, Internal Revenue Service, 1998.

across brackets associated with different marginal tax rates at the federal level. We also consider the distribution of dividends and interest received across these income brackets. We assign weights to different marginal tax rates in proportion to dividends or interest received by individuals in the corresponding income brackets. We then take a weighted average of marginal tax rates to obtain the average marginal tax rate at the federal level.[2]

As an illustration, we consider the calculation of the average marginal tax rate for 1995. In table 3.2 we present the distribution of AGI across income brackets corresponding to different marginal tax rates at the federal level. Table 3.3 gives the distribution of this income and the associated distributions of interest and dividends received. The distribution of wages and salaries will be used below in calculating the average marginal tax rate on labor income. The total in table 3.2 is less than that in table 3.3, since table 3.2 excludes tax returns with income below the amount exempt from tax, including those with a deficit. To eliminate this discrepancy we first compute the total of positive AGI in all returns by adding the deficits to total income. Then we calculate the total of positive AGI in nontaxable

Table 3.3
Distribution of AGI, wages and salaries, interest, and dividends, 1995 (millions of dollars)

Size of AGI (thousand $)	AGI Less deficit	Salaries and wages	Interest	Dividends
All returns	4,189,354	3,201,457	203,299	94,592
no AGI	–55,254	7,019	4,759	1,063
under 5	37,605	32,697	2,875	1,483
5–10	104,603	78,275	7,029	2,457
10–15	169,317	125,644	10,270	3,141
15–20	198,418	151,480	11,651	3,328
20–25	223,400	182,785	8,158	2,959
25–30	215,200	174,597	8,171	3,040
30–40	430,491	363,703	14,248	4,957
40–50	406,639	338,902	12,701	5,128
50–75	828,349	685,129	26,239	12,690
75–100	458,506	371,177	16,491	8,228
100–200	532,030	384,653	26,895	15,335
200–500	292,118	174,551	20,543	11,203
500–1000	120,347	60,204	10,151	5,841
1000 or more	227,583	70,641	23,117	13,740

Source: *Statistics of Income: Individual Income Tax Returns*, 1995, Internal Revenue Service, 1998.

returns by subtracting total income in table 3.2 from the total of positive income in all returns.

We assign the total of positive AGI in the nontaxable returns to the zero marginal tax rate bracket in table 3.3. This involves allocating the income in the first two size categories given in table 3.3 to the zero tax bracket. At this point, the total of the remaining positive income in table 3.3 is equal to the total income in table 3.2. The next step is to fill the tax brackets corresponding to positive marginal tax rates with the remaining positive income in table 3.3. We assume that the distributions of income from taxable returns and from all returns are monotone in the marginal tax rates. Next we allocate the interest and dividends received in table 3.3 to each of the tax brackets in proportion to AGI. Interest and dividends received from returns with a deficit are allocated to the tax bracket with a zero marginal tax rate.

Finally, state and local individual income taxes are deductible from revenue in defining income for federal tax purposes. We adjust the federal tax rates for state and local individual income taxes to obtain the average marginal tax rate at both levels. For this purpose we

Table 3.4
Average marginal tax rates on interest and dividends

	Interest		Dividends	
Year	Federal (t_p^{df})	Federal, state, and local (t_p^d)	Federal (t_p^{ef})	Federal, state, and local (t_p^e)
1970	0.2585	0.2814	0.3874	0.4152
1971	0.2460	0.2720	0.3779	0.4101
1972	0.2508	0.2809	0.3815	0.4185
1973	0.2596	0.2912	0.3942	0.4326
1974	0.2714	0.3019	0.4044	0.4407
1975	0.2691	0.3037	0.4094	0.4508
1976	0.2756	0.3106	0.4196	0.4612
1977	0.2803	0.3158	0.4213	0.4632
1978	0.2796	0.3146	0.4190	0.4603
1979	0.2959	0.3292	0.4383	0.4768
1980	0.3144	0.3489	0.4496	0.4883
1981	0.3240	0.3578	0.4370	0.4743
1982	0.2886	0.3225	0.3711	0.4092
1983	0.2607	0.2975	0.3517	0.3945
1984	0.2595	0.2996	0.3458	0.3922
1985	0.2621	0.3009	0.3410	0.3854
1986	0.2560	0.2958	0.3479	0.3944
1987	0.2419	0.2799	0.2779	0.3192
1988	0.2193	0.2555	0.2452	0.2841
1989	0.2248	0.2619	0.2474	0.2869
1990	0.2236	0.2608	0.2455	0.2850
1991	0.2219	0.2609	0.2460	0.2877
1992	0.2196	0.2598	0.2448	0.2879
1993	0.2398	0.2819	0.2625	0.3069
1994	0.2425	0.2843	0.2635	0.3075
1995	0.2484	0.2904	0.2718	0.3161
1996	0.2484	0.2879	0.2717	0.3134

Source: *Statistics of Income Bulletin*, *Statistics of Income*, various issues.

multiply the federal tax rates by the ratio of the sum of federal and state and local individual income tax revenues to federal income tax revenue, adjusted for the investment tax credit and the deductibility of state and local income taxes. The resulting average marginal tax rates are given in columns 2 and 4 of table 3.4 and figure 3.2 for the federal income tax and columns 3 and 5 of this table for federal and state and local income taxes combined.

Capital gains on corporate equities held by households are subject to taxation only when the gains are realized and not when they are

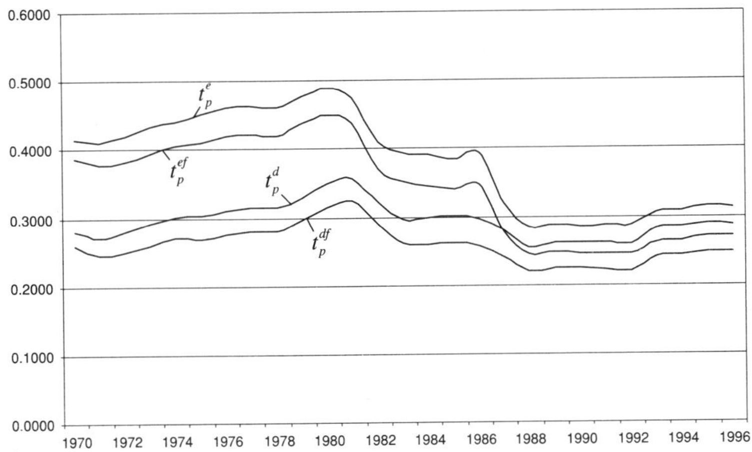

Notes: t_p^e: Tax rate on dividends, federal, state, and local; t_p^{ef}: Tax rate on dividends, federal; t_p^d: Tax rate on interest, federal, state, and local; t_p^{df}: Tax rate on interest, federal

Figure 3.2
Average marginal tax rates on interest and dividends.

accrued. Until 1978, 50 percent of net capital gains, defined as long-term gains less short-term losses, were excluded from income for tax purposes. After 1978, 60 percent of net capital gains were excluded from income. The Tax Reform Act of 1986 abolished this exclusion. We assume that deferral of tax liabilities due to taxation of realized capital gains reduces the effective tax rate on accrued capital gains by 50 percent.[3] Second, we assume that elimination of tax liabilities for capital gains prior to the death of the owner of assets included in a bequest reduces the effective tax rate by an additional 50 percent. Under these assumptions the effective tax rate on capital gains t_h^{gq} is

$$t_h^{gq} = 0.25(1 - E)t_h^{eq}, \tag{3.2}$$

were E is the proportion of net capital gains excluded for individual income tax purposes, and t_h^{eq} is the average marginal tax rate on individual income in the form of corporate dividends, adjusted for non-taxable services of commercial and savings banks described below.

We have now completed the discussion of corporate and individual income tax rates. Tax exempt owners include private pension funds, the pension business of life insurance companies, state and local government retirement funds, and nonprofit institutions. Although income received by pension funds is not tax exempt, the returns to assets held in the pension funds are not taxable until they are distributed to the beneficiary. Deferral of taxes and the possibility of low tax rates after retirement reduce the effective rate of taxation on these returns to negligible levels, so that we assume that returns to assets held by pension funds are tax-free. A similar argument applies to the assets held by the state and local government retirement funds.[4]

The final ownership category for assets owned by individuals consists of insurance companies. Under the Life Insurance Income Tax Act of 1959 the income of life insurance companies was taxed in two phases. First, taxable income was defined as the lesser of the gain from operations and investment income. Second, if the gain from operations exceeded investment income, one-half of the excess was taxable. Since gains from operations are approximately equal to the total of investment income and income from underwriting, a company subject to excess taxation was taxed on the sum of its investment income and one-half of its underwriting income. The remaining half of the excess became part of the policyholders' surplus account. This was taxed only when distributed to stockholders or upon dissolution of the company.

The Deficit Reduction Act of 1984 (DEFRA) repealed the provisions of the 1959 Act. Under DEFRA taxation of life insurance companies was consolidated into a single phase. Compared to prior law, as amended by the Tax Equity and Fiscal Responsibility Act of 1982 (TEFRA), this change increased the taxable income of insurance companies substantially. In order to shield insurance companies from a sudden and substantial increase in taxes, DEFRA allowed a special life insurance company deduction for 20 percent of taxable income. This special deduction was repealed in the Tax Reform Act of 1986.

We assume that dividends and interest received by life insurance companies were taxed under the 1959 Act on gross investment income. Taxable income is the sum of interest, dividends, rents, short-term capital gains, less investment expenses, income on reserves necessary to meet future insurance obligations, the company's share of tax-exempt interest, and 85 percent of intercorporate dividends, reduced to 80 percent by the Tax Reform Act of 1986. Deductions of income on reserves was determined by the "10-for-1" Menge formula, $iR^*(1-10(i-i^*))$, where i is the company's adjusted reserve rate in decimal fraction, R^* is the reserve required to meet future insurance obligations, and i^* is the rate of return in decimal fraction assumed in determining the required reserve, R^*.[5] Thus the tax liability is $t_q[iR - iR^*(1 - 10(i - i^*))]$, where R is the total assets of the company.

We assume that total assets of an insurance company are equal to the reserves required to meet future insurance obligations. Under this assumption the marginal tax rate on interest income from one dollar's worth of additional assets is $10t_q(i - i^*)$. Since the assumed rate of return has been three percent, we estimate the marginal tax rate on interest received by life insurance companies to be $t_{LI}^d = 10t_q(i - 0.03)$, through 1981, $t_{LI}^d = t_q(1 - 0.9^{100(i-0.03)})$ for 1982–1983 and 1987–1996, and $t_{LI}^d = t_q(1 - 0.9^{100(i-0.03)})(1 - 0.2)$ for 1984–1986, where i is set equal to the interest rate on Baa class corporate bonds. We assume further that the company's share of intercorporate dividends is the same as the corresponding share of interest. We estimate that the marginal tax rate on dividends received by the life insurance companies is $10t_q(i - 0.03)(1 - \text{ICDD})$,[6] where ICDD is the rate of the intercorporate dividend deduction, 0.85 until 1986 and 0.80 from 1987 to 1996.

In summary, we estimate that the marginal tax rate for interest income was $10t_q(i - 0.03)$ for 1958–1981. We calculate the marginal tax rates using the geometric version of the Menge formula for 1982–1986. The marginal tax rate on interest is calculated according to the formula $t_q(1 - 0.9^{100*(i-0.03)})$ for 1982–1983 and 1987–1996 and $t_q(1 - 0.9^{100*(i-0.03)})(1 - 0.2)$ for 1984–1986. The marginal tax rate on dividends is adjusted for the intercorporate dividend deduction on the company's share. We set the marginal tax rate on dividends equal to 15 percent of the marginal tax rate on interest income for the period of 1970–1986 and 20 percent for 1987–1996.

Non-life insurance companies are taxed like other corporations. The marginal tax rate on interest received by non-life insurance companies is $t_{OI}^d = t_q$. The marginal tax rate for dividend income t_{OI}^e is estimated to be $(1 - 0.85)t_q$ for 1970–1986 and $(1 - 0.80)t_q$ for 1987–1996, due to the deduction for intercorporate dividends. The marginal tax rate on capital gains is the same as for insurance companies as for other corporations. We have ignored the tax liabilities that might arise at the individual level when benefits are distributed to the insured. This reflects the effects of tax deferral, lower personal tax rates after retirement, and the possibility of death of the insured in the case of life insurance companies. We have now completed the derivation of marginal tax rates at the corporate and individual levels for all three categories of ownership.

Table 3.5
Ownership distribution of corporate equity (billions of dollars)

Year	Total	Households	Tax-exempt institutions	Insurance companies
1970	724.3	579.0	121.2	24.1
1971	849.1	662.5	155.2	31.4
1972	1054.1	818.4	194.7	41.0
1973	805.7	604.5	163.2	38.0
1974	534.8	383.0	123.8	28.0
1975	717.0	507.7	176.2	33.0
1976	891.5	640.3	212.3	38.9
1977	787.2	545.8	203.8	37.5
1978	830.0	553.0	236.3	40.7
1979	996.3	672.5	276.5	47.3
1980	1300.9	891.0	352.3	57.6
1981	1199.4	797.6	345.4	56.4
1982	1361.2	865.5	431.8	63.8
1983	1617.1	997.7	543.2	76.1
1984	1563.2	938.5	554.8	69.9
1985	1996.8	1171.6	732.3	92.9
1986	2381.0	1494.3	791.5	95.2
1987	2405.9	1485.7	818.6	101.6
1988	2716.0	1734.5	872.8	108.7
1989	3331.0	2108.3	1095.9	126.8
1990	3088.5	1928.9	1042.2	117.3
1991	4312.4	2740.7	1419.3	152.4
1992	4889.6	3156.6	1572.6	160.4
1993	5669.6	3641.4	1844.9	183.3
1994	5670.9	3598.5	1862.7	209.8
1995	7573.0	4877.2	2430.4	265.5
1996	9167.7	5857.5	3003.7	306.5

Source: Board of Governors of the Federal Reserve System, *Flow of Funds Accounts*.

3.2 Distribution of Assets

Our next objective is to determine the distribution of corporate equity among the institutions through which individuals own claims on these assets. We also determine the distribution of debt for households, noncorporate and corporate businesses, and the government sector. For this purpose we utilize data from the U.S. Flow of Funds Accounts. These Accounts provide the distribution of corporate equity among the various ownership categories. However the "Households" sector includes both individuals and nonprofit institutions.

We allocate seven percent of the corporate equity held by households to nonprofit institutions.[7] Corporate equity held by life insur-

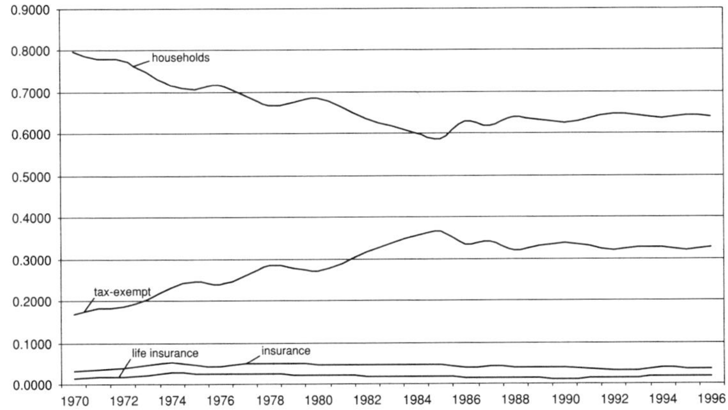

Figure 3.3
Ownership distribution of corporate equity.

ance companies must be divided between insurance business and pension business. We allocate the corporate equity held by life insurance companies in proportion to pension and life insurance reserves. Table 3.5 shows the ownership distribution of corporate equity and figure 3.3 and table A3.1 (see appendix) show the ownership composition of corporate equity. Table A3.2 (see appendix) breaks down the equity held by the households into equity held by individuals, commercial banks, savings institutions, and mutual funds.

Data from the Flow of Fund Accounts include the assets and liabilities of corporate and noncorporate sectors of nonfarm nonfinancial business and farm businesses. These accounts do not provide a breakdown of farm businesses between corporate and noncorporate sectors, so that we allocate the assets and liabilities of farm businesses between corporate and noncorporate sectors in proportion to depreciable capital stocks in the two farm sectors. We estimate the stocks of depreciable capital for corporate and noncorporate farm businesses, using investment data from the Bureau of Economic Analysis described in more detail in section 3.4 below.

Corporate financial assets include demand deposits and currency, time deposits, security repurchase agreements, U.S. government securities, state and local government obligations, commercial paper, consumer credit, trade credit, and miscellaneous assets. Liabilities include corporate bonds (including tax exempt bonds), mortgages—home, multi-family, commercial, and farm—bank loans, commercial paper,

Table 3.6
Ownership distribution of corporate net debt (billions of dollars)

Year	Total	Households	Tax-exempt institutions	Insurance companies
1970	292.5	145.8	77.6	69.1
1971	314.0	159.3	82.7	72.1
1972	343.0	179.7	89.4	74.0
1973	399.0	216.8	99.8	82.4
1974	446.8	252.6	108.1	86.1
1975	459.2	245.7	123.3	90.3
1976	484.2	253.4	132.8	98.1
1977	546.5	276.1	156.6	113.8
1978	606.5	296.3	185.4	124.8
1979	673.8	331.6	211.2	131.0
1980	728.1	346.3	249.3	132.5
1981	827.2	405.6	282.7	138.9
1982	872.1	422.8	315.1	134.2
1983	943.0	471.8	337.4	133.8
1984	1100.1	579.4	381.7	139.0
1985	1233.1	684.2	364.9	184.0
1986	1417.3	806.1	415.7	195.5
1987	1579.2	926.4	425.6	227.2
1988	1734.7	999.8	489.8	245.1
1989	1893.3	1081.4	547.5	264.4
1990	1947.4	1098.5	579.3	269.6
1991	1930.1	1096.8	560.5	272.8
1992	1950.4	1071.1	606.3	273.0
1993	1968.5	1064.2	630.6	273.7
1994	2067.0	1123.1	655.5	288.4
1995	2227.5	1240.2	687.8	299.5
1996	2332.1	1278.3	723.9	329.9

Source: See table 3.5.

banker's acceptances, finance company loans, U.S. government loans, trade debt and miscellaneous liabilities.

In computing the distribution of corporate net debt we exclude government securities and loans, net trade credit, and miscellaneous assets and liabilities. We then determine the distribution of each category of assets and liabilities among the ownership categories. On the asset side we allocate demand deposits and currency between the liabilities of commercial banks and savings institutions in proportion to the relative shares of total demand deposits and currency held in commercial banks and savings institutions. We allocate time deposits between these two ownership categories in the same way. We allocate

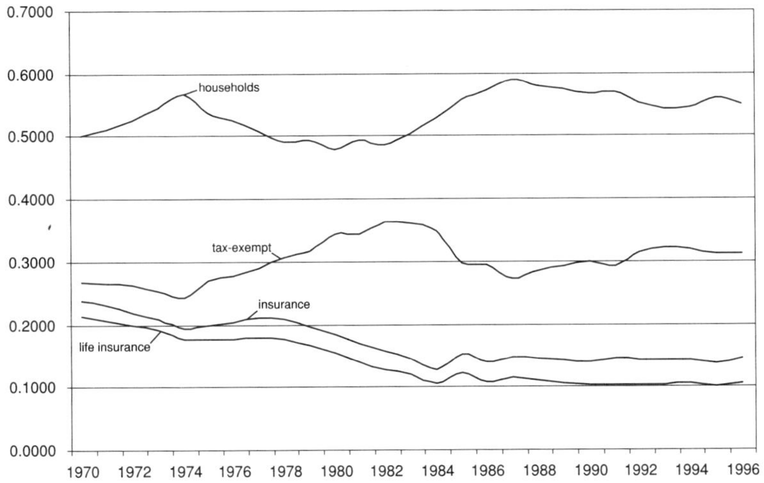

Figure 3.4
Ownership distribution of corporate net debt.

commercial paper to finance companies and consumer credit to individuals.

On the liabilities side we allocate corporate bonds, including a small amount of tax exempt bonds, in proportion to the distribution of corporate and foreign bonds among households, savings institutions, life insurance companies, pension funds, state and local government retirement funds, other insurance companies, and mutual funds. Similarly, we allocate the four types of mortgages among households, mortgage pools, commercial banks, savings institutions, life insurance companies, private pension funds, state and local government retirement funds, finance companies, and real estate investment trusts.

Since nonprofit institutions hold a very small fraction of corporate debt, we allocate the entire corporate debt held by the "Households" sector of the Flow of Funds Accounts to individuals. The debt allocated to insurance companies is further divided between life insurance business and pension business in proportion to the reserves attributable to the two businesses. Finally, we allocate bank loans and banker's acceptances to commercial banks and we allocate commercial paper and finance company loans to finance companies. Whenever the net liability of an ownership category is negative we replace the value of net debt with zero and assign zero weight to it. The

Table 3.7
Ownership distribution of noncorporate net debt (billions of dollars)

Year	Total	Households	Tax-exempt institutions	Insurance companies
1970	122.5	86.8	11.9	23.8
1971	144.7	105.8	13.3	25.7
1972	175.4	133.2	14.6	27.7
1973	197.0	155.5	14.5	27.0
1974	234.8	185.1	17.4	32.2
1975	252.7	198.0	20.4	34.3
1976	274.8	217.0	23.2	34.6
1977	305.8	243.9	26.0	36.0
1978	350.4	280.9	30.7	38.8
1979	414.6	331.5	38.8	44.2
1980	470.4	369.5	50.0	50.9
1981	512.0	399.9	58.7	53.4
1982	581.4	444.1	77.7	59.5
1983	640.6	498.0	85.0	57.6
1984	736.0	584.7	94.0	57.3
1985	828.6	651.1	100.2	77.3
1986	898.5	709.0	112.1	77.4
1987	939.5	750.2	109.5	79.7
1988	1005.2	794.4	130.3	80.5
1989	1067.9	845.2	141.1	81.6
1990	1075.4	837.8	154.1	83.4
1991	1064.1	830.8	152.1	81.2
1992	1045.5	828.5	143.5	73.5
1993	1043.1	843.1	134.2	65.7
1994	1038.7	853.4	124.4	60.9
1995	1056.2	880.9	119.7	55.5
1996	1096.3	929.9	112.8	53.6

Source: See table 3.5.

results are shown in table 3.6, figure 3.4 and table A3.3 (see appendix) show the ownership composition of corporate net debt and table A3.4 (see appendix) gives the corporate net debt held by individuals and financial institutions through which households own corporate net debt.

Assets of the noncorporate sector include demand deposits and currency, consumer credit, trade credit, and miscellaneous assets. Liabilities include mortgages—home, multi-family, commercial, and farm—bank loans, U.S. government loans, trade debt, and miscellaneous liabilities. We exclude government liabilities, net trade debt and miscellaneous assets and liabilities. We follow the same procedures for allocating noncorporate net debt among ownership categories as for

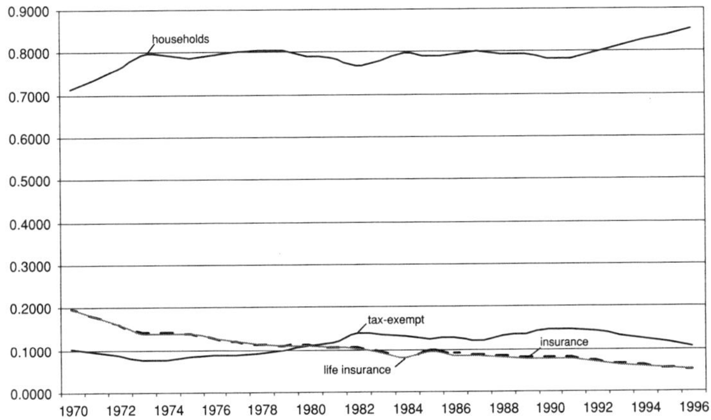

Figure 3.5
Ownership distribution of noncorporate net debt.

corporate net debt. When an ownership category shows a net asset position or negative net debt, we set net debt equal to zero and assign zero weight to it. The results are shown in tables 3.7, A3.5, A3.6 (see appendix), and figure 3.5. Finally, we employ the same procedures for allocating government net debt among ownership categories. The results are shown in tables 3.8, A3.7, A3.8 (see appendix), and figure 3.6.

Household assets include demand deposits and currency, time and savings deposits, money market fund shares, U.S. government securities, corporate bonds, mortgages, corporate equities, life insurance and pension reserves, and miscellaneous assets. Household liabilities include home mortgages, consumer installment credit, bank loans, trade debt, and miscellaneous liabilities. Among these assets and liabilities we consider consumer installment credit and mortgages as most relevant to the financing of household assets. We include the credit obtained from commercial banks, savings and loan associations, mutual savings banks, credit unions, and finance companies in consumer installment credit and exclude the credit obtained from the nonfinancial corporate and nonfarm noncorporate business.

Mortgages, which include home mortgages and small amounts of other mortgages, are allocated among individuals, mortgage pools, commercial banks, savings institutions, life insurance companies, mutual funds, state and local government retirement funds, finance companies, and real estate investment trusts in proportion to the

Table 3.8
Ownership distribution of government securities (billions of dollars)

Year	Total	Households	Tax-exempt institutions	Insurance companies
1970	203.3	177.9	17.0	8.5
1971	203.0	179.7	14.9	8.4
1972	213.6	187.3	17.8	8.5
1973	224.8	194.9	21.6	8.3
1974	241.1	205.3	27.0	8.7
1975	302.3	255.2	34.8	12.2
1976	337.8	277.2	44.4	16.2
1977	361.8	285.5	56.3	20.0
1978	382.9	293.9	66.8	22.2
1979	459.1	349.4	84.8	24.9
1980	547.4	409.8	109.9	27.7
1981	616.1	443.7	140.2	32.1
1982	792.5	544.4	208.6	39.5
1983	987.3	669.3	265.4	52.6
1984	1158.4	759.9	328.7	69.8
1985	1310.1	820.0	390.0	100.1
1986	1503.9	976.7	409.3	117.9
1987	1691.5	1108.1	453.8	129.6
1988	1844.4	1213.5	492.3	138.6
1989	1934.3	1205.6	570.0	158.8
1990	2254.8	1415.3	659.8	179.8
1991	2527.1	1561.1	729.4	236.6
1992	2880.3	1861.0	765.9	253.4
1993	3107.4	1985.1	835.7	286.6
1994	3504.2	2306.5	896.5	301.2
1995	3576.0	2315.2	956.1	304.7
1996	3718.4	2441.5	983.1	293.7

Source: See table 3.5.

distribution of home mortgages. Mortgages allocated to life insurance companies are further divided between the life insurance reserves and pension funds reserves. The results are presented in tables 3.9, A3.9, A3.10 (see appendix) and figure 3.7.

Our next objective is to calculate averages of the marginal tax rates for households, tax exempt institutions and insurance companies. First, we adjust the marginal tax rate on the assets held by households

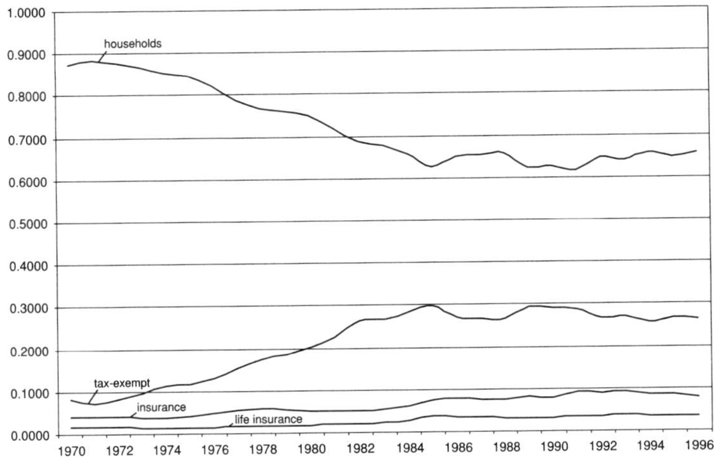

Figure 3.6
Ownership distribution of government securities.

for the fact that demand deposits and currency held in the commercial banks and savings institutions yield returns in the form of services that are not taxable. Commercial banks and savings institutions hold only a minuscule amount of corporate equity, but they hold substantial amounts of corporate, noncorporate, household, and government debt. We adjust the marginal tax rates for the assets held by households through these two financial institutions.

We first calculate the ratio of currency and demand deposits held in commercial banks to the total liabilities of the commercial banks. We assume that this ratio represents the proportion of debt held in commercial banks and balanced by liabilities of commercial banks in the form of demand deposits. We adjust the marginal tax rate on dividends and interest received by individuals for demand deposits and currency held in commercial banks to obtain the marginal tax rate of the entire household ownership category. We make a similar adjustment for demand deposits held in savings institutions.

Specifically, for the marginal tax rate on dividends received by households we make the following adjustment

$$t_h^{eq} = t_p^e\left(1 - \frac{E_b^q R_b + E_s^q R_s}{E_h^q}\right),$$

where t_p^e is the marginal individual tax rate on dividends, E_b^q and E_s^q

Table 3.9
Ownership distribution of household net debt (billions of dollars)

Year	Total	Households	Tax-exempt institutions	Insurance companies
1970	399.3	365.3	12.3	21.8
1971	435.9	404.6	11.7	19.5
1972	490.9	462.8	10.9	17.2
1973	553.0	527.1	10.3	15.6
1974	591.9	567.3	10.1	14.5
1975	633.4	610.4	9.9	13.1
1976	714.0	693.0	9.7	11.3
1977	840.1	820.6	9.6	10.0
1978	991.8	972.2	10.1	9.5
1979	1146.9	1124.5	12.1	10.3
1980	1245.6	1220.1	14.6	10.9
1981	1331.5	1306.0	15.4	10.1
1982	1381.3	1354.0	18.1	9.1
1983	1523.2	1498.4	17.0	7.8
1984	1733.8	1708.8	18.2	6.8
1985	2003.3	1979.3	17.0	7.0
1986	2254.2	2231.5	16.2	6.5
1987	2505.1	2484.6	13.7	6.8
1988	2773.1	2753.3	14.5	5.3
1989	2993.5	2969.8	18.2	5.5
1990	3235.7	3210.8	19.3	5.6
1991	3380.3	3359.0	16.7	4.6
1992	3532.5	3511.4	16.2	4.8
1993	3734.9	3716.8	14.4	3.6
1994	4021.2	4004.4	13.9	2.9
1995	4287.5	4269.5	15.0	3.0
1996	4569.2	4550.8	15.6	2.9

Source: See table 3.5.

are corporate equity held through commercial banks and savings institutions, E_h^q is the corporate equity held in the household ownership category, R_b and R_s are the ratios of checkable deposits plus currency and total liabilities in commercial banks and savings institutions, respectively.

We make similar adjustments for the marginal tax rate on interest received by the household ownership category, namely,

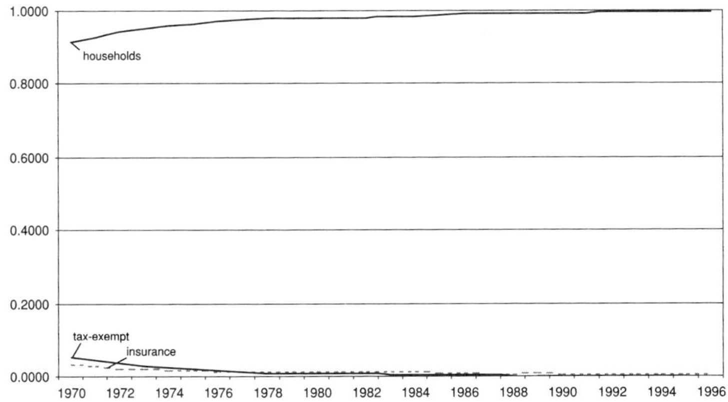

Note: Insurance companies include life insurance companies only.

Figure 3.7
Ownership distribution of household net debt.

$$t_h^{dq} = t_p^d\left(1 - \frac{B_b^q R_b + B_s^q R_s}{B_h^q}\right),$$

$$t_h^{dm} = t_p^d\left(1 - \frac{B_b^m R_b + B_s^m R_s}{B_h^m}\right),$$

$$t_h^{dh} = t_p^d\left(1 - \frac{B_b^h R_b + B_s^h R_s}{B_h^h}\right),$$

and

$$t_h^{dg} = t_p^d\left(1 - \frac{B_b^g R_b + B_s^g R_s}{B_h^g}\right).$$

In these formulas t_p^d is the marginal individual tax rate on interest received. The debt of sector i held through commercial banks and savings institutions is B_b^i and B_s^i, respectively, and the debt of sector i held by the household ownership category is B_h^i. The subscript i runs through corporate, noncorporate, household, and government sectors. Table 3.10 and figure 3.8 show the average marginal tax rates on dividends and interest income received by households.

We next calculate average marginal tax rates for returns to corporate equity and the debt of corporate, noncorporate, household, and government sectors. We combine the distribution of the financial

Table 3.10
Average marginal tax rates on household income

Year	Corporate dividends t_h^{eq}	Corporate interest t_h^{dq}	Noncorporate interest t_h^{dm}	Household interest t_h^{dh}	Government interest t_h^{dg}
1970	0.4152	0.2262	0.2548	0.2496	0.2369
1971	0.4101	0.2223	0.2475	0.2424	0.2282
1972	0.4185	0.2310	0.2556	0.2512	0.2364
1973	0.4326	0.2419	0.2623	0.2621	0.2508
1974	0.4407	0.2541	0.2715	0.2745	0.2656
1975	0.4508	0.2611	0.2732	0.2772	0.2642
1976	0.4611	0.2710	0.2795	0.2848	0.2686
1977	0.4631	0.2750	0.2846	0.2902	0.2761
1978	0.4603	0.2746	0.2838	0.2901	0.2786
1979	0.4767	0.2863	0.2966	0.3044	0.2964
1980	0.4883	0.3035	0.3162	0.3250	0.3158
1981	0.4743	0.3145	0.3230	0.3335	0.3255
1982	0.4092	0.2814	0.2912	0.3006	0.2955
1983	0.3944	0.2601	0.2703	0.2777	0.2729
1984	0.3922	0.2649	0.2717	0.2797	0.2780
1985	0.3853	0.2698	0.2719	0.2810	0.2800
1986	0.3943	0.2613	0.2629	0.2750	0.2729
1987	0.3191	0.2510	0.2502	0.2620	0.2603
1988	0.2840	0.2307	0.2294	0.2393	0.2389
1989	0.2867	0.2393	0.2365	0.2462	0.2451
1990	0.2849	0.2396	0.2348	0.2454	0.2449
1991	0.2875	0.2413	0.2325	0.2444	0.2425
1992	0.2877	0.2396	0.2288	0.2423	0.2397
1993	0.3068	0.2610	0.2476	0.2618	0.2586
1994	0.3073	0.2645	0.2525	0.2653	0.2662
1995	0.3159	0.2726	0.2604	0.2721	0.2730
1996	0.3133	0.2719	0.2606	0.2702	0.2723

assets across the various ownership categories and the marginal tax rates for each ownership category on dividends, interest, and capital gains on corporate equity. The average marginal tax rate on dividends t_q^e is a weighted average of the marginal tax rates on dividends for households, life insurance companies, other insurance companies and tax exempt owners,

$$t_q^e = w_h^{eq} t_h^{eq} + w_{LI}^{eq} t_{LI}^e + t_{OI}^{eq} t_{OI}^e ,$$

where the marginal tax rate of the tax exempt institutions is zero by definition. In this formula the weights w_i^{eq} are the proportions of corporate equity held by sector i, where the subscript i runs through household, life insurance, and other insurance companies.

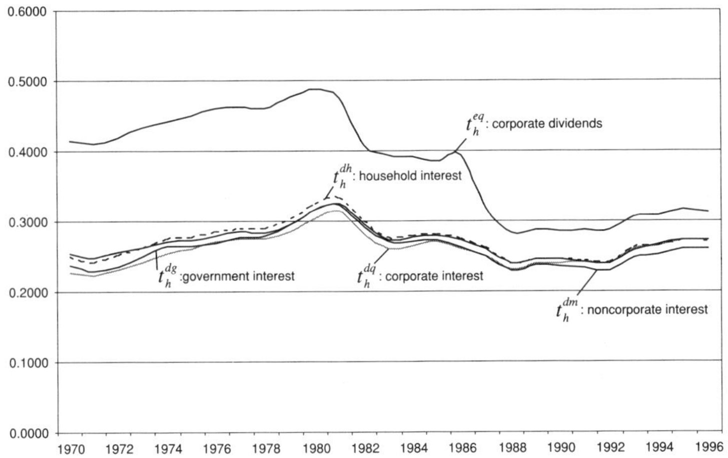

Figure 3.8
Average marginal tax rates on household income.

We calculate average marginal tax rates on corporate capital gains and interest income from corporate, noncorporate, household, and government debt in the same way. The average marginal tax rate on corporate capital gains t_q^g is a weighted average of the marginal tax rates on capital gains

$$t_q^g = w_h^{eq} t_h^{gq} + (w_{LI}^{eq} + w_{OI}^{eq}) t_q^{gq} \ .$$

The average marginal tax rate on corporate interest t_q^d is a weighted average of the marginal tax rates on interest income from corporate debt

$$t_q^d = w_h^{dq} t_h^{dq} + w_{LI}^{dq} t_{LI}^d + w_{OI}^{dq} t_{OI}^d \ .$$

The weights are the proportions of corporate debt held by each ownership category. The expressions for the average marginal tax rates on noncorporate, household, and government interest income are strictly analogous.

We do not have separate estimates of average marginal tax rates on returns to noncorporate equity. We assume that the average marginal tax rate on income from noncorporate equity is the same as the rate on interest income accruing to individuals given in table 3.4, i.e., $t_m^e = t_p^d$. While income from household equity is not subject to tax, household interest and property tax payments are deductible from revenue under the individual income tax. We take the average marginal tax rate for these deductions to be the same as the rate on interest income, i.e., $t_h^e = t_p^d$.

The accrual based average marginal tax rate on capital gains on noncorporate equity is set at one quarter of the tax rate on other income on noncorporate equity:

$$t_m^g = 0.25(1 - E)t_m^e\ , \qquad (3.3)$$

where E is the proportion of net capital gains excluded for individual income tax purposes. We set the marginal tax rate of capital gains on household equity at zero, i.e., $t_h^g = 0$. The generous "roll over" provisions for capital gains on owner-occupied residential real estate and the effects of tax deferral combine to lower the effective tax rate on these capital gains virtually to zero. Average marginal tax rates for all forms of income from capital are summarized in tables 3.11, 3.12, and 3.13 and figures 3.9, 3.10 and 3.11.

In the household sector property taxes include taxes on owner-occupied farm and nonfarm dwellings, automobile use taxes, state and local personal motor vehicle licenses, state and local personal property taxes, and other state and local personal taxes. Noncorporate property taxes include state and local noncorporate business property taxes, the noncorporate part of the state and local business motor vehicle licenses, and the noncorporate part of other state and local business taxes. Finally, corporate property taxes include the corporate part of state and local business property taxes, state and local business motor vehicle licenses, and the other state and local taxes. Average property tax rates for all three sectors are shown in table 3.14 and figure 3.12.

3.3 Vintage Price Functions

Perfect substitutability among durable goods of different vintages implies the existence of a *vintage price function,* for each durable good. This presents the price of acquisition as a function of age or vintage and the price of a new durable good of the same type, expressed as a

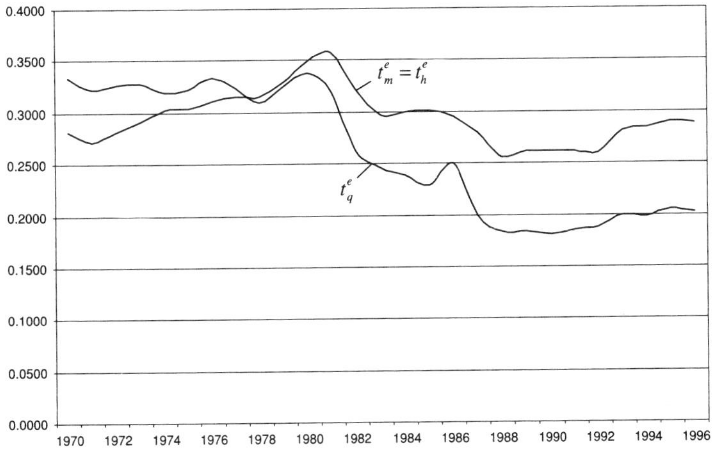

Notes: t_q^e: Corporate; t_m^e: Noncorporate; t_h^e: Household

Figure 3.9
Average marginal tax rates on equity income.

Table 3.11
Average marginal tax rates on equity income

Year	Corporate t_q^e	Noncorporate t_m^e	Household t_h^e
1970	0.3340	0.2814	0.2814
1971	0.3222	0.2720	0.2720
1972	0.3272	0.2809	0.2809
1973	0.3273	0.2912	0.2912
1974	0.3189	0.3019	0.3019
1975	0.3223	0.3037	0.3037
1976	0.3339	0.3106	0.3106
1977	0.3240	0.3158	0.3158
1978	0.3098	0.3146	0.3146
1979	0.3249	0.3292	0.3292
1980	0.3378	0.3489	0.3489
1981	0.3194	0.3578	0.3578
1982	0.2634	0.3225	0.3225
1983	0.2465	0.2975	0.2975
1984	0.2383	0.2996	0.2996
1985	0.2290	0.3009	0.3009
1986	0.2499	0.2958	0.2958
1987	0.1998	0.2799	0.2799
1988	0.1840	0.2555	0.2555
1989	0.1839	0.2619	0.2619
1990	0.1804	0.2608	0.2608

Table 3.11 (continued)

Year	Corporate t_q^e	Noncorporate t_m^e	Household t_h^e
1991	0.1849	0.2609	0.2609
1992	0.1877	0.2598	0.2598
1993	0.1989	0.2819	0.2819
1994	0.1972	0.2843	0.2843
1995	0.2055	0.2904	0.2904
1996	0.2020	0.2879	0.2879

Table 3.12
Average marginal tax rates on capital gains

Year	Corporate t_q^g	Noncorporate t_m^g	Household t_h^g
1970	0.0468	0.0352	0.0000
1971	0.0459	0.0340	0.0000
1972	0.0468	0.0351	0.0000
1973	0.0481	0.0364	0.0000
1974	0.0478	0.0377	0.0000
1975	0.0473	0.0380	0.0000
1976	0.0484	0.0388	0.0000
1977	0.0478	0.0395	0.0000
1978	0.0462	0.0393	0.0000
1979	0.0393	0.0329	0.0000
1980	0.0402	0.0349	0.0000
1981	0.0387	0.0358	0.0000
1982	0.0333	0.0323	0.0000
1983	0.0316	0.0298	0.0000
1984	0.0304	0.0300	0.0000
1985	0.0298	0.0301	0.0000
1986	0.0311	0.0296	0.0000
1987	0.0560	0.0700	0.0000
1988	0.0518	0.0639	0.0000
1989	0.0514	0.0655	0.0000
1990	0.0504	0.0652	0.0000
1991	0.0513	0.0652	0.0000
1992	0.0516	0.0649	0.0000
1993	0.0543	0.0705	0.0000
1994	0.0545	0.0711	0.0000
1995	0.0563	0.0726	0.0000
1996	0.0552	0.0720	0.0000

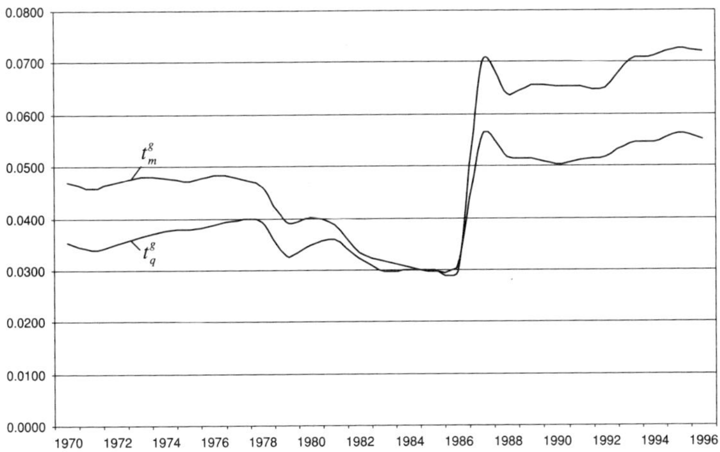

Notes: $t_h^g = 0.0$; t_q^g: Corporate; t_m^g: Noncorporate; t_h^g: Household

Figure 3.10
Average marginal tax rates on capital gains.

Table 3.13
Average marginal tax rates on interest income

Year	Corporate t_q^d	Noncorporate t_m^d	Households t_h^d	Government t_g^d
1970	0.1929	0.2424	0.2456	0.2255
1971	0.1833	0.2312	0.2377	0.2193
1972	0.1829	0.2358	0.2460	0.2238
1973	0.1908	0.2437	0.2573	0.2328
1974	0.2111	0.2598	0.2712	0.2424
1975	0.2193	0.2672	0.2752	0.2422
1976	0.2167	0.2645	0.2819	0.2426
1977	0.2095	0.2634	0.2871	0.2431
1978	0.2082	0.2645	0.2876	0.2404
1979	0.2186	0.2779	0.3018	0.2504
1980	0.2402	0.3059	0.3231	0.2623
1981	0.2594	0.3203	0.3321	0.2635
1982	0.1987	0.2617	0.2972	0.2256

Table 3.13 (continued)

Year	Corporate t_q^d	Noncorporate t_m^d	Households t_h^d	Government t_g^d
1983	0.1822	0.2411	0.2749	0.2078
1984	0.1802	0.2383	0.2768	0.2065
1985	0.1955	0.2387	0.2786	0.2048
1986	0.1892	0.2279	0.2729	0.2076
1987	0.1835	0.2186	0.2605	0.1945
1988	0.1695	0.1995	0.2380	0.1812
1989	0.1716	0.2035	0.2447	0.1785
1990	0.1701	0.1996	0.2439	0.1787
1991	0.1725	0.1973	0.2431	0.1791
1992	0.1645	0.1947	0.2411	0.1814
1993	0.1720	0.2108	0.2607	0.1925
1994	0.1761	0.2182	0.2644	0.2012
1995	0.1818	0.2262	0.2710	0.2020
1996	0.1804	0.2292	0.2692	0.2020

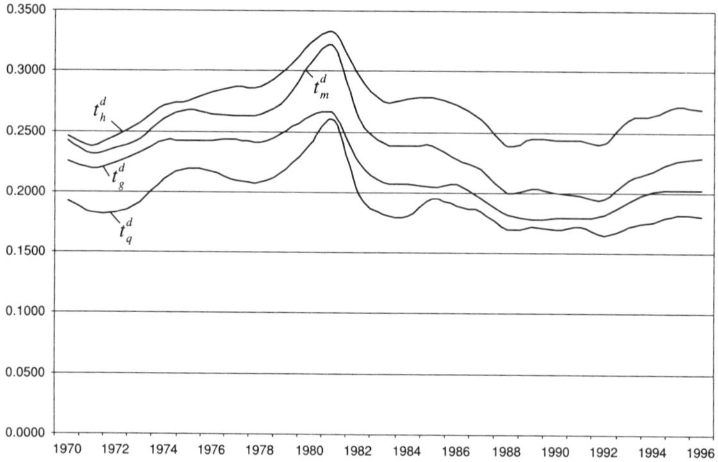

Notes: t_q^d: Corporate; t_m^d: Noncorporate; t_h^d: Household; t_g^d: Government

Figure 3.11
Average marginal tax rates on interest income.

Table 3.14
Property tax rates

Year	Corporate t_q^p	Noncorporate t_m^p	Household t_h^p
1970	0.0147	0.0173	0.0135
1971	0.0152	0.0178	0.0138
1972	0.0150	0.0180	0.0136
1973	0.0145	0.0169	0.0131
1974	0.0136	0.0158	0.0125
1975	0.0132	0.0167	0.0129
1976	0.0125	0.0159	0.0125
1977	0.0122	0.0158	0.0124
1978	0.0111	0.0142	0.0112
1979	0.0101	0.0127	0.0100
1980	0.0096	0.0114	0.0096
1981	0.0096	0.0114	0.0094
1982	0.0091	0.0108	0.0092
1983	0.0090	0.0109	0.0093
1984	0.0096	0.0115	0.0095
1985	0.0096	0.0112	0.0093
1986	0.0092	0.0104	0.0088
1987	0.0092	0.0105	0.0086
1988	0.0093	0.0100	0.0083
1989	0.0096	0.0104	0.0084
1990	0.0096	0.0104	0.0083
1991	0.0099	0.0111	0.0087
1992	0.0104	0.0115	0.0090
1993	0.0113	0.0112	0.0092
1994	0.0116	0.0117	0.0093
1995	0.0117	0.0121	0.0094
1996	0.0120	0.0114	0.0091

function of time. The price of acquisition of new investment goods q_t is a weighted sum of the present values of future rentals $\{c_t\}$. With a constant rate of decline in efficiency the rental price becomes:

$$c_t = q_{t-1}r_t + \delta q_t - (q_t - q_{t-1}) , \tag{3.4}$$

where r_t is the discount rate. Depreciation $q_{D,t}$ is proportional to the acquisition price:

$$q_{D,t} = \delta q_t . \tag{3.5}$$

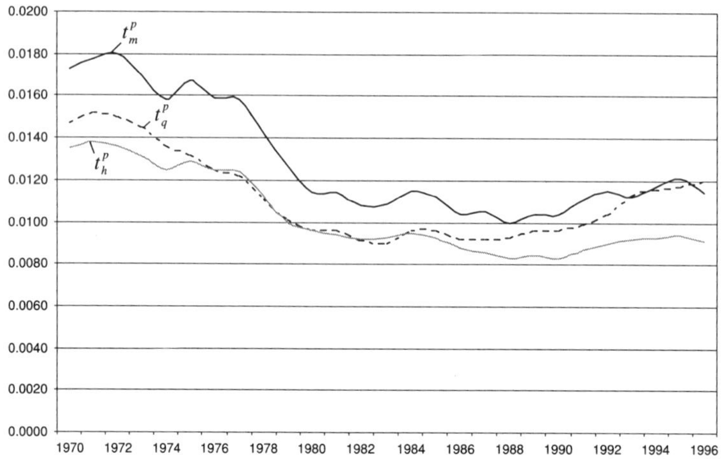

Notes: t_q^p: Corporate; t_m^p: Noncorporate; t_h^p: Household

Figure 3.12
Property tax rates.

Finally, the acquisition price of investment goods of age v at time t, say $q_{t,v}$ is:

$$q_{t,v} = (1-\delta)^v q_t \ . \tag{3.6}$$

Under the assumption that the decline in efficiency of a durable good is geometric, the vintage price system depends on the price for acquisition of new capital goods q_t. At each point of time the prices for acquisition of capital goods of age v, say $\{q_{t,v}\}$, are proportional to the price for new capital goods. The constants of proportionality decline geometrically at the rate δ. The rate of decline can be treated as an unknown parameter in an econometric model and estimated from a sample of prices for acquisition of capital goods of different vintages.

We obtain an econometric model for vintage price functions by taking logarithms of the acquisition prices $\{q_{t,v}\}$ and adding a random disturbance term:

$$\begin{aligned} \ln q_{t,v} &= \ln q_0 + \ln(1-\delta)v + \ln(1+\gamma)t + \varepsilon_{t,v} \ , \\ &= \alpha_0 + \beta_v v + \beta_t t + \varepsilon_{t,v} \ , \qquad (t = 1, 2 \ldots T;\ v = 0, 1 \ldots) \ , \end{aligned} \tag{3.7}$$

where the rate of decline in efficiency δ and the rate of inflation in the price of the asset γ are unknown parameters and $\varepsilon_{t,v}$ is an unobservable random disturbance.

We assume that the disturbance term has expected value equal to zero and constant variance, say σ^2, so that:

$$E(\varepsilon_{t,v}) = 0\,, \tag{3.8}$$

$$V(\varepsilon_{t,v}) = \sigma^2\,, \qquad (t = 1, 2 \ldots T;\; v = 0, 1 \ldots)\,. \tag{3.9}$$

We also assume that disturbances corresponding to distinct observations are uncorrelated:

$$C(\varepsilon_{t,v}, \varepsilon_{t',v'}) = 0\,, \qquad (t \neq t', v \neq v')\,. \tag{3.10}$$

Under these assumptions the unknown parameters of the econometric model can be estimated by linear regression methods.

The econometric model for vintage price functions can be generalized in several directions. First, the age of the durable good v and the time period t can enter nonlinearly into the vintage price function. Hall (1971) has proposed an analysis of variance model for the vintage price function. In this model each age is represented by a dummy variable equal to one for that age and zero otherwise. Similarly, each time period can be represented by a dummy variable equal to one for that time period and zero otherwise.

Hall's analysis of variance model for vintage price functions can be written:

$$\ln q_{t,v} = \alpha_0 + \beta_v{}'D_v + \beta_t{}'D_t + \varepsilon_{t,v}\; (t = 1, 2 \ldots T;\; v = 0, 1 \ldots)\,, \tag{3.11}$$

where D_v is a vector of dummy variables for age v and D_t is a vector of dummy variables for time t; β_v and β_t are the corresponding vectors of parameters. In the estimation of this model dummy variables for one vintage and one time period can be dropped in order to obtain a matrix of observations on the independent variables of full rank.

Hulten and Wykoff (1981b) have proposed an alternative approach to nonlinearity. They transform the prices of acquisition $\{q_{t,v}\}$, age v, and time t by means of the Box-Cox transformation, obtaining:

$$q^*_{t,v} = (q^{\theta_q}_{t,v} - 1)/\theta_q,\; v^* = (v^{\theta_v} - 1)/\theta_v,\; t^* = (t^{\theta_t} - 1)/\theta_t\,, \tag{3.12}$$

where the parameters θ_q, θ_v, and θ_t can be estimated by nonlinear regression methods from the model for vintage price functions:

$$q^*_{t,v} = \alpha_0 + \beta_v v^* + \beta_t t^* + \varepsilon_{t,v} , \quad (t = 1, 2 \ldots ; v = 0, 1 \ldots) . \tag{3.13}$$

The model giving the logarithm of an asset price as a linear function of age v and time period t is a limiting case of the Hulten-Wykoff model with parameter values:

$$\theta_q = 0 , \quad \theta_v = 1 , \quad \theta_t = 1 . \tag{3.14}$$

A third approach to nonlinearity has been introduced by Oliner (1993). He proposes to augment the linear model by introducing polynomials in age and time. For example, a quadratic model can be represented by:

$$\ln q_{t,v} = \alpha_0 + \beta_{1,v} v + \beta_{2,v} v^2 + \beta_{1,t} t + \beta_{2,t} t^2 + \beta_{v,t} v \ t + \varepsilon_{t,v} , \\ (t = 1, 2 \ldots T; v = 0, 1 \ldots) . \tag{3.15}$$

This has the advantage of flexibility in the representation of time and age effects, but economizes on the number of unknown parameters.

A further generalization of the econometric model of vintage price functions has been proposed by Hall (1971). This is appropriate for durable goods with a number of different models that are perfect substitutes in production. Each model is characterized by a number of technical characteristics that affect relative efficiency. We can express the price for acquisition of new capital goods at time zero as a function of the characteristics:

$$\ln q_0 = \alpha_0 + \beta_c{}'C , \tag{3.16}$$

where C is a vector of characteristics and β_c is the corresponding vector of parameters.

An econometric model of prices of new capital goods makes it possible to correct these prices for quality change. Changes in quality can be incorporated into price indices for capital goods by means of the "hedonic technique" originated by Waugh (1929) in dealing with the heterogeneity of agricultural commodities. This approach was first applied to capital goods in an important study of automobile prices by Court (1939). A seminal article by Griliches (1961) revived the hedonic methodology and applied it to postwar automobile prices. Chow (1967) first applied this methodology to computer prices in research conducted at IBM.[8]

Cole, Chen, Barquin-Stolleman, Dulberger, Helvacian, and Hodge (1986) reported the results of a joint project conducted by the Bureau of Economic Analysis (BEA) of the Department of Commerce and IBM to construct a constant quality price index for computers. Triplett (1986) discussed the economic interpretation of constant quality price indices in an accompanying article. Subsequently, BEA (1986) described the introduction of constant quality price indices for computers into the U.S. National Income and Product Accounts. A more detailed report on the BEA-IBM research on computer processors is presented by Dulberger (1989), who employs speed of processing and main memory as technical characteristics in modeling the prices of processors. An extensive survey of research on hedonic price indices for computers is given by Triplett (1989).[9]

Hall's (1971) methodology provides a means for determining both a quality-corrected price index for new capital goods and relative efficiencies for different vintages of capital goods. Substituting the "hedonic" model of prices of net assets into the econometric model of vintage price functions:

$$\ln q_{t,v} = \alpha_0 + \beta_v' D_v + \beta_t' D_t + \beta_c' C + \varepsilon_{t,v}, \quad (t = 1, 2 \ldots T;\ v = 0, 1 \ldots). \quad (3.17)$$

The unknown parameters of this model can be estimated by linear regression methods. Hall's methodology has been applied to prices of mainframe computers and computer peripherals by Oliner (1993, 1994). In Oliner's applications the chronological age of assets is replaced by the "model" age, that is, the time that a model has been available from the manufacturer.

An alternative approach is to substitute observations on the price of new capital goods q_0 into the econometric model, so that the dependent variable is the difference between the logarithms of new and used assets:

$$\ln q_{t,v} - \ln q_0 = \alpha_0 + \beta_v' D_v + \beta_t' D_t + \varepsilon_{t,v} \quad (t = 1, 2 \ldots T;\ v = 0, 1 \ldots). \quad (3.18)$$

This makes it possible to separate the modeling of the vintage price function and the quality-corrected price index of new capital goods. Hulten, Robertson, and Wykoff (1989), Wykoff (1989), and OTA (1990, 1991a, 1991b) have employed this approach.

A further decomposition of the econometric model of asset prices has been suggested by Biorn (1998). In order to isolate the vintage effect from the other determinants of asset prices, Biorn proposes to substitute observations on the prices of new capital goods in each time period q_t into the econometric model:

$$\ln q_{t,v} - \ln q_t = \alpha_0 + \beta_v' D_v + \varepsilon_{t,v} \quad (t = 1, 2 \ldots T;\ v = 0, 1 \ldots)\,. \tag{3.19}$$

This decomposition is implicit in the vintage price model originated by Terborgh (1954). The decomposition of vintage price functions is discussed in more detail by Biorn (1998).

3.4 Capital Cost Recovery

The Haig-Simons definition of taxable income requires that capital cost recovery must equal economic depreciation. Capital cost recovery for tax purposes has diverged from economic depreciation whenever capital consumption allowances and the investment tax credit have been utilized in providing tax incentives for private investment. Second, capital consumption allowances are based on the original acquisition price of an asset rather than current acquisition cost. The original acquisition price and the current acquisition cost differ by the cumulative inflation that has taken place since the original acquisition.

To illustrate the measurement of economic depreciation we consider an empirical study by Hulten and Wykoff (1981b) for eight categories of assets in the United States. This study includes tractors, construction machinery, metalworking machinery, general industrial equipment, trucks, autos, industrial buildings, and commercial buildings. In 1977 investment expenditures on these categories amounted to fifty-five percent of spending on producers' durable equipment and forty-two percent of spending on nonresidential structures.[10]

In the estimation of econometric models of vintage price functions, the sample of used asset prices is "censored" by the retirement of assets. The price of acquisition for assets that have been retired is equal to zero. If only observations on surviving assets are included in a sample of used asset prices, estimates of depreciation are biased by excluding observations on assets that have been retired. In order to correct this bias Hulten and Wykoff (1981b) multiply the prices of surviving assets of each vintage by the probability of survival, expressed as a function of age.

Finally, the rate of economic depreciation for each class of assets is tabulated as a function of the age of the asset. The natural logarithm of the price is regressed on age and time to obtain an average rate of depreciation, which Hulten and Wykoff refer to as the best geometric average (BGA). Hulten and Wykoff (1981b, p. 387) conclude that "... *a constant rate of depreciation can serve as a reasonable statistical approxima-*

tion to the underlying Box-Cox rates even though the latter are not geometric [their italics]. This result, in turn, supports those who use the single parameter depreciation approach in calculating capital stocks using the "perpetual inventory method."

After 1973 energy prices increased sharply and productivity growth rates declined dramatically at both aggregate and sectoral levels. Baily (1981) attributed part of the slowdown in economic growth to a decline in relative efficiencies of older capital goods resulting from higher energy prices. Hulten, Robertson, and Wykoff (1989) have tested the stability of vintage price functions during the 1970s. Wykoff (1989) has analyzed price data for four models of business-use automobiles collected from a large leasing company, applying the Hulten-Wykoff methodology.

Hulten, Robertson, and Wykoff (1989, p. 255) have carefully documented the fact that the relative efficiency functions for nine types of producers' durable equipment were unaffected by higher energy prices: "While depreciation almost certainly varies from year to year in response to a variety of factors, we have found that a major event like the energy crises, which had the potential of significantly increasing the rate of obsolescence, did not in fact result in a systematic change in age-price profiles." They also conclude that "the use of a single number to characterize the process of economic depreciation [of a given type of asset] seems justified in light of the results ... "

Hulten and Wykoff (1981b) have compared the best geometric depreciation rates with depreciation rates employed by the Bureau of Economic Analysis (1977) in estimating capital stock. The Hulten-Wykoff rate for equipment averages 0.133, while the BEA rate averages 0.141, so that the two rates are very similar. The Hulten-Wykoff rate for structures is 0.037, while the BEA rate is 0.060, so that these rates are substantially different.

The distribution of retirements used by Hulten and Wykoff (1981b) to correct for censored sample bias are based on the Winfrey (1935) S–3 curve with BEA (1977) lifetimes. These lifetimes are taken, in turn, from *Bulletin F*, compiled by the Internal Revenue Service and published in 1942. Between 1971 and 1981 the Office of Industrial Economics (OIE) conducted 46 studies of survival probabilities, based on vintage accounts for assets reported under the Asset Depreciation Range System introduced in 1962. The results of 27 of these studies have been summarized by Brazell, Dworin, and Walsh (1989). These results provide estimates of the distribution of useful lives based on the actual retention periods for the assets examined. A very important objective for future research on vintage price functions is to incorporate information from the OIE studies into corrections for sample selection bias.

Before 1981 tax law had linked tax depreciation to retirement of assets. Between 1981 and 1986 the Accelerated Cost Recovery System severed the link between tax depreciation and economic depreciation altogether. The Tax Reform Act of 1986 re-instituted tax depreciation based on economic depreciation.[11] Under the 1986 Act the Office of Tax Analysis (OTA) was mandated by the Congress to undertake empirical studies of economic depreciation, including "the anticipated decline in value over time",[12] and report the results in the form of a useful life. This is the lifetime for straight-line depreciation that yields the same present value as economic depreciation. For this purpose OTA (1990, 1991a, 1991b) conducted major surveys of used asset prices and retirements for scientific instruments, business-use passenger cars, and business-use light trucks and analyzed the results.

Oliner (1996) has conducted an extensive survey of used asset prices and retirement patterns for machine tools with the assistance of the Machinery Dealers National Association. He compares his results with those from previous empirical studies of economic depreciation for this industry, including those of Beidleman (1976) and Hulten and Wykoff (1981b). Finally, he compares estimates of depreciation and capital stock with those of the BEA (1987) Capital Stock Study. Oliner's study, like those of OTA, combines information on used asset prices and retirements for the same or similar populations of assets. This is an important advance over previous studies based on the vintage price approach.

Oliner (1993) has collected and analyzed used asset prices for IBM mainframe computers and has estimated constant-quality price change and economic depreciation simultaneously. Previous studies of computer prices, such as the studies surveyed by Triplett (1989), had been limited to constant-quality price change. The primary data source for computer prices used by Oliner is the *Computer Price Guide*, published by Computer Merchants, Inc. The data on retirement patterns are obtained from data on the installed stock of IBM computers tabulated by the International Data Corporation. Oliner (1994) has conducted a similar study of computer peripherals—large and intermediate disk drives, printers, displays, and card readers and punches. The prices of used assets are based on *Computer Price Guide* and estimates of retirement patterns are inferred from the duration of price listings.

The Bureau of Economic Analysis has employed constant quality price indices for computers in the U.S. National Accounts since 1986. For the measurement of depreciation in the national accounts BEA has adopted geometric rates based on the acquisition prices for used capital goods for all categories of assets except for computers and automobiles.[13] We have estimated best geometric rates for these two assets from the efficiency profiles employed by BEA. We have employed the BEA geometric rates for the remaining forty-nine categories of business assets given in table 3.15. BEA economic depreciation rates for consumer durables are presented in table 3.16.

We have now completed the presentation of economic depreciation rates. We next consider capital consumption allowances for tax purposes under U.S. tax law. Since the Internal Revenue Service introduced *Bulletin F* lifetimes in 1942, tax policy on capital cost recovery has undergone a number of substantial changes. The first significant change was the adoption of double declining balance and sum of the years digits methods for cost recovery in 1954 as alternatives to the traditional straight-line method for new investments. In 1962 the Internal Revenue Service introduced Guideline lifetimes for machinery and equipment, which were 30 to 40 percent shorter than the *Bulletin F* lifetimes.

The Revenue Act of 1971 introduced the Asset Depreciation Range (ADR) system, which permitted taxpayers to use lifetimes 20 percent above or below the Guideline lifetimes. Two depreciation methods were permitted under the ADR system: the straight-line method and the declining balance method with an optimal switch to straight-line. Taxpayers were assumed to recover part of their investment through disposal of the scrap. They were allowed to claim depreciation allowances equal to the value of investment net of the scrap value. The rate of declining balance under DBM was increased from 150 percent to 200 percent in 1954. In 1970 this rate was reduced to 150 percent for real property. A half-year convention applied to all asset categories; half of the first year's depreciation was allowed during the year the asset was acquired.[14]

The Economic Recovery Tax Act (ERTA) of 1981 introduced the Accelerated Cost Recovery System (ACRS), further liberalizing tax deductions for capital cost recovery. ACRS distinguished real property with a recovery period of 15 years and four classes of personal

Table 3.15
Economic depreciation rates: Business assets

	Asset	Life year	Depreciation rate
1.	Household furniture and fixtures	12	0.1375
2.	Other furniture	14	0.1179
3.	Fabricated metal products	18	0.0917
4.	Steam engines and turbines	32	0.0516
5.	Internal combustion engines	8	0.2063
6	Farm tractors	9	0.1452
7.	Construction tractors	8	0.1633
8.	Agricultural machinery	14	0.1179
9.	Construction machinery	10	0.1722
10.	Mining and oilfield machinery	11	0.1500
11.	Metalworking machinery	16	0.1225
12.	Special industry machinery	16	0.1031
13.	General industrial	16	0.1225
14.	Office, computing, accounting mach.	8	0.2729
15.	Service industry machinery	10	0.1650
16.	Communication equipment	15	0.1100
17.	Electrical transmission	33	0.0500
18.	Household appliances	10	0.1651
19.	Other electrical equipment	9	0.1834
20.	Trucks, buses and truck trailers	9	0.2537
21.	Autos	10	0.3333
22.	Aircraft	16	0.1833
23.	Ships and boats	27	0.0611
24.	Railroad equipment	30	0.0550
25.	Scientific and engineering instruments	12	0.1350
26.	Photocopy and related equipment	9	0.1800
27.	Other nonresidential equipment	11	0.1473
28.	Industrial buildings	31	0.0361
29.	Mobile offices	16	0.0556
30.	Office buildings	36	0.0247
31.	Commercial warehouses	40	0.0222
32.	Other commercial buildings	34	0.0262
33.	Religious buildings	48	0.0188
34.	Educational buildings	48	0.0188
35.	Hospital and institutional buildings	48	0.0233
36.	Hotels and motels	32	0.0247
37.	Amusement and recreational	30	0.0469
38.	Other nonfarm buildings	38	0.0370
39.	Railroad structures	54	0.0166
40.	Telephone and telegraph structures	40	0.0225
41.	Electric light and power structures	40	0.0225
42.	Gas structures	40	0.0225

Table 3.15 (continued)

	Asset	Life year	Depreciation rate
43.	Local transit	38	0.0450
44.	Petroleum pipelines	40	0.0450
45.	Farm structures	38	0.0237
46.	Petroleum and natural gas	16	0.0563
47.	Other mining exploration	16	0.0563
48.	Other nonresidential structures	40	0.0225
49.	Railraod replacement track	38	0.0236
50.	Nuclear fuel	6	0.2500
51.	Residential structure	–	0.0130

Sources: Hulten and Wykoff (1981), Jorgenson and Sullivan (1981), adjusted by the authors for the reclassification of assets and the revision of the asset lives by the Bureau of Economic Analysis (*Survey of Current Business*, July 1985, Jan. 1986).

Table 3.16
Economic depreciation rates: Consumer durables

	Asset	Depreciation rate
1.	Autos	0.2550
2.	Trucks	0.1996
3.	Other (RVs)	0.1996
4.	Furniture, including matresses and bedsprings	0.1268
5.	Kitchen and other household appliances	0.1570
6.	China, glassware, tableware, and utensils	0.1943
7.	Other durable house furnishings	0.1786
8.	Computing equipment	0.2729
9.	Video and audio equipment and musical instruments	0.1949
10.	Jewelry and watches	0.1540
11.	Ophthalmic products and orthopedic appliances	0.3027
12.	Books and maps	0.1855
13.	Wheel goods, sport and photo equipment, boats, aircraft	0.1649

Source: Bureau of Economic Analysis.

property with recovery periods of 3, 5, 10, and 15 years. Personal property was depreciated according to the 150 percent declining balance method with an optimal switchover to the straight-line method. Real property was depreciated according to the 175 percent declining balance method with an optimal switchover. A half-year convention was applied to both personal and real property; for personal property this was applied during the year the asset was acquired, while it applied at both ends of the recovery period for real property.

The prospect of an unacceptably large Federal budget deficit resulted in the Tax Equity and Fiscal Responsibility Act of 1982 (TEFRA). This Act repealed the provisions of ERTA for phasing in a more accelerated cost recovery system for personal property placed in service in 1985 and after. The tax life of real property was increased from 15 years to 18 years in 1984 and then to 19 years in 1985. Under TEFRA the basis for depreciation was reduced by 50 percent of the investment tax credit for assets acquired in 1983–1985.[15]

The Tax Reform Act of 1986 modified ACRS by increasing the number of asset classes from five to eight and lengthening the capital cost recovery periods. Under the 1986 Act the recovery periods were 3, 5, 7, 10, 15, and 20 years for personal property, 27.5 for residential rental property, and 31.5 years for nonresidential real property. Property with recovery periods of 3, 5, 7, and 10 years was depreciated according to the 200 percent declining balance method with an optimal switchover to the straight-line method. Property with recovery periods of 15 and 20 years, primarily public utility property, was subject to the 150 percent declining balance method with optimal switchover. Other real property was depreciated by the straight-line method. The recovery period of 31.5 years was increased to 39 years in 1993.[16]

Jorgenson and Sullivan (1981) conducted a detailed simulation study of the tax provisions for capital cost recovery through 1980. This study reproduced the capital consumption allowances actually claimed by corporate taxpayers over the period 1946–1980 on the basis of assumptions about formulas for cost recovery, tax lifetimes, and salvage values. The study also estimated effective rates of the investment tax credit for these same types of assets for the period 1970–1980. Jorgenson and Sullivan estimated the average lifetimes for 35 asset categories; we map their asset classification into our system of 51 asset categories. They also estimated the proportion of assets recovered through the accelerated depreciation method and found that 68–75 percent of assets were recovered through the declining balance method with the proportion increasing monotonically through time during the period 1970–1980. Under the declining balance method the optimal switchover to straight-line is when 55 percent of the tax lifetime has elapsed for 200 percent declining balance and 40 percent of the lifetime for 150 percent declining balance. The salvage value was estimated to be one percent for real property; for personal property the salvage value was three percent for 1970–1976 and one percent thereafter.

For the period 1970–1980, we begin with estimates of capital cost recovery schedules and salvage values by Jorgenson and Sullivan. We assign the schedule for capital consumption allowances for office buildings to hotels and motels. Similarly, we assume that schedules for assets in the classes of railroad replacement track (class 49) and nuclear fuel (class 50) are the same as those for railroad structures (class 39) and aircraft (class 22), respectively.

For 1981–1996 we use the capital cost recovery rules mandated by legislation, tables A3.12 and A3.13a,b (see appendix). One problem however is that the average taxlife of an asset category does not always correspond to a statutory cost recovery class. For the asset category whose average recovery period coincides with a statory recovery period, we assume that all the assets in that category belong to the corresponding statutory recovery class. For an asset category whose average recovery period does not coincide with any statutory recovery period, we assume that it consists of assets in the two adjacent statutory recovery classes. For example, the average recovery period of asset category 3 (fabricated metal product) is 5.4 years under ACRS and the two adjacent statutory recovery periods are 5 and 10 years. We assume that the average recovery period is a weighted average of the two statutory recovery periods where the capital stock is used as the weights. We then estimate the shares of capital stock in the 5-year and 10-year recovery classes. The results are shown in tables A3.14 and A3.15 in the appendix.

We summarize tax provisions for capital cost recovery in terms of the present value of tax deductions for capital consumption allowances and the investment tax credit. In computing the present value of capital consumption allowances, we use the interest rate on corporate bonds of the Baa class after corporate taxes. For an asset category whose average recovery period does not coincide with any statutory recovery period, we calculate the weighted average of the present values of depreciation allowances for assets in the two adjacent recovery classes. Table 3.17 presents the present value of capital consumption allowances for selected years. This completes our discussion of capital consumption allowances for tax purposes under U.S. tax law. We now turn our attention to the investment tax credit, which can also be regarded as a form of capital cost recovery.

The investment tax credit was first introduced in 1962. This credit was allowed for equipment and special purpose structures such as research facilities and certain storage facilities. The investment tax credit was eliminated in April 1969 and reinstated by the Revenue Act of 1971. The Tax Revenue Act of 1975 temporarily increased the regular credit from 7 to 10 percent and the credit for eligible public utility property from 4 to 10 percent. The temporary credit was to expire at the end of 1980, but the Revenue Act of 1978 made the 10 percent credit permanent.

The Economic Recovery Tax Act of 1981 increased the rates of the investment tax credit. Under prior law the 10 percent regular credit was allowed for assets with a useful lifetime of seven years or more, two-thirds for assets with a useful lifetime of 5–6 years, and one-third for assets with a useful lifetime of 3–4 years. ERTA made the 10 percent credit available for personal property with 5-year, 10-year, 15-year tax lifetimes and other tangible assets such as elevators. It also increased the credit for property with a 3-year tax lifetime to 60 percent of the regular credit. The Tax Reform Act of 1986 repealed the investment tax credit for assets acquired after December 31, 1985.

Fullerton, Gillette and Mackie (1987) estimated effective rates of the investment tax credit for the 51 classes of depreciable assets prior to the 1986 Tax Act. For 1970–1985 we assign appropriate rates of the investment tax credit to each class. We also make some specific adjustments to reflect the changes in the composition in certain classes of

Table 3.17
Present value of capital consumption allowances (z)

Asset	1970	1975	1980	1985	1990	1996
1	0.8061	0.8081	0.7892	0.8387	0.8937	0.9161
2	0.8061	0.8081	0.7892	0.8387	0.8564	0.8858
3	0.7739	0.7741	0.7482	0.8311	0.8669	0.8944
4	0.7391	0.7320	0.7020	0.7323	0.6744	0.7325
5	0.7391	0.7320	0.7020	0.7814	0.7588	0.8043
6	0.9096	0.8860	0.8796	0.8387	0.8663	0.8939
7	0.9096	0.8860	0.8796	0.8387	0.8947	0.9169

Table 3.17 (continued)

Asset	1970	1975	1980	1985	1990	1996
8	0.8026	0.8081	0.7892	0.8387	0.8564	0.8858
9	0.8150	0.8067	0.7909	0.8387	0.8903	0.9134
10	0.8208	0.8123	0.7987	0.8387	0.8564	0.8858
11	0.7739	0.7666	0.7435	0.8544	0.8800	0.9050
12	0.7773	0.7691	0.7435	0.8423	0.8646	0.8926
13	0.7879	0.7753	0.7513	0.8348	0.8515	0.8818
14	0.8208	0.8081	0.7892	0.8387	0.8978	0.9194
15	0.8150	0.8027	0.7842	0.8364	0.8928	0.9154
16	0.7818	0.7765	0.7498	0.7867	0.8003	0.8395
17	0.7818	0.7765	0.7498	0.7869	0.7918	0.8324
18	0.7818	0.7765	0.7498	0.8387	0.8978	0.9194
19	0.7818	0.7765	0.7498	0.8387	0.8930	0.9156
20	0.8748	0.8739	0.8776	0.8880	0.8978	0.9194
21	0.9082	0.9211	0.9259	0.9073	0.8978	0.9194
22	0.8695	0.8657	0.8554	0.8387	0.8564	0.8858
23	0.7089	0.7026	0.6653	0.8387	0.8023	0.8412
24	0.7340	0.7377	0.7103	0.8387	0.8564	0.8858
25	0.8061	0.7989	0.7792	0.8135	0.8417	0.8738
26	0.8061	0.7989	0.7792	0.8392	0.8937	0.9161
27	0.8150	0.8054	0.7858	0.8387	0.8912	0.9140
28	0.6147	0.5908	0.5148	0.6816	0.5262	0.5668
29	0.4801	0.4496	0.3719	0.6575	0.4385	0.4516
30	0.4801	0.4496	0.3719	0.6575	0.4385	0.4516
31	0.4801	0.4496	0.3719	0.6575	0.4385	0.4516
32	0.4801	0.4496	0.3719	0.7628	0.6948	0.7499
33	0.4649	0.4438	0.3677	0.6575	0.4385	0.4516
34	0.4649	0.4438	0.3677	0.6575	0.4385	0.4516
35	0.4649	0.4438	0.3677	0.6575	0.4385	0.4516
36	0.4801	0.4496	0.3719	0.6575	0.4385	0.4516
37	0.5915	0.5694	0.4924	0.7434	0.7159	0.7679
38	0.5915	0.5694	0.4924	0.6575	0.4385	0.4516
39	0.5720	0.5808	0.5044	0.8387	0.8564	0.8858
40	0.6268	0.6095	0.5348	0.7434	0.7372	0.7860
41	0.6233	0.6095	0.5348	0.6936	0.6353	0.6977
42	0.6484	0.6405	0.5683	0.7142	0.6031	0.6677
43	0.6731	0.6629	0.5930	0.8387	0.8978	0.9194
44	0.6731	0.6629	0.5930	0.8387	0.6787	0.7364
45	0.6268	0.6303	0.5573	0.6575	0.6063	0.6719
46	0.8542	0.8711	0.8384	0.8387	0.8564	0.8858
47	0.8542	0.8711	0.8384	0.8387	0.8564	0.8858
48	0.5837	0.5917	0.5197	0.6575	0.4385	0.4516
49	0.5720	0.5808	0.5044	0.8387	0.8564	0.8858
50	0.8751	0.8695	0.8384	0.8387	0.8978	0.9194
51	0.5931	0.5790	0.5025	0.6577	0.4800	0.5557

Note: Asset numbers are the same as in table 3.15.

assets in the more detailed classification scheme used by Fullerton, Gillette, and Mackie. Table 3.18 shows the rates of the investment tax credit for the 51 depreciable assets for selected years.

3.5 Financial Structure

We next consider the impact of the financial policy of firms and households on the cost of capital. The most important features of the financial structure are the ratios of debt to the value of capital stock for firms and households and the dividend pay-out ratio for corporations. We begin by describing the estimation of capital stock in households and noncorporate and corporate businesses. We describe the construction of estimates for depreciable and nondepreciable assets separately.

For depreciable assets we employ investment data from the Bureau of Economic Analysis, which include investment expenditures in current and constant prices for 50 categories of nonresidential business assets and 22 categories of residential assets in the corporate, noncorporate, and household sectors. These data also include investment expenditures for thirteen categories of consumer durables in the household sector. We first aggregate the 22 categories of residential assets into a single category. At this level of aggregation we construct price indexes for investment expenditures for 64 categories of assets by dividing the current dollar values of investment by the corresponding constant dollar values. The 64 categories of assets include 50 categories of nonresidential business assets, one category of residential assets, and thirteen categories of consumer durables.

We assume that existing capital goods and new capital goods are perfect substitutes in production, as in the model of capital as a factor of production presented in chapter 2. The rates of substitution can be

Table 3.18
Investment tax credits (k)

Asset	1971	1975	1980	1985
1	0.0480	0.0830	0.0920	0.1000
2	0.0480	0.0830	0.0920	0.1000
3	0.0430	0.0830	0.0920	0.1000
4	0.0280	0.0830	0.0920	0.1000
5	0.0280	0.0830	0.0920	0.1000
6	0.0330	0.0550	0.0610	0.1000
7	0.0330	0.0550	0.0610	0.1000

Table 3.18 (continued)

Asset	1971	1975	1980	1985
8	0.0490	0.0830	0.0920	0.1000
9	0.0470	0.0830	0.0920	0.1000
10	0.0490	0.0830	0.0920	0.1000
11	0.0490	0.0830	0.0920	0.0910
12	0.0490	0.0830	0.0920	0.0980
13	0.0450	0.0830	0.0920	0.0980
14	0.0480	0.0830	0.0920	0.1000
15	0.0470	0.0830	0.0920	0.1000
16	0.0400	0.0830	0.0920	0.1000
17	0.0400	0.0830	0.0920	0.0990
18	0.0400	0.0830	0.0920	0.1000
19	0.0400	0.0830	0.0920	0.1000
20	0.0230	0.0410	0.0460	0.0710
21	0.0160	0.0280	0.0310	0.0600
22	0.0440	0.0750	0.0830	0.1000
23	0.0490	0.0830	0.0920	0.1000
24	0.0490	0.0830	0.0920	0.1000
25	0.0460	0.0830	0.0920	0.1000
26	0.0460	0.0830	0.0920	0.1000
27	0.0490	0.0830	0.0920	0.1000
28	0.0080	0.0210	0.0230	0.0250
29	0.0000	0.0000	0.0000	0.0000
30	0.0000	0.0000	0.0000	0.0000
31	0.0000	0.0000	0.0000	0.0000
32	0.0210	0.0550	0.0620	0.0670
33	0.0000	0.0000	0.0000	0.0000
34	0.0000	0.0000	0.0000	0.0000
35	0.0000	0.0000	0.0000	0.0000
36	0.0000	0.0000	0.0000	0.0000
37	0.0320	0.0830	0.0920	0.1000
38	0.0000	0.0000	0.0000	0.0000
39	0.0140	0.0830	0.0920	0.1000
40	0.0100	0.0630	0.0700	0.0760
41	0.0140	0.0830	0.0920	0.1000
42	0.0080	0.0470	0.0520	0.0570
43	0.0140	0.0830	0.0920	0.1000
44	0.0140	0.0830	0.0920	0.1000
45	0.0000	0.0000	0.0000	0.0000
46	0.0210	0.0550	0.0610	0.1000
47	0.0210	0.0550	0.0610	0.1000
48	0.0000	0.0000	0.0000	0.0000
49	0.0320	0.0830	0.0920	0.1000
50	0.0320	0.0830	0.0920	0.1000
51	0.0000	0.0000	0.0000	0.0010

Note: Asset numbers are the same as in table 3.15.

determined from the relative efficiencies of capital goods of different ages. In measuring capital stock for each category of assets we utilize the rates of economic depreciation in tables 3.15 and 3.16 as rates of replacement. Rates of depreciation and replacement are identical under the assumption that relative efficiencies of capital goods decline geometrically with age of the asset. The current value of capital stock is the product of capital stock and the corresponding acquisition price of investment goods.

Nondepreciable assets include farm inventories, nonfarm inventories and land. Our data on inventories are taken from the Bureau of Economic Analysis. Inventories are divided among three categories—farm, nonfarm corporate, and nonfarm noncorporate inventories. We allocate farm inventories to the noncorporate sector. We construct price and quantity indexes for land in the corporate, noncorporate, and household sectors by combining the current values of land in these sectors with sales and purchase values of land by federal and state and local governments.[17] To provide some ideas about the composition of capital stock in the U.S., tables A3.16a and A3.16b in the appendix show the composition of capital stock in producer durable equipment (PDE) and nonresidential structures (NRS) in the corporate, noncorporate, and household sectors and table A3.16c shows the composition of consumer durables (CD) in the household sector. Table A3.17 shows the size and composition of capital stock in the short-lived and long-lived asset categories of the corporate, noncorporate, and household sectors, and figures A3.1 and A3.2 show in pie charts the composition of capital stock in the short-lived and long-lived asset categories, respectively.

We define the dividend pay-out ratio of the corporate sector as the ratio of dividend payments to income from corporate equity.[18] Income from corporate equity is defined as total remuneration of corporate capital inputs, less economic depreciation, less real interest expenses, less federal and state and local income taxes, and less property taxes. Table 3.19 shows dividends paid, income from corporate equity, and the dividend pay-out ratio and figure 3.13 shows the dividend pay-out ratio.

We describe the capital structures of the household, noncorporate and corporate sectors in terms of ratios of the value of outstanding liabilities to the value of capital stock. To estimate debt/capital ratios for the noncorporate and corporate sectors, we first convert the book values of financial assets and liabilities to market values by applying

Table 3.19
After-tax corporate profits and dividend payments

Year	Dividends	After-tax profits	Pay-out ratio (α)
1970	22.5	48.2	0.4658
1971	22.9	58.0	0.3949
1972	24.4	70.0	0.3493
1973	27.0	72.8	0.3717
1974	29.7	62.4	0.4771
1975	29.6	89.2	0.3318
1976	34.6	88.4	0.3920
1977	39.5	118.6	0.3329
1978	44.7	139.8	0.3200
1979	50.1	144.4	0.3469
1980	54.7	125.3	0.4368
1981	63.6	166.3	0.3824
1982	66.9	137.5	0.4862
1983	71.5	160.0	0.4470
1984	79.0	227.5	0.3474
1985	83.3	258.9	0.3216
1986	91.3	236.1	0.3867
1987	98.2	262.6	0.3738
1988	115.3	319.0	0.3616
1989	134.6	338.4	0.3976
1990	153.4	306.5	0.5007
1991	160.0	301.9	0.5299
1992	169.5	298.6	0.5676
1993	195.8	335.8	0.5830
1994	216.2	415.9	0.5199
1995	264.4	489.3	0.5403
1996	304.8	561.8	0.5425

market-to-par indexes for long-term debt instruments estimated by Strong (1989). We then allocate net liabilities—total liabilities less total financial assets—of farm businesses between corporate and noncorporate sectors in proportion to the stocks of depreciable assets in these sectors. Assuming that debt claims on assets are equal to net financial liabilities, we calculate debt/capital ratios for the corporate and noncorporate sectors by dividing the market value of the net financial liabilities by the value of tangible assets. The value of depreciable assets for these sectors is net of the investment tax credit and the present value of tax deductions for capital consumption.

Although income from equity in household assets is not taxed, interest payments corresponding to financial liabilities of the house-

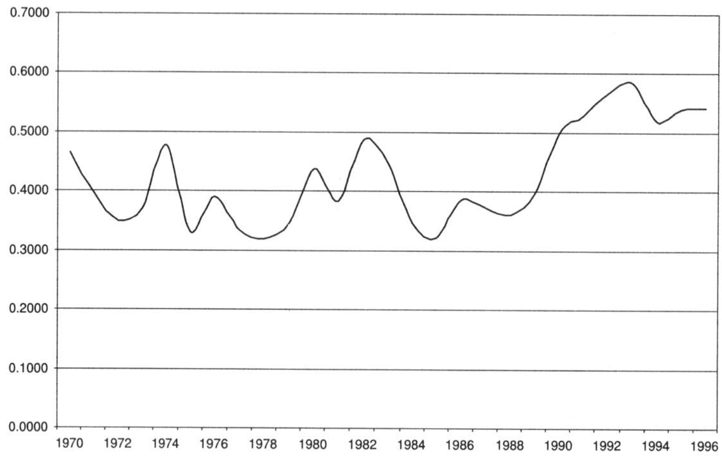

Figure 3.13
Corporate dividend pay-out ratio (α).

hold sector are deductible from revenue in defining taxable income at the individual level. However, not all of the outstanding household liabilities are associated with the financing of household assets. We consider mortgages, and installment credit from commercial banks, savings and loan associations, mutual savings banks, credit unions, and finance companies as household liabilities associated with the acquisition of household assets. We define the capital structure of the household sector as the ratio of these liabilities to the value of household assets. Estimates of the debt/capital ratios for household, noncorporate and corporate sectors are shown in table 3.20 and figure 3.14.

3.6 Alternative Approaches

In this chapter we have presented a quantitative description of the U.S. tax system. For this purpose we have developed estimates of income and property tax rates for assets utilized by households and noncorporate and corporate businesses. We have represented the corporate income tax as a flat rate tax on income from corporate assets. By contrast the personal income tax is progressive. Tax liabilities increase as a proportion of the income of each taxpayer. We have characterized the personal income tax schedule by means of average marginal tax rates for each category of income. Finally, we have

Table 3.20
Debt/asset ratios

Year	Corporate β_q	Noncorporate β_m	Household β_h
1970	0.1335	0.1582	0.2545
1971	0.1495	0.1746	0.2652
1972	0.1324	0.1807	0.2640
1973	0.1297	0.1914	0.2596
1974	0.0574	0.2292	0.2544
1975	0.1827	0.2196	0.2362
1976	0.2057	0.2436	0.2556
1977	0.2083	0.2462	0.2685
1978	0.2024	0.2434	0.2765
1979	0.1930	0.2458	0.2795
1980	0.1736	0.2345	0.2587
1981	0.1803	0.1841	0.2199
1982	0.2074	0.1923	0.2185
1983	0.1916	0.2111	0.2471
1984	0.1794	0.1981	0.2514
1985	0.2055	0.2000	0.2743
1986	0.1889	0.1933	0.2827
1987	0.1589	0.1894	0.2949
1988	0.1510	0.1827	0.3013
1989	0.1575	0.1826	0.3037
1990	0.1659	0.1814	0.3206
1991	0.1589	0.1815	0.3289
1992	0.1773	0.1802	0.3383
1993	0.1621	0.1820	0.3504
1994	0.1501	0.1779	0.3687
1995	0.1385	0.1721	0.3773
1996	0.1199	0.1695	0.3839

represented the property tax as a flat tax on the value of assets held by each legal form of organization.

Corporate income is the base for the corporate income tax and personal income is the base for the individual income tax. However, income defined for tax purposes differs substantially from the economic concept of income. Tax provisions for capital cost recovery are an important source of these differences. We have presented data on capital consumption allowances and the investment tax credit for all

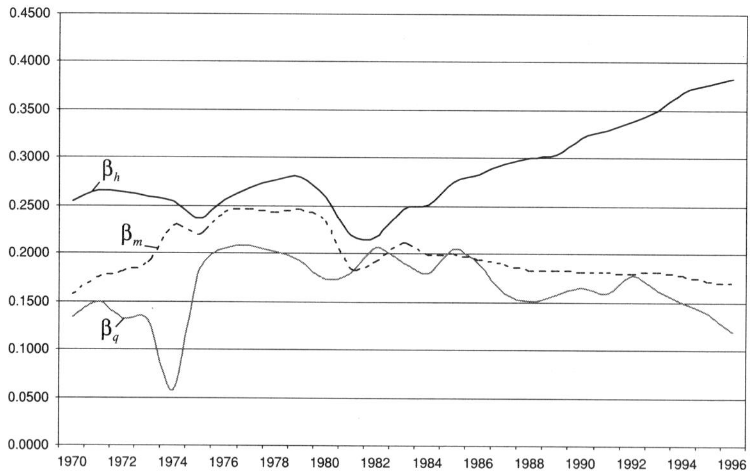

Notes: β_q: Corporate; β_m: Noncorporate; β_h: Household

Figure 3.14
Debt/asset ratios.

categories of depreciable assets utilized in noncorporate and corporate businesses. We have also presented estimates of economic depreciation, based on the estimates given in the U.S. National Income and Product Accounts.

An alternative to the vintage price approach that underlies the depreciation estimates in the U.S. National Accounts is to employ rental prices rather than prices of acquisition to estimate the pattern of decline in efficiency.[19] This approach has been employed by Malpezzi, Ozanne, and Thibodeau (1987) to analyze rental price data on residential structures and by Taubman and Rasche (1969) to study rental price data on commercial structures. While leases on residential property are very frequently one year or less in duration, leases on commercial property are typically for much longer periods of time. Since the rental prices are constant over the period of the lease, estimates based on annual rental prices for commercial property are biased toward the one-hoss-shay pattern found by Taubman and Rasche; Malpezzi, Ozanne, and Thibodeau find rental price profiles for residential property that decline with age.

A second alternative to the vintage price approach is to analyze investment for replacement purposes. This was originated by Meyer and Kuh (1957) and has been employed by Eisner (1972), Feldstein and Foot (1974), and Coen (1975, 1980). Coen (1980) compares the explanatory power of alternative patterns of decline in efficiency in a model of investment behavior that also includes the price of capital services. For equipment he finds that eleven of twenty-one two-digit manufacturing industries are characterized by geometric decline in efficiency, three by sum of the years' digits and seven by straight-line. For structures he finds that fourteen industries are characterized by geometric decline, five by straight-line and two by one-hoss-shay patterns. Hulten and Wykoff (1981c, p. 110) conclude that: "The weight of Coen's study is evidently on the side of the geometric and near-geometric forms of depreciation."

Alternative approaches for analyzing investment for replacement purposes have been introduced to Pakes and Griliches (1984) and Doms (1996). Pakes and Griliches have related profits for U.S. manufacturing firms to past investment expenditures. The weights on investments of different ages can be interpreted as relative efficiencies of these assets. Doms has included a weighted average of past investment expenditures in a production function. Treating the weights as unknown parameters to be estimated, he obtains estimates of relative efficiences of assets. While Pakes and Griliches find patterns of relative efficiencies that rise and then decline, Doms obtains relative efficiencies that decline geometrically.

We conclude that satisfactory empirical estimates of economic depreciation are available in the U.S. National Income and Product Accounts. These estimates are based on the extensive research of Hulten and Wykoff (1981a, 1981b, 1981c), Hulten, Robertson, and Wykoff (1989), and Wykoff (1989). Important additional studies have been completed by OTA (1990, 1991a, 1991b) and Oliner (1993, 1994, 1996). Finally, estimates of retirement distributions required for correcting sample selection bias have been completed by OIE and summarized by Brazell, Dworin, and Walsh (1989). Taken together, these empirical studies provide the information needed for measuring depreciation empirically.

The model of capital as a factor of production presented in chapter 2 is simplified by assuming that the decline in efficiency of durable goods is geometric. However, this assumption is inessential to the model. Biorn (1989) has developed appropriate concepts of the cost of capital, the rate of return, and effective tax rates for a model of capital as a factor of production that does not require geometric decline in efficiency. He has also developed similar concepts for putty-clay technologies where substitution among inputs is limited to the *ex ante* representation of technology before an investment has been made. After capital goods have been put in place the *ex post* representation of this technology is characterized by fixed input proportions.

We have estimated present values of capital consumption allowances and effective rates of the investment tax credit for both corporate and noncorporate sectors in Jorgenson and Yun (1991b). Our estimates are closely related to that of Fullerton, Gillette, and Mackie (1987), since we use the same classification of assets in describing economic depreciation and provisions for capital cost recovery for the business sector. Fullerton (1987) employs a classification of assets based on that of Hulten and Wykoff (1981b) and Jorgenson and Sullivan (1981).[20]

The final step in describing the U.S. tax structure is to estimate the proportions of debt and equity in the value of capital for households and noncorporate and corporate businesses. For this purpose we have presented data on the value of capital in each legal form of organization. These data are based on the model of capital as a factor of production presented in chapter 2 and utilize rates of economic depreciation based on those of the Bureau of Economic Analysis. We have estimated the value of debt for each form of organization. We have also estimated the dividend pay-out ratio for the corporate sector from dividend payments and the income from assets utilized in that sector.

In chapter 4 we analyze the impact of tax policy on the cost of capital and the rate of return by means of the concept of the marginal effective tax rate presented in chapter 2. For this purpose we utilize the information on tax rates, provisions for capital cost recovery, and the financial structure of corporate and noncorporate businesses and households presented in this chapter to estimate private and social returns for all assets in the private sector of the U.S. economy. We estimate effective tax rates for these assets and employ these tax rates to assess the impact of the U.S. tax structure on the efficiency of capital allocation.

Appendix

Table A3.1
Ownership composition of corporate equity

Year	Households	Tax-exempt institutions	Insurance companies		
			Total	Life	Other
1970	0.7993	0.1673	0.0333	0.0151	0.0182
1971	0.7802	0.1828	0.0369	0.0174	0.0195
1972	0.7764	0.1847	0.0389	0.0182	0.0207
1973	0.7503	0.2026	0.0472	0.0227	0.0244
1974	0.7161	0.2315	0.0524	0.0284	0.0239
1975	0.7081	0.2458	0.0461	0.0263	0.0198
1976	0.7182	0.2382	0.0436	0.0247	0.0190
1977	0.6934	0.2590	0.0476	0.0259	0.0217
1978	0.6663	0.2847	0.0490	0.0256	0.0234
1979	0.6750	0.2775	0.0475	0.0226	0.0249
1980	0.6849	0.2708	0.0443	0.0194	0.0248
1981	0.6650	0.2880	0.0470	0.0200	0.0270
1982	0.6358	0.3173	0.0469	0.0186	0.0283
1983	0.6170	0.3359	0.0471	0.0173	0.0298
1984	0.6004	0.3549	0.0447	0.0161	0.0286
1985	0.5867	0.3667	0.0465	0.0180	0.0285
1986	0.6276	0.3324	0.0400	0.0143	0.0257
1987	0.6175	0.3403	0.0422	0.0152	0.0270
1988	0.6386	0.3213	0.0400	0.0137	0.0263
1989	0.6329	0.3290	0.0381	0.0128	0.0252
1990	0.6246	0.3375	0.0380	0.0121	0.0259
1991	0.6355	0.3291	0.0353	0.0135	0.0218
1992	0.6456	0.3216	0.0328	0.0129	0.0199
1993	0.6423	0.3254	0.0323	0.0141	0.0182
1994	0.6346	0.3285	0.0370	0.0172	0.0198
1995	0.6440	0.3209	0.0351	0.0159	0.0191
1996	0.6389	0.3276	0.0334	0.0172	0.0162

Source: See table 3.5.

Table A3.2
Household ownership distribution of corporate equity (billions of dollars)

Year	Households total	Individuals	Commercial banks	Savings institutions	Mutual funds
1970	579.0	536.4	0.1	2.8	39.7
1971	662.5	610.3	0.1	3.5	48.6
1972	818.4	762.0	0.1	4.5	51.7
1973	604.5	561.9	0.2	4.2	38.3
1974	383.0	352.7	0.2	3.7	26.4
1975	507.7	469.5	0.2	4.4	33.7
1976	640.3	598.4	0.2	4.4	37.3
1977	545.8	508.9	0.3	4.8	31.9
1978	553.0	516.5	0.1	4.8	31.7
1979	672.5	632.2	0.1	4.7	35.4
1980	891.0	844.3	0.1	4.2	42.5
1981	797.6	756.9	0.1	3.2	37.4
1982	865.5	812.7	0.1	3.3	49.4
1983	997.7	919.0	0.1	4.3	74.4
1984	938.5	853.7	0.0	4.1	80.6
1985	1171.6	1052.5	0.1	5.2	113.7
1986	1494.3	1326.0	0.1	7.0	161.2
1987	1485.7	1297.0	0.0	7.0	181.7
1988	1734.5	1538.4	0.0	8.5	187.6
1989	2108.3	1842.1	4.7	11.0	250.5
1990	1928.9	1684.8	2.2	8.8	233.2
1991	2740.7	2417.7	3.8	10.3	308.9
1992	3156.6	2740.7	3.4	11.2	401.3
1993	3641.4	3017.1	4.3	12.5	607.4
1994	3598.5	2875.7	2.9	10.4	709.5
1995	4877.2	3833.0	5.0	14.3	1024.9
1996	5857.5	4362.7	6.8	17.9	1470.0

Source: See table 3.5.

Table A3.3
Ownership composition of corporate net debt

Year	Households	Tax-exempt institutions	Insurance companies		
			Total	Life	Other
1970	0.4985	0.2654	0.2361	0.2105	0.0256
1971	0.5072	0.2632	0.2295	0.2050	0.0245
1972	0.5238	0.2605	0.2157	0.1955	0.0202
1973	0.5433	0.2501	0.2066	0.1895	0.0171
1974	0.5654	0.2419	0.1927	0.1738	0.0189
1975	0.5350	0.2685	0.1965	0.1746	0.0220
1976	0.5233	0.2742	0.2025	0.1755	0.0270
1977	0.5052	0.2866	0.2082	0.1775	0.0307
1978	0.4885	0.3057	0.2057	0.1750	0.0307
1979	0.4922	0.3134	0.1944	0.1634	0.0311
1980	0.4757	0.3424	0.1819	0.1519	0.0301
1981	0.4903	0.3417	0.1679	0.1371	0.0308
1982	0.4848	0.3613	0.1539	0.1244	0.0295
1983	0.5003	0.3578	0.1419	0.1188	0.0231
1984	0.5267	0.3470	0.1263	0.1028	0.0235
1985	0.5549	0.2959	0.1492	0.1213	0.0279
1986	0.5687	0.2933	0.1379	0.1057	0.0322
1987	0.5866	0.2695	0.1439	0.1121	0.0317
1988	0.5764	0.2823	0.1413	0.1078	0.0335
1989	0.5712	0.2892	0.1396	0.1037	0.0359
1990	0.5641	0.2975	0.1384	0.1010	0.0374
1991	0.5683	0.2904	0.1413	0.1013	0.0401
1992	0.5492	0.3108	0.1400	0.1013	0.0386
1993	0.5406	0.3204	0.1391	0.1012	0.0378
1994	0.5434	0.3171	0.1395	0.1025	0.0370
1995	0.5568	0.3088	0.1345	0.0983	0.0361
1996	0.5481	0.3104	0.1415	0.1033	0.0382

Source: See table 3.5.

Table A3.4
Household ownership distribution of corporate net debt (billions of dollars)

Year	Total	Individuals	Commercial banks	Savings institutions	Mutual funds	Finance companies
1970	145.8	20.3	77.8	25.4	3.0	17.8
1971	159.3	22.3	83.9	30.8	3.1	16.7
1972	179.7	22.9	96.9	34.2	3.5	18.5
1973	216.8	25.0	120.5	37.2	3.6	24.0
1974	252.6	32.2	143.3	35.9	4.1	31.0
1975	245.7	38.9	124.6	32.3	4.6	39.5
1976	253.4	42.5	120.9	34.5	4.8	46.2
1977	276.1	35.5	139.1	29.9	5.9	61.7
1978	296.3	26.1	157.1	29.2	5.4	74.6
1979	331.6	20.2	184.7	23.9	6.3	92.9
1980	346.3	7.5	202.6	26.3	7.7	98.9
1981	405.6	6.7	232.4	30.0	9.5	124.2
1982	422.8	0.6	263.6	26.0	10.0	119.4
1983	471.8	–1.5	299.2	32.0	12.7	125.4
1984	579.4	–5.1	349.2	47.8	13.9	169.0
1985	684.2	48.8	369.3	40.4	22.1	198.2
1986	806.1	69.1	448.2	38.7	39.5	203.5
1987	926.4	74.4	492.0	69.9	40.9	240.6
1988	999.8	61.0	523.5	83.2	42.9	279.6
1989	1081.4	83.1	548.1	73.7	45.6	320.4
1990	1098.5	106.6	528.7	58.2	47.2	346.3
1991	1096.8	175.8	471.4	46.1	68.2	323.1
1992	1071.1	164.5	422.7	51.3	89.6	330.5
1993	1064.2	172.2	386.7	47.1	120.2	324.7
1994	1123.1	152.2	423.0	45.2	118.0	370.2
1995	1240.2	179.5	474.4	32.8	126.1	411.7
1996	1278.3	175.9	509.2	13.0	143.8	418.8

Source: See table 3.5.

Table A3.5
Ownership composition of noncorporate net debt

Year	Households	Tax-exempt institutions	Insurance companies		
			Total	Life	Other
1970	0.7085	0.0970	0.1945	0.1938	0.0007
1971	0.7308	0.0919	0.1774	0.1768	0.0005
1972	0.7591	0.0831	0.1577	0.1573	0.0004
1973	0.7891	0.0737	0.1372	0.1370	0.0002
1974	0.7886	0.0742	0.1372	0.1370	0.0002
1975	0.7836	0.0807	0.1357	0.1354	0.0003
1976	0.7897	0.0845	0.1257	0.1254	0.0004
1977	0.7974	0.0849	0.1177	0.1172	0.0005
1978	0.8017	0.0877	0.1106	0.1102	0.0004
1979	0.7996	0.0936	0.1067	0.1060	0.0007
1980	0.7854	0.1064	0.1082	0.1070	0.0012
1981	0.7812	0.1146	0.1042	0.1027	0.0015
1982	0.7640	0.1336	0.1024	0.1003	0.0021
1983	0.7774	0.1327	0.0899	0.0873	0.0025
1984	0.7945	0.1277	0.0778	0.0752	0.0026
1985	0.7857	0.1210	0.0933	0.0900	0.0033
1986	0.7891	0.1248	0.0861	0.0823	0.0038
1987	0.7986	0.1165	0.0849	0.0811	0.0038
1988	0.7903	0.1296	0.0801	0.0762	0.0039
1989	0.7915	0.1321	0.0764	0.0723	0.0041
1990	0.7791	0.1433	0.0776	0.0732	0.0044
1991	0.7808	0.1429	0.0763	0.0721	0.0042
1992	0.7925	0.1373	0.0703	0.0664	0.0039
1993	0.8083	0.1287	0.0630	0.0601	0.0029
1994	0.8216	0.1198	0.0586	0.0563	0.0023
1995	0.8341	0.1133	0.0526	0.0510	0.0016
1996	0.8482	0.1029	0.0489	0.0477	0.0012

Source: See table 3.5.

Table A3.6
Household ownership distribution of noncorporate net debt (billions of dollars)

Year	Household total	Individuals	Commercial banks	Savings institutions	Finance companies	Mortgage pools
1970	86.8	25.2	22.2	33.9	1.2	2.4
1971	105.8	25.5	27.2	43.9	2.6	3.3
1972	133.2	27.9	36.1	55.0	3.7	4.4
1973	155.5	27.7	50.3	59.3	4.2	5.2
1974	185.1	31.3	66.3	68.4	3.4	5.8
1975	198.0	31.7	71.3	78.2	2.8	6.1
1976	217.0	35.7	80.5	86.1	2.2	7.0
1977	243.9	41.2	92.5	95.2	2.9	8.0
1978	280.9	46.8	112.9	104.5	3.4	9.9
1979	331.5	57.3	137.8	116.0	4.3	12.9
1980	369.5	66.0	152.6	127.6	5.1	15.2
1981	399.9	70.5	175.7	133.0	5.5	13.3
1982	444.1	72.2	196.8	148.2	6.4	18.4
1983	498.0	75.2	207.7	176.4	6.6	29.9
1984	584.7	68.2	254.7	216.4	7.5	34.7
1985	651.1	58.4	287.9	248.6	8.5	42.3
1986	709.0	50.2	327.3	256.9	9.7	59.6
1987	750.2	46.0	358.0	267.7	8.2	64.4
1988	794.4	37.6	384.4	273.7	9.2	82.2
1989	845.2	40.0	420.5	266.5	9.8	101.5
1990	837.8	35.4	438.3	233.6	11.6	112.4
1991	830.8	36.1	449.8	204.5	11.7	122.5
1992	828.5	36.9	451.6	180.0	13.1	137.9
1993	843.1	40.0	453.8	172.2	13.6	153.7
1994	853.4	39.3	467.4	160.0	13.6	158.1
1995	880.9	40.4	497.7	147.1	15.1	163.6
1996	929.9	41.6	520.8	140.1	32.8	174.2

Source: See table 3.5.

Table A3.7
Ownership composition of government securities

Year	Households	Tax-exempt institutions	Insurance companies		
			Total	Life	Other
1970	0.8748	0.0836	0.0416	0.0169	0.0247
1971	0.8852	0.0736	0.0412	0.0162	0.0250
1972	0.8768	0.0835	0.0398	0.0155	0.0243
1973	0.8671	0.0962	0.0367	0.0138	0.0229
1974	0.8517	0.1121	0.0361	0.0131	0.0230
1975	0.8444	0.1150	0.0405	0.0140	0.0265
1976	0.8206	0.1315	0.0479	0.0149	0.0330
1977	0.7891	0.1555	0.0554	0.0162	0.0391
1978	0.7675	0.1745	0.0580	0.0180	0.0401
1979	0.7611	0.1846	0.0543	0.0180	0.0362
1980	0.7487	0.2007	0.0506	0.0170	0.0337
1981	0.7202	0.2276	0.0522	0.0190	0.0332
1982	0.6869	0.2633	0.0498	0.0212	0.0285
1983	0.6779	0.2688	0.0533	0.0249	0.0284
1984	0.6560	0.2837	0.0603	0.0282	0.0321
1985	0.6259	0.2977	0.0764	0.0375	0.0389
1986	0.6494	0.2722	0.0784	0.0353	0.0431
1987	0.6551	0.2683	0.0766	0.0333	0.0434
1988	0.6579	0.2669	0.0752	0.0304	0.0448
1989	0.6232	0.2947	0.0821	0.0320	0.0502
1990	0.6277	0.2926	0.0797	0.0305	0.0492
1991	0.6177	0.2886	0.0936	0.0358	0.0578
1992	0.6461	0.2659	0.0880	0.0354	0.0526
1993	0.6388	0.2689	0.0922	0.0379	0.0544
1994	0.6582	0.2558	0.0859	0.0349	0.0510
1995	0.6474	0.2674	0.0852	0.0344	0.0508
1996	0.6566	0.2644	0.0790	0.0328	0.0462

Source: See table 3.5.

Table A3.8
Household ownership distribution of government securities (billions of dollars)

Year	Household total	Commercial banks	Saving institutions	Mutual funds	Money market funds
1970	177.9	76.4	17.8	0.9	0.0
1971	179.7	83.6	21.4	0.6	0.0
1972	187.3	90.1	24.9	0.7	0.0
1973	194.9	88.8	25.9	0.7	0.0
1974	205.3	88.3	26.4	1.1	0.1
1975	255.2	119.9	38.0	1.1	0.9
1976	277.2	140.3	45.8	1.1	1.1
1977	285.5	139.5	54.8	1.8	0.9
1978	293.9	139.6	57.5	1.6	1.5
1979	349.4	147.6	59.9	1.5	5.6
1980	409.8	173.3	72.6	1.9	8.2
1981	443.7	185.4	80.6	2.8	31.9
1982	544.4	212.9	113.2	5.1	54.6
1983	669.3	259.5	167.8	5.7	36.2
1984	759.9	260.4	193.0	12.0	42.1
1985	820.0	266.9	194.4	64.9	42.4
1986	976.7	312.8	247.8	134.6	42.8
1987	1108.1	338.9	304.2	150.3	40.9
1988	1213.5	360.6	313.7	143.1	29.6
1989	1205.6	395.8	254.1	145.9	35.4
1990	1415.3	456.9	234.5	159.7	81.3
1991	1561.1	568.2	203.7	200.6	118.9
1992	1861.0	672.9	225.6	257.4	132.7
1993	1985.1	745.4	234.4	306.6	147.2
1994	2306.5	719.2	250.0	296.2	143.3
1995	2315.2	746.1	247.0	315.1	160.8
1996	2441.5	757.3	241.5	330.2	192.0

Source: See table 3.5.

Table A3.9
Ownership composition of household net debt

Year	Households	Tax-exempt institutions	Insurance companies		
			Total	Life	Other
1970	0.9148	0.0307	0.0545	0.0545	0.0000
1971	0.9282	0.0269	0.0448	0.0448	0.0000
1972	0.9428	0.0222	0.0350	0.0350	0.0000
1973	0.9531	0.0187	0.0282	0.0282	0.0000
1974	0.9585	0.0171	0.0244	0.0244	0.0000
1975	0.9637	0.0156	0.0208	0.0208	0.0000
1976	0.9705	0.0136	0.0159	0.0159	0.0000
1977	0.9767	0.0114	0.0119	0.0119	0.0000
1978	0.9802	0.0102	0.0096	0.0096	0.0000
1979	0.9805	0.0106	0.0090	0.0090	0.0000
1980	0.9795	0.0117	0.0088	0.0088	0.0000
1981	0.9808	0.0116	0.0076	0.0076	0.0000
1982	0.9803	0.0131	0.0066	0.0066	0.0000
1983	0.9837	0.0112	0.0051	0.0051	0.0000
1984	0.9855	0.0105	0.0039	0.0039	0.0000
1985	0.9880	0.0085	0.0035	0.0035	0.0000
1986	0.9899	0.0072	0.0029	0.0029	0.0000
1987	0.9918	0.0055	0.0027	0.0027	0.0000
1988	0.9929	0.0052	0.0019	0.0019	0.0000
1989	0.9921	0.0061	0.0018	0.0018	0.0000
1990	0.9923	0.0060	0.0017	0.0017	0.0000
1991	0.9937	0.0049	0.0014	0.0014	0.0000
1992	0.9940	0.0046	0.0014	0.0014	0.0000
1993	0.9952	0.0039	0.0010	0.0010	0.0000
1994	0.9958	0.0034	0.0007	0.0007	0.0000
1995	0.9958	0.0035	0.0007	0.0007	0.0000
1996	0.9960	0.0034	0.0006	0.0006	0.0000

Source: See table 3.5.

Table A3.10
Household ownership distribution of household net debt (billions of dollars)

Year	Households total	Commercial banks	Savings institutions	Mortgage pools
1970	365.3	111.5	195.2	3.3
1971	404.6	126.0	213.0	7.9
1972	462.8	147.7	241.8	12.3
1973	527.1	171.7	273.3	15.6
1974	567.3	182.6	294.0	19.2
1975	610.4	189.9	328.3	27.6
1976	693.0	210.9	372.7	40.1
1977	820.6	253.1	434.3	56.8
1978	972.2	306.6	501.6	70.9
1979	1124.5	349.9	562.7	97.1
1980	1220.1	359.0	600.0	119.4
1981	1306.0	376.9	630.6	141.4
1982	1354.0	388.9	595.3	198.6
1983	1498.4	419.2	632.1	269.8
1984	1708.8	486.8	725.7	326.9
1985	1979.3	547.1	787.5	422.2
1986	2231.5	590.6	785.9	590.6
1987	2484.6	650.9	794.3	739.2
1988	2753.3	753.1	885.2	823.4
1989	2969.8	825.9	864.6	950.1
1990	3210.8	906.0	821.4	1123.3
1991	3359.0	935.0	756.1	1309.4
1992	3511.4	967.3	703.6	1470.5
1993	3716.8	1061.7	694.3	1575.1
1994	4004.4	1181.6	715.4	1691.8
1995	4269.5	1288.3	734.4	1799.5
1996	4550.8	1348.4	791.2	1968.6

Source: See table 3.5.

Table A3.11
Capital cost recovery periods by asset class

		Recovery periods	
Asset	1980	ACRS (1981–1986)[1]	MACRS (1987–)[2]
A. Producer Durable Equipment			
1	9.2	5.00	5.20
2	9.2	5.00	7.00
3	11.5	5.40	6.49
4	14.4	10.67	15.30
5	14.4	8.01	11.70
6	5.0	5.00	6.52
7	5.0	5.00	5.15
8	9.2	5.00	7.00
9	9.1	5.00	5.36
10	8.9	5.00	7.00
11	11.8	4.53	5.86
12	11.8	4.89	6.60
13	11.3	5.25	7.26
14	9.2	5.00	5.00
15	9.5	5.12	5.24
16	11.4	7.73	9.99
17	11.4	7.74	10.34
18	11.4	5.00	5.00
19	11.4	5.00	5.23
20	5.1	3.56	5.00
21	2.8	3.00	5.00
22	6.0	5.00	7.00
23	16.6	5.00	9.88
24	13.8	5.00	7.00
25	9.86	6.32	7.78
26	9.8	4.98	5.20
27	9.4	5.00	5.32

Table A3.11 (continued)

		Recovery periods	
Asset	1980	ACRS (1981–1986)[1]	MACRS (1987–)[2]
B. Nonresidential Structures			
28	25.6	15.51	25.49
29	42.4	19.00	31.50
30	42.4	19.00	31.50
31	42.4	19.00	31.50
32	42.4	9.67	14.34
33	42.8	19.00	31.50
34	42.8	19.00	31.50
35	42.8	19.00	31.50
36	42.4	19.00	31.50
37	27.6	10.00	13.47
38	27.6	19.00	31.50
39	26.7	5.00	7.00
40	24.0	10.56	12.59
41	24.0	13.00	18.00
42	21.3	12.71	20.22
43	19.6	5.00	5.00
44	19.6	5.00	15.00
45	22.3	19.00	20.00
46	6.0	5.00	7.00
47	6.0	5.00	7.00
48	25.1	19.00	31.50
49	26.7	5.00	7.00
50	6.0	5.00	5.00
C. Residential Structures			
51	26.9	18.94	27.45

Notes:
1. ERTA of 1981 and TEFRA of 1982 prescribed new depreciation schedules (ACRS) and investment tax credits. ERTA was effective after December 31, 1980 and the basis adjustment of TEFRA went into effect on January 1, 1983. Recovery period of nonresidential real property was increased from 15 to 18 years on March 15, 1984, and then to 19 years on May 8, 1985.
2. In 1986, the Tax Reform Act of 1986 introduced the MACRS (modified ACRS). The Tax Reform Act of 1986 lowered tax rates (1987), abolished investment tax credits (1986) and increased recovery period of assets. The recovery period of nonresidential real property was increased from 31.5 to 39 years on May 13, 1993.
Source: 1980 figures are from Jorgenson and Sullivan (1981) and the recovery period under the ACRS and the MACRS are from Fullerton, Gillette, and Mackie (1987), p.138.

Table A3.12
Depreciation schedule by recovery class under ACRS: 1981–1986

Age of Asset	Recovery period (years) Personal property				Real property		
	3	5	10	15	15	18	19
1	0.25	0.15	0.08	0.05	0.06	0.05	0.05
2	0.38	0.22	0.14	0.10	0.11	0.09	0.09
3	0.37	0.21	0.12	0.09	0.10	0.08	0.08
4		0.21	0.10	0.08	0.09	0.08	0.07
5		0.21	0.10	0.07	0.08	0.07	0.07
6			0.10	0.07	0.07	0.06	0.06
7			0.09	0.06	0.06	0.06	0.06
8			0.09	0.06	0.05	0.05	0.05
9			0.09	0.06	0.05	0.05	0.05
10			0.09	0.06	0.05	0.05	0.04
11				0.06	0.05	0.05	0.04
12				0.06	0.05	0.05	0.04
13				0.06	0.05	0.04	0.04
14				0.06	0.05	0.04	0.04
15				0.06	0.05	0.04	0.04
16					0.03	0.04	0.04
17						0.04	0.04
18						0.04	0.04
19						0.02	0.04
20							0.02

Note: The depreciation schedule for personal (3-,5-,10-,15 year) property follows 150% declining balance method with an optimal switchover to straight-line method. Real property follows 175% declining balance method with an optimal switchover to straight-line method.

Table A3.13a
Depreciation schedules by recovery period under the modified ACRS: 1987–

Age of Asset	Recovery period (years)—personal property					
	3	5	7	10	15	20
1	0.3333	0.2000	0.1429	0.1000	0.0500	0.0375
2	0.4444	0.3200	0.2449	0.1800	0.0950	0.0722
3	0.1481	0.1920	0.1749	0.1440	0.0855	0.0668
4	0.0742	0.1152	0.1249	0.1152	0.0770	0.0618
5		0.1152	0.0892	0.0922	0.0693	0.0571
6		0.0576	0.0892	0.0737	0.0623	0.0528
7			0.0892	0.0655	0.0590	0.0489
8			0.0448	0.0655	0.0590	0.0452
9				0.0655	0.0590	0.0446
10				0.0655	0.0590	0.0446
11				0.0329	0.0590	0.0446
12					0.0590	0.0446
13					0.0590	0.0446
14					0.0590	0.0446
15					0.0590	0.0446
16					0.0299	0.0446
17						0.0446
18						0.0446
19						0.0446
20						0.0446
21						0.0225

Table A3.13b
Depreciation schedules under modified ACRS: 1989

Age of Asset	Recovery period (years)—real property		
	27.5	31.5	39.0 (1993–)
1	0.0182	0.0159	0.0128
2	0.0364	0.0318	0.0257
3	0.0364	0.0317	0.0256
4	0.0364	0.0318	0.0257
5	0.0364	0.0317	0.0256
6	0.0364	0.0318	0.0257
7	0.0364	0.0317	0.0256
8	0.0364	0.0318	0.0257
9	0.0364	0.0317	0.0256
10	0.0363	0.0318	0.0257
11	0.0364	0.0317	0.0256
12	0.0363	0.0318	0.0257
13	0.0364	0.0317	0.0256
14	0.0363	0.0318	0.0257
15	0.0364	0.0317	0.0256
16	0.0363	0.0318	0.0257
17	0.0364	0.0317	0.0256
18	0.0363	0.0318	0.0257
19	0.0364	0.0317	0.0256
20	0.0363	0.0318	0.0257′
21	0.0364	0.0317	0.0256
22	0.0363	0.0318	0.0257
23	0.0364	0.0317	0.0256
24	0.0363	0.0318	0.0257
26	0.0363	0.0318	0.0257
27	0.0364	0.0317	0.0256
28	0.0363	0.0318	0.0257
29		0.0317	0.0256
30		0.0317	0.0257
31		0.0317	0.0256
32		0.0317	0.0257
33			0.0256
34			0.0256
35			0.0256
36			0.0256
37			0.0256
38			0.0256
39			0.0256
40			0.0128

Notes: Recovery period of nonresidential structures was extended from 31.5 to 39 years in 1993.

Table A3.14
Proportion of capital stock and investment in the lower recovery class: ACRS (1981–1986)

Asset Category	Recovery period			Weight	
	Lower	Average	Upper	Capital	Investment
A. Producer Durable Equipment					
1	5.0	5.00	10.0	1.0000	1.0000
2	5.0	5.00	10.0	1.0000	1.0000
3	5.0	5.40	10.0	0.9200	0.9548
4	10.0	10.67	15.0	0.8660	0.9071
5	5.0	8.01	10.0	0.3980	0.5669
6	5.0	5.00	10.0	1.0000	1.0000
7	5.0	5.00	10.0	1.0000	1.0000
8	5.0	5.00	10.0	1.0000	1.0000
9	5.0	5.00	10.0	1.0000	1.0000
10	5.0	5.00	10.0	1.0000	1.0000
11	3.0	4.53	5.0	0.2350	0.3217
12	3.0	4.89	5.0	0.0550	0.0837
13	5.0	5.25	10.0	0.9500	0.9679
14	5.0	5.00	10.0	1.0000	1.0000
15	5.0	5.12	10.0	0.9760	0.9863
16	5.0	7.73	10.0	0.4540	0.5807
17	5.0	7.74	10.0	0.4520	0.5736
18	5.0	5.00	10.0	1.0000	1.0000
19	5.0	5.00	10.0	1.0000	1.0000
20	3.0	3.56	5.0	0.7200	0.7944
21	3.0	3.00	5.0	1.0000	1.0000
22	5.0	5.00	10.0	1.0000	1.0000
23	5.0	5.00	10.0	1.0000	1.0000
24	5.0	5.00	10.0	1.0000	1.0000
25	5.0	6.32	10.0	0.7360	0.8395
26	3.0	4.98	5.0	0.0100	0.0161
27	5.0	5.00	10.0	1.0000	1.0000

Table A3.14 (continued)

Asset Category	Recovery period			Weight	
	Lower	Average	Upper	Capital	Investment
B. Nonresidential Structures					
28	15.0	15.51	19.0	0.8725	0.8886
29	15.0	19.00	19.0	0.0000	0.0000
30	15.0	19.00	19.0	0.0000	0.0000
31	15.0	19.00	19.0	0.0000	0.0000
32	5.0	9.67	10.0	0.0660	0.0950
33	15.0	19.00	19.0	0.0000	0.0000
34	15.0	19.00	19.0	0.0000	0.0000
35	15.0	19.00	19.0	0.0000	0.0000
36	15.0	19.00	19.0	0.0000	0.0000
37	10.0	10.00	15.0	1.0000	1.0000
38	15.0	19.00	19.0	0.0000	0.0000
39	5.0	5.00	10.0	1.0000	1.0000
40	10.0	10.56	15.0	0.8880	0.9042
41	10.0	13.00	15.0	0.4000	0.4959
42	10.0	12.71	15.0	0.4580	0.5492
43	5.0	5.00	10.0	1.0000	1.0000
44	5.0	5.00	10.0	1.0000	1.0000
45	15.0	19.00	19.0	0.0000	0.0000
46	5.0	5.00	10.0	1.0000	1.0000
47	5.0	5.00	10.0	1.0000	1.0000
48	15.0	19.00	19.0	0.0000	0.0000
49	5.0	5.00	10.0	1.0000	1.0000
50	5.0	5.00	10.0	1.0000	1.0000
C. Residential Structures					
51	15.0	18.94	19.0	0.0150	0.0166

Notes:
1. When the average recovery period coincides with one of the statutory recovery periods, a weight of 1.0 is assigned to the statutory recovery class.
2. A recovery period of 19 years (1986 value) is used for real property.
3. "Lower" and "upper" stand for the statutory recovery periods that bracket the average recovery period from below and from above, respectively.
4. The average recovery periods are from table A3.11. For calculation of capital stock weights, see chapter 3, and for calculation of investment weights, see chapter 8.

Table A3.15
Proportion of capital stock and investment in the lower recovery class: MACRS (1987–)

Asset Category	Recovery period Lower	Average	Upper	Weight Capital	Investment
A. Producer Durable Equipment					
1	5.0	5.20	7.0	0.9000	0.9235
2	7.0	7.00	10.0	1.0000	1.0000
3	5.0	6.49	7.0	0.2550	0.3166
4	15.0	15.30	20.0	0.9400	0.9543
5	10.0	11.70	15.0	0.6600	0.7370
6	5.0	6.52	7.0	0.2400	0.2989
7	5.0	5.15	7.0	0.9250	0.9444
8	7.0	7.00	10.0	1.0000	1.0000
9	5.0	5.36	7.0	0.8200	0.8547
10	7.0	7.00	10.0	1.0000	1.0000
11	5.0	5.86	.0	0.5700	0.6355
12	5.0	6.60	7.0	0.2000	0.2511
13	7.0	7.26	10.0	0.9133	0.9310
14	5.0	5.00	7.0	1.0000	1.0000
15	5.0	5.24	7.0	0.8800	0.9070
16	7.0	9.99	10.0	0.0033	0.0042
17	10.0	10.34	15.0	0.9320	0.9458
18	5.0	5.00	7.0	1.0000	1.0000
19	5.0	5.23	7.0	0.8850	0.9130
20	5.0	5.00	7.0	1.0000	1.0000
21	5.0	5.00	7.0	1.0000	1.0000
22	7.0	7.00	10.0	1.0000	1.0000
23	7.0	9.88	10.0	0.0400	0.0693
24	7.0	7.00	10.0	1.0000	1.0000
25	7.0	7.78	10.0	0.7400	0.7940
26	5.0	5.20	7.0	0.9000	0.9246
27	5.0	5.32	7.0	0.8400	0.8750

Table A3.15 (continued)

Asset Category	Recovery period Lower	Average	Upper	Weight Capital	Investment
B. Nonresidential Structures					
28	20.0	25.49	31.5	0.5226	0.6258
29	20.0	31.50	31.5	0.0000	0.0000
30	20.0	31.50	31.5	0.0000	0.0000
31	20.0	31.50	31.5	0.0000	0.0000
32	10.0	14.34	15.0	0.1320	0.1586
33	20.0	31.50	31.5	0.0000	0.0000
34	20.0	31.50	31.5	0.0000	0.0000
35	20.0	31.50	31.5	0.0000	0.0000
36	20.0	31.50	31.5	0.0000	0.0000
37	10.0	13.47	15.0	0.3060	0.3469
38	20.0	31.50	31.5	0.0000	0.0000
39	7.0	7.00	10.0	1.0000	1.0000
40	10.0	12.59	15.0	0.4820	0.5304
41	15.0	18.00	20.0	0.4000	0.4664
42	20.0	20.22	31.5	0.9809	0.9888
43	5.0	5.00	7.0	1.0000	1.0000
44	15.0	15.00	20.0	1.0000	1.0000
45	20.0	20.00	31.5	1.0000	1.0000
46	7.0	7.00	10.0	1.0000	1.0000
47	7.0	7.00	10.0	1.0000	1.0000
48	20.0	31.50	31.5	0.0000	0.0000
49	7.0	7.00	10.0	1.0000	1.0000
50	5.0	5.00	10.0	1.0000	1.0000
C. Residential Structures					
51	20.0	27.45	27.5	0.0067	0.0076

Notes:
1) For residential structures (asset number 51), the statutory recovery period bracket of 20–27.5 year is used. Since the 27.5-year recovery period is for residential structures only, for other real property, the 20–31.5-year bracket is used.
2) For other notes, see table A3.14.

Table A3.16a
Capital stock composition (1996)—Producer durable equipment (PDE)

Asset	Corporate	Noncorporate	Household
1	0.0021	0.0078	0.0171
2	0.0596	0.0611	0.0637
3	0.0396	0.0198	0.0298
4	0.0202	0.0047	0.0150
5	0.0014	0.0040	0.0072
6	0.0089	0.0607	0.0126
7	0.0046	0.0041	0.0037
8	0.0116	0.1005	0.0033
9	0.0246	0.0208	0.0028
10	0.0051	0.0028	0.0000
11	0.0725	0.0206	0.0244
12	0.0869	0.0381	0.0692
13	0.0682	0.0349	0.0309
14	0.0646	0.0400	0.0168
15	0.0228	0.0376	0.0394
16	0.1354	0.1028	0.0986
17	0.1026	0.0231	0.0338
18	0.0017	0.0023	0.0039
19	0.0126	0.0258	0.0528
20	0.0708	0.1028	0.0096
21	0.0187	0.0265	0.0005
22	0.0277	0.0131	0.0013
23	0.0157	0.0127	0.0002
24	0.0330	0.0118	0.0000
25	0.0323	0.0761	0.2138
26	0.0297	0.0279	0.0323
27	0.0272	0.1176	0.2175
Total	1.0000	1.0000	1.0000

Note: Asset numbers are the same as in table 3.15.

Table A3.16b
Capital stock composition (1996)—Nonresidential structures (NRS)

Asset	Corporate	Noncorporate	Household
28	0.1883	0.0186	0.0000
29	0.0021	0.0016	0.0000
30	0.1490	0.2419	0.0168
31	0.0000	0.0000	0.0000
32	0.1565	0.2849	0.0184
33	0.0000	0.0000	0.2336
34	0.0008	0.0010	0.2163
35	0.0083	0.0151	0.4223
36	0.0264	0.0969	0.0000
37	0.0095	0.0120	0.0346
38	0.0050	0.0339	0.0000
39	0.0896	0.0000	0.0000
40	0.0665	0.0075	0.0046
41	0.1278	0.0030	0.0534
42	0.0521	0.0000	0.0000
43	0.0000	0.0000	0.0000
44	0.0072	0.0000	0.0000
45	0.0041	0.1983	0.0000
46	0.0710	0.0394	0.0000
47	0.0080	0.0015	0.0000
48	0.0277	0.0445	0.0000
49	0.0000	0.0000	0.0000
50	0.0000	0.0000	0.0000
Total	1.0000	1.0000	1.0000

Note: Asset numbers are the same as in table 3.15.

Table A3.16c
Capital stock composition (1996)—Consumer durables (CD)

Asset	Corporate	Noncorporate	Household
1			0.2339
2			0.1172
3			0.0240
4			0.1198
5			0.0532
6			0.0408
7			0.0962
8			0.0135
9			0.0920
10			0.0817
11			0.0155
12			0.0390
13			0.0732
Total			1.0000

Note: Asset numbers are the same as in table 3.16.

Table A3.17
Composition of short-lived and long-lived assets (1996)

A. Capital stock (billions of 1996 dollars)			
	Corporate	Noncorporate	Household
1. Short-lived Assets			
CD	0.0	0.0	2820.8
PDE	2574.6	480.0	146.8
Total	2574.6	480.0	2967.6
2. Long-lived Assets			
NRS	3534.1	968.5	621.5
RS	101.3	2135.0	6052.1
FINV	10.8	91.8	0.0
NFINV	1121.2	70.8	0.0
LAND	1106.3	1561.9	1980.2
Total	5873.7	4828.0	8653.8

Table A3.17 (continued)

B. Composition of Capital Stock	Corporate	Noncorporate	Household
1. Short-lived Assets			
CD	0.0000	0.0000	0.9505
PDE	1.0000	1.0000	0.0495
Total	1.0000	1.0000	1.0000
2. Long-lived Assets			
NRS	0.6017	0.2006	0.0718
RS	0.0172	0.4422	0.6994
FINV	0.0018	0.0190	0.0000
NFINV	0.1909	0.0147	0.0000
LAND	0.1884	0.3235	0.2288
Total	1.0000	1.0000	1.0000

Notations:
CD: Consumer durables
PDE: Producer durable equipment
NRS: Nonresidential structures
RS: Residential structures
FINV: Farm inventories
NFINV: Nonfarm inventories
Land: Land

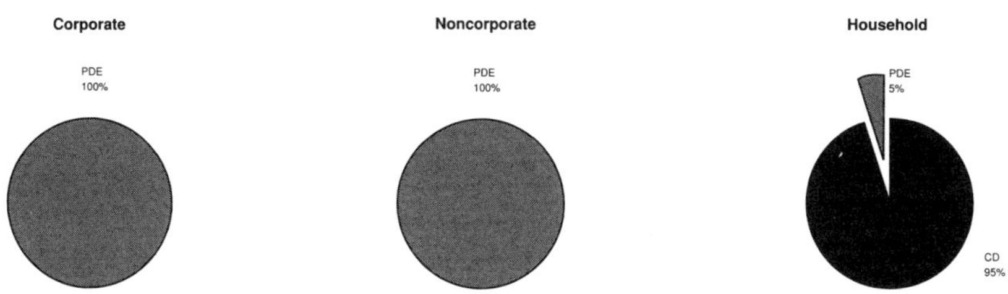

Figure A3.1
Composition of capital stock: Short-lived assets.

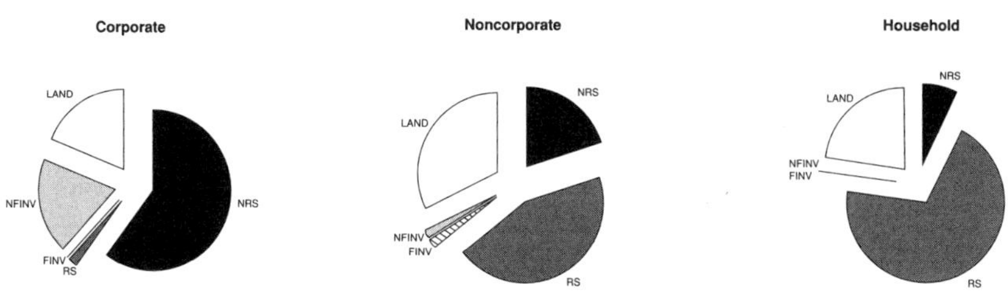

Figure A3.2
Composition of capital stock: Long-lived assets.

Notes

1. These forms of ownership are distinguished, for example, by King and Fullerton (1984) and Jorgenson and Yun (1991b).
2. This method of estimation of average marginal tax rates was introduced by Barro and Sahasakul (1983, 1985) and employed by Jorgenson and Yun (1991b).
3. This assumption is employed, for example, by Bailey (1969), King and Fullerton (1984), and Jorgenson and Yun (1991b).
4. See Feldstein and Summers (1979), King and Fullerton (1984), and Jorgenson and Yun (1991b).
5. In 1982 TEFRA changed the formula to a geometric 10-for-1 formula to provide a better approximation to the deduction when the rate of inflation is high. The geometric version of the formula is $i\,R^*\;0.9^{100(i-i^*)}$.
6. King and Fullerton (1984), p. 227, and table 6.13, p. 234, estimate that the marginal tax rate on dividends is 0.15 t_q, which is equivalent to assuming that all intercorporate dividends are allocated to the company. However, the dividends received by the company are included in gross investment income and are divided between the company and the policyholders in accord with the Menge formula.
7. This allocation is employed by Feldstein and Summers (1979), Feldstein, Poterba, and Dicks-Mireaux (1983), and Jorgenson and Yun (1991b).
8. Surveys of the hedonic technique are given by Triplett (1975, 1987, 1990).
9. Gordon (1989) has presented an alternative constant quality price index for computers. This was incorporated into Gordon's (1990) study of constant quality price indices for all components of producers' durable equipment in the U.S. National Accounts.
10. Hulten and Wykoff (1980) estimated vintage price functions for structures from a sample of 8066 observations on market transactions in used structures. These data were collected by the Office of Industrial Economics of the U.S. Department of the Treasury in 1972 and were published in *Business Building Statistics* (1975). They estimated vintage price functions for equipment from prices of machine tools collected by Beidleman (1976) and prices of other types of equipment collected from used equipment dealers and auction reports of the U.S. General Services Administration.
11. Detailed histories of U.S. tax policy for capital recovery are presented by Brazell, Dworin, and Walsh (1989) and Jorgenson and Yun (1991b).
12. Joint Committee on taxation (1986), p. 103.
13. See Fraumeni (1997) for a description of the BEA estimates.
14. For tax lives by asset class prior to the ERTA of 1981, see column 1 of table A3.11.
15. For tax lives by asset class under the ERTA of 1981, see column 2 of table A3.11. For depreciation schedules by recovery class under the ACRS, see table A3.12.
16. For tax lives by asset class under the modified ACRS, see column 3 of table A3.11. For depreciation schedules by recovery period under the modified ACRS, see tables A3.13a,b.
17. Data for current values of land are from *The Balance Sheet for the U.S. Economy*, published annually by the Board of Governors of the Federal Reserve System. Data for sales and purchases of land are from *Survey of Current Business*, July 1987, table 3.17B and table 3.18, and various other issues.
18. Dividend data are from Bureau of Economic Analysis (1977), National Income and Product Accounts: 1929–1974, and various issues of the *Survey of Current Business*.
19. Hulten and Wykoff (1981c) summarize studies of economic depreciation completed prior to their own study. Vintage Price functions have provided the most common methodology for such studies.
20. Fullerton (1987), pp. 30–35, presents a detailed description of the data employed in his study. A similar description is given by Fullerton, Gillette, and Mackie (1987), pp. 135–142, for the data used in their study.

4 Effective Tax Rates

In this chapter we summarize the tax burden on capital income by means of the marginal effective tax rate, introduced by Auerbach and Jorgenson (1980). An effective tax rate represents the complex provisions of tax law in terms of a single *ad valorem* rate. This tax rate is based on the social rate of return, defined as income per dollar of capital, adjusted for inflation and depreciation, but not for taxes. This social rate of return can be compared with the corresponding private rate of return, which excludes all tax liabilities at both corporate and individual levels. The effective tax rate is defined as the difference between the social and private rates of return, divided by the social rate of return, net of inflation.

We calculate private and social rates of return for assets in the corporate, noncorporate, and household sectors. Private rates of return on capital differ among sectors, since they depend on the debt/capital ratio of each sector. However, these rates of return are the same for all types of assets within a given sector. The social rates of return depend on asset specific provisions of U.S. tax law, such as the rate of the investment tax credit and the present value of tax deductions for capital consumption allowances, and may differ among assets within a sector. We also present marginal effective tax rates, defined as ratios of the tax wedges to the social rates of return, net of inflation, for all types of assets.

In section 4.1 we estimate social rates of return for 67 types of assets—the 51 types of depreciable business assets listed in table 3.15, the 13 types of consumer durables listed in table 3.16, and three types of nondepreciable assets—farm inventories, nonfarm inventories, and land—in the household, noncorporate, and corporate sectors. We assume that interest rates on net debt in the household, noncorporate, and corporate sectors are equal to the interest rate on corporate bonds of the Baa class. We also assume that nominal private rates of return on equity are the same in all three sectors.

In order to establish a basis for comparison among sectors and time periods we calculate the social rate of return and the effective tax rate for an after-tax corporate rate of return on corporate capital, $r^c - \pi$, of 6.50 percent per year and a dividend pay-out ratio, α, of 42.62 percent. These values are set at their averages for 1970–1996. We can solve for the nominal private rate of return on equity ρ^e from the definition of the weighted average rate of return to corporate capital, adjusted for inflation, presented in chapter 2.

For each class of assets in the corporate and noncorporate sectors, we calculate weighted averages of social rates of return, where the values of the assets are used as weights. Due to sectoral differences in the capital structure, the ownership distribution of financial claims, and the tax treatment of different owners, the private and social rates of return for an asset may depend on the sector in which it is employed. We present social rates of return and effective tax rates, defined as ratios of the tax wedges to the social rates of return, net of inflation, for assets employed in the corporate, noncorporate and household sectors in section 4.2.

In section 4.3 we discuss discrepancies in tax burdens among different assets within a given sector and the same asset in different sectors. Differences among social rates of return provide a means of quantifying the impact of distortions in the allocation of capital. For example, suppose that the social rates of return on two assets differ by, say, five percent and that the private rate of return is five percent. If tax policy can be changed so that one dollar's worth of capital is transferred from the lightly taxed asset to the heavily taxed asset, the yield at the margin is five cents. At a private rate of return of five percent, this addition to the stream of income is worth one dollar. Wealth is one dollar before the transfer and two dollars after the transfer, so that the national wealth can be doubled at the margin by changing tax policy.

Finally, the effective tax rates for the corporate sector presented in this chapter are based on the "traditional" view of corporate income taxation discussed in chapter 2. We also distinguish marginal effective tax rates based on the cost of capital from average effective tax rates. Average effective tax rates are based on comparisons of corporate tax liabilities with corporate income from both new and existing assets. It is marginal rather than average tax rates that are relevant to comparisons of resource allocation under alternative tax policies. Effective tax rates for the corporate sector have also been calculated on the basis of the "new" view outlined in section 2.8. In section 4.4 we compare these alternative approaches.

4.1 Economic Impact of U.S. Tax Law

The effective tax rate on an asset depends on provisions of U.S. tax law as well as factors not determined by the tax law that affect the economic impact of the tax system. The tax provisions include the definitions of taxable income, rate schedules for the various types of income, and rules for capital cost recovery, such as the rate of the investment tax credit and formulas for calculating capital consumption allowances. Other determinants of effective tax rates include the rate of inflation, the interest rate, the rate of return to equity, the dividend pay-out ratio in the corporate sector, and the distributions of financial assets among owners with different tax statuses.

The analytical framework presented in chapter 2 makes it possible to show how the rate of interest and the rate of inflation interact in determining effective tax rates. For example, if the marginal tax rate of a firm is greater than that of the individual who holds the debt of the firm, inflation can reduce the tax burden on income from capital by increasing nominal interest rates. An increase in nominal interest rates raises deductions for interest expenses at the level of the firm and increases tax liabilities for interest income at the level of the individual by the same amount. The reduction in taxes resulting from the deductibility of nominal interest expenses outweighs the increased tax liability for interest income.[1]

Since capital consumption allowances are based on the original acquisition cost of investment goods, nominal interest rates affect the present value of capital consumption allowances. To the extent that inflation increases the nominal interest rate, it can raise the tax burden on assets by reducing the present value of capital consumption allowances, inflating nominal capital gains, and pushing taxpayers into higher marginal tax brackets. Column 1 of table 4.1 and figure 4.1a show the rate of inflation in the acquisition price of tangible assets in the United States for the period 1970–1996. The nominal interest rate has increased substantially over the postwar period, reaching a peak of 16.11 percent in 1982. This trend in the nominal interest rate affects costs of capital, social rates of return, and effective tax rates. Table 4.1 and figures 4.1a, b, and c show nominal interest rate,

Table 4.1
Rates of inflation and interest, discount rates, and private rates of return

Year	π	i	$r^q - \pi$	$r^m - \pi$	$r^h - \pi$	$\rho^b - \pi$	$\rho^q - \pi$	$\rho^m - \pi$	$\rho^h - \pi$
1970	0.0411	0.0911	0.0592	0.0502	0.0459	0.0506	0.0512	0.0496	0.0467
1971	0.0503	0.0856	0.0592	0.0504	0.0447	0.0504	0.0510	0.0495	0.0454
1972	0.0834	0.0816	0.0587	0.0477	0.0376	0.0475	0.0486	0.0459	0.0383
1973	0.0809	0.0824	0.0594	0.0461	0.0370	0.0470	0.0487	0.0444	0.0377
1974	0.0320	0.0950	0.0587	0.0505	0.0482	0.0511	0.0518	0.0503	0.0490
1975	0.1255	0.1061	0.0618	0.0324	0.0261	0.0406	0.0472	0.0296	0.0269
1976	0.0655	0.0975	0.0558	0.0467	0.0438	0.0474	0.0485	0.0457	0.0445
1977	0.0968	0.0897	0.0554	0.0436	0.0395	0.0447	0.0464	0.0418	0.0401
1978	0.1083	0.0949	0.0548	0.0431	0.0374	0.0443	0.0462	0.0410	0.0381
1979	0.1194	0.1069	0.0543	0.0415	0.0348	0.0435	0.0456	0.0399	0.0356
1980	0.1089	0.1367	0.0518	0.0411	0.0356	0.0431	0.0451	0.0397	0.0366
1981	0.1128	0.1604	0.0510	0.0417	0.0370	0.0432	0.0452	0.0400	0.0381
1982	0.0517	0.1611	0.0502	0.0497	0.0487	0.0512	0.0518	0.0501	0.0496
1983	0.0218	0.1355	0.0507	0.0511	0.0513	0.0534	0.0542	0.0520	0.0520
1984	0.0610	0.1419	0.0512	0.0506	0.0487	0.0520	0.0527	0.0510	0.0495
1985	0.0816	0.1272	0.0534	0.0506	0.0459	0.0513	0.0520	0.0502	0.0466
1986	0.0462	0.1039	0.0539	0.0522	0.0488	0.0529	0.0532	0.0525	0.0495
1987	0.0465	0.1058	0.0572	0.0535	0.0485	0.0526	0.0529	0.0521	0.0491
1988	0.0605	0.1083	0.0583	0.0537	0.0466	0.0526	0.0532	0.0517	0.0472
1989	0.0597	0.1018	0.0591	0.0538	0.0455	0.0527	0.0534	0.0517	0.0461

Table 4.1 (continued)

Year	π	i	$r^q - \pi$	$r^m - \pi$	$r^h - \pi$	$\rho^b - \pi$	$\rho^q - \pi$	$\rho^m - \pi$	$\rho^h - \pi$
1990	0.0081	0.1036	0.0588	0.0559	0.0574	0.0566	0.0566	0.0566	0.0579
1991	0.0054	0.0980	0.0587	0.0556	0.0573	0.0565	0.0566	0.0565	0.0579
1992	-0.0034	0.0898	0.0595	0.0561	0.0587	0.0573	0.0573	0.0573	0.0593
1993	-0.0015	0.0793	0.0595	0.0551	0.0558	0.0565	0.0567	0.0562	0.0564
1994	-0.0017	0.0863	0.0595	0.0553	0.0571	0.0566	0.0567	0.0565	0.0577
1995	0.0303	0.0820	0.0602	0.0541	0.0466	0.0540	0.0544	0.0532	0.0472
1996	0.0295	0.0805	0.0606	0.0543	0.0464	0.0542	0.0547	0.0533	0.0470

Notes:
The rate of return on corporate capital after corporate taxes, $r^c - \pi$, and the dividend pay-out ratio, α, are set at the 1970–1996 averages, 6.50% and 42.62%, respectively.
π: Rate of inflation in the price of assets
i: Rate of interest on Baa class corporate bonds
$r^q - \pi$: Discount rate for corporate investment
$r^m - \pi$: Discount rate for noncorporate investment
$r^h - \pi$: Discount rate for household investment
$\rho^b - \pi$: Private rate of return on business investment
$\rho^q - \pi$: Private rate of return on corporate investment
$\rho^m - \pi$: Private rate of return on noncorporate investment
$\rho^h - \pi$: Private rate of return on household investment

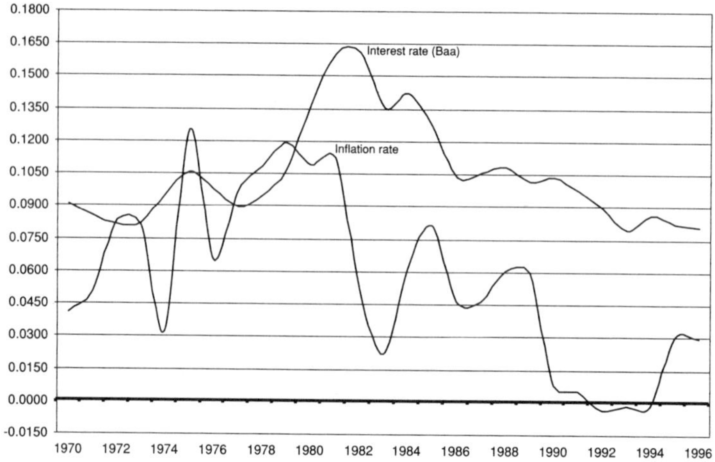

Figure 4.1a
Nominal interest rate and inflation in the price of asset.

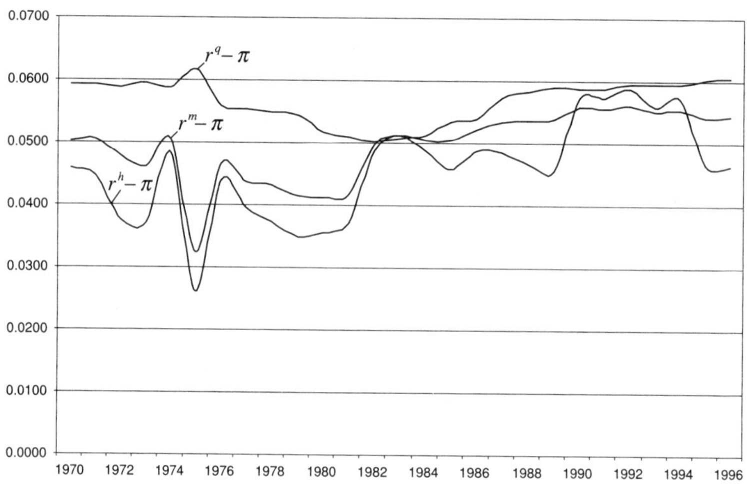

Notes: $r^q - \pi$: Corporate; $r^m - \pi$: Noncorporate; $r^h - \pi$: Household

Figure 4.1b
Discount rates for investment income.

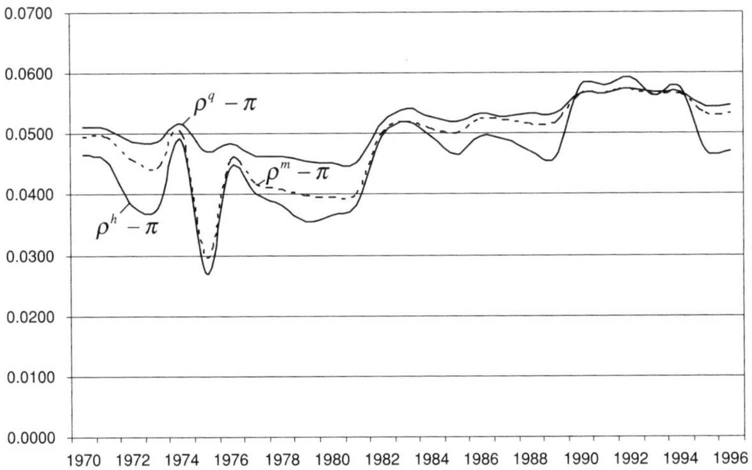

Notes: $\rho^q - \pi$: Corporate; $\rho^m - \pi$: Noncorporate; $\rho^h - \pi$: Household

Figure 4.1c
Private rates of return.

discount rates, and private rates of return in the corporate, noncorporate, and household sectors.

Changes in the distribution of financial assets affect the tax burden on income from capital through changes in average tax rates. In the case of corporate equity the share of households declined steadily from 79.93 percent in 1970 to 58.67 percent in 1985. In the same period the share of tax-exempt owners increased from 16.73 percent to 36.67 percent and that of insurance companies fluctuated between 3.33 and 4.90 percent. These changes in the distribution of corporate equity among owners with different tax statuses, together with the decline in statutory tax rates, underlie the downward trend in average marginal tax rates on dividends and capital gains. We could conduct a parallel analysis for the debt of the corporate, noncorporate, and household sectors. Changes in the distribution of debt had major impacts on the marginal tax rates on interest income.

Since the introduction of accelerated depreciation in 1954, most of the significant changes in the treatment of income from capital U.S. tax law have been directed toward providing tax incentives for private investment. In the years of tax reductions—1954, 1962, 1966, 1969, 1971, 1975, 1981—unemployment peaked. We conclude that past changes in tax law have been motivated in part by the objective of counteracting the fluctuations of the U.S. economy. The effects of changes in tax policy are most visible in the case of short-lived assets. This is not surprising since most of the tax changes were targeted at short-lived assets, particularly through the liberalization of the investment tax credit and capital consumption allowances.

4.2 Effective Tax Rates

In order to condense the presentation of effective tax rates we aggregate the assets within each sector into larger groups. We aggregate the corporate and noncorporate assets into producer's durable equipment (PDE), nonresidential structures (NRS), residential structures (RS), and nondepreciable assets (ND). We also aggregate the assets into the short-lived depreciable assets (SD), long-lived depreciable assets (LD), short-lived assets (S), long-lived assets (L), depreciable assets (D), nondepreciable assets (ND), and all assets (A). PDE includes the first 27 types of assets in table 3.15, NRS includes the next 23 types of assets, and RS is the remaining asset type included in this table.

We use names of the asset groups to indicate the criterion for asset classification. Short-lived depreciable assets (SD) and short-lived assets (S) include PDE only. Long-lived depreciable assets (LD) include NRS and RS, and long-lived assets also include nondepreciable assets (ND), which in turn include inventories and land. Depreciable assets (D) include SD and LD and all assets (A) include S and L or equivalently D and ND. For household assets there are no asset specific tax provisions; therefore, we group all the household assets into a single category. In table 4.2 and figures 4.2a–d we present the social rates of return and effective tax rates of assets in the business sector.

In 1954 accelerated depreciation was made available for all new investment goods and the proportion of new investment using accelerated depreciation methods began to increase rapidly. Jorgenson and Sullivan (1981) estimate that the proportion of new investment using accelerated depreciation was only 9 percent in 1953. This proportion jumped to 52 percent in 1955 and rose to 85 percent by 1978. However, the effects of this tax reduction were not sufficient to offset the effects of rising interest rates and increases in tax rates.

In 1968 the 10 percent Vietnam War tax surcharge was imposed. The investment tax credit was abolished in April 1969. Capital consumption allowances for structures signed into contract after July 24, 1969, were restricted to the 150 percent declining balance method.

Table 4.2
Effective tax rates on business assets

	(1) PDE=SD=S		(2) NRS		(3) RS	
Year	$\sigma^b - \pi$	e^b	$\sigma^b - \pi$	e^b	$\sigma^b - \pi$	e^b
1970	0.1003	0.4958	0.0994	0.4915	0.0779	0.3507
1971	0.1067	0.5276	0.1039	0.5149	0.0796	0.3670
1972	0.0895	0.4691	0.1001	0.5253	0.0767	0.3806
1973	0.0825	0.4305	0.0978	0.5200	0.0739	0.3646
1974	0.0815	0.3725	0.0970	0.4725	0.0778	0.3428
1975	0.0844	0.5192	0.0985	0.5882	0.0601	0.3248
1976	0.0751	0.3685	0.0919	0.4837	0.0756	0.3720
1977	0.0691	0.3525	0.0884	0.4940	0.0715	0.3746
1978	0.0621	0.2869	0.0845	0.4760	0.0687	0.3555
1979	0.0606	0.2820	0.0819	0.4694	0.0664	0.3455
1980	0.0615	0.2996	0.0819	0.4746	0.0666	0.3539
1981	0.0667	0.3522	0.0863	0.4995	0.0699	0.3825
1982	0.0513	0.0031	0.0705	0.2743	0.0714	0.2828
1983	0.0519	−0.0292	0.0706	0.2445	0.0718	0.2570
1984	0.0561	0.0728	0.0716	0.2733	0.0710	0.2666
1985	0.0588	0.1269	0.0752	0.3181	0.0723	0.2908
1986	0.0575	0.0799	0.0750	0.2944	0.0728	0.2728
1987	0.0777	0.3237	0.0765	0.3125	0.0720	0.2701
1988	0.0834	0.3694	0.0854	0.3839	0.0766	0.3134
1989	0.0845	0.3762	0.0864	0.3899	0.0777	0.3211
1990	0.0832	0.3198	0.0857	0.3394	0.0794	0.2871
1991	0.0840	0.3267	0.0865	0.3463	0.0799	0.2927
1992	0.0843	0.3203	0.0871	0.3419	0.0804	0.2875
1993	0.0844	0.3304	0.0874	0.3532	0.0798	0.2913
1994	0.0832	0.3196	0.0870	0.3488	0.0795	0.2877
1995	0.0850	0.3650	0.0889	0.3934	0.0797	0.3227
1996	0.0850	0.3627	0.0891	0.3916	0.0787	0.3113

Notes: Property taxes are included in the calculation and the after-corporate-tax real rate of return, $r^c - \pi$, and the corporate dividend pay-out ratio, α, are set at their sample averages, 6.50 and 42.62%, respectively.

PDE: Producer durable equipment
NRS: Non-residential structures
RS: Residential structures
SD: Short-lived depreciable assets
S: Short-lived assets
$\sigma^b - \pi$: Social rate of return
e^b: Effective tax rate

Table 4.2 (continued)

	(4) LD		(5) L		(6) D	
Year	$\sigma^b - \pi$	e^b	$\sigma^b - \pi$	e^b	$\sigma^b - \pi$	e^b
1970	0.0921	0.4511	0.1011	0.4999	0.0946	0.4654
1971	0.0959	0.4741	0.1027	0.5093	0.0991	0.4915
1972	0.0924	0.4857	0.0997	0.5234	0.0915	0.4809
1973	0.0899	0.4777	0.0979	0.5205	0.0877	0.4646
1974	0.0906	0.4352	0.0992	0.4844	0.0879	0.4183
1975	0.0861	0.5290	0.0939	0.5680	0.0856	0.5262
1976	0.0868	0.4531	0.0942	0.4962	0.0833	0.4301
1977	0.0831	0.4615	0.0913	0.5099	0.0788	0.4320
1978	0.0794	0.4425	0.0881	0.4977	0.0740	0.4018
1979	0.0769	0.4346	0.0850	0.4883	0.0718	0.3946
1980	0.0769	0.4398	0.0840	0.4877	0.0721	0.4031
1981	0.0807	0.4651	0.0865	0.5009	0.0764	0.4348
1982	0.0708	0.2772	0.0811	0.3687	0.0649	0.2112
1983	0.0710	0.2486	0.0809	0.3403	0.0653	0.182
1984	0.0714	0.2711	0.0815	0.3617	0.0668	0.2208
1985	0.0743	0.3094	0.0852	0.3975	0.0696	0.2628
1986	0.0743	0.2875	0.0868	0.3902	0.0692	0.2357
1987	0.0750	0.2991	0.0832	0.3678	0.0758	0.3067
1988	0.0825	0.3619	0.0875	0.3989	0.0828	0.3642
1989	0.0835	0.3687	0.0886	0.4049	0.0838	0.3710
1990	0.0836	0.3231	0.0891	0.3649	0.0835	0.3221
1991	0.0844	0.3298	0.0896	0.3694	0.0842	0.3289
1992	0.0849	0.3253	0.0904	0.3661	0.0847	0.3238
1993	0.0849	0.3343	0.0909	0.3779	0.0848	0.3331
1994	0.0845	0.3300	0.0906	0.3748	0.0841	0.3268
1995	0.0859	0.3717	0.0912	0.4085	0.0856	0.3697
1996	0.0856	0.3671	0.0912	0.4059	0.0855	0.3658

Notes:
LD: Long-lived depreciable assets (NRS + RS)
L: Long-lived assets (NRS + RS + inventories + land)
D: Depreciable assets (PDE + NRS + RS)

Table 4.2 (continued)

	(7) ND		(8) A	
Year	$\sigma^b - \pi$	e^b	$\sigma^b - \pi$	e^b
1970	0.1154	0.5617	0.1009	0.4991
1971	0.1141	0.5584	0.1036	0.5133
1972	0.1125	0.5777	0.0975	0.5128
1973	0.1110	0.5767	0.0948	0.5045
1974	0.1127	0.5463	0.0957	0.4653
1975	0.1101	0.6316	0.0919	0.5583
1976	0.1095	0.5669	0.0899	0.4722
1977	0.1078	0.5852	0.0862	0.4808
1978	0.1048	0.5778	0.0821	0.4611
1979	0.0999	0.5647	0.0794	0.4526
1980	0.0970	0.5563	0.0790	0.4552
1981	0.0973	0.5564	0.0821	0.4738
1982	0.0998	0.4872	0.0745	0.3133
1983	0.1001	0.4670	0.0745	0.2837
1984	0.1010	0.4846	0.0759	0.3144
1985	0.1033	0.5033	0.0795	0.3549
1986	0.1046	0.4940	0.0809	0.3458
1987	0.0943	0.4428	0.0821	0.3594
1988	0.0941	0.4411	0.0867	0.3932
1989	0.0950	0.4450	0.0878	0.3996
1990	0.0956	0.4082	0.0880	0.3568
1991	0.0964	0.4135	0.0885	0.3614
1992	0.0977	0.4134	0.0892	0.3574
1993	0.0992	0.4300	0.0896	0.3686
1994	0.1001	0.4344	0.0890	0.3638
1995	0.1006	0.4639	0.0898	0.3994
1996	0.1010	0.4636	0.0899	0.3968

Notes:
ND: Non-depreciable assets (inventories + land)
A: All assets (PDE + NRS + RS + inventories + land)

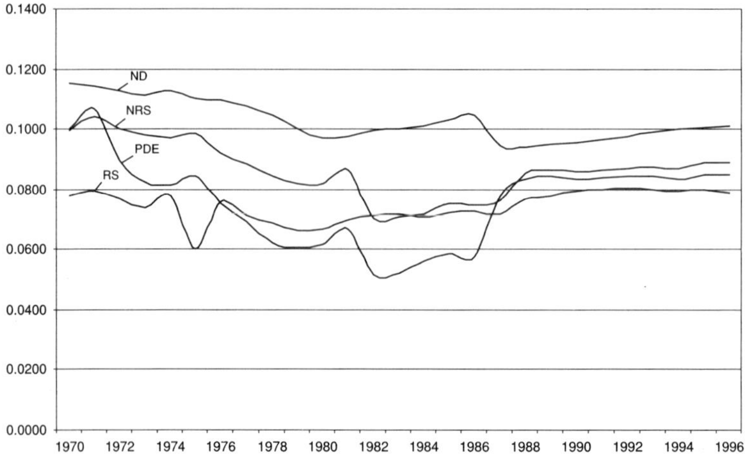

Notes: PDE: Producer's durable equipment; NRS: Nonresidential structures; RS: Residential structures; ND: Nondepreciable assets.

Figure 4.2a
Social rates of return on business assets ($\sigma^b - \pi$): PDE, NRS, RS, ND.

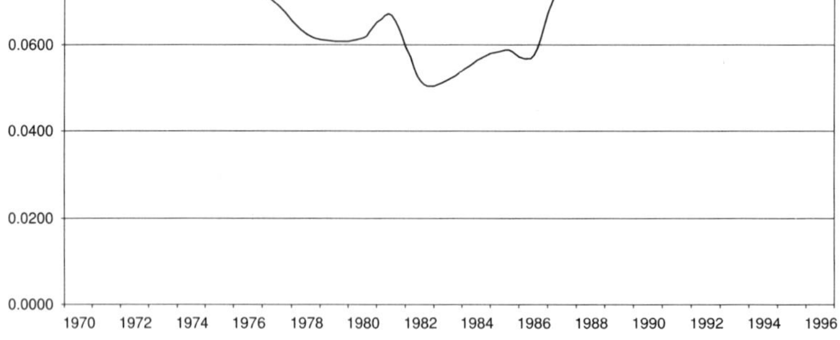

Notes: S: Short-lived assets; L: Long-lived assets; A: All assets.

Figure 4.2b
Social rates of return on business assets ($\sigma^b - \pi$): S, L, A.

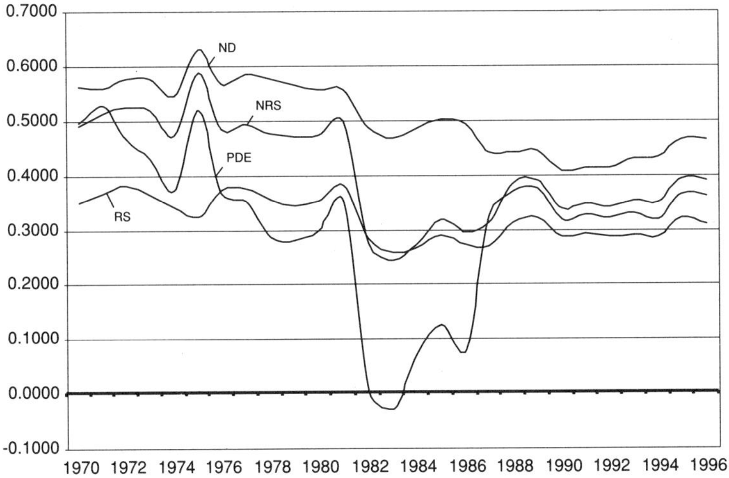

Notes: PDE: Producer's durable equipment; NRS: Nonresidential structures; RS: Residential structures; ND: Nondepreciable assets.

Figure 4.2c
Effective tax rates on business assets (e^b): PDE, NRS, RS, ND.

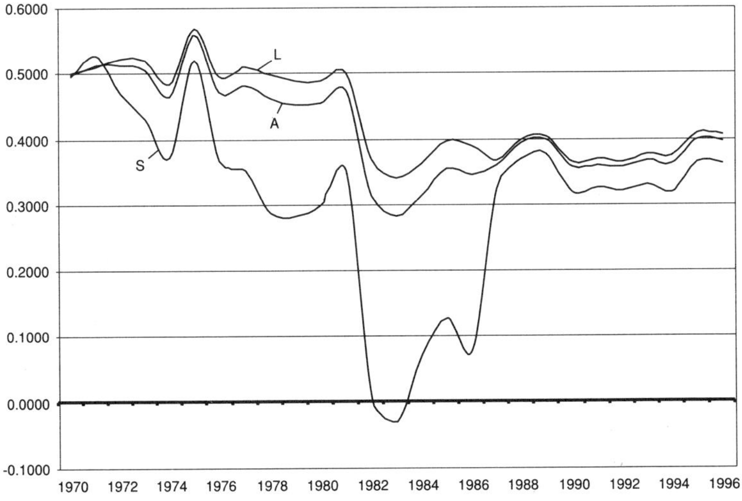

Notes: S: Short-lived assets; L: Long-lived assets; A: All assets.

Figure 4.2d
Effective tax rates on business assets (e^b): S, L, A.

These changes in the tax law, coupled with rising nominal interest rates and increasing tax rates at individual and corporate levels, raised the effective tax rate on depreciable business assets. By 1971 the effective tax rate on the short-lived assets had risen to 52.76 percent and that on long-lived depreciable assets had risen to 47.41 percent. In 1970 the Vietnam War tax surcharge was reduced to 2.5 percent. The surcharge was phased out in 1971.

The Revenue Act of 1971 reinstated the investment tax credit and reduced the lifetimes used in calculating capital consumption allowances for tax purposes. This Revenue Act also introduced the Asset Depreciation Range System. The effects of this series of changes in tax policy on effective tax rates are clearly visible in the case of short-lived assets. The effective tax rate on short-lived assets fell from 52.76 percent in 1971 to 43.05 percent in 1973. For other categories of assets the rise in inflation rates and the increase in nominal interest rates more than offset the effects of the tax cut.

The Revenue Reduction Act of 1975 liberalized the investment tax credit. This resulted in a drop in the effective tax rate on depreciable assets. The effective tax rate on short-lived assets dropped from 51.92 percent in 1975 to 36.85 percent in 1976 and that on long-lived depreciable assets dropped from 52.90 to 45.31 percent in the same period. Part of the decline in effective tax rates is attributable to changes in the rate of inflation and the nominal interest rate. Effective tax rates on residential structures and nondepreciable assets decreased in the same period. In 1979 the maximum Federal corporate tax rate was reduced from 48 to 46 percent.

The Economic Recovery Tax Act (ERTA) of 1981 was one of the largest tax reductions in U.S. history. There are three areas in which ERTA introduced important changes. First, ERTA reduced the maximum marginal tax rate for individuals from 70 to 50 percent. Second, ERTA introduced the Accelerated Cost Recovery System (ACRS), which drastically cut asset lifetimes for capital cost recovery. ERTA also introduced new schedules for capital consumption allowances on personal and real property. Finally, ERTA liberalized the investment tax credit by reducing the tax lifetime of assets eligible for the 10 percent regular credit. The result was a dramatic reduction in effective tax rates, as shown in table 4.2 and figures 4.2a–4.2d. The effective tax rate on short-lived assets dropped from 35.22 percent in 1981 to a negative 2.92 percent in 1983. In the same period the effective tax rate on long-lived depreciable assets declined from 46.51 to 24.86 percent and that on nondepreciable assets dropped from 55.64 to 46.70 percent.

For household assets there are no asset specific tax provisions, so that all household assets bear the same tax burden. Table 4.3 and figures 4.3a–d show social rates of return and effective tax rates for various categories of assets in the corporate sector, while table 4.4 and figures 4.4a–d give the corresponding information for the noncorporate sector. For household assets there are no asset specific tax provisions, so that all household assets bear the same tax burden. Table 4.5 and figures 4.5a–b give social rates of return and effective tax rates for the household sector. Finally, table 4.6 and figures 4.6a–b give these rates for the private sector of the U.S. economy.

The effective tax rates on all private assets was reduced sharply by ERTA. This tax rate dropped from 37.23 percent in 1981 to 21.81 percent in 1983. The reduction for household assets from 11.57 percent to 10.15 percent was relatively modest. By contrast the fall in the tax rate for noncorporate assets was from 42.26 to 27.43 percent and the decline for corporate assets was from 49.82 to 28.91 percent. The large gap between effective tax rates on household and business assets was essentially unaffected by the ERTA legislation or by the subsequent Tax Reform Act of 1986. However, the gap between tax rates for corporate and noncorporate businesses declined considerably.

The tax wedge between social and private rates of return on all forms of capital results in distortions of resource allocation over time. The average intertemporal tax wedges on assets in the business, corporate, noncorporate, household, and all private sectors are equal to the social rates of return multiplied by the corresponding effective tax rates shown in tables 4.2–4.6. In the corporate sector this tax wedge was in the range of 2.20–6.66 percent during the period 1970–1996. In the same period the corresponding ranges were 1.97–3.24 percent and 0.50–0.93 percent in the noncorporate and household sectors, respectively.

In the period 1970–1996 private rates of return ranged from 4.51–5.73 percent, 3.97–5.73 percent, and 2.69–5.93 percent in the corporate, noncorporate, and household sectors, respectively. The welfare costs of tax distortion in the intertemporal allocation of resources is potentially very important. However, it is important to bear in mind that tax distortions are inevitable. If the tax on income from capital were to be cut, the tax revenue loss would have to be made up by

Table 4.3
Effective tax rates on corporate assets

	(1) PDE=SD=S		(2) NRS		(3) RS	
Year	$\sigma^q - \pi$	e^q	$\sigma^q - \pi$	e^q	$\sigma^q - \pi$	e^q
1970	0.1059	0.5166	0.1048	0.5117	0.1014	0.4954
1971	0.1126	0.5471	0.1099	0.5357	0.1050	0.5143
1972	0.0948	0.4876	0.1061	0.5421	0.1033	0.5296
1973	0.0876	0.4442	0.1042	0.5328	0.1020	0.5227
1974	0.0856	0.3950	0.1020	0.4923	0.1001	0.4831
1975	0.0927	0.4909	0.1088	0.5665	0.1068	0.5585
1976	0.0790	0.3867	0.0960	0.4952	0.0994	0.5125
1977	0.0730	0.3636	0.0927	0.4989	0.0973	0.5227
1978	0.0654	0.2942	0.0885	0.4784	0.0934	0.5058
1979	0.0640	0.2873	0.0859	0.4689	0.0907	0.4972
1980	0.0651	0.3060	0.0857	0.4734	0.0899	0.4979
1981	0.0704	0.3588	0.0903	0.4996	0.0934	0.5165
1982	0.0526	0.0141	0.0712	0.2720	0.0820	0.3676
1983	0.0530	−0.0237	0.0713	0.2402	0.0823	0.3410
1984	0.0578	0.0881	0.0726	0.2743	0.0811	0.3502
1985	0.0609	0.1468	0.0769	0.3237	0.0873	0.4046
1986	0.0594	0.1046	0.0765	0.3050	0.0880	0.3953
1987	0.0790	0.3302	0.0778	0.3201	0.0796	0.3359
1988	0.0855	0.3776	0.0882	0.3965	0.0915	0.4184
1989	0.0866	0.3832	0.0892	0.4012	0.0926	0.4231
1990	0.0847	0.3325	0.0877	0.3553	0.0910	0.3786
1991	0.0855	0.3384	0.0886	0.3617	0.0919	0.3847
1992	0.0858	0.3327	0.0892	0.3582	0.0925	0.3808
1993	0.0861	0.3411	0.0898	0.3684	0.0930	0.3898
1994	0.0847	0.3303	0.0891	0.3635	0.0915	0.3800
1995	0.0867	0.3724	0.0915	0.4052	0.0934	0.4174
1996	0.0870	0.3708	0.0920	0.4049	0.0938	0.4163

Note: The superscript q stands for the corporate sector. Other notations are the same as in table 4.2.

Table 4.3 (continued)

	(4) LD		(5) L	
Year	$\sigma^q - \pi$	e^q	$\sigma^q - \pi$	e^q
1970	0.1047	0.5111	0.1177	0.5652
1971	0.1097	0.5350	0.1195	0.5732
1972	0.1060	0.5416	0.1166	0.5836
1973	0.1041	0.5324	0.1161	0.5806
1974	0.1019	0.4920	0.1143	0.5471
1975	0.1087	0.5662	0.1197	0.6059
1976	0.0961	0.4958	0.1067	0.5458
1977	0.0928	0.4997	0.1045	0.5558
1978	0.0886	0.4793	0.1012	0.5438
1979	0.0861	0.4698	0.0975	0.5322
1980	0.0859	0.4742	0.0959	0.5294
1981	0.0904	0.5002	0.0983	0.5407
1982	0.0716	0.2754	0.0862	0.3983
1983	0.0717	0.2436	0.0858	0.3686
1984	0.0729	0.2769	0.0873	0.3963
1985	0.0772	0.3264	0.0929	0.4405
1986	0.0769	0.3080	0.0952	0.4413
1987	0.0778	0.3206	0.0883	0.4008
1988	0.0883	0.3971	0.0954	0.4419
1989	0.0893	0.4019	0.0964	0.4458
1990	0.0878	0.3560	0.0953	0.4065
1991	0.0887	0.3624	0.0959	0.4103
1992	0.0893	0.3588	0.0967	0.4080
1993	0.0899	0.3690	0.0978	0.4199
1994	0.0892	0.3640	0.0971	0.4156
1995	0.0916	0.4056	0.0984	0.4471
1996	0.0920	0.4052	0.0992	0.4483

Table 4.3 (continued)

	(6) D		(7) ND		(8) A	
Year	$\sigma^q - \pi$	e^q	$\sigma^q - \pi$	e^q	$\sigma^q - \pi$	e^q
1970	0.1052	0.5133	0.1381	0.6292	0.1144	0.5526
1971	0.1108	0.5398	0.1356	0.6239	0.1176	0.5661
1972	0.1017	0.5222	0.1352	0.6408	0.1104	0.5601
1973	0.0978	0.5022	0.1357	0.6412	0.1082	0.5500
1974	0.0957	0.4589	0.1338	0.6131	0.1064	0.5137
1975	0.1027	0.5408	0.1404	0.6641	0.1121	0.5791
1976	0.0895	0.4587	0.1275	0.6200	0.0985	0.5082
1977	0.0850	0.4536	0.1269	0.6340	0.0951	0.5116
1978	0.0793	0.4184	0.1238	0.6273	0.0904	0.4897
1979	0.0772	0.4092	0.1176	0.6120	0.0875	0.4787
1980	0.0776	0.4180	0.1130	0.6005	0.0869	0.4802
1981	0.0823	0.4516	0.1120	0.5967	0.0900	0.4982
1982	0.0640	0.1902	0.1111	0.5333	0.0763	0.3206
1983	0.0644	0.1581	0.1118	0.5153	0.0762	0.2891
1984	0.0669	0.2128	0.1133	0.5349	0.0786	0.3297
1985	0.0708	0.2654	0.1181	0.5596	0.0838	0.3793
1986	0.0700	0.2399	0.1214	0.5619	0.0853	0.3764
1987	0.0783	0.3245	0.1027	0.4851	0.0857	0.3826
1988	0.0872	0.3894	0.1046	0.4913	0.0926	0.4254
1989	0.0882	0.3945	0.1054	0.4931	0.0937	0.4300
1990	0.0866	0.3468	0.1044	0.4584	0.0925	0.3882
1991	0.0874	0.3530	0.1053	0.4629	0.0931	0.3921
1992	0.0879	0.3485	0.1069	0.4641	0.0937	0.3886
1993	0.0884	0.3578	0.1090	0.4794	0.0944	0.3991
1994	0.0874	0.3507	0.1093	0.4808	0.0934	0.3928
1995	0.0896	0.3925	0.1099	0.5048	0.0949	0.4265
1996	0.0900	0.3916	0.1111	0.5073	0.0955	0.4269

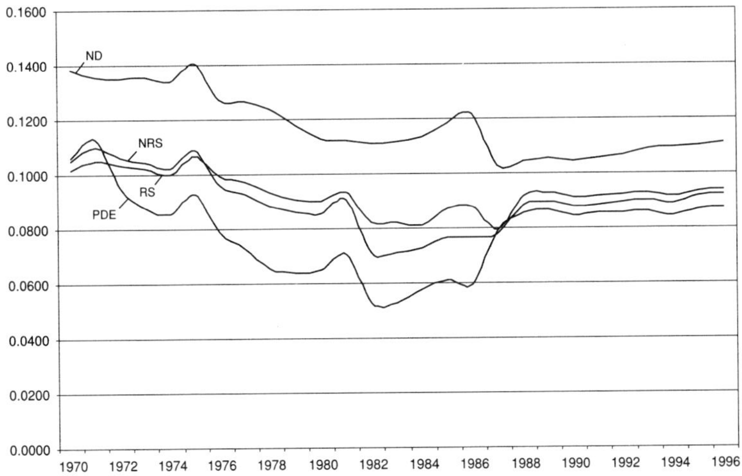

Notes: PDE: Producer's durable equipment; NRS: Nonresidential structures; RS: Residential structures; ND: Nondepreciable assets

Figure 4.3a
Social rates of return on corporate assets ($\sigma^q - \pi$): PDE, NRS, RS, ND.

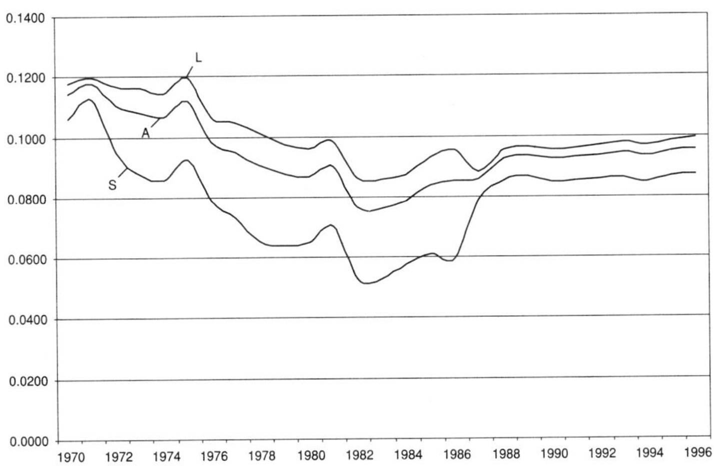

Notes: S: Short-lived assets; L: Long-lived assets; A: All assets.

Figure 4.3b
Social rates of return on corporate assets ($\sigma^b - \pi$): S, L, A.

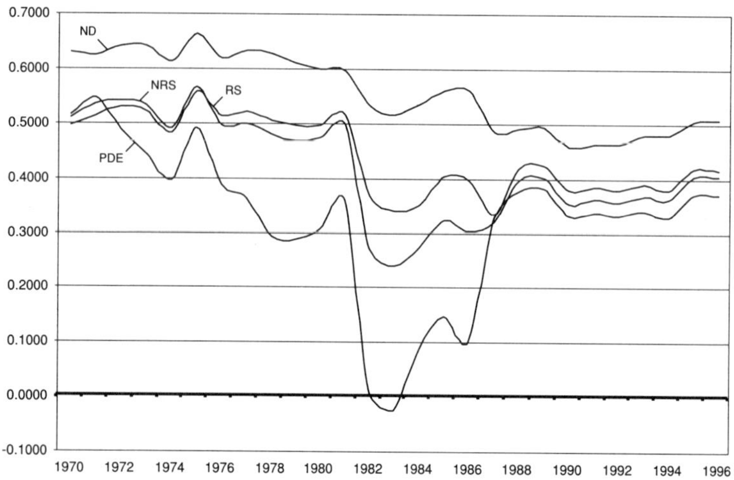

Notes: PDE: Producer's durable equipment; NRS: Nonresidential structures; RS: Residential structures; ND: Nondepreciable assets.

Figure 4.3c
Effective tax rates on corporate assets (e^q): PDE, NRS, RS, ND.

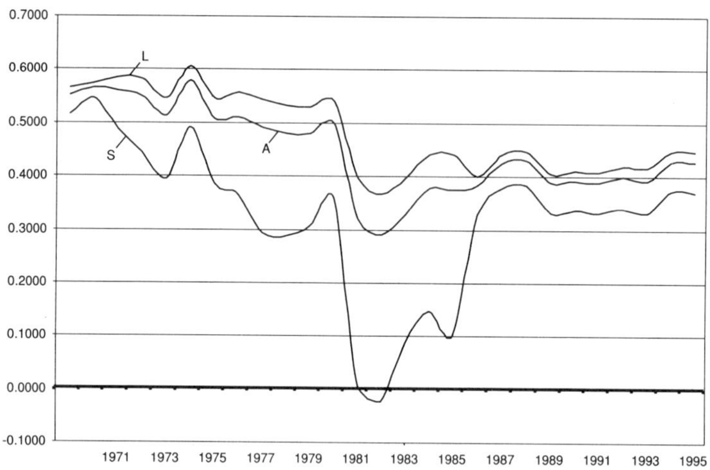

Notes: S: Short-lived assets; L: Long-lived assets; A: All assets.

Figure 4.3d
Effective tax rates on corporate assets (e^q): S, L, A.

Table 4.4
Effective tax rates on noncorporate assets

	(1) PDE=SD=S		(2) NRS		(3) RS	
Year	$\sigma^m - \pi$	e^m	$\sigma^m - \pi$	e^m	$\sigma^m - \pi$	e^m
1970	0.0767	0.3532	0.0788	0.3704	0.0763	0.3495
1971	0.0815	0.3929	0.0811	0.3898	0.0779	0.3652
1972	0.0670	0.3147	0.0775	0.4078	0.0750	0.3878
1973	0.0603	0.2636	0.0746	0.4045	0.0721	0.3842
1974	0.0640	0.2146	0.0789	0.3634	0.0764	0.3424
1975	0.0481	0.3836	0.0599	0.5051	0.0572	0.4817
1976	0.0575	0.2046	0.0760	0.3985	0.0741	0.3826
1977	0.0512	0.1827	0.0716	0.4161	0.0700	0.4024
1978	0.0466	0.1186	0.0685	0.4011	0.0672	0.3890
1979	0.0445	0.1038	0.0665	0.3998	0.0650	0.3861
1980	0.0454	0.1261	0.0672	0.4101	0.0653	0.3927
1981	0.0495	0.1917	0.0710	0.4373	0.0686	0.4173
1982	0.0456	–0.0982	0.0679	0.2620	0.0708	0.2922
1983	0.0468	–0.1102	0.0680	0.2353	0.0713	0.2702
1984	0.0486	–0.0504	0.0679	0.2491	0.0704	0.2757
1985	0.0486	–0.0329	0.0691	0.2732	0.0716	0.2984
1986	0.0484	–0.0839	0.0693	0.2429	0.0720	0.2706
1987	0.0717	0.2733	0.0718	0.2740	0.0716	0.2726
1988	0.0733	0.2943	0.0757	0.3166	0.0759	0.3180
1989	0.0743	0.3039	0.0767	0.3259	0.0769	0.3273
1990	0.0756	0.2510	0.0785	0.2787	0.0788	0.2812
1991	0.0762	0.2587	0.0791	0.2856	0.0793	0.2880
1992	0.0766	0.2510	0.0796	0.2791	0.0798	0.2815
1993	0.0756	0.2565	0.0789	0.2871	0.0791	0.2893
1994	0.0753	0.2507	0.0792	0.2870	0.0789	0.2846
1995	0.7575	0.2969	0.0797	0.3328	0.0790	0.3266
1996	0.0747	0.2853	0.0787	0.3219	0.0780	0.3159

Note: The superscript m stands for the noncorporate sector. Other notations are the same as in table 4.2.

Table 4.4 (continued)

Year	(4) LD		(5) L	
	$\sigma^m - \pi$	e^m	$\sigma^m - \pi$	e^m
1970	0.0770	0.3559	0.0809	0.3870
1971	0.0789	0.3730	0.0819	0.3961
1972	0.0757	0.3942	0.0788	0.4178
1973	0.0729	0.3908	0.0764	0.4186
1974	0.0772	0.3491	0.0814	0.3830
1975	0.0580	0.4894	0.0596	0.5027
1976	0.0747	0.3878	0.0775	0.4098
1977	0.0705	0.4068	0.0733	0.4295
1978	0.0676	0.3929	0.0707	0.4192
1979	0.0654	0.3904	0.0685	0.4176
1980	0.0659	0.3981	0.0688	0.4234
1981	0.0693	0.4235	0.0716	0.4415
1982	0.0699	0.2832	0.0746	0.3288
1983	0.0702	0.2596	0.0745	0.3023
1984	0.0696	0.2676	0.0742	0.3127
1985	0.0708	0.2907	0.0754	0.3344
1986	0.0711	0.2620	0.0767	0.3154
1987	0.0717	0.2731	0.0772	0.3253
1988	0.0758	0.3176	0.0786	0.3416
1989	0.0769	0.3268	0.0797	0.3512
1990	0.0787	0.2804	0.0821	0.3102
1991	0.0792	0.2872	0.0824	0.3146
1992	0.0797	0.2807	0.0830	0.3094
1993	0.0790	0.2886	0.0828	0.3210
1994	0.0790	0.2854	0.0828	0.3184
1995	0.0792	0.3286	0.0824	0.3543
1996	0.0782	0.3178	0.0815	0.3450

Table 4.4 (continued)

	(6) D		(7) ND		(8) A	
Year	$\sigma^m - \pi$	e^m	$\sigma^m - \pi$	e^m	$\sigma^m - \pi$	e^m
1970	0.0770	0.3555	0.0872	0.4312	0.0805	0.3837
1971	0.0793	0.3761	0.0870	0.4314	0.0819	0.3958
1972	0.0744	0.3833	0.0842	0.4553	0.0776	0.4086
1973	0.0710	0.3749	0.0819	0.4582	0.0748	0.4066
1974	0.0753	0.3327	0.0881	0.4293	0.0798	0.3705
1975	0.0566	0.4764	0.0633	0.5315	0.0584	0.4923
1976	0.0721	0.3657	0.0836	0.4531	0.0753	0.3927
1977	0.0675	0.3806	0.0794	0.4737	0.0708	0.4097
1978	0.0644	0.3624	0.0770	0.4673	0.0680	0.3967
1979	0.0622	0.3590	0.0746	0.4652	0.0659	0.3948
1980	0.0628	0.3682	0.0745	0.4674	0.0663	0.4018
1981	0.0664	0.3977	0.0763	0.4758	0.0692	0.4226
1982	0.0663	0.2446	0.0841	0.4041	0.0717	0.3008
1983	0.0668	0.2218	0.0836	0.3779	0.0717	0.2743
1984	0.0666	0.2337	0.0837	0.3908	0.0716	0.2872
1985	0.0676	0.2570	0.0836	0.3997	0.0728	0.3105
1986	0.0679	0.2273	0.0845	0.3790	0.0742	0.2926
1987	0.0717	0.2731	0.0847	0.3851	0.0767	0.3212
1988	0.0755	0.3145	0.0822	0.3706	0.0782	0.3380
1989	0.0765	0.3238	0.0833	0.3791	0.0793	0.3476
1990	0.0783	0.2765	0.0860	0.3416	0.0816	0.3059
1991	0.0788	0.2835	0.0864	0.3459	0.0819	0.3104
1992	0.0793	0.2768	0.0873	0.3435	0.0825	0.3050
1993	0.0786	0.2844	0.0880	0.3610	0.0822	0.3161
1994	0.0785	0.2810	0.0890	0.3656	0.0822	0.3131
1995	0.0788	0.3245	0.0884	0.3979	0.0818	0.3494
1996	0.0777	0.3136	0.0876	0.3911	0.0808	0.3400

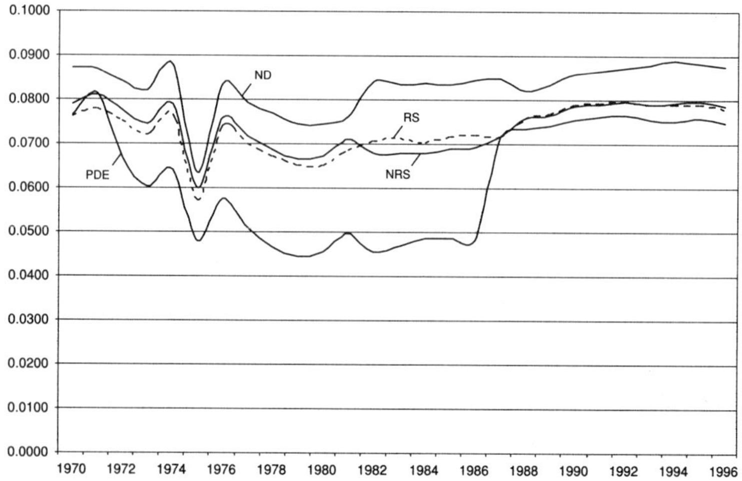

Notes: PDE: Producer's durable equipment; NRS: Nonresidential structures: RS: Residential structures; ND: Nondepreciable assets.

Figure 4.4a
Social rates of return on noncorporate assets ($\sigma^m - \pi$): PDE, NRS, RS, ND.

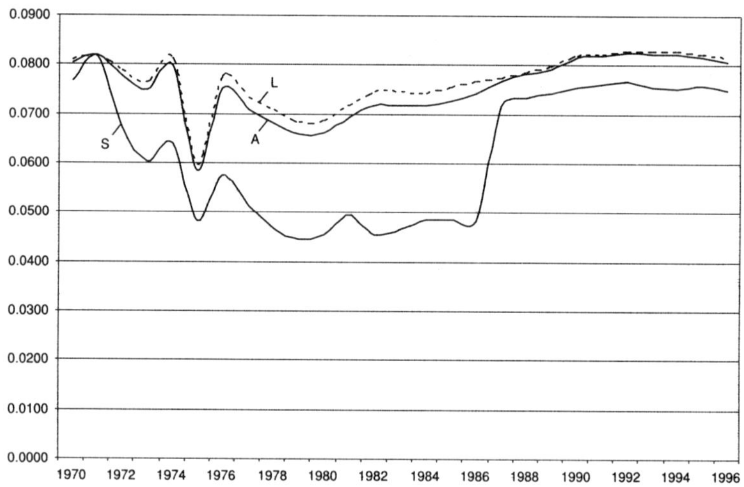

Notes: S: Short-lived assets; L: Long-lived assets; A: All assets.

Figure 4.4b
Social rates of return on noncorporate assets ($\sigma^m - \pi$): S, L, A.

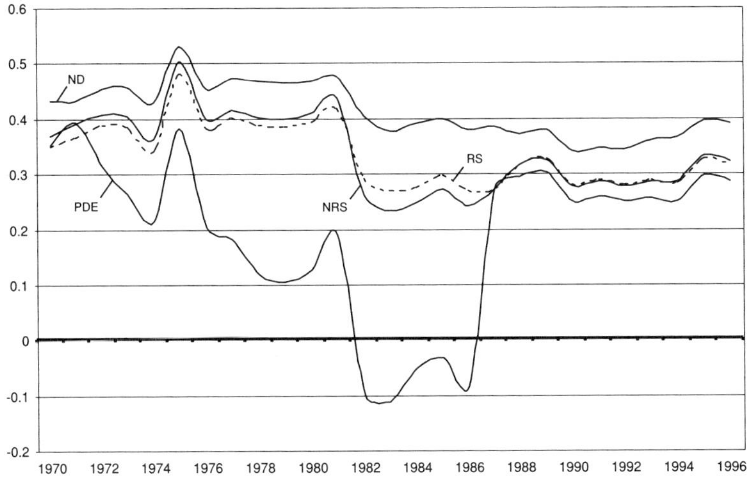

Notes: PDE: Producer's durable equipment; NRS: Nonresidential structures: RS: Residential structures; ND: Nondepreciable assets.

Figure 4.4c
Effective tax rates on noncorporate assets (e^m): PDE, NRS, RS, ND.

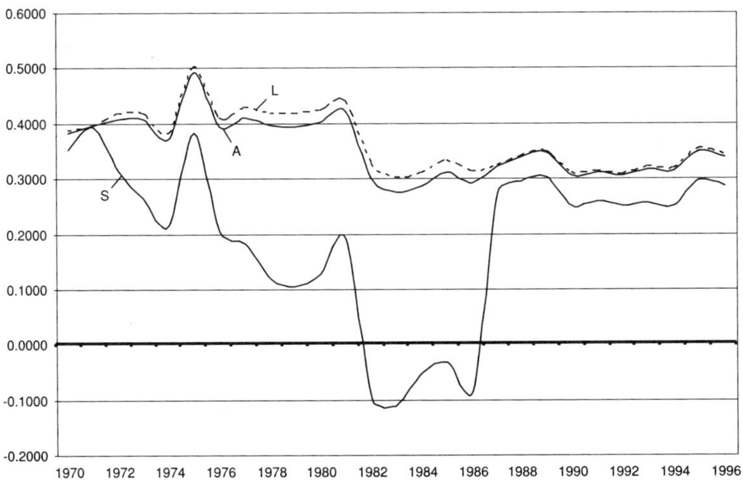

Notes: S: Short-lived assets; L: Long-lived assets; A: All assets.

Figure 4.4d
Effective tax rates on noncorporate assets (e^m): S, L, A.

Table 4.5
Effective tax rates on household assets

Year	$\sigma^h - \pi$	e^h
1970	0.0555	0.1584
1971	0.0548	0.1702
1972	0.0474	0.1912
1973	0.0462	0.1848
1974	0.0569	0.1398
1975	0.0351	0.2347
1976	0.0525	0.1517
1977	0.0479	0.1630
1978	0.0451	0.1549
1979	0.0415	0.1424
1980	0.0419	0.1255
1981	0.0431	0.1157
1982	0.0549	0.0975
1983	0.0578	0.1015
1984	0.0554	0.1064
1985	0.0524	0.1107
1986	0.0551	0.1011
1987	0.0547	0.1023
1988	0.0528	0.1063
1989	0.0518	0.1097
1990	0.0635	0.0880
1991	0.0637	0.0916
1992	0.0654	0.0933
1993	0.0624	0.0967
1994	0.0638	0.0955
1995	0.0533	0.1148
1996	0.0529	0.1120

Note: There are no interasset tax wedges in the household sector.

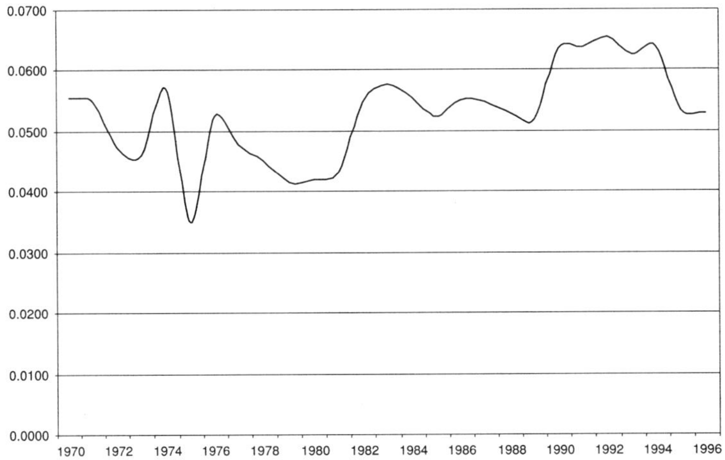

Figure 4.5a
Social rates of return on household assets ($\sigma^h - \pi$).

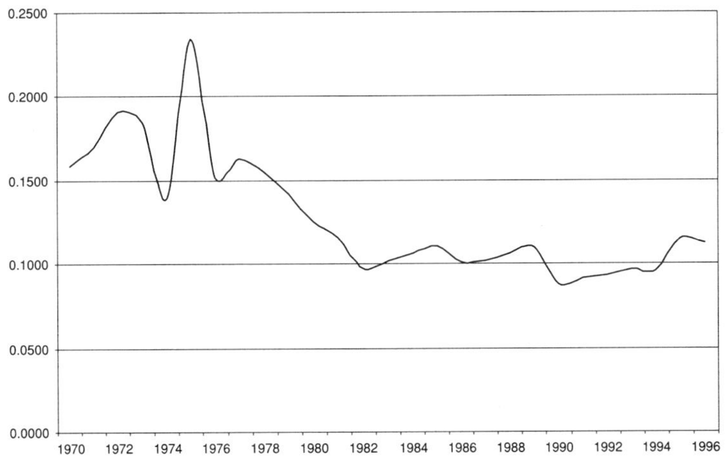

Figure 4.5b
Effective tax rates on household assets (e^h).

Table 4.6
Effective tax rates on all private assets

Year	$\sigma^a - \pi$	e^a
1970	0.0810	0.3967
1971	0.0823	0.4139
1972	0.0756	0.4248
1973	0.0735	0.4165
1974	0.0787	0.3624
1975	0.0673	0.4853
1976	0.0738	0.3741
1977	0.0696	0.3858
1978	0.0659	0.3695
1979	0.0628	0.3625
1980	0.0629	0.3599
1981	0.0653	0.3723
1982	0.0663	0.2377
1983	0.0675	0.2181
1984	0.0672	0.2417
1985	0.0680	0.2748
1986	0.0698	0.2633
1987	0.0702	0.2724
1988	0.0718	0.3005
1989	0.0719	0.3077
1990	0.0772	0.2589
1991	0.0775	0.2629
1992	0.0786	0.2593
1993	0.0774	0.2699
1994	0.0776	0.2637
1995	0.0732	0.3047
1996	0.0729	0.3022

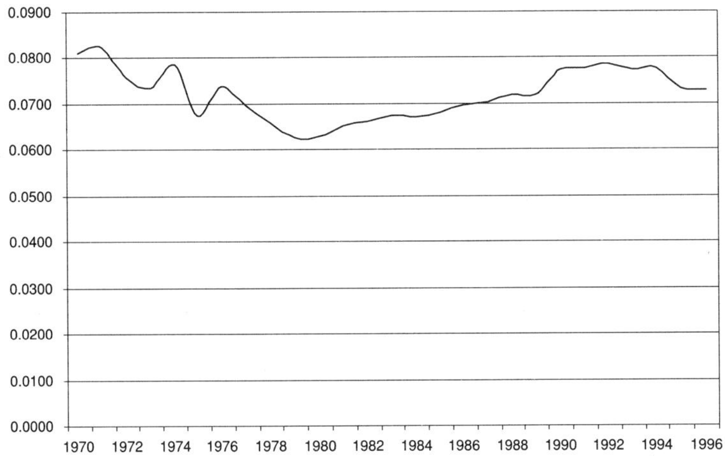

Figure 4.6a
Social rates of return on all private assets ($\sigma^a - \pi$).

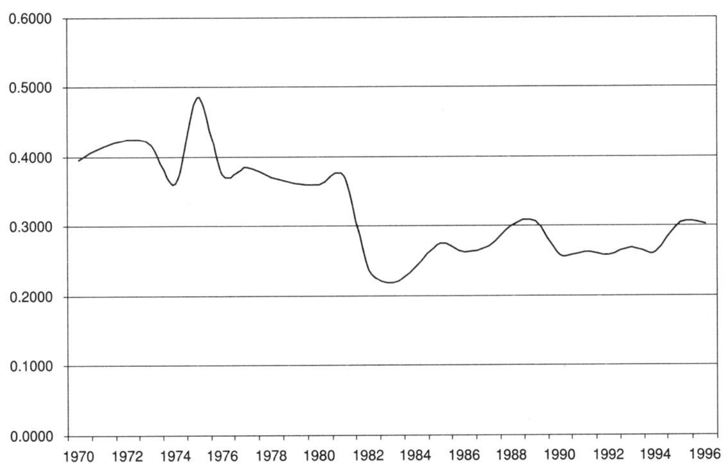

Figure 4.6b
Effective tax rates on all private assets (e^a).

other taxes. Hence, the issue is how to minimize the total welfare loss from taxation, not how to eliminate intertemporal tax distortions.

4.3 Differences in Effective Tax Rates

We next discuss inequalities in tax burdens born by assets within each sector and the same asset in different sectors. Table 4.7 and figures 4.7a and 4.7b show differences between social rates of return on different assets in the corporate and noncorporate sectors. Social rates of return on depreciable and nondepreciable assets differed substantially throughout the period 1970–1996; however, these differences were reduced by the Tax Reform Act of 1986. By contrast the differences between short-lived and long-lived depreciable assets were nearly eliminated by this legislation.

To quantify the potential distortions in the allocation of capital due to tax policy, we consider social rates of return for assets utilized in the corporate sector presented in table 4.7. In 1986 the social rate of return for short-lived assets was 1.75 percent less than for long-lived depreciable assets. In 1987 short-lived assets had a social rate of return that was only 0.11 percent higher than the return on long-lived assets, as a consequence of the Tax Reform Act of 1986. Similarly, the social rate of return on nondepreciable assets exceeded that for depreciable assets by 5.14 percent in 1986, but the gap shrank to 2.44 percent in 1987 and 1.75 percent in 1988. The reductions in differences in social rates of return within the noncorporate sector were similar, but less dramatic.

If we were to transfer $1.00 from depreciable to nondepreciable assets within the corporate sector in 1986, national income would have increased by 5.14 cents per year. Considering the fact that private rates of return were in the range of 4.95–5.32 percent with an average of 5.14 percent in 1986, these gains correspond to very substantial increases in the national wealth. For example, the transfer of each dollar with a perpetual return of 5.14 percent results in an increase in national wealth of 97 cents at a corporate rate of return of 5.32 percent. We conclude that national wealth could have been almost doubled at the margin by transferring capital to heavily taxed nondepreciable assets from less heavily taxed depreciable assets within the corporate sector.

Differences between social rates of return for assets held in the household, noncorporate, and corporate sectors are given in tables 4.8, 4.9, and 4.10 and figures 4.8, 4.9, and 4.10. These differences are given

Table 4.7
Interasset tax wedges

Year	Corporate			Noncorporate		
	SD–LD	S–L	D–ND	SD–LD	S–L	D–ND
1970	0.0012	–0.0118	–0.0329	–0.0003	–0.0042	–0.0102
1971	0.0029	–0.0069	–0.0248	0.0026	–0.0004	–0.0077
1972	–0.0112	–0.0218	–0.0336	–0.0088	–0.0119	–0.0098
1973	–0.0165	–0.0285	–0.0379	–0.0126	–0.0161	–0.0109
1974	–0.0163	–0.0287	–0.0381	–0.0132	–0.0175	–0.0127
1975	–0.0161	–0.0270	–0.0377	–0.0100	–0.0115	–0.0067
1976	–0.0171	–0.0277	–0.0380	–0.0172	–0.0200	–0.0115
1977	–0.0198	–0.0316	–0.0419	–0.0193	–0.0221	–0.0119
1978	–0.0232	–0.0358	–0.0445	–0.0210	–0.0241	–0.0127
1979	–0.0220	–0.0335	–0.0404	–0.0209	–0.0240	–0.0124
1980	–0.0208	–0.0309	–0.0354	–0.0205	–0.0234	–0.0117
1981	–0.0199	–0.0279	–0.0296	–0.0199	–0.0221	–0.0099
1982	–0.0190	–0.0336	–0.0471	–0.0243	–0.0290	–0.0178
1983	–0.0187	–0.0329	–0.0475	–0.0234	–0.0277	–0.0168
1984	–0.0151	–0.0295	–0.0463	–0.0211	–0.0257	–0.0172
1985	–0.0163	–0.0320	–0.0473	–0.0222	–0.0268	–0.0161
1986	–0.0175	–0.0358	–0.0514	–0.0227	–0.0282	–0.0166
1987	0.0011	–0.0093	–0.0244	0.0000	–0.0055	–0.0131
1988	–0.0028	–0.0099	–0.0175	–0.0025	–0.0053	–0.0067
1989	–0.0027	–0.0098	–0.0171	–0.0025	–0.0054	–0.0068
1990	–0.0031	–0.0106	–0.0178	–0.0031	–0.0065	–0.0077
1991	–0.0032	–0.0104	–0.0179	–0.0030	–0.0062	–0.0075
1992	–0.0035	–0.0109	–0.0190	–0.0032	–0.0065	–0.0080
1993	–0.0038	–0.0117	–0.0206	–0.0034	–0.0072	–0.0094
1994	–0.0045	–0.0124	–0.0219	–0.0037	–0.0075	–0.0105
1995	–0.0048	–0.0117	–0.0203	–0.0036	–0.0067	–0.0096
1996	–0.0050	–0.0122	–0.0211	–0.0035	–0.0068	–0.0099

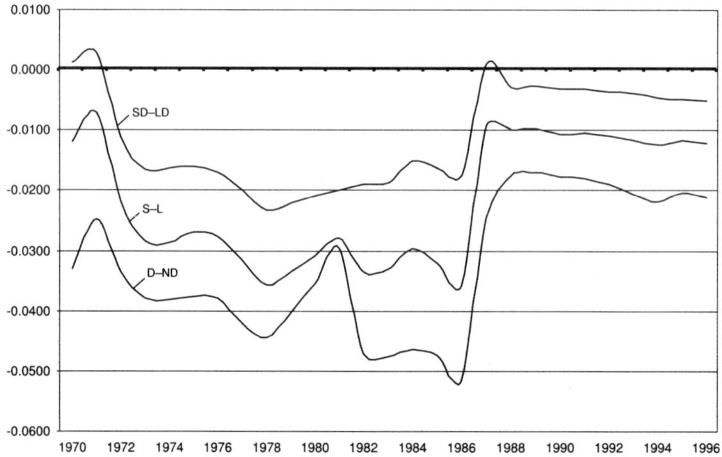

Notes: SD–LD: Short-lived depreciable–long-lived depreciable assets; S–L: Short-lived–long-lived assets; D–ND: Depreciable–non-depreciable assets.

Figure 4.7a
Interasset tax wedge: Corporate.

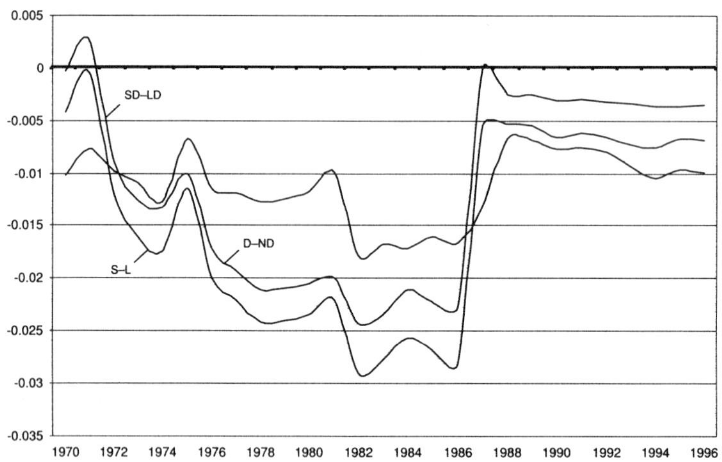

Notes: SD–LD: Short-lived depreciable–long-lived depreciable assets; S–L: Short-lived–long-lived assets; D–ND: Depreciable–non-depreciable assets.

Figure 4.7b
Interasset tax wedge: Noncorporate.

Table 4.8
Intersectoral tax wedges: Corporate—noncorporate

Year	SD=S	LD	L	D	ND	A
1970	0.0292	0.0277	0.0368	0.0282	0.0509	0.0339
1971	0.0312	0.0308	0.0376	0.0315	0.0486	0.0357
1972	0.0278	0.0302	0.0378	0.0272	0.0510	0.0328
1973	0.0273	0.0313	0.0397	0.0268	0.0538	0.0334
1974	0.0216	0.0247	0.0329	0.0204	0.0457	0.0266
1975	0.0446	0.0507	0.0601	0.0461	0.0772	0.0537
1976	0.0215	0.0214	0.0292	0.0174	0.0439	0.0232
1977	0.0218	0.0223	0.0312	0.0175	0.0474	0.0243
1978	0.0188	0.0210	0.0305	0.0150	0.0468	0.0224
1979	0.0195	0.0206	0.0290	0.0150	0.0430	0.0216
1980	0.0197	0.0200	0.0272	0.0148	0.0385	0.0206
1981	0.0210	0.0210	0.0267	0.0160	0.0357	0.0208
1982	0.0070	0.0017	0.0115	−0.0023	0.0270	0.0047
1983	0.0061	0.0014	0.0113	−0.0024	0.0282	0.0046
1984	0.0092	0.0032	0.0131	0.0004	0.0295	0.0070
1985	0.0124	0.0064	0.0175	0.0032	0.0345	0.0110
1986	0.0110	0.0057	0.0185	0.0020	0.0369	0.0111
1987	0.0073	0.0062	0.0110	0.0066	0.0180	0.0089
1988	0.0122	0.0125	0.0168	0.0117	0.0224	0.0145
1989	0.0123	0.0124	0.0166	0.0117	0.0220	0.0144
1990	0.0091	0.0091	0.0132	0.0083	0.0184	0.0109
1991	0.0093	0.0095	0.0135	0.0086	0.0190	0.0111
1992	0.0093	0.0096	0.0137	0.0086	0.0195	0.0112
1993	0.0105	0.0109	0.0150	0.0098	0.0210	0.0122
1994	0.0094	0.0102	0.0142	0.0089	0.0203	0.0113
1995	0.0111	0.0123	0.0160	0.0108	0.0215	0.0131
1996	0.0123	0.0138	0.0178	0.0122	0.0235	0.0147

Table 4.9
Intersectoral tax wedges: Corporate—household

Year	SD=S	LD	L	D	ND	A
1970	0.0504	0.0492	0.0622	0.0496	0.0825	0.0589
1971	0.0579	0.0549	0.0648	0.0561	0.0809	0.0628
1972	0.0474	0.0586	0.0692	0.0543	0.0878	0.0630
1973	0.0414	0.0579	0.0699	0.0516	0.0895	0.0620
1974	0.0286	0.0450	0.0574	0.0387	0.0769	0.0495
1975	0.0575	0.0736	0.0845	0.0676	0.1053	0.0769
1976	0.0266	0.0437	0.0542	0.0371	0.0751	0.0461
1977	0.0250	0.0449	0.0566	0.0371	0.0790	0.0472
1978	0.0203	0.0436	0.0561	0.0343	0.0787	0.0453
1979	0.0225	0.0446	0.0560	0.0357	0.0761	0.0460
1980	0.0232	0.0440	0.0541	0.0357	0.0711	0.0450
1981	0.0273	0.0473	0.0552	0.0392	0.0689	0.0469
1982	–0.0024	0.0166	0.0312	0.0091	0.0562	0.0214
1983	–0.0049	0.0138	0.0280	0.0066	0.0540	0.0184
1984	0.0024	0.0175	0.0319	0.0116	0.0579	0.0232
1985	0.0085	0.0248	0.0405	0.0184	0.0657	0.0314
1986	0.0043	0.0218	0.0402	0.0149	0.0664	0.0302
1987	0.0243	0.0232	0.0336	0.0236	0.0480	0.0310
1988	0.0327	0.0355	0.0426	0.0344	0.0518	0.0398
1989	0.0348	0.0375	0.0446	0.0365	0.0536	0.0419
1990	0.0212	0.0243	0.0318	0.0231	0.0409	0.0289
1991	0.0218	0.0250	0.0322	0.0237	0.0416	0.0293
1992	0.0204	0.0239	0.0314	0.0225	0.0415	0.0283
1993	0.0237	0.0275	0.0354	0.0259	0.0466	0.0320
1994	0.0210	0.0254	0.0333	0.0236	0.0455	0.0297
1995	0.0334	0.0382	0.0451	0.0363	0.0566	0.0416
1996	0.0341	0.0391	0.0463	0.0371	0.0582	0.0426

Table 4.10
Intersectoral tax wedges: Noncorporate—households

Year	SD=S	LD	L	D	ND	A
1970	0.0212	0.0215	0.0254	0.0214	0.0317	0.0250
1971	0.0267	0.0241	0.0272	0.0245	0.0322	0.0271
1972	0.0196	0.0284	0.0314	0.0270	0.0368	0.0302
1973	0.0140	0.0266	0.0301	0.0248	0.0357	0.0286
1974	0.0071	0.0203	0.0245	0.0184	0.0311	0.0229
1975	0.0130	0.0229	0.0245	0.0215	0.0281	0.0232
1976	0.0050	0.0223	0.0250	0.0197	0.0312	0.0229
1977	0.0032	0.0226	0.0254	0.0196	0.0315	0.0229
1978	0.0015	0.0225	0.0256	0.0193	0.0320	0.0230
1979	0.0030	0.0240	0.0270	0.0207	0.0331	0.0244
1980	0.0035	0.0240	0.0269	0.0209	0.0326	0.0244
1981	0.0064	0.0262	0.0285	0.0233	0.0332	0.0261
1982	–0.0093	0.0149	0.0197	0.0114	0.0291	0.0167
1983	–0.0110	0.0124	0.0167	0.0090	0.0258	0.0138
1984	–0.0068	0.0143	0.0188	0.0112	0.0284	0.0162
1985	–0.0038	0.0184	0.0230	0.0152	0.0312	0.0204
1986	–0.0066	0.0161	0.0216	0.0129	0.0295	0.0191
1987	0.0170	0.0170	0.0225	0.0170	0.0301	0.0221
1988	0.0205	0.0230	0.0258	0.0227	0.0294	0.0254
1989	0.0226	0.0251	0.0280	0.0248	0.0316	0.0276
1990	0.0121	0.0152	0.0186	0.0148	0.0225	0.0181
1991	0.0125	0.0155	0.0187	0.0151	0.0226	0.0182
1992	0.0112	0.0143	0.0177	0.0139	0.0220	0.0171
1993	0.0132	0.0166	0.0204	0.0161	0.0256	0.0198
1994	0.0116	0.0152	0.0191	0.0147	0.0252	0.0184
1995	0.0224	0.0259	0.0291	0.0254	0.0350	0.0285
1996	0.0217	0.0253	0.0285	0.0248	0.0347	0.0279

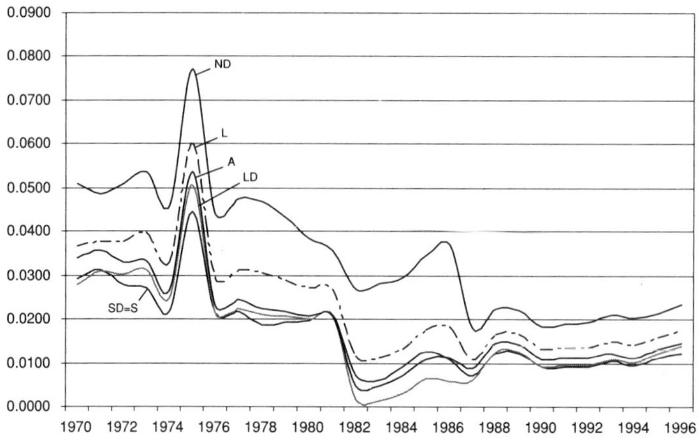

Figure 4.8
Intersectoral tax wedges: Corporate—noncorporate.

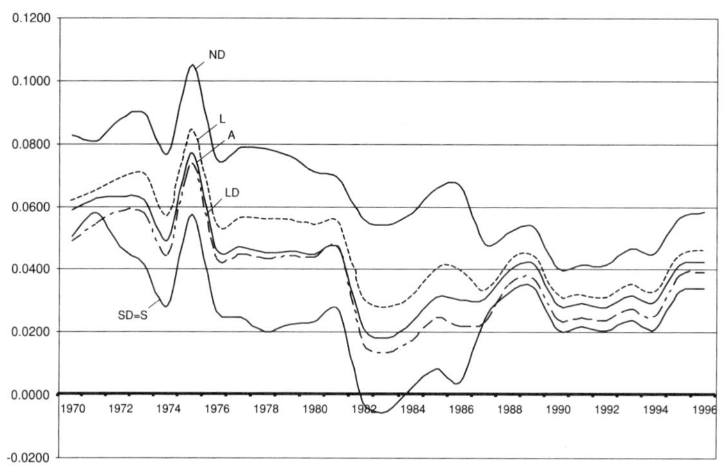

Figure 4.9
Intersectoral tax wedges: Corporate—household.

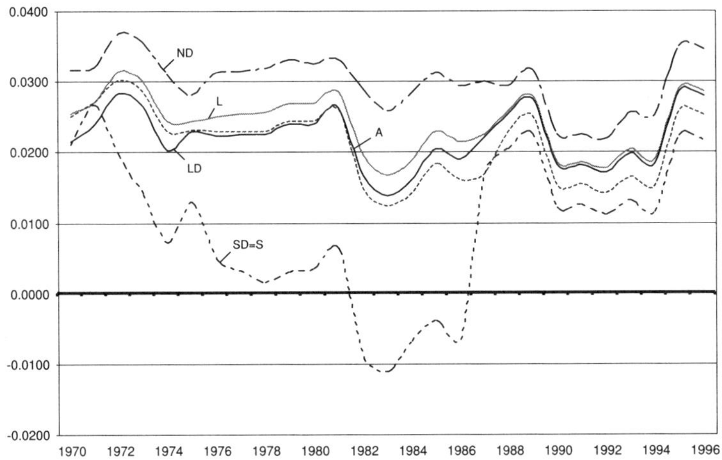

Figure 4.10
Intersectoral tax wedges: Noncorporate—household.

separately for short-lived and long-lived depreciable assets, all short-lived and long-lived assets, depreciable and nondepreciable assets, and all assets. Since corporate assets are usually the most heavily taxed and those in the household sector are the most lightly taxed, the largest differences were usually between the corporate and household sectors. However, the differences between corporate and noncorporate sectors and between assets in the noncorporate and household sectors were also large and economically significant.

Our results show that discrepancies in tax burdens are greatest between nondepreciable assets in the corporate and household sectors. This can be attributed to the fact that nondepreciable assets are not eligible for the investment tax credit and accelerated capital consumption allowances. These provisions for capital cost recovery have tended to reduce the tax burden. For example, in 1986 the difference between social rates of return on nondepreciable assets in the corporate and household sectors was 6.64 percent, which is greater than the private rates of return in the corporate and household sectors in the same year. In the same year the difference between social rates of return on these assets in the corporate and noncorporate sectors was 3.69 percent.

The Tax Reform Act of 1986 significantly reduced differences in social rates of return among corporate, noncorporate, and household sectors. However, substantial differences between household and corporate sectors remained, especially for nondepreciable assets. We conclude that interasset and intersectoral differences in social rates of return have been very substantial, relative to the private rate of return to capital. The potential loss of economic welfare due to the misallocation of capital is very great. It is important to consider the distortions caused by the interasset differences as well as intersectoral differences in analyzing the distortion of capital allocation due to the taxation of income from capital.

4.4 Alternative Approaches

In this chapter we have implemented the cost of capital approach for the analysis of taxation of income from capital in the United States. We have found that changes in tax policies have had significant effects on the tax burden of income from capital. In addition to provisions of the tax law, there are other factors that play an important role in determining the tax burden of assets. These include the rate of inflation, the interest rate, financial policy of corporate and noncorporate businesses and households, and the distribution of debt and equity claims among owners with different tax statuses.

Our most significant findings are, first, that there have been very substantial differences in the tax treatment of assets within the corporate and noncorporate sectors. These differences have resulted in severe distortions in the allocation of capital within these sectors. Second, there are important differences in the tax treatment of the same type of assets in different sectors. These differences are attributable to the distribution of financial claims among taxpayers subject to different tax treatment, the financial policies of the taxpayers, and the fact that the tax treatment of an asset depends on the legal form of organization in which the asset is employed.

Our estimates of tax wedges and effective tax rates are based on the concept of the marginal effective tax rate, introduced by Auerbach and Jorgenson (1980). The marginal effective tax rate is based on provisions of tax law that are applicable to new assets. Auerbach and Jorgenson have presented marginal effective corporate tax rates for different types of assets within the corporate sector. Jorgenson and Sullivan (1981) have given marginal effective corporate tax rates for the thirty-five categories of assets. They have also given these tax rates for forty-four industrial groups, covering the whole of the U.S. economy. Both sets of effective tax rates cover the period 1946–1980.[2]

Tax wedges and marginal effective tax rates incorporating provisions of both corporate and individual income taxes were introduced by Boadway, Bruce, and Mintz (1984) and King and Fullerton (1984). Under our assumption that the private rate of return is the same for all assets in the corporate sector, differences in effective tax rates among assets are due entirely to differences in the marginal effective corporate tax rates considered by Auerbach and Jorgenson. However, comparisons of marginal effective tax rates among corporate, noncorporate, and household sectors obviously require both corporate and individual tax wedges for the corporate sector. We have presented marginal effective tax rates for all three sectors in Jorgenson and Yun (1986b, 1991b). Our effective tax rates for the corporate sector are based on the "traditional" view of corporate income taxation presented in chapter 2.

The marginal effective tax rates presented by Boadway, Bruce, and Mintz and King and Fullerton are limited to the corporate sector. However, the King-Fullerton methodology has been extended to the noncorporate sector and owner-occupied housing by Fullerton (1987) and Fullerton, Gillette, and Mackie (1987). This methodology incorporates the "new" view of corporate taxation, discussed in section 2.8. The weighted average rate of return for the corporate sector is based on the relative proportions of new issues of equity, retained earnings, and new issues of debt in financing corporate investment. Since retained earnings greatly predominate over new issues of equity, the resulting rate of return is very similar to a weighted average of rates of return for retained earnings and debt alone, which would be consistent with the new view as presented by King (1977), Auerbach (1979), and Bradford (1981b).[3]

The marginal effective tax rates that we have presented in this chapter must be carefully distinguished from the average effective tax rates introduced by Harberger (1962, 1966). Marginal and average tax rates differ substantially, since changes in tax laws usually apply only to new assets. Since new and existing assets are perfect substitutes in production in the model of capital as a factor of production presented in chapter 1, it is marginal rather than the average rates that are relevant to measuring distortions in the allocation of capital. Rosenberg (1969) has presented a set of average effective tax rates for the United States for the period 1953–1959 that includes a breakdown by forty-five industry groups. The average effective tax rates presented by Harberger and Rosenberg include corporate income taxes and property taxes, but do not incorporate individual taxes on distributions from corporate and noncorporate business.

Feldstein and Summers (1979) have presented average effective tax rates for the corporate sector that incorporate individual as well as corporate income tax liabilities. These tax rates are based on the "traditional" rather than the "new" view of corporate taxation and include taxes on dividends paid by the corporate sector as well as taxes on capital gains realized by holders of corporate equity. The estimates of Feldstein and Summers cover the period 1954–1977 and are given separately for twenty two-digit industries within manufacturing. The estimates for the corporate sector as a whole have been updated and revised to cover the period 1953–1979 by Feldstein, Poterba, and Dicks-Mireaux (1983) and the period 1953–1984 by Feldstein and Jun (1987).[4]

It must be emphasized, however, that effective tax rates or tax wedges do not provide a complete analysis of the distortionary effects of capital income taxation. The distortion of resource allocation depends on substitutability between assets as well as the tax wedges. As an example, consider the allocation of capital between short-lived and long-lived depreciable assets in the corporate sector. Even if the interasset difference in tax treatment is large, the distortion of capital allocation can be small if the services of the two types of assets are not substitutable. Similarly, the distortion in the allocation of resources for consumption over time can be small if intertemporal substitutability in consumption is small.

In chapter 5, we discuss applications of the cost of capital approach in modeling economic behavior. A general equilibrium analysis of the atemporal as well as the intertemporal effects of tax policy is required to measure the impact of tax induced distortions in capital allocation. The model of capital as a factor of production presented in chapter 2 is the key to dynamic general equilibrium modeling of the economic impact of tax policy.

Notes

1. A more detailed discussion of the effect of inflation on the taxation of income from capital is given by Feldstein (1983).

2. Marginal effective corporate tax rates are also presented by Bradford and Fullerton (1981), Gravelle (1981), and Hall (1981) and, subsequently, by Auerbach (1983, 1987), Hulten and Robertson (1984), and many others.

3. Scott (1987) has suggested a modification of the King-Fullerton approach along these lines. Ballentine (1987) lists a number of important features of the 1986 Tax Act that are not modeled in effective tax rate calculations, such as those we have presented and those given by Fullerton, Gillette, and Mackie (1987). Fullerton, Gillette, and Mackie (1987), pp. 165–167, provide an assessment of the sensitivity of their results to these omissions and conclude that the effects are small.

4. Fullerton (1984) has discussed the distinction between average and marginal effective tax rates and concludes that empirical measures of effective tax rates based on these two different concepts are not closely related. King and Fullerton (1984), table 6.34, p. 265, provide an estimate of the average effective tax rate for the United States in 1978–1980 and the accompanying text provides comparisons with the results of Feldstein, Poterba, and Dicks-Mireaux, and the earlier work of Rosenberg.

5 Dynamic General Equilibrium Model

The purpose of this chapter is to present a dynamic general equilibrium model for evaluating the impact of tax policy on U.S. economic growth. Tax induced distortions in private decisions can have a substantial impact on the rate of investment and the allocation of capital among different types of assets. These distortions result from the tax wedges that we have identified in the preceding chapter. However, the effects of these tax wedges depend on the elasticities of substitution along all the relevant margins.

The intertemporal margin, involving the allocation of resources between present and future consumption, is particularly critical to the analysis of tax policy. The key dynamic relationships are included in the model of capital as a factor of production presented in chapter 2. The cost of capital affects the demand for capital services, which is essential in simulating the impact of tax policies on investment. The effects of tax policy on future costs of capital are incorporated into the price of investment goods.

In Jorgenson and Yun (1986a), we constructed a dynamic general equilibrium model of the U.S. economy. We employed this model in evaluating the economic impact of the U.S. tax reforms of 1981 in Jorgenson and Yun (1986b). In this chapter we present a new version of our dynamic general equilibrium model. This model incorporates the detailed description of the U.S. tax system given in chapter 3. In the following chapter we present econometric models of producer and consumer behavior based on data for the U.S. economy covering the period 1970–1996.

The plan of this chapter is as follows: In section 5.1 we present a system of notation for demands and supplies of the four commodity groups included in our model—capital and labor services and consumption and investment goods. Equilibrium is characterized by an intertemporal price system. At each point of time this price system links the past and the future through markets for investment goods and capital services. Assets are accumulated as a result of past investments, while asset prices are equal to present values of future capital services. The price system clears the markets for all four commodity groups in every time period.

In section 5.2 we present a model of producer behavior based on a production possibility frontier for the representative producer and the corresponding objective function. The first stage of the producer's optimization problem is to choose appropriate levels for outputs of investment and consumption goods and inputs of capital and labor services. In our model inputs of corporate and noncorporate capital services are treated separately. The second stage is to allocate capital services within each of these sectors between long-lived and short-lived assets.

In section 5.3 we present a model of household behavior based on an intertemporal welfare function for the representative consumer and the corresponding budget constraint. The first stage of the consumer's optimization problem is to allocate wealth among levels of consumption in all time periods. The second stage is to allocate consumption in each time period among capital services, other goods and services, and leisure. We derive labor supply by subtracting leisure demand from the total time endowment. The third and final stage is to allocate capital services between the services of long-lived and short-lived assets within the household sector.

In section 5.4 we present accounts for the government and rest-of-the-world sectors based on identities between income and expenditure. We first outline the generation of government revenue from taxes on transactions in consumption and investment goods and capital and labor services. We complete the government budget by generating government purchases of consumption and investment goods and labor services. The deficit of the government sector is the difference between expenditure and revenue. Similarly, net foreign investment is equal to the difference between U.S. imports and U.S. exports to the rest of the world.

Finally, we describe intertemporal equilibrium in our model in section 5.5. Equilibrium requires that supply must be equal to demand for each of the four commodity groups included in the model—consumption goods, investment goods, capital services, and labor services. We show that demand and supply functions satisfy Walras' Law, so that one of the four market clearing conditions is implied by the three remaining conditions, together with identities between income and expenditure for the household, business, government, and rest-of-the-world sectors. In addition, the equations of the model are homogeneous of degree zero in prices and nominal magnitudes such as income and wealth.

5.1 Commodities

In our model the U.S. economy is divided into household, business, government, and rest-of-the-world sectors. As in chapter 2, the household sector includes both households and nonprofit institutions. Similarly, the business sector includes both corporate and noncorporate businesses. Although we do not model production in the corporate and noncorporate sectors separately, we distinguish between assets and capital services in these two sectors. The government sector includes general government and government enterprises. Finally, the rest-of-the-world sector encompasses transactions between the U.S. economy and the rest of the world.

Our model includes four commodity groups—consumption goods, investment goods, capital services, and labor services. To represent the quantities of these commodity groups we introduce the following notation:

C—personal consumption expenditures, excluding household capital services.

I—gross private domestic investment, including purchases of consumers' durables.

K—private national capital stock, including the stock of household capital.

L—labor services.

Consumption and investment correspond closely to the concepts employed in the U.S. National Income and Product Accounts. However, purchases of consumers' durables are included in personal consumption expenditures and excluded from gross private domestic investment in the U.S. national accounts. Our accounting system treats consumers' durables symmetrically with other forms of capital. To denote prices we place a P before the corresponding symbol for quantity. For example, PC is the price of private national consumption, excluding household capital services.

We require notation for the supply and demand of consumption goods, investment goods, and labor services by all four sectors. Private national consumption C represents purchases of consumption goods by the household sector. The remaining components of supply and demand for consumption goods are as follows:

CG—government purchases of consumption goods.

CR—rest-of-the-world purchases of consumption goods.

CS—supply of consumption goods by private enterprises.

CE—supply of consumption goods by government enterprises.

Similarly, gross private domestic investment I represents purchases of investment goods by the business and household sectors. The remaining components of supply and demand for investment goods are as follows:

IG—government purchases of investment goods.

IR—rest-of-the-world purchases of investment goods.

IS—supply of investment goods by private enterprise.

As in chapter 4, we treat assets and capital services in the corporate, noncorporate, and household sectors separately. We further distinguish between short-lived and long-lived assets within each sector. Short-lived assets include producers' and consumers' durable equipment, while long-lived assets include residential structures, nonresidential structures, inventories, and land. Altogether, we represent six types of assets, cross-classified by legal form of organization and durability, in the model.

The classification of assets by legal form of organization enables us to model differences in the tax treatment of capital income in the corporate, noncorporate, and household sectors. The classification of assets differing in durability is useful in introducing the effects of asset-specific tax rules, such as the investment tax credit and capital consumption allowances. Ignoring the interasset tax wedges within the corporate and noncorporate sectors would omit an important source of tax distortions. Similarly, a classification of assets based only on differences in durability would neglect the impact of intersectoral tax wedges. Our two-way classification of assets encompasses both sources of tax distortions.

We employ the cost of capital approach presented in chapter 2 in modeling the taxation of income from capital. We have shown how past and current tax rules for the definition of capital income can be incorporated into the cost of capital. The cost of capital can also be used in representing recent proposals for taxation of income from capital. These proposals include indexing capital gains, interest income, and interest expenses for inflation, integrating corporate and individual income taxation, and eliminating deductibility of state and local taxes under the federal income tax.

Using the cost of capital approach presented in chapter 2, we can distinguish between debt and equity claims on capital income for corporate, noncorporate, and household sectors. We take the debt-equity ratios to be fixed exogenously for all three sectors. Financial market equilibrium requires that after-tax rates of return to equity are equalized across the three sectors. In addition, rates of return on debt issued by the private sectors and the government must equal the market interest rate. Conditions for financial market equilibrium determine the allocation of capital among the sectors and the allocation of financial claims between debt and equity.

We have simplified the representation of technology in our model by introducing a single stock of capital at each point of time. Capital is perfectly malleable and allocated so as to equalize after-tax rates of return to equity in the corporate, noncorporate, and household sectors. Capital services, say KD, are proportional to private national capital stock K. A complete system of notation that includes the six classes of assets in our model is as follows:

HD—household capital services.

HL—household capital services from long-lived assets.

HS—household capital services from short-lived assets.

MD—noncorporate capital services.

ML—noncorporate capital services from long-lived assets.

MS—noncorporate capital services from short-lived assets.

QD—corporate capital services.

QL—corporate capital services from long-lived assets.

QS—corporate capital services from short-lived assets.

The household sector is the only sector with a time endowment. Part of this endowment is consumed as leisure by the household sector. The rest is supplied as labor services to the business, government, and rest-of-the-world sectors. The components of demand and supply for labor services are as follows:

LH—time endowment.

LJ—leisure time.

LD—private enterprise purchases of labor services.

LE—government enterprise purchases of labor services.

LG—general government purchases of labor services.

LR—rest-of-the-world purchases of labor services.

5.2 Producer Behavior

The business sector includes both corporate and noncorporate enterprises. Instead of modeling corporate and noncorporate businesses as separate production units, we have divided the flow of business capital services between corporate and noncorporate capital services. Similarly, to capture differences in the tax treatment of income from long-lived and short-lived assets, we have divided capital services in the corporate and noncorporate sectors between long-lived and short-lived components. We model the tax treatment of capital income by incorporating specific features of the tax structure that are applicable to each component into the cost of capital.

Our model provides a highly schematic representation of the U.S. economy. A single representative producer employs capital and labor services to produce outputs of consumption and investment goods. The objective of the representative producer is to maximize profits. Our model of producer behavior is based on two-stage allocation.[1] At the first stage the value of output is allocated between consumption and investment goods and among corporate and noncorporate capital services and labor services. At the second stage the values of both types of capital services are allocated between long-lived and short-lived assets.

To represent our model of producer behavior we first require some notation. We denote the shares of outputs and inputs in the value of labor input as follows:

$$v_{CS} = \frac{PCS \cdot CS}{PLD \cdot LD}, \quad v_{IS} = \frac{PIS \cdot IS}{PLD \cdot LD}, \quad v_{MD} = -\frac{PMD \cdot MD}{PLD \cdot LD},$$
$$v_{QD} = -\frac{PQD \cdot QD}{PLD \cdot LD}.$$

The value shares for outputs are positive, while the value share for inputs are negative. We find it convenient to introduce the following additional notation:

v = $(v_{CS}, v_{IS}, v_{MD}, v_{QD})$—vector of value shares.

$\ln P = (\ln PCS, \ln PIS, \ln PMD, \ln PQD)$—vector of logarithms of prices of outputs and inputs.

We characterize the technology of the business sector in terms of labor requirements. The labor services required for production are a function of consumption and investment goods outputs and corporate and noncorporate capital services inputs. This technology is characterized by constant returns to scale, so that any production plan proportional to a feasible plan is also feasible. By modeling the substitution between consumption and investment goods in production, we introduce costs of adjustment in the response of investment to changes in tax policy.[2]

Under constant returns to scale we can represent the technology of the business sector in dual form through the price function, giving the price of labor services as a function of the prices of consumption and investment goods, corporate and noncorporate capital services, and time as an index of technology. The price function must be homogeneous of degree one, nondecreasing in the prices of outputs and nonincreasing in the prices of inputs, and convex in the prices of outputs and inputs. We have incorporated these restrictions into the system of supply and demand functions presented in the following chapter. The rate of productivity growth is endogenous and depends on the prices of inputs and outputs.[3]

We employ the transcendental logarithmic or translog form for the price function:[4]

$$\ln PLD = \ln P'\alpha_P + \alpha_T T + \frac{1}{2} \ln P' B_{PP} \ln P + \ln P'\beta_{PT} T + \beta_{TT} T^2 . \tag{5.1}$$

In this representation the scalars $\{\alpha_T, \beta_{TT}\}$, the vectors $\{\alpha_P, \beta_{PT}\}$, and the matrix $\{B_{PP}\}$ are constant parameters. The dual representation of technology facilitates the expression of demands and supplies as explicit functions of prices of inputs and outputs. The parameters of these functions embody the elasticities of demand and supply that are critical for the evaluation of alternative tax policies.

A model of producer behavior based on the translog price function has an important advantage over models based on Cobb-Douglas or constant elasticity of substitution production functions. Although explicit demand and supply functions can be derived from these production functions, the elasticities must satisfy arbitrary restrictions, such as the restriction that all elasticities of substitution must be same.[5] This frustrates the basic objective of determining the elasticities of demand and supply empirically in order to model the response of producer behavior to changes in tax policy.

The value shares for outputs and inputs can be expressed in terms of the logarithmic derivatives of the price function with respect to the logarithms of the prices of the output and input prices:

$$v = \alpha_P + B_{PP} \ln P + \beta_{PT} T . \tag{5.2}$$

The parameters $\{B_{PP}\}$ can be interpreted as *share elasticities* and represent the degree of substitutability among inputs and outputs, while the parameters $\{\beta_{PT}\}$ are *biases of productivity growth* and represent the impact of changes in productivity on the value shares.[6]

Similarly, the rate of productivity growth, say v_T, is the negative of the growth of the price of labor input, holding the prices of outputs and inputs constant:

$$-v_T = \alpha_T + \beta_{PT} \ln P + \beta_{TT} T . \tag{5.3}$$

The parameter β_{TT} is the *deceleration* of productivity growth. Since Harrod-neutrality of productivity growth is required for the existence of a balanced growth equilibrium of our model, we impose the following restrictions:

$$\beta_{PT} = 0 , \quad \beta_{TT} = 0 .$$

Under these restrictions, productivity growth is labor-augmenting and takes place at a constant rate. This completes the description of the first stage of our model of producer behavior.

We have assumed that production decisions can be separated into two stages. At the first stage the value of output is divided between consumption and investment goods outputs and among corporate and noncorporate capital inputs and labor inputs. At the second stage corporate and noncorporate capital services are allocated between their long-lived and short-lived components. To complete our model of producer behavior we require a model of this second stage.

We first require some additional notation. We denote the shares of long-lived and short-lived assets in the value of noncorporate and corporate capital as follows:

$$v_{ML} = \frac{PML \cdot ML}{PMD \cdot MD}, \; v_{MS} = \frac{PMS \cdot MS}{PMD \cdot MD}, \; v_{QL} = \frac{PQL \cdot QL}{PQD \cdot QD},$$
$$v_{QS} = \frac{PQS \cdot QS}{PQD \cdot QD}.$$

These value shares are positive. We also find it convenient to introduce the notation:

$v_M = (v_{ML}, v_{MS})$—vector of value shares in noncorporate capital input.

$v_Q = (v_{QL}, v_{QS})$—vector of value shares in corporate capital input.

$\ln PM = (\ln PML, \ln PMS)$—vector of logarithms of prices of capital inputs in the noncorporate sector.

$\ln PQ = (\ln PQL, \ln PQS)$—vector of logarithms of prices of capital input in the corporate sector.

We can represent the technology of the second stage of our model of producer behavior by expressing the prices of corporate and noncorporate capital services as functions of the prices of their long-lived and short-lived components. These price functions must be homogeneous of degree one, nondecreasing in the prices of inputs, and concave in the input prices. We have incorporated these restrictions into the demand functions presented in the following chapter.

As before, we employ the translog form for the price functions:

$$\ln PMD = \ln PM'\alpha_{PM} + \frac{1}{2}\ln PM' B_{PM} \ln PM, \tag{5.4}$$
$$\ln PQD = \ln PQ'\alpha_{PQ} + \frac{1}{2}\ln PQ' B_{PQ} \ln PQ.$$

In this representation the matrices $\{B_{PM}, B_{PQ}\}$ are constant parameters that embody the elasticities of demand for capital inputs that are needed for analyzing the response of producer behavior to changes in tax policy.

The value shares can be expressed in terms of the logarithmic derivatives of the price functions with respect to the logarithms of the prices:

$$v_M = \alpha_{PM} + B_{PM} \ln PM\,, \qquad (5.5)$$
$$v_Q = \alpha_{PQ} + B_{PQ} \ln PQ\,.$$

The *share elasticities* $\{B_{PM}, B_{PQ}\}$ represent the degree of substitutability between the capital services of short-lived and long-lived assets within the noncorporate and corporate sectors. There is no role for productivity growth in the second stage of our model of producer behavior.

5.3 Consumer Behavior

The household sector includes both households and nonprofit institutions. This sector owns all the private capital in the U.S. economy and also owns claims on government and the rest of the world. Claims on the government sector represent liabilities owed by the government to its own citizens. Similarly, claims on the rest of the world correspond to liabilities owed by the rest of the world sector to the household sector. The wealth of the household sector is the sum of tangible capital in the private sector and claims on the government and rest-of-the-world sectors.

A portion of the services generated by private capital is consumed by the household sector itself. The rest is supplied to the business sector in the form of corporate and noncorporate capital services. We have divided the capital services in the household sector between long-lived and short-lived components in order to capture differences in the tax treatment of income from these assets. We model the tax treatment of capital income in the household sector by incorporating features of the tax structure that are specific to household assets into the cost of capital.

Our model of consumer behavior is based on a representative consumer who takes prices and rates of return as given. We also assume that the representative consumer has an infinite time horizon. This assumption appears to be a viable alternative to the life-cycle theory in modeling consumer behavior.[7] Barro (1974) has provided a rationale for the infinite horizon representative consumer model in terms of intergenerational altruism. Intergenerational altruism has implications that are very different from those of the life-cycle theory, based on a finite lifetime for each consumer.[8]

The objective of the representative consumer is to maximize welfare through allocation of lifetime wealth among time periods. Our model is based on an intertemporally additive utility function that depends on levels of full consumption in all time periods. Full consumption is an aggregate of consumption goods, household capital services, and leisure. To simplify the representation of preferences we endow the representative consumer with perfect foresight about future prices and rates of return.[9]

To represent our model of consumer behavior we introduce the following notation:

F_t—full consumption per capita with population measured in efficiency units.

PF_t—price of full consumption per capita.

n—rate of population growth.

$-\alpha_T$—rate of labor-augmenting productivity growth.

ρ—nominal private rate of return.

Labor-augmenting productivity growth is incorporated into our representation of the technology of the business sector. Since full consumption includes consumption goods, household capital services, and leisure, an important issue is how to incorporate productivity growth into our representation of the preferences of the household sector. We take the rate of labor-augmenting productivity growth in both sectors to be the same. This assumption is required in order to assure the existence of a balanced growth equilibrium for our model of the U.S. economy. We find it convenient to represent full consumption per capita in a time-invariant form by defining population in efficiency units. In terms of these units the population is equal to the number of individuals, augmented by growth in productivity.

In our model of consumer behavior the representative consumer maximizes the *intertemporal welfare function*:

$$V = \frac{1}{(1-\sigma)} \sum_{t=0}^{\infty} \left(\frac{1+n}{1+\gamma} \right)^t U_t^{1-\sigma} . \tag{5.6}$$

where σ is the inverse of the intertemporal elasticity of substitution and γ is the subjective rate of time preference. These two parameters describe the preferences of the representative consumer. The intertemporal welfare function is a discounted sum of products of total population, which grows at the constant rate n, and per capita atemporal welfare functions $U_t(t = 0, 1, \ldots)$. These welfare functions depend on full consumption per capita F_t with population measured in efficiency units:

$$U_t = F_t(1-\alpha_T)^t, \quad (t = 0, 1, \dots). \tag{5.7}$$

In this expression the term $(1-\alpha_T)^t$, involving the constant rate of labor-augmenting productivity growth, converts the population from efficiency units to natural units.

The representative consumer maximizes the welfare function (5.6), subject to the *intertemporal budget constraint*:

$$W = \sum_{t=0}^{\infty} \frac{PF_t F_t (1-\alpha_T)^t (1+n)^t}{\prod_{s=0}^{t}(1+\rho_s)}, \tag{5.8}$$

where W is full wealth. Full wealth is the present value of full consumption over the whole future of the U.S. economy. The current value of full consumption is discounted at the nominal private rate of return ρ.

The intertemporal welfare function V is additively separable in the atemporal welfare functions $U_t(t = 0, 1, \dots)$. These functions depend on the consumption of leisure, consumption goods, and capital services in each period, so that we can divide the representative consumer's optimization problem into two stages. In the first stage, the consumer allocates full wealth among consumption levels of different time periods. In the second stage, the consumer allocates full consumption among leisure, consumption goods, and household capital services in each period.

The necessary conditions for a maximum of the intertemporal utility function, subject to the constraint on full wealth, are given by the discrete time Euler equation:

$$\frac{F_t}{F_{t-1}} = \left[\frac{PF_{t-1}}{PF_t} \cdot \frac{1+\rho_t}{(1+\gamma)(1-\alpha_T)^{\sigma}}\right]^{\frac{1}{\sigma}}, \quad (t = 1, 2, \dots). \tag{5.9}$$

This equation describes the optimal time path of full consumption, given the sequence of prices of full consumption and nominal rates of return. We refer this equation as the *transition equation* for full consumption. The growth rate of full consumption is uniquely determined by the transition equation, so that we only need to determine the level of full consumption in any one period in order to find the whole optimal time path.

In a steady state with no inflation, the level of full consumption per capita with population measured in efficiency units is constant. Therefore, the only private nominal rate of return consistent with the steady state, say $\tilde{\rho}$, is

$$\tilde{\rho} = (1+\gamma)(1-\alpha_T)^{\sigma} - 1 . \tag{5.10}$$

This rate of return depends on the rate of labor-augmenting productivity growth and the parameters of the intertemporal welfare function, but is independent of tax policy.

We denote the rate of inflation in the price of full consumption by π_t, where:

$$\pi_t = \frac{PF_t}{PF_{t-1}} - 1 , \qquad (t = 1, 2 \ldots) .$$

In a steady state with a constant rate of inflation, say $\tilde{\pi}$, the nominal private rate of return is:

$$\tilde{\rho} = (1+\gamma)(1-\alpha_T)^{\sigma}(1+\tilde{\pi}) - 1. \tag{5.11}$$

If we denote the real private rate of return by r_t, where:

$$r_t = \frac{PF_{t-1}}{PF_t}(1+\rho_t) - 1, \qquad (t = 1, 2 \ldots) ,$$

the steady-state real private rate of return, say $\tilde{r}$, is:

$$\tilde{r} = (1+\gamma)(1-\alpha_T)^{\sigma} - 1 . \tag{5.12}$$

This rate of return is independent of tax policy and the rate of inflation.

The transition equation for full consumption implies that if the real private rate of return exceeds the steady-state rate of return, full consumption rises; conversely, if the rate of return is below its steady-state value, full consumption falls. To show this we take the logarithm of both sides of the transition equation, obtaining:

$$\ln \frac{F_t}{F_{t-1}} = \frac{1}{\sigma}\left[\ln(1+r) - \ln(1+\tilde{r})\right] . \tag{5.13}$$

To a first-order approximation, the growth rate of full consumption is proportional to the difference between the real private rate of return and its steady-state value.[10] The constant of proportionality is the intertemporal elasticity of substitution $1/\sigma$. The greater this elasticity, the more rapidly full consumption approaches its steady-state level.

We have assumed that consumption decisions can be separated into three stages. At the first stage the value of full wealth is allocated among levels of full consumption in different time periods. At the second stage full consumption is allocated among nondurable consumption goods, household capital services, and leisure. The third stage involves the allocation of household capital services between the services of long-lived and short-lived assets.

To complete the representation of preferences of the household sector we require some additional notation. We denote the shares of consumption goods, household capital services, and leisure in full consumption as follows:

$$v_C = \frac{PC \cdot C}{PF \cdot F}, \quad v_{HD} = \frac{PHD \cdot HD}{PF \cdot F}, \quad v_{LJ} = \frac{PLJ \cdot LJ}{PF \cdot F}.$$

Similarly, we denote the shares of long-lived and short-lived assets in household capital services as follows:

$$v_{HL} = \frac{PHL \cdot HL}{PHD \cdot HD}, \quad v_{HS} = \frac{PHS \cdot HS}{PHD \cdot HD}.$$

These value shares are positive. We find it convenient to introduce the notation:

$v_D = (v_C, v_{HD}, v_{LJ})$—vector of value shares of full consumption.

$v_H = (v_{HL}, v_{HS})$—vector of value shares of household capital input.

$\ln PD = (\ln PC, \ln PHD, \ln PLJ^*)$—vector of logarithms of prices of consumption goods, household capital services, and leisure, where PLJ^* is the price of leisure, defined in terms of labor measured in efficiency units.

$\ln PH = (\ln PHL, \ln PHS)$—vector of logarithms of prices of capital inputs in the household sector.

Taking the preferences of the household sector to be homothetic, we can represent the preferences of the second stage of our model of consumer behavior by expressing the price of full consumption as a function of the prices of nondurable consumption goods, household capital services, and leisure. This price function must be homogeneous of degree one, nondecreasing in the prices of the three commodity groups, and concave in these prices. We have incorporated these restrictions into the demand functions presented in the following chapter.

As before, we employ the translog form for the price function:[11]

$$\ln PF = \ln PD'\alpha_{PD} + \frac{1}{2}\ln PD'B_{PD}\ln PD\,. \tag{5.14}$$

In this representation the matrix B_{PD} is constant. The parameters embody elasticities of demand needed for analyzing the response of consumer behavior to changes in tax policy.

Similarly, we can express the price of household capital services as a function of its long-lived and short-lived components. This price function must also be homogeneous of degree one, nondecreasing in the prices of the two components, and concave in these prices. We incorporate these restrictions into the demand functions presented in chapter 6. Employing the translog form for this price function:

$$\ln PHD = \ln PH'\alpha_{PH} + \frac{1}{2}\ln PH'B_{PH}\ln PH\,. \tag{5.15}$$

The matrix B_{PH} is constant and embodies elasticities of demand for household capital services.

The value shares can be expressed in terms of logarithmic derivatives of the price functions with respect to the logarithms of the prices:

$$\begin{aligned} v_D &= \alpha_{PD} + B_{PD}\ln PD\,, \\ v_H &= \alpha_{PH} + B_{PH}\ln PH\,. \end{aligned} \tag{5.16}$$

The *share elasticities* B_{PD}, B_{PH} represent the degree of substitutability among commodity groups within the household sector.

5.4 Government and Rest of the World

We consolidate federal and the state and local governments into a single government sector. The government collects taxes from the household and business sectors, issues government debt to households to finance deficits, and spends its revenues on consumption goods, investment goods, labor services, interest on the government debt, and transfer payments to households and the rest of the world. Similarly, we consolidate the federal and state and local government enterprises into a single government enterprise sector. Government enterprises purchase labor services to produce consumption goods and turn over any surplus to the general government.

5.4.1 Government revenue

To represent the tax revenues of the government sector we introduce some additional notation. We use the symbol R for government revenues and the symbol t for tax rates. For sales taxes our notation is as follows:

R_C—sales tax revenues from consumption goods;

R_I—sales tax revenues from investment goods;

t_C—sales tax rate on consumption goods;

t_I—sales tax rate on investment goods.

Government revenues from taxes on consumption goods and investment goods are generated by the following equations:

$$R_C = t_C \; PCS \cdot CS \,, \qquad (5.17)$$
$$R_I = t_I \; PIS \cdot IS \,.$$

Property taxes are levied on the lagged values of assets, so that we require the following notation:

R_q^p, R_m^p, R_h^p—property tax revenues from corporate, noncorporate, and household assets;

t_q^p, t_m^p, t_h^p—property tax rates on corporate, noncorporate, and household assets;

VQL, VML, VHL—lagged values of corporate, noncorporate, and household assets;

VGL, VRL—lagged values of claims on government and rest of the world.

Government revenues from property taxes are generated by:

$$R_q^p = t_q^p VQL \,, \qquad (5.18)$$
$$R_m^p = t_m^p VML \,,$$
$$R_h^p = t_h^p VHL \,.$$

Wealth taxes include federal estate and gift taxes and state and local death and gift taxes. These taxes are levied on the lagged value of wealth, so that we require the notation:

R_w—wealth tax revenues;

WL—lagged value of wealth;

t_w—wealth tax rate.

The lagged value of wealth is the sum of the lagged values of corporate, noncorporate, and household assets, together with the lagged values of claims on government and rest-of-the-world sectors:

$$WL = VQL + VML + VHL + VGL + VRL .$$

Wealth tax revenues are generated by:

$$R_w = t_w WL . \quad (5.19)$$

5.4.2 Corporate income tax

Income from corporate capital is taxed both at the corporate level and the individual level. The base of the corporate income tax is corporate property compensation less depreciation allowances. At the federal level this is reduced by tax deductions for interest expenses, state and local property taxes, and state and local corporate income taxes. During part of the period covered by our study, tax liabilities were reduced by the investment tax credit.

Replicating the actual practice for calculating capital consumption allowances would require a detailed description of tax law and vintage accounts of all depreciable assets. Similarly, reproducing the calculation of the investment tax credit would require a mechanism for allocating investment expenditure among various categories of assets. However, we can approximate the economic effects of these tax provisions very accurately by introducing the concepts of imputed capital consumption allowances and investment tax credits. Imputed capital consumption allowances convert the present value of these allowances into a current flow that is proportional to the flow of capital services; imputed investment tax credits are defined similarly.

To represent the corporate income tax we require the following notation:

α—dividend pay-out rate;

β_q—debt-capital ratio of the corporate sector;

δ_q^s, δ_q^l—economic depreciation rates on short-lived and long-lived corporate assets;

DC—proportion of nominal capital gains excluded from the individual income tax base;

DI—proportion of interest deduction for indexation for inflation;

DD—proportion of dividend deduction for corporate income tax purpose;

DQ—imputed corporate capital consumption allowances;

DSLI—deduction of state and local income taxes for federal tax purposes;

DSLQ—deduction of state and local taxes on corporate property for federal tax purposes;

i—interest rate;

k_q^s, k_q^l—corporate investment tax credit rates on short-lived and long-lived assets;

ITCQ—imputed corporate investment tax credit rate;

r^e—real rate of return on corporate equity after corporate taxes;

r^q—nominal discount rate for corporate investment;

ρ^e—nominal private rate of return on equity;

t_q^e—marginal tax rate on corporate dividends;

t_q^g—marginal tax rate on capital gains on corporate equity;

t_q—corporate income tax rate;

t_q^f, t_q^s—corporate income tax rates, federal and state and local;

VQL^s, VQL^l—lagged values of corporate capital stock of short-lived and long-lived assets;

z_q^s, z_q^l—present values of corporate capital consumption allowances on short-lived and long-lived assets.

The base of corporate income tax *BQ* is defined as

$$BQ = PQD \cdot QD - DQ - [\beta_q(1 - DI)i + \alpha \cdot DD(1 - \beta_q)r^e]VQL - [t_q^s + t_q^f(DSLQ - DSLI\ t_q^s)]R_q^p/t_q, \quad (5.20)$$

where imputed corporate capital consumption allowances *DQ* are:[12]

$$DQ = z_q^s[r^q - \pi + (1 + \pi)\delta_q^s]VQL^s + z_q^l[r^q - \pi + (1 + \pi)\delta_q^l]VQL^l .$$

The real rate of return on corporate equity after taxes is:

$$r^e = \frac{\rho^e - \pi[1-(1-DC)t_q^g]}{1-[\alpha t_q^e + (1-\alpha)t_q^g]} \,.$$

Equation (5.20) shows how the tax treatment of various types of corporate expenses affects the corporate tax burden. For example, when state and local taxes are fully deductible at the federal level, the term involving revenue from taxes on corporate property reduces to R_q^p. Similarly, if interest expenses are not indexed for inflation, so that DI is equal to zero, all of nominal interest payments are deductible. Finally, tax revenues from corporate taxes R_q are generated by:

$$R_q = t_q \cdot BQ - ITCQ \,, \tag{5.21}$$

where the imputed corporate investment tax credit $ITCQ$ is defined as:

$$ITCQ = k_q^s[r^q - \pi + (1+\pi)\delta_q^s]VQL^s + k_q^l[r^q - \pi + (1+\pi)\delta_q^l]VQL^l \,.$$

5.4.3 Individual income tax

To represent the individual income tax we require the following notation:

β_m, β_h—debt-capital ratios of the noncorporate and household sectors;

δ_m^s, δ_m^l—economic depreciation rates on short-lived and long-lived noncorporate assets;

DHI—proportion of household interest expense deductible for tax purposes;

DM—imputed noncorporate capital consumption allowances;

$DSLM$—deduction of state and local taxes on noncorporate property for federal tax purposes;

$DSLH$—deduction of state and local taxes on household property for federal tax purposes;

HDI—proportion of the household interest payments deducted for indexation for inflation;

r^m—nominal discount rate for noncorporate investment;

t_m^e—marginal tax rate on income from noncorporate equity;

t_m^{ef}, t_m^{es} —marginal tax rates on income from noncorporate equity, federal and state and local;

t_h^e—marginal tax rate for deductions from household equity income;

t_h^{ef}, t_h^{es}—marginal tax rates for deductions from household equity income, federal and state and local.

t_m^g—marginal tax rate on capital gains on noncorporate assets;

t_h^g—marginal tax rate on capital gains on household assets;

VDQ—economic depreciation on corporate assets;

VML^s, VML^l—lagged values of noncorporate capital stock of short-lived and long-lived assets;

z_m^s, z_m^l—present values of noncorporate capital consumption allowances on short-lived and long-lived assets.

In modeling the taxation of individual income, we distinguish between income from labor and capital, since these incomes can be taxed differently. All labor compensation is included in the individual income tax base BL, defined as:

$$BL = PLD \cdot LD + PLE \cdot LE + PLG \cdot LG + PLR \cdot LR . \tag{5.22}$$

Interest income is the sum of interest earned on corporate, noncorporate, and household debt and on claims on government and the rest of the world. We assume that households own claims on the rest of the world through U.S. corporations and that these corporations pay income taxes to the host countries on the earnings of U.S. assets abroad. We assume, further, that the rate of return on these claims after corporate taxes is the same as on domestic corporate capital. Interest originating in the household sector is taxable to the creditor and deductible from the income of the debtor. Under these assumptions the interest income of individuals BD is:

$$BD = [\beta_q(VQL + VRL) + \beta_m VML + \beta_h VHL + VGL](1 - DI)i , \tag{5.23}$$

where VQL is the value of lagged capital stock of both short-lived and long-lived corporate assets and VML and VHL are the values of lagged capital stock of the corresponding noncorporate and household assets, respectively.

Income from equity includes income from corporate and noncorporate assets. Income from equity in household assets is not taxed, but interest expenses and property taxes on these assets are deductible from the income of the owner. Since nominal capital gains on assets are taxed only on realization, we define the marginal tax rate on capital gains in such a way as to convert accrued capital gains to a realization basis.[13]

Taxable income from equity BE includes corporate profits after taxes, together with earnings on claims on the rest of the world. This income also includes noncorporate property compensation—net of interest expenses, property taxes, and depreciation allowances—less property taxes and interest expenses on household assets. Finally, income from equity includes nominal capital gains on private capital. Taxable income from equity is defined as

$$\begin{aligned} BE = {} & PQD \cdot QD - R_q^p - R_q + (1-\beta_q) r^e \cdot VRL - \beta_q (i - \pi) VQL - VDQ \\ & + PMD \cdot MD - DM - \beta_m \, VML \cdot (1 - DI) i - [t_m^{es} + t_m^{ef} (DSLM \\ & - DSLI \cdot t_m^{es})] R_m^p / t_m^e - DHI \cdot \beta_h \, (1 - HDI) VHL \cdot i - [t_h^{es} + t_h^{ef} (DSLH \\ & - DSLI \cdot t_h^{es})] R_h^p / t_h^e + [(1-\beta_q)(VQL + VRL) t_q^g / t_q^e \\ & + (1-\beta_m) VML \, t_m^g / t_m^e + (1-\beta_h) VHL \, t_h^g / t_h^e](1 - DC)\pi , \end{aligned} \tag{5.24}$$

where economic depreciation on corporate assets VDQ is defined as:

$$VDQ = (1+\pi)[\delta_q^s VQL^s + \delta_q^l VQL^l] ,$$

and imputed noncorporate capital consumption allowances DM are defined as:

$$DM = z_m^s [r^m - \pi + (1+\pi)\delta_m^s] VML^s + z_m^l [r^m - \pi + (1+\pi)\delta_m^l] VML^l .$$

To complete the representation of the individual income tax we require the following notation:

$ITCH$—imputed household investment tax credit;

$ITCM$—imputed noncorporate investment tax credit;

k_h^s, k_h^l—household investment tax credit rates on short-lived and long-lived assets;

k_m^s, k_m^l—noncorporate investment tax credit rates on short-lived and long-lived assets;

R_l—tax revenues from labor income;

R_e—tax revenues from equity income;

R_d—tax revenues from interest income;

t_L^a—average tax rate on labor income;

t_e^a—average tax rate on equity income;

t_d^a—average tax rate on interest income.

Tax revenues from individual income taxes are generated by:

$$R_l = t_L^a BL \,,$$
$$R_e = t_e^a BE - ITCM - ITCH \,,$$
$$R_d = t_d^a BD \,, \tag{5.25}$$

where the imputed household and noncorporate investment tax credits $ITCH$ and $ITCM$ are defined as:

$$ITCH = k_h^s\,[r^h - \pi + (1+\pi)\delta_h^s]VHL^s + k_h^s[r^h - \pi + (1+\pi)\delta_h^l]VHL^l \,.$$
$$ITCM = k_m^s[r^m - \pi + (1+\pi)\delta_m^s]VML^s + k_m^s[r^m - \pi + (1+\pi)\delta_m^l]VML^l \,.$$

Ordinarily, average tax rates on equity and interest incomes are the same.

To represent the government budget we require the following notation:

t_L^m—marginal tax rate on labor income;

t_g^d—marginal tax rate on government interest payments;

t_t—effective rate of non-tax payments;

DG—government deficit;

EL—government transfers to households;

ER—government transfers to foreigners;

GS—real government expenditures, net of interest payments;

PGS—price deflator, government expenditures;

R—government revenue;

R_{ge}—surplus of government enterprises;

R_t—revenue from non-tax payments;

R_{lum}—government revenues from a lump sum tax;

$SGOV$—share of government expenditures in GDP;

SCE—proportion of consumption goods produced by government enterprises to business sector production;

SLE—proportion of the labor compensation of government enterprises in the value of labor supply;

SCG—proportion of government purchases of consumption goods in government expenditures, net of interest payments;

SIG—proportion of government purchases of investment goods in government expenditures, net of interest payments;

SLG—proportion of government purchases of labor services in government expenditures, net of interest payments;

SEL—proportion of transfers to households in government expenditures, net of interest payments;

SER—proportion of transfers to foreigners in government expenditures, net of interest payments;

XPND—government expenditures, including interest payments.

To complete the specification of the government budget we must determine revenues from non-tax payments and government enterprises, as well as government expenditures. We assume that federal and state and local personal non-tax payments are given as a proportion of before-tax labor income, so that revenue from non-tax payments is generated by:

$$R_t = t_t BL. \tag{5.26}$$

We assume that the value of labor compensation from government enterprises is given as a proportion of the value of total labor compensation:

$$PLE \cdot LE = SLE \frac{PLH \cdot LH - PLJ \cdot LJ}{1 - t_L^m}. \tag{5.27}$$

Government enterprises employ labor to produce consumption goods; surpluses of these enterprises are revenues of the general government. We assume that the production of consumption goods by government enterprises *CE* is proportional to business production of these goods:

$$CE = SCE \cdot CS. \tag{5.28}$$

The surplus of government enterprises R_{ge} is the difference between the value of output and labor compensation:

$$R_{ge} = PC \cdot CE - PLE \cdot LE. \tag{5.29}$$

We assume that the government allocates total expenditures, net of interest payments on government debt, among consumption goods, investment goods, labor services, and transfer payments to the household and rest-of-the-world sectors in the following proportions:

$$\begin{aligned} &PC \cdot CG = SCG(XPND - VGL \cdot i)\,, \\ &PI \cdot IG = SIG(XPND - VGL \cdot i)\,, \\ &PLG \cdot LG = SLG(XPND - VGL \cdot i)\,, \\ &EL = SEL(XPND - VGL \cdot i)\,, \\ &ER = SER(XPND - VGL \cdot i)\,. \end{aligned} \tag{5.30}$$

Under our assumptions on the allocation of government expenditures, we can aggregate the five categories of government expenditures by means of a linear logarithmic or Cobb-Douglas price function. The price index for government expenditures is defined as:

$$\ln PGS = SCG \cdot \ln(PCG) + SIG \cdot \ln(PIG) + SLG \cdot \ln(PLG)\,, \tag{5.31}$$

where the price indexes of transfer payments to households and the rest of the world are equal to unity. The quantity of government expenditures net of interest payments is then defined as

$$GS = \frac{XPND - VGL \cdot i}{PGS}\,. \tag{5.32}$$

In some experiments with alternative tax policies, we control the paths of real government expenditures and government debt and use a "lump sum tax" levied on the household sector to generate government revenue. We can express the the revenue of the government as the sum of tax revenues, including this lump sum tax, non-tax receipts, and the surplus of government enterprises. Government revenue is defined as:

$$\begin{aligned} R = {} & R_C + R_I + R_q + R_l + R_e + R_d + R_{ge} + R_q^p + R_m^p + R_h^p + R_t \\ & + R_w + R_{lum}. \end{aligned} \tag{5.33}$$

We assume that government expenditures are a constant proportion of gross domestic product (*GDP*):

$$XPND = SGOV \cdot GDP\,, \tag{5.34}$$

where GDP is defined below. The government budget constraint, including the government deficit, is defined by:

$$XPND = R + DG \,. \tag{5.35}$$

5.4.4 Rest of the world

To represent the rest-of-the-world sector we require the following notation:

DR—current account deficit of the rest of the world;

SCR—proportion of purchases of consumption goods by the rest of the world to domestic purchases;

SLR—proportion of purchases of labor services by the rest of the world in the value of labor supply;

SIR—proportion of purchases of investment goods by the rest of the world to domestic supply;

We assume that purchases of consumption goods, labor services, and investment goods by the rest of the world are given by:

$$CR = SCR(C + CG)\,,$$
$$IR = SIR \cdot IS\,,$$
$$PLR \cdot LR = SLR\,\frac{PLH \cdot LH - PLJ \cdot LJ}{1 - t_L^m}\,. \tag{5.36}$$

The value of net exports from the U.S., together with earnings from claims on the rest of the world, net of the government transfers to foreigners, is added to the U.S. claims on the rest of the world. The current account deficit of the rest of the world or surplus of the U.S. is given by:

$$DR = PC \cdot CR + PI \cdot IR + PLR \cdot LR + [(1 - \beta_q)r^e + \beta_q(i - \pi)]VRL - ER\,. \tag{5.37}$$

5.4.5 National Income and Wealth

To represent the national income and product accounts we require the following notation:

D—economic depreciation;

GDP—gross domestic product;

GNP—gross national product;

S—gross private national saving;

V—revaluation of domestic capital;

VK—value of private domestic capital;

Y—gross private national income;

We define gross domestic product GDP as the market value of goods and services produced domestically, which is equal to the sum of the value of domestically employed labor and capital services, indirect taxes, and the surplus of government enterprises. Gross national product GNP is defined as the sum of GDP and the value of labor and capital services employed abroad:

$$\begin{aligned} GDP &= PLD \cdot LD + PLG \cdot LG + PLE \cdot LE \\ &\quad + PQD \cdot QD + PMD \cdot MD + PHD \cdot HD + R_C + R_I + R_{ge} , \\ GNP &= GDP + PLR \cdot LR + [(1-\beta_q)r^e + \beta_q(i-\pi)]VRL . \end{aligned} \tag{5.38}$$

Gross private national income Y is the sum of labor and capital incomes after taxes:

$$\begin{aligned} Y = {} & PLD \cdot LD + PLG \cdot LG + PLE \cdot LE + PLR \cdot LR - R_l \\ & + PQD \cdot QD + PMD \cdot MD + PHD \cdot HD \\ & + [(1-\beta_q)r^e + \beta_q(i-\pi)]VRL + VGL \cdot i \\ & - (R_q^p + R_m^p + R_h^p + R_q + R_e + R_d + R_w + R_t + R_{lum}) . \end{aligned} \tag{5.39}$$

Gross private domestic saving S is defined as gross private national income plus government transfers to households, less household expenditures on consumption goods and capital services:

$$S = Y + EL - (PC \cdot C + PHD \cdot HD) . \tag{5.40}$$

Saving is used to finance gross private domestic investment and the deficits of the government and rest of the world:

$$S = PI \cdot ID + DG + DR . \tag{5.41}$$

Private domestic investment is allocated among the six categories of private assets—short-lived and long-lived assets in the corporate, noncorporate, and household sectors. We assume that tangible assets are perfectly malleable and can be transformed from one category to another. Under this assumption we can represent the accumulation of capital by:

$$VK = VKL + PI \cdot ID - D + V \,, \tag{5.42}$$

where VK is the current value of capital stock and VKL is the lagged value. For each asset category the value of economic depreciation is the product of the rate of economic depreciation and the current value of lagged capital stock and revaluation is the difference between the current and lagged values of the lagged capital stock.

The accumulation of nominal government debt is represented as

$$VG = DG + VGL \,, \tag{5.43}$$

where VG is the current value of outstanding government debt. Similarly, the accumulation of claims on the rest of the world is represented as

$$VR = DR + (1+\pi)VRL \,, \tag{5.44}$$

where VR is the current value of claims on the rest of the world.

5.5 Market Equilibrium

We represent markets in the U.S. economy corresponding to consumption goods, investment goods, labor services, and capital services. The business sector and government enterprises supply the consumption goods purchased by the household, government, and rest-of-the-world sectors. The value of consumption goods supplied is equal to the value demanded:

$$(1+t_C)PCS \cdot CS + PC \cdot CE = PC \cdot (C + CG + CR) \,. \tag{5.45}$$

We assume, further, that the products of the business sector and government enterprises are homogenous, so that balance between supply and demand implies:

$$CS + CE = C + CG + CR \,. \tag{5.46}$$

Equivalently, we can replace this equation with the relationship between the producer and consumer prices:

$$PC = (1 + t_C)\ PCS\ .$$

We use the price deflator PC for consumption goods produced by government enterprises and for purchases by the household, government, and rest-of-the-world sectors.

The business sector supplies the investment goods purchased by the household, government and rest-of-the-world sectors. Since private domestic saving is used to finance private investment, as well as the deficits of government and rest-of-the-world sectors, the demand for private investment is given by:

$$PI \cdot ID = S - DG - DR\ . \tag{5.47}$$

The value of investment goods supplied is equal to the value demanded:

$$(1 + t_I)PIS \cdot IS = PI \cdot (ID + IG + IR)\ , \tag{5.48}$$

and the balance between supply and demand implies:

$$IS = ID + IG + IR\ . \tag{5.49}$$

As before, we can replace this equation with the relationship between the producer and consumer prices:

$$PI = (1 + t_I)PIS\ . \tag{5.50}$$

We assume that the consumer is endowed with a fixed amount of time, fourteen hours per day, that can be consumed as leisure or supplied as labor services. The remaining ten hours per day are required for personal maintenance and is not available for other uses. Labor supply is the difference between the time endowment of the household sector and the consumption of leisure. This supply is allocated among the business, government, government enterprise, and rest-of-the-world sectors. For the economy as a whole, we distinguish among individuals by sex, level of education, and age and allow for the fact that wage rates vary among individuals. Since the composition of the time endowment, leisure, and employment in the various sectors of the economy differs, we use separate price indexes for the time endowment and its various uses.

Demand for labor originates from businesses, governments, government enterprises, and the rest of the world. The value of labor supplied is equal to the value demanded:

$$PLH \cdot LH - PLJ \cdot LJ = (PLD \cdot LD + PLG \cdot LG + PLE \cdot LE + PLR \cdot LR)(1 - t_L^m). \tag{5.51}$$

Since we have no mechanism to determine the relative prices of the time endowment, the consumption of leisure, and labor demanded, we take the relative prices to be exogenous. We find it convenient to express the prices of labor in terms of the price for labor demanded by the business sector:

$$\begin{aligned} PLH &= (1 - t_L^m) A_{LH} \cdot PLD, \\ PLJ &= (1 - t_L^m) A_{LJ} \cdot PLD, \\ PLG &= A_{LG} \cdot PLD, \\ PLE &= A_{LE} \cdot PLD, \\ PLR &= A_{LR} \cdot PLD, \end{aligned} \tag{5.52}$$

where the factors of proportionality—A_{LH}, A_{LJ}, A_{LG}, A_{LE}, A_{LR}—are given exogenously.

Households are the sole suppliers of capital services and own all private capital. The demand side of the market includes corporate and noncorporate businesses, as well as households. As in the case of labor services, we take the relative prices of the six types of capital assets to be exogenous. Under the assumption of perfect malleability of capital any type of capital can be converted into any other type of capital with rates of transformation given by the relative prices. In order to describe the equilibrium of capital market, we introduce the following notations:

K_{QS}: quantity of short-lived corporate capital stock.

K_{QL}: quantity of long-lived corporate capital stock.

K_{MS}: quantity of short-lived noncorporate capital stock.

K_{ML}: quantity of long-lived noncorporate capital stock.

K_{HS}: quantity of short-lived household capital stock.

K_{HL}: quantity of long-lived household capital stock.

We define capital services and capital stock in such a way that one unit of each of the six categories of capital stock generates one unit of capital services. The quantity index of the demand for capital services of a particular category is equal to the quantity index of the capital stock necessary to meet the demand for capital services, i.e., $K_{QS} = QS$, $K_{QL} = QL$, $K_{MS} = MS$, $K_{ML} = ML$, $K_{HS} = HS$, and $K_{HL} = HL$. Given differences in tax rates, investment tax credits, capital consumption allowances, and economic rates of depreciation, a dollar's worth of assets in different categories of capital generates different amounts of capital services.

Equilibrium in the market for capital services is achieved when the total value of capital stock required to meet the demands for all six categories of capital services is equal to the value of the capital stock available:

$$\begin{aligned} PK_{QS} \cdot QS + PK_{QL} \cdot QL + PK_{MS} \cdot MS + PK_{ML} \cdot ML \\ + PK_{HS} \cdot HS + PK_{HL} \cdot HL = (1+\pi)VKL \end{aligned} \tag{5.53}$$

where π is the rate of inflation in the price of capital assets, PK_{QS} is the current price of short-lived corporate capital stock and PK_{QL}, the current price of long-lived corporate capital stock, and so on.

The equilibrium values of economic depreciation D and revaluation V are based on the allocation of capital among the six categories of assets.

In order to express Walras' Law we can define the value of excess demand, say SXD, as the sum of differences between the values of supply and demand in each of the four markets. Substituting the definitions of tax revenues and the surplus of government enterprises, we obtain the following expression for the value of excess demands:

$$\begin{aligned} SXD = {} & PC(C+CG-CE) - (PCS \cdot CS + R_C) + PI(ID+IG) - (PIS \cdot IS + R_I) \\ & + (PLD \cdot LD + PLE \cdot LE + PLG \cdot LG) \\ & - \left[\frac{PLH \cdot LH - PLJ \cdot LJ}{1-t_L^m}(1-t_L^a) + R_l \right] \\ & + (PQD \cdot QD + PMD \cdot MD + PHD \cdot HD) \\ & - (PQS \cdot K_{QS} + PQL \cdot K_{QL} + PMS \cdot K_{MS} + PML \cdot K_{ML} \\ & + PHS \cdot K_{HS} + PHL \cdot K_{HL}) . \end{aligned} \tag{5.54}$$

where $K_{QS} = QS$, $K_{QL} = QL$, $K_{MS} = MS$, $K_{ML} = ML$, $K_{HS} = HS$, and K_{HL} are substituted from (5.53).

By successive substitutions we arrive at the following expression for the value of excess demand:

$$SXD = (PQD \cdot QD + PMD \cdot MD + PLD \cdot LD) - (PIS \cdot IS + PCS \cdot CS),$$

which is the zero profit condition of the business sector. Walras' Law implies that the market clearing condition for one market is implied by the conditions for the other three markets and the budget constraints of the household, business, government, and rest-of-the-world sectors. In solving the model, we drop the condition for equilibrium of the labor market.

In modeling the allocation of full consumption, production, and the allocation of demand for capital services, we have imposed homogeneity of degree one on the price functions. For each of the six categories of capital services the price of capital services is homogeneous of degree one in the current and lagged prices of capital stock, given the rate of revaluation and the nominal rate of return. Finally, gross private national income and savings are homogenous of degree one in prices, given the nominal rate of return. We conclude that the model is homogeneous of degree zero in the prices and the nominal magnitudes, such as income and wealth, given the rate of inflation and the real private rate of return.

We normalize the prices by setting the current price of capital assets and investment goods and, therefore, the rate of inflation exogenously. Under this normalization, it is natural to define the rate of inflation as the rate of change in the price of capital assets and investment goods. As a consequence, we use the terms "rate of inflation" and "rate of revaluation" for capital stock interchangeably.

Notes

1. Two-stage allocation in the context of producer behavior is discussed in more detail by Jorgenson (1986).
2. For alternative approaches to costs of adjustment, see Summers (1981) and Auerbach (1989b).
3. Our approach to endogenous productivity growth was originated by Jorgenson and Fraumeni (1981).
4. The translog price function was introduced by Christensen, Jorgenson, and Lau (1971, 1973).
5. McFadden (1963) and Uzawa (1962) have shown that this restriction is implicit in constant elasticity of substitution production functions. For further discussion, see Fuss, McFadden, and Mundlak (1978) and Jorgenson (1986).
6. For further discussion of share elasticities and biases of productivity growth, see Jorgenson (1986).
7. For example, Kotlikoff and Summers (1981) have suggested that life-cycle saving accounts for only a small fraction of the total saving, so that a significant fraction of saving is motivated by bequests. See also Kotlikoff (1988), Modigliani (1988), and Gale and Scholz (1994).

8. A few examples are implications of distortions in intertemporal consumption due to the Social Security System, considered by Feldstein (1974), the burden of the national debt, analyzed by Barro (1974), and the intergenerational distribution of the tax burden, studied by Auerbach and Kotlikoff (1987) and Auerbach (1989a).

9. Perfect foresight models of tax incidence are presented by Hall (1971), Chamley (1981), Judd (1987), Sinn (1987), Lucas (1990), and many others.

10. Chamley (1981) derives this formula in a continuous time framework with a single good and fixed labor supply.

11. The translog indirect utility function was introduced by Christensen, Jorgenson, and Lau (1975). Jorgenson and Lau (1975) show that under homotheticity this function can be represented by means of a translog price function.

12. Additional details are given in chapter 2, especially section 2.7.

13. Further details are given in chapter 2.

6 Estimating the Parameters

The purpose of this chapter is to estimate the parameters of the dynamic general equilibrium model of the U.S. economy presented in chapter 5. The dominant methodology for assigning parameter values is calibration to a single data point. The econometric methods we employ are more burdensome from the computational point of view, but incorporate considerably more information. These methods facilitate the use of more flexible descriptions of technology and preferences and generate more reliable estimates of the responses of producers and consumers to changes in tax policy.

Our model of consumer behavior is divided into three stages. The first stage combines the transition equation for full consumption (5.9) with the lifetime budget constraint (5.8) to allocate household sector wealth over time. The second stage determines the distribution of full consumption among goods, leisure, and household capital services within each time period. We employ share equations derived from the price function for full consumption (5.14) for this purpose. Finally, the third stage allocates household capital services between short-lived and long-lived assets, using share equations derived from the price function for capital services (5.15).

Our model of producer behavior involves two separate stages. At the first stage labor services and capital services from the corporate and noncorporate sectors are used to produce outputs of consumption and investment goods. Share equations derived from the price function for labor input (5.1) are used to model the production process. At the second stage capital services in both sectors are allocated between short-lived and long-lived assets. We employ price functions for corporate and noncorporate capital services (5.4) to generate the share equations for this purpose.

The plan of this chapter is as follows: In order to estimate the parameters describing preferences, we begin by specifying econometric models corresponding to the transition equation for full consumption and the share equations for allocating full consumption and household capital services within each time period. We impose the restrictions required for concavity of the underlying price functions at all data points in our sample. We combine the transition equation and the two sets of share equations and estimate the parameters simultaneously. The resulting parameter estimates generate the econometric model of consumer behavior presented in section 6.1.

We follow a similar strategy in estimating the parameters that describe technology. We first specify an econometric model corresponding to the share equations for outputs of consumption and investment goods and inputs of capital services from corporate and noncorporate assets. We then specify the share equations for allocating corporate and noncorporate capital services between short-lived and long-lived assets separately. We impose curvature restrictions on the underlying price functions at all data points in our sample. We estimate the three sets of equations simultaneously. The resulting estimates generate the econometric model of producer behavior presented in section 6.2.

In section 6.3 we describe our econometric models of consumer and producer behavior in terms of price elasticities of demand and supply. We present estimates of own-price and cross-price elasticities for each model. We also provide an estimate of the compensated elasticity of labor supply in our model of consumer behavior, holding consumer welfare constant. Finally, we provide estimates of the elasticities of substitution for both consumer and producer models. The intertemporal elasticity of substitution of full consumption is a constant parameter and we present an estimate of this elasticity as well.

In section 6.4 we assign values to the remaining parameters employed in our dynamic general equilibrium model. We employ historic averages to represent debt/asset ratios in corporate, noncorporate, and household sectors, the dividend pay-out ratio in the corporate sector, and the real interest rate. We use similar averages for the shares of different commodity groups in government expenditure and the shares of the labor force employed by the rest-of-the world and government enterprises. Finally, we choose relative prices of different types of capital assets and investment goods and relative prices of different types of labor to coincide with historical relationships.

We choose values for the parameters that determine steady-state values for the debt of the government and rest-of-the-world sectors to assure the existence of a viable long-run equilibrium of the U.S. economy. The key parameter for the government sector is the share of government expenditures in gross domestic product (GDP). For the rest of the world the key parameters are net exports of consumption and investment goods as proportions of the domestic demand for consumption goods and domestic production of investment goods, respectively. Finally, we present the historical data for the period 1970–1996 used in the estimation of our model in the appendix to this chapter.

6.1 Consumer Behavior

The lifetime budget constraint and the transition equation for full consumption determine the allocation of the household sector's wealth over time. To generate an econometric model for this allocation we add a disturbance term to the transition equation (5.13), obtaining:

$$\ln \frac{F_t}{F_{t-1}} = \frac{1}{\sigma}\,[\ln(1+r_t) - \ln(1+\tilde{r})] + \varepsilon_{Ft}, \quad t = 1, 2, \ldots, T, \tag{6.1}$$

where r_t is the real private rate of return

$$r_t = \frac{PF_{t-1}}{PF_t}\,(1+\rho_t) - 1,$$

and $\tilde{r}$ is the steady-state value of this rate of return

$$\tilde{r} = (1+\gamma)(1-\alpha_T)^{\sigma} - 1.$$

The parameter σ is the inverse of the intertemporal elasticity of substitution and the parameter γ is the subjective rate of time preference. We estimate the parameter α_T, the negative of the rate of labor-augmenting productivity growth, as part of the model of producer behavior described below.

The variables F_t and r_t in the transition equation (6.1) both have time subscripts. The disturbances ε_{Ft} correspond to random deviations from the optimal allocation of full consumption as well as errors in measurement of the growth rate of consumption. We assume that the disturbance term is distributed independently over time with expected value zero and constant variance.

Under homotheticity of preferences we can describe the allocation of full consumption among different commodity groups by means of the price function (5.14). The value shares (5.16) sum to unity, since this function is homogeneous of degree one in the prices. In addition, the matrix of share elasticities B_{PD} must be symmetric. We refer to these as the *summability* and *symmetry* restrictions.

The theory of consumer behavior implies two additional sets of restrictions on the model for the allocation of full consumption among commodity groups. First, the value shares must be *nonnegative,* since the price function is nondecreasing in the prices of the commodity groups. Second, the price function must be *concave* to guarantee the appropriate curvature.

To generate an econometric model for the allocation of full consumption we add a vector of random disturbances ε_{Dt} to the equations for the value shares (5.16), obtaining:

$$v_{Dt} = \alpha_{PD} + B_{PD} \ln PD_t + \varepsilon_{Dt} , \quad t = 1, 2, \ldots, T , \tag{6.2}$$

where the parameters α_{PD} and B_{PD} are the same as in (5.16), the variables v_{Dt} and $\ln PD_t$ now have time subscripts, and the vector of disturbances ε_{Dt} takes the form:

$$\varepsilon_{Dt} = \begin{bmatrix} \varepsilon_{Ct} \\ \varepsilon_{LJt} \\ \varepsilon_{HDt} \end{bmatrix} . \tag{6.3}$$

The disturbance vector corresponds to random deviations from the optimal allocation of full consumption within each time period and errors in measuring the value shares. We assume that the expected value of this vector is zero,

$$E(\varepsilon_{Dt}) = 0, \quad t = 1, 2, \ldots, T , \tag{6.4}$$

and the covariance matrix

$$V(\varepsilon_{Dt}) = \Sigma, \quad t = 1, 2, \ldots, T , \tag{6.5}$$

is constant. We also assume that the disturbances of any two distinct time periods are distributed independently.

The summability restrictions imply that the value shares sum to unity, so that the sum of the corresponding disturbance terms must be zero.

$$i'\varepsilon_{Dt} = 0 \quad t = 1, 2, \ldots, T\,, \tag{6.6}$$

and the covariance matrix Σ must be singular. We assume that this third-order matrix has rank two.

In the unrestricted form of our econometric model for the allocation of full consumption (6.2), there are twelve parameters to be estimated. Symmetry of the matrix B_{PD} reduces this number to nine and summability restrictions reduce the number to five. These restrictions also imply that the contemporaneous disturbances are linearly dependent and the covariance matrix is singular. Therefore we drop the share equation for consumption goods and estimate the parameters of the remaining two equations. Estimates of the parameters of the equation for consumption goods can be recovered from the symmetry and summability conditions.[1]

We incorporate symmetry and summability restrictions into our model of consumer behavior by imposing these restrictions on parameter estimates for the share equations. Since we can always choose a set of non-zero prices for which at least one of the shares is negative, nonnegativity restrictions cannot be imposed on the parameters and must be checked at each data point. To impose the concavity restrictions on the price function for full consumption, we first consider the following transformation of the Hessian of the price function:

$$\frac{1}{PF} P'\, HP = B_{PD} + v_D v_D{}' - V_D\,, \tag{6.7}$$

where H is the Hessian and P is a diagonal matrix with prices of the three commodity groups along the main diagonal:

$$P = \begin{bmatrix} PC & 0 & 0 \\ 0 & PHD & 0 \\ 0 & 0 & PLJ \end{bmatrix},$$

v_D is the vector of value shares of full consumption and V_D is a diagonal matrix with these value shares along the main diagonal:

$$V_D = \begin{bmatrix} v_C & 0 & 0 \\ 0 & v_{HD} & 0 \\ 0 & 0 & v_{LJ} \end{bmatrix}.$$

Since the prices are nonnegative, the Hessian H is negative semi-definite if, and only if, the expression on the right-hand side of equation (6.7) is negative semi-definite.[2]

Prices are the independent variables in our econometric models of producer and consumer behavior. In our complete model of the U.S. economy these prices are endogenously determined by the interaction of supply and demand. We use the instrumental variables listed in table A6.1 of the appendix to this chapter to obtain consistent estimates. With these instrumental variables the method of nonlinear three-stage least-squares (NL3SLS) is consistent and asymptotically efficient in the class of minimum distance estimators that employ the same set of instruments.[3] The nonlinear three-stage least-squares estimator is invariant with respect to the choice of an equation to be dropped under the summability conditions.

Our strategy is to estimate the share equations with the parameters constrained so that concavity holds at all data points. We require that the transformation of the Hessian of the price function given in equation (6.7) must be negative semi-definite for each data point. We represent this transformation of the Hessian in terms of its Cholesky factorization

$$B_{PD} + v_D v_D' - V_D = LDL' \tag{6.8}$$

where L is a lower triangular matrix and D is a diagonal matrix.

Under concavity the diagonal elements of the matrix D, the so-called *Cholesky values*, must be less than or equal to zero. We choose the Cholesky values in the base year 1992 for our price system so that Cholesky values for all data points satisfy these nonnegativity restrictions. Since one of the Cholesky values is zero by summability, only inequality constraints corresponding to the two remaining values must be imposed. We consider four combinations of restrictions on the Cholesky values in the base year: (1) neither parameter is constrained; (2) the first is constrained; (3) the second is constrained; (4) both are constrained. We choose the set of estimates with the lowest sum of squared residuals.

The parameters of our econometric model for the allocation of full consumption, α_{PD} and B_{PD}, are estimated with the consumer prices of consumption goods, leisure, and household capital services normalized at unity in 1992, the base year for estimation. Under these normalizations, the vector of value shares of full consumption in 1992, $v_{D,1992}$, is equal to α_{PD}, which is convenient for representing the concavity restrictions for 1992. In the simulations with our dynamic general equilibrium model, however, we use a different normalization for the price system. Accordingly, we adjust the estimates of α_{PD} for the shift of base year using the following relationship:

$$\nu_{D,1992} = \alpha_{PD} = \alpha^*_{PD} + \ln PD^*_{1992} B_{PD}$$

where the superscript * indicates that the price system used in the value share equation is the one consistent with our dynamic general equilibrium model. The estimate of B_{PD} is not affected by the shift of base year.

Given the prices of consumption goods, leisure, and household capital services, the knowledge of α^*_{PD} and B_{PD} is sufficient to determine the value shares of full consumption, but the price level of full consumption is still indeterminate. To fix the price level of full consumption, we add a constant term α_0^{PD} to the logarithmic price function of full consumption, and set its value at the average of

$$\ln PF^* - \ln PD^{*'} \alpha^*_{PD} - \frac{1}{2} \ln PD^{*'} B_{PD} \ln PD^*$$

for our sample period 1970–1996, where $\ln PF^*$ and $\ln PD^*$ are based on the price system consistent with our model. This procedure enables the fitted value of full consumption price to track the historical path closely.[4]

The parameter estimates for our econometric model for the allocation of full consumption are given in table 6.1, together with estimates of the Cholesky values for the base year 1992 and the sum of squared residuals. The estimated Cholesky values for each data point during the period 1970–1996 are also given in table 6.2 and are nonpositive. The fitted shares of the three commodity groups in full consumption are nonnegative. The model satisfies the symmetry, summability, nonnegativity, and concavity conditions required by the price function (5.14) of chapter 5 at every data point. The data used in the estimation of the consumer model are presented in tables A6.3c, A6.4, A6.6, and A6.7. The instrumental variables are presented in table A6.1 (see appendix).

Finally, we must estimate the parameters of the price function (5.15) that determine the allocation of household capital services between short-lived and long-lived components. As before, the value shares (5.16) sum to unity, since this function is homogeneous of degree one in the prices. In addition, the matrix of share elasticities B_{PH} must be symmetric. These are the summability and symmetry restrictions for

Table 6.1
Allocation of full consumption: Parameter estimates

Parameter	Estimate	Standard Error	t-Statistic
α_C	0.242349	0.000685	353.5
α_L	0.681565	0.001588	428.9
α_H	0.076086	0.000958	79.4
β_{CC}	0.119251	0.006838	17.4
β_{CL}	–0.101220	0.009187	–11.0
β_{CH}	–0.018031	0.007364	–2.4
β_{LC}	–0.101220	0.009187	–11.0
β_{LL}	0.140383	0.017934	7.8
β_{LH}	–0.039163	0.010467	–3.7
β_{HC}	–0.018031	0.007364	–2.4
β_{HL}	–0.039163	0.010467	–3.7
β_{HH}	0.057195	0.003201	17.8
δ_L	–0.076651	0.017853	–4.2
λ_{LH}	–0.165608	0.100844	–1.6
δ_H	–0.011000	0.0	0.0
α_0^{PD}	0.21075		
α_L^*	0.72357		
α_H^*	0.064366		
α_C^*	0.21206		
SSR	1.75442		

Note: δ_H is constrained at –.011.

the price function. In addition, the value shares must be nonnegative, since the price function is nondecreasing, and this function must be concave.

To generate an econometric model for the allocation of household capital services we add a vector of random disturbances ε_{Ht} to the equations for the value shares (5.16), obtaining

$$v_{Ht} = \alpha_{PH} + B_{PH} \ln PH_t + \varepsilon_{Ht}, \quad t = 1, 2, \ldots, T, \tag{6.9}$$

where the parameters α_{PH} and B_{PH} are the same as in (5.16), the variables v_{Ht} and $\ln PH_t$ have time subscripts, and the vector of disturbances ε_{Ht} takes the form

$$\varepsilon_{Ht} = \begin{bmatrix} \varepsilon_{HLt} \\ \varepsilon_{HSt} \end{bmatrix}. \tag{6.10}$$

Table 6.2
Allocation of full consumption: Local Cholesky values

Year	δ_L	δ_H
1970	–0.069943	–0.008739
1971	–0.071206	–0.009596
1972	–0.072857	–0.010105
1973	–0.074210	–0.010057
1974	–0.073214	–0.008936
1975	–0.071933	–0.001301
1976	–0.077169	–0.011919
1977	–0.079238	–0.013582
1978	–0.079392	–0.014085
1979	–0.078158	–0.011239
1980	–0.076611	–0.007459
1981	–0.077982	–0.008987
1982	–0.075193	–0.010667
1983	–0.077913	–0.014006
1984	–0.080787	–0.016443
1985	–0.079862	–0.014235
1986	–0.080172	–0.014338
1987	–0.075992	–0.012556
1988	–0.076207	–0.011618
1989	–0.077235	–0.010995
1990	–0.078444	–0.013592
1991	–0.076110	–0.011020
1992	–0.076651	–0.011000
1993	–0.076536	–0.010548
1994	–0.076765	–0.012402
1995	–0.074995	–0.009010
1996	–0.075155	–0.009391

The disturbance vector corresponds to random deviations from the optimal allocation of household capital services within each time period, as well as errors in measuring the value shares. We assume that the expected value of this vector is zero, the covariance matrix is constant, and the disturbances from distinct time periods are distributed independently. Summability implies that the value shares must sum to one, so that the disturbances must sum to zero and the covariance matrix is singular; we assume that this second-order matrix must have rank one.

In the unrestricted form of our econometric model for the allocation of household capital services (6.9) there are six parameters to be estimated. Symmetry of the matrix B_{PH} reduces this number to five and summability reduces the number to two. We drop the share equation for long-lived assets and estimate the parameters of the remaining equation; estimates of the parameters of the equation for long-lived assets can be recovered from the symmetry and summability conditions.

Nonnegativity restrictions cannot be imposed on the parameters; to impose concavity restrictions we consider a transformation of the Hessian of the price function analogous to (6.7) above. As before, our strategy is to estimate the share equation with the parameters constrained to satisfy concavity at all data points in the sample, using the Cholesky factorization of the transformed Hessian. Since one of the two Cholesky values is equal to zero by summability, only the inequality restriction on the remaining Cholesky value must be imposed.

We estimate the econometric models for allocation of full consumption and household capital services simultaneously. The advantages of this approach arise from pooling the information from both sets of equations and allowing for non-zero covariances among the disturbances. As before, we employ the instrumental variables listed in appendix table A6.1 to obtain consistent estimates.

The parameter estimates of our econometric models are given in table 6.3, together with estimates of the Cholesky values for the base year 1992 and the corresponding sum of squared residuals. The estimated Cholesky values are given in table 6.4 and are nonpositive at all data points. The fitted value shares for both models are nonnegative at all data points. The models satisfies the symmetry, summability, nonnegativity, and concavity conditions required for the price functions (5.14) and (5.15) of chapter 5.

Finally, we estimate all three components of our econometric model of consumer behavior simultaneously. The first corresponds to the intertemporal allocation of lifetime wealth, the second to the allocation of full consumption among leisure, consumption goods, and household capital services, and the third to allocation of capital services between short-lived and long-lived assets. The advantages of estimating the three components simultaneously arise from pooling the information from all three sets of equations and allowing for non-zero covariances among the disturbances in these equations.

As before, we require that parameter estimates for the two sets of share equations must satisfy nonnegativity and concavity conditions at all data points. We also impose symmetry and summability restric-

Table 6.3
Allocation of full consumption and household capital services: Parameter estimates

Parameter	Estimate	Standard Error	t-Statistic
α_C	0.242373	0.000683	354.4
α_L	0.681514	0.001526	446.4
α_H	0.076113	0.000897	84.8
β_{CC}	0.116165	0.006969	16.6
β_{CL}	–0.103010	0.008173	–12.6
β_{CH}	–0.013155	0.005031	–2.6
β_{LC}	–0.103010	0.008173	–12.6
β_{LL}	0.147987	0.012553	11.7
β_{LH}	–0.044977	0.006205	–7.2
β_{HC}	–0.013155	0.005031	–2.6
β_{HL}	–0.044977	0.006205	–7.2
β_{HH}	0.058132	0.001390	41.8
δ_L	–0.069066	0.012529	–5.5
λ_{LH}	–0.099838	0.074801	–1.3
δ_H	–0.011500	0.0	0.0
α_0^{PD}	0.21107		
α_L^*	0.72580		
α_H^*	0.062654		
α_C^*	0.21155		
α_S^H	0.512204	0.003787	135.2
α_L^H	0.487796	0.003787	128.8
β_{SS}^H	0.166370	0.004706	35.3
β_{SL}^H	–0.166370	0.004706	–35.3
β_{LL}^H	0.166370	0.004706	35.3
δ_S^H	–0.083481	0.004678	–17.8
α_0^{PH}	–0.0012771		
SSR	2.79935		

Notes:
1) δ_H is constrained at –0.0115
2) α_0^{PH} is set at the average of $\ln PHD * - \ln PH *' \alpha_{PH} - \frac{1}{2} \ln PH *' B_{PH} \ln PH *$ for 1970–1996.

Table 6.4
Allocation of full consumption and household capital services: Local Cholesky values

Year	δ_L	δ_H	δ_S^H
1970	–0.062184	–0.009048	–0.062652
1971	–0.063516	–0.010036	–0.063697
1972	–0.065225	–0.010624	–0.064993
1973	–0.066588	–0.010544	–0.067599
1974	–0.065485	–0.009175	–0.070379
1975	–0.063873	–0.000572	–0.052235
1976	–0.069696	–0.012696	–0.070519
1977	–0.071877	–0.014587	–0.072669
1978	–0.072040	–0.015109	–0.075016
1979	–0.070653	–0.011901	–0.073559
1980	–0.068901	–0.007605	–0.070689
1981	–0.070379	–0.009391	–0.073109
1982	–0.067570	–0.011121	–0.078488
1983	–0.070491	–0.014902	–0.080803
1984	–0.073524	–0.017655	–0.081821
1985	–0.072478	–0.015164	–0.081529
1986	–0.072796	–0.015277	–0.082144
1987	–0.068431	–0.013164	–0.082744
1988	–0.068604	–0.012098	–0.082672
1989	–0.069630	–0.011422	–0.082652
1990	–0.071039	–0.014508	–0.083593
1991	–0.068513	–0.011509	–0.083494
1992	–0.069066	–0.011500	–0.083481
1993	–0.068923	–0.010975	–0.083435
1994	–0.069272	–0.013145	–0.083621
1995	–0.067247	–0.009128	–0.083291
1996	–0.067459	–0.009643	–0.083523

tions on the parameter estimates. The complete system of equations consists of the transition equation (6.1), two of the three equations for the allocation of full consumption (6.2), and one of the two equations for the allocation of household capital services (6.9).

A total of twenty parameters must be estimated in our econometric model of consumer behavior—two in the transition equation, twelve in the allocation of full consumption, and six in the allocation of household capital services. The symmetry and summability restrictions reduce the number of parameters in the four estimating equations to only nine. Imposing concavity restrictions on the two sets of share equations does not reduce the number of parameters to be estimated.

Table 6.5
Allocation of lifetime wealth, full consumption, and household capital services: Parameter estimates

Parameter	Estimate	Standard Error	t-Statistic
α_C	0.242199	0.000715	338.4
α_L	0.681746	0.001550	439.7
α_H	0.076055	0.000889	85.4
β_{CC}	0.105804	0.006487	16.3
β_{CL}	–0.097349	0.007368	–13.2
β_{CH}	–0.008455	0.004970	–1.7
β_{LC}	–0.097349	0.007368	–13.2
β_{LL}	0.146566	0.011135	13.1
β_{LH}	–0.049217	0.005443	–9.0
β_{HC}	–0.008455	0.004970	–1.7
β_{HL}	–0.049217	0.005443	–9.0
β_{HH}	0.057672	0.000880	65.5
δ_L	–0.070403	0.011093	–6.3
λ_{LH}	–0.037398	0.071565	–0.5
δ_H	–0.012500	0.0	0.0
α_0^{PD}	0.21108		
α_L^*	0.72560		
α_H^*	0.061327		
α_C^*	0.21307		
α_S^H	0.513615	0.003643	140.9
α_L^H	0.486385	0.003643	133.5
β_{SS}^H	0.161082	0.004603	34.9
β_{SL}^H	–0.161082	0.004603	–34.9
β_{LL}^H	0.161082	0.004603	34.9
δ_S^H	–0.088733	0.004569	–19.4
α_0^{PH}	–0.0011957		
σ	2.55462	0.439428	5.8
γ	0.021500	0.008958	2.4
SSR	3.54101		

Notes:

1) δ_H is constrained at –0.0125

2) α_0^{PH} is set at the average of $\ln PHD^* - \ln PH^{*\prime}\,\alpha_{PH} - \frac{1}{2}\ln PH^{*\prime}\,B_{PH}\ln PH^*$ for 1970–1996.

Table 6.6
Allocation of lifetime wealth, full consumption, and household capital services: Local Cholesky values

Year	δ_L	δ_H	δ_S^H
1970	–0.063677	–0.009488	–0.068745
1971	–0.065008	–0.010637	–0.069737
1972	–0.066675	–0.011355	–0.070969
1973	–0.067975	–0.011334	–0.073445
1974	–0.066847	–0.009799	–0.076092
1975	–0.064851	–0.000425	–0.058867
1976	–0.071068	–0.013813	–0.076225
1977	–0.073257	–0.015950	–0.078275
1978	–0.073443	–0.016524	–0.080516
1979	–0.071944	–0.013012	–0.079125
1980	–0.070043	–0.008328	–0.076388
1981	–0.071554	–0.010326	–0.078694
1982	–0.068955	–0.012027	–0.083845
1983	–0.071956	–0.016250	–0.086079
1984	–0.075002	–0.019334	–0.087071
1985	–0.073866	–0.016605	–0.086786
1986	–0.074175	–0.016739	–0.087388
1987	–0.069890	–0.014282	–0.087981
1988	–0.069996	–0.013129	–0.087909
1989	–0.070941	–0.012451	–0.087889
1990	–0.072452	–0.015831	–0.088859
1991	–0.069874	–0.012482	–0.088747
1992	–0.070403	–0.012500	–0.088733
1993	–0.070238	–0.011928	–0.088683
1994	–0.070688	–0.014283	–0.088896
1995	–0.068536	–0.009854	–0.088534
1996	–0.068765	–0.010417	–0.088779

We estimate our econometric model of consumer behavior by the method of nonlinear three-stage least-squares (NL3SLS), using the instrumental variables presented in table A6.1. The results are summarized in table 6.5 and are used in our dynamic general equilibrium model. The price function for household capital services satisfies the conditions for local concavity without imposing restrictions on the parameters. Cholesky values at each data point in the sample are given in table 6.6. The nonnegativity conditions hold at every data point in the sample. To provide an interpretation of the implications of our estimates for consumer behavior we present price elasticities of demand and elasticities of substitution for this model in section 6.3 below.

6.2 Producer Behavior

There are many similarities between our model for describing the technology of the business sector and the model we have developed for representing the preferences of the household sector. We describe technology in terms of the labor requirements for producing outputs of consumption and investment goods, given inputs of corporate and noncorporate capital services. Our description of technology also expresses inputs of corporate and noncorporate capital services as functions of their long-lived and short-lived components.

Our representation of household preferences is time invariant and depends only on prices and quantities. In order to capture changes in productivity we introduce a time trend into our description of technology. Finally, we impose conditions on the description of technology that imply the existence of a balanced growth equilibrium for our dynamic general equilibrium model of the U.S. economy. These conditions imply that productivity growth is Harrod-neutral.

Under constant returns to scale we can describe the technology of the business sector through the price function for labor input (5.1). The value shares (5.2) derived from this price function sum to unity, since the function is homogeneous of degree one. The interpretation of this condition is that the value of the products is exhausted by the value of the factors of production. In addition, the matrix of share elasticities B_{PP} must be symmetric. We refer to these as the *product exhaustion* and *symmetry* restrictions.

The theory of producer behavior implies two additional sets of restrictions on our description of technology. First, the value shares of outputs of consumption and investment goods must be nonnegative and the shares of inputs of corporate and noncorporate capital services must be nonpositive, since the price function is nondecreasing in the prices of outputs and nonincreasing in the prices of inputs. Second, the price function must be *convex* in order to guarantee the appropriate curvature.

To generate an econometric model for the outputs of consumption and investment goods and inputs of corporate and noncorporate capital services we add a vector of random disturbances ε_t to the equations for the value shares (5.2), obtaining:

$$v_t = \alpha_P + B_{PP} \ln P_t + \beta_{PT} T + \varepsilon_t \,, \tag{6.11}$$

where the parameters α_P, B_{PP}, and β_{PT} are the same as in (5.2), the variables v_t and $\ln P_t$ now have time subscripts, and the vector of disturbances ε_t takes the form:

$$\varepsilon_t = \begin{bmatrix} \varepsilon_{CSt} \\ \varepsilon_{ISt} \\ \varepsilon_{MDt} \\ \varepsilon_{QDt} \end{bmatrix}. \tag{6.12}$$

The disturbance vector corresponds to random deviations from the optimal allocation of outputs and inputs and errors in measuring the value shares. We assume that the expected value of this vector is zero, the covariance matrix is constant, and the disturbances corresponding to any two distinct time periods are distributed independently. The product exhaustion condition implies that the value shares sum to unity, so that the sum of the corresponding disturbance terms must be zero and the covariance matrix must be singular. We assume that this fourth-order matrix has rank three.

The rate of productivity growth v_T is the negative of the growth rate of the price of labor input, holding the prices of the two outputs and the two capital inputs constant. To generate an econometric model for the rate of productivity growth we add a random disturbance ε_{Tt} to equation (5.3):

$$-v_{Tt} = \alpha_T + \beta_{PT} \ln P_t + \beta_{TT} T + \varepsilon_{Tt}, \tag{6.13}$$

where the parameters α_T, β_{PT}, and β_{TT} are the same as in (5.3) and the variables v_{Tt} and $\ln P_t$ have time subscripts.

The disturbance ε_{Tt} corresponds to random shocks in the rate of productivity growth and errors in measurement in this growth rate. Harrod-neutrality of productivity growth is required for the existence of a balanced growth equilibrium of our model, so that the parameters β_{PT} and β_{TT} must be equal to zero in (6.11) and (6.13). These are the *balanced growth* restrictions.

There are twenty-one parameters to be estimated in the equations for the value shares and the rate of productivity growth. Symmetry of the matrix B_{PP} reduces this number to fifteen and product exhaustion reduces the number to ten. These restrictions also imply that the contemporaneous disturbances are linearly dependent and the covariance matrix is singular. Therefore we drop the share equation for the output of consumption goods and estimate the parameters of the remaining four equations. Estimates of the parameters for the share equation for consumption goods can be recovered from the symmetry and product exhaustion conditions.[5] As before, we employ the method of nonlinear three-stage least-squares to obtain consistent estimates, using the instrumental variables.

We incorporate symmetry, product exhaustion, and balanced growth restrictions into our parameter estimates. The nonnegativity and nonpositivity restrictions on the share equations must be checked at each data point. To impose convexity restrictions on the price function for labor input, we consider the following transformation of the Hessian of the price function

$$\left(\frac{1}{PLD}\right)P'HP = B_{PP} + vv' - V\,, \tag{6.14}$$

where H is the Hessian and P is a diagonal matrix with prices of the four inputs and outputs along the main diagonal

$$P = \begin{bmatrix} PCS & 0 & 0 & 0 \\ 0 & PIS & 0 & 0 \\ 0 & 0 & PMD & 0 \\ 0 & 0 & 0 & PQD \end{bmatrix},$$

v is the vector of value shares of the outputs and inputs and V is a diagonal matrix with these value shares along the main diagonal

$$V = \begin{bmatrix} v_{CS} & 0 & 0 & 0 \\ 0 & v_{IS} & 0 & 0 \\ 0 & 0 & v_{MD} & 0 \\ 0 & 0 & 0 & v_{QD} \end{bmatrix}.$$

Our strategy for imposing convexity on the price function for labor input is similar to the approach we have employed for imposing concavity in our model of consumer behavior. We constrain the parameters of the share equations so that convexity holds at all data points in the sample. To impose convexity we require that the Hessian of the price function is positive semi-definite. We represent the transformation of the Hessian (6.14) in terms of its Cholesky factorization

$$B_{PP} + v\,v' - V = LDL' , \tag{6.15}$$

where L is a lower triangular matrix and D is a diagonal matrix.

Under convexity the diagonal elements of the matrix D, the Cholesky values, must be greater than or equal to zero. Since one of the Cholesky values is zero by product exhaustion, we impose inequality constraints on the three remaining values in the base year 1992 in such a way that convexity restrictions are satisfied at all data points. We consider eight combinations of restrictions on the Cholesky values: none of the parameters is constrained; only one of the parameters is contrained; the parameters are constrained two at a time; all three of the parameters are constrained. Finally, we choose the set of estimates with the lowest sum of squared residuals.

The rate of productivity growth cannot be measured directly. However, the translog price function (5.1) implies that the rate of productivity growth in any two periods can be expressed as an *exact index number*:

$$\begin{aligned} \bar{v}_{Tt} = {} & \Delta \ln PLD_t - \bar{v}_{Ct} \Delta \ln PCS_t - \bar{v}_{It} \Delta \ln PIS_t \\ & - \bar{v}_{Qt} \Delta \ln PQD_t - \bar{v}_{Mt} \Delta \ln PMD_t . \end{aligned} \tag{6.16}$$

The average rate of productivity growth in any two periods is the difference between the growth rate of the price of labor input and a weighted average of the growth rates of consumption and investment goods outputs and corporate and noncorporate capital inputs. The weights are unweighted averages of the value shares of the outputs and inputs in the two periods.[6]

Under the balanced growth restrictions the negative of the average rate of productivity growth (6.16) in any two periods can be expressed as a constant plus the average of the disturbance terms in the two periods:

$$-\bar{v}_{Tt} = \alpha_T + \bar{\varepsilon}_{Tt} , \tag{6.17}$$

so that the covariance matrix of the transformed disturbances is the Laurent matrix:

$$\Omega = \begin{bmatrix} \frac{1}{2} & \frac{1}{4} & 0 & \dots & 0 \\ \frac{1}{4} & \frac{1}{2} & \frac{1}{4} & \dots & 0 \\ 0 & \frac{1}{4} & \frac{1}{2} & \dots & 0 \\ \dots & \dots & \dots & \dots & \dots \\ 0 & 0 & 0 & \dots & \frac{1}{2} \end{bmatrix}.$$

The subdiagonals above and below the main diagonal of this matrix reflect the serial correlation induced by averaging the rate of productivity growth. To eliminate this serial correlation we express the matrix Ω^{-1} in terms of the Cholesky factorization

$$\Omega^{-1} = LDL',$$

where L is a unit lower triangular matrix and D is a diagonal matrix.

We transform the matrix Ω by premultiplying this matrix by the matrix square-root of Ω^{-1}:

$$D^{1/2} L' \Omega L D^{1/2} = I,$$

where I is an identity matrix of order $T - 1$. We can transform the vector of observations in the equation for the average rate of productivity growth (6.17) by means of this matrix square-root to eliminate serial correlation.

We treat the share equations (6.11) symmetrically with the average rate of productivity growth (6.17) by expressing the average of the value shares in any two periods as a function of the average of the logarithm of the prices in the two periods:

$$\bar{v}_t = \alpha_P + \beta_{PP} \overline{\ln P}_t + \bar{\varepsilon}_t .$$

This transformation induces serial correlation that can be eliminated by multiplying the vector of observations by the matrix square-root of the matrix Ω^{-1}.

Our strategy for estimation of the model of producer behavior is similar to the one we have used for the model of consumer behavior. However, we require that the price function for labor input is convex; we must also take account of serial correlation induced by construction of the exact index number for productivity growth. First, we construct the variables by calculating two-year averages of the value shares, the rate of productivity growth, and the logarithms of prices. Second, we transform the vector of dependent and independent variables by the matrix square-root given above. Third, we drop the share equation for consumption goods in order to incorporate the product exhaustion restrictions.

In estimating the parameters of producer behavior, α_P, α_T, and B_{PP}, we normalize the producer prices of consumption goods, investment goods, corporate and noncorporate capital services at unity in 1992, and simplify representation of the convexity restrictions. Under these normalizations, the vector of value shares of labor input for 1992, v_{1992}, is equal to α_P. In the simulations with our dynamic general equilibrium model, however, we use a different normalization for the producer prices. Accordingly, we adjust the estimates of α_P for the shift of base year using the following relationship:

$$v_{1992} = \alpha_P = \alpha_P^* + \ln P_{1992}^* B_{PP}$$

where the superscript * indicates that the price system used in the value share equation is the one used in our dynamic general equilibrium model. The estimate of B_{PP} is not affected by the shift of base year. To fix the level of producer price of labor services, we add a constant term α_0^P to the logarithmic producer price function of labor services, and set its value at the average of

$$\ln PLD^* - \ln P^{*\prime} \alpha_P^* - \alpha_T T - \frac{1}{2} \ln P^{*\prime}, B_{PP} \ln P^*$$

for 1970–1996, where $\ln PLD^*$ and $\ln P^*$ are based on the price system used in our dynamic general equilibrium model. This procedure enables the fitted value of labor price to track the historical path closely.

Table 6.7 reports the results of estimation under local convexity, together with estimates of the Cholesky values for the base year 1992 and the sum of squared residuals. Table 6.8 gives the local Cholesky values for all observations in our sample period. The fitted value shares satisfy the appropriate nonnegativity and nonpositivity conditions for all data points. The model satisfies the symmetry, summability, nonnegativity, and convexity conditions required by the price function (5.1) of chapter 5 at every data point. The data used in the estimation of the producer model are presented in tables A6.3a, A6.3b,

Table 6.7
Production frontier: Parameter estimates

Parameter	Estimate	Standard Error	t-Statistic
α_C	1.03269	0.008927	115.6
α_I	0.447221	0.003229	138.4
α_Q	−0.323446	0.006176	−52.3
α_M	−0.156465	0.002570	−60.8
α_T	0.00931499	0.014574	0.6
β_{CC}	0.645518	0.106687	6.0
β_{CI}	−0.512108	0.032377	−15.8
β_{CQ}	−0.106783	0.071318	−1.4
β_{CM}	−0.026628	0.032022	−0.8
β_{IC}	−0.512108	0.032377	−15.8
β_{II}	0.263214	0.000340	771.9
β_{IQ}	0.190167	0.023417	8.1
β_{IM}	0.058727	0.012845	4.5
β_{QC}	−0.106783	0.071318	−1.4
β_{QI}	0.190167	0.023417	8.1
β_{QQ}	−0.113208	0.056752	−1.9
β_{QM}	0.029824	0.021655	1.3
β_{MC}	−0.026628	0.032022	−0.8
β_{MI}	0.058727	0.012845	4.5
β_{MQ}	0.029824	0.021655	1.3
β_{MM}	−0.061923	0.011514	−5.3
δ_I	0.016000	0.0	0.0
λ_{IQ}	2.84466	1.47999	1.9
λ_{IM}	−0.702968	0.781605	−0.8
δ_Q	0.185382	0.169159	1.0
λ_{QM}	0.606465	0.544440	1.1
δ_M	0.042933	0.076420	0.5
α_0^P	0.096506		
α_I^*	0.43324		
α_Q^*	−0.31876		
α_M^*	−0.15466		
α_C^*	1.04019		
SSR	2.99809		

Note: δ_I is constrained at 0.016, δ_Q and δ_M are not constrained.

Table 6.8
Production frontier: Local Cholesky values

Year	δ_I	δ_Q	δ_M
1970	0.014755	0.22337	0.043245
1971	0.014224	0.19866	0.040659
1972	0.014929	0.22792	0.043216
1973	0.014804	0.23623	0.044133
1974	0.013720	0.19078	0.038325
1975	0.013320	0.15843	0.040357
1976	0.013867	0.19219	0.041869
1977	0.015374	0.22674	0.041891
1978	0.016093	0.24788	0.044073
1979	0.015487	0.23358	0.041709
1980	0.014061	0.18011	0.034044
1981	0.013789	0.16183	0.029969
1982	0.013717	0.14390	0.017350
1983	0.013432	0.13341	0.003584
1984	0.013687	0.19283	0.022752
1985	0.013672	0.21564	0.027529
1986	0.013279	0.19638	0.021825
1987	0.013220	0.19469	0.016941
1988	0.013215	0.21649	0.022121
1989	0.013256	0.22549	0.028048
1990	0.013589	0.21297	0.027910
1991	0.014551	0.19464	0.032471
1992	0.016000	0.18538	0.042933
1993	0.016609	0.19696	0.050869
1994	0.015655	0.22926	0.052775
1995	0.015043	0.25964	0.055544
1996	0.015038	0.28209	0.060455

A6.5, A6.6, and A6.7. The instrumental variables are presented in table A6.1 (see appendix).

We follow the estimation procedure employed for household capital services in section 6.1 in estimating our models for allocation of capital services between long-lived and short-lived assets in the corporate and noncorporate sectors. We estimate the share equations under symmetry and local concavity. We pool the three components of our model of producer behavior by estimating the parameters simultaneously. By pooling observations we are able to exploit the information in all three components of our producer model and take account of non-zero covariances among the disturbances in these models.

In order to take account of the serial correlation induced by averaging the rate of productivity growth, we employ two-year averages of both dependent and independent variables in all equations and eliminate the resulting serial correlation by transforming these averaged observations. Table 6.9 summarizes the estimates, which are used in our dynamic general equilibrium model.. Table 6.10 gives the Cholesky values at each data point. As before, the fitted value shares satisfy appropriate nonnegativity conditions for all data points.

Table 6.9
Production frontier and the allocation of corporate and noncorporate capital services: Parameter estimates

Parameter	Estimate	Standard Error	*t*-Statistic
α_C	1.03401	0.008777	117.7
α_I	0.441526	0.002420	182.3
α_Q	–0.317819	0.005315	–59.7
α_M	–0.157714	0.002964	–53.2
α_T	0.00875502	0.014573	0.6
β_{CC}	0.675587	0.114317	5.9
β_{CI}	–0.587580	0.025456	–23.0
β_{CQ}	–0.035933	0.065687	–0.5
β_{CM}	–0.052074	0.037038	–1.4
β_{IC}	–0.587580	0.025456	–23.0
β_{II}	0.288581	0.000283	1019.2
β_{IQ}	0.219402	0.016649	13.1
β_{IM}	0.079597	0.009901	8.0
β_{QC}	–0.035933	0.065687	–0.5
β_{QI}	0.219402	0.016649	13.1
β_{QQ}	–0.203933	0.039113	–5.2
β_{QM}	0.020463	0.022485	0.9
β_{MC}	–0.052074	0.037038	–1.4
β_{MI}	0.079597	0.009901	8.0
β_{MQ}	0.020463	0.022485	0.9
β_{MM}	–0.047986	0.013307	–3.6

Table 6.9 (continued)

Parameter	Estimate	Standard Error	t-Statistic
δ_I	0.042000	0.0	0.0
λ_{IQ}	1.88278	0.374683	5.0
λ_{IM}	0.237193	0.223282	1.0
δ_Q	0.066010	0.067347	0.9
λ_{QM}	0.785197	0.465279	1.6
δ_M	0.091540	0.023477	3.8
α_0^P	0.091077		
α_I^*	0.42473		
α_Q^*	–0.30751		
α_M^*	–0.15617		
α_C^*	1.03895		
α_S^Q	0.422196	0.003772	111.9
α_L^Q	0.577804	0.003772	153.1
β_{SS}^Q	–0.081301	0.020329	–3.9
β_{SL}^Q	0.081301	0.020329	3.9
β_{LL}^Q	–0.081301	0.020329	–3.9
δ_S^Q	–0.325247	0.020589	–15.7
α_0^{PQ}	–0.00079730		
α_S^M	0.183052	0.002358	77.6
α_L^M	0.816948	0.002358	346.4
β_{SS}^M	0.111681	0.007244	15.4
β_{SL}^M	–0.111681	0.007244	–15.4
β_{LL}^M	0.111681	0.007244	15.4
δ_S^M	–0.037863	0.008260	–4.5
α_0^{PM}	0.00025284		
SSR	4.88279		

Notes:

1) δ_I is constrained at 0.042, and δ_Q, δ_M, δ_S^Q and δ_S^M are not constrained.

2) α_0^{PQ}, and α_0^{PM} are set at the averages of $\ln PQD* - \ln PQ*' \alpha_{PQ} - \frac{1}{2} \ln PQ*' B_{PQ} \ln PQ*$, and $\ln PMD* - \ln PM*' \alpha_{PM} - \frac{1}{2} \ln PM*' B_{PM} \ln PM*$, respectively for 1970–1996.

Table 6.10
Production frontier and the allocation of corporate and noncorporate capital: Local Cholesky values

Year	δ_I	δ_Q	δ_M	δ_S^Q	δ_S^M
1970	0.040266	0.10979	0.070219	–0.32037	–0.072971
1971	0.039625	0.07938	0.068881	–0.31925	–0.074675
1972	0.040538	0.11807	0.072050	–0.32076	–0.069952
1973	0.040418	0.12948	0.074853	–0.32263	–0.063017
1974	0.039086	0.07364	0.072460	–0.32290	–0.060663
1975	0.038620	0.02995	0.064072	–0.32225	–0.071191
1976	0.039148	0.06816	0.064771	–0.32227	–0.072869
1977	0.041104	0.11829	0.072463	–0.32305	–0.063178
1978	0.042065	0.14761	0.075539	–0.32403	–0.059107
1979	0.041295	0.12824	0.075470	–0.32436	–0.056772
1980	0.039472	0.06108	0.068737	–0.32374	–0.059300
1981	0.039149	0.04030	0.063380	–0.32341	–0.060481
1982	0.039104	0.02372	0.044602	–0.32375	–0.056790
1983	0.038811	0.01654	0.014447	–0.32441	–0.052095
1984	0.039182	0.08545	0.078236	–0.32518	–0.047688
1985	0.039192	0.11278	0.085011	–0.32570	–0.043786
1986	0.038669	0.09029	0.083215	–0.32605	–0.040249
1987	0.038594	0.09018	0.084578	–0.32547	–0.039639
1988	0.038589	0.11699	0.092183	–0.32494	–0.039863
1989	0.038608	0.12709	0.096264	–0.32535	–0.037745
1990	0.038967	0.11146	0.096400	–0.32556	–0.035345
1991	0.040143	0.08513	0.093747	–0.32546	–0.035596
1992	0.042000	0.06601	0.091540	–0.32525	–0.037863
1993	0.042742	0.07685	0.097752	–0.32547	–0.037733
1994	0.041432	0.12088	0.10673	–0.32613	–0.034914
1995	0.040615	0.16052	0.11198	–0.32667	–0.033053
1996	0.040572	0.18774	0.11579	–0.32717	–0.031283

6.3 Elasticities

The estimated values of the parameters in our models of consumer and producer behavior provide important information on the responses of consumers and producers to changes in tax policy. In this section we supplement this information by deriving price elasticities of demand and supply implied by our parameter estimates, including the compensated price elasticity of supply for labor services. We also provide elasticities of substitution in consumption and production, including the intertemporal elasticity of substitution, a constant parameter in our model of consumer behavior.

6.3.1 Consumer behavior

In our model for consumer behavior the quantity index of full consumption is an index of consumer welfare. The compensated demand functions for the three components of full consumption are obtained by solving the share equations (5.16) for the quantities demanded as functions of full consumption and the prices. As an illustration, we consider the compensated demand for consumption goods:

$$C = F \cdot \frac{PF}{PC} v_C ,$$

where v_C is the share of consumption goods in full consumption. We obtain the compensated own-price elasticity of demand for consumption goods, say ε_{CC}:

$$\varepsilon_{CC} = v_C + \frac{\beta_{CC}}{v_C} - 1 . \tag{6.18}$$

Similarly, we obtain the cross-price elasticities of demand:

$$\varepsilon_{CL} = v_{LJ} + \frac{\beta_{CL}}{v_C} ,$$
$$\varepsilon_{CH} = v_{HD} + \frac{\beta_{CH}}{v_C} ,$$

where ε_{CL} is the elasticity of demand for consumption goods with respect to the price of leisure and ε_{CH} is the elasticity of demand with respect to the price of household capital services. We calculate similar own-price and cross-price elasticities of demand for leisure and household capital services, using pooled estimates for our model of consumer behavior and average shares for the period 1970–1996. The results are presented in panel 2 of table 6.11.

The average share of leisure is more than sixty-eight percent of full consumption, while the share of consumption goods and services is slightly more than twenty-four percent and the share of household capital services is around seven and a half percent. The own-price elasticity of demand for consumption goods and services is around a third, while the own-price elasticity of demand for leisure is only 0.10 and the elasticity of demand for capital services is 0.17. Cross-

Table 6.11
Elasticities of consumer behavior

1. **Basic Information**	
A. *Average shares*: 1970–1996	
$v_C =$	0.24120
$v_{LJ} =$	0.68263
$v_{HD} =$	0.07617
$v_{HS} =$	0.56948
B. *Second-order coefficients*	
$\beta_{CC} =$	0.10580
$\beta_{CL} =$	–0.097349
$\beta_{CH} =$	–0.0084549
$\beta_{LL} =$	0.14657
$\beta_{LH} =$	–0.049217
$\beta_{HH} =$	0.057672
$\beta_{SS}^{H} =$	0.161082
2. **Compensated Elasticities** (with constant full consumption)	
A. *Elasticities of demand*	
$\varepsilon_{CC} =$	–0.32015
$\varepsilon_{CL} =$	0.27904
$\varepsilon_{CH} =$	0.041112
$\varepsilon_{LC} =$	0.098596
$\varepsilon_{LL} =$	–0.10266
$\varepsilon_{LH} =$	0.0040659
$\varepsilon_{HC} =$	0.13020
$\varepsilon_{HL} =$	0.036441
$\varepsilon_{HH} =$	–0.16664
B. *Elasticity of labor supply*	
$\varepsilon_{LL}^{S} =$	0.31653
3. **Elasticity of Intertemporal Substitution**	
$\sigma^{-1} =$	0.39145
4. **Elasticities of Intratemporal Substitution**	
$e_{CL} =$	–0.40907
$e_{CH} =$	–0.26597
$e_{LH} =$	–0.16753
$e_{HD} =$	–0.34299

elasticities of demand are substantial, especially the cross-elasticity of demand for goods with respect to the price of leisure of 0.28; the three commodity groups are substitutes rather than complements.

The compensated elasticity of labor supply is, perhaps, a more familiar parameter than the elasticity of demand for leisure. To derive the compensated elasticity of labor supply, we first consider the following identity for the value of the time endowment $PLH \cdot LH$:

$$PLH \cdot LH - PLJ \cdot LJ = (1 - t_L^m)(PLD \cdot LD + PLG \cdot LG + PLE \cdot LE + PLR \cdot LR) .$$

Defining the value of labor supply $PL \cdot L$ as follows:

$$PL . L = PLD \cdot LD + PLG \cdot LG + PLE \cdot LE + PLR \cdot LR ,$$

we obtain:

$$PLH \cdot LH - PLJ \cdot LJ = (1 - t_L^m) PL \cdot L .$$

Under the assumption that relative prices of the time endowment, leisure, labor supply, and the components of labor demand are fixed, we obtain the following expression for the compensated elasticity of labor supply, say ε_{LL}^S,

$$\varepsilon_{LL}^S = - \varepsilon_{LL} \frac{PLJ \cdot LJ}{PLH \cdot LH - PLJ \cdot LJ} . \tag{6.19}$$

We employ the average ratio of the values of leisure and labor supply for the period 1970–1996 in estimating this elasticity; the result, given at the bottom of panel 2, table 6.11, is 0.31653. The elasticity of intertemporal substitution in consumption is the inverse of σ, estimated from the transition equation for full consumption (6.1). The estimate of this elasticity, reported in panel 3 of table 6.11, is 0.39145. This parameter describes the rate of adjustment of full consumption to the difference between the real private rate of return and its long-run equilibrium value.

The elasticity of substitution between two consumption goods is defined as the ratio of the proportional change in the ratio of the quantities consumed relative to the proportional change in the corresponding price ratio. The prices of other components are held constant, while the quantities are allowed to adjust to relative price changes. Our estimates of elasticities of substitution are based on parameter values from the pooled estimation of the model of consumer behavior, using average shares for the 1970-1996 period.

We first consider substitution between consumption goods and leisure. Using the share equation for consumption goods we can express the elasticity of substitution, say e_{CL}, as follows:

$$e_{CL} = -1 + \frac{\partial \ln v_C}{\partial \ln\left(\frac{PC}{PLJ}\right)} - \frac{\partial \ln v_{LJ}}{\partial \ln\left(\frac{PC}{PLJ}\right)}.$$

Since we are holding the price of household capital services *PHD* constant, we can rewrite this elasticity in the form:

$$e_{CL} = -1 + \frac{\beta_{CC}}{v_C} - \frac{\beta_{CL}}{v_{LJ}} - \left(\frac{\beta_{CH}}{v_C} - \frac{\beta_{LH}}{v_{LJ}}\right)\left(\frac{\partial \ln PLJ}{\partial \ln \frac{PC}{PLJ}}\right).$$

Differentiating $\ln\left(\frac{PF}{PLJ}\right)$ with respect to $\partial \ln\left(\frac{PC}{PLJ}\right)$ while holding *PF* and *PHD* constant, we obtain

$$\frac{\partial \ln PLJ}{\partial \ln\left(\frac{PC}{PLJ}\right)} = \frac{v_C}{v_{HD} - 1}.$$

Substituting this expression into our formula for the elasticity of substitution, we obtain:

$$e_{CL} = (\varepsilon_{CC} - \varepsilon_{LC}) - (\varepsilon_{CH} - \varepsilon_{LH})\frac{v_C}{v_{HD} - 1}. \tag{6.20}$$

Similarly

$$e_{CH} = (\varepsilon_{CC} - \varepsilon_{HC}) - (\varepsilon_{CL} - \varepsilon_{HL})\frac{v_C}{v_{LJ} - 1},$$

and:

$$e_{LH} = (\varepsilon_{LL} - \varepsilon_{HL}) - (\varepsilon_{LC} - \varepsilon_{HC})\frac{v_{LJ}}{v_C - 1}.$$

We report estimates of the elasticities of substitution in panel 4 of table 6.11. By definition these elasticities are symmetric. The elasticity of substitution between the services of the long-lived and short-lived household assets e_{HD} can be derived along similar lines and estimates are presented at the bottom of panel 4, table 6.11. All of these elasticities are considerably less than one, so that the corresponding value shares rise with an increase in price.

6.3.2 Producer behavior

As in our model of consumer behavior, we can define elasticities of substitution in production by allowing the relative quantities to adjust to changes in relative prices, while holding the prices of other inputs and outputs constant. We derive the formulas for the elasticities of substitution in production and estimate these elasticities, based on parameter values from the pooled estimation of our model of producer behavior and the average value shares for the 1970-1996 period.

We first consider the elasticity of substitution between labor input and consumption goods output, defined as[7]

$$e_{CL} = -1 + \frac{\partial \ln v_{CS}}{\partial \ln (PCS/PLD)},$$

where the other prices—*PIS*, *PQD*, *PMD*—are held constant. Making use of the share equation for the output of consumption goods, this elasticity of substitution can be rewritten as:

$$e_{CL} = -1 + \frac{1}{v_{CS}} \beta_{CC} \frac{\partial \ln PCS}{\partial \ln (PCS/PLD)}.$$

where

$$\frac{\partial \ln PCS}{\partial \ln (PCS/PLD)} = \frac{1}{1 - v_{CS}},$$

so that

$$e_{CL} = -1 + \frac{\beta_{CC}}{v_{CS}(1 - v_{CS})}. \tag{6.21}$$

Similarly, we can derive elasticities of substitution between labor input and investment goods output and between labor and capital services inputs from corporate and noncorporate assets:

$$e_{IL} = -1 + \frac{\beta_{II}}{v_{IS}(1 - v_{IS})},$$

$$e_{QL} = -1 + \frac{\beta_{QQ}}{v_{QD}(1 - v_{QD})},$$

$$e_{ML} = -1 + \frac{\beta_{MM}}{v_{MD}(1 - v_{MD})}.$$

The formulas for the elasticities of substitution between outputs and inputs other than labor can be derived along the same lines as for substitution in consumption. It is convenient at this point to introduce symbols for price elasticities of factor demand and product supply, for example:

$$\varepsilon_{II} = v_{IS} + \frac{\beta_{II}}{v_{IS}} - 1, \tag{6.22}$$

and

$$\varepsilon_{IC} = v_{CS} + \frac{\beta_{IC}}{v_{IS}}.$$

As an illustration, the elasticity of substitution between consumption and investment goods outputs is defined by

$$e_{CI} = -1 + \frac{\partial \ln v_{CS}}{\partial \ln (PCS/PIS)} - \frac{\partial \ln v_{IS}}{\partial \ln (PCS/PIS)}.$$

Holding the prices PQD and PMD constant, we can rewrite this elasticity as follows:

$$e_{CI} = (\varepsilon_{CC} - \varepsilon_{IC}) - (\varepsilon_{CQ} + \varepsilon_{CM} - \varepsilon_{IQ} - \varepsilon_{IM}) \frac{\partial \ln PIS}{\partial \ln (PCS/PIS)},$$

where

$$\frac{\partial \ln PIS}{\partial \ln (PCS/PIS)} = -\frac{v_{CS}}{v_{CS} + v_{IS}}.$$

We report the results in panel 2 of table 6.12. We also give the elasticities of substitution between the capital services from the short-lived and long-lived assets in the corporate and noncorporate sectors, e_{QD} and e_{MD}. The relative value shares of labor and the two capital inputs rise with a price increase if these elasticities of substitution are less than unity and fall with a price increase if the elasticities are greater

Table 6.12
Elasticities of producer behavior

1. **Basic Information** (1970–1996)	
A. *Average shares*	
v_{CS} =	0.94256
v_{IS} =	0.50597
v_{QD} =	–0.30931
v_{MD} =	–0.13897
v_{QS} =	0.41891
v_{MS} =	0.20617
B. *Second-order coefficients*	
β_{CC} =	0.67559
β_{CI} =	–0.58758
β_{CQ} =	–0.035933
β_{CM} =	–0.052074
β_{II} =	0.28858
β_{IQ} =	0.21940
β_{IM} =	0.079597
β_{QQ} =	–0.20393
β_{QM} =	0.020463
β_{MM} =	–0.047986
β_{SS}^{Q} =	–0.081301
β_{SS}^{M} =	0.11168
2. **Elasticities of Substitution**	
e_{CL}	11.47882
e_{IL}	0.15449
e_{QL}	–0.49644
e_{ML}	–0.69683
e_{CI}	0.43277
e_{CQ}	–0.25525
e_{CM}	–0.58933
e_{IQ}	–2.43209
e_{IM}	–1.17369
e_{QM}	–0.46605
e_{QD}	–1.33399
e_{MD}	–0.31762

than unity. The elasticities of substitution among inputs are less than unity; for example, the elasticities of substitution between labor and corporate capital and between the two types of capital are around a half, while the elasticity of substitution between labor and noncorporate capital is about 0.7.

6.4 Other Parameters

We conclude this chapter by assigning values to the parameters of our dynamic general equilibrium model of the U.S. economy that cannot be estimated from our econometric models of consumer and producer behavior. These include the ratio of government expenditures to gross domestic product, $SGOV$, the share of unemployed labor time in total labor supply, SLU, and the shares of government expenditures, net of interest payments on government debt—SCG, SIG, SLG, SEL, SER. These parameters are given in the first three panels of table 6.13.

The next group of parameters includes the proportions of labor employed by government enterprises and net exports of labor services to the total labor supply—SLE and SLR. It also includes the production of consumption goods by government enterprises as a proportion of the total consumption goods produced by the business sector, SCE. Finally, it includes net exports of consumption goods as a proportion of the total domestic demand for consumption goods, SCR, and net exports of investment goods as a proportion of the total domestic production of investment goods, SIR. This group of parameters is given in the fourth and fifth panels of table 6.13.

The third group of parameters includes the dividend pay-out ratio of the corporate sector, α, the debt/asset ratios of the corporate, noncorporate, and household sectors, β_q, β_m, and β_h, and the real interest rate. This group of parameters is given in the sixth panel of table 6.13. The parameters—$SGOV$, SCR, SIR— are used to calibrate the size of government debt and claims on the rest world in the steady state of our model of the U.S. economy. All other parameter values are set at the averages for the sample period, 1970–1996.

The fourth group of parameters is given in panels 7 and 8 of table 6.13. These are important determinants of the size and rate of growth of the U.S. economy. These include the time endowment, LH, and its growth rate, n. They also include steady-state values of government debt and claims on the rest of the world, relative to the U.S. gross domestic product. The time endowment is set at the historical value in

Table 6.13
Non-tax parameters

1. Size of Government

SGOV = 0.2132	government expenditure including debt service/gross domestic product

2. Unemployment

SLU = 0.0	share of unemployed time in total labor supply

3. Allocation of Government Expenditure, Net of Interest Payments (1970–1996 averages)

SCG = 0.1738	share of consumption goods
SIG = 0.1837	share of investment goods
SLG = 0.4889	share of labor services
SEL = 0.1450	share of transfer payments
SER = 0.0085	share of transfer to foreigners

4. Government Enterprises (1970–1996 averages)

SLE = 0.0198	share of labor used by government enterprises
SCE = 0.0298	ratio of consumption goods produced by government enterprises and the private sector

5. Export—Import

SCR = –0.0103	net export of consumption goods as a fraction of total domestic demand for consumption goods
SIR = 0.0128	net export of investment goods as a fraction of total domestic production of investment goods
SLR = –0.0001	share of exported labor

6. Financial Variables (1970–1996 averages)

$\alpha = 0.42620$	dividend pay-out ratio
$\beta_q = 0.16524$	debt/capital ratio in the corporate sector
$\beta_m = 0.19798$	debt/capital ratio in the noncorporate sector
$\beta_h = 0.28647$	debt/capital ratio in the household sector
$i_0 = 0.048604$	real interest rate

7. Other Parameters

LH = 17571	total time endowment in efficiency units of 1997
n = 0.01	growth rate of time endowment

8. Wealth Composition (steady state)
Government Debt/GDP = 0.20
Claims on the Rest of the World/GDP = 0.10

9. Rates of Economic Depreciation (1996 values)

$\delta_q^S = 0.1367$	short-lived corporate asset
$\delta_q^L = 0.0175$	long-lived corporate asset
$\delta_m^S = 0.1533$	short-lived noncorporate asset
$\delta_m^L = 0.0112$	long-lived noncorporate asset
$\delta_h^S = 0.1918$	short-lived household asset
$\delta_h^L = 0.0107$	long-lived household asset

Table 6.13 (continued)

10. Prices of Assets and Investment Goods (1997 values)	
$PK_{QS} = 4.8798$	short-lived corporate asset
$PK_{QL} = 10.5343$	long-lived corporate asset
$PK_{MS} = 4.8316$	short-lived noncorporate asset
$PK_{ML} = 12.5564$	long-lived noncorporate asset
$PK_{HS} = 4.3224$	short-lived household asset
$PK_{HL} = 15.6756$	long-lived household asset
$PI = 1.0683$	investment goods
11. Relative Prices of Labor (1980–1996 averages, relative to PLD)	
$A_{LH} = 1.0101$	time endowment (before tax)
$A_{LJ} = 1.0044$	leisure (before tax)
$A_{LG} = 1.0049$	labor employed in general government
$A_{LE} = 0.9824$	labor employed in government enterprises
$A_{LR} = 1.0$	exported labor (assumption)
$A_{LU} = 1.0$	unemployed time (assumption)

1997; the growth of the time endowment reflects the growth of population as well as changes in the quality of labor.[8]

During our sample period, 1970–1996, the average annual growth rate of the U.S. time endowment was 1.72 percent per year. However, we assume that population growth and changes in labor quality will decline in the future and set the growth rate, n, at one percent per year. The initial values of the quantity indexes of the capital stock, government debt, and claims on the rest of the world are set at their historical values in 1997. This procedure guarantees that the size of our simulated economy is equal to that of the U.S. economy in 1997.

The ratio of government debt to the U.S. gross domestic product has shown a distinct downward trend after the two World Wars. The recent increase in this ratio may be seen as an aberration from the longer-term perspective. Accordingly, we set the steady-state ratio of government debt to the gross domestic product at 0.2, close to the post-war low. On similar grounds we set the steady-state ratio of the U.S. claims on the rest of the world to the gross domestic product at 0.10. We treat the paths of government debt and claims on the rest of the world as exogenous.

Our fifth group of parameters includes the rates of economic depreciation. We distinguish among corporate, noncorporate and household sectors and two types of assets, short-lived and long-lived, within each sector. For the corporate and noncorporate sectors the short-lived asset includes producers' durable equipment, while the long-lived asset includes structures, inventories, and land. For the household sector the short-lived asset includes thirteen types of consumers' durables, while the long-lived asset includes structures and land.

The rates of economic depreciation of the six classes of assets, two classes within each of the three sectors, are weighted averages of their components with capital stocks at the end of 1996 as weights. For example, the rate of economic depreciation of the long-lived corporate asset is the average depreciation rate of twenty-three categories of non-residential structures, residential structures, non-farm inventories, and land employed in the corporate sector. Economic depreciation rates for the six categories of assets are shown in panel 9 of table 6.13.

Finally, we present two sets of relative prices in panels 10 and 11 of table 6.13. The relative prices of the six categories of assets in the corporate, noncorporate, and household sectors and the price of investment goods are the first of these. We set the relative prices of the six categories of assets and investment goods at their 1996 values, adjusted for the inflation of 1997. The relative prices of the time endowment, leisure, and labor employed in the various sectors of the economy and the rest of the world are set at historical averages for the period 1980–1996.

Notes

1. Additional details are given by Jorgenson (1986).
2. Further details are given by Jorgenson (1986).
3. See Jorgenson and Laffont (1974) and Amemiya (1977).
4. We similarly determine the levels of estimated logarithmic price functions for capital services of the household, corporate, and noncorporate sectors, and labor requirement in the business sector.
5. Additional details are given by Jorgenson (1986).
6. See Jorgenson (1986) for further details.
7. We treat inputs and outputs symmetrically and do not distinguish among substitution between inputs, substitution between outputs, and transformation from inputs to outputs.
8. Changes in the quality of the time endowment are due to changes in the composition in the population by age, sex, education, and class of employment. We define separate quality indexes for the time endowment, leisure, labor employed in the business, government, government enterprises, and rest-of-the-world sectors. Further details are given by Jorgenson, Gollop, and Fraumeni (1987).

Appendix

Table A6.1
Instrumental variables

Year	t_L^m	t_q	t_q^e	t_C	LH	PC(−1)
1970	0.2510	0.5198	0.3340	0.0629	10900.4	0.2615
1971	0.2470	0.5089	0.3222	0.0640	11117.2	0.2753
1972	0.2548	0.5114	0.3272	0.0602	11352.9	0.2880
1973	0.2650	0.5100	0.3273	0.0608	11597.1	0.2993
1974	0.2729	0.5118	0.3189	0.0627	11840.0	0.3182
1975	0.2860	0.5140	0.3223	0.0613	12091.3	0.3551
1976	0.2964	0.5151	0.3339	0.0584	12350.0	0.3840
1977	0.3064	0.5164	0.3240	0.0560	12612.1	0.4056
1978	0.3065	0.5135	0.3098	0.0544	12878.4	0.4334
1979	0.3124	0.4955	0.3249	0.0530	13149.4	0.4662
1980	0.3305	0.4991	0.3378	0.0565	13413.5	0.5106
1981	0.3398	0.5017	0.3194	0.0613	13668.0	0.5688
1982	0.3184	0.5078	0.2634	0.0574	13917.1	0.6206
1983	0.3038	0.5066	0.2465	0.0561	14197.4	0.6562
1984	0.3011	0.5058	0.2383	0.0568	14500.8	0.6876
1985	0.3013	0.5082	0.2290	0.0566	14754.4	0.7152
1986	0.3019	0.5198	0.2499	0.0547	15000.2	0.7426
1987	0.2736	0.3882	0.1998	0.0534	15221.7	0.7630
1988	0.2572	0.3887	0.1840	0.0534	15433.5	0.7924
1989	0.2585	0.3833	0.1839	0.0533	15647.7	0.8282
1990	0.2580	0.3802	0.1804	0.0542	15853.6	0.8732
1991	0.2576	0.3849	0.1849	0.0583	16061.7	0.9230
1992	0.2586	0.3831	0.1877	0.0578	16260.7	0.9653
1993	0.2641	0.3914	0.1989	0.0576	16419.5	1.0000
1994	0.2640	0.3907	0.1972	0.0601	16650.7	1.0287
1995	0.2669	0.3867	0.2055	0.0585	16838.2	1.0536
1996	0.2645	0.3880	0.2020	0.0580	16999.1	1.0830

Notes:
1. One of the instrumental variables is a vector of 1's and is not included in the table.
2. LH and PLD are in natural unit, while PLJ is in efficiency unit.
3. $W(-1)$ is the lagged value of private wealth and CLDA is the logarithmic level of labor efficiency.

Table A6.1 (continued)

Year	PLJ(–1)	PHD(–1)	EXP(CLDA)	PLD(–1)	F(–1)	W(–1)
1970	0.2150	0.2801	0.8007	0.2398	6996.4	3401.9
1971	0.2346	0.2892	0.8359	0.2623	7236.4	3647.9
1972	0.2403	0.3046	0.8729	0.2808	7664.7	3945.8
1973	0.2415	0.3125	0.8938	0.2990	8115.7	4387.8
1974	0.2483	0.3230	0.8550	0.3237	8447.6	4899.3
1975	0.2808	0.3535	0.8590	0.3522	8372.8	5214.0
1976	0.2933	0.3101	0.9031	0.3964	8667.6	5999.8
1977	0.2995	0.4146	0.9309	0.4191	9211.1	6596.4
1978	0.3084	0.4503	0.9388	0.4482	9628.7	7475.1
1979	0.3321	0.4919	0.9180	0.4810	9903.8	8536.3
1980	0.3651	0.4995	0.8853	0.5264	9957.4	9811.6
1981	0.4087	0.5069	0.8901	0.5751	9926.4	11055.0
1982	0.4367	0.5655	0.8585	0.6174	10138.3	12495.1
1983	0.5029	0.6676	0.8977	0.6448	10132.5	13401.4
1984	0.5089	0.7472	0.9417	0.6792	10698.5	14202.3
1985	0.5031	0.8003	0.9504	0.7042	11252.9	15499.0
1986	0.5232	0.7797	0.9757	0.7384	11595.8	17287.4
1987	0.5337	0.7987	0.9688	0.7838	12098.5	18676.1
1988	0.6067	0.8494	0.9843	0.7850	12266.5	19978.5
1989	0.6247	0.8540	0.9933	0.8188	12635.7	21719.0
1990	0.6378	0.8629	0.9921	0.8651	12919.0	23471.4
1991	0.6707	0.9760	0.9697	0.9078	13105.3	24135.9
1992	0.7256	0.9765	1.0000	0.9367	13039.4	24665.3
1993	0.7414	1.0000	1.0027	1.0000	13498.0	25069.8
1994	0.7615	1.0151	1.0120	1.0142	13723.0	25893.6
1995	0.7898	1.1051	1.0020	1.0107	14029.4	26580.6
1996	0.8210	1.0453	1.0150	1.0185	14152.4	27940.5

Table A6.2a
Capital stock: Corporate

Year	Short-lived		Long-lived	
	PK_{QS}	K_{QS}	PK_{QL}	K_{QL}
1970	0.3616	866.6	0.2525	3136.2
1971	0.3761	902.7	0.2663	3208.5
1972	0.3839	953.6	0.2889	3300.3
1973	0.3947	1024.6	0.3147	3414.5
1974	0.4302	1091.1	0.3385	3531.6
1975	0.5017	1128.1	0.3806	3570.5
1976	0.5407	1169.6	0.4032	3670.1
1977	0.5773	1232.2	0.4404	3768.9
1978	0.6144	1311.2	0.4870	3888.5
1979	0.6601	1390.9	0.5507	4005.6
1980	0.7290	1454.0	0.6082	4100.9
1981	0.7930	1514.2	0.6834	4229.2
1982	0.8305	1549.2	0.7190	4342.3
1983	0.8434	1587.9	0.7265	4424.4
1984	0.8492	1662.1	0.7656	4596.4
1985	0.8545	1740.5	0.8237	4713.2
1986	0.8735	1806.9	0.8485	4793.0
1987	0.8919	1857.3	0.8792	4878.6
1988	0.9152	1914.2	0.9410	4958.5
1989	0.9427	1974.8	0.9982	5038.0
1990	0.9684	2027.4	1.0089	5105.2
1991	0.9892	2056.9	1.0096	5144.4
1992	1.0000	2107.4	1.0000	5182.2
1993	1.0057	2174.5	0.9982	5251.4
1994	1.0151	2266.0	0.9991	5340.1
1995	1.0235	2380.9	1.0324	5423.9
1996	1.0230	2516.8	1.0687	5496.3

Notations:
K_{QS}, K_{QL}: Corporate capital stock in short-lived and long-lived assets
PK_{QS}, PK_{QL}: Price indexes of K_{QS} and K_{QL}

Table A6.2b
Capital stock: Noncorporate

Year	Short-lived		Long-lived	
	PK_{MS}	K_{MS}	PK_{ML}	K_{ML}
1970	0.3365	219.4	0.2066	3093.0
1971	0.3488	227.7	0.2180	3178.6
1972	0.3555	238.6	0.2463	3258.7
1973	0.3648	255.6	0.2735	3337.3
1974	0.4025	265.3	0.2656	3373.5
1975	0.4636	268.5	0.2991	3403.4
1976	0.4976	274.8	0.3179	3434.7
1977	0.5313	287.0	0.3552	3499.5
1978	0.5655	308.0	0.4048	3574.1
1979	0.6154	331.8	0.4619	3718.5
1980	0.6862	340.1	0.5147	3832.6
1981	0.7570	348.5	0.5777	3972.5
1982	0.8056	349.0	0.6090	3988.4
1983	0.8254	352.1	0.6267	4021.1
1984	0.8380	362.8	0.6859	4100.6
1985	0.8431	368.9	0.7736	4192.1
1986	0.8637	375.8	0.8238	4242.3
1987	0.8824	382.8	0.8753	4293.6
1988	0.9059	392.5	0.9435	4331.4
1989	0.9339	403.1	1.0169	4381.1
1990	0.9588	404.3	1.0144	4409.8
1991	0.9824	406.7	1.0127	4431.9
1992	1.0000	403.2	1.0000	4458.5
1993	1.0128	410.9	0.9834	4482.9
1994	1.0268	424.6	0.9620	4538.6
1995	1.0380	440.4	0.9997	4572.7
1996	1.0441	459.7	1.0439	4624.9

Notations:
K_{MS}, K_{ML}: Noncorporate capital stock in short-lived and long-lived assets
PK_{MS}, PK_{ML}: Price indexes of K_{MS} and K_{ML}

Table A6.2c
Capital stock: Households

Year	Short-lived		Long-lived	
	PK_{HS}	K_{HS}	PK_{HL}	K_{HL}
1970	0.4318	902.9	0.2169	4671.2
1971	0.4485	949.3	0.2283	4811.9
1972	0.4543	1014.3	0.2523	4978.6
1973	0.4628	1091.1	0.2771	5146.7
1974	0.4930	1134.9	0.2785	5286.3
1975	0.5385	1170.8	0.3130	5397.6
1976	0.5693	1231.1	0.3350	5550.1
1977	0.5941	1305.9	0.3756	5740.0
1978	0.6282	1384.1	0.4240	5933.6
1979	0.6725	1445.5	0.4801	6037.6
1980	0.7331	1469.8	0.5360	6085.4
1981	0.7854	1492.8	0.6008	6128.2
1982	0.8191	1511.0	0.6328	6195.7
1983	0.8384	1568.3	0.6503	6322.7
1984	0.8502	1663.7	0.7040	6463.5
1985	0.8612	1778.5	0.7799	6584.6
1986	0.8744	1907.5	0.8300	6745.8
1987	0.9013	2017.4	0.8777	6899.7
1988	0.9209	2136.3	0.9356	7042.6
1989	0.9425	2244.7	0.9995	7179.9
1990	0.9595	2330.0	1.0033	7302.0
1991	0.9810	2364.5	1.0059	7397.0
1992	1.0000	2419.3	1.0000	7517.5
1993	1.0157	2498.6	0.9993	7644.3
1994	1.0384	2599.2	0.9952	7793.6
1995	1.0529	2701.0	1.0317	7935.0
1996	1.0565	2808.9	1.0699	8088.4

Notations:
K_{HS}, K_{HL}: Household capital stock in short-lived and long-lived assets
PK_{HS}, PK_{HL}: Price indexes of K_{HS} and K_{HL}

Table A6.3a
Capital services: Corporate

Year	Short-lived		Long-lived		All	
	PQS	*QS*	*PQL*	*QL*	*PQD*	*QD*
1970	0.4173	153.0	0.2794	311.8	0.3287	459.3
1971	0.4508	160.1	0.3095	319.1	0.3603	474.6
1972	0.4439	167.5	0.3541	326.7	0.3877	490.1
1973	0.4393	178.7	0.3811	336.1	0.4041	511.3
1974	0.4413	193.9	0.3650	347.9	0.3942	539.1
1975	0.5108	207.6	0.4068	360.0	0.4463	565.7
1976	0.5542	214.3	0.4594	364.3	0.4956	577.2
1977	0.5987	223.0	0.5290	374.7	0.5560	596.6
1978	0.6272	237.0	0.5962	385.0	0.6087	621.3
1979	0.6501	254.8	0.6028	397.5	0.6216	651.9
1980	0.6783	271.4	0.5894	410.0	0.6246	681.6
1981	0.7626	283.4	0.6750	420.5	0.7097	704.5
1982	0.7356	296.3	0.6708	434.5	0.6963	731.6
1983	0.7783	303.7	0.7578	446.6	0.7653	751.2
1984	0.8408	314.4	0.8628	455.0	0.8529	770.3
1985	0.8322	333.4	0.8798	473.4	0.8593	807.6
1986	0.8122	353.5	0.8844	485.5	0.8537	839.2
1987	0.9221	370.4	0.8859	493.7	0.9012	864.2
1988	0.9599	382.2	0.9607	502.4	0.9601	884.9
1989	0.9769	395.6	1.0014	510.8	0.9905	906.6
1990	0.9787	408.6	1.0131	519.2	0.9979	927.9
1991	0.9897	420.1	0.9988	526.6	0.9947	946.8
1992	1.0000	427.0	1.0000	531.2	1.0000	958.2
1993	1.0342	439.4	1.0809	535.4	1.0600	974.6
1994	1.0860	456.3	1.2123	542.5	1.1552	998.2
1995	1.1215	479.9	1.2895	551.7	1.2133	1029.9
1996	1.1425	508.3	1.3984	560.4	1.2810	1065.1

Notations:
QS, *QL*, *QD*: Capital services from short-lived, long-lived and all assets in the corporate sector
PQS, *PQL*, *PQD*: Price indexes of *QS*, *QL*, *QD*

Table A6.3b
Capital services: Noncorporate

Year	Short-lived		Long-lived		All	
	PMS	*MS*	*PML*	*ML*	*PMD*	*MD*
1970	0.3487	44.0	0.1947	252.2	0.2203	292.6
1971	0.3729	45.7	0.2138	257.1	0.2404	299.5
1972	0.3687	47.5	0.2427	264.4	0.2645	308.7
1973	0.3645	50.0	0.2635	271.2	0.2817	318.4
1974	0.3822	53.7	0.2714	278.0	0.2912	329.6
1975	0.4067	55.6	0.2070	281.6	0.2412	335.6
1976	0.4751	55.9	0.3183	284.3	0.3458	338.5
1977	0.5102	57.2	0.3604	287.1	0.3870	342.8
1978	0.5418	60.1	0.4139	292.6	0.4370	351.7
1979	0.5678	65.1	0.4318	299.2	0.4563	364.1
1980	0.6037	70.3	0.4258	311.5	0.4579	382.3
1981	0.6851	71.7	0.5017	321.8	0.5347	393.8
1982	0.7132	73.3	0.5655	334.2	0.5920	407.5
1983	0.7614	73.2	0.6446	336.1	0.6657	409.2
1984	0.8132	74.2	0.7363	339.0	0.7502	413.1
1985	0.8022	76.8	0.7618	345.8	0.7691	422.6
1986	0.7919	78.4	0.7940	353.7	0.7936	432.1
1987	0.9112	80.3	0.8806	358.1	0.8861	438.4
1988	0.9311	82.0	0.9277	362.7	0.9282	444.7
1989	0.9509	84.2	0.9759	366.3	0.9712	450.6
1990	0.9676	86.5	1.0312	370.8	1.0192	457.3
1991	0.9826	86.8	1.0014	373.4	0.9978	460.2
1992	1.0000	87.5	1.0000	375.4	1.0000	463.0
1993	1.0299	87.2	1.0534	377.6	1.0490	464.9
1994	1.0867	89.2	1.1761	379.7	1.1592	468.8
1995	1.1150	92.9	1.2009	384.3	1.1847	477.0
1996	1.1333	96.9	1.2876	387.2	1.2580	483.7

Notations:
MS, ML, MD: Capital services from short-lived, long-lived and all all assets in the noncorporate sector
PMS, PML, PMD: Price indexes of *MS, ML, MD*

Table A6.3c
Capital services: Households

Year	Short-lived		Long-lived		All	
	PHS	*HS*	*PHL*	*HL*	*PHD*	*HD*
1970	0.4077	221.7	0.1837	308.1	0.2892	508.2
1971	0.4258	229.6	0.1961	315.4	0.3046	524.1
1972	0.4320	241.6	0.2047	325.5	0.3125	547.2
1973	0.4363	258.4	0.2194	337.4	0.3230	578.1
1974	0.4644	277.9	0.2502	349.5	0.3535	612.5
1975	0.4661	287.6	0.1729	359.9	0.3101	632.9
1976	0.5442	295.5	0.2942	367.8	0.4146	648.9
1977	0.5771	310.6	0.3310	378.6	0.4503	676.2
1978	0.6118	329.5	0.3769	392.0	0.4919	710.1
1979	0.6330	348.9	0.3727	405.6	0.4995	744.8
1980	0.6631	363.5	0.3602	413.1	0.5069	769.0
1981	0.7208	368.2	0.4187	416.6	0.5655	777.7
1982	0.7873	373.0	0.5506	419.7	0.6676	786.0
1983	0.8377	377.1	0.6548	424.6	0.7472	794.8
1984	0.8704	391.8	0.7253	433.6	0.8003	819.2
1985	0.8560	416.8	0.6993	443.7	0.7797	855.5
1986	0.8591	446.8	0.7333	452.5	0.7987	896.1
1987	0.8916	480.2	0.8023	464.3	0.8494	942.6
1988	0.8994	507.5	0.8036	475.6	0.8540	981.9
1989	0.9096	537.5	0.8110	486.2	0.8629	1023.5
1990	0.9593	564.1	0.9952	496.3	0.9760	1060.5
1991	0.9750	585.0	0.9782	505.4	0.9765	1090.4
1992	1.0000	591.8	1.0000	512.4	1.0000	1104.2
1993	1.0201	604.2	1.0093	521.3	1.0151	1125.5
1994	1.0770	623.4	1.1379	530.5	1.1051	1153.8
1995	1.0629	648.0	1.0241	541.4	1.0453	1189.3
1996	1.0790	672.4	1.0912	551.6	1.0845	1224.0

Notations:
HS, HL, HD: Capital services from short-lived, long-lived and all assets in the household sector
PHS, PHL, PHD: Price indexes of *HS, HL, HD*

Table A6.4
Time endowment and leisure (in natural units)

Year	Time endowment		Leisure	
	PLH	*LH*	*PLJ*	*LJ*
1970	0.1899	10900.4	0.1878	8150.6
1971	0.2037	11117.2	0.2009	8349.0
1972	0.2140	11352.9	0.2108	8508.7
1973	0.2264	11597.1	0.2219	8661.5
1974	0.2446	11840.0	0.2400	8879.3
1975	0.2593	12091.3	0.2520	9077.0
1976	0.2766	12350.0	0.2705	9282.3
1977	0.2933	12612.1	0.2871	9462.8
1978	0.3181	12878.4	0.3118	9623.9
1979	0.3427	13149.4	0.3352	9784.2
1980	0.3686	13413.5	0.3618	10016.1
1981	0.3950	13668.0	0.3887	10217.1
1982	0.4364	13917.1	0.4317	10462.2
1983	0.4628	14197.4	0.4568	10658.3
1984	0.4807	14500.8	0.4738	10830.0
1985	0.5047	14754.4	0.4972	11006.0
1986	0.5293	15000.2	0.5207	11220.5
1987	0.5880	15221.7	0.5878	11379.8
1988	0.6187	15433.5	0.6149	11526.0
1989	0.6420	15647.7	0.6336	11658.0
1990	0.6726	15853.6	0.6654	11777.9
1991	0.7039	16061.7	0.7036	11872.1
1992	0.7414	16260.7	0.7414	11966.2
1993	0.7633	16419.5	0.7636	12120.3
1994	0.7923	16650.7	0.7993	12289.1
1995	0.8140	16838.2	0.8226	12451.1
1996	0.8453	16999.1	0.8558	12581.1

Notations:
LH: Total time endowment in natural unit
LJ: Leisure consumed
PLH, *PLJ*: Price indexes of *LH* and *LJ*

Table A6.5
Labor inputs (in natural units)

Year	Business		Government		Gov't enterprises	
	PLD	*LD*	*PLG*	*LG*	*PLE*	*LE*
1970	0.2623	2106.2	0.2325	513.5	0.2332	55.2
1971	0.2808	2099.0	0.2553	512.8	0.2527	55.7
1972	0.2990	2168.0	0.2766	517.4	0.2751	55.4
1973	0.3237	2281.5	0.2967	523.7	0.2987	56.1
1974	0.3522	2283.6	0.3175	534.5	0.3338	57.8
1975	0.3964	2210.6	0.3465	546.8	0.3797	58.5
1976	0.4191	2286.3	0.3730	553.1	0.4109	58.4
1977	0.4482	2378.4	0.4027	558.4	0.4510	57.5
1978	0.4810	2519.7	0.4282	571.0	0.4819	59.1
1979	0.5264	2625.7	0.4631	575.0	0.5094	61.3
1980	0.5751	2610.1	0.5149	574.1	0.5226	68.4
1981	0.6174	2644.1	0.5741	566.5	0.5919	68.7
1982	0.6448	2586.6	0.6200	569.5	0.6203	68.9
1983	0.6792	2635.3	0.6596	569.7	0.6768	68.0
1984	0.7042	2807.1	0.7095	579.3	0.7030	70.2
1985	0.7384	2880.5	0.7487	593.5	0.7346	72.8
1986	0.7838	2896.1	0.7756	607.4	0.7340	75.6
1987	0.7850	3010.9	0.8066	620.8	0.7538	78.1
1988	0.8188	3101.1	0.8377	634.1	0.8031	79.6
1989	0.8651	3196.4	0.8667	652.6	0.8247	81.3
1990	0.9078	3214.3	0.9141	665.2	0.8947	81.9
1991	0.9367	3192.8	0.9649	667.8	0.9353	81.8
1992	1.0000	3225.4	1.0000	670.8	1.0000	81.1
1993	1.0142	3331.2	1.0337	671.6	1.0038	81.3
1994	1.0107	3465.8	1.0580	675.3	1.0331	83.4
1995	1.0185	3574.3	1.0851	678.7	1.0445	85.1
1996	1.0319	3665.8	1.1279	677.3	1.0628	86.0

Notations:
LD: Labor demand of business sector
LG: Labor demand of government
LE: Labor demand of public enterprises
PLD, *PLG*, *PLE*: Price indexes of *LD*, *LG*, and *LE*

Table A6.6
Consumption and investment goods

Year	Consumption Goods: Consumption		Consumption Goods: Production		Investment Goods Production	
	PC	*C*	*PCS*	*CS*	*PIS*	*IS*
1970	0.2753	1822.6	0.2702	1819.8	0.3573	772.7
1971	0.2880	1869.0	0.2820	1865.6	0.3743	818.8
1972	0.2993	1961.5	0.2939	1948.3	0.3858	901.2
1973	0.3182	2036.1	0.3126	2032.1	0.4017	996.3
1974	0.3551	2029.9	0.3422	2045.7	0.4396	939.9
1975	0.3840	2082.5	0.3709	2115.3	0.4922	864.1
1976	0.4056	2182.7	0.3907	2196.5	0.5210	967.2
1977	0.4334	2264.3	0.4153	2272.2	0.5521	1063.9
1978	0.4662	2353.9	0.4490	2367.4	0.5901	1155.2
1979	0.5106	2411.2	0.4892	2433.2	0.6450	1184.9
1980	0.5688	2415.0	0.5364	2478.6	0.7034	1099.3
1981	0.6206	2438.0	0.5840	2516.4	0.7681	1137.9
1982	0.6562	2470.4	0.6227	2553.7	0.8114	1021.2
1983	0.6876	2578.7	0.6557	2648.8	0.8188	1099.2
1984	0.7152	2679.6	0.6797	2732.4	0.8311	1307.1
1985	0.7426	2792.1	0.7072	2847.1	0.8424	1344.3
1986	0.7630	2890.1	0.7301	2963.2	0.8515	1369.8
1987	0.7924	2984.7	0.7577	3054.3	0.8643	1407.7
1988	0.8282	3087.0	0.7940	3167.8	0.8793	1464.4
1989	0.8732	3149.8	0.8351	3252.3	0.9034	1533.6
1990	0.9230	3211.9	0.8776	3325.0	0.9227	1508.9
1991	0.9653	3212.0	0.9149	3347.3	0.9381	1416.9
1992	1.0000	3287.0	0.9454	3428.3	0.9454	1486.6
1993	1.0287	3371.0	0.9736	3497.0	0.9591	1558.9
1994	1.0536	3463.8	0.9953	3586.6	0.9744	1673.0
1995	1.0830	3541.8	1.0264	3674.5	0.9868	1706.4
1996	1.1128	3627.9	1.0530	3757.9	0.9913	1814.0

Notations:
C: Household demand for consumption goods and services
CS: Business production of consumption goods and services
IS: Business production of investment goods
PC, *PCS*, *PIS*: Price indexes of *C*, *CS*, and *IS*

Table A6.7
Full consumption, nominal rate of return on private wealth, and technical change

Year	Full consumption		Private rate of return	Technical change	
	PF	*F*	*PRORN*	*DLDA*	*CLDA*
1970	0.3048	7236.4	0.080527	0.00243	−0.22221
1971	0.3144	7664.7	0.089854	0.04302	−0.17919
1972	0.3187	8115.7	0.12156	0.04326	−0.13593
1973	0.3304	8447.6	0.11876	0.02369	−0.11224
1974	0.3716	8372.8	0.073783	−0.04444	−0.15668
1975	0.3870	8667.6	0.14732	0.00465	−0.15203
1976	0.4054	9211.1	0.10758	0.05016	−0.10187
1977	0.4228	9628.7	0.13937	0.03028	−0.07159
1978	0.4557	9903.8	0.15418	0.00849	−0.06310
1979	0.4975	9957.4	0.16013	−0.02242	−0.08553
1980	0.5522	9926.4	0.14332	−0.03634	−0.12187
1981	0.5950	10138.3	0.15003	0.00550	−0.11637
1982	0.6723	10132.5	0.099811	−0.03621	−0.15258
1983	0.6915	10698.5	0.078390	0.04468	−0.10789
1984	0.6966	11252.9	0.12152	0.04782	−0.06007
1985	0.7203	11595.8	0.13348	0.00916	−0.05091
1986	0.7363	12098.5	0.095799	0.02635	−0.02456
1987	0.8146	12266.5	0.098337	−0.00710	−0.03167
1988	0.8402	12635.7	0.10913	0.01589	−0.01578
1989	0.8639	12919.0	0.10554	0.00910	−0.00668
1990	0.9150	13105.3	0.062986	−0.00128	−0.00796
1991	0.9752	13039.4	0.058506	−0.02276	−0.03072
1992	1.0000	13498.0	0.050571	0.03072	0.00000
1993	1.0266	13723.0	0.053396	0.00267	0.00267
1994	1.0657	14029.4	0.061721	0.00929	0.01196
1995	1.0961	14152.4	0.086249	−0.01000	0.00196
1996	1.1269	14486.0	0.088291	0.01288	0.01484

Notations:
F: Full consumption
PRORN: After-tax nominal rate of return on private wealth
DLDA: Rate of technical change (logarithmic)
CLDA: Level of technology (sum of DLDA normalized at zero in the base year)

7 Economic Impact of Tax Reform

Analyzing differences in effective tax rates, as we did in chapter 4, can identify potential sources of inefficiency. However, the tax wedges that underlie these effective tax rates are incomplete indicators of the welfare costs of a given tax policy. Similarly, the response of the tax wedges to a change in tax policy is an imperfect guide to the economic effects of a policy change. The welfare costs of taxation depend not only on the tax wedges, but also on the elasticities of substitution along the relevant margins.

The taxation of income from capital drives a wedge between the marginal rate of substitution in consumption between goods at two different points of time and the marginal rate of transformation in production. This raises the issue of intertemporal efficiency in the allocation of resources. One way to achieve intertemporal efficiency is to require zero marginal effective tax rates on all forms of income from capital. An obvious way of imposing a zero tax rate on capital is to eliminate capital income taxes.

Since the U.S. tax system fails to impose a uniform effective tax rate on all forms of income from capital, it can be argued that this system is flawed. However, this argument holds only in a partial equilibrium context or under the restrictive assumption that the allocation of capital among alternative uses is separable from the allocation of other resources. Equality of effective tax rates is not required for allocative efficiency in a more general setting.

The taxation of labor income also has important implications for welfare through its impact on the choice between leisure and labor. This has received much less attention than the taxation of capital income as a source of allocative inefficiency. However, labor income accounts for roughly sixty percent of private national income and much of the government's revenue is collected from taxes on labor. Furthermore, even though the price elasticity of labor supply is very low,[1] there is a substitution effect of a change in the after-tax wage rate, almost equal in magnitude to the income effect, but opposite in sign.

As an illustration, suppose that household preferences are linear logarithmic in consumption and leisure and that labor is the only source of income. Then labor supply is completely inelastic with respect to a change in the after tax wage. However, underlying the zero price elasticity of supply are substitution and income effects that are equal in magnitude but opposite in sign. Only the substitution effect, not the total price effect, is relevant to measuring the distortion of resource allocation by labor income taxes.

The first objective of this chapter is to develop a methodology for evaluating the welfare effects of tax reform. For this purpose we design a computational algorithm for determining the time path of the economy following the reform. This algorithm is composed of two parts. First, we solve for the unique steady state of the economy corresponding to any tax policy. We then determine the unique transition path that is consistent with both the steady state and the initial conditions. We describe the dynamics of our dynamic general equilibrium model of the U.S. economy in terms of the saddle point configuration of this transition path.

Our next objective is to evaluate the welfare effects of alternative tax reform proposals. In addition, we attempt to identify the sources of tax distortions more precisely in order to determine possible directions for future reforms. With these objectives in mind we find it useful to analyze the likely economic impact of recent tax reform proposals. Many of these proposals involve shifting the tax base from income to consumption. However, we also consider reforms of the income tax that would leave the tax base unchanged.

The efficiency cost of taxation is a central concept in public finance. This concept has its most straightforward application in the cost-benefit analysis of public expenditure, where the benefits of a public program must be balanced against the social costs of financing it. The concept also plays an important role in optimal taxation, where the government maximizes the social welfare resulting from tax policy, subject to the government budget constraint. The efficiency cost of a tax program is a measure of the social cost incurred in raising a dollar of tax revenue. Our final objective is to assess the efficiency cost of the existing U.S. tax system.

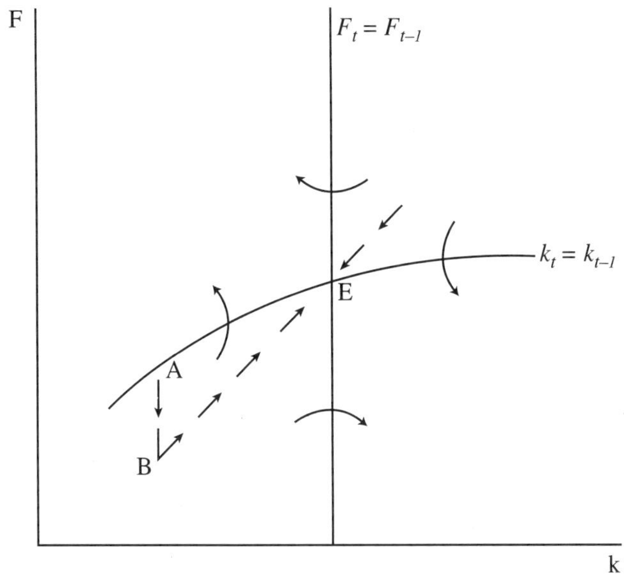

Figure 7.1
Transition path under perfect foresight.

The plan of this chapter is as follows. In section 7.1 we describe the dynamics of our model of the U.S. economy. In section 7.2 we present a methodology for comparing welfare levels associated with alternative tax policies. In section 7.3 we outline our computational algorithm for determining the transition path to a new balanced growth equilibrium following tax reform. In section 7.4 we evaluate the economic impact of alternative tax reform proposals. In section 7.5 we present a methodology for analyzing the efficiency cost of alternative taxes. In section 7.6 we analyze the efficiency cost of different components of the U.S. tax system. In section 7.7 we compare our results with those obtained by alternative approaches. Finally, in section 7.8 we present our conclusions.

7.1 Perfect Foresight Dynamics

In a world of perfect foresight the transition path of the economy from an initial state to the steady state is unique. It is also self-validating in the sense that expectations on the future course of the economy are actually realized. Suppose that the economy is initially at a steady state, indicated by point A in figure 7.1. At the steady state, the real private rate of return on capital $\tilde{r}$ is constant at the value determined by (5.12)

$$\tilde{r} = (1+\gamma)(1-\alpha_T)^{\sigma} - 1\,, \tag{7.1}$$

where γ is the rate of time preference, $-\alpha_T$ is the rate of labor-augmenting productivity growth, and σ is the inverse of intertemporal elasticity of substitution. The steady-state value of the rate of return is independent of tax policy.

For expository purposes we first assume that the supply of labor is fixed and that full consumption includes only a single homogeneous good, measured in the same units as capital. We also assume that government rebates all the tax revenues to the household sector and that net exports are zero. We suppose that a new tax policy is introduced in order to improve the efficiency of capital allocation. The short-run impact of this policy is that the nominal rate of return ρ rises above the steady-state level $\tilde{\rho}$.

The transition path for full consumption is described by equation (5.9), so that:

$$F_t = F_{t-1}\left[\frac{PF_{t-1}}{PF_t}\cdot\frac{1+\rho_t}{(1+\gamma)(1-\alpha_T)^{\sigma}}\right]^{\frac{1}{\sigma}}, \tag{7.2}$$

where F is full consumption per capita with population expressed in efficiency units and PF is the price of full consumption. Immediately after the introduction of the new policy the level of full consumption rises over time. The intuition is that with a higher rate of return future consumption is cheaper relative to current consumption, so that the consumer can attain a higher level of welfare by saving more now in order to consume more in the future.

When the rate of return exceeds its long-run equilibrium level, capital intensity in the new steady state is higher than in the initial state. As the economy moves along the transition path, capital intensity rises and the rate of return is brought down, gradually, to the steady-state level. In the new steady state, represented by point E in figure 7.1, both the level of full consumption and capital intensity are higher than at the starting point of the transition path, given by point B.

In order to understand the dynamics of the transition to a new steady state, it is useful to examine changes in the level of full consumption and capital intensity. At the beginning of period t the capital stock is the sum of capital stock at the beginning of period $t-1$ and investment during period $t-1$. In period t, this capital stock must be allocated among the total labor force. As a consequence, *capital intensity*, defined as the ratio of capital stock to labor in efficiency units, grows according to the equation:

$$k_t = \frac{[k_{t-1} + h(k_{t-1}) - F_t]}{(1-\alpha_T)(1+n)}, \tag{7.3}$$

where k_{t-1} is the capital intensity at the end of period $t-1$, h is the production function in intensive form, representing output per capita as a function of capital intensity, and n is the rate of population growth.

The locus of points at which capital intensity remains constant is characterized by $k_t = k_{t-1}$. By substituting this condition into (7.3), we obtain

$$F_t = h(k_{t-1}) - ((1-\alpha_T)(1+n)-1)\, k_{t-1}\,. \tag{7.4}$$

Similarly, the locus of the points at which full consumption per capita remains constant is obtained by substituting $F_t = F_{t-1}$ into (7.2):

$$\tilde{\rho}_t = \rho_t\,. \tag{7.5}$$

Making use of equations (7.2)–(7.5), we can illustrate the dynamics of our model of the U.S. economy. In figure 7.1 the arrows indicate directions of movement. If the new policy improves efficiency of the economy, the locus of $k_t = k_{t-1}$ shifts upward and the initial steady state at point A lies below the curve along which capital intensity is constant under the new policy. At the beginning of the transition the economy has to jump to point B by adjusting the level of full consumption downward. Once this level of full consumption is known, we can describe the entire transition path of the economy with equations (7.2) and (7.3). The only path that leads to the new steady state is $\overline{BE}$. Along this transition path thc markets for goods and for labor and capital services clear in each period.

7.2 Comparison of Welfare Levels

In order to evaluate alternative tax policies, we compare the levels of social welfare associated with each of these policies. We can translate welfare comparisons into monetary terms by introducing the intertemporal counterpart of Hicks's equivalent variation. For this purpose we express the full wealth required to achieve a given level of welfare in terms of the time path of all future prices of full consumption and rates of return. Since full wealth is the present value of full consumption over the whole future of the U.S. economy, we refer to this expression as the *intertemporal expenditure function.* Using the expenditure function, we can express differences in welfare in terms of differences in wealth.

To derive the intertemporal expenditure function we first express the time path of full consumption in terms of the initial level and future real private rates of return:

$$\frac{F_t}{F_0} = \prod_{s=0}^{t} \left[\frac{1+r_s}{(1+\gamma)(1-\alpha_T)^{\sigma}} \right]^{\frac{1}{\sigma}}, \qquad (t = 1, 2, \ldots). \tag{7.6}$$

Using this expression, we can write the intertemporal welfare function as:

$$V = \frac{F_0^{1-\sigma}}{1-\sigma} D, \tag{7.7}$$

where

$$D = \sum_{t=0}^{\infty} \left[\frac{1+n}{(1+\gamma)^{\frac{1}{\sigma}}} \right]^t \prod_{s=0}^{t} (1+r_s)^{\frac{1-\sigma}{\sigma}}.$$

The function D summarizes the effect of all future prices and rates of return on the initial level of full consumption F_0 associated with a given level of welfare V.

Since the optimal time path for full consumption must satisfy the intertemporal budget constraint, we can express the initial level of full consumption in terms of full wealth and all future real private rates of return

$$F_0 = \frac{W}{PF_0} \frac{1}{D}.$$

Combining this expression with (7.7) and solving for full wealth, we obtain the intertemporal expenditure function, say $W(PF_0, D, V)$, where

$$W(PF_0, D, V) = PF_0 \left[\frac{(1-\sigma)\, V}{D^{\sigma}} \right]^{\frac{1}{1-\sigma}} . \tag{7.8}$$

We employ the intertemporal expenditure function to provide a money measure of differences in levels of welfare associated with alternative tax policies. For this purpose we first calculate the solution to our dynamic general equilibrium model of the U.S. economy for the reference tax policy. We denote the resulting prices and discount rates by PF_0 and D_0 and the corresponding level of welfare by V_0. We then solve the model for an alternative tax policy and denote the resulting level of welfare by V_1. Finally, we calculate the *equivalent variation in full wealth*, say ΔW, where

$$\begin{aligned} \Delta W &= W(PF_0, D_0, V_1) - W(PF_0, D_0, V_0), \\ &= W(PF_0, D_0, V_1) - W_0 . \end{aligned} \tag{7.9}$$

The equivalent variation in full wealth (7.9) is the difference between the wealth required to attain the level of welfare associated with the alternative tax policy at prices of the reference policy $W(PF_0, D_0, V_1)$ less the wealth required for the reference policy W_0. If the equivalent variation is positive, a change in policy produces a gain in welfare; otherwise, the policy change results in a welfare loss. The equivalent variations in full wealth enable us to rank the reference policy and any number of alternative policies in terms of a money metric of the corresponding welfare levels.

Obviously, there are many different ways of expressing welfare comparisons among alternative tax policies. The approach proposed by Ballard, Fullerton, Shoven and Whalley (1985, chap. 7) is based on the difference between present values of time paths of full consumption associated with alternative tax policies, rather than the equivalent variation in full wealth. Although there are important similarities between comparisons of present values of full consumption and the equivalent variation, the two approaches do not coincide. Only comparisons based on the equivalent variation provide a money metric of intertemporal welfare useful in ranking alternative tax policies.

The first proposal of Ballard *et al.*, is to calculate the present value of differences in full consumption at prices of the reference tax policy. This amounts to replacing the present value of the full consumption $W(PF_0, D_0, V_1)$ required for the level of welfare under the alternative tax policy (7.9) with the present value of the time path of full consumption associated with that policy. Since the representative consumer minimizes the present value of the full consumption required to attain any level of welfare, this overstates welfare gains and understates welfare losses. The second proposal of Ballard *et al.*, is to calculate the present value of differences in full consumption at prices of the alternative tax policy. This measure understates welfare gains and overstates welfare losses and has the added disadvantage of producing welfare comparisons among alternative tax policies that are not transitive.

7.3 Computational Algorithm

The computational algorithm for determining the solution of our dynamic general equilibrium model of the U.S. economy has two stages. In the first stage we determine the steady state consistent with a given tax policy. In the second stage we find the transition path that is consistent with this steady state and the initial conditions at the time the tax policy is introduced. The evolution of the economy from one period to the next is determined by the transition equation for full consumption and the accumulation equations for capital stock, government debt, and claims on the rest of the world. Since the paths of government debt and claims on the rest of the world are predetermined and the initial value of capital stock is given, the second stage reduces to finding the initial level of full consumption that is consistent with convergence to the steady state of the economy.

Along the transition path, as well as in the steady state, the time endowment in efficiency units grows at the constant rate $(1-\alpha_T)(1+n)-1$. We find it convenient to use the property of constant returns in order to scale the solution of the model to the time endowment. When the economy moves from one period to the next, we rescale the economy by dividing the three stock variables—capital stock, government debt, and claims on the rest of the world—at the end of the period by the factor $(1-\alpha_T)(1+n)$ in order to obtain the stocks available at the beginning of the next period.

With a rate of inflation different from zero it is convenient to normalize the price system in each period by first setting price levels for the six categories of assets, investment goods, capital stock, government debt, and claims on the rest of the world. We set the prices of the six categories of assets and the price of investment goods at the values shown in panel 10 of table 6.13. For capital stock, government debt, and claims on the rest of the world, we set the current prices at unity and the lagged prices at $1/(1+\pi)$. Once the normalized equilibrium of the economy is determined, conversion to the actual size of the economy with the absolute price level is straightforward.

We turn next to the algorithm for finding the equilibrium for our model of the U.S. economy. The model is in balanced growth equilibrium when all the quantities grow at the same rate $(1-\alpha_T)(1+n)$ and relative prices are constant. This is a steady state in the sense that the relative prices and quantities per unit of labor expressed in efficiency units are constant. In each period the relative prices and the allocation of the capital stock and the time endowment are determined so that all the markets clear, producers maximize profit, and consumers maximize utility.

We can characterize the steady state of the economy by three conditions: First, capital stock, government debt, and claims on the rest of the world grow at the same rate as the time endowment:

$$VK = VKL - D + V + (S - DG - DR) = VKL(1-\alpha_T)(1+n)(1+\pi)\,, \qquad (7.10a)$$

$$VG = VGL + DG = VGL(1-\alpha_T)(1+n)(1+\pi)\,, \qquad (7.10b)$$

$$VR = VRL(1+\pi) + DR = VRL(1-\alpha_T)(1+n)(1+\pi)\,. \qquad (7.10c)$$

Equation (7.10a) shows that the nominal value of private capital decreases by the value of depreciation (D) and increases by revaluation of the capital remaining (V) and gross investment. Investment equals gross private saving (S), net of the accumulation of government debt (DG) and claims on the rest of the world (DR). Equation (7.10b) shows that the outstanding government debt grows at the rate of government budget deficit of the rest of the world (DG). Equation (7.10c) shows that growth of the claims on the rest of the world is the sum of the current account deficit of the rest of the world (DR) and the revaluation of the outstanding claims. In a steady state with a constant rate of inflation, the nominal value of private capital (VKL), government debt (VGL), and claims on the rest of the world (VRL) all grow at the same rate and the quantities of these variables per unit of labor in efficiency units remain constant.

Second, full consumption per unit of labor in efficiency units remains constant:

$$F_t = F_{t-1}\,. \qquad (7.11)$$

Together with (7.1) and (7.2), Equation (7.11) implies that the nominal rate of return ρ is equal to its steady state value $\tilde{\rho}$.

Finally, every market must clear in the steady state. By invoking Walras' Law we can ignore the labor market and consider clearing of markets for consumption goods, investment goods, and capital services. The market clearing condition for consumption goods from chapter 5 is:

$$PC(C + CG + CR - CE) = (1 + t_C)PCS \cdot CS\,, \tag{7.12}$$

where $PC = (1 + t_C)PCS$. Similarly, the market clearing conditions for the investment goods is

$$PI(ID + IG + IR) = (1 + t_I)PIS \cdot IS\,, \tag{7.13}$$

where $PI = (1 + t_I)PIS$. Finally, the market clearing condition for the capital services is (5.53):

$$\begin{aligned} &PK_{QS}QS + PK_{QL}QL + PK_{MS}MS + PK_{ML}ML \\ &\qquad + PK_{HS}HS + PK_{HL}HL = (1 + \pi)VKL\,. \end{aligned} \tag{7.14}$$

In the steady state all the endogenous variables can be expressed in terms of the seven variables—F, KL, GL, RL , PC, PLD, LD—where KL, GL, and RL are quantity indexes of capital stock, government debt, and claims on the rest of the world, respectively.[2] Note that both the price and quantity indexes of labor demand by the business sector are included, since we do not make use of the labor market clearing condition. Thus, we have seven unknowns and six equations, (7.10a)–(7.10c) and (7.12)–(7.14). The system is closed by the price possibility frontier (5.1) of the business sector:

$$\ln PLD = \ln P'\alpha_P + \alpha_T \cdot T + \frac{1}{2} \ln P' B_{PP} \ln P\,. \tag{7.15}$$

This form of the price possibility frontier is consistent with the existence of a balanced growth equilibrium.

Making use of (7.15), we can eliminate PLD and reduce the number of unknowns and the number of equations to six. We solve for the variables— FSL, KL, GL, RL, PC, LD—where FSL is the lagged value of FS, defined as a function of F and PF

$$FS = F \cdot PF^{\frac{1}{\sigma}} . \tag{7.16}$$

Since PF can be expressed in terms of PC and other variables that are known and F can be determined from (7.2), replacing F with FSL leaves the solution to the model unchanged. We can solve the equation systems (7.10a)–(7.10c) and (7.12)–(7.14) by Newton's method.

To solve for the steady state, we set the prices of investment goods, capital stock, government debt, and claims on the rest of the world exogenously. The prices of aggregate capital stock, government debt, and claims on the rest of the world are set at unity. The producers' price of investment goods is obtained from:

$$PIS = \frac{PI}{1+t_I} .$$

Since the real private rate of return r is equal to the value $\tilde{r}$ in the steady state, the nominal private rate of return is defined as

$$\rho = (1+\tilde{r})(1+\pi)-1 , \tag{7.17}$$

and the nominal private rate of return on equity, say ρ^e, is obtained from the definition of ρ:

$$\rho(VKL+VGL+VRL) = ((1-\beta)\rho^e+\beta i_k)(VKL+VRL)+i_g \cdot VGL . \tag{7.18}$$

where β is the average debt-asset ratio of private national wealth, including private assets and claims on the rest of the world, i_k is the average after-tax nominal interest rate on private national wealth, and i_g is the after-tax nominal interest rate on government debt, defined as

$$i_g = [1-(1-DI)t_g^d] \cdot i .$$

The nominal interest rate i is determined according to the strict version of Fisher's law:

$$i = i_0 + \pi ,$$

where i_0 is the real interest rate, given exogenously. Given the nominal private rate of return to equity, the nominal discount rates for investments in the corporate, noncorporate, and household sectors (r^q, r^m, r^h) can be calculated from the equations given in chapter 2:

$$
\begin{aligned}
r^q - \pi &= (1-\beta_q)\frac{[\rho^e - \pi(1-(1-DC)t_q^g](1-\alpha \cdot DD \cdot t_q)}{1-[\alpha t_q^e + (1-\alpha)t_q^g]} \\
&\quad + \beta_q[(1-(1-DI)t_q)i - \pi], \qquad (7.19a) \\
r^m - \pi &= (1-\beta_m)[\rho^e - \pi(1-(1-DC)t_m^g)] \\
&\quad + \beta_m[(1-(1-DI)t_m^e)\, i - \pi], \qquad (7.19b) \\
r^h - \pi &= (1-\beta_h)[\rho^e - \pi(1-(1-DC)t_h^g)] \\
&\quad + \beta[(1-DHI(1-HDI)t_h^e)\, i - \pi]. \qquad (7.19c)
\end{aligned}
$$

The nominal private rate of return on equity ρ^e can be calculated from (7.18) if the average debt-asset ratio of private national wealth β and the average after-tax nominal interest rate i_k are known. However, β and i_k depend on the allocation of capital among the corporate, noncorporate and household sectors, which in turn depends on ρ^e through the discount rates for investment in the three private sectors as defined in (7.19a)–(7.19c). In order to cut through this interdependence and simplify the algorithm, we include the nominal private rate of return to equity ρ^e in the list of unknowns and equation (7.18) to the simultaneous equation system to be solved. The computational procedure for applying Newton's method to our seven equation system for the steady state under the reference policy, or the *base case*, is summarized in the following steps; the variables in parenthesis at the end of each step are those determined in that step:

(1) Start with an initial guess of the vector of the seven unknowns $(FSL, KL, GL, RL, \rho^e, PC, LD)$.

(2) Set the current prices of capital assets in the three private sectors. Lagged prices of capital assets are obtained by deflating the current prices with $1+\pi$, where π is the rate of inflation in asset prices. Also set the purchasers' price of investment goods, and the current and lagged prices of the aggregate capital stock, government debt and the claims on the rest of the world. Compute the producer's prices of consumption and investment goods from $PCS = PC/(1+t_C)$ and $PIS = PI/(1+t_I)$ $(PK_{QS}, PK_{QL}, PK_{MS}, PK_{ML}, PK_{HS}, PK_{HL}, PI, PK, PKL, PG, PGL, PR, PRL, PCS, PIS)$.

(3) Making use of (7.19a), (7.19b), and (7.19c), compute the discount rates for investment in the corporate, noncorporate, and household sectors (r^q, r^m, r^h).

(4) Compute the prices of capital services from the formulas given in chapter 2 $(PQS, PQL, PMS, PML, PHS, PHL)$.

(5) Using the price functions for capital services in each sector, (5.4) and (5.15), compute the service prices (PQD, PMD, PHD).

(6) Making use of the share equations (5.5) and (5.16), compute the value shares of the capital services for short-lived and long-lived assets in the corporate, noncorporate, and household sectors $(v_{QL}, v_{QS}, v_{ML}, v_{MS}, v_{HL}, v_{HS})$.

(7) From the price function for labor in the business sector (5.1) and the corresponding share equations (5.2), compute the purchaser's price of labor services and the value shares of the outputs and inputs relative to the value of labor input $(PLD, v_{CS}, v_{IS}, v_{QD}, v_{MD})$.

(8) Making use of (5.52), compute the prices of time endowment, leisure, and the labor employed in the government, government enterprises, and the rest of the world $(PLH, PLJ, PLG, PLE, PLR)$.

(9) Making use of the price function for full consumption (5.14) and the corresponding share equations (5.16), compute the price of full consumption and the value shares of consumption goods, capital services, and leisure in full consumption $(PF, v_C, v_{HD}, v_{LJ})$.

(10) Making use of the fact that, in a steady state, the rate of inflation in asset price is equal to the rate of inflation in the price of full consumption, compute the lagged value of full consumption from (7.2) and set it to be equal to its current value (F).

(11) Combining F, PF, v_C, v_{HD}, v_{LJ}, PC, PLJ, and PHD, compute the household demands for consumption goods, leisure and capital services (C, LJ, HD).

(12) Making use of (5.51), compute the total value of labor supply. Then, from (5.27), compute the labor employed by the government enterprises (VLS, LE).

(13) Combining the value shares obtained in step (7) and the value of labor demanded by the business sector $(PLD \cdot LD)$, compute the supplies of consumption and investment goods and the demands for the corporate and noncorporate capital services by this sector. Note that LD is taken as given in the initial guess for the iteration and does not interact with the supply side of the labor market in the iteration process (CS, IS, QD, MD).

(14) Combining the value shares of the capital services from the short-lived and long-lived assets, sectoral demands for aggregate capital services, and their prices $(QD, MD, HD, PQD, PMD, PHD)$, compute the

demands for the six classes of capital services (QL, QS, ML, MS, HL, HS).

(15) From the allocation of capital in step (14), compute economic depreciation and revaluation of capital. Then compute the imputed capital consumption allowances in the corporate and noncorporate sectors and the imputed investment tax credits in the corporate, noncorporate, and household sectors ($D, V, DQ, DM, ITCQ, ITCM, ITCH$).

(16) From (5.28) compute the amount of consumption goods produced by government enterprises (CE).

(17) Making use of (5.17)–(5.19), (5.21), (5.25)–(5.26), and (5.29), compute the revenues from sales taxes on consumption and investment goods, income on labor and capital income, the surplus of government enterprises, property taxes, non-tax payments, and wealth taxes. Generate government revenue according to (5.33)

$$(R, R_C, R_I, R_q, R_l, R_e, R_d, R_{ge}, R_q^p, R_m^p, R_h^p, R_t, R_w). \tag{7.20}$$

(18) Compute the gross domestic product, gross national product, and private national income defined by (5.38) and (5.39) (GDP, GNP, Y).

(19) Making use of (5.30), (5.34), and (5.35), compute the government deficit, government spending, and its allocation among consumption goods, investment goods, labor, and transfer payments (DG, $XPND$, CG, IG, LG, EL, ER).

(20) Making use of (5.31) and (5.32), compute the price and quantity indexes of the aggregate government spending (PGS, GS).

(21) Making use of (5.36) and (5.37), compute the net exports of consumption goods, investment goods, labor services, and the deficit of the rest of the world (CR, IR, LR, DR).

(22) Making use of (5.40), compute gross private saving (S).

(23) Making use of (5.41), compute gross private domestic investment (ID).

(24) Evaluate both sides of (7.10a)–(7.10c), (7.12)–(7.14) and (7.18) and revise the vector of unknowns with the information derived in steps (1)–(23).

(25) Repeat the steps (2)–(24) until a solution is obtained.

(26) Check if GL and RL are roughly 20% and 10% of GDP, respectively. If not, adjust $SGOV$, SCR, and SIR and repeat steps (1)–(25).

The remaining problem is to find the transition path consistent with the steady state and the initial conditions of the economy. Once the steady state of the economy under the reference policy is determined, we constrain government debt and claims on the rest of the world in such a way that they converge to their steady-state values along smooth transition paths. Capital stock and full consumption remain the essential determinants of the dynamics of the economy along the transition path. Given the level of full consumption in the first year on the transition path, the complete time path of full consumption is determined by the model.

It is convenient to reformulate the problem by assuming that the economy has been under a new policy regime in period 0, one period before the new policy is actually introduced. Then we can characterize the starting point of the transition with the variables FS_0, K_0, G_0, R_0, where the subscript indicates the time period. Since K_0, G_0, R_0 are already known from the initial conditions, the only problem is to find FS_0. For this purpose we employ the method of multiple shooting.[3]

Suppose we start with an initial guess of FS_0. Then we have all the initial conditions for the period 1 (FS_0, K_0, G_0, R_0). The next step is to find the equilibrium of the economy in period 1 such that consumer maximizes utility and the producer maximizes profits. For period 1 all the endogenous variables can be expressed in terms of the elements of the vector (ρ_1^e, PC_1, LD_1), given the initial conditions of the economy. However (7.2) shows that F_1 depends upon PF_1 and ρ_1^e and ρ_1^e in turn is affected by F_1. We simplify the algorithm by including F in the list of unknowns and adding (7.2) to the simultaneous equation system to be solved. Thus we have a vector of four unknowns $(F_1, \rho_1^e, PC_1, LD_1)$ and three market conditions (7.8), (7.9) and (7.10) plus one transition equation for full consumption (7.2).

The computational procedures are similar to those of the steady-state solution except that we now take the full consumption (F_1) as one of the unknowns and FS_0, K_0, G_0, R_0 as given. The current and lagged prices of assets, and the producer and purchaser's price of investment goods are determined as before. We summarize the iterative process of Newton's method in the following steps:

(1) Start with an initial guess of the unknowns (F, ρ^e, PC, LD).

(2) Repeat steps (2)–(23) for the steady-state solution with the following modifications: Since full consumption F is treated as an unknown, step (10) is no longer necessary. The government deficit (DG) and

deficit of the rest of the world (DR) are obtained from (5.43) and (5.44). Government expenditure is set equal to the sum of tax revenues and the budget deficit, and the government spending is net of interest payments. Finally, there is no guarantee that the net exports of consumption goods (CR), investment goods (IR), and labor services (LR) determined as in the steady-state solution are consistent with the predetermined path of the deficit of the rest of the world (DR). We adjust these variables in proportion to their absolute values so that net exports are consistent with the time path of the claims on the rest of the world.

(3) Evaluate both sides of (7.2), (7.12), (7.13), and (7.14) with the information derived so far, and revise the initial guess of the vector $(F, \rho^e, PC, LD))$.

(4) Repeat the process until a solution is found.

After the equilibrium of period 1 is found, we move on to the next period. The initial conditions of the period 2 are obtained from

$$FSL = F_1\left(\frac{PF_1}{1+\pi}\right)^{\frac{1}{\sigma}}, \tag{7.21a}$$

$$KL = \frac{K_0 + (PI \cdot ID_1 - D_1)/PK}{(1-\alpha_T)(1+n)}. \tag{7.21b}$$

In (7.21a), PF_1 is deflated by $1+\pi$, since the entire price system is renormalized in period 2.

After equilibrium in period 2 is obtained we proceed to period 3, and so on. We assume that the economy reaches the steady state in 100 years. In most cases the economy comes very close to the steady state within 30–35 years after the introduction of a new policy. Hence, our time horizon is sufficiently long for practical purposes. However, if we actually solve the economy forward for 100 years, even a very small error in FS_0 will be quickly magnified, so that the computation will break down. In order to control the iterative process, we divide the 100-year period into intervals and introduce starting values of FS and K for each interval. We find that setting the number of intervals at ten is sufficient to control the explosiveness of the iterative process.

In general the welfare level of an economy depends upon both private consumption and government spending. In chapter 5 we did not include government spending in the intertemporal utility function. When we compare the performance of tax policy alternatives in terms of levels of welfare attainable by the economy, it is essential to control the size and composition of government spending so that the benefits from government spending are the same for all the policies compared.

We have assumed that the allocation of total government expenditure, net of the interest payments on government debt, among consumption goods (CG), investment goods (IG), labor (LG), and transfer payments to U.S. citizens (EL) and to foreigners (ER) can be represented by a Cobb-Douglas price function (5.31):

$$\ln PGS = SCG \ln PC + SIG \ln PI + SLG \ln PLG + SEL \ln PEL + SER \ln PER ,$$

where PGS is the price index of aggregate government spending, and SCG, SIG, SLG, SEL and SER are the exogenously given shares of government expenditure. We set the prices of transfer payments at unity:

$$PEL = PER = 1 .$$

Under a proper normalization of the indirect utility function of the government, the benefits derived from government spending are equal to the quantity of government spending (GS).

Under the reference policy, we set the steady-state level of government equal to a fixed proportion $SGOV$ of the gross domestic product. Along the transition path the level of government spending is determined as the sum of the tax revenue and budget deficit. When we solve the model under the alternative policy, we control the level of welfare derived from government spending by setting the quantity of government spending in each period at the value under the reference policy.

On the receipt side of the government budget taxation and borrowing from the public are the two alternative means of raising revenues. In a dynamic setting the budget constraint of the government takes the form that the present value of government spending equals the present value of government receipts plus the net worth of the government. Under this budget constraint, the government can finance a given amount of spending either by taxation or by issuing debt, followed by a tax increase to service and eventually repay the debt. However, this is not to say that tax financing and debt financing are equivalent.

In our model, Ricardian equivalence of taxation and borrowing does not hold because taxes are not distortion-free. Therefore, it matters whether a given amount of revenue is raised by taxation or borrowing. In order to take account of this aspect of the revenue side of the government budget, we require the budget deficit of the government and government tax revenue must follow the same path under all the policies being compared. We assume that the level of government debt reaches its steady-state value in thirty-nine years after the introduction of the new policy. We close the gap between the initial and the steady-state levels of the government debts at the annual rate of 1/34 during the first twenty-nine years and then at the annual rate of 1/68 for the remaining ten years. The steady-state value is reached in year 40. We apply the same procedure to determine the path of claims on the rest of the world. Table A7.1 and figure A7.3 in the appendix to this chapter present the transition paths of real government spending net of interest payments, government debt, and claims on the rest of the world. In the same appendix, table A7.2 shows the base case paths of gross domestic product, full consumption, labor supply, capital stock, and the average private rate of return to all assets.[4]

Since the time paths of real government spending and the government budget deficit are predetermined, the level of tax revenue under an alternative tax policy must be adjusted to meet the budget constraint. In order to adjust the tax revenues, we consider four alternative approaches. These include the adjustments of a hypothetical lump sum tax, sales taxes, the labor income tax, and the individual income tax. This procedure requires that in each period we have to find the size of tax adjustment along with other endogenous variables. When the lump sum tax is adjusted to meet the government budget constraint, R_{lum} is added to government tax revenue and is subtracted from private national income.

Under the labor income tax adjustment we adjust the average and marginal tax rates on labor income by the same percentage points or by the same proportion. These adjustment methods are referred to the *additive adjustment* and *proportional adjustment*, respectively. Under the sales tax adjustment, we adjust the tax rates on consumption goods and investment goods by the same percentage points. When the sales taxes are flat and the tax rates are the same, additive and proportional adjustments are equivalent. Finally, when the individual income tax is adjusted, we adjust the average and marginal tax rates on labor income either by the same percentage points or by the same proportion.

If the average and marginal tax rates on labor income are adjusted by the same percentage points, the average tax rate on capital income is also adjusted by the same percentage points, but the marginal tax rates on capital income are adjusted in the same proportion as the marginal tax rate on labor income. If the average and marginal tax rates on labor income are adjusted by the same proportion, the average and marginal tax rates on capital income are also adjusted in the same proportion. We represent the size of tax adjustment by ADJ, and to close the equation system for the equilibrium of the economy, we add the budget constraint of the government (5.35) as one of the balancing equations.

The algorithm used to solve for the steady state under an alternative tax policy is similar to the one used for the steady state under the reference policy. The steady-state values of GL, RL, GS, DG, and DR are the same as those under the reference policy. This implies that we must adjust tax revenues and net exports in order to satisfy the budget constraints on the government and the rest of the world. The adjustment of net exports is simple enough so that we can eliminate it. By contrast with the reference policy, we can eliminate GL and RL from the list of unknowns and add the tax adjustment to the list.

Once the steady-state solution for the alternative policy is found, the next step is to find the transition path between the initial and the steady states of the economy. The computational algorithm is similar to the one used for the reference policy. For the intertemporal part of the problem, we solve for the paths of FSL and KL, since the paths of GL and RL are the same as those under the reference policy. For the atemporal part of the problem, we solve for the variables (F, ρ^e, PC, LD) and the tax adjustment ADJ.

In our model of the U.S. economy trade with the rest of the world need not be balanced. From the viewpoint of an individual, it does not matter whether a given amount of saving is invested domestically or abroad. However, for the economy as a whole it makes a difference for at least two reasons. First, capital employed abroad does not generate corporate tax revenues. Second, this capital is not combined with domestic labor in production, so that domestic labor productivity is unaffected. Therefore we control the path of the claims on the rest of the world in the same way as we control the path of government debt. In order to keep the trade deficit on a path implied by claims on the rest of the world, we adjust net exports of consumption and investment goods and labor services.

There is no reason to believe that the actual levels of the government budget deficit and the deficit of the rest of the world will follow the time paths used in our simulations. The purpose of controlling government budget deficit and the deficit of the rest of the world sector is to isolate the effects of tax policy changes. Our projections of the future paths of the two deficits is of secondary importance in comparing alternative tax policies.

7.4 Welfare Effects of Tax Reform

The effects of taxation on the allocation of resources depend not only on the size of the tax wedges imposed on transactions but also on the elasticities of substitution along the relevant margins. Moreover, tax distortion of resource allocation at one margin has further impacts at other margins. The analysis of taxation in terms of effective tax rates and tax wedges may be suggestive but incomplete as an economic analysis of the tax distortion of resource allocation—in certain contexts, it may even be inappropriate due to the limitation of the typically static and partial equilibrium nature of the analysis. In this section, we employ the dynamic general equilibrium model which we have presented in chapters 5 and 6 in order to evaluate the potential welfare impacts of alternative tax reform proposals.

In evaluating the welfare effects of various tax policies we require a reference economy with which the resource allocation and welfare under alternative tax policies can be compared. We take the U.S. economy under the tax laws effective in 1996 as the reference economy. The simulated dynamic path of the reference economy with an annual inflation rate of four percent is the "base case" for our simulation analysis. Since the base case serves as the reference for the evaluation of the performance of the economy under alternative tax policies, it is useful to describe its main characteristics. We describe the construction of the base case by presenting the exogenous variables that are common to all the simulations we consider.

We take January 1, 1997, as the starting point for all the simulations we consider. The main role of the initial year of the simulation is to determine the initial values of the stock variables and the scale of the economy. The stock variables determined by the starting year are the total time endowment (LH), capital stock (KL), and the claims on the government and the rest of the world (GL and RL). In our simulations, the starting values of LH, KL, GL, and RL are set in their historical values. Specifically, in 1997, LH = \$17,571 billion, KL = \$25,847 billion, GL = \$3,784 billion. Since inflation is assumed to be 4 percent per year in the base case, we set *PKL*, *PGL*, and *PRL* at $(1+0.04)^{-1}$ = 0.96154 dollars per unit.

After 1997, we assume that the distribution of individuals among the categories distinguished by age, sex, and level of education will stabilize and hence the quality of time endowment, leisure, and the labor employed in the various sectors of the economy will not change. This implies that the growth rate of the total effective time endowment will be the same as the growth rate of population. We assume that population will grow at an annual rate of one percent per year and the efficiency of labor improves at the rate of productivity growth we estimated by pooling the entire producer model.

In table 7.1 we present the tax rates that describe the U.S. tax system in 1996. These include the marginal tax rates on individual capital income, the corporate income tax rate, the marginal tax rate on labor income and the average tax rate on personal income. The tax rates also include sales and property taxes, personal non-taxes, and wealth taxes. We have described the estimation of marginal tax rates on capital income in chapter 3. Given the definitions of the tax rates in chapter 5, the data on tax revenues, production of consumption and investment goods, employment and compensation of labor from the National Income and Product Accounts, and our estimates of capital stock in the three private sectors, the estimation of the sales tax rates, property tax rates, and the rate of non-tax payment and wealth tax rate are straightforward.

We estimate the marginal tax rate on labor income t_L^m in exactly the same way as the average marginal tax rates on interest income and dividends, t_P^d and t_P^e of table 3.4. To estimate the average tax rates on labor and capital income of individuals, we use tables 7.2 and 7.3 based on Internal Revenue Service, *Statistics of Income–1996, Individual Income Tax Returns*. First, we reconcile the total adjusted gross income (*AGI*) in the two tables by creating a zero tax rate bracket in table 7.3 and allocating the excess of total positive *AGI* in table 7.2 over that of table 7.3 ($4,536.0–4,439.7 + $54.6 = $150.9 billion dollars) to the zero tax rate bracket.

Second, assuming that the marginal tax rate increases with the *AGI* bracket in table 7.2, we allocate the tax revenue of table 7.3 across the positive *AGI* brackets of table 7.2. We then allocate the tax revenue in each *AGI* bracket of table 7.2 between labor and nonlabor income, using the share of labor income in each *AGI* bracket (see column 3 of table 7.3). Third, we calculate the average federal labor income tax rate t_L^{af} by dividing the total tax revenue allocated to wages and salaries with the total wages and salaries in AGI. Similarly, we calculate the average federal nonlabor income tax rate and interpret it as the average federal income tax rate on individual capital income t_K^{af}. The results are: $t_L^{af} = 0.12970$ and $t_K^{af} = 0.18757$.

Table 7.1
Inflation and tax rates (1996)

1. *Marginal Tax Rates on Individual Capital Income*			
Inflation Rate	0.0	0.04	0.08
t_q^e	0.20166	0.20203	0.20228
t_m^e	0.28786	0.28786	0.28786
t_h^e	0.28786	0.28786	0.28786
t_q^g	0.05589	0.05589	0.05589
t_m^g	0.07196	0.07196	0.07196
t_h^g	0.00000	0.00000	0.00000
t_q^d	0.17096	0.18228	0.18971
t_m^d	0.22480	0.23003	0.23346
t_h^d	0.26910	0.26917	0.26921
t_g^d	0.19893	0.20252	0.20488
2. *Corporate Income Tax Rate*			
	t_q		0.38799
3. *Marginal Tax Rate on Labor Income*			
	t_L^m		0.26447
4. *Average Tax Rate on Personal Income*			
	t_L^a		0.12657
	t_e^a		0.18304
	t_d^a		0.18304
5. *Sales Tax*			
	t_C		0.05800
	t_I		0.05800
6. *Property Tax*			
	t_q^p		0.01201
	t_m^p		0.01137
	t_h^p		0.00912
7. *Others*			
	t_t		0.00675
	t_w		0.00083

Table 7.1 (continued)

Notations:

Note: We set $t_h^e = t_m^e$ and $t_h^g = 0$.

t_q^e, t_m^e, t_h^e:	Average marginal tax rates of individual income accruing to corporate, noncorporate and household equities, respectively
t_q^g, t_m^g, t_h^g:	Average marginal tax rates of capital gains accruing to corporate, noncorporate and household equities, respectively
$t_q^d, t_m^d, t_h^d, t_g^d$:	Average marginal tax rats of interest income accruing to corporate, noncorporate, household, and government debts, respectively
t_q:	Corporate income tax rate (federal + state and local)
t_L^m:	Average marginal tax rate of labor income
t_L^a:	Average tax rate of labor income
t_e^a, t_d^a:	Average tax rates of personal capital income from equity and debt
t_c, t_I:	Sales tax rates of consumption and investment goods
t_q^p, t_m^p, t_h^p:	Property tax rates of corporate, noncorporate and household assets, respectively
t_t:	Rate of personal non-taxes
t_w:	Effective rate of wealth taxation

We note that our approach has a number of shortcomings. For example, *AGI* does not include income not reported in the tax returns; *AGI* excludes tax-exempt income; labor income of the self-employed is included in nonlabor income; and nonlabor income includes income other than capital income such as alimony, social security benefits, unemployment compensation, gambling earnings, etc. To offset some biases that may be caused by these factors, we calculate the federal and state and local average tax rates on labor and capital income as:

$$t_L^a = \frac{t_P^a \cdot t_L^{af}}{t_P^{af}}$$

$$t_K^a = \frac{t_P^a \cdot t_K^{af}}{t_P^{af}},$$

Table 7.2
Adjusted gross income and wages and salaries

Size of AGI (1,000 dollar)	AGI	W (billions of dollar)	S
No AGI	– 54.6	7.2	—
under 5	38.3	33.8	0.88045
5–10	102.1	75.4	0.73816
10–15	165.2	122.0	0.73874
15–20	202.3	154.1	0.76212
20–25	217.9	176.0	0.80738
25–30	221.1	181.2	0.81975
30–40	436.4	362.3	0.83017
40–50	426.8	353.8	0.82907
50–75	871.8	715.5	0.82074
75–100	498.4	394.9	0.79240
100–200	603.7	433.7	0.71840
200–500	347.4	204.7	0.58926
500–1000	144.8	70.5	0.48675
1000 or more	314.4	91.7	0.29181
All Returns, Total	4536.0	3376.9	0.74446

Note:
1) AGI is net of deficit
2) All figures are estimates based on samples

Notations:
AGI: Adjusted gross income
W: Wages and salaries
S: Share of wages and salaries in AGI (S/AGI)

Source: Internal Revenue Service, *Statistics of Income—1996, Individual Income Tax Returns*, table 1.4.

where t_P^{af} is the average federal tax rate defined as the total tax revenue of 7.3 divided by the total positive *AGI* of 7.2, and t_P^a is the federal and state and local average personal income tax rates estimated from the National Income and Product Accounts. We estimate that $t_P^{af} = 0.14449$ and $t_P^a = 0.141$ for 1996. We assume the average tax rates are the same for dividends and interest income. The results are $t_L^a = 0.12657$ and $t_e^a = t_d^a = 0.18304$ as shown in table 7.1.

Table 7.3
Tax generated at all rates by marginal tax rate (unit: %, billions of dollars)

Marginal tax rate	AGI	Tax generated at all rates, after credit
0.0	(150.9)	0.0
15.0	1681.8	128.9
28.0	1625.7	235.7
31.0	355.0	70.0
36.0	249.2	59.0
39.6	527.9	161.8
Total	4439.7	655.4

Source: Internal Revenue Service, *Statistics of Income—1996, Individual Income Tax Returns*, table 1.4.

Capital consumption allowances are allowed only for corporate and noncorporate business sectors. In table 7.2 we present the present value of these allowances for short-lived and long-lived assets under three alternative rates of inflation. We begin the calculation of the capital consumption allowances with the statutory depreciation schedules given in table A3.13 and the capital stock weights given in table A3.15.

We employ the after-tax nominal interest rate for discounting depreciation allowances. The nominal interest rate is the sum of the real interest rate and the inflation rate. The real interest rate is set equal to the average of the Baa corporate bond rate for our sample period 1970–1996, 0.048604. The rate of inflation varies with the simu-

Table 7.4
Present value of capital consumption allowances (1996)

Inflation rate	Corporate		Noncorporate	
	Short	Long	Short	Long
0.00	0.9299	0.5418	0.9347	0.4962
0.04	0.8801	0.4574	0.8878	0.3909
0.08	0.8360	0.3982	0.8460	0.3197

lation scenario and takes the values of zero, four, and eight percent per year. The after-tax nominal interest rate is calculated as $i \cdot (1-t_q)$, where t_q is the corporate tax rate given in table 7.1. After the present values of depreciation allowances for the 51 depreciable asset classes are calculated, we use the same procedure as the one employed for the average depreciation rates in chapter 6. The only difference is that the weight is now the value of capital stock, adjusted for economic depreciation, inflation, and the after-tax discount rate for investment. These adjustments are necessary to make the sum of the value of capital services from these asset categories equal to the value of aggregate capital services.

In our model, the time horizon of the consumer is infinite and the model is consistent with a wide range of the steady-state configurations of the economy. From a practical point of view, this implies that the steady-state configuration of the economy can be very different from the initial conditions of the economy. We estimate the welfare effects of the alternative tax reform proposals under three alternative assumptions on the rate of inflation and four alternative methods of adjusting tax revenues. The adjustment of tax revenues is necessary to keep the government's real budgetary position on the same path as in the base case economy. This approach ensures that the government budget does not affect the measured differential welfare effects either through expenditures or through budget deficits/surpluses. However, it should be noted that when the revenue adjustment involves changes in the marginal rate of the adjusted tax, there will be substitution effects.

Under the 1996 tax law, inflation increases the tax burden of corporate assets faster than that of noncorporate assets and the burden of noncorporate assets faster than that of household assets. But inflation has mixed effects on the absolute size of the intersectoral tax wedges where the tax wedges have negative sign. Table 7.5 shows the impact of inflation on the performance of the U.S. economy under the 1996 tax law. An increase in the rate of inflation reduces welfare under a lump sum tax adjustment, but enhances welfare under labor income tax, sales tax, and individual income tax adjustments.

The welfare cost of the distortion of resource allocation by taxes can be measured as the improvement in the economic welfare of the economy when the tax wedges are eliminated. We first analyze the impact of distortions resulting from the taxation of income from capital. We

Table 7.5
Welfare effects of inflation under the 1996 law
(billions of 1997 dollars)

Rate of inflation	Revenue adjustment	Welfare effect
0%	Lump sum tax	482.4
	Labor income tax	–89.5
	Sales tax	–96.8
	Individual income tax	-89.2
4%	Lump sum tax	0.0
	Labor income tax	0.0
	Sales tax	0.0
	Individual income tax	0.0
8%	Lump sum tax	–407.0
	Labor income tax	15.6
	Sales tax	31.6
	Individual income tax	19.0

Note: In 1997, the national wealth (beginning of the year) and GDP were $25,378 and $8,111 billion dollars, respectively.

consider the elimination of interasset, intersector, and intertemporal tax wedges. Specifically, we measure the efficiency gains from the following changes in the 1996 tax system:

(1) Eliminate intra-sectoral tax wedges between short-lived and long-lived assets.

(2) Eliminate intersectoral tax wedges for short-lived and long-lived assets in the business sector—corporate and noncorporate.

(3) Eliminate intersectoral tax wedges among all private sectors—corporate, noncorporate, and household.

(4) Eliminate intersectoral and intra-sectoral tax wedges in the business sector.

(5) Eliminate intersectoral and intra-sectoral tax wedges in the private sector.

(6) Corporate tax integration.

(7) Eliminate taxation of income from capital.

(8) Eliminate capital income taxes and the sales tax on investment goods.

Table 7.6
Steady state of the base case (rate of inflation: 4%)

	Corporate		Noncorporate		Household	
	Short	Long	Short	Long	Short	Long
w	0.0868	0.2430	0.0178	0.2076	0.0968	0.3480
z	0.8801	0.4574	0.8878	0.3909	0.0000	0.0000
δ	0.1367	0.0175	0.1533	0.0112	0.1918	0.0107
PKS	0.2211	0.1066	0.2276	0.0849	0.2486	0.0602

Notations:
w: Share of capital stock
z: Present value of consumption allowances
δ: Economic depreciation rate
PKS: Price of capital services

(9) Eliminate capital income taxes and property taxes.

(10) Eliminate capital income taxes, the sales tax on investment goods, and property taxes.

In order to eliminate tax wedges between a set of asset categories, we set their social rates of return to be equal. We achieve this objective by assigning an appropriate investment tax credit for each category. The rate of the tax credit required is calculated using the cost of capital formulas presented in chapter 2. Note that equalizing social rates of return across sectors is not equivalent to equalizing effective tax rates, since the private rate of return varies with the capital structure of each sector. However, equalizing the social rates of return to short-lived and long-lived assets within a given sector is equivalent to equalizing their effective tax rates. Table 7.6 shows the present value of capital consumption allowances z and the rates of economic depreciation δ. It also shows the allocation of capital stock w and the prices of capital services *PKS* in the steady state of the base case corresponding to the 1996 tax system.

The tax credits required for the first six sets of changes in the 1996 tax system given above are presented in panel 2 of table 7.7, along with the corresponding social rates of return and effective tax rates. Base case figures are presented in panel 1 for comparison. In the first tax change we equalize the social rates of return to short-lived and long-lived assets within each sector, by setting the social rates of return for short-lived and long-lived assets at their sectoral average in the steady state of base case, where the composition of capital stock in

Table 7.7
Elimination of interasset and intersectoral tax wedges (rate of inflation: 4%)

	Corporate		Noncorporate		Household	
	Short	Long	Short	Long	Short	Long
1. Base Case						
$\sigma - \pi$	0.0789	0.0884	0.0681	0.0733	0.0491	0.0491
e	0.3983	0.4625	0.3240	0.3715	0.1223	0.1223
k	0.0000	0.0000	0.0000	0.0000	0.0000	0.0000
2. Alternative Policies						
(1) *No interasset wedges: Corporate and noncorporate sectors*						
$\sigma - \pi$	0.0859	0.0859	0.0729	0.0729	0.0491	0.0491
e	0.4470	0.4470	0.3680	0.3680	0.1223	0.1223
k	–0.0219	0.0216	-0.0163	0.0049	0.0000	0.0000
(2) *No intersector wedges: Corporate and noncorporate sectors*						
$\sigma - \pi$	0.0771	0.0814	0.0771	0.0814	0.0491	0.0491
e	0.3840	0.4167	0.4025	0.4342	0.1223	0.1223
k	0.0058	0.0604	–0.0308	–0.0981	0.0000	0.0000
(3) *No intersector wedges: All sectors*						
$\sigma - \pi$	0.0636	0.0673	0.0636	0.0673	0.0636	0.0673
e	0.2538	0.2947	0.2762	0.3159	0.3227	0.3599
k	0.0481	0.1829	0.0155	0.0718	–0.0600	–0.3392
(4) *No interasset and intersector wedges: All assets, corporate and noncorporate sectors*						
$\sigma - \pi$	0.0806	0.0806	0.0806	0.0806	0.0491	0.0491
e	0.4108	0.4108	0.4285	0.4285	0.1223	0.1223
k	–0.0053	0.0675	–0.0429	–0.0883	0.0000	0.0000
(5) *No interasset and intersector wedges: All assets, all sectors*						
$\sigma - \pi$	0.0666	0.0666	0.0666	0.0666	0.0666	0.0666
e	0.2868	0.2868	0.3083	0.3083	0.3528	0.3528
k	0.0388	0.1893	0.0053	0.0808	–0.0722	–0.3253
(6) *Corporate tax integration*						
$\sigma - \pi$	0.0681	0.0733	0.0681	0.0733	0.0491	0.0491
e	0.3030	0.3520	0.3240	0.3715	0.1223	0.1223
k	0.0340	0.1311	0.0000	0.0000	0.0000	0.0000

Notes:
$\sigma - \pi$: Social rate of return
e: Effective tax rate
k: Investment tax credit
π: Rate of inflation

the steady state of base case in table 7.6 is used as the weight. Once the social rate of return for an asset is determined, the required rate of investment tax credit can be solved from the cost of capital formula.

There is, of course, no interasset tax wedge within the household sector, since no tax is levied on the income of the household sector and property tax rates are the same for short-lived and long-lived assets. In this tax change the intersectoral tax wedges among corporate, noncorporate, and household sectors are maintained. In the second tax change we follow the same procedure and equalize social rates of return of short-lived assets in the corporate and noncorporate sectors and similarly for long-lived assets, but the interasset wedges remain the same. The third tax change extends this analysis to the household sector. In the fourth tax change both interasset and intersectoral tax wedges in the business sectors are eliminated and the fifth extends the analysis to the household sector.

We eliminate tax wedges in the first five tax changes given above by setting the relevant social rates of return at the average value in the steady state of the base case corresponding to the 1996 tax law. This assures that the resulting tax change will be approximately revenue neutral. We implement corporate tax integration, the sixth tax change given above, by setting the social rates of return for short-lived and long-lived assets in the corporate sector equal to their values in the noncorporate sector. This is not, of course, revenue neutral. In the appendix, figures A7.1a–A7.1g and figures A7.2a–A7.2g present the social rates of return and the effective tax rates for the six asset categories under the seven tax policy regimes of table 7.7, including the base case.

In the seventh through tenth tax changes we evaluate the potential welfare gains from the elimination of intertemporal tax wedges. These are determined by capital income taxes, sales taxes on investment goods, and property taxes. The seventh tax change measures the welfare gain from elimination of the taxation of capital income for both individuals and corporations. We then move step-by-step to eliminate intertemporal tax wedges. In the eighth tax change we eliminate the sales tax on investment goods, as well as capital income taxes. In the ninth tax change we also eliminate property taxes. Finally, in the tenth change we eliminate capital income taxes, sales taxes on investment goods, and property taxes.

The welfare effects of the ten simulations are summarized in table 7.8. Beginning with the simulations with a lump sum tax adjustment,

Table 7.8
Welfare effects of tax distortion: 1996 tax law (billions of 1997 dollars)

Eliminated wedges and method of revenue adjustment	Welfare effect	
	Additive	Proportional
(1) *Within Sector Interasset Distortion*		
Lump sum tax adjustment	182.1	182.1
Labor income tax adjustment	193.4	266.5
Sales tax adjustment	185.5	185.5
Individual income tax adjustment	184.6	252.0
(2) *Intersector Distortion: Corporate and Noncorporate Sectors*		
Lump sum tax adjustment	45.1	45.1
Labor income tax adjustment	–25.3	–59.0
Sales tax adjustment	–31.4	–31.4
Individual income tax adjustment	–32.2	–48.4
(3) *Intersector Distortion: All Sectors*		
Lump sum tax adjustment	1616.8	1616.8
Labor income tax adjustment	1716.8	1906.8
Sales tax adjustment	1709.5	1709.5
Individual income tax adjustment	1701.5	1849.6
(4) *Interasset and Intersector Distortion: Corporate and Noncorporate Sectors, all Assets*		
Lump sum tax adjustment	127.6	127.6
Labor income tax adjustment	80.4	67.0
Sales tax adjustment	70.5	70.5
Individual income tax adjustment	70.1	72.3
(5) *Interasset and Intersector Distortion: All sectors, all Assets*		
Lump sum tax adjustment	1692.7	1692.7
Labor income tax adjustment	1810.2	2015.0
Sales tax adjustment	1800.3	1800.3
Individual income tax adjustment	1789.6	1949.9
(6) *Corporate Tax Integration (Set $\sigma^q = \sigma^m$)*		
Lump sum tax adjustment	1067.4	1067.4
Labor income tax adjustment	282.8	–976.2
Sales tax adjustment	250.3	250.3
Individual income tax adjustment	280.4	–595.2
(7) *Capital Income Taxes (Business and Personal)*		
Lump sum tax adjustment	2691.5	2691.4
Labor income tax adjustment	362.9	–5480.2
Sales tax adjustment	493.0	493.0
Individual income tax adjustment	362.9	–5480.2
(8) *Capital Income Taxes and Sales Tax on Investment Goods*		
Lump sum tax adjustment	3367.4	3367.4
Labor income tax adjustment	383.6	–8957.9
Sales tax adjustment	710.2	710.3
Individual income tax adjustment	383.6	–8957.9

Table 7.8 (continued)

Eliminated wedges and method of revenue adjustment	Welfare effect Additive	Proportional
(9) *Capital Income Taxes and Property Taxes*		
Lump sum tax adjustment	3723.2	3723.3
Labor income tax adjustment	–1085.0	—
Sales tax adjustment	-554.0	–554.0
Individual income tax adjustment	–1085.0	—
(10) *Capital Income Taxes, Sales Tax on Investment Goods, and Property Taxes*		
Lump sum tax adjustment	4309.5	4309.3
Labor income tax adjustment	–1101.0	—
Sales tax adjustment	–237.8	–237.9
Individual income tax adjustment	–1101.0	—

Notes:
1. Inflation is fixed at 4% per year.
2. Under the additive tax adjustment, the average and marginal tax rates of labor income and the average tax rates of individual capital income are adjusted in the same percentage points. The marginal tax rates of individual capital income are adjusted in the same proportion as the marginal tax rate of labor income.
3. Under the proportional tax adjustment, average and marginal tax rates are adjusted in the same proportion.

we find that the welfare gain from the elimination of the interasset tax wedges within sectors are $182.1 billion under the 1996 Tax Law. Under the lump sum tax adjustment, elimination of intersectoral wedges between the corporate and noncorporate assets yields a welfare gain of $45.1 billion.

The result of the third simulation suggests that there is potentially a very large welfare gain to be realized from eliminating the intersectoral wedges between the business and household sectors. The estimated gains are $1,616.8 billion under the 1996 Tax Law. This result is not surprising, given the large tax wedges between business and household assets. The welfare gains from eliminating the interasset and intersectoral wedges among business assets are estimated to be $127.6 billion under the 1996 Tax Law. The welfare gain from eliminating all the atemporal tax wedges in the entire private economy is estimated to be $1,692.7 billion under the 1996 Tax Law. Most of this welfare gain can be attributed to the elimination of the tax wedges between business and household sectors.

In the sixth simulation we eliminate the intersectoral tax wedges between the assets in the corporate and noncorporate assets by setting the social rates of return of corporate assets to be equal to the corresponding rates of return of the noncorporate assets in the reference case. The tax burdens on the corporate assets are unambiguously reduced without an offsetting increase in other marginal tax rates. The estimated welfare gains from this experiment are $1,067.4 billion under the 1996 Tax Law. These welfare gains are more than half of those attainable by eliminating all the atemporal tax wedges.

In the first six simulations we focused on the distortionary effects of atemporal tax wedges. However, in the following four simulations, we estimate the welfare cost of intertemporal tax distortions. For this purpose we measure the welfare gains from eliminating the distortions caused by the taxes on capital income, including property taxes and sales taxes on investment goods. In the seventh simulation we set the effective tax rates on all forms of capital equal to be zero. Social rates of return are not equalized across sectors, due to the differences in the debt/asset ratios and the property tax rates.

We find that elimination of capital income taxes at both individual and corporate levels generates a welfare gain of $2.691.5 billion under the 1996 Tax Law. Eliminating sales taxes on investment goods as well increases this gain to $3,367.4 billion. Eliminating capital income taxes and property taxes produces a gain of $3,723.2, while eliminating taxes on investments goods as well generates a gain of $4,309.5 billion. If we start with the 1996 Tax Law and eliminate all intertemporal tax wedges, the welfare gain is as large 53.1% of the U.S. *GDP* and 16.8% of the private national wealth in 1997.

Table 7.8 shows that the magnitudes of welfare gains under the distortionary tax adjustments are substantially different from those under the lump sum tax adjustment. Since the elimination of the tax wedges are not calibrated to be revenue neutral, the changes in the marginal tax rates due to the revenue adjustments can generate significant substitution effects. We find that the welfare effects from the elimination of tax wedges are very sensitive to the choice of the revenue adjustment method. The welfare effects are most sensitive to the choice between the lump sum tax adjustment and the distortionary tax adjustments. The results are also somewhat sensitive to the choice among the distortionary tax adjustments, especially when the size of the required revenue is large.

Note that when elimination of tax wedges implies tax cuts at the relevant margins, the welfare gains under the distortionary tax adjustments are substantially smaller than the corresponding gains under the lump sum tax adjustment. The logic underlying this observation is straightforward. The excess burden tends to increase more than proportionally with the required revenue increase. When elimination of tax wedges involves tax cuts with substantial revenue impacts, the welfare measures under the lump sum tax adjustment are best interpreted as the upper bounds of the welfare gains. Lowering marginal tax rates coupled with broadening the tax base is a successful strategy for improving the efficiency of resource allocation.

The fact that the estimated welfare gains from the elimination of the intertemporal tax wedges is in the range of $2,691.5–4,309.5 billion suggests that the potential welfare gain from replacing the current income taxes with consumption based individual taxes is potentially very large. At the same time, welfare gains under the distortionary tax adjustments are much smaller, indicating that improvements in the efficiency of resource allocation can be best achieved by reducing distortions at the atemporal margins of resource allocation.

Our final simulation is intended to measure the distortions associated with progressivity of the tax on labor income. This produces marginal tax rates far in excess of average tax rates. Our point of departure is the elimination of all intersectoral and interasset tax distortions in Panel (5) of table 7.8. In table 7.9, we replace the progressive labor income tax by a flat labor income tax with the same average tax rate. Under a lump sum tax adjustment this generates a welfare gain of $4,585.9 billion, relative to 1996 Tax Law. We conclude that elimination of the progressive labor income tax, together with elimination of all intersectoral and interasset tax distortions, would produce the largest welfare gains of all the tax changes we have considered. These gains are even larger with distortionary tax adjustments as the lower marginal tax rate on labor income improves resource allocation and allows the marginal tax rates of the adjusted taxes to be lowered.

7.5 Efficiency Costs of Taxation

If the government could employ nondistorting or lump sum taxes, the social value of a dollar in the private sector and the social cost of raising a dollar of tax revenue would be the same. However, lump sum taxes are not available in practice, so that the government must use distorting taxes to raise revenue. Even under an optimal tax policy, the social value of a dollar in the private sector and the cost of a dollar of public funds raised through taxation will differ.[5] Measurement of the social cost of tax distortions has attracted the attention of public

Table 7.9
Welfare cost of labor tax progressivity under efficient capital allocation (billions of 1997 dollars)

	Progressive		Proportional
Revenue adjustment	Additive	Proportional	Additive
Lump sum tax	1692.7	1692.7	4585.9
Labor income tax	1810.2	2015.0	4823.0
Sales tax	1800.3	1800.3	4899.9
Individual income tax	1789.6	1949.9	4857.8

Notes
1. Inflation is fixed at 4% per year
2. Under the additive tax adjustment, the average and marginal tax rates of labor income and the average tax rates of individual capital income are adjusted in the same percentage points. The marginal tax rates of individual capital income are adjusted in the same proportion as the marginal tax rate of labor income.
3. Under the proportional tax adjustment, average and marginal tax rates are adjusted in the same proportion.
4. The figures for the progressive labor income tax are the same as in Panel (5) of table 7.8.
5. Under the proportional labor income tax, additive and proportional tax adjustments are equivalent.

finance economists and significant progress has been made.[6] The final objective of this chapter is to employ our model of the U.S. economy to measure the social cost of different tax programs, including the existing tax law and alternative tax reform programs.

To fix ideas we first consider an economy with only two goods, say X and Y. Under the *reference tax policy*, only good X is taxed. In figure 7.2 AD is the budget line of the consumer under the reference tax policy and AA is the budget line when there is no tax on good X. The consumer is in equilibrium at E^0 and the level of utility is U^0. The line LL passes through E^0 and is parallel to AA. Therefore LL represents the locus of points with equal tax revenue at prices before taxes. It may also be interpreted as the budget line of the consumer under a lump sum tax that generates the same revenue as the reference tax policy.

Now, suppose that the government reduces the tax on good X. There are a number of budgetary alternatives we could consider. For example, the government could reduce expenditures, it could maintain the level of expenditures and finance the reduction in the tax revenues by issuing bonds, or it could introduce a new tax on good Y. In order to isolate the distorting effect of the tax on X, we hold the level

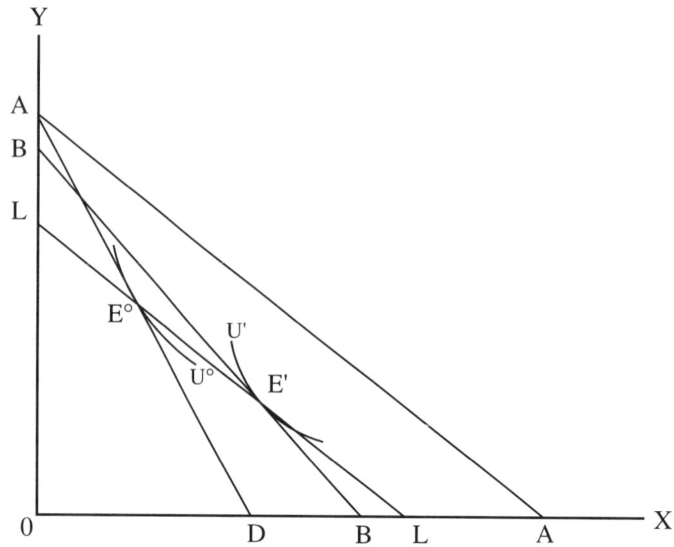

Figure 7.2
Efficiency cost of taxation.

of government expenditures constant and make up the lost revenue by levying a lump sum tax on the consumer. This is the *alternative tax policy*.

The alternative tax policy consists of a lower tax on good X and a lump sum tax. Under this policy consumer equilibrium is at E^1 in figure 7.2, where AB represents the lump sum tax and the indifference curve U^1 is tangent to the new budget constraint BB. At E^1 the consumer is enjoying a higher level of utility $(U^1 > U^0)$ and the government is collecting the same revenue as at E^0. The reduction of the tax on X has improved the efficiency of resource allocation and the welfare of the consumer.

Our objective is to measure the welfare loss attributable to the distorting tax on good X. Equivalently, we are interested in measuring the welfare gain achieved by replacing part of the tax on X with a lump sum tax. Let $e(P,U)$ be the expenditure function which gives the minimum amount of expenditure required to attain the utility level U at prices given by the vector P. Making use of the expenditure function we can measure the welfare cost of tax distortion in terms of either the Hicksian equivalent variation or compensating variation.

The equivalent variation, say EV, is the welfare cost attributable to the part of the tax we have replaced with a lump sum tax. This is implicitly defined by (with sign reversion) $U^1 = V(P^0, Y^0 + EV)$ or, equivalently,

$$Y^0 + EV = e(P^0, U^1), \tag{7.22}$$

where V is the indirect utility function and Y^0 equals OA in figure 7.2. Furthermore, $U^0 = V(P^0, Y^0)$, or:

$$Y^0 = e(P^0, U^0). \tag{7.23}$$

Combining (7.22) and (7.23), we have the equivalent variation, say EV:

$$EV = e(P^0, U^1) - e(P^0, U^0). \tag{7.24}$$

The equivalent variation EV is a money measure of the tax distortion, based on the prices under the reference tax policy. This is represented in figure 7.2 by the difference between the indifference curves U^1 and U^0.

Similarly, the compensating variation, say CV, is defined by (with sign reversion) $U^0 = V(P^1, Y^0 - TLUMP - CV)$, where $TLUMP$ equals the lump sum tax AB in figure 7.2. Equivalently,

$$CV = Y^0 - TLUMP - e(P^1, U^0)\,, \tag{7.25}$$

Since, from $U^1 = V(P^1, Y^0 - TLUMP)$ and $Y^0 - TLUMP = e(P^1, U^1)$, equation (7.25) can be rewritten as

$$CV = e(P^1, U^1) - e(P^1, U^0). \tag{7.26}$$

Equation (7.26) shows that CV is a money measure of the welfare cost of tax distortion, based on the prices under the alternative policy. Comparison of (7.25) and (7.26) confirms the well-known fact that the difference between EV and CV lies in the prices used in converting the utility measure into a money measure of welfare.

When we compare a single alternative policy with the reference policy, both the equivalent and the compensating variation give the same ranking. With more than one alternative policy to compare with the reference policy, only the equivalent variation gives a transitive ordering, since all comparisons involve prices under the reference policy. The compensating variation employs prices under each of the alternative policies and, hence, does not provide a transitive ordering. Therefore, we employ the equivalent variation in measuring the welfare effects of tax policy changes.[7]

Since the total revenue of the government is held constant, the reduction in the revenue from the distorting tax on X is precisely equal to the additional revenue from the lump sum tax, say TLUMP. Hence, we define the equivalent variation measure of the *average efficiency cost*, say AEC, per dollar of tax revenue replaced by the lump sum tax as:

$$AEC = \frac{EV}{TLUMP} . \tag{7.27}$$

Alternatively, if we consider a small change in the tax on X, we can measure the *marginal efficiency cost*, say MEC, of dollar of tax revenue, defined as

$$MEC = \frac{\Delta EV}{\Delta TLUMP} , \tag{7.28}$$

where ΔEV and $\Delta TLUMP$ denote changes in EV and $TLUMP$ corresponding to a small change in the rate of tax on good X.

Next, we generalize the above example to our dynamic general equilibrium model of the U.S. economy. First, we replace the expenditure function of the static model with the intertemporal expenditure function introduced in section 7.2. At the same time we replace the utility index by the intertemporal utility function of chapter 5. In order to assure transitivity of the welfare comparisons we evaluate the intertemporal expenditure function at the prices of full consumption under the reference tax policy.

We reduce tax rates in part or all of the tax system and employ lump sum tax adjustments so that the time paths of real government spending and government debt are unaffected by the tax reductions. Finally, to calculate the present value of lump sum taxes under the alternative tax policies, we convert these taxes into full consumption units. We add the time path of the taxes to the time path of full consumption under the reference policy. We employ the intertemporal expenditure function to evaluate the composite time path. The difference between the present value of the composite path and the time path of full consumption under the reference tax policy represents the present value of the lump sum taxes, discounted at the marginal rates of substitution of full consumption in different time periods.

The steps outlined above enable us to generalize the example of tax reduction in the static two-good model to our dynamic general equilibrium model of the U.S. economy. Using the intertemporal expenditure function (7.8), we can express the equivalent variation as:

$$EV = [W(D_0, V_1) - W(D_0, V_0)]PF_0 , \tag{7.29}$$

where V_1 and V_0 are the levels of intertemporal utility under the alternative and the reference policies, respectively, and all the other symbols are as defined in section 7.2. Similarly the present value of the stream of lump sum taxes can be calculated as

$$TLUMP = [W(D_0, V_2) - W(D_0, V_0)]PF_0 , \tag{7.30}$$

where V_2 is the level of intertemporal utility attainable with the composite path of the lump sum taxes and full consumption under the reference policy. As in the example of the static two-good model, we can define the *AEC* of the tax revenue raised by distorting taxes and replaced by the lump sum tax as:

$$AEC = \frac{EV}{TLUMP} , \tag{7.31}$$

where *EV* and *TLUMP* are defined by (7.29) and (7.30), respectively. Similarly, we can represent the *MEC* of the tax revenue raised by the distorting taxes as

$$MEC = \frac{\Delta EV}{\Delta TLUMP} . \tag{7.32}$$

7.6 Efficiency Costs under the 1996 Tax Law

In this section, we estimate the efficiency costs for various components of the U.S. tax system under the 1996 Tax Law and for several fundamental tax reforms. For this purpose, we employ our dynamic general equilibrium model to simulate the U.S. economy under hypothetical tax policies that replace parts of the U.S. tax system by a hypothetical nondistorting tax.

We carry out tax policy simulations for ten components of the U.S. tax system. The first is the corporate income tax. The second is capital income taxes at the individual level, including taxation of noncorporate capital income as well as the individual capital income originating from the corporate sector. The third is property taxes on corporate, noncorporate, and household assets. The fourth is capital income taxes at both the corporate and individual levels. The fifth is labor income taxes. The sixth is all taxes on capital and labor income. The seventh is the individual income tax. The eighth is sales taxes on consumption and investment goods. The ninth is the combination of all taxes, except property taxes. The tenth is all taxes.

The tax rates corresponding to each of the components of the tax system are (1) corporate tax rate (t_q), (2) marginal and average tax rates of individual capital income (t_q^e, t_m^e, t_h^e, t_q^d, t_m^d, t_h^d, t_g^d, t_e^a, t_d^a), (3) property tax rates in the corporate, noncorporate, and household sectors (t_q^p, t_m^p, t_h^p), (4) corporate income tax rate and the average and marginal tax rates on individual capital income, equivalent to the combination of (1) and (2), (5) average and marginal tax rates on labor income (t_L^m and t_L^a), (6) the combination of (4) and (5), (7) the combination of (2) and (5), (8) sales tax rates of consumption and investment goods (t_C and t_I), (9) the combination of (1), (2), (5) and (8), and finally, (10) the combination of (1), (2), (3), (5), and (8).

In each simulation we reduce the tax rates,[8] by five percent, ten percent, and then by ten percent intervals until the tax rates are reduced to zero. These reductions are distributed evenly, except for the first two reductions of five percent each. We then evaluate the *MEC* and *AEC* of raising tax revenues for all eleven reductions between the reference tax policy and the tax system with tax rates reduced to zero.

In the first set of simulations we evaluate the efficiency cost of U.S. tax policy under the tax law in 1996. We take tax policy under this law as the reference policy. We then lower the average and marginal tax rates sequentially. For each alternative tax policy we evaluate the *AEC* for the tax revenue replaced by a hypothetical nondistorting lump sum tax. Since the economy under the 1996 Tax Law is the reference, the present value of the stream of lump sum taxes is discounted at the marginal rate of substitution of full consumption between the initial time period and the relevant time period along the consumption path.

Table 7.10 and figure 7.3 present the *AEC* and *MEC* of the various parts of the U.S. tax system under the 1996 Tax Law. For example, in the case of corporate income tax, *MEC* is 0.279 when the corporate income tax rate is increased from 95% to 100% of their 1996 levels. This implies that if the government increases the corporate income tax rate proportionally, the burden to the economy in excess of the tax revenue is 27.9 cents per dollar of the extra tax revenue. Conversely, if the corporate tax rate is reduced by 5% and the revenue loss is made up for by lump sum tax, the economy will gain 27.9 cents per dollar of

Table 7.10
Efficiency cost of taxation in the United States: 1996 Tax Law

Taxes	Reduction in Tax Rates (%)										
	5	10	20	30	40	50	60	70	80	90	100
1. *Corporate Income Tax*											
MEC	0.279	0.273	0.264	0.254	0.245	0.237	0.229	0.222	0.216	0.211	0.205
AEC	0.279	0.276	0.270	0.266	0.261	0.257	0.254	0.250	0.247	0.245	0.242
2. *Individual Capital Income Tax*											
MEC	0.257	0.251	0.241	0.230	0.219	0.208	0.198	0.188	0.178	0.169	0.160
AEC	0.257	0.254	0.248	0.242	0.236	0.231	0.226	0.221	0.216	0.211	0.206
3. *Property Tax*											
MEC	0.139	0.137	0.135	0.133	0.130	0.128	0.125	0.123	0.120	0.118	0.115
AEC	0.139	0.138	0.137	0.135	0.134	0.133	0.132	0.130	0.129	0.128	0.126
4. *Capital Income Tax*											
MEC	0.264	0.253	0.238	0.219	0.202	0.185	0.170	0.156	0.142	0.130	0.118
AEC	0.264	0.259	0.249	0.239	0.231	0.223	0.215	0.208	0.201	0.195	0.189
5. *Labor Income Tax*											
MEC	0.404	0.384	0.357	0.323	0.293	0.265	0.240	0.218	0.198	0.179	0.162
AEC	0.404	0.394	0.375	0.358	0.342	0.328	0.314	0.301	0.289	0.277	0.267

Table 7.10 (continued)

Taxes	Reduction in Tax Rates (%)										
	5	10	20	30	40	50	60	70	80	90	100
6. *Capital and Labor Income Tax* (1 + 2 + 5 = 4 + 5)											
MEC	0.334	0.314	0.287	0.252	0.221	0.191	0.164	0.139	0.115	0.093	0.073
AEC	0.334	0.324	0.306	0.289	0.273	0.258	0.244	0.231	0.218	0.206	0.195
7. *Individual Income Tax*											
MEC	0.352	0.333	0.307	0.274	0.244	0.216	0.189	0.165	0.142	0.120	0.100
AEC	0.352	0.343	0.325	0.308	0.293	0.278	0.264	0.251	0.239	0.227	0.215
8. *Sales Tax*											
MEC	0.175	0.176	0.173	0.170	0.166	0.163	0.159	0.156	0.153	0.149	0.146
AEC	0.175	0.175	0.174	0.173	0.171	0.169	0.168	0.166	0.164	0.163	0.161
9. *All Taxes, Except for Property Tax*											
MEC	0.291	0.274	0.246	0.211	0.180	0.150	0.123	0.099	0.076	0.055	0.035
AEC	0.291	0.283	0.264	0.247	0.231	0.216	0.202	0.189	0.176	0.164	0.153
10. *All Taxes*											
MEC	0.266	0.246	0.217	0.182	0.150	0.120	0.093	0.067	0.044	0.023	0.003
AEC	0.266	0.256	0.237	0.219	0.202	0.186	0.171	0.157	0.144	0.132	0.120

Note:
1. Inflation is fixed at 4% per year.

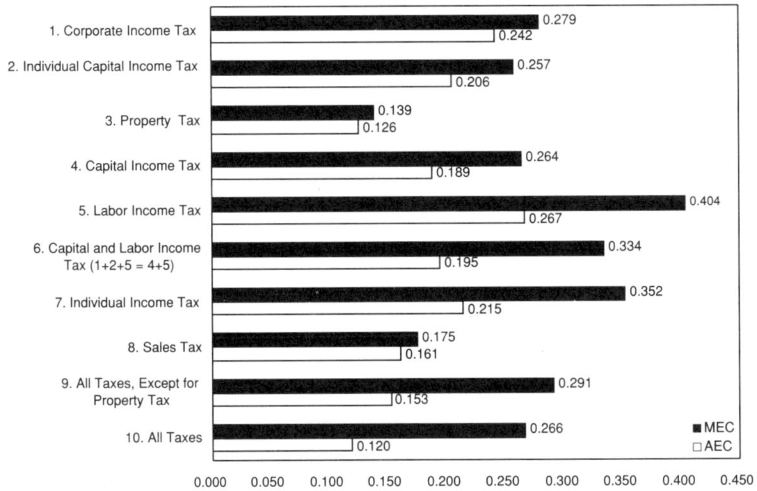

Figure 7.3
Efficiency cost of taxation in the United States: 1996 Tax Law.

the corporate income tax revenue which is replaced by the lump sum tax. Since the first column of table 7.10 represents the efficiency costs measured from the first tax reduction, the estimated *MEC* and *AEC* are the same. The *MEC* in figure 7.3 represents the marginal efficiency cost estimated from the first 5% tax reduction from the 1996 tax system (see *MEC* in column 1 of table 7.10).

Now consider the last column of table 7.10. For the corporate income tax, *MEC* is 0.205 meaning that the efficiency cost is 20.5 cents per dollar of tax revenue raised by increasing the tax rate from 0 to 10% of the 1996 levels. On the other hand that *AEC* is 0.242 implies that the efficiency cost is 24.2 cents per dollar for the entire revenue raised by the corporate income tax of 1996. To be precise, our measure of *AEC* may be referred to as the local *AEC* which includes the concepts of deadweight loss employed by Hausman (1981, 1985) and the average welfare cost of Ballard *et al.* (1985a,b) as special cases. In fact our measure of the *AEC*s in column 11 of table 7.10 are exactly the same as the concepts employed by Hausman and Ballard, *et al.* The *AEC* in figure 7.3 represents the average efficiency cost estimated from complete elimination of the relevant part of the 1996 tax system (see *AEC* in column 11 of table 7.10).

For the tax programs we consider the *MEC* declines with the size of tax reduction, so that the *MEC* is lower than the *AEC*, except for the first tax reduction in each set. In particular, the *MEC* of the actual tax system in column 1 is always greater than the *AEC* in column 11. This simply confirms the standard result that total welfare cost increases more than in proportional to the tax rate.

Second, except for the reduction of all the taxes, the *MEC* is substantially greater than zero, even when the relevant tax rates are close to zero.[9] For example, in the taxation of corporate income and individual capital income, the *MEC*s are 0.205 and 0.160, respectively, even when the tax rates are reduced to zero from 10% of the 1996 levels. This suggests that there are significant interactions between taxes in the allocation of resources. The *MEC* for mutually exclusive components of the tax system are not additive. The results of a partial equilibrium analysis of tax distortions can be grossly misleading. For example, starting with initial tax rates at ten percent of those under the 1996 tax system, the complete elimination of distorting taxes brings about a welfare gain of 0.3 cents per dollar of replaced revenue while the elimination of any subset of the taxes brings about much larger welfare gain per dollar of revenue reduction.[10]

Another example is the interaction between the taxation of capital and labor incomes. The *MEC* in column 11 are 0.118 for capital income and 0.162 for labor income. But the *MEC* of capital and labor incomes combined is only 0.073. Similarly, the *MEC* of the individual income tax (0.100) is smaller than those of individual capital income (0.160) and labor income (0.162) taxes. The *MEC* of a given set of taxes is likely to be higher if the rates of other taxes are higher. This underlines the importance of distortions due to other taxes in analyzing the welfare effects of a given subset of taxes.

The *MEC* of the entire U.S. tax system is 0.266, suggesting that there are large potential welfare gains to be realized through the reduction of marginal tax rates. In particular the *MEC* of labor income is as high as 40.4 cents per dollar of tax revenue, so that one dollar of revenue collected from individual labor income taxes incurs an additional burden of about 40 percent of the tax revenue.

The marginal efficiency cost of the labor income tax is considerably greater than might be implied by the marginal tax rate and the own- and cross-elasticities of labor supply. In table 7.10 the average and marginal tax rates on labor income are reduced in the same proportion, so that the welfare cost depends on the change in the average tax rate as well as the marginal rate. In the reference case the marginal and average tax rates on labor income are 0.264 and 0.127, respectively.[11] A ten percent reduction in these tax rates implies a cut of 2.64 percent for the marginal tax rate, but only 1.27 percent for the average tax rate. By contrast the individual marginal tax rates for corporate dividends and interest income are 0.202 and 0.182, respectively, while the average tax rate is 0.183 for both types of income. The marginal efficiency cost for taxation of labor income is higher due to greater progressivity.

To obtain additional perspectives on the efficiency costs of taxation and tax reform in the United States, it is useful to analyze the structure of efficiency costs of tax revenue for alternative tax systems. In particular, for a large-scale tax reform like the fundamental tax reforms we discuss in chapter 8, one may identify basic components of the proposal and evaluate their economic impacts individually or jointly. We shift our reference from the 1996 tax law to the tax policies of Panel 5 in table 7.8, where all interasset and intersector tax wedges for capital allocation are eliminated. We estimate the efficiency costs of taxation for two tax policy regimes, one of which is obtained by eliminating tax wedges for capital allocation under the additive adjustment of labor income tax and the other, under the proportional adjustment of labor income tax. To extend our analysis of the welfare cost of progressivity in labor income taxation, we also consider the tax policy regime where the capital income tax of panel 5 of table 7.8 is combined with a proportional tax on labor income.

The labor income tax rates of the tax policy regimes for which we estimate the efficiency costs of tax revenue are represented by the three sets of time paths of tax rates shown in table 7.11 and figure 7.4. All the other tax rates are the same as in the 1996 tax law. To reduce a subset of tax rates, we cut the relevant average and marginal tax rates and the investment tax credits by the same proportion throughout the transition period and in the steady state.

Tables 7.12a and 7.12b show the average and marginal efficiency costs of tax revenue for the tax systems with progressive labor income tax. Comparison of tables 7.12a and 7.12b with table 7.10 reveals that the *MEC* and *AEC* of corporate and individual capital income taxes are reduced dramatically by the elimination of interasset and intersector tax wedges for capital allocation. If labor income tax rates are adjusted additively for the reference tax policy regime, table 7.12a shows that *MEC* is reduced from 0.264 to 0.087 for capital income tax and from 0.266 to 0.197 for all taxes. If proportional tax adjustment is used for the reference tax policy regime, table 7.12b shows that *MEC* is

Table 7.11
Transition paths of labor income tax rates under efficient capital allocation

	Progressive Labor Tax				Proportional Labor Tax
	Additive		Proportional		Additive
Year	t_L^a	t_L^m	t_L^a	t_L^m	$t_L^a = t_L^m$
1	0.1210	0.2589	0.1198	0.2504	0.1033
2	0.1211	0.2590	0.1200	0.2507	0.1039
3	0.1212	0.2591	0.1201	0.2510	0.1044
4	0.1213	0.2592	0.1203	0.2513	0.1053
5	0.1213	0.2592	0.1204	0.2516	0.1053
6	0.1214	0.2593	0.1205	0.2518	0.1056
7	0.1215	0.2594	0.1206	0.2520	0.1060
8	0.1216	0.2595	0.1207	0.2522	0.1063
9	0.1216	0.2595	0.1208	0.2524	0.1066
10	0.1216	0.2595	0.1208	0.2526	0.1068
12	0.1216	0.2595	0.1209	0.2528	0.1072
14	0.1218	0.2597	0.1211	0.2530	0.1076
16	0.1219	0.2598	0.1212	0.2532	0.1079
18	0.1219	0.2599	0.1212	0.2533	0.1082
20	0.1219	0.2598	0.1213	0.2535	0.1084
25	0.1221	0.2600	0.1214	0.2637	0.1087
30	0.1221	0.2600	0.1214	0.2537	0.1091
35	0.1220	0.2599	0.1214	0.2537	0.1092
40	0.1221	0.2600	0.1214	0.2537	0.1094
45	0.1220	0.2599	0.1214	0.2536	0.1094
50	0.1219	0.2598	0.1213	0.2536	0.1094
60	0.1219	0.2598	0.1214	0.2536	0.1094
70	0.1220	0.2599	0.1213	0.2536	0.1094
80	0.1220	0.2599	0.1213	0.2536	0.1094
90	0.1220	0.2599	0.1213	0.2536	0.1094
100	0.1220	0.2599	0.1213	0.2536	0.1094

Notes:
1. All the other tax rates are the same as in the base case.
2. Under additive tax adjustment, the average and marginal tax rates are adjusted in the same percentage points. Under proportional tax adjustment, the average and marginal tax rates are adjusted in the same proportion.
3. Under proportional labor income tax, additive and proportional tax adjustments are equivalent.

Notations:
t_L^m: Marginal tax rate of labor income
t_L^a: Average tax rate of labor income

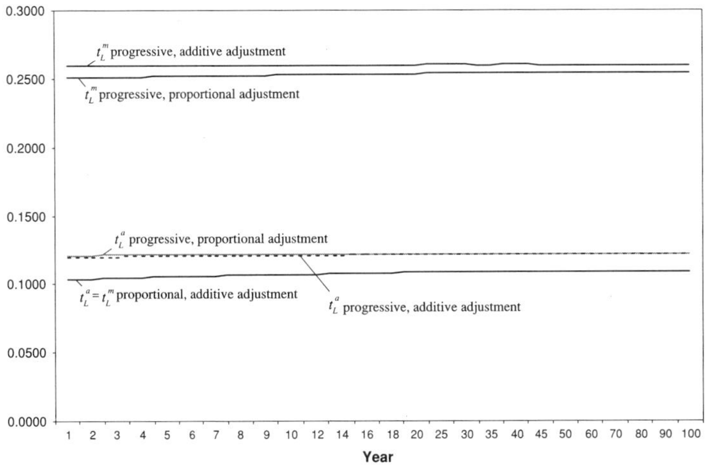

Figure 7.4
Transition paths of labor income tax rates under efficient capital allocation.

reduced from 0.264 to 0.085 for capital income tax and from 0.266 to 0.189 for all taxes. One interesting aspect of the simulation is that the *MEC* and *AEC* of corporate income tax increase with tax reduction as the simultaneous reduction of the tax rate and investment tax credit increase effective tax burden on corporate investment.

Table 7.12c shows the efficiency costs of tax revenues for the policy regime that combines capital income tax policy of Panel 5 of table 7.8 and the proportional labor income tax. The effects of flattening the labor income tax is striking. The *MEC* drops from 0.404 to 0.073 for labor income tax, and from 0.266 to 0.076 for all taxes. Figures 7.5 and 7.6 compare the marginal and average efficiency costs for the three tax policy regimes. For ease of comparison, we also present the *MEC* and *AEC* for the 1996 tax law.

7.7 Alternative Approaches

At this point we find it useful to compare our estimates of the *AEC* and the *MEC* with estimates obtained in other studies. Table 7.13 summarizes key features of the alternative approaches. It also gives the central estimates of the efficiency costs of distorting taxes obtained in previous studies.[12]

The studies of Browning (1976) and Hausman (1981) are based on partial equilibrium analysis and estimate the efficiency cost of taxes on

Table 7.12a
Efficiency cost of taxation: Efficient capital allocation with progressive labor income tax and additive labor tax adjustment

	Reduction in Tax Rates and Investment Tax Credits (%)										
Taxes	5	10	20	30	40	50	60	70	80	90	100
1.*Corporate Income Tax*											
MEC	0.149	0.150	0.150	0.150	0.151	0.152	0.153	0.154	0.156	0.157	0.158
AEC	0.149	0.149	0.149	0.150	0.150	0.151	0.151	0.152	0.152	0.153	0.154
2. *Individual Capital Income Tax*											
MEC	0.090	0.087	0.084	0.079	0.075	0.070	0.066	0.062	0.059	0.055	0.051
AEC	0.090	0.088	0.086	0.084	0.081	0.079	0.077	0.075	0.073	0.071	0.069
3. *Property Tax*											
MEC	0.124	0.123	0.121	0.118	0.114	0.111	0.108	0.105	0.102	0.099	0.095
AEC	0.124	0.124	0.122	0.121	0.119	0.117	0.116	0.114	0.113	0.111	0.109
4. *Capital Income Tax*											
MEC	0.087	0.084	0.080	0.075	0.070	0.066	0.062	0.057	0.053	0.049	0.046
AEC	0.087	0.086	0.083	0.080	0.078	0.075	0.073	0.071	0.069	0.067	0.065
5. *Labor Income Tax*											
MEC	0.368	0.348	0.321	0.287	0.255	0.227	0.200	0.176	0.154	0.134	0.115
AEC	0.368	0.358	0.339	0.322	0.306	0.291	0.276	0.263	0.250	0.238	0.227

Table 7.12a (continued)

	Reduction in Tax Rates and Investment Tax Credits (%)										
Taxes	5	10	20	30	40	50	60	70	80	90	100
6. *Capital and Labor Income Tax* (1 + 2 + 5 = 4 + 5)											
MEC	0.240	0.226	0.206	0.180	0.157	0.136	0.116	0.098	0.082	0.067	0.053
AEC	0.240	0.233	0.219	0.207	0.195	0.184	0.173	0.163	0.154	0.145	0.137
7. *Individual Income Tax*											
MEC	0.238	0.223	0.203	0.177	0.154	0.132	0.112	0.094	0.077	0.062	0.047
AEC	0.238	0.231	0.217	0.204	0.192	0.180	0.170	0.159	0.150	0.141	0.132
8. *Sales Tax*											
MEC	0.149	0.150	0.147	0.144	0.141	0.138	0.135	0.131	0.128	0.125	0.122
AEC	0.149	0.149	0.148	0.147	0.145	0.144	0.142	0.141	0.139	0.137	0.136
9. *All Taxes, Except for Property Tax*											
MEC	0.213	0.201	0.181	0.155	0.132	0.110	0.091	0.073	0.056	0.041	0.027
AEC	0.213	0.207	0.194	0.181	0.169	0.158	0.147	0.137	0.128	0.119	0.111
10. *All Taxes*											
MEC	0.197	0.182	0.161	0.135	0.111	0.088	0.068	0.049	0.031	0.016	0.002
AEC	0.197	0.190	0.176	0.162	0.150	0.138	0.126	0.115	0.105	0.096	0.087

Notes:
1. In the case of corporate income tax, #MEC# and #AEC# increase with tax reduction because proportional reduction of the tax rates and investment tax credit increases the tax burden on corporate capital.
2. Inflation is fixed at 4% per year.

Table 7.12b
Efficiency cost of taxation: Efficient capital allocation with progressive labor income tax and proportional labor tax adjustment

	Reduction in Tax Rates and Investment Tax Credits (%)										
Taxes	5	10	20	30	40	50	60	70	80	90	100
1. *Corporate Income Tax*											
MEC	0.146	0.147	0.147	0.148	0.149	0.150	0.151	0.152	0.154	0.155	0.156
AEC	0.146	0.147	0.147	0.148	0.148	0.148	0.149	0.150	0.150	0.151	0.151
2. *Individual Capital Income Tax*											
MEC	0.088	0.086	0.082	0.077	0.073	0.069	0.065	0.061	0.057	0.053	0.050
AEC	0.088	0.087	0.084	0.082	0.080	0.078	0.075	0.073	0.071	0.069	0.067
3. *Property Tax*											
MEC	0.123	0.121	0.119	0.116	0.113	0.110	0.107	0.103	0.100	0.097	0.094
AEC	0.123	0.122	0.120	0.119	0.117	0.116	0.114	0.113	0.111	0.109	0.108
4. *Capital Income Tax*											
MEC	0.085	0.083	0.079	0.073	0.069	0.064	0.060	0.056	0.052	0.048	0.044
AEC	0.085	0.084	0.081	0.079	0.076	0.074	0.072	0.069	0.067	0.065	0.063
5. *Labor Income Tax*											
MEC	0.347	0.329	0.304	0.272	0.243	0.217	0.192	0.170	0.149	0.130	0.112
AEC	0.347	0.338	0.321	0.305	0.290	0.276	0.262	0.250	0.238	0.227	0.216

Table 7.12b (continued)

Taxes	Reduction in Tax Rates and Investment Tax Credits (%)										
	5	10	20	30	40	50	60	70	80	90	100
6. *Capital and Labor Income Tax* (1+2+5 = 4+5)											
MEC	0.228	0.215	0.196	0.172	0.150	0.130	0.112	0.094	0.079	0.064	0.051
AEC	0.228	0.222	0.209	0.197	0.186	0.175	0.165	0.156	0.147	0.139	0.131
7. *Individual Income Tax*											
MEC	0.226	0.213	0.194	0.170	0.147	0.127	0.108	0.090	0.074	0.060	0.046
AEC	0.226	0.220	0.207	0.195	0.183	0.172	0.162	0.152	0.143	0.135	0.127
8. Sales Tax											
MEC	0.147	0.147	0.145	0.142	0.138	0.135	0.132	0.129	0.126	0.123	0.119
AEC	0.147	0.147	0.146	0.144	0.143	0.141	0.140	0.138	0.137	0.135	0.133
9. *All Taxes, Except for Property Tax*											
MEC	0.204	0.192	0.173	0.149	0.127	0.106	0.087	0.070	0.054	0.040	0.027
AEC	0.204	0.198	0.186	0.174	0.162	0.152	0.142	0.132	0.123	0.114	0.107
10. *All Taxes*											
MEC	0.189	0.175	0.155	0.130	0.107	0.085	0.065	0.047	0.030	0.015	0.002
AEC	0.189	0.182	0.169	0.156	0.144	0.132	0.121	0.111	0.101	0.092	0.084

Note: See table 7.12a.

Table 7.12c
Efficiency cost of taxation: Efficient capital allocation with proportional labor income tax and additive labor tax adjustment

	Reduction in Tax Rates and Investment Tax Credits (%)										
Taxes	5	10	20	30	40	50	60	70	80	90	100
1. *Corporate Income Tax*											
MEC	0.104	0.105	0.105	0.106	0.106	0.107	0.108	0.109	0.110	0.112	0.112
AEC	0.104	0.105	0.105	0.105	0.105	0.106	0.106	0.107	0.107	0.108	0.108
2. *Individual Capital Income Tax*											
MEC	0.057	0.055	0.051	0.047	0.043	0.039	0.035	0.031	0.028	0.024	0.021
AEC	0.057	0.056	0.054	0.051	0.049	0.047	0.045	0.043	0.041	0.039	0.038
3. *Property Tax*											
MEC	0.091	0.089	0.087	0.084	0.081	0.078	0.075	0.071	0.068	0.065	0.062
AEC	0.091	0.090	0.089	0.087	0.085	0.084	0.082	0.081	0.079	0.077	0.076
4. *Capital Income Tax*											
MEC	0.055	0.052	0.048	0.044	0.040	0.035	0.032	0.028	0.024	0.021	0.018
AEC	0.055	0.054	0.051	0.049	0.046	0.044	0.042	0.040	0.038	0.037	0.035
5. *Labor Income Tax*											
MEC	0.073	0.072	0.069	0.065	0.062	0.059	0.056	0.052	0.049	0.046	0.044
AEC	0.073	0.072	0.071	0.069	0.067	0.066	0.064	0.062	0.061	0.059	0.058

Table 7.12c (continued)

Taxes	Reduction in Tax Rates and Investment Tax Credits (%)										
	5	10	20	30	40	50	60	70	80	90	100
6. *Capital and Labor Income Tax* (1+2+5 = 4+5)											
MEC	0.065	0.062	0.057	0.052	0.046	0.041	0.037	0.032	0.028	0.024	0.020
AEC	0.065	0.063	0.060	0.057	0.055	0.052	0.050	0.047	0.045	0.043	0.041
7. *Individual Income Tax*											
MEC	0.066	0.062	0.058	0.052	0.047	0.041	0.037	0.032	0.027	0.023	0.019
AEC	0.066	0.064	0.061	0.058	0.055	0.053	0.050	0.047	0.045	0.043	0.040
8. *Sales Tax*											
MEC	0.100	0.100	0.098	0.095	0.092	0.090	0.087	0.084	0.081	0.078	0.075
AEC	0.100	0.100	0.099	0.098	0.097	0.095	0.094	0.092	0.091	0.089	0.088
9. *All Taxes, Except for Property Tax*											
MEC	0.072	0.070	0.064	0.056	0.049	0.042	0.036	0.030	0.025	0.020	0.015
AEC	0.072	0.071	0.067	0.064	0.060	0.057	0.053	0.050	0.047	0.044	0.041
10. *All Taxes*											
MEC	0.076	0.071	0.063	0.054	0.044	0.036	0.027	0.019	0.012	0.005	–0.002
AEC	0.076	0.073	0.068	0.063	0.059	0.054	0.049	0.045	0.041	0.037	0.033

Note: See table 7.12a.

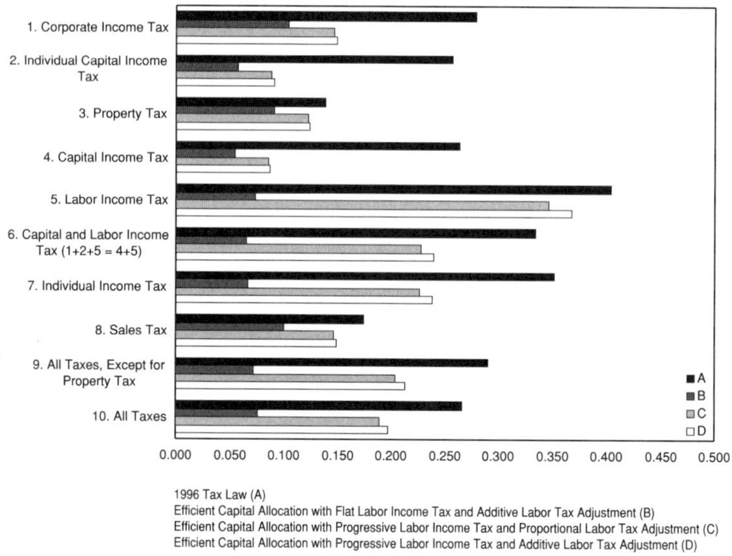

Figure 7.5
Marginal efficiency cost of taxation in the United States.

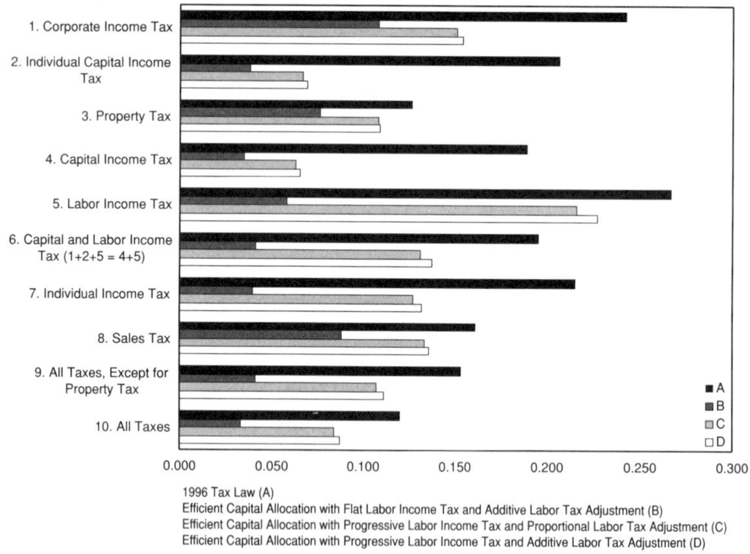

Figure 7.6
Average efficiency cost of taxation in the United States.

Table 7.13
Efficiency costs of taxation: Comparison with other studies

Author(s)	Key Features	Central Results
Browning (1976)	Partial equilibrium model (tax on labor, U.S.)	MEC = 0.09–0.16
Stuart (1984)	Simple static general general equilibrium model, (tax on labor, U.S.)	MEC = 0.207
Hausman (1981)	Partial equilibrium model (tax on labor, U.S.)	AEC = 0.221 for prime age male, 0.184 for wives
Ballard, Shoven and Whalley (1985a,b)	Dynamic general equilibrium model (U.S. tax system, 1973)	MEC = 0.332, AEC = 0.238 for the tax system
Hanson and Stuart (1985)	Two-sector static general equilibrium model, taxes on capital and labor (Sweden, marginal tax rate on labor is 0.7)	MEC = 0.69–1.29
Jorgenson and Yun	Dynamic general equilibrium model (U.S. tax system, 1996)	MEC = 0.266, AEC = 0.120 for the tax system MEC = 0.404, AEC = 0.267 for tax on labor

Note: Hausman's results are quoted from Hausman (1985).

labor income in the United States. Hausman estimates only the *AEC*. Stuart (1984) employs a static general equilibrium model to estimate the *MEC* of taxes on labor income in the United States. Similarly Hansson and Stuart (1985) use a static general equilibrium model to estimate the *MEC* of the Swedish tax system. In their study, the Swedish tax system is represented by separate taxes on capital and labor incomes and the average and marginal tax rates are carefully distinguished. Finally Ballard, Shoven and Whalley (BSW) use a dynamic general equilibrium model of the United States to estimate *MEC* (1985a) and *AEC* (1985b) of various components of the U.S. tax system.

Compared with the results of Browning (1976), Hausman (1981), and Stuart (1984) our estimates of the *AEC* (0.267) and the *MEC* (0.404) for taxes on labor income are higher. The differences can be attributed to many factors. Some of these include the differences in modeling the economy, the representation of the tax system, or the

Table 7.14
Comparison with Ballard-Shoven-Whalley

Author(s)	Taxes	MEC	AEC
Ballard, Shoven and Whalley 1985a,b)	all taxes	0.332	0.238
	capital taxes at industry level	0.463	0.355
	labor taxes at industry level	0.230	0.145
	consumer sales taxes	0.388	0.208
	sales taxes on commodities other than alcohol, tobacco, and gasoline	0.115	0.087
	income taxes	0.314	0.374
	output taxes	0.279	0.194
Jorgenson and Yun	all taxes	0.266	0.120
	corporate income tax	0.279	0.242
	capital income taxes, corporate and individual	0.264	0.189
	property taxes	0.139	0.126
	labor income tax	0.404	0.267
	sales tax	0.175	0.161
	individual income tax	0.352	0.215

selection of parameters describing substitution in consumption and production.

Another interesting comparison is between the results of our study and *BSW*, which is also based on a dynamic general equilibrium model of the United States. Table 7.14 compares our results with the central estimates of the *AEC* and *MEC* by *BSW*. Since the classifications of taxes in the two studies are different it is impossible to make a precise comparison. Overall, our estimates of the *AEC* and the *MEC* are lower than those of *BSW*. In particular, our estimate of the *MEC* and *AEC* of corporate income tax are 0.279 and 0.242, respectively, while estimates of the *MEC* and *AEC* for capital taxes at industry level by *BSW*[13] are 0.463 and 0.355, respectively. The differences in the estimated efficiency costs appear to be even larger when the taxes on capital income is defined to include both corporate income tax and taxes on capital income at the individual level. In this case, our estimates of the *MEC* and the *AEC* are 0.264 and 0.189, respectively.

BSWs estimates of the welfare costs of labor taxes at the industry level and our results for the labor income tax are not comparable. *BSW*'s labor taxes represent social security taxes, unemployment insurance, and workman's compensation, while our labor income tax represents the portion of individual income tax attributable to labor income. For the individual income tax, our estimate of the *MEC* is larger than of *BSW*, but our estimate of the *AEC* is smaller than that of *BSW*. It is surprising that the estimate of the *AEC* by *BSW* is larger than the estimate of the *MEC*.

Major differences between our study and that of *BSW* include the structure of models representing the economy, the treatment of the U.S. tax system, the choice of parameter values describing technology and preferences, and assumptions about expectations. It is difficult to allocate the differences between the estimates of efficiency costs among the many possible sources. However, differences between the treatments of the tax system appear to be an important factor in explaining differences between the estimated efficiency costs.

For example, *BSW* treat the corporate income tax as an *ad valorem* tax on capital inputs. They do not distinguish between the average and marginal tax rates and represent the individual income tax by a linear income tax. By contrast, we distinguish average and marginal tax rates for firms and individuals. We distinguish the average and marginal tax rates for firms by recognizing the difference between the effective marginal tax rates and the statutory tax rates. We model average income tax rates for individuals as part of the process for generating government revenues, while marginal tax rates are used in determining the relative prices at the relevant margins of substitution.

At the individual level we have separate average tax rates for labor income and capital income, and separate marginal tax rates for labor income, dividends, noncorporate equity income, interest income originating from the corporate, noncorporate, household, and goverment sectors, capital gains, and the marginal tax rates of the household equity owners. In addition, our representation of the economy and the tax system is designed to capture the major sources of tax distortions in the allocation of capital. As we have seen in chapter 4, the U.S. tax system derives large tax wedges between the short-lived and long-lived assets and between corporate, noncorporate, and household sectors. By ignoring interasset and intersector differences in the taxes on income from capital, *BSW* have left out these important tax wedges.

An important factor in measuring distortions in the allocation of labor is the compensated elasticity of labor supply. In the central case of *BSW*, the uncompensated elasticity of labor supply is 0.15. Since *BSW* do not report the income elasticity of labor supply, this cannot be compared with our estimate of the compensated elasticity of 0.31653.[14] Whatever the difference, the compensated elasticities of labor supply can explain only part of the differences in the estimated *AEC* and *MEC*. There are important interactions between labor supply and other parts of the economy and between taxes on labor income and other taxes.

Eliminating the intersectoral tax wedges between the assets in the corporate and noncorporate sectors may worsen the resource allocation if the wedges are removed through a intersectoral redistribution of the tax burdens. On the other hand, if the intersectoral tax wedges are removed through the reduction of tax burden on the corporate assets, substantial welfare gains are possible under the lump sum tax adjustment. However, under a more realistic distortionary tax adjustment, the welfare gains are much smaller. Much larger welfare gains can be attained if the tax burden of the business capital is redistributed evenly across all private capital. However there are many political and technical difficulties in redistributing the tax burden from business assets to household assets and thus such a reform remains only as a remote possibility.

Replacing the current income tax system with a consumption-based individual tax system may be more realistic strategy than equalizing the tax burdens between business and household assets. This still implies radical changes in the U.S. tax policy. Under the lump sum tax adjustment, replacing the current income tax system with a consumption-based tax system can generate a welfare gain in the range of $2,691.5–4,309.5 billion dollars. However, such a tax reform effectively excludes capital income from the tax base. Since lump sum taxes are not available, the welfare gain from switching from a income-based tax system to a consumption-based system would be substantially smaller.

In this chapter we have estimated the efficiency costs of various components of the U.S. tax system under the 1996 Tax Law and a number of hypothetical tax reforms. We find that the efficiency cost of taxation under the 1996 Tax Law is substantial. There still appear to be large potential welfare gains that could be exploited through tax reform aimed at lowering marginal tax rates.

The most important differences between our study and other studies are in the representation of the U.S. economy and the U.S. tax system. Our study differs in key parameter values describing producer and consumer behavior, in assumptions about expectations, in simulation methods, and in the definition of efficiency costs. Not surprisingly, our results are different from those obtained in other studies. Our conclusion that reducing marginal tax rates can bring about large welfare gains. is supported by estimates of the *MEC* by alternative approaches.

Notes

1. The elasticity of labor supply is typically estimated to be close to zero for primary workers, while the elasticity for secondary workers is close to unity. See Hausman (1981, 1985). For the effects of recent tax reforms on labor supply, see Eissa (1996).
2. The quantity indexes are implicitly defined by *VKL* = *KL*. *PKL*, *VGL* = *GL*. *PGL*, and *VRL* = *RL*. *PRL*
3. For a systematic treatment of the multiple shooting technique, see Lipton, Poterba, Sachs, and Summers (1982).
4. In the appendix to chapter 8, we compare the base case transition paths of these endogenous variables with those for alternative tax policies. We also compare the steady-state values of tax parameters and other selected variables for the base case and alternative tax policies. See tables A8.1, A8.2, A8.7–A8.10 and figures A8.1–A8.4.
5. Diamond and Mirrlees (1971a,b), Stiglitz and Dasgupta (1971).
6. Harberger (1966), Diamond and McFadden (1974), Kay (1980), Browning (1976), Stuart (1984), Ballard *et al.* (1985a), Hansson and Stuart (1985), Shoven (1976), Triest (1990), Mayshar (1990, 1991), and Fullerton (1991).
7. See Kay (1980).
8. When the corporate income tax is reduced, we also reduce the tax credits on corporate investment in the same proportion. Similarly, when the capital income tax at the individual level is reduced, we reduce the tax credits on noncorporate investments in the same proportion.
9. See column 11.
10. See the *MEC* in column 11 of table 7.10.
11. See table 7.1.
12. In this section, the *AEC* of our study refers to the average efficiency cost of the revenue raised by the taxes in question. Estimates for our study are from column 11 of table 7.10.
13. In BSW, capital taxes at industry level include corporate taxes, corporate franchise taxes, and property taxes on business capital.
14. See table 6.11.

Appendix

Table A7.1
Dynamic paths of variables controlled across simulations (billions of units)

YEAR	GS	GL	RL
1	1298.7	3783.6	291.4
2	1300.8	3714.5	304.0
3	1302.9	3645.5	316.6
4	1304.8	3576.4	329.2
5	1306.7	3507.4	341.8
6	1308.5	3438.3	354.4
7	1310.1	3369.3	367.0
8	1311.8	3300.3	379.6
9	1313.3	3231.2	392.2
10	1314.8	3162.2	404.8
11	1316.3	3093.1	417.4
12	1317.6	3024.1	430.0
13	1318.9	2955.0	442.6
14	1320.3	2886.0	455.2
15	1321.6	2816.9	467.8
16	1322.8	2747.9	480.4
17	1324.0	2678.8	493.0
18	1325.2	2609.8	505.6
19	1326.3	2540.7	518.2
20	1327.5	2471.7	530.8
21	1328.6	2402.6	543.4
22	1329.6	2333.6	556.0
23	1330.7	2264.6	568.5
24	1331.7	2195.5	581.1
25	1332.8	2126.5	593.7
26	1333.8	2057.4	606.3
28	1335.7	1919.3	631.5
30	1374.2	1781.2	656.7
32	1375.4	1712.2	669.3
34	1376.5	1643.1	681.9
36	1377.6	1574.1	694.5
38	1378.6	1505.0	707.1
40	1416.1	1436.0	719.7
42	1416.4	1436.0	719.7
44	1416.6	1436.0	719.7
46	1416.8	1436.0	719.7
48	1417.0	1436.0	719.7
50	1417.1	1436.0	719.7
55	1417.4	1436.0	719.7
60	1417.5	1436.0	719.7
65	1417.6	1436.0	719.7
70	1417.7	1436.0	719.7
75	1417.7	1436.0	719.7

Table A7.1 (continued)

YEAR	GS	GL	RL
80	1417.7	1436.0	719.7
85	1417.7	1436.0	719.7
90	1417.6	1436.0	719.7
95	1417.7	1436.0	719.7
100	1417.7	1436.0	719.7

Notes:
1. The variables are generated in the simulation under the 1996 laws, the reference case.
GS — Real government spending
GL — Real government debt, beginning of the period
RL — Real claims on the rest of the world, beginning of the period

Table A7.2
Dynamic paths of selected variables: Base case (billions of units)

YEAR	GDP	F	L	KL1	r^P
1	7165.3	14740	4175.1	25847	0.039762
2	7166.0	14727	4183.9	25751	0.040148
3	7166.4	14715	4191.9	25663	0.040503
4	7166.7	14704	4199.3	25584	0.040827
5	7166.8	14694	4206.1	25512	0.041125
6	7166.8	14685	4212.4	25447	0.041398
7	7166.6	14676	4218.1	25388	0.041647
8	7166.3	14669	4223.4	25334	0.041875
9	7165.9	14661	4228.3	25286	0.042084
10	7165.4	14655	4232.7	25242	0.042274
11	7164.8	14649	4236.9	25203	0.042447
12	7163.9	14644	4240.7	25167	0.042605
13	7163.2	14639	4244.2	25134	0.042749
14	7162.6	14634	4247.4	25105	0.042879
15	7161.7	14630	4250.4	25079	0.042997
16	7160.7	14626	4253.2	25056	0.043103
17	7159.6	14623	4255.8	25035	0.043199
18	7158.5	14620	4258.2	25016	0.043285
19	7157.3	14617	4260.4	25000	0.043361
20	7156.0	14614	4262.5	24985	0.043429
21	7154.6	14612	4264.5	24972	0.043489
22	7153.2	14610	4266.3	24960	0.043540
23	7151.6	14608	4268.1	24951	0.043585
24	7150.0	14606	4269.8	24942	0.043621
25	7148.2	14603	4272.9	24929	0.043674
28	7142.1	14600	4275.8	24920	0.043698
30	7160.7	14584	4290.1	24915	0.043760
32	7159.0	14581	4292.7	24897	0.043841

Table A7.2 (continued)

YEAR	GDP	F	L	KL1	r^P
34	7157.0	14578	4295.0	24883	0.043898
36	7154.7	14576	4297.2	24872	0.043934
38	7151.9	14574	4299.2	24865	0.043948
40	7172.1	14559	4312.5	24861	0.044009
42	7172.2	14557	4314.2	24842	0.044095
44	7172.4	14554	4315.6	24826	0.044166
46	7172.4	14553	4316.7	24813	0.044224
48	7172.5	14551	4317.7	24802	0.044273
50	7172.6	14550	4318.5	24794	0.044313
55	7172.7	14548	4319.9	24778	0.044385
60	7172.7	14546	4320.8	24768	0.044429
65	7172.8	14545	4321.4	24762	0.044458
70	7172.8	14545	4321.7	24758	0.044475
75	7172.8	14545	4321.9	24756	0.044485
80	7172.8	14544	4322.0	24754	0.044491
85	7172.8	14544	4322.2	24753	0.044496
95	7172.7	14544	4322.2	24753	0.044496
100	7172.5	14544	4322.3	24753	0.044493

Notes:
1. The variables are generated in the simulation under the 1996 laws, the reference case.
GDP — Gross national product, nominal
F — Full consumption, real
L — Labor supply, real
KL1 — Total capital stock, beginning of the period, real
r^P — Real private rate of return, all assets

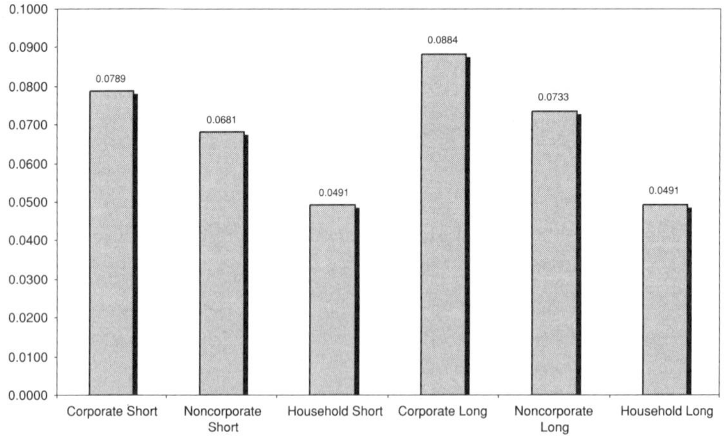

Figure A7.1a
Social rates of return: Base case.

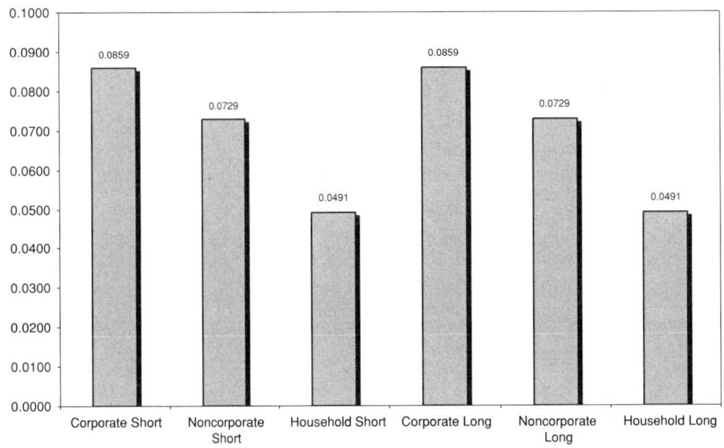

Figure A7.1b
Social rates of return. No interasset wedges: Corporate and noncorporate sectors.

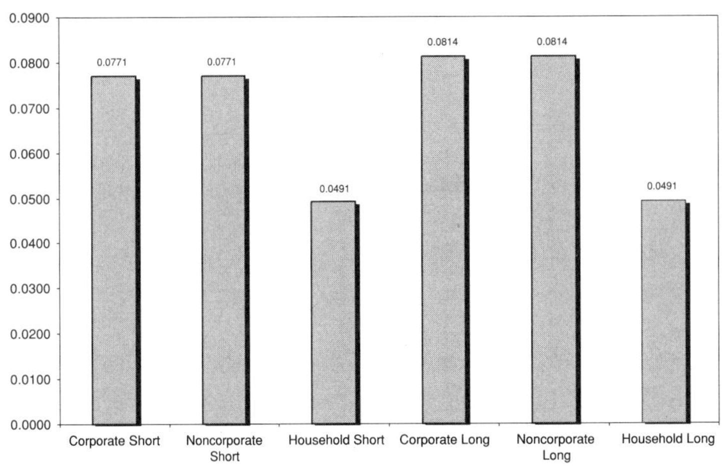

Figure A7.1c
Social rates of return. No intersector wedges: Corporate and noncorporate sectors.

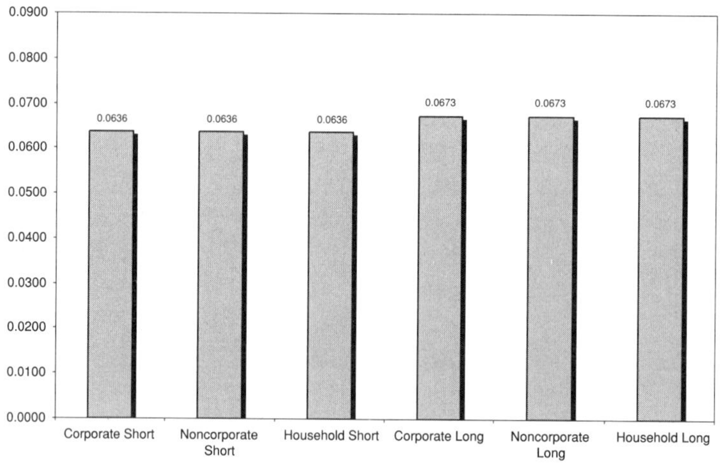

Figure A7.1d
Social rates of return. No intersector wedges: All sectors.

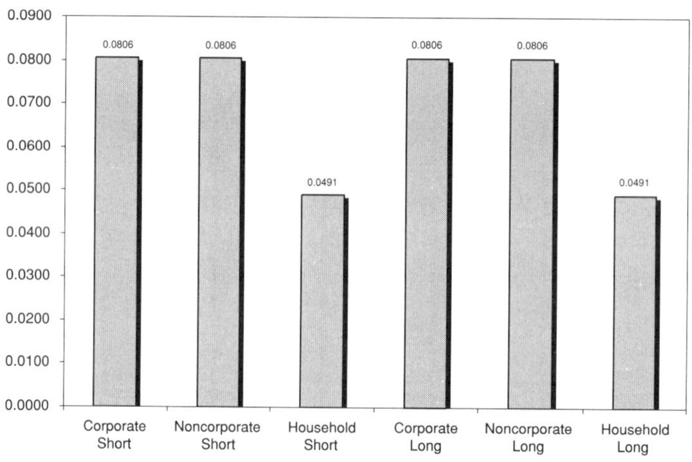

Figure A7.1e
Social rates of return. No interasset and intersector wedges: All assets, corporate and noncorporate sectors.

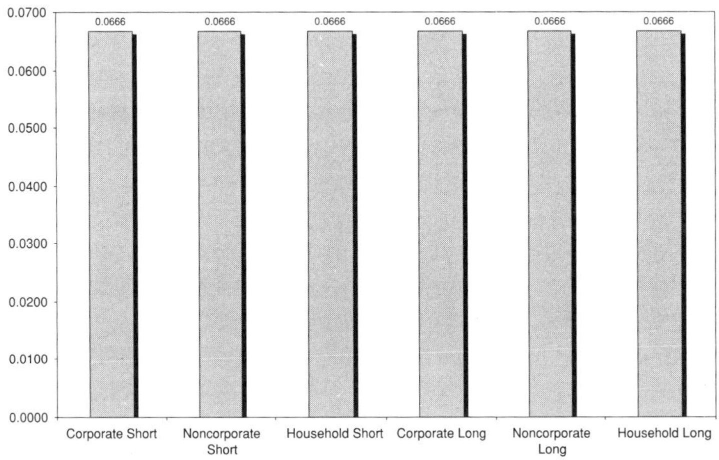

Figure A7.1f
Social rates of return. No interasset and intersector wedges: All assets, all sectors.

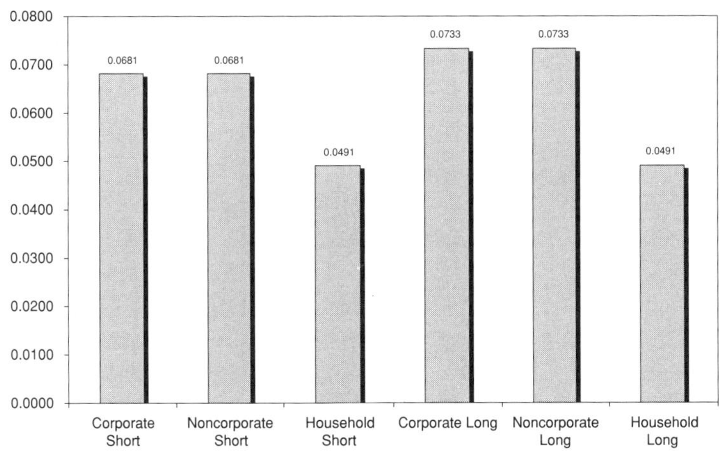

Figure A7.1g
Social rates of return. Corporate tax integration.

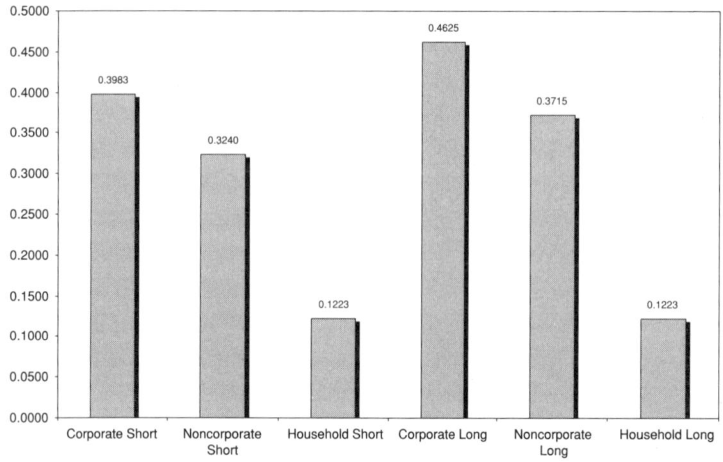

Figure A7.2a
Effective tax rates: Base case.

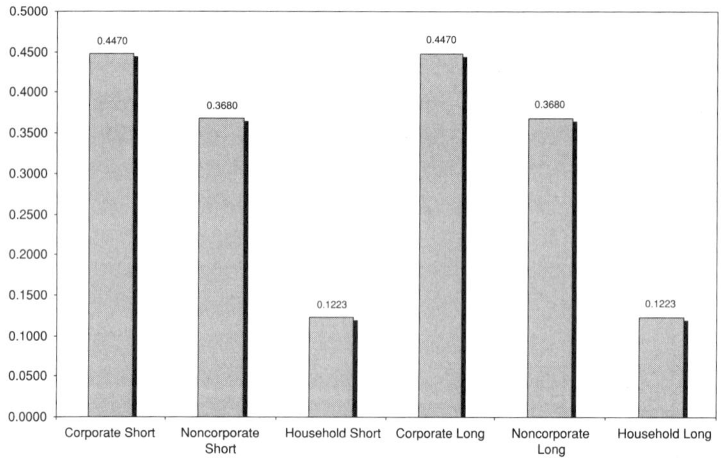

Figure A7.2b
Effective tax rates. No interasset wedges: Corporate and noncorporate sectors.

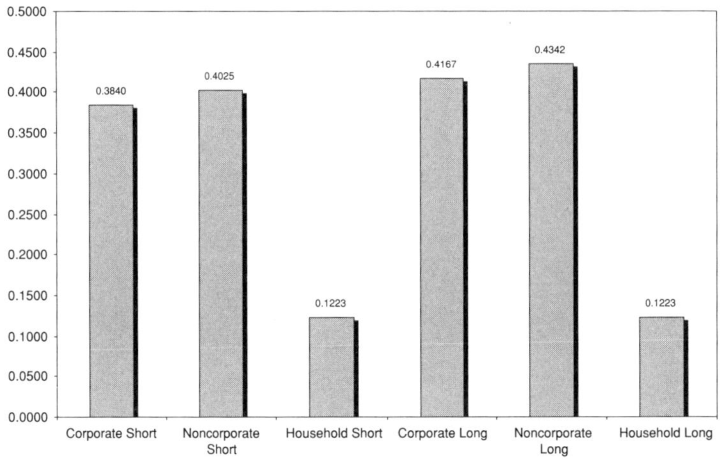

Figure A7.2c
Effective tax rates. No intersector wedges: Corporate and noncorporate sectors.

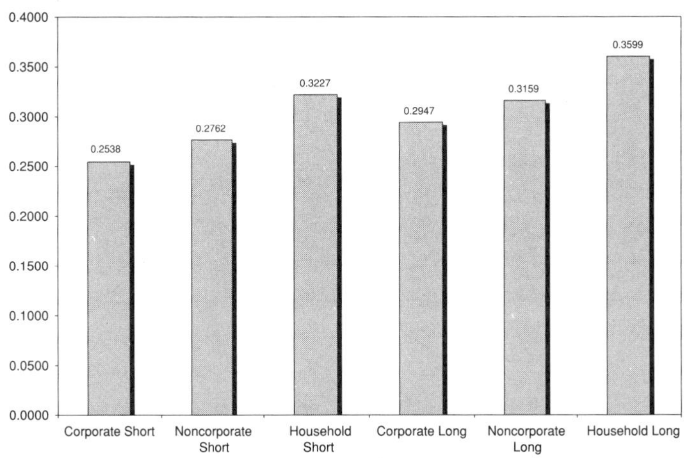

Figure A7.2d
Effective tax rates. No intersector wedges: All sectors.

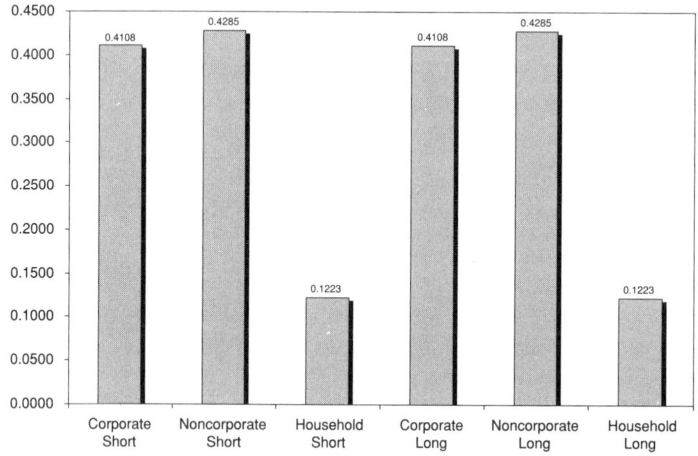

Figure A7.2e
Effective tax rates. No interasset and intersector wedges: All assets, corporate and noncorporate sectors.

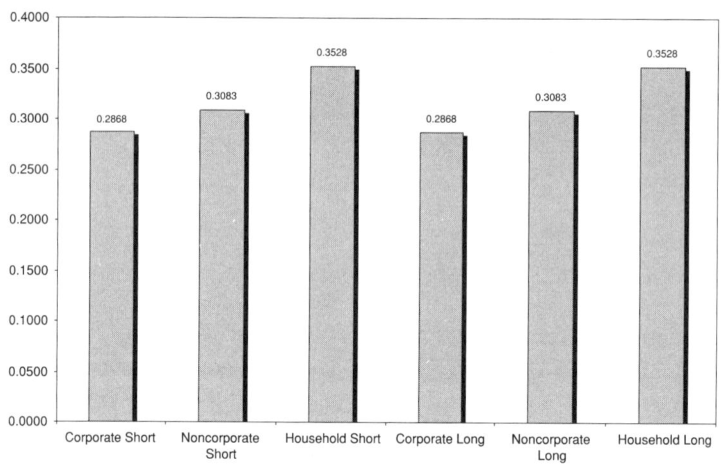

Figure A7.2f
Effective tax rates. No interasset and intersector wedges: All assets, all sectors.

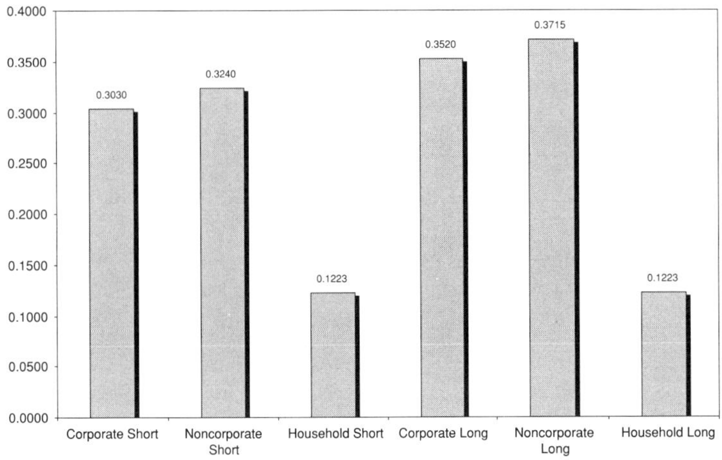

Figure A7.2g
Effective tax rates. Corporate tax integration.

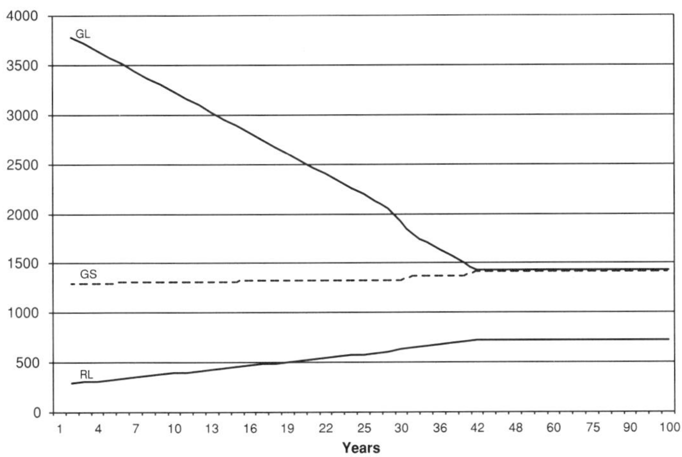

Figure A7.3
Dynamic paths of variables controlled across simulations.

8 Fundamental Tax Reform

We have considered the economic impacts of reforms of the U.S. system for capital income taxation in chapter 7. For this purpose we have simulated the effects of proposals that would equalize the burden of taxation among assets—plant, equipment, inventories, and land—among sectors—corporate and noncorporate business and households—and among all assets and all sectors. The welfare gains could be substantial, amounting to 1.7–2.0 trillion dollars or more than twenty percent of U.S. gross domestic product in 1997, the reference year for our simulations.

The largest gains from capital tax reform are associated with equalizing tax burdens on all assets and all sectors. These gains produce a better balance of the tax burden between household assets, especially owner-occupied residential real estate, and business assets, especially plant and equipment in the corporate sector. We have considered only tax reforms that are *revenue neutral* in the sense that the time path of the government deficit is the same before and after the reform. This implies that revenues lost by lowering taxes on some assets are precisely equal to revenues gained by raising taxes on others.

In this chapter we extend our investigations of reform of the U.S. tax system by simulating the economic impact of changing the base for taxation from income to consumption. This has been a major thrust of reform proposals considered by tax economists and tax policymakers in recent years. Substitution of consumption for income as a tax base would have the effect of eliminating capital income taxes altogether, so that tax burdens would be equalized among all assets and all sectors, as in the reforms we have considered in chapter 7. In addition, distortions of inter-temporal allocation, resulting from the tax wedge between earnings on investments and returns to savings, would be removed.

Three alternative methods for implementing a consumption tax have emerged, corresponding to three alternative and equivalent definitions of the concept of consumption. The first definition is the difference between value-added and investment, where value-added is the sum of capital and labor income. The second definition is the difference between business receipts and purchases from other businesses, including purchases of investment goods. The third definition is retail sales to consumers, including sales of services, consumers' durables, and new residential real estate.

The three principal methods for implementing a consumption tax correspond to the three definitions of the tax base:

1. *The subtraction method.* Business purchases from other businesses, including investment goods, would be subtracted from business receipts, including proceeds from the sale of assets. This method can be implemented within the framework of the existing U.S. tax system by first integrating individual and corporate taxes along the lines we have outlined in chapter 7. The second step would be to allow full expensing of the purchases of investment goods in the year they are acquired. If no business receipts were excluded and no deductions and tax credits were permitted, the tax return could be reduced to the now-familiar postcard size, as in the Flat Tax proposal of Hall and Rabushka (1995). Enforcement problems would be reduced by drastically simplifying the tax rules, but the principal method of enforcement, auditing of taxpayer records by the Internal Revenue Service, would remain unchanged.

2. *The credit method.* Business purchases would produce a credit against tax liabilities for value-added taxes paid on goods and services received. This method is used in Canada and all European countries that impose a value-added tax. From the point of view of tax administration, the credit method has the advantage that both purchases and sales generate records of all tax credits. The idea of substituting a value-added tax for existing income taxes would be an innovation, since European and Canadian value-added taxes were added to preexisting income taxes. In Canada and many other countries, the value-added tax replaced an earlier and more complex system of retail and wholesale sales taxes. The credit method would require substantial modification of U.S. tax collection procedures, but decades of experience in Europe have ironed out many of the wrinkles.

3. *National retail sales tax.* Like state sales taxes, a national retail sales

tax would be collected by retail establishments, including service providers and real estate developers, possibly by subcontracting the actual collection to existing state agencies. Enforcement procedures would be similar to those used by the states and the Internal Revenue Service would be transformed into an agency that would subcontract collections. Alternatively, a new agency could be created for this purpose and the IRS abolished.

The crucial point is that all three methods for implementing a consumption tax are based on the same definition of the tax base. This greatly simplifies the task for tax analysis, since the economic impact is independent of the specific method of implementation. Furthermore, the alternative approaches have distinct advantages and disadvantages in terms of administrative feasibility and enforcement, so that the selection of the appropriate method could balance the economic impacts against the other criteria that are important in choosing a tax policy. Combinations of the different approaches could be considered as a means of achieving the most appropriate balance.

From the economic point of view, the definition of consumption is straightforward. A useful starting point is Personal Consumption Expenditures (PCE) as defined in the U.S. National Income and Product Accounts (NIPA). However, the taxation of services poses important administrative problems reviewed in the U.S. Treasury (1984) monograph on the value-added tax. First, PCE includes the rental equivalent value of owner-occupied housing, but does not include the services of consumers' durables. Both are substantial in magnitude, as we have seen in chapter 7, but could be taxed by the "prepayment method" described by Bradford (1986)[1]. In this approach, taxes on the consumption of services would be prepaid by including investment rather than consumption in the tax base.

The prepayment of taxes on services of owner-occupied housing would remove an important political obstacle to substitution of a consumption tax for existing income taxes. At the time the substitution takes place, all owner-occupiers would be treated as having prepaid all future taxes on the services of their dwellings. This is equivalent to excluding not only mortgage interest from the tax base, but also returns to equity, which might be taxed upon the sale of a residence with no corresponding purchase of residential property of equal or greater value. Of course, this argument is vulnerable to the specious criticism that home owners should be allowed to take the mortgage deduction twice—when they are deemed to have paid all future taxes and, again, when tax liabilities are actually assessed on the services of household capital.

Under the prepayment method, purchases of consumers' durables by households for their own use would be subject to tax. This would include automobiles, appliances, home furnishings, and the like. In addition, new construction of owner-occupied housing would be subject to tax, as would sales of existing renter-occupied housing to owner occupiers. These are politically sensitive issues and it is important to be clear about the implications of prepayment as the debate proceeds. Housing and consumers' durables must be included in the tax base in order to reap the substantial economic benefits of substituting consumption for income as a basis for taxation.

Other purchases of services that are especially problematical under a consumption tax would include services provided by nonprofit institutions, such as schools and colleges, hospitals, and religious and eleemosynary institutions. The traditional, tax-favored status of these forms of consumption would be tenaciously defended by recipients of the services and, even more tenaciously, by the providers. For example, elegant, and sometimes persuasive arguments can be made that schools and colleges provide services that represent investment in human capital rather than consumption. However, consumption of the resulting enhancements in human capital often takes the form of leisure time, which would remain the principal untaxed form of consumption. Taxes could be prepaid by including educational services in the tax base.

Finally, any definition of a consumption tax base must distinguish between consumption for personal and business purposes. Ongoing disputes over exclusion of home offices, business-provided automobiles, equipment, and clothing, as well as business-related lodging, entertainment, and meals would continue to plague tax officials, the entertainment and hospitality industries, and users of expense accounts. In short, substitution of a consumption tax for the existing income tax system would not eliminate the practical issues that arise from the necessity of distinguishing between business and personal activities in defining consumption. However, these issues are common to the two tax bases.

The first issue that will surface in the tax reform debate is *progressivity* or use of the tax system to redistribute economic resources. We consider alternative tax reform proposals that differ in their impact on the distribution of resources. However, our simulations are limited to the efficiency impacts of these proposals.[2] One of our most important findings is that redistribution through tax policy is very costly in terms of efficiency. Unfortunately, there is no agreed-upon economic methodology for trading off efficiency and equity. It is, nonetheless, important to quantify the impact of alternative tax policies on the efficiency of resource allocation.

The second issue to be debated is *fiscal federalism*, or the role of state and local governments. Since state and local income taxes usually employ the same tax bases as the corresponding federal taxes, it is reasonable to assume that the substitution of a consumption tax for income taxes at the federal level would be followed by similar substitutions at the state and local level. For simplicity, we consider the economic effect of substitutions at all levels simultaneously. Since an important advantage of fundamental tax reform is the possibility, at least at the outset, of radically simplifying tax rules, it makes little sense to assume that these rules would continue to govern state and local income taxes, even if federal income taxes were abolished.

The third issue in the debate will be the impact of the *federal deficit*. Nearly two decades of economic disputation over this issue have failed to produce a clear resolution. No doubt this dispute will continue to occupy the next generation of fiscal economists, as it has the previous generation. An effective device for insulating the discussion of fundamental tax reform from the budget debate is to limit consideration to revenue neutral proposals, as we did in chapter 7. This device was critical to the eventual enactment of the Tax Reform Act of 1986 and is, we believe, essential to progress in the debate over fundamental tax reform.

8.1 Tax Reform Proposals

The subtraction method for implementing a consumption tax is the basis for the ingenious Flat Tax proposed by Hall and Rabushka (1995). The Hall-Rabushka (HR) proposal divides tax collections between firms and households. Firms would expense the cost of all purchases from other businesses, including purchases of investment goods, as in the subtraction method for implementing a consumption tax. However, firms would also deduct all purchases of labor services, so that labor compensation—wages and salaries, health insurance, pension contributions, and other supplements—would be taxed at the individual level. This would permit the introduction of allowances for low-income taxpayers in order to redistribute economic resources through the Flat Tax.

Taxation of business firms under the HR proposal is different from the current income tax system in three ways. First, a flat rate is applied to the tax base, hence the identification of this proposal as the Flat Tax. Second, interest paid by the firm is treated as part of property income and is no longer deducted from the tax base. Third, investment spending is recovered through immediate write-offs rather than depreciation over time, so that the effective tax rate on capital is zero. The inclusion of interest payments in the tax base eliminates the differential tax treatment of debt and equity, insuring the financial neutrality of the tax system.

The federal tax rate proposed by HR is 19% for both businesses and individuals. However, if unused depreciation from capital accumulation predating the tax reform is allowed as a deduction from the tax base, the tax rate will rise to 20.1%. Personal allowances under the Hall-Rabushka proposal for 1995 are $16,500 for married taxpayers filing jointly, $14,000 for head of household, and $9,500 for single taxpayer. The allowance for each dependent is $4,500. A family of four with two adults filing jointly, for example, is entitled to a deduction of $25,500. Personal allowances are indexed to the Consumer Price Index (Hall-Rabushka, 1995, p. 144).

The Armey-Shelby (AS) proposal, introduced in the 104th Congress by Representative Dick Armey and Senator Richard Shelby, is best considered as a variant of the HR Flat Tax proposal. The principal differences between HR and AS are the Flat Tax rate and the level of personal allowances. The AS Flat Tax rate is 20% for the first two years and 17% thereafter. Compared with the HR tax rate of 19%, the AS rate is higher during the first two years by one percentage point, but lower by two percentage points thereafter. Personal allowances under AS are $21,400 for married taxpayers filing jointly, $14,000 for head of household, and $10,700 for single taxpayers. The allowance for each dependent is $5,000, so that a family of our with two adults filing jointly would be entitled to a deduction of $31,400.

The AS proposal is more generous to the taxpayer than the HR proposal in the sense that the Flat Tax rate is lower after the first two years and the family allowances are higher. The natural question is, would the AS proposal raise sufficient tax revenue to replace the income tax system? Since Hall and Rabushka have calibrated their proposal to the National Income and Product Accounts of 1993 and set the Flat Tax rate to make the HR proposal revenue neutral, it is clear that tax revenue under the AS would fall short of the level required for neutrality. We will show, however, that revenues raised under either Flat Tax proposal would be substantially below this level.

A proposal for replacing the income tax system with a National Retail Sales Tax has been introduced by Representatives Dan Schaefer, Bill Tauzin (ST), and others.[3] The ST proposal replaces personal and corporate income taxes, estate and gift taxes, and some excise taxes with a 15% national retail sales tax on a tax-inclusive consumption base. On this definition the tax base would include sales tax revenues as well as the value of retail sales to consumers. The tax rate would be lower on a tax-inclusive basis than a tax-exclusive basis, that is, where the sales tax base excludes the tax revenues. The tax rate under the ST proposal would be 17.6% on a tax-exclusive base. The ST proposal allows for a family consumption refund for qualified family units in order to redistribute economic resources.[4]

Americans for Fair Taxation (AFT) have advanced an alternative proposal for a National Retail Sales Tax. The AFT proposal replaces personal and corporate income taxes, estate and gift taxes, and the payroll tax with a 23% national retail sales tax on a tax-inclusive base similar to that of the ST proposal (29.9% on a tax exclusive base). The AFT proposal is more ambitious than the ST proposal in that it replaces the payroll tax, used to fund entitlements such as Social Security and Medicare, as well as the income tax system. This has two important implications. The first is that the unfunded liabilities of the entitlement systems would ultimately have to be funded through the sales tax. The second is that a revenue neutral tax rate would be very high.

Gale (1999) estimates that, assuming perfect compliance and no politically motivated erosion of the statutory tax base, the tax-exclusive sales tax rate has to be as high a 31.6% for the ST proposal and 53.6% for the AFT proposal to achieve revenue neutrality.[5] Comparison of these tax rates with the proposed rates of 17.6% and 29.9% reveals the dimensions of the potential revenue shortfall. Furthermore, if state and local income taxes are replaced along with the federal taxes, the tax rates have to be about 30% higher for the AFT proposal and 50% higher for the ST proposal.

A very high tax rate of the National Retail Sales Tax provides powerful incentives for tax evasion and renders effective tax administration difficult. Although it is possible to mitigate compliance problems, controlling the erosion of the tax base within a tolerable limit appears to be more problematical.[6] To achieve revenue neutrality through a National Retail Sales Tax, we consider a number of alternatives to the ST and AFT proposals. In all of these alternatives, the capital income tax would be eliminated. We construct a prototype NRST and then develop alternative proposals by varying the degree of progressivity and the division of revenues between a labor income tax and a sales tax. Both the sales tax and the labor income tax may be flat, that is, proportional to the tax base, or may be made progressive by introducing a system of family allowances.

8.2 Modeling the Tax Reform Proposals

We maintain the role of the property tax in the existing U.S. tax system in all of our simulations. However, we consider alternative treatments of existing sales taxes on consumption and investment goods. The key tax parameter of the HR and AS proposals is the Flat Tax rate. If investment is expensed, the effective tax rate on capital income is equal to zero, whatever the Flat Tax rate, so that the choice of this rate does not affect inter-temporal resource allocation. On the other hand, the Flat Tax rate plays a very important role in the labor-leisure choice of households. It also affects the tax burden on capital assets already accumulated at the time of the tax reform.

Provided that the value added by a business firm is greater than its compensation for labor input, the marginal and average tax rates are the same as the statutory flat rate. However, a large number of households are exempt from taxation due to personal allowances. For tax-exempt households, the average tax rate is zero and for most of them the marginal tax rate is zero as well. We represent the distribution of marginal tax rates between zero and the Flat Tax rate by the average marginal tax rate for labor income. At the same time, we measure the average tax burden on labor income by the average tax rate.

Under the HR proposal the statutory Flat Tax rate is 19%. Under the AS proposal a Flat Tax rate of 20% applies in the first two years after the tax reform, followed by a lower rate of 17% thereafter. These rates are chosen in order to replace federal tax revenues. In our model all three levels of government—federal, state, and local—are combined into a single government sector. If the federal income tax is replaced by a Flat Tax, we assume that the state and local income taxes are also replaced by a Flat Tax. In addition, we assume that the state and local

Flat Tax is deductible at the federal level. We then calibrate the Flat Tax system to the 1996 federal and state and local income tax revenues.

Specifically, we assume that the federal and state and local Flat Tax revenues are generated according to the equations

$$R_F^f = (B - R_F^s) \cdot t_F^f \tag{8.1}$$

$$R_F^s = B \cdot t_F^s \tag{8.2}$$

where B is the state and local flat tax base, t_F^f and t_F^s are the federal and the state and local Flat Tax rates and R_F^f and R_F^s are the corresponding tax revenues. The Flat Tax rate for the government sector, t_F, is defined as

$$t_F = t_F^s + t_F^f(1 - t_F^s) \tag{8.3}$$

where the expression in the parenthesis reflects the deduction of state and local taxes at the federal level.

Since the federal Flat Tax rate, t_F^f, is known, we first set federal and state and local revenues, R_F^f and R_F^s, equal to the federal and the state and local corporate income tax revenues of 1996, \$194.5 billion and \$34.5 billion, respectively. We then solve equations (8.1) and (8.2) for the state and local Flat Tax rate, t_F^s, and obtain the overall Flat Tax rate, t_F, from equation (8.3). The resulting Flat Tax rates are $t_F = 0.2164$ for the HR proposal and $t_F = 0.1943$ for the AS proposal. These rates may be compared with the corporate income tax rate $t_q = 0.3880$ at federal, state, and local levels, corresponding to the federal corporate income tax rate of 0.35 under the 1996 Tax Law.

The average marginal tax rate for labor income is defined as a weighted average of the marginal tax rates of individual taxpayers, where the share of labor income for each taxpayer in total labor income is used as the weight. The average tax rate is simply the total tax revenue divided by total labor income. Using the same National Income and Product Accounts for 1993 as Hall and Rabushka (1995, p. 57, table 3.1), we estimate that the average labor income tax rate is 0.0855 for the HR Flat Tax proposal.

In order to determine the average marginal tax rates for the HR and AS proposals on a consistent basis, we require the distribution of labor income by the marginal tax rate of the individual taxpayer. We use the 1996 Current Population Survey to estimate the average and the average marginal tax rates on labor income for both the HR and AS Flat Tax proposals.[7] We find that the average tax rates on labor income at the federal level, t_L^{af}, are 0.1232 for HR and 0.0961 for AS, and the corresponding average marginal tax rates, t_L^{mf}, are 0.1797 and 0.1551, respectively.

In order to determine the average marginal tax rate on labor income for the government sector as a whole, we follow the same procedure as in calculating the marginal rate t_F. In place of the corporate income tax revenues, we use the individual income tax revenues for 1996. The results are that the average marginal tax rate, t_L^m, is 0.2114 for HR and 0.1834 for AS. The corresponding figure for the Tax Law of 1996 is 0.2645. We could have used a similar approach for estimating the average tax rates for the government sector. However, in order to reflect the realities of tax administration, we estimate the average tax rate, t_L^a, as

$$t_L^a = \frac{t_L^{af} \cdot t_{P96}^a}{t_{P96}^{af}},$$

where t_{P96}^a is the average tax rate of individual income in 1996 and t_{P96}^{af} is the average federal tax rate on individual income in the same year.[8] Our estimate of t_L^a is 0.1202 for HR and 0.0938 for AS. These figures may be compared with the corresponding figure of 0.1266 for the 1996 Tax Law, or with the federal tax rate of 0.0855 estimated by Hall and Rabushka.

We can summarize the tax rates as follows:

Hall-Rabushka

Business tax rate, average and marginal: $t_F = 0.2164$

Labor income tax rate, marginal: $t_L^m = 0.2114$

Labor income tax rate, average: $t_L^a = 0.1202$

Armey-Shelby

Business tax rate, average and marginal: $t_F = 0.1943$

Labor income tax rate, marginal: $t_L^m = 0.1834$

Labor income tax rate, average: $t_L^a = 0.0938$

Tax Law of 1996

Corporate income tax rate: $t_q = 0.3880$

Labor income tax rate, marginal: $t_L^m = 0.2645$

Labor income tax rate, average: $t_L^a = 0.1266$

We develop a number of alternative plans for the NRST by combining a sales tax on consumption and a labor income tax. In all of the alternative plans the capital income tax is eliminated. Although the existing sales taxes on investment spending may or may not be abolished, we prefer the policies with no sales tax on investment. As before, property taxes are left unchanged in our simulations. The alternative proposals differ in progressivity. They also differ in the division of revenue-raising roles between the sales tax and the labor income tax. This division has the effect of altering the relative tax burden between labor income and capital accumulated prior to the tax reform.

In order to develop alternative plans, we first construct a prototype sales tax and a prototype labor income tax. The labor income tax is based on the HR Flat Tax proposal. The sales tax has a flat tax rate with personal exemptions. We set the proportion of total exemptions in retail sales equal to the proportion of total exemptions in HR, which is 0.3516. Assuming that the federal sales tax rate is 17% as in Aaron and Gale (1996), table 1.1, we estimate that the corresponding average tax rate is 11.02%. In order to represent the current sales taxes, used mainly by the state and local governments, we add a flat tax of 5.8% to the progressive tax system we have derived. At this point, we have a progressive NRST with a marginal tax rate of 22.80% and an average tax rate of 16.82%.

We construct eight alternative NRST plans. Each plan consists of two parts—a sales tax and a labor income tax. The first two plans are limited to a sales tax, while the last two consist of a labor income tax alone. Although these two plans are not sales taxes in the usual sense, they provide benchmarks for analyzing the effects of the NRST plans on resource allocation and economic welfare. We evaluate the efficiency of resource allocation under all of the eight plans. However, we consider plans involving a sales tax as the most interesting proposals for implementing the NRST.

In Plan 1, a progressive NRST replaces the capital and labor income taxes. Since the revenue requirement is very large in relation to the sales tax base, we start with tax rates twice as high as those of the prototype, that is

$$t_C = 2 * (0.17 + 0.058) = 0.4560 \text{ ,}$$

and

$$t_C^a = 2 * (0.1102 + 0.058) = 0.3365 ,$$
$$t_L^m = t_L^a = 0 ,$$

where t_C is the average marginal tax rate and t_C^a is the average tax rate. These sales tax rates serve as the starting values for our simulations and will be adjusted to meet the budget constraints of the government sector.

In Plan 2, we remove the progressivity from the sales tax of Plan 1 and set the marginal tax rate equal to the average tax rate, so that

$$t_C = t_C^a = 0.3365 ,$$
$$t_L^m = t_L^a = 0 .$$

In Plan 3, we introduce the prototype labor income tax from the HR Flat Tax proposal and combine it with the prototype sales tax with the progressivity removed. As a consequence, the sales tax is flat while the labor income tax has the same progressivity as HR. Compared with Plan 1, the role of the sales tax as an instrument for tax collection and redistribution is substantially reduced. Specifically, we set

$$t_C = t_L^a = 0.1682 ,$$
$$t_L^m = 0.2114 ,$$
$$t_L^a = 0.1202 .$$

In Plan 4, we replace the current income tax system with the combination of a flat sales tax and a flat labor income tax. Since no attempt is made to redistribute economic resources through the tax system, this plan may be politically unpopular. On the other hand, the efficiency loss is minimal. In this sense, Plan 4 provides a useful benchmark for the possible trade-offs between equity and efficiency. The sales tax rate is set at the average tax rate of the prototype NRST and the labor income tax rate is set at the average tax rate of the HR proposal, so that

$$t_C = t_C^a = 0.1682 ,$$
$$t_L^m = t_L^a = 0.1202 .$$

Plan 5 combines a progressive sales tax with a flat labor income tax. Although the sales tax redistributes economic resources, the revenue-raising function is shared with the flat labor tax and there is less redistribution than in Plan 1. The sales tax is the same as in the prototype sales tax plan and the rate of the labor income tax is set at the average tax rate of the HR proposal, so that

$$t_C = 0.2280 ,$$
$$t_C^a = 0.1682 ,$$
$$t_L^m = t_L^a = 0.1202 .$$

Plan 6 combines the prototype sales tax with the labor income tax of the HR proposal. Since both segments of the plan are progressive, the sacrifice of efficiency may be substantial. The tax parameters are

$$t_C = 0.2280 ,$$
$$t_C^a = 0.1682 ,$$
$$t_L^m = 0.2114 ,$$
$$t_L^a = 0.1202 .$$

In Plan 7, the labor income tax is flat and there is no sales tax. The average and the average marginal tax rates of labor income are equal. Since all the replacement tax revenue is raised by the tax on labor, we start with a labor income tax rate twice that of the HR Flat Tax proposal

$$t_C = t_C^a = 0 ,$$
$$t_L^m = t_L^a = 0.2404 .$$

Finally, in Plan 8, we introduce an element of progressivity into Plan 7 by setting the average marginal tax rate of labor income at the twice the level in the HR proposal

$$t_C = t_C^a = 0 ,$$
$$t_L^m = 0.4228 ,$$
$$t_L^a = 0.2404 .$$

Business investment is expensed in the HR and AS Flat Tax proposals. In the NRST proposals household investment is taxed as consumption, which may be interpreted as a prepayment of taxes on the services of household capital. To represent the Flat Tax proposals of HR and AS and the various NRST plans, we must determine the allocation of gross private investment among the three private sectors—corporate, noncorporate, and household. To determine the investment in each of these sectors, we first allocate the total value of net investment among the six asset categories in proportion to the capital stock. This is equivalent to assuming that the capital stocks in the three private sectors grow at the same rate.

Next we add the current value of economic depreciation to obtain the gross investment, VIG_i, in asset category i, so that

$$VIG_i = \left(\delta_i + \frac{VIN}{VK}\right)VK_i$$

where δ_i is the economic depreciation rate, VIN is the total value of net private investment, VK is the total current value of lagged private capital stock, and VK_i is the current value of lagged capital stock in asset category i. In this expression VIN and VK are defined as

$$VIN = (IS - IG - IR) \cdot PI - D$$
$$VK = VKL(1 + \pi)$$

where IS is the total supply of investment goods, IG is the government demand for investment goods, IR is the demand from the rest of the world, PI is the price of investment goods, and D is economic depreciation on private capital. In a steady state the allocation of gross investment across the asset categories takes a simpler form:

$$VIG_i = [(1 - \alpha_T)(1 + n) - (1 - \delta_i)]VK_i$$

where $-\alpha_T$ is the rate of technical change, and n is the growth rate of time endowment.

We preserve revenue neutrality by requiring the government sector to follow the same time paths of real spending and government debt under all the tax reform proposals. We also fix the time path of the claims on the rest of the world. These assumptions are necessary to separate the economic impacts of alternative tax policies from the effects of changes in the government budget and the balance of payments. Government revenues must be adjusted through changes in the tax policy instruments in order to satisfy the government budget constraints in every period along the transition path to a steady state.

In some simulations we take Flat Tax rate in the HR and AS proposals or the sales tax or labor income tax rates in the NRST plans to be fixed and vary other taxes in order to meet the government budget constraints. In other simulations we vary the tax rates themselves to meet these constraints, so that the rates we have derived serve only as starting values. For example, in the case of the HR and AS proposals, the simulation with adjustment of the Flat Tax rate, where t_F, t_L^m, and t_L^a are adjusted simultaneously and in the same proportion, will generate a configuration of the U.S. tax system that is revenue neutral. Similarly, in the analysis of an NRST plan, adjustment of the sales tax and the labor income tax rates achieves revenue neutrality. In the sales tax adjustment, t_C and t_C^a are adjusted in the same proportion; in the labor income tax adjustment, t_L^m and t_L^a are adjusted similarly.

In the HR and AS proposals the effective tax rate on investment is zero, reducing the tax wedge between returns to investors and earnings of savers. The remaining distortion at the inter-temporal margin of resource allocation is due to the property tax and the sales tax on investment goods. In the NRST all taxes on capital income are abolished and the sales tax on investment goods is abolished as well in some of the alternatives we consider. The only remaining source of inter-temporal distortions is the property tax. In our model the sales tax on investment goods affects the producer price of investment goods. Therefore, formulas for the cost of capital are not affected by the tax.

The price of capital services from one unit of capital, P_j, is:

$$P_j = \left[RD_j + \frac{1 - D \cdot t_F}{1 - t_F} \cdot t_s^P \right] \cdot q_j , \qquad j = QS, QL, MS, ML \tag{8.4}$$

$$P_j = [RD_j + (1 - D \cdot t_L^m) t_s^P] \cdot q_j , \qquad j = HS, HL \tag{8.5}$$

where RD is the gross discount rate, t_F is the Flat Tax rate, t_s^P is the property tax rate, q_j is the lagged price of a capital asset, the subscript j stands for the short-lived and long-lived assets in the corporate, noncorporate, and household sectors, and s stands for the three private sectors. Thus $s = q$ if $j = QS, QL$; $s = m$ if $j = MS, ML$; and $s = h$ if $j = HS, HL$. $D = 1$ if property tax is deductible and $D = 0$, otherwise.

In the HR and AS Flat Tax proposals, the labor income tax is the only tax, other than property tax, that is collected directly from the household sector. Hence, we allow the property tax as a deduction from labor income. The gross discount rate, RD_j, is defined as the sum of the after-tax real discount rate and the economic depreciation rate adjusted for inflation:

$$RD_j = (1-\beta_s)(\rho^e - \pi) + \beta_s(i-\pi) + (1+\pi)\delta_j\ , \quad j = QS, QL, MS, ML, HS, HL \text{ and } s = q, m, h \tag{8.6}$$

where ρ^e is the after-tax nominal rate of return to equity, i is the nominal interest rate, β_s is the debt/asset ratio, π is inflation rate, and δ_j is the rate of economic depreciation.

Equations (8.4)–(8.6) apply to the HR and AS proposals, as well as the NRST. However equation (8.5) must be interpreted with some care. Investment spending on household assets is included in the sales tax base under the NRST. The most important type of investment spending is the purchase of owner-occupied housing. We model the sales tax on household investment by imposing taxes on sales to the household sector. At the same time we increase the price of capital services by the amount of the sales tax. This treatment of the sales tax on household investment is equivalent to prepayment of the consumption tax on household capital services. Thus, we may interpret (8.5) as the "producer" price of household capital services, while the corresponding "consumer" price is defined as:

$$P_j^C = (1+t_C)[RD_j + t_h^P] \cdot q_j\ , \quad j = HS, HL \tag{8.5'}$$

where we set $D = 0$.

8.3 Welfare Impacts of Fundamental Tax Reform

Table 8.1 summarizes the key tax parameters of the fundamental tax reform proposals and tables 8.2a and 8.2b report the estimated welfare effects. In table 8.2a, we present two sets of results. In the first set of simulations the corporate and individual income taxes of 1996 are replaced by the HR or AS Flat Tax, while sales taxes on consumption and investment goods remain unchanged (column 2). In the second set of simulations we replace the sales taxes as well, so that $t_C = t_C^a = t_I = 0$ (column 3). In the second set of simulations, all the inter-temporal distortions, except for the property tax, are eliminated since $t_I = 0$.

With the initial Flat Tax rates both the HR and the AS proposals fall short of revenue neutrality. The welfare impact of these proposals depends on the tax instrument chosen for raising the necessary revenue. If sales taxes on consumption goods and investment goods are maintained, the welfare gains are in the ranges of \$2.06–3.64 trillion for HR and \$1.23–4.17 trillion for AS, measured in 1997 dollars.

Table 8.1
Tax parameters of fundamental tax reform proposals—Lump sum tax adjustment, central cases

Tax Reform Proposal	t_q or t_F	t_L^m	t_L^a	t_C	t_C^a	t_I
1. Base Case						
(1) Tax Law of 1996	0.3880	0.2645	0.1265	0.0580	0.0580	0.0580
2. Flat Tax						
(1) Hall-Rabushka	0.2164	0.2114	0.1202	0.0580	0.0580	0.0580
(2) Armey-Shelby	0.1943	0.1834	0.0938	0.0580	0.0580	0.0580
3. National Retail Sales Tax						
(1) Progressive Sales Tax and No Labor Income Tax	0.0	0.0	0.0	0.4560	0.3365	0.0
(2) Proportional Sales Tax and No Labor Income Tax	0.0	0.0	0.0	0.3365	0.3365	0.0
(3) Proportional Sales Tax and Progressive Labor Income Tax	0.0	0.2114	0.1202	0.1682	0.1682	0.0
(4) Proportional Sales Tax and Proportional Labor Income Tax	0.0	0.1202	0.1202	0.1682	0.1682	0.0
(5) Progressive Sales Tax and Proportional Labor Income Tax	0.0	0.1202	0.1202	0.2280	0.1682	0.0
(6) Progressive Sales Tax and Progressive Labor Income Tax	0.0	0.2114	0.1202	0.2280	0.1682	0.0
(7) No Sales Tax, Proportional Labor Income Tax	0.0	0.2404	0.2404	0.0	0.0	0.0
(8) No Sales Tax, Progressive Labor Income Tax	0.0	0.4228	0.2404	0.0	0.0	0.0

Notes:
1. In the central case, $t_C = t_C^a = t_I = 0.058$ for the flat tax (HR and AS), and $t_I = 0$ for the NRST.
2. In the cases of flat tax adjustment, the values of t_F, t_L^m, and t_L^a in the table are used as the starting values for iteration. Similarly for sales tax and labor income tax adjustment.

t_F: flat tax rate
t_L^m: average marginal tax rate of labor income
t_L^a: average tax rate on labor income
t_C: average marginal tax rate on retail sales
t_C^a: average tax rate on retail sales
t_I: sales tax rate on investment spending

Table 8.2a
Welfare effects of fundamental tax reform—Flat tax (billions of 1997 dollars)

Tax reform proposal and revenue adjustment	Welfare effect	
	$t_C = t_C^a = t_I = 0.058$	$t_C = t_C^a = t_I = 0$
1. *Hall-Rabushka*		
Lump sum tax	3637.3	4991.6
Flat tax	2056.2	814.9
Sales taxes	2582.2	—
Flat tax and sales taxes	2240.1	—
2. *Armey-Shelby*		
Lump sum tax	4173.0	5392.2
Flat tax	1229.3	–756.0
Sales taxes	2476.2	—
Flat tax and sales taxes	1772.7	—

Note: Inflation is fixed at 4% per year.
t_C: Marginal sales tax rate on consumption goods
t_C^a: Average sales tax rate on consumption goods
t_I: Flat sales tax rate on investment goods

Table 8.2b
Welfare effects of fundamental tax reform—National Retail Sales Tax (billions of 1997 dollars)

Tax reform proposal and revenue adjustment	Welfare effect	
	$t_I = 0.058$	$t_I = 0$
1. *Progressive Sales, no Labor Income Tax*		
Lump sum tax	1830.1	2583.9
Labor income tax	—	—
Sales taxes	3268.5	3323.6
Labor income tax and sales taxes	—	—
2. *Flat Sales, no Labor Income Tax*		
Lump sum tax	3500.8	4115.6
Labor income tax	—	—
Sales taxes	4540.8	4686.8
Labor income tax and sales taxes	—	—
3. *Flat Sales Tax, Progressive Labor Income Tax*		
Lump sum tax	1924.0	2678.3
Labor income tax	3413.0	3086.9
Sales taxes	2686.1	2871.3
Labor income tax and sales taxes	2992.9	2965.8

Table 8.2b (continued)

Tax reform proposal and revenue adjustment	Welfare effect	
	$t_I = 0.058$	$t_I = 0$
4. *Flat Sales, Flat Labor Income Tax*		
Lump sum tax	3838.3	4427.8
Labor income tax	4504.9	4697.3
Sales taxes	4545.5	4696.5
Labor income tax and sales taxes	4530.8	4697.3
5. *Progressive Sales Tax, Flat Labor Income Tax*		
Lump sum tax	2965.1	3633.8
Labor income tax	3666.8	3868.9
Sales taxes	3888.8	3946.0
Labor income tax and sales taxes	3796.9	3910.1
6. *Progressive Sales Tax, Progressive Labor Income Tax*		
Lump sum tax	769.3	1609.3
Labor income tax	2233.3	1802.7
Sales taxes	1694.0	1737.5
Labor income tax and sales taxes	1921.3	1766.5
7. *No Sales, Flat Labor Income Tax*		
Lump sum tax	4106.1	4664.3
Labor income tax	4354.6	4527.8
Sales taxes	—	—
Labor income tax and sales taxes	—	—
8. *No Sales, Progressive Labor Tax*		
Lump sum tax	–1806.8	–818.2
Labor income tax	-2869.3	–4447.9
Sales taxes	—	—
Labor income tax and sales taxes	—	—

Note: 1. Inflation is fixed at 4% per year.
t_I: Sales tax rate on investment goods

Converted into annual flows at the long run real private rate of return of 4.45%, the welfare gains are in the range of $92–162 billion for HR and $55–186 billion for AS.

The largest welfare gains are obtained when a lump sum tax is used to compensate for the revenue shortfall. Since the lump sum tax is not available in practice, the welfare gains for the lump sum tax adjustment may be interpreted as the potential gains in welfare from a Flat Tax proposal. If both income taxes and sales taxes are replaced by a Flat Tax and a lump sum tax is used to compensate for the revenue shortfall, the welfare gains are very substantial, $3.64 trillion for HR and $4.17 trillion for AS. If sales taxes, as well as corporate and individual income taxes, are replaced with a Flat Tax and a lump sum tax is used to raise the additional revenue, the gains are even larger, almost $5 trillion for HR and $5.39 trillion for AS.

The welfare gains from the Flat Tax proposals are lower when distorting taxes are increased to meet the revenue requirement. The actual welfare gain depends critically on the taxes that are replaced and the tax distortions introduced to meet the revenue requirement. If the Flat Tax rate is adjusted to make up the revenue shortfall, substitution of the HR Flat Tax for corporate and individual income taxes would produce a welfare gain of only $2.06 trillion. If sales taxes are also replaced the gain falls to $0.81 trillion. The corresponding welfare gains for the AS Flat Tax are $1.23 trillion for replacement of income taxes and a negative $0.76 trillion for replacement of sales taxes as well. These results imply that the distortions resulting from the Flat Tax are worse than those from the sales tax at the margin.

The most interesting cases in table 8.2a are the simulations where personal allowances are held fixed and the Flat Tax rate is adjusted to make up lost revenue. The welfare gains are $2.06 trillion for the HR proposal and $1.23 trillion for AS proposal. The reason for the relatively poor performance of the AS proposal is the higher marginal tax rate on labor.[9] Recall that that the HR proposal has a higher tax rate than the AS proposal. However, given the constraint imposed by fixed time paths of government debt and real government spending, the more generous personal allowances in the AS proposal imply a higher tax rate. This point is corroborated in table 8.3 and figures 8.1a and 8.1b, where the transition paths of the Flat Tax rate and the average and marginal tax rates of the labor income tax are given.[10]

Table 8.2b reports the welfare effects of the six plans for replacing the corporate and individual income taxes with an NRST and the two additional plans for replacing income taxes with a labor income tax. We present two sets of simulations—one with the sales tax on investment goods and the other without. First, note that the case without a sales tax on investment goods is more in the spirit of the NRST, which exempts sales of investment goods from taxation. Unsurprisingly, the cases with sales taxes on investment removed are generally more efficient than those with sales taxes unchanged ($t_I = 0.058$).

Second, in Plans 1 through 6 where a sales tax is included as a part of the replacement tax policy, the tax parameters in Panel 3 of table 8.1, together with sales taxes on investment goods ($t_I = 0.058$ or $t_I = 0$), generate revenue surpluses and require either a negative lump sum tax or a decrease in tax rates. This explains the fact that welfare

Table 8.3
Transition paths of tax rates: Flat taxes ($t_C = t_C^a = t_I = 0.058$)

	1. Hall-Rabushka				2. Armey-Shelby			
Year	t_F	t_L^a	t_L^m	ADJ	t_F	t_L^a	t_L^m	ADJ
1	0.2872	0.1595	0.2805	0.3273	0.3244	0.1566	0.3063	0.6699
2	0.2872	0.1595	0.2805	0.3272	0.3244	0.1566	0.3063	0.6700
3	0.2871	0.1595	0.2805	0.3270	0.3244	0.1566	0.3062	0.6698
4	0.2870	0.1594	0.2804	0.3266	0.3243	0.1565	0.3062	0.6694
5	0.2869	0.1594	0.2803	0.3260	0.3242	0.1565	0.3061	0.6688
6	0.2868	0.1593	0.2801	0.3254	0.3241	0.1564	0.3059	0.6680
7	0.2866	0.1592	0.2800	0.3246	0.3239	0.1563	0.3058	0.6672
8	0.2864	0.1591	0.2798	0.3237	0.3237	0.1562	0.3056	0.6661
9	0.2862	0.1590	0.2796	0.3227	0.3234	0.1561	0.3053	0.6649
10	0.2860	0.1589	0.2794	0.3217	0.3232	0.1560	0.3051	0.6637
12	0.2854	0.1586	0.2788	0.3192	0.3226	0.1557	0.3046	0.6606
14	0.2849	0.1583	0.2783	0.3167	0.3220	0.1554	0.3040	0.6576
16	0.2843	0.1579	0.2777	0.3139	0.3213	0.1551	0.3034	0.6541
18	0.2837	0.1576	0.2771	0.3109	0.3206	0.1548	0.3027	0.6504
20	0.2830	0.1572	0.2764	0.3078	0.3199	0.1544	0.3020	0.6465
25	0.2812	0.1562	0.2747	0.2997	0.3179	0.1534	0.3001	0.6364
30	0.2782	0.1545	0.2717	0.2857	0.3144	0.1518	0.2968	0.6185
35	0.2774	0.1541	0.2710	0.2822	0.3136	0.1514	0.2960	0.6142
40	0.2754	0.1530	0.2690	0.2729	0.3113	0.1502	0.2938	0.6022
45	0.2756	0.1531	0.2692	0.2738	0.3115	0.1504	0.2941	0.6035
50	0.2758	0.1532	0.2694	0.2745	0.3117	0.1504	0.2942	0.6042
60	0.2759	0.1532	0.2695	0.2751	0.3118	0.1505	0.2944	0.6050
70	0.2760	0.1533	0.2696	0.2753	0.3119	0.1505	0.2944	0.6053
80	0.2760	0.1533	0.2696	0.2754	0.3119	0.1505	0.2944	0.6054
90	0.2760	0.1533	0.2696	0.2753	0.3119	0.1505	0.2944	0.6053
100	0.2759	0.1532	0.2695	0.2749	0.3118	0.1505	0.2943	0.6048

Note: The flat tax rate is adjusted for revenue neutrality.
t_C: Marginal sales tax rate on consumption goods
t_C^a: Average sales tax rate on consumption goods
t_I: Sales tax rate on investment goods
t_F: Flat tax rate of the business sector
t_L^m: Marginal tax rate on labor income
t_L^a: Average tax rate on labor income
ADJ: Adjustment factor for tax rates

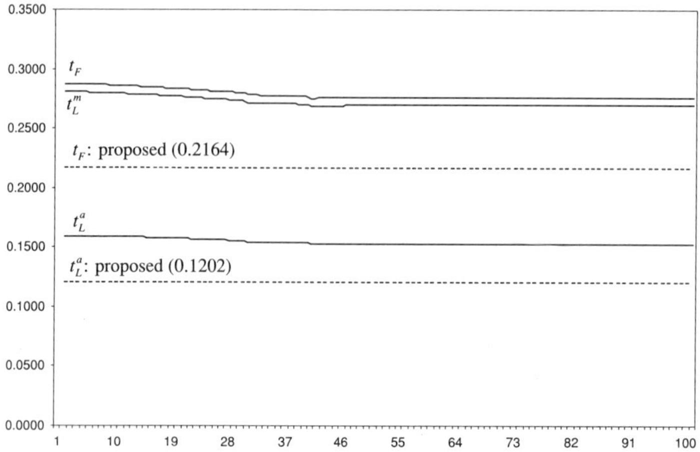

Notes: t_F: Flat tax rate; t_L^m: Marginal tax rate on labor income; t_L^a: Average tax rate on labor income. Sales taxes on consumption goods and investment goods are set at 5.8%. For calculation of the proposed tax rates, see text.

Figure 8.1a
Transition paths of tax rates: Flat tax, Hall-Rabushka.

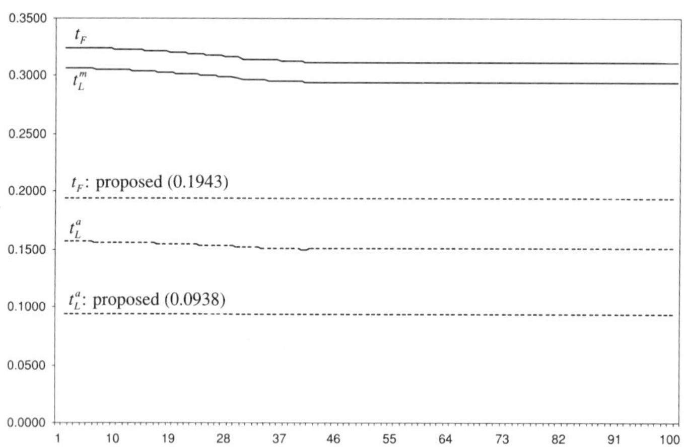

Notes: t_F: Flat tax rate; t_L^m : Marginal tax rate on labor income; t_L^a: Average tax rate on labor income. Sales taxes on consumption goods and investment goods are set at 5.8%. For calculation of the proposed tax rates, see text.

Figure 8.1b
Transition paths of tax rates: Flat tax, Armey-Shelby.

gains under the lump sum tax adjustment are lower than under other tax adjustments.[11] Third, except for Plan 8 and possibly for Plan 6, the welfare gains are impressive. Plan 4 with flat sales and labor income taxes and no tax on investment goods ($t_I = 0$) attains a welfare gain of $4.70 trillion, more than five times the corresponding gain for the HR Flat Tax proposal. However, Plan 2 and Plan 7 are not far behind in terms of gains in welfare. Finally, the welfare gains attainable with the progressive Plans 1, 3, 5 are also much higher than those of the HR and AS Flat Tax proposals.

A second set of comparisons that is highly relevant to deliberations about tax reform is the cost of progressivity. One of the most attractive features of the HR and AS Flat Tax proposals is the possibility of introducing a system of family allowances in order to preserve the important function of the existing U.S. tax system in redistributing economic resources. Plan 1 for the NRST also retains this feature of the tax system, but generates welfare gains of $3.32 trillion, exceeding those of the HR Flat Tax proposal by more than fifty percent. Of course, a sales tax can be employed to compensate for the revenue shortfall of the HR Flat Tax, reducing the difference between the welfare gains. However, the NRST is clearly superior to the Flat Tax as an approach to tax reform when both retain an element of progressivity.

The costs of progressivity can be ascertained by comparing the welfare gains between Plan 1, a progressive sales tax, with Plan 2, a flat sales tax. With no sales tax on investment goods and adjustment of the sales tax on consumption goods to achieve revenue neutrality, the gain in welfare from eliminating progressivity is $1.36 trillion, added to the welfare gain of a progressive sales tax of $3.32 trillion for an overall gain of $4.69 trillion. Similar comparisons can be made between Plan 3 with a flat sales tax and a progressive labor income tax and Plan 4 with flat sales and labor income taxes. The welfare gains from eliminating progressivity are $1.61 trillion when the labor income tax is used to achieve revenue neutrality and $1.83 trillion when the sales tax is used for this purpose. Other comparisons between progressive and flat versions of the NRST given in table 8.2b generate estimates of the cost of progressivity that are similar in magnitude.

Since taxes distort resource allocation, a critical requirement for a fair comparison among alternative tax reform proposals is that all proposals must raise the same amount of revenue. It is well known that the ST and AFT sales tax proposals fail to achieve revenue neutrality and tax rates must be increased substantially above the levels proposed by the authors of the plans.[12] The authors of the HR Flat Tax proposal have calibrated their tax rates to the National Income and Product Accounts for 1993 in such a way that the resulting tax regime is revenue neutral. It is clear that the AS proposal falls short of revenue neutrality because it is more generous in personal allowances and applies a lower tax rate than the HR proposal. As it turns out, however, the HR proposal also raises too little revenue to be neutral.

Based on the federal Flat Tax rate proposed by Hall and Rabushka, we have estimated three tax rates under the assumption that the state and local income taxes are also replaced by a Flat Tax. Specifically, we start with the Flat Tax rate $t_F = 0.2164$, the marginal tax rate on labor income $t_L^m = 0.2114$, and the average tax rate on labor income $t_L^a = 0.1202$ (see table 8.1). In order to meet the government sector revenue requirement, these tax rates must be increased by a factor of 0.27–0.33 (column 5, table 8.3). It follows that the statutory federal Flat Tax rate must be increased from 19% to 24–25%. The problem is even severer with the AS proposal, where the tax rates must be increased by a factor of 0.60–0.67 (column 9, table 8.3), implying that the proposed federal Flat Tax rate must be increased from 17% to 27–28%.

The need for a major upward adjustment in the Flat Tax rate conflicts with the fact that HR is originally designed to be revenue neutral. The explanation is that the data set employed by Hall and Rabushka, the U.S. National Income and Product Accounts of 1993, was generated under a tax system with a significant tax burden on capital.[13] Unsurprisingly, they found a large tax base in the business sector.[14] Although the Flat Tax imposes a lump sum tax on "old" capital accumulated before the tax reform, the Flat Tax does not impose any tax burden on "new" capital accumulated through investment after the reform. The tax base of the business portion of the tax shrinks dramatically and a large revenue shortfall emerges, requiring an increase in the Flat Tax rate.

In table 8.4 we report the transition paths of the tax rates for four NRST plans with no sales tax on investment goods ($t_I = 0$)—Plans 1,2 4, and 5. In addition, we present the transition paths of tax rates for plan 7. The transition paths of the tax rates are also shown in figures 8.2a and 8.2b. In order to make the plans revenue neutral, we adjust the sales tax rates of Plans 1 and 2 proportionally. For Plans 4 and 5, where the sales tax is combined with a flat labor income tax, the sales tax rate and the labor income tax rate are adjusted simultaneously and

Table 8.4
Transition paths of tax rates: National retail sales tax

	Plan 1. Progressive Sales Tax No Labor Income Tax ($t_F = t_L^a = t_L^m = t_I = 0.0$)		Plan 2. Flat Sales Tax No Labor Income Tax ($t_F = t_L^a = t_L^m = t_I = 0.0$)	Plan 4. Flat Sales Tax Flat Labor Income Tax ($t_F = t_I = 0.0$)	
Year	t_C^a	t_C	$t_C^a = t_C$	$t_L^a = t_L^m$	$t_C = t_C^a$
1	0.2976	0.4034	0.2874	0.1132	0.1585
2	0.2977	0.4035	0.2875	0.1132	0.1584
3	0.2978	0.4036	0.2875	0.1132	0.1584
4	0.2978	0.4036	0.2875	0.1131	0.1583
5	0.2978	0.4036	0.2874	0.1131	0.1583
6	0.2978	0.4036	0.2874	0.1131	0.1582
7	0.2977	0.4035	0.2873	0.1130	0.1582
8	0.2977	0.4034	0.2872	0.1130	0.1581
9	0.2976	0.4033	0.2871	0.1129	0.1580
10	0.2975	0.4032	0.2870	0.1128	0.1579
12	0.2972	0.4028	0.2867	0.1127	0.1577
14	0.2970	0.4025	0.2864	0.1125	0.1575
16	0.2966	0.4020	0.2861	0.1124	0.1573
18	0.2963	0.4015	0.2858	0.1122	0.1570
20	0.2959	0.4010	0.2854	0.1120	0.1568
25	0.2948	0.3996	0.2843	0.1115	0.1561
30	0.2948	0.3996	0.2843	0.1111	0.1555
35	0.2944	0.3990	0.2838	0.1109	0.1552
40	0.2951	0.4000	0.2844	0.1108	0.1550
45	0.2953	0.4003	0.2846	0.1108	0.1551
50	0.2954	0.4004	0.2847	0.1109	0.1552
60	0.2956	0.4006	0.2848	0.1109	0.1552
70	0.2956	0.4007	0.2849	0.1109	0.1553
80	0.2957	0.4007	0.2849	0.1109	0.1553
90	0.2956	0.4007	0.2849	0.1109	0.1552
100	0.2959	0.4011	0.2851	0.1110	0.1553

Note:
For revenue neutrality, the sales tax rate is adjusted for Plans 1 and 2. For Plans 4 and 5, both the sales tax and the labor income tax rates are adjusted in the same proportion.

Notations:
t_F: Flat tax rate of the business sector
t_L^m: Marginal tax rate on labor income
t_L^a: Average tax rate on labor income
t_C: Marginal sales tax rate on consumption goods
t_C^a: Average sales tax rate on consumption goods
t_I: Sales tax rate on investment goods

Table 8.4 (continued)

	Plan 5. Progressive Sales Tax Flat Labor Income Tax ($t_F = t_I = 0.0$)			Plan 7. Flat Labor Income Tax ($t_F = t_I = t_C^a = t_C = 0.0$)
Year	$t_L^a = t_L^m$	t_C^a	t_C	$t_L^a = t_L^m$
1	0.1153	0.1614	0.2188	0.2533
2	0.1153	0.1614	0.2188	0.2532
3	0.1153	0.1614	0.2187	0.2530
4	0.1153	0.1613	0.2187	0.2529
5	0.1153	0.1613	0.2186	0.2527
6	0.1152	0.1612	0.2186	0.2526
7	0.1152	0.1612	0.2185	0.2524
8	0.1151	0.1611	0.2184	0.2522
9	0.1151	0.1610	0.2183	0.2520
10	0.1150	0.1610	0.2182	0.2518
12	0.1149	0.1608	0.2179	0.2514
14	0.1147	0.1606	0.2176	0.2510
16	0.1146	0.1603	0.2173	0.2506
18	0.1144	0.1601	0.2170	0.2501
20	0.1142	0.1598	0.2167	0.2496
25	0.1137	0.1592	0.2157	0.2483
30	0.1133	0.1585	0.2149	0.2463
35	0.1131	0.1582	0.2145	0.2457
40	0.1129	0.1580	0.2142	0.2443
45	0.1130	0.1581	0.2144	0.2445
50	0.1131	0.1582	0.2144	0.2445
60	0.1131	0.1583	0.2145	0.2446
70	0.1131	0.1583	0.2146	0.2447
80	0.1131	0.1583	0.2146	0.2447
90	0.1131	0.1583	0.2146	0.2447
100	0.1132	0.1584	0.2146	0.2447

by the same proportion. For Plan 7, we adjust the labor income tax rates. In Plan 1, the closest to the ST version of the NRST, we find that the marginal tax rate must be raised to about 40% and the average tax rate to about 30%. By contrast, the sales tax rate proposed in ST is 15% on a tax-inclusive base, which is equivalent to 17.6% on a tax-exclusive basis.

We take the 1996 composition of the corporate and individual income tax revenues as the benchmark. We then multiply the ST tax rate by the ratio of the income tax revenues of the federal, state, and local governments to the revenues of the federal government alone to obtain the ST tax rate for the government sector. In 1996, corporate income taxes were $194.5 billion at the federal level and $34.5 billion

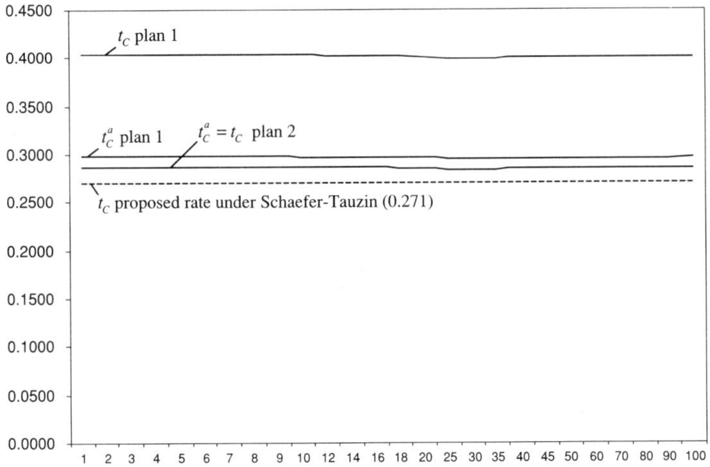

Notes: t_C : marginal sales tax; t_C^a: average sales tax
Plan 1: Progressive sales tax with no labor income tax.
Plan 2: Flat sales tax with no labor income tax.
The proposed marginal sales tax rate of 27.1% is obtained by adding the sales tax rate 5.8% of the 1996 tax system to the Schaefer-Tauzin sales tax rate of 21.3% intended to replace income taxes. We note however that the Schaefer-Tauzin proposal replaces estate and gift taxes and some excise taxes as well as income taxes.

Figure 8.2a
Transition paths of tax rates: Plans 1 and 2 of NRST.

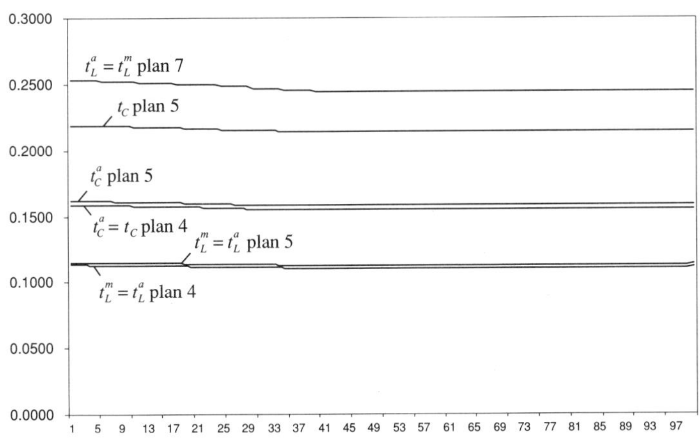

Notes: t_C: marginal sales tax; t_C^a: average sales tax; t_L^a: average tax rate on labor income; t_L^m: marginal tax rate on labor income.
Plan 4: flat sales tax and flat labor income tax.
Plan 5: progressive sales tax and flat labor income tax.
Plan 7: flat labor income tax with no sales tax.

Figure 8.2b
Transition paths of tax rates: Plans 4, 5, and 7 of NRST

at the state and local level. In the same year, individual income taxes were $666.7 billion at the federal level and $149.1 billion at the state and local level. We multiply the ST tax rate by 1.213 to obtain 21.3% ($= 17.6 * 1.213$) as the ST tax rate for the government sector on a tax-exclusive basis. We find that the ST tax rate is only about half the rate required for revenue neutrality. It is also lower than the revenue neutral average tax rates of Plan 1 and Plan 2 reported in table 8.4, suggesting strongly that the ST proposal falls far short of revenue neutrality.[15]

Sales tax rates decline slowly with time, reflecting the fact that capital stock grows in response to the elimination of income taxes on capital, raising output and, ultimately, consumption. We also note that the tax rate of Plan 2 is lower than the average tax rate of Plan 1 by about one percentage point, reflecting the greater efficiency of Plan 2. If the revenue-raising role is shared between the sales tax and the flat labor income tax, the required marginal sales tax rate is 15.5–15.9% for Plan 4 and 15.8–16.1 for Plan 5. The required average tax rate on labor income t_L^a, which is equal to the required marginal tax rate t_L^m, is 11.1–11.3% in Plan 4, and 11.3–11.5% in Plan 5.

From the point of view of efficiency the most attractive approach to tax reform we have considered is Plan 4 for the NRST, which combines a flat sales tax with a flat labor income tax and eliminates sales taxes on investment goods. Table 8.4 shows that an initial sales tax rate of 15.9 percent and a labor income tax rate of 11.3 percent are required, with both rates gradually declining over time. The welfare gain would be diminished relatively little by shifting the burden toward the labor income tax, as in Plan 7. The combination of an NRST collected at the retail level and a labor income tax collected as at present would be administratively attractive and would generate welfare gains amounting to more than half of the gross domestic product in 1997, the benchmark year for our simulations.

The Flat Tax proposals of HR and AS have attracted a great deal of attention. An important transition issue is whether depreciation allowances on "old" assets, that is, assets placed in service prior to the tax reform, would be allowed to continue. We consider a scenario in which depreciation allowances continue in accord with depreciation schedules provided in the tax laws prior to reform. An alternative might be to permit an immediate write-off of the unused depreciation allowances. This could be justified on the grounds that taxpayers would demand compensation for the lost reductions in tax liabilities.

In the HR and AS Flat Tax proposals the effective tax rate on investment is zero, but there is a lump sum tax on "old" capital. It follows that the deduction of depreciation allowances would not affect the price of capital services and has no impact on resource allocation. If we were to allow taxpayers to deduct unused depreciation allowances on "old" capital and make up for the lost tax revenue through a lump sum tax, resource allocation would also be unaffected. However, if a distorting tax is raised in order to compensate for revenue losses, allowing depreciation deductions on "old" capital would affect resource allocation.

We estimate the amount of unused capital consumption allowances on "old" capital by combining investment in each asset category with the depreciation schedules effective at the time of investment. We start with time series for investment in the 51 categories of depreciable assets in the corporate and noncorporate sectors and reallocate them into the statutory recovery classes.[16] The capital consumption allowances deductible after the tax reform are then calculated by applying the relevant depreciation schedules to the annual investments in each statutory recovery class.

By the end of 1996, producer durable equipment placed in service prior to 1970 had already been completely depreciated and accelerated depreciation, inflation, and economic growth had dramatically reduced the importance of unused capital consumption allowances on long-lived assets placed in service prior to 1970.[17] For our purposes, it is sufficient to consider capital consumption allowances on assets placed in service since 1970. During this period, the cost recovery system evolved from the Asset Depreciation Range (ADR) system to the Accelerated Cost Recovery System (ACRS) in 1981, and then to the modified ACRS (MACRS) in 1987.

For investment made in the 1970–1980, we follow Jorgenson and Sullivan (1981) and apply the depreciation schedules under the ADR system. Under the ADR system, straight line method and declining balance method with an optimal switch to straight line method were available. Prior to 1970, the rate of declining balance was 200%. In 1970 it was lowered to 150% for real property (asset 28–51 in table A3.11). Jorgenson and Sullivan estimated that, in 1970–1980, 68–76% of asset was depreciated through the accelerated depreciation method, with the proportion increasing over time. Salvage value was estimated to be 1% for real property. For personal property, it was estimated to be 3% for 1970–1976 and 1% thereafter. They also found that the optimal switch point to the straight line method was when 55% of the

Table 8.5a
Investment in the corporate sector (billions of dollars)

Year	PDE	NRS	RS	VSUM
1970	51.4	28.0	0.5	25.8
1971	53.5	28.8	0.6	27.0
1972	61.7	32.1	0.7	29.9
1973	74.6	37.2	0.7	34.6
1974	83.5	44.0	0.5	39.6
1975	86.3	44.8	0.4	38.8
1976	97.1	48.7	0.5	41.4
1977	119.0	53.3	0.7	44.3
1978	141.7	64.2	0.9	53.1
1979	161.3	84.1	2.1	69.2
1980	172.8	96.4	2.2	76.0
1981	191.9	118.1	2.0	
1982	188.0	126.7	1.1	
1983	196.8	109.6	1.3	
1984	233.8	126.9	1.6	
1985	250.4	138.9	2.0	
1986	257.6	121.7	1.7	
1987	258.1	115.4	1.7	
1988	277.4	121.7	1.8	
1989	296.5	130.2	1.5	
1990	302.7	141.4	1.2	
1991	292.0	130.5	1.2	
1992	318.7	124.0	1.4	
1993	345.1	127.9	1.8	
1994	384.3	133.6	2.1	
1995	424.1	147.2	2.1	
1996	460.1	154.2	2.3	

Notation:
PDE: Producer durable equipment
NRS: Nonresidential structures
RS: Residential structures
VSUM: Total value of investment in the 22 asset classes with tax life of 17 years or more in 1980

Table 8.5b
Investment in the noncorporate sector (billions of dollars)

Year	PDE	NRS	RS	VSUM
1970	13.7	7.1	11.8	18.7
1971	14.3	8.1	14.7	22.6
1972	15.9	8.8	18.5	27.1
1973	19.2	11.3	17.3	28.3
1974	19.3	10.7	13.1	23.3
1975	19.7	10.0	12.2	21.1
1976	22.6	9.9	14.3	23.1
1977	27.7	13.5	19.6	30.9
1978	35.6	19.6	25.3	40.8
1979	42.7	21.6	62.4	81.1
1980	39.3	27.4	64.9	86.3
1981	44.2	35.0	62.4	
1982	41.4	34.6	28.4	
1983	44.4	28.1	34.8	
1984	52.0	34.1	44.2	
1985	50.1	38.6	54.3	
1986	53.0	37.6	41.6	
1987	55.3	39.1	46.2	
1988	60.2	40.9	49.1	
1989	64.3	42.2	42.7	
1990	58.2	39.0	34.9	
1991	60.8	31.1	35.6	
1992	56.4	24.2	42.6	
1993	68.3	26.1	56.7	
1994	76.9	27.8	64.6	
1995	82.6	30.1	64.3	
1996	89.2	35.3	69.8	

Notation: See table 8.5a.

recovery period elapsed for the 200% declining balance method, and when 40% of the recovery period elapsed for the 150% declining balance method. We assume that taxpayers chose the depreciation method that minimized tax burden.

The recovery period of assets in table A3.11 does not necessary coincide with one of the statutory recovery periods under ACRS (1981–1996) and the modified ACRS (1987–1996). Indeed the recovery period for an asset category in table A3.11 is the average of statutory recovery periods for the assets in the same category, where capital stock is used as the weight. If the recovery period for an asset category in table A3.11 coincides with one of the statutory recovery periods, we assume that all the assets in that category have the same recovery period. Otherwise, we allocate the investment in that asset category between the two adjacent statutory recovery classes whose recovery periods bracket the average recovery period. To determine the investment composition of an asset category, we start with the capital stock composition implied by the average recovery period of the asset category.

We make three assumptions to estimate investment composition of an asset category. First, we assume that in any of the 51 depreciable business asset categories, the composition of capital stock by statutory recovery period remains constant over time. It follows

$$\frac{I \cdot w_I - \delta_1 \cdot K \cdot w_K}{I \cdot (1 - w_I) - \delta_2 \cdot K \cdot (1 - w_K)} = \frac{w_K}{1 - w_K} \tag{8.7}$$

where δ_1 and δ_2 are the economic depreciation rates of the asset in the statutory recovery classes whose recovery periods bracket the average recovery period from below and from above, respectively, w_I and w_K are the proportions of investment and capital stock in the statutory recovery class with the shorter recovery period, and I and K are total investment and capital stock in the asset category in 1996. Second, we assume the rate of declining balance is the same for all assets in the same asset category. In particular, we assume

$$\delta_i = \frac{R_{DB}}{L_i}, \quad i = 1, 2 \tag{8.8}$$

where R_{DB} is the rate of declining balance of the asset category and L_i is the economic life of the asset in the statutory recovery class I. Finally, we assume that the ratio between economic life and statutory recovery period is the same for all assets in the same category. In particular, we assume

$$\frac{L_i}{L} = \frac{T_i}{T}, \quad i = 1, 2 \tag{8.9}$$

where T_i is the statutory recovery period of recovery class i, and L and T are the economic life and average recovery period for the asset category. Making use of (8.8) and (8.9), we can express δ_1 and δ_2 as

$$\delta_i = \frac{R_{DB} \cdot T}{L \cdot T_i}, \quad i = 1, 2\,. \tag{8.10}$$

Substituting (8.10) into (8.7) and rearranging terms, we obtain

$$w_I = w_K\left[1+(1-w_K)\cdot(\delta_1-\delta_2)\cdot\frac{K}{I}\right]. \tag{8.11}$$

Column 6 of table A3.14 and table A3.15 show the share of investment allocated to the statutory recovery class with the shorter recovery period.

With the investment in the 51 asset classes allocated to the appropriate statutory recovery classes, it is straightforward to calculate the unused depreciation allowances for "old" capital stock at the end of 1996. We first apply the statutory depreciation schedule to the annual investment in each statutory recovery class and calculate the corresponding stream of depreciation allowances. Then we add the scheduled depreciation allowances from all the statutory recovery classes for years 1997 and beyond. Tables 8.6a and 8.6b show the capital consumption allowances for corporate and noncorporate sectors by assets placed in service in 1970–1980, 1981–1986, and 1987–1996. The corporate and noncorporate totals of capital allowances on the assets existing at the time of tax reform are also shown in figure 8.3.

Table 8.6a
Unused depreciation allowances on capital stock of 1996: Corporate (billions of dollars)

Year	Total	1970–1980 (ADR)	1981–1986 (ACRS)	1987–1996 (MACRS)
1997	437.3	13.1	13.5	410.7
1998	318.8	12.3	10.6	295.9
1999	239.8	11.4	8.0	220.4
2000	186.3	10.4	6.0	170.0
2001	137.8	9.3	4.3	124.2
2002	103.3	8.2	3.7	91.4
2003	81.4	7.0	2.9	71.5
2004	65.6	5.7	2.1	57.8
2005	55.5	4.5	0.8	50.2
2006	45.8	3.6	0.0	42.2
2007	39.9	3.3	0.0	36.6
2008	36.8	3.2	0.0	33.6
2009	33.5	3.2	0.0	30.3
2010	29.8	3.2	0.0	26.6
2011	25.8	3.2	0.0	22.6

Table 8.6a (continued)

Year	Total	1970–1980 (ADR)	1981–1986 (ACRS)	1987–1996 (MACRS)
2012	23.0	3.2	0.0	19.8
2013	21.5	3.0	0.0	18.5
2014	20.0	2.9	0.0	17.2
2015	18.4	2.6	0.0	15.8
2016	16.7	2.4	0.0	14.3
2017	15.6	2.1	0.0	13.5
2018	15.4	1.9	0.0	13.5
2019	13.8	1.6	0.0	12.2
2020	12.1	1.3	0.0	10.8
2021	10.3	1.0	0.0	9.3
2022	8.2	0.5	0.0	7.7
2023	6.2	0.0	0.0	6.2
2024	4.8	0.0	0.0	4.8
2025	4.3	0.0	0.0	4.3
2026	4.3	0.0	0.0	4.3
2027	4.3	0.0	0.0	4.3
2028	4.3	0.0	0.0	4.3
2029	4.3	0.0	0.0	4.3
2030	4.3	0.0	0.0	4.3
2031	4.3	0.0	0.0	4.3
2032	4.0	0.0	0.0	4.0
2033	3.1	0.0	0.0	3.1
2034	1.9	0.0	0.0	1.9
2035	0.7	0.0	0.0	0.7
2036	0.0	0.0	0.0	0.0
2037	0.0	0.0	0.0	0.0
2038	0.0	0.0	0.0	0.0
2039	0.0	0.0	0.0	0.0
2040	0.0	0.0	0.0	0.0
Total	2063.4	124.3	51.8	1887.2

Note: Column 3 is for investment made in 1970–1980 under the ADR system. Similarly for columns 4 and 5.

Table 8.6b
Unused depreciation allowances on capital stock of 1996: Noncorporate (billions of dollars)

Year	Total	1970–1980 (ADR)	1981–1986 (ACRS)	1987–1996 (MACRS)
1997	125.5	12.3	12.7	100.5
1998	99.6	11.7	10.2	77.7
1999	82.1	10.9	8.4	62.9
2000	71.1	10.1	7.9	53.1
2001	61.2	9.3	7.8	44.1
2002	53.1	8.6	6.8	37.7
2003	47.2	8.0	5.2	34.0
2004	42.3	7.3	3.6	31.3
2005	37.6	6.5	1.3	29.8
2006	33.1	4.8	0.0	28.3
2007	29.9	2.6	0.0	27.3
2008	28.4	1.7	0.0	26.7
2009	27.8	1.7	0.0	26.1
2010	27.0	1.7	0.0	25.3
2011	26.2	1.7	0.0	24.5
2012	25.7	1.7	0.0	24.1
2013	25.5	1.6	0.0	23.9
2014	25.2	1.5	0.0	23.7
2015	23.2	1.3	0.0	21.9
2016	21.1	1.2	0.0	19.9
2017	19.4	1.1	0.0	18.3
2018	18.0	0.9	0.0	17.0
2019	16.0	0.9	0.0	15.1
2020	13.6	0.7	0.0	12.8
2021	10.6	0.5	0.0	10.1
2022	7.4	0.3	0.0	7.1
2023	4.2	0.0	0.0	4.2
2024	1.4	0.0	0.0	1.4
2025	1.2	0.0	0.0	1.2
2026	1.2	0.0	0.0	1.2
2027	1.2	0.0	0.0	1.2
2028	1.2	0.0	0.0	1.2
2029	1.2	0.0	0.0	1.2
2030	1.2	0.0	0.0	1.2

Table 8.6b (continued)

Year	Total	1970–1980 (ADR)	1981–1986 (ACRS)	1987–1996 (MACRS)
2031	1.2	0.0	0.0	1.2
2032	1.1	0.0	0.0	1.1
2033	0.9	0.0	0.0	0.9
2034	0.6	0.0	0.0	0.6
2035	0.2	0.0	0.0	0.2
2036	0.0	0.0	0.0	0.0
2037	0.0	0.0	0.0	0.0
2038	0.0	0.0	0.0	0.0
2039	0.0	0.0	0.0	0.0
2040	0.0	0.0	0.0	0.0
Total	1014.8	110.4	63.9	840.5

Note: Column 3 is for investment made in 1970–1980 under the ADR system. Similarly for columns 4 and 5.

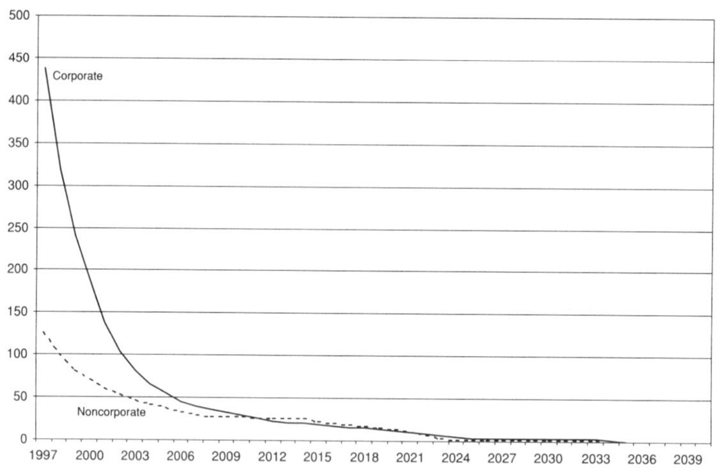

Figure 8.3
Unused depreciation allowances on capital stock of 1996 (billions of dollars).

In simulating the impact of deductions for unused depreciation allowances and property taxes we take revenue-neutral versions of the HR and AS Flat Tax proposals as our point of departure. Specifically, we constrain the three tax rates—t_F, t_L^a, and t_L^m—to follow the paths reported in table 8.3. and figures 8.1a and 8.1b Reductions in tax revenue due to the deductions are offset by one of our methods for revenue adjustment. The upper panel in table 8.7 confirms that, if a lump sum tax is used to meet the government budget constraints, there is no effect on resource allocation or the level of economic welfare. However, if the revenue losses due to deductions for unused depreciation allowances are compensated by an increase in distorting taxes, efficiency declines.

Another interesting issue is the deduction of property taxes for the purpose of the flat tax. The deduction of property taxes on "old" assets is not distorting by itself. However, the deduction of property taxes applies to "new" assets as well and is not transitory in nature. It is straightforward to implement the property tax deduction for firms. We simply deduct the property taxes paid from the flat tax base. However, the only direct tax in the household sector is the labor income tax.

Although it may appear rather artificial to deduct property taxes from labor income, this appears to be the only practical approach.

The second panel of table 8.7 shows the welfare effects of property tax deductions. When property tax deductions are allowed and a lump sum tax is used to compensate for the revenue loss, the welfare gain is \$0.5 trillion for HR and \$0.6 trillion for AS. However, if the revenue loss is offset by an increase in distorting taxes, the welfare effect is a loss in the range of \$0.2–0.7 trillion for HR and \$0.2–1.1 trillion for AS. Adding the deduction of depreciation allowances does not affect resource allocation under the lump sum tax adjustment. Under a distorting tax adjustment, the combined welfare effect of property tax deduction and the deduction of depreciation allowances is \$0.3–1.0 trillion for HR and \$0.3–1.8 for AS.

8.4 Equivalence of Consumption and Labor Income Taxes

In a closed economy where labor is the only factor of production and government does not participate in the markets for goods and services, a flat sales tax on consumption is equivalent to a flat labor income tax. However, the equivalence breaks down if capital is used

Table 8.7
Welfare effects of continued deduction of depreciation allowances and property taxes under the Flat Tax (billions of 1997 dollars)

Policy Alternatives and Method of Revenue Adjustment	Hall-Rabushka	Armey-Shelby
1. *No more deduction of property taxes*		
a. No more depreciation allowances (reference case)	0.0	0.0
b. Depreciation allowances continue		
Lump sum tax adjustment	0.0	0.0
Flat tax adjustment	–263.2	–383.7
Sales tax adjustment	–121.4	–151.0
Flat tax and sales tax adj.	–223.2	–317.6
c. Depreciation balance is expensed		
Lump sum tax adjustment	0.0	0.0
Flat tax adjustment	–366.6	–536.7
Sales tax adjustment	–176.8	–219.8
Flat tax and sales tax adj.	–312.6	–446.2
2. *Deduction of Property Taxes Continues*		
a. No more depreciation allowances		
Lump sum tax adjustment	479.1	616.5
Flat tax adjustment	–615.4	–1065.1
sales tax adjustment	–153.9	–175.6
Flat tax and sales tax adj.	–474.9	–781.9
b. Depreciation allowances continue		
Lump sum tax adjustment	479.3	616.9
Flat tax adjustment	–1043.4	–1776.4
Sales tax adjustment	–286.5	–340.4
Flat tax and sales tax adj.	–795.3	–1280.4
c. Depreciation balance is expensed		
Lump sum tax adjustment	479.2	616.7
Flat tax adjustment	–1209.1	–2064.9
Sales tax adjustment	–344.8	–413.1
Flat tax and sales tax adj.	–920.0	–1479.0

Note:
1. t_F, t_L^a, t_L^m are set at their transition paths of table 8.3.
2. t_C, t_C^a, and t_I are set at 0.058.
3. Inflation is fixed at 4% per year.

in production or if government participates in the market as a buyer or a seller. Since capital is a factor of production in our model, the equivalence does not hold in its strict form. Nevertheless table 8.2b shows that the welfare gains from replacing the current income tax with a flat sales tax on consumption, a flat labor income tax, or a hybrid of the two, are remarkably close: When the current income tax system is replaced by a flat sales tax on consumption and the sales tax on investment goods is eliminated ($t_I = 0$), the present value of welfare gain is estimated to be $4686.8 billion (Panel 2, column 2). For a similar switch to a hybrid system of flat sales tax on consumption and flat income tax on labor, the welfare gain is $4697.3 billion. For a switch to a flat labor income tax, the gain is $4527.8 billion. The pattern of relative welfare gains does not seem to be sensitive to the presence of a sales tax on investment (column 1, $t_I = 5.8\%$).

Although the exact equivalence between the flat sales tax and the flat labor income tax is invalidated by the presence of capital as a factor of production, a government sector, and a rest of the world sector, table 8.2b indicates that the equivalence may be a good approximation. First, consider a stripped-down version of our model where capital and labor are used to produce investment and consumption goods.[18]

The household budget constraint and the condition for goods market equilibrium in a closed economy take the form

$$C + S = Y = rK + wL$$
$$S = I$$

where C is consumption expenditure, S is saving, Y is income, r is the rate of return to capital (net of depreciation), K is capital input, w is wage rate, L is labor input, and I is investment.

Combining the two equations, we can express the income-expenditure relationship of the economy as:

$$C + I = Y = rK + wL\ .$$

Making use of the income-expenditure identity, we can derive a number of tax equivalence results. For example, with a uniform sales tax on consumption and investment the identity can be rewritten as

$$(1 + t_o)(C + I) = Y = rK + wL \tag{8.12}$$

where t_o is the tax rate on output. Dividing both sides of (8.12) by $(1+t_o)$, we can rewrite the income-expenditure identity as

$$C+I=\frac{rK+wL}{1+t_o}=(rK+wL)(1-\tau_i)$$

where $1-\tau_i\equiv 1/(1+t_o)$. It follows that a uniform output tax on consumption and investment goods is equivalent to a uniform input tax on capital and labor.

Similarly, it can be shown that a flat consumption tax is equivalent to a flat tax on income net of investment. We can also confirm that with no capital input ($I=K=0$), a flat consumption tax is equivalent to a flat labor income tax. How well does the equivalence of consumption and labor income taxation approximate the resource allocation in the presence of capital as a factor of production? To analyze this issue in a dynamic setting, we can rewrite the income-expenditure identity in the absence of taxation as

$$C_t+I_t=Y_t=r_t(K_t^O+K_t^N)+w_tL_t \tag{8.13}$$

where K_t^O is the capital stock accumulated prior to the tax reform, K_t^N is the capital stock accumulated after the tax reform, and t is the time subscript.

Multiplying the income-expenditure identity by the discount factor

$$\exp\left[\int_0^t -r_s\,ds\right]$$

and integrating over $t=[0,\infty)$, we obtain:

$$Z_0=K_0^O+H_0 \tag{8.14}$$

where

$$Z_0=\int_0^\infty \exp\left[\int_0^t -r_s\,ds\right]C_t\,dt$$

is the present value of the consumption stream, K_0^O is the value of capital stock at the time of tax reform, and

$$H_0 = \int_0^\infty \exp\left[\int_0^t -r_s \, ds\right] w_t L_t \, dt$$

is the present value of the labor income stream. To obtain the present value income-expenditure equation, we have used

$$K_t^N = \int_0^t I_s \, ds$$

and

$$\int_0^\infty r_t K_t^N \exp\left[\int_0^t -r_v \, dv\right] dt = \int_0^\infty \int_0^t I_s r_t \exp\left[\int_0^t -r_v \, dv\right] ds dt$$

$$= \int_0^\infty I_s \int_s^\infty r_t \exp\left[\int_0^t -r_v \, dv\right] dt ds$$

$$= \int_0^\infty I_s \exp\left[\int_0^s -r_v \, dv\right] ds \, .$$

Next, we assume that a permanent sales tax on consumption is introduced. Then the present value income-expenditure identity can be written as

$$(1 + t_c) Z_0 = K_0^O + H_0$$

where t_C is the tax rate. It follows immediately that a permanent flat sales tax on consumption is equivalent to a permanent uniform flat tax on the incomes from "old" capital and labor. Similarly, a permanent flat tax on labor income is equivalent to a flat tax on consumption net of the income from "old" capital. The difference between a flat sales tax on consumption and a flat labor income tax boils down to the taxation of the capital accumulated prior to the tax reform.

If we let $1 - \tau \equiv 1/(1 + t_c)$, as before, then the flat sales tax is equivalent to a uniform flat tax of τ on the incomes from "old" capital and labor. Further, let the labor income tax rate be τ_L. Then a comparison of the flat sales tax and the flat labor income tax is equivalent to a comparison of the uniform tax τ on the incomes from "old" capital and labor and the flat tax on labor income only. Since the tax on "old" capital is a lump sum tax, under the equal-revenue restriction, the flat sales tax is more efficient than the flat labor income tax.

To examine this issue from another perspective, we consider a transition from the uniform tax on labor and "old" capital to the flat labor tax. Revenue neutrality requires that the tax rate on labor income has to be increased from τ to τ_L, while the lump sum tax on "old" capital is eliminated. In the process, the efficiency of resource allocation must worsen as the distorting tax on labor is increased. The welfare cost of replacing the flat sales tax with the flat labor tax, ΔW, may be approximated by multiplying the present value of the lump sum tax by the marginal efficiency cost of labor income tax:

$$\Delta W = \tau K_0^O MEC_L \tag{8.15}$$

where MEC_L is the marginal efficiency cost of labor income tax for the tax rate in the range of τ and τ_L.

In our simulations, K_0^O = \$25,847 billion 1997 dollars. In the steady state of the economy under the flat sales tax, the sales tax rate is 0.28511. Hence $\tau = 1-(1+0.28511)^{-1} = 0.2219$. Under the flat labor income tax, the steady-state labor income tax rate is 0.2447. The welfare gains from replacing the flat labor income tax with the flat sales tax are due to the reduction of labor income tax rate from 0.2447 to 0.2219, which is a cut of approximately ten percent in the tax rate. We use the average efficiency cost *AEC* for a 10% labor income tax cut in table 8.11e, below, as the relevant marginal efficiency cost, that is, $MEC_L = 0.084$.

Making use of these figures, we estimate ΔW = \$481.8 billion dollars. This is larger than the welfare difference between Panels 2 and 7 of column 2, table 8.2, which is \$4,686.8–4,527.8 = \$159.0 billion dollars. Although the difference of \$322.8 (= 481.8–159.0) billion dollars in present value is small given the size of the U.S. economy, it seems to be too large to be attributable to the nonlinearity of the model and the associated numerical inaccuracy of a linear approximation. On the other hand, such a discrepancy is not surprising given that (8.15) is derived from an income-expenditure identity that abstracts from government and the rest of the world.

To add realism to the analysis, we consider the tax base of the flat sales tax in our model, which is defined as

$$BS \equiv PCS(CS + CE) + PHD \cdot HD/(1 + t_C) \, .$$

Making use of the zero-profit condition of the business sector, the definitions of the surplus of government enterprises and the base of labor income tax, and the market clearing conditions for labor and investment goods, we have

$$\begin{aligned} BS &= (BL - PLG \cdot LG - PLR \cdot LR) - PIS(IS - IG - IR) \\ &\quad + PQD \cdot QD + PMD \cdot MD + \frac{PHD \cdot HD}{1 + t_C} + \tilde{RE} \end{aligned} \tag{8.16}$$

where $\tilde{RE}$ is the surplus of government enterprises, net of sales tax

$$\tilde{RE} \equiv PCS \cdot CE - PLE \cdot LE = RE - PCS \cdot CE \cdot t_C \, .$$

Since the total labor supply is allocated to the business sector, government enterprises, general government, and the rest of the world, the first parenthesis on the RHS represents the labor employed in the business sector and government enterprises, and the second parenthesis, gross investment in the private sector. Making use of the cost of capital formulas and the relationship between private saving and capital accumulation, we can rewrite (8.16) as

$$\begin{aligned} BS &= BL - [PLG \cdot LG + PLR \cdot LR + PIS(IG + IR)] + \tilde{RE} \\ &\quad + VKL\left[r^p - \{(1 + g_K)(1 + n)(1 - \alpha_T) - 1\}(1 + \pi)\right] + R^P \end{aligned} \tag{8.17}$$

where r^p is the after-tax real rate of return to capital, g_K is the growth rate of capital-labor ratio, n is the rate of population growth, $-\alpha_T$ is the rate of technical change, and R^P is property tax revenue ($\equiv R_q^P + R_m^P + R_h^P$). All the variables are scaled to the initial time endowment in efficiency unit. In the steady state, $g_K = 0$.

The difference between BS and BL is small. In the steady state under the flat sales tax, $BS - BL$ = \$-77.4 (= \$4,370.0–4,447.4) billion dollars, –31.7 (= \$4,412.5–4,444.2) billion dollars under the flat labor income tax, and -\$57.9 (= \$4,388.5–4,446.4) billion dollars under the hybrid flat sales and labor income taxes. The transition path of the economy under the flat taxes is very close to a balanced growth path. Table 8.8 shows that the range of variation is less than 2.5%

Table 8.8
Variation of economic variables during transition

A. Flat Sales Tax on Consumption (Plan 2, NRST)

	Low	High	STD	(H-L)/STD
F	14617	14739	14695	0.008
C	3821.4	3872.4	3859.2	0.013
LJ	13171	13243	13205	0.005
HD	1070.7	1092.	1089.4	0.020
LD	3679.6	3769.7	3685.7	0.024
L	4445.2	4517.6	4482.3	0.016
KL	25847	26962	26863	0.042
r^P	0.044101	0.049792	0.044499	0.128
t_C	0.28352	0.28754	0.28513	0.014
t_L^m	—	—	—	—

B. Hybrid of Flat Sales and Flat Labor Taxes (Plan 4, NRST)

	Low	High	STD	(H-L)/STD
F	14614	14738	14698	0.008
C	3850.1	3858.5	3847.8	0.002
LJ	13186	13258	13220	0.005
HD	1069.3	1092.4	1089.	0.021
LD	3679.5	3767.0	3684.5	0.024
L	4430.0	4501.8	4467.2	0.016
KL	25847	27000	26923	0.043
r^P	0.044159	0.049913	0.044498	0.129
t_C	0.15499	0.15850	0.15535	0.023
t_L^m	0.11076	0.11327	0.11102	0.023

Table 8.8 (continued)

C. Flat Labor Income Tax (Plan 7, NRST)

	Low	High	STD	(H-L)/STD
F	14608	14734	14698	0.009
C	3777.7	3833.7	3828.1	0.015
LJ	13212	13281	13242	0.005
1067.0	1090.9	1088.9	0.022	
LD	3679.3	3758.74	3681.7	0.022
L	4406.7	4476.1	4445.9	0.016
KL	25847	27039	26994	0.044
r^P	0.044296	0.050041	0.044504	0.129
t_C	—	—	—	—
t_L^m	0.24436	0.25333	0.24473	0.037

Notations:
Low: Lowest value in the transition path
High: Highest value in the transition path
STD: Steady state value
(H-L)/STD: Ratio of High-Low and STD
F: Full consumption (billion unit)
C: Consumption of consumption goods
LJ: Leisure consumed
HD: Household capital services
LD: Labor demand by business
L: Total labor supply
KL: Quantity of capital stock
r^P: Real private rate of return to capital
t_C: Sales tax rate
t_L^m: Labor income tax rate

of the respective steady-state value for most quantity variables. The only exception is capital stock with a variation of 4.2–4.4% of the steady-state value. The after-tax real rate of return to capital starts at a level considerably higher than its steady-state value, which is consistent with the fact that capital stock is larger in the steady state than in the initial state. However, it comes within 2.5% of its steady-state values in 15–20 years, indicating a fairly rapid approach to the steady state.

We conclude that the steady-state configuration of the economy provides a good approximation of the economy in transition. Although capital is present in our model, the equivalence between the flat sales tax and the flat labor income tax seems to hold quite closely as an approximation. Obviously, this result is not general and depends critically upon the particular set of parameters used in our simulations. To understand the factors that drive this approximate equivalence result, it is useful to evaluate the terms in (8.17) that constitute the difference between *BS* and *BL*. In the steady state under the flat sales tax on consumption,

$$PLG \cdot LG + PIS \cdot IG = 968.7$$

$$PLR \cdot LR + PIS \cdot IR = 29.2$$

$$\tilde{RE} = 6.2$$

$$VKL[r^P - \{(1+n)(1-\alpha_T) - 1\}(1+\pi)] = 638.0$$

$$R^P = 276.2.$$

The presence of capital as a factor of production drives wedges between the bases of flat sales tax and flat labor income tax by generating income net of investment and property taxes. If we interpret $\tilde{RE}$ as the returns to capital in government enterprises, the difference between *BS* and *BL* explained by the presence of capital amounts to 21.1% $(= (6.2 + 638.0 + 276.2)/4370.0)$ of *BS*. However, the effects of capital are offset by the labor and investment goods purchased by government and the rest of the world $(968.7 + 29.2)$. In a dynamic context, flat sales tax can still be interpreted partly as a lump sum tax on "old" capital (K_0^O) and a flat tax on labor income (H_0). However, the tax base is affected by property taxes, surplus of government enterprises, and labor and investment good demands by government and the rest of the world.

Equality of sales tax and labor income tax bases is a necessary but not sufficient condition for equivalence. Even if the two tax bases were the same, relative prices and the distribution of tax burden among the household, government, and the rest of the world may vary.[19] To focus on the income effect, consider the budget constraint of the household. Since part of the sales taxes are paid by the government and the rest of the world, the labor income tax collected from households under the labor income tax cannot be equivalent to the sales tax paid by households under the flat sales tax. Although, part of the labor income tax may be interpreted as paid by the government when it purchases labor at the tax inclusive price, there is no guarantee that the sales tax paid by the government is equivalent to the labor tax it pays under the labor income tax. Indeed, in 1970–1996, consumption goods account for on average 17.4% of government spending net of interest payments while labor purchases account for 48.9%.

Substitution effects are also important determinants of resource allocation. Although the sales tax does not necessarily make consumption goods more expensive, it does affect the relative prices, and similarly for labor income tax. Table 8.9 shows that, for the general government, consumption good is relatively more expensive under the sales tax, while labor is relatively more expensive under the labor income tax. This result is related to the fact that, in our model, the general government pays the tax-inclusive prices for consumption goods and labor, and tax is shifted by less than 100%. For the household sector, although consumption good and household capital services are more expensive under the sales tax and leisure is cheaper under the labor income tax, the consumption good is cheaper, relative to leisure, under the sales tax than under the labor income tax. For the business sector, consumption good is cheaper, relative to investment good, under the sales tax than under the labor income tax. The steady-state prices of investment good and the capital services are constant.

We conclude that in a closed economy where labor is the only factor of production and government demands for goods and labor services are zero, a flat sales tax is equivalent to a flat labor income tax. If capital is introduced as an additional factor of production, a flat sales tax is equivalent to a flat tax on "old" capital and labor income. However, these equivalence results are invalidated by the presence of government and the rest of the world in the goods and factor markets. Even if the tax bases of the two flat taxes have the same size, the income and substitution effects would still invalidate the equivalence proposition. Nevertheless our simulation results suggest that, in the United States, a flat sales tax and a flat labor income tax would generate similar efficiency effects under revenue neutrality. We have shown that this result is an artifact of the parameters of the U.S. economy and no generalization is warranted.

Table 8.9
Relative prices under the flat taxes—steady state

	Flat Sales Tax (Plan 2)	Hybrid Tax (Plan 4)	Flat Labor Tax (Plan 7)
A. General Government			
PC	1.0309	0.9302	0.8091
PI	1.0683	1.0683	1.0683
PLG	0.9744	0.9775	0.9817
PEL	1.0	1.0	1.0
PER	1.0	1.0	1.0
B. Household			
PC	1.0309	0.9302	0.8091
PLJ	0.9962	0.8884	0.7581
PHD	1.3043	1.1726	1.0150
PLJ/PC	0.9663	0.9551	0.9369
PHD/PC	1.2652	1.2606	1.2545
C. Business			
PCS	0.8022	0.8051	0.8091
PIS	1.0683	1.0683	1.0683
PLD	0.9918	0.9950	0.9992
PQD	0.8200	0.8200	0.8200
PMD	0.8448	0.8448	0.8448
D. Tax Rates			
t_C	0.2851	0.1553	—
t_L^m	—	0.1110	0.2447

Notations:
PC: Consumer price of consumption goods
PI: Investor price of investment goods
PLG: Price of labor purchased by government
PEL: Price index of transfer to households
PER: Price index of transfer to foreigners
PLJ: Price of leisure
PHD: Price of household capital services
PCS: Producer price of consumption goods
PIS: Producer price of investment goods
PLD: Producer price of labor
PQD: Price of corporate capital service
PMD: Price of non-corporate capital service
t_C: Flat sales tax rate
t_L^m: Flat labor income tax rate

8.5 Efficiency Costs of Taxation

In order to provide more details about the performance of the alternative tax reform proposals, we estimate the marginal and average efficiency costs of tax revenue. We have selected seven tax policy regimes—the HR and AS Flat Tax proposals and Plans 1, 2, 4, 5 and 7 of NRST. All of these tax reform proposals are made revenue neutral by adjusting the appropriate tax rates. Specifically, the Flat Tax rates are adjusted for HR and AS and the sale tax rates are adjusted for Plans 1 and 2 of NRST. For Plans 4 and 5 of NRST, sales tax and labor income tax rates are adjusted in the same proportion. Finally, labor income tax is adjusted for Plan 7. In other words, we constrain the relevant tax rates to follow the paths given in tables 8.3 and 8.4.

We conduct the simulations for each tax system and also for subsets of the tax system. For the HR and AS Flat Tax proposals we consider the property tax, the flat tax, the sales tax, and combinations of the property tax, the Flat Tax and the sales tax. We consider the property tax and the sales tax as the subsets of the tax system for Plans 1 and 2, and the property tax, labor income tax, and the sales tax for Plans 4 and 5. Finally, we choose the property tax and the labor income tax as the subset of the tax system for Plan 7. In Plans 1 and 2, labor income is not taxed and in Plan 7, sales tax is not imposed.

Tables 8.10 and 8.11 show the marginal and average efficiency costs of tax revenue for the HR and AS proposals, and figures 8.4a and 8.4b compare them. Tables 8.12a–8.12e show the marginal and average efficiency costs of tax revenue for Plans 1, 2, 4, 5,and 7 of NRST, and figures 8.5a and 8.5b compare them.

Comparison with table 7.10 of chapter 7 reveals that each of the tax reform proposals reduces the efficiency costs of the U.S. tax system considerably. In the cases of the HR and AS Flat Tax proposals, the marginal efficiency cost (*MEC*) of the tax system is reduced from 0.266 in table 7.10 to 0.178 and 0.211, respectively. The improvement in efficiency is more dramatic for the NRST proposals. For example, Plans 2 and 4 reduce the *MEC* to 0.077 and 0.076, respectively, by replacing income tax and excise taxes with a flat sales tax or a combination of a flat sales tax and a flat labor income tax. Plans 1 and 5, which incorporate progressivity, reduce the *MEC* to 0.131 and 0.107.

The most dramatic reduction in efficiency cost occurs in labor income taxation. For example, the *MEC* for labor income tax is reduced from 0.404 to 0.219 for the HR proposal, to 0.272 for the AS

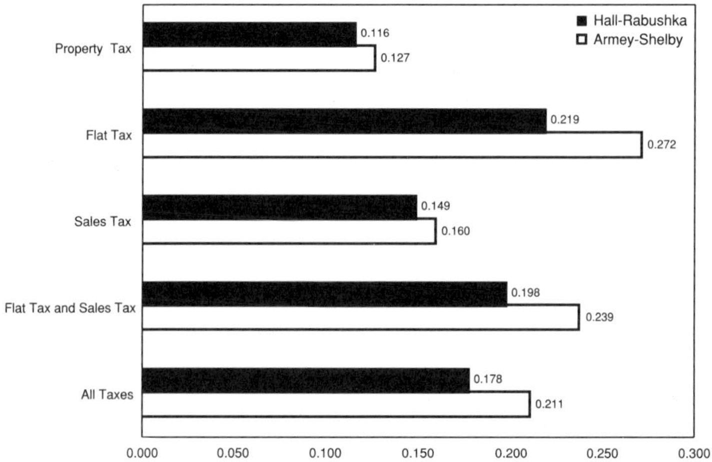

Figure 8.4a
Marginal efficiency cost of flat tax: Hall-Rabushka and Armey-Shelby.

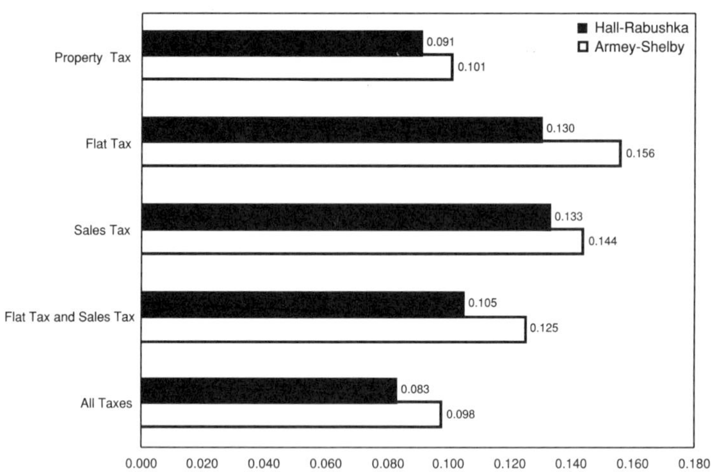

Figure 8.4b
Average efficiency cost of flat tax: Hall-Rabushka and Armey-Shelby.

Table 8.10
Efficiency cost of taxation under reform proposals—Hall-Rabushka with flat tax adjustment

	Reduction in Tax Rates (%)										
Taxes	5	10	20	30	40	50	60	70	80	90	100
1. *Property Tax*											
MEC	0.116	0.113	0.110	0.105	0.100	0.095	0.090	0.085	0.080	0.075	0.069
AEC	0.116	0.114	0.112	0.110	0.107	0.105	0.102	0.100	0.097	0.094	0.091
2. *Flat Tax*											
MEC	0.219	0.207	0.189	0.167	0.147	0.128	0.111	0.095	0.081	0.068	0.055
AEC	0.219	0.213	0.201	0.190	0.180	0.170	0.161	0.152	0.144	0.137	0.130
3. *Sales Tax*											
MEC	0.149	0.147	0.145	0.142	0.138	0.135	0.132	0.129	0.126	0.123	0.119
AEC	0.149	0.148	0.146	0.145	0.143	0.142	0.140	0.138	0.137	0.135	0.133
4. *Flat Tax and Sales Tax (All Taxes, Except for Property Tax)*											
MEC	0.198	0.187	0.168	0.145	0.124	0.105	0.087	0.071	0.056	0.042	0.030
AEC	0.198	0.192	0.181	0.169	0.158	0.148	0.139	0.129	0.121	0.113	0.105
5. *All Taxes*											
MEC	0.178	0.165	0.146	0.122	0.100	0.081	0.063	0.047	0.032	0.019	0.007
AEC	0.178	0.171	0.159	0.147	0.136	0.125	0.115	0.106	0.098	0.090	0.083

Notes:
1. The tax rates associated with the experiments are as follows:
   Property tax: t_q^P, t_m^P, t_h^P
   Flat tax: t_F, t_L^a, t_L^m
   Sales tax: t_C^a, t_C, t_I
2. Inflation is fixed at 4% per year.

Table 8.11
Efficiency cost of taxation under reform proposals—Armey-Shelby with flat tax adjustment

	Reduction in Tax Rates (%)										
Taxes	5	10	20	30	40	50	60	70	80	90	100
1. *Property Tax*											
MEC	0.127	0.124	0.120	0.115	0.110	0.105	0.100	0.094	0.089	0.083	0.078
AEC	0.127	0.126	0.123	0.120	0.118	0.115	0.112	0.110	0.107	0.104	0.101
2. *Flat Tax*											
MEC	0.272	0.255	0.232	0.203	0.177	0.153	0.131	0.112	0.093	0.077	0.062
AEC	0.272	0.263	0.248	0.233	0.220	0.207	0.196	0.185	0.174	0.165	0.156
3. *Sales Tax*											
MEC	0.160	0.158	0.155	0.152	0.149	0.146	0.142	0.139	0.136	0.133	0.130
AEC	0.160	0.159	0.157	0.155	0.154	0.152	0.150	0.149	0.147	0.146	0.144
4. Flat Tax and Sales Tax (All Taxes, Except for Property Tax)											
MEC	0.239	0.225	0.201	0.173	0.147	0.123	0.101	0.081	0.063	0.047	0.032
AEC	0.239	0.232	0.217	0.202	0.189	0.176	0.165	0.154	0.143	0.134	0.125
5. *All Taxes*											
MEC	0.211	0.195	0.172	0.143	0.117	0.094	0.073	0.054	0.036	0.021	0.007
AEC	0.211	0.203	0.188	0.173	0.160	0.147	0.136	0.125	0.115	0.106	0.098

Note: See table 8.10.

Table 8.12a
Efficiency cost of taxation under reform proposals—Plan 1, NRST: Progressive Sales Tax, No Labor Income Tax with sales tax adjustment

	Reduction in Tax Rates (%)										
Taxes	5	10	20	30	40	50	60	70	80	90	100
1. *Property Tax*											
MEC	0.107	0.105	0.102	0.098	0.094	0.090	0.086	0.081	0.077	0.073	0.069
AEC	0.107	0.106	0.104	0.102	0.100	0.098	0.095	0.093	0.091	0.089	0.087
2. *Labor Income Tax*											
MEC						N.A.					
AEC											
3. *Sales Tax*											
MEC	0.140	0.133	0.124	0.111	0.098	0.085	0.073	0.061	0.048	0.037	0.025
AEC	0.140	0.137	0.130	0.123	0.117	0.110	0.103	0.097	0.090	0.083	0.076
4. Labor and Sales Tax (All Taxes, Except for Property Tax)											
MEC						N.A.					
AEC											
5. *Sales and Property Taxes (All Taxes)*											
MEC	0.131	0.124	0.112	0.097	0.083	0.069	0.055	0.042	0.029	0.017	0.006
AEC	0.131	0.127	0.120	0.112	0.104	0.097	0.089	0.082	0.074	0.067	0.060

Notes:
1. The tax rates associated with the experiments are as follows:
   Property tax: t_q^P, t_m^P, t_h^P
   Sales tax: t_C^a, t_C
2. Inflation is fixed at 4% per year.

Table 8.12b
Efficiency cost of taxation under reform proposals—Plan 2, NRST: Flat Sales tax, no Labor Income Tax with sales tax adjustment

	Reduction in Tax Rates (%)										
Taxes	5	10	20	30	40	50	60	70	80	90	100
1. *Property Tax*											
MEC	0.078	0.076	0.073	0.070	0.066	0.062	0.059	0.055	0.051	0.047	0.043
AEC	0.078	0.077	0.075	0.073	0.072	0.070	0.068	0.066	0.064	0.062	0.060
2. *Labor Income Tax*											
MEC						N.A.					
AEC											
3. *Sales Tax*											
MEC	0.077	0.074	0.069	0.062	0.056	0.049	0.042	0.036	0.030	0.024	0.017
AEC	0.077	0.076	0.072	0.069	0.065	0.062	0.058	0.055	0.052	0.048	0.045
4. Labor and Sales Tax (All Taxes, Except for Property Tax)											
MEC						N.A.					
AEC											
5. *Sales and Property Taxes (All Taxes)*											
MEC	0.077	0.072	0.066	0.057	0.048	0.040	0.032	0.024	0.017	0.010	0.003
AEC	0.077	0.075	0.070	0.066	0.061	0.057	0.052	0.048	0.044	0.040	0.036

Note: See table 8.12a.

Table 8.12c
Efficiency cost of taxation under reform proposals—Plan 4: Flat Sales Tax and Flat Labor Income Tax with sales tax and labor income tax adjustment

	Reduction in Tax Rates (%)										
Taxes	5	10	20	30	40	50	60	70	80	90	100
1. *Property Tax*											
MEC	0.074	0.072	0.069	0.066	0.062	0.059	0.055	0.052	0.048	0.044	0.041
AEC	0.074	0.073	0.071	0.069	0.068	0.066	0.064	0.062	0.060	0.058	0.056
2. *Labor Income Tax*											
MEC	0.080	0.078	0.075	0.071	0.068	0.064	0.061	0.057	0.054	0.051	0.048
AEC	0.080	0.079	0.077	0.075	0.073	0.071	0.070	0.068	0.066	0.065	0.063
3. *Sales Tax*											
MEC	0.078	0.075	0.072	0.068	0.064	0.060	0.056	0.052	0.048	0.043	0.039
AEC	0.078	0.077	0.074	0.072	0.070	0.068	0.066	0.064	0.062	0.060	0.057
4. *Labor and Sales Tax (All Taxes, Except for Property Tax)*											
MEC	0.076	0.074	0.068	0.061	0.054	0.047	0.040	0.034	0.028	0.022	0.017
AEC	0.076	0.075	0.072	0.068	0.064	0.061	0.057	0.054	0.051	0.048	0.044
5. *Labor, Sales, and Property Taxes (All Taxes)*											
MEC	0.076	0.071	0.064	0.055	0.047	0.038	0.030	0.023	0.015	0.009	0.002
AEC	0.076	0.074	0.069	0.064	0.060	0.055	0.051	0.047	0.043	0.039	0.035

Notes:
1. The tax rates associated with the experiments are as follows:
   Property tax: t_q^P, t_m^P, t_h^P
   Labor income tax: t_L^m
   Sales tax: t_C^a, t_C
2. Inflation is fixed at 4% per year.

Table 8.12d
Efficiency cost of taxation under reform proposals—Plan 5: Progressive Sales Tax and Flat Labor Income Tax with sales tax and labor income tax adjustment

	Reduction in Tax Rates (%)										
Taxes	5	10	20	30	40	50	60	70	80	90	100
1. *Property Tax*											
MEC	0.090	0.088	0.085	0.082	0.078	0.074	0.071	0.067	0.063	0.059	0.055
AEC	0.090	0.089	0.087	0.085	0.083	0.082	0.080	0.078	0.076	0.074	0.072
2. *Labor Income Tax*											
MEC	0.099	0.097	0.094	0.089	0.085	0.081	0.078	0.074	0.070	0.067	0.063
AEC	0.099	0.098	0.096	0.094	0.092	0.090	0.088	0.086	0.084	0.082	0.080
3. *Sales Tax*											
MEC	0.128	0.124	0.118	0.110	0.102	0.094	0.087	0.079	0.071	0.063	0.055
AEC	0.128	0.126	0.122	0.118	0.114	0.110	0.106	0.102	0.098	0.093	0.089
4.*Labor and Sales Tax (All Taxes, Except for Property Tax)*											
MEC	0.112	0.108	0.099	0.088	0.077	0.067	0.057	0.047	0.038	0.029	0.021
AEC	0.112	0.110	0.104	0.099	0.093	0.088	0.083	0.077	0.072	0.067	0.063
5. *Labor, Sales, and Property Taxes (All Taxes)*											
MEC	0.107	0.101	0.091	0.078	0.065	0.054	0.043	0.032	0.022	0.012	0.004
AEC	0.107	0.104	0.097	0.091	0.084	0.078	0.072	0.066	0.060	0.055	0.049

Note: See table 8.12c.

Table 8.12e
Efficiency cost of taxation under reform proposals—Plan 7: Flat Labor Income Tax and No Sales Tax, with labor income tax adjustment

Taxes	Reduction in Tax Rates (%)										
	5	10	20	30	40	50	60	70	80	90	100
1. *Property Tax*											
MEC	0.068	0.067	0.064	0.061	0.058	0.055	0.051	0.048	0.044	0.041	0.038
AEC	0.068	0.068	0.066	0.064	0.063	0.061	0.059	0.058	0.056	0.054	0.052
2. *Labor Income Tax*											
MEC	0.087	0.082	0.074	0.065	0.056	0.048	0.041	0.034	0.027	0.021	0.016
AEC	0.087	0.084	0.079	0.075	0.070	0.066	0.062	0.058	0.055	0.051	0.048
3. *Sales Tax*											
MEC	N.A.										
AEC											
4. *Labor and Sales Tax (All Taxes, Except for Property Tax)*											
MEC	N.A.										
AEC											
5. *Labor and Property Taxes (All Taxes)*											
MEC	0.083	0.077	0.068	0.068	0.048	0.038	0.030	0.022	0.015	0.008	0.002
AEC	0.083	0.080	0.074	0.069	0.064	0.059	0.054	0.050	0.046	0.042	0.038

Note: See table 8.12c.

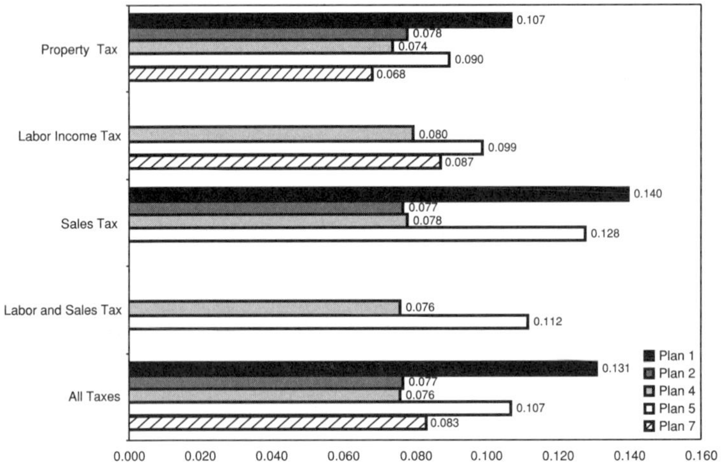

Figure 8.5a
Marginal efficiency cost of national retail sales tax: Plans 1, 2, 4, 5, and 7.

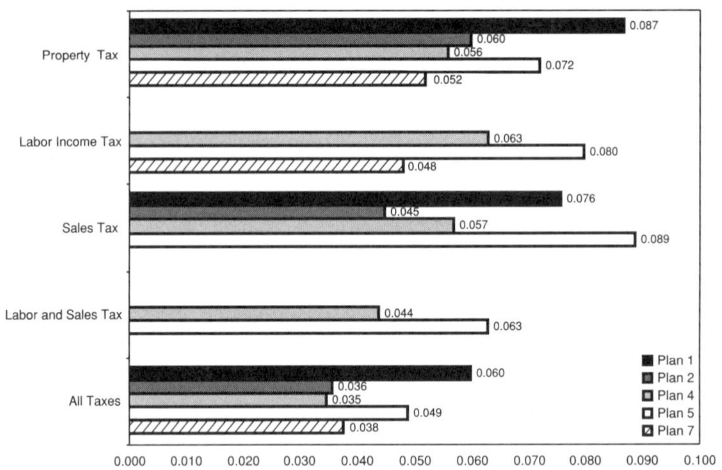

Figure 8.5b
Average efficiency cost of national retail sales tax: Plans 1, 2, 4, 5, and 7.

proposal, and to surprisingly low levels of 0.080 and 0.099 in Plans 4 and 5 of the NRST. In Plan 7 of the NRST where the corporate and individual income taxes are replaced by a proportional labor income tax, the *MEC* for labor income tax is reduced to 0.087. The efficiency cost of sales taxes is reduced more effectively by the NRST, especially when the replacement tax is a flat sales tax (Plan 2 and 4). Due to interactions among the subsets of the tax system, the efficiency costs of taxes not directly affected by the tax reform are also reduced. For example, the HR proposal reduces the *MEC* of the property tax from 0.139 to 0.116 and that of sales tax, from 0.175 to 0.149.

The overall level and the differences among the *MEC*s are useful in understanding the welfare impact of the alternative tax reform programs. For example, the AS proposal has the highest *MEC* overall and performs worst in terms of welfare gain among the reform programs considered in tables 8.10, 8.11, and 8.12a–8.12e. By contrast Plan 4 of the NRST has the lowest overall *MEC* with very little variation among the *MEC*s and performs best with the welfare gain of $4.7 trillion. Plan 2 of NRST shows almost equally strong performance. Not surprisingly, the *MEC*s are uniform and nearly as low as those of Plan 4. By comparing the configurations of the *MEC*s, we can also derive the efficiency costs of policies for redistributing income.

8.6 Alternative Approaches

Estimates of the economic impact of fundamental tax reform depend critically on the structure and parameters of the model used for analyzing tax policy. One way of assessing the robustness of our results is to study their sensitivity to specific assumptions and particular parameter estimates. An alternative approach is to compare the results with those from other studies. Since there are many alternative analyses of the fundamental tax reform proposals, we need to be selective. We have chosen to compare our simulation results with those of David Altig, Alan Auerbach, Lawrence Kotlikoff, Kent Smetters, and Jan Walliser (AAKSW, 1999) and Diane Lim Rogers (1997). [20]

Our primary focus is on the impact of fundamental tax reform on overall economic efficiency and long-run resource allocation. We first compare the effects of replacing the current U.S. income tax system with a consumption-based system. Second, we compare the effects of maintaining current depreciation rules for business assets during the transition from the income tax to a consumption-based flat tax of the type proposed by Hall and Rabushka. Since Rogers does not provide any comparable simulations of this transition relief, we compare our results with those of AAKSW. Third, we compare the simulated effects of replacing the U.S. income tax system with a proportional labor income tax. Since AAKSW do not provide a comparable simulation, we compare our results with those of Rogers.

AAKSW (1999) employ an enhanced version of Auerbach-Kotlikoff (1987) model and Rogers (1997) uses an updated version of Fullerton-Rogers model (1993). Although there are a number of potentially important differences between our model and these alternative models, there are also sufficient similarities to warrant comparison of the results. In particular, all three models focus on resource allocation in dynamic setting. They also have detailed representations of the current U.S. tax system and the proposed reform proposals. The differences among the models are helpful in understanding the implication of alternative assumptions, parameter values, and simulation strategies.

Although we do not attempt to trace the differences among the three models to their sources, we do emphasize that there are substantial differences in the structure of the models. These differences are found in the number of consumer groups, the modeling of the production sector, the representation of tax system, formation of expectations, and so on. For example, Auerbach and Kotlikoff and Fullerton and Rogers distinguish twelve income classes while our model is based on a representative consumer. Fullerton and Rogers and our model incorporate detailed representations of capital income taxation, while Auerbach and Kotlikoff rely heavily on average marginal tax rates to summarizes the effects of capital taxes. The Fullerton and Rogers model is based on myopic expectations while the Auerbach and Kotlikoff model and our model employ perfect foresight.

Table 8.13 provides a comparison of simulation results from the three models. The change in policy is to replace the current U.S. income tax system with a consumption tax. The consumption tax is either proportional or progressive. AAKSW replace the federal income taxes with a consumption tax. The pre-reform consumption tax of 8.8%, representing indirect business taxes and excise taxes, as well as the proportional state income tax of 3.7%, are kept intact. They implement a proportional consumption tax by applying a flat tax rate on all income net of investment.

AAKSW also simulate a progressive consumption tax, referred to as a "flat tax." This is implemented by allowing a standard deduction of

Table 8.13
Transition to consumption tax: Welfare effects and long-run resource allocation in alternative models. Percentage changes from the base case

	Proportional Tax				Progressive Tax				
	AK	FR High	FR Low	JY NRST-2	AK	FR High	FR Low	JY HR	JY NRST-1
output	—	6.0	1.8	—	—	5.8	1.7	—	—
cons. goods	—	—	—	8.3	—	—	—	3.9	5.5
inv. goods	—	—	—	3.5	—	—	—	3.1	1.7
national income	9.4	—	—	—	4.5	—	—	—	—
consumption/GDP	—	1.0	0.4	—	—	0.9	0.4	—	—
net invest./GDP	—	19.6	3.5	—	—	21.5	3.5	—	—
net saving rate[1] (5.1)	5.9	—	—	—	5.6	—	—	—	—
net investment	—	—	—	8.5	—	—	—	4.6	6.0
capital stock	25.4	22.5	5.2	8.5	15.0	23.8	5.2	4.6	6.0
residential	—	4.4	–5.4	–2.4	—	–4.4	–5.6	–2.9	–3.5
labor supply	4.6	0.5	0.0	3.7	1.3	0.0	–0.1	0.7	2.3
real wage[2]	4.6	—	—	15.0	3.2	—	—	9.5	15.2
net wage[2]	13.7	24.6	18.7	28.7	2.7	18.7	13.4	8.8	18.3
interest rate[1] (8.3)	7.3	—	—	—	8.0	—	—	—	—

Table 8.13 (continued)

	Proportional Tax				Progressive Tax				
	AK	FR High	FR Low	JY NRST-2	AK	FR High	FR Low	JY HR	JY NRST-1
social rates of return[1]									
corporate									
short(7.9)	—	—	—	5.6	—	—	—	6.1	5.6
long(8.8)	—	—	—	5.6	—	—	—	6.1	5.6
noncorporate									
short (6.8)	—	—	—	5.6	—	—	—	6.0	5.6
long (7.3)	—	—	—	5.6	—	—	—	6.0	5.6
household									
short (4.9)	—	—	—	5.4	—	—	—	5.4	5.4
long (4.9)	—	—	—	5.4	—	—	—	5.4	5.4
after-tax rate of return	—	0.5	21.7	0.0	—	8.7	16.2	0.0	0.0
marginal tax rate [3]	12.7	14.0	14.0	22.2	19.9	20.0	20.0	27.0	28.6
efficiency gain[4]	—	0.97	–0.05	2.81	—	0.96	–0.04	1.23	1.99

Table 8.13 (continued)

Notes:

AK: Figures are from Altig, Auerbach, Kotlikoff, Smetters, an Walliser (1999) based on an enhanced version of the Auerbach-Kotlikoff model (1987). Federal Income taxes are replaced. Among the remaining taxes are a consumption tax of 8.8%, representing indirect business and excise taxes, and a proportional state income tax of 3.7%.

FR: Figures are from Diane Rogers (1997) based on the Fullerton-Rogers model (1993). "High" indicates that 0.5 is used for the intertemporal and intratemporal elasticities of substitution in consumption. In the "Low" elasticity cases, 0.15 is used for the elasticities. Corporate and personal income taxes are replaced and sales and product taxes remain unaffected.

JY: Calculation by the authors. HR stands for the Hall-Rabushka proposal and NRST, the national retail sales tax. Under HR, corporate and personal income taxes are replaced, and deduction of property tax is eliminated. The pre-reform sales taxes on consumption and investment goods remain in effect under HR, but replaced under NRST. Housing services are not taxed under the HR. Under NRST, sales tax is levied on new housing, which is equivalent to taxing housing services from new housing.

[1] Absolute value in percent. In the parentheses are the base case values.

[2] In JY, real wage is calculated as the producer price of labor service divided by the producer price of consumption good, and net wage, as the price of leisure divided by the consumer price of consumption good.

[3] For NRST and FR, tax inclusive rate in percent, and for HR and labor income tax, marginal tax rate on labor income. For AK, statutory federal rate on labor income.

[4] For FR, percent of lifetime income, and for JY, percent of the present value of the steady-state labor income in the base case.

$9,500 per household and exempting housing wealth from taxation. The amount of the standard deduction is equal to the personal allowance for the single taxpayer under the flat tax proposal of Hall and Rabushka. Columns 1 and 5, under the heading AK for simplicity, show the simulation results. The relatively low marginal tax rates reflect the fact that only federal income taxes are replaced. The proportional consumption tax induces strong responses from capital stock, net wages, and national income. Although the overall impact on the efficiency of the economy is not reported, the large increase in national income suggests that overall efficiency in resource allocation will improve in the long run. Comparison of columns 1 and 5 reveals the effects of a higher marginal tax rates under the flat tax. Progressivity substantially dampens the responses of capital stock, labor supply, net wage, and national income.

Rogers replaces the federal and state income taxes with a consumption tax while maintaining the pre-reform sales taxes included in consumer prices and the output taxes—excise tax plus indirect business tax net of property tax and motor vehicle taxes—included in producer prices. The consumption tax is collected at the point of purchase and progressivity is modeled by means of a lump sum exemption of $10,000 per household. The simulation results under the heading FR in columns 2, 3, 6, and 7 are sensitive to the elasticity of substitution. If a high elasticity of 0.5 is assumed for both intratemporal and intertemporal substitution in consumption, a proportional consumption tax induces strong responses for capital stock and net investment. Even residential capital stock increases by 4.4% relative to the base case.

By contrast, labor supply increases only 0.5% despite the 24.6% gain in net wages. Although total output increases in the long run by 6%, the efficiency gain is only 0.97% of lifetime income. If a low elasticity of substitution of 0.15 is used, despite the substantial increases in net wages and the after-tax rate of return to capital, long-run responses of labor supply, capital stock, and total output are modest at best. Rather surprisingly, efficiency gains are negative, as the gains to the young and to future generations are overshadowed by losses of the old generation at the time of the tax reform. It is also noteworthy that Rogers' results are not sensitive to the marginal tax rate on consumption. This is because a higher consumption tax rate worsens efficiency by distorting labor supply and, at the same time, improves efficiency by redistributing income from the old to the young.[21]

We replace the federal and state income taxes with two alternative consumption-based taxes—a flat tax and a national retail sales tax (NRST). For a proportional consumption tax we use the flat NRST (Plan 2) as the replacement tax, and for the progressive consumption tax replacement, we use the Hall-Rabushka proposal (HR) and the progressive NRST (Plan 1). Under the NRST plans, the pre-reform indirect tax on investment goods is abolished and the indirect tax on consumption goods is subsumed in the new consumption tax. Investment in owner-occupied housing is taxed at the rate of the national sale tax, which is equivalent to a prepayment of consumption tax on the capital services generated by household assets placed in service after the tax reform.

Under HR the pre-reform indirect taxes on investment goods and consumption goods remain in force and the deduction of property taxes is disallowed. Compared with AAKSW, our results show smaller quantity responses and larger price responses. This is consistent with the fact that our intratemporal elasticities of substitution in consumption and production are relatively low.[22] In addition, the long run after-tax rate of return to private wealth (4.45%) is constant and the effective tax rate on private capital is quite high in the base case (30.2% in 1996, table 4.6). In the AAKSW simulations, the long-run interest rate depends on the replacement tax policy and the decline is relatively small. By contrast, the decline in the average long-run social rate of return in our simulations is proportionally larger and the long-run social rates of return to capital are independent of the type of consumption tax.

Under the HR flat tax proposal social rates of return to business assets are higher than under the NRST only because property taxes are not deductible. If property taxes are allowed as a deduction under HR, the property tax raises the social rate of return point for point and social rates of return under the NRST and HR are equalized.[23] The strong convergence of social rates of return under NRST and HR is another important feature of our results, indicating improvement in capital allocation. On top of the increased labor supply and capital stock, improved capital allocation provides additional efficiency gains in resource allocation. Our estimate of efficiency gains from a proportional consumption tax is as large as 2.8% of the base case labor income. The efficiency gain from the HR proposal and the progressive NRST are smaller, due to higher marginal tax rates. Rogers' results generally show smaller efficiency gains, especially with her "low" elasticity case, where the efficiency gains are negative.

We next compare the long-run effects of transition relief designed to moderate the economic losses to asset owners from replacing income taxes with a flat tax. A widely discussed relief measure is maintaining pre-reform depreciation rules for assets in place at the time of the tax reform. Based on their estimate that the present value of the depreciation allowances equals roughly 50% of the nonresidential capital stock, AAKSW implement the transition relief by cutting the effective cash-flow tax rate in half. We estimate that the total balance of unused depreciation allowances is, before discounting, $3.1 trillion in 1996 (see tables 8.6a and 8.6b). For the same year, capital stock in the business sector is estimated to be $13.8 trillion, of which depreciable assets account for $9.8 trillion. We find that AAKSW have overestimated the balance of unused depreciation allowances.

Table 8.14 shows substantial differences between our results and those of AAKSW. In the AK model, where consumers have finite time horizon, transitional policy can affect long-run resource allocation. In the AAKSW simulation transition relief has large negative long-run impacts on national income, capital stock, labor supply, and the marginal tax rate. By contrast the transition relief does not affect the long-run resource allocation in our simulation, although it reduces the total efficiency gains from the tax reform. One obvious explanation of the large impacts of the transition relief is that AAKSW overestimate the value of transition relief. Since transition relief is equivalent to replacing a lump sum tax with a distortionary tax of equal revenue, the efficiency loss is likely to be a fraction of the revenue involved. The AAKSW findings that transition relief lowers the long-run national income by 2.6% and that the flat tax rate must be increased by 2.7% for revenue neutrality appear to be very large.

Lastly we compare our simulations with those of Rogers where the U.S. income tax system is replaced with a proportional wage tax. Although the proportional consumption tax of table 8.13 is not equivalent to the proportional wage tax in table 8.15, the economic effects are similar. One well known reason for the efficiency improvement resulting from a proportional consumption tax is that it levies a lump sum tax on the capital in place at the time of the tax reform.

We have now completed our simulations of the economic impact of changing the base for the U.S. tax system from income to consumption. Despite the fact that all of the tax reform proposals we have considered in this chapter employ a consumption tax base, there are very important differences in the economic effects. To put all the pro-

Table 8.14
Long-run effects of transition relief under flat tax: Auerbach-Kotlikoff vs. Jorgenson-Yun. Percentage changes from the base case

	Auerback-Kotlikoff (Flat Tax)		Jorgenson-Yun (Hall-Rabushka)	
	Standard	With relief	Standard	With relief
output	—	—	—	—
cons. goods	—	—	3.9	3.9
inv. goods	—	—	3.1	3.1
national income	4.5	1.9	—	—
net saving rate (5.1)[1]	5.6	5.5	—	—
net investment	—	—	4.6	4.6
capital stock	15.0	8.3	4.6	4.6
residential	—	—	–2.9	–2.9
labor supply	1.3	–0.2	0.7	0.7
real wage[2]	3.2	2.1	9.5	9.5
net wages[2]	2.7	–2.1	8.8	8.8
interest rate[1] (8.3)	8.0	7.8	—	—
social rates of return[1]				
corporate				
short(7.9)	—	—	6.1	6.1
(8.8)	—	—	6.1	6.1
noncorporate				
short (6.8)	—	—	6.0	6.0
long (7.3)	—	—	6.0	6.0
household				
short (4.9)	—	—	5.4	5.4
long (4.9)	—	—	5.4	5.4
marginal tax rate [3]	19.9	22.6	27.0	27.0
efficiency gain[4]	—	—	1.23	1.08

Note: See table 8.13.

posals onto an equal footing we have imposed the requirement that each proposal must be revenue neutral. More precisely, we have held the time path of real government spending and the outstanding debt of the government sector, as well as the balance of payments, fixed throughout all simulations. We have found, perhaps surprisingly, that none of the tax reform proposals actually under consideration in the U.S. Congress comes close to revenue neutrality.

We have imposed the requirement that all the tax reform proposals must be revenue neutral by adjusting the tax rates that define the pro-

Table 8.15
Transition to proportional wage taxes: Fullerton-Rogers vs. Jorgenson-Yun (Long-Run). Percentage changes from the base case

	Fullerton-Rogers		Jorgenson-Yun
	High	Low	
output	5.4	2.4	—
cons. goods	—	—	8.8
inv. goods	—	—	3.1
consumption/GDP	0.9	0.4	—
net invest./GDP	17.8	7.2	—
net saving rate[1] (5.1)	5.6	5.5	—
net investment	—	—	9.1
capital stock	20.2	8.7	9.1
residential	4.0	–3.0	–2.4
labor supply	0.3	–0.1	2.9
real wage[2]	—	—	14.9
net wages[2]	20.2	17.1	24.8
social rates of return[1]			
corporate			
short (7.9)	—	—	5.6
long (8.8)	—	—	5.6
noncorporate			
short (6.8)	—	—	5.6
long (7.3)	—	—	5.6
household			
short (4.9)	—	—	5.4
long (4.9)	—	—	5.4
after-tax rate of return	18.8	35.2	0.0
marginal tax rate[3]	18.0	17.0	24.5
efficiency gain[4]	0.86	–0.20	2.71

Note: See table 8.13.

posal, such as the Flat Tax rate in the HR and AS proposals or the sales tax rate in the National Retail Sales Tax. We have also introduced changes in other tax instruments, such as sales and income taxes, in order to make up the revenue shortfalls. Finally, we have considered a hypothetical lump sum tax as a means of raising revenue in order to achieve neutrality. This is useful chiefly as a means of assessing the potential for gains in efficiency. Conversion of the potential gains into actual gains requires losses in efficiency from tax distortions that must be balanced against efficiency gains from tax reform.

Our first conclusion is that the consumption tax proposals generate greater welfare gains than the capital income tax reforms we have considered in chapter 7. In particular, the HR and AS Flat Tax proposals have a clear edge over a reformed capital income tax, even with equal burdens for all assets and all sectors. However, this edge could easily disappear if depreciation on "old" capital, accumulated prior to the tax reform, were allowed to continue after the tax reform. If property tax deductions were allowed as well, a reformed capital income tax would be superior to either the HR or AS Flat Tax in terms of economic efficiency.

Our second conclusion is that the NRST proposals offer a significant advantage over the Flat Tax proposals with similar progressivity. The NRST proposals could generate gains in efficiency that are fifty percent greater than Flat Tax proposals. This is due to the greater distortions resulting from the Flat Tax. Further, eliminating sales taxes on investment goods in the NRST would produce substantial gains in efficiency. This reduces inter-temporal distortions due to reduction of the tax wedge between the returns to investors and the earnings of savers.

Our third, and final, conclusion is that the efficiency cost of progressive taxation is very substantial. Shifting from a sales tax with a system of family allowances to a flat sales tax would generate sizable gains in efficiency. Similarly, the combination of a flat sales tax and a flat labor income tax is far superior in terms of efficiency to a similar combination with a system of family allowances. The cost of progressivity, even on the limited scale contemplated in the HR and AS Flat Tax proposals, amounts to around 1.5 trillion dollars with gains that depend on specific features of the proposal. We conclude that the efficiency costs of progressivity should be carefully assessed as part of any future deliberations about fundamental tax reform.

We have quantified the economic impact of tax reform in terms of gains in economic welfare. An alternative perspective is provided by the marginal efficiency cost (*MEC*) of specific tax provisions. These costs must be reduced as much as possible and variations among the costs of different components of the tax system must be minimized. We find that the flat sales tax version of the NRST would achieve the smallest cost of taxation at the margin. This would be as little as a quarter of the marginal cost of taxation of the 1996 Tax Law that we have estimated in chapter 7. This quantifies, very dramatically, the potential gains in economic efficiency from fundamental tax reform.

Appendix

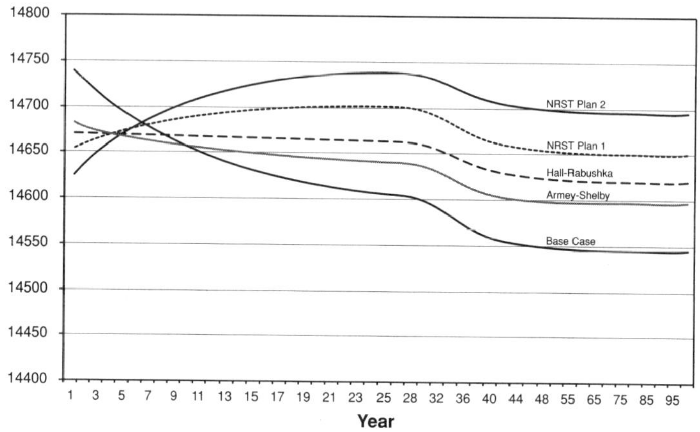

Figure A8.1
Dynamic paths of full consumption (billions of units).

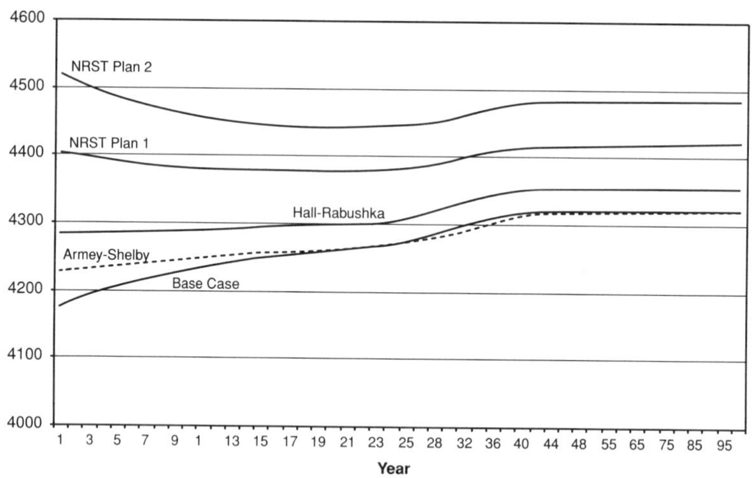

Figure A8.2
Dynamic paths of labor supply (billions of units).

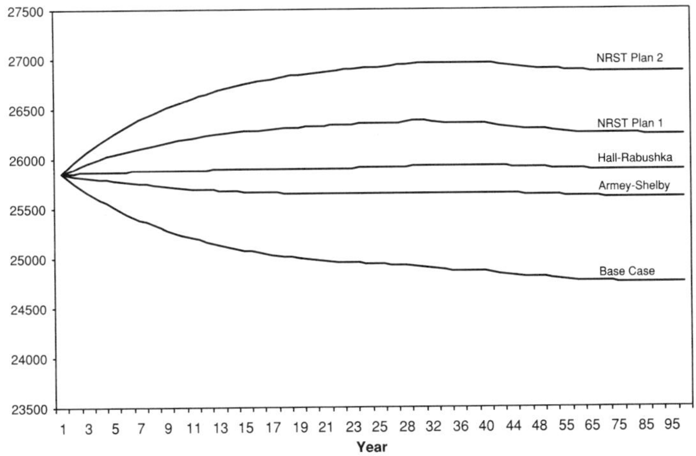

Figure A8.3
Dynamic paths of total capital stock (billions of units).

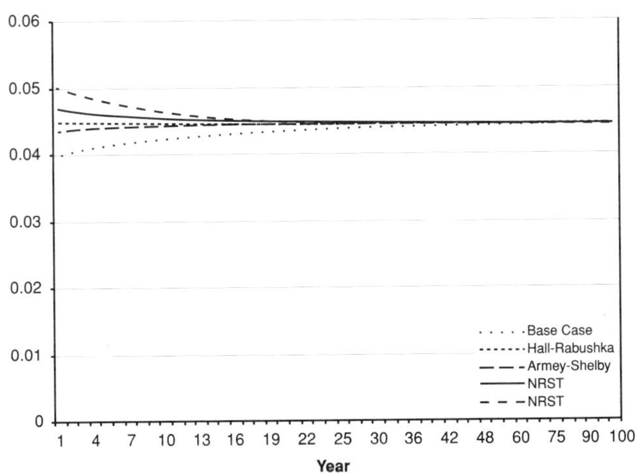

Figure A8.4
Dynamic paths of real private rate of return, all assets.

Table A8.1
Steady-state tax parameters under alternative policies

	Base Case	Efficient Cap. Alloc.	Hall-Rabushka	Armey-Shelby	NRST[2] Plan 1	NRST[3] Plan 2	NRST[4] Plan 4	NRST[5] Plan 5	NRST[6] Plan 7
1. *Capital Income Taxes/Flat Tax*									
t_q or t_f	0.3880	0.3880	0.2759	0.3118	—	—	—	—	—
t_q^e	0.2020	0.1964	—	—	—	—	—	—	—
t_m^e	0.2879	0.2798	—	—	—	—	—	—	—
t_h^e	0.2879	0.2798	—	—	—	—	—	—	—
t_q^g	0.0559	0.0543	—	—	—	—	—	—	—
t_m^g	0.0720	0.0699	—	—	—	—	—	—	—
t_h^g	0.0	0.0	—	—	—	—	—	—	—
t_q^d	0.1823	0.1772	—	—	—	—	—	—	—
t_m^d	0.2300	0.2236	—	—	—	—	—	—	—
t_h^d	0.2693	0.2616	—	—	—	—	—	—	—
t_g^d	0.2025	0.1968	—	—	—	—	—	—	—
$t_e^a = t_d^a$	0.1830	0.1779	—	—	—	—	—	—	—
2. *Present Value of Depreciation Allowances*									
z_q^s	0.8801	0.8801	1.0	1.0	—	—	—	—	—
z_q^l	0.4574	0.4574	1.0	1.0	—	—	—	—	—
z_m^s	0.8878	0.8878	1.0	1.0	—	—	—	—	—
z_m^l	0.3909	0.3909	1.0	1.0	—	—	—	—	—
z_h^s	—	—	—	—	—	—	—	—	—
z_h^l	—	—	—	—	—	—	—	—	—

Table A8.1 (continued)

	Base Case	Efficient Cap. Alloc.	Hall-Rabushka	Armey-Shelby	NRST[2] Plan 1	NRST[3] Plan 2	NRST[4] Plan 4	NRST[5] Plan 5	NRST[6] Plan 7
3. *Investment Tax Credit*									
k_q^s	—	0.0388	—	—	—	—	—	—	—
k_q^l	—	0.1893	—	—	—	—	—	—	—
k_m^s	—	0.0053	—	—	—	—	—	—	—
k_m^l	—	0.0808	—	—	—	—	—	—	—
k_h^e	—	–0.0722	—	—	—	—	—	—	—
k_h^l	—	–0.3253	—	—	—	—	—	—	—
4. *Labor Income Tax*									
t_L^m	0.2645	0.2570	0.2695	0.2944	—	—	0.1110	0.1132	0.2447
t_L^a	0.1266	0.1230	0.1533	0.1505	—	—	0.1110	0.1132	0.2447
5. *Sales Taxes*									
t_C	0.058	0.058	0.058	0.058	0.4011	0.2851	0.1553	0.2147	—
t_C^a	0.058	0.058	0.058	0.058	0.2959	0.2851	0.1553	0.1584	—
t_I	0.058	0.058	0.058	0.058	0.0	0.0	0.0	0.0	—
6. *Property Tax*									
t_q^P	0.0120		same as left						
t_m^P	0.0114		same as left						
t_h^P	0.0091		same as left						

Table A8.1 (continued)

	Base Case	Efficient Cap. Alloc.	Hall-Rabushka	Armey-Shelby	NRST[2] Plan 1	NRST[3] Plan 2	NRST[4] Plan 4	NRST[5] Plan 5	NRST[6] Plan 7
7. *Other Taxes*									
t_t	0.0068		same as left						
t_w	0.0008		same as left						
8. *Property Tax Deduction*									
	Yes	Yes	No		No	No	No	No	No
9. *Adjusted Taxes for Revenue Neutrality*[7]									
	—	Individual Income Tax	Flat Tax	Flat Tax	NRST	NRST		NRST&Labor	

Notes:
1. In the case of efficient capital allocation, the social rates of return to short-lived and long-lived assets in the corporate, noncorporate, and household sectors are equalized.
2. NRST Plan 1: Progressive Sales Tax and No Tax on Labor Income
3. NRST Plan 2: Flat Sales Tax with No Tax on Labor Income
4. NRST Plan 4: Flat sales Tax with Flat Labor Income Tax
5. NRST Plan 5: Progressive Sales Tax with Flat Labor Income Tax
6. NRST Plan 7: Flat Labor Income Tax
7. Tax rates are adjusted proportionally to balance government budget
8. See table 7.1 for notation.
9. Inflation is fixed at 4% per year.

Table A8.2
Steady-state resource allocation under alternative policies

	Base Case	Efficient Cap. Alloc.	Hall-Rabushka	Armey-Shelby	NRST 1	NRST 2	NRST 4	NRST 5	NRST 7
1. *Household Behavior (billion units)*									
F	14544	14601	14620	14596	14651	14695	14698	14672	14698
C	3539	3661	3664	3620	3766	3859	3848	3791	3828
LJ	13365	13342	13335	13365	13266	13205	13220	13258	13242
HD	1104	1065	1084	1079	1077	1089	1089	1082	1089
L	4322	4345	4352	4322	4421	4482	4467	4429	4446
2. *Business Production (billion units)*									
LD	3531	3560	3567	3537	3613	3686	3685	3640	3682
QD	1012	1068	1067	1054	1073	1106	1110	1089	1114
MD	500	529	542	533	567	586	588	577	592
CS	3647	3777	3791	3747	3848	3952	3960	3896	3969
IS	1707	1706	1713	1700	1737	1767	1765	1746	1761
3. *Government Spending (billion units)*									
CG	256	270	278	277	227	243	265	255	298
IG	242	239	235	235	250	248	244	245	238
LG	705	698	698	699	719	707	693	700	675
EL	204	201	198	198	211	209	205	206	201
ER	12.0	11.9	11.7	11.7	12.4	12.3	12.1	12.1	11.8
GS	1418	same as in the base case							

Table A8.2 (continued)

	Base Case	Efficient Cap. Alloc.	Hall-Rabushka	Armey-Shelby	NRST 1	NRST 2	NRST 4	NRST 5	NRST 7
4. *Capital Allocation (billions of 1997 dollars)*									
VKL	23800	24336	24889	24623	25231	25829	25887	25524	25956
VQL	7851	8636	8718	8596	8854	9127	9157	8990	9197
VML	5363	5692	5843	5745	6118	6322	6349	6224	6385
VHL	10587	10008	10328	10283	10258	10379	10379	10309	10374
5. *Prices (1997 dollar per unit)*									
PF	0.9655	0.9682	0.9285	0.9064	1.284	1.2626	1.1295	1.1385	0.9689
PC	0.9558	0.8953	0.8573	0.8594	1.1122	1.0309	0.9302	0.9718	0.8091
PLJ	0.7175	0.7232	0.7000	0.6752	0.9873	0.9962	0.8884	0.8814	0.7581
PHD	0.9705	1.1362	1.0148	1.0148	1.4219	1.3043	1.1726	1.2328	1.0150
PI	1.0683	same as in the base case							
PCS	0.9034	0.8462	0.8104	0.8123	0.7938	0.8022	0.8051	0.8001	0.8091
PIS	1.0097	1.0097	1.0097	1.0097	1.0683	1.0683	1.0683	1.0683	1.0683
PQD	1.0615	0.9023	0.8575	0.8645	0.8200	0.8200	0.8200	0.8200	0.8200
PMD	1.0312	0.9556	0.8914	0.9002	0.8448	0.8448	0.8448	0.8448	0.8448
PLD	0.9711	0.9690	0.9540	0.9526	0.9829	0.9918	0.9950	0.9950	0.9992
PGS	0.9923	0.9801	0.9653	0.9650	1.0249	1.0159	0.9994	1.0044	0.9776
6. *Welfare Differential (billions of 1997 dollars)*									
ΔW	0.0	1949.9	2056.2	1229.3	3323.6	4686.8	4697.3	3910.1	4527.8

Table A8.2 (continued)

Notes:
1. For explanation of alternative policies, see table A8.1.
2. Inflation is fixed at 4% per year.

F: Full consumption
C: Nondurable goods and services
LJ: Leisure
HD: Household capital services
L: Labor supply
LD: Labor used in the business sector
QD: Corporate capital services
MD: Noncorporate capital services
CS: Production of consumption goods
IS: Production of investment goods
CG: Government demand, consumption goods
IG: Government demand, investment goods
LG: Government demand, labor
EL: Transfer to households
ER: Transfer to the rest of the world
GS: Real government spending

VKL: Lagged value of private capital stock (VQL+VML+VHL
VQL: Lagged value of corporate capital stock
VML: Lagged value of noncorporate capital stock
VHL: Lagged value of Household capital stock
PF: Price of full consumption
PC: Price of consumption goods (nondurables)
PLJ: Imputed price of leisure
PHD: Price of household capital services
PI: Price of investment goods, inclusive of sales tax
PCS: Producer price of consumption goods, exclusive of sales tax
PIS: Producer price of investment goods, exclusive of sales tax
PQD: Price of corporate capital services
PMD: Price of noncorporate capital services
PLD: producer price of labor services
PGS: Price index of GS
ΔW: Welfare gains from tax reform.

Table A8.3
Dynamic paths of selected variables: Hall-Rabushka (billions of units)

YEAR	GDP	F	L	KL1	RSPA
1	6884.8	14670	4283.8	25847	0.044902
2	6886.3	14670	4283.9	25855	0.044865
3	6887.7	14670	4284.1	25861	0.044835
4	6889.1	14670	4284.4	25867	0.044810
5	6890.4	14670	4284.8	25872	0.044790
6	6891.8	14670	4285.3	25875	0.044773
7	6893.1	14670	4285.9	25879	0.044760
8	6894.4	14669	4286.5	25881	0.044750
9	6895.6	14669	4287.2	25884	0.044741
10	6896.9	14669	4288.0	25885	0.044734
11	6898.1	14668	4288.8	25887	0.044729
12	6899.1	14668	4289.7	25888	0.044724
13	6900.2	14668	4290.6	25890	0.044718
14	6901.4	14667	4291.4	25891	0.044714
15	6902.4	14667	4292.4	25892	0.044709
16	6903.4	14666	4293.3	25893	0.044703
17	6904.3	14666	4294.3	25894	0.044697
18	6905.1	14665	4295.4	25896	0.044689
19	6905.8	14665	4296.4	25897	0.044679
20	6906.5	14665	4297.5	25898	0.044667
21	6907.1	14664	4298.6	25900	0.044653
22	6907.5	14664	4299.7	25902	0.044637
23	6907.8	14663	4300.8	25904	0.044617
24	6908.0	14663	4302.0	25906	0.044593
25	6908.1	14662	4303.2	25909	0.044565
26	6907.9	14662	4304.5	25912	0.044532
28	6907.0	14661	4307.2	25919	0.044449
30	6927.0	14646	4325.1	25927	0.044418
32	6927.0	14645	4326.7	25925	0.044407
34	6926.7	14644	4328.3	25925	0.044386
36	6925.9	14643	4329.9	25925	0.044348
38	6924.4	14642	4331.7	25927	0.044290
40	6944.1	14626	4348.6	25931	0.044290
42	6944.2	14625	4349.1	25924	0.044321
44	6944.2	14624	4349.6	25918	0.044348
46	6944.2	14624	4349.9	25912	0.044371
48	6944.3	14623	4350.3	25908	0.044391

Table A8.3 (continued)

YEAR	GDP	F	L	KL1	RSPA
50	6944.3	14623	4350.5	25904	0.044408
55	6944.4	14622	4351.1	25897	0.044440
60	6944.4	14621	4351.4	25892	0.044462
65	6944.4	14620	4351.6	25889	0.044475
70	6944.4	14620	4351.8	25886	0.044485
75	6944.5	14620	4351.9	25885	0.044492
80	6944.5	14620	4352.0	25884	0.044496
85	6944.5	14620	4352.0	25883	0.044500
90	6944.6	14620	4352.0	25883	0.044504
95	6944.8	14620	4352.0	25883	0.044509
100	6945.0	14620	4352.2	25882	0.044518

Note: See table A7.2.

Table A8.4
Dynamic paths of selected variables: Armey-Shelby (billions of units)

YEAR	GDP	F	L	KL1	RSPA
1	6831.3	14682	4228.5	25847	0.043621
2	6833.0	14678	4230.7	25826	0.043707
3	6834.7	14675	4232.9	25807	0.043788
4	6836.3	14672	4235.0	25790	0.043864
5	6837.9	14669	4237.1	25773	0.043936
6	6839.4	14667	4239.1	25758	0.044004
7	6840.9	14664	4241.0	25744	0.044067
8	6842.4	14662	4242.9	25731	0.044126
9	6843.8	14660	4244.8	25719	0.044181
10	6845.2	14658	4246.6	25708	0.044232
11	6846.5	14656	4248.4	25698	0.044277
12	6847.7	14654	4250.2	25689	0.044319
13	6848.9	14653	4251.8	25681	0.044357
14	6850.2	14651	4253.4	25674	0.044391
15	6851.3	14650	4255.1	25668	0.044422
16	6852.4	14649	4256.6	25662	0.044449
17	6853.4	14647	4258.2	25657	0.044471
18	6854.3	14646	4259.8	25653	0.044490
19	6855.2	14645	4261.3	25650	0.044505

Table A8.4 (continued)

YEAR	GDP	F	L	KL1	RSPA
20	6856.0	14644	4262.8	25647	0.044515
21	6856.6	14643	4264.3	25645	0.044521
22	6857.2	14642	4265.8	25643	0.044522
23	6857.6	14642	4267.3	25642	0.044518
24	6857.9	14641	4268.8	25642	0.044509
25	6858.1	14640	4270.3	25642	0.044495
26	6858.0	14639	4271.8	25643	0.044474
28	6857.3	14638	4274.9	25646	0.044411
30	6877.6	14622	4294.0	25652	0.044402
32	6877.7	14621	4295.8	25649	0.044398
34	6877.4	14620	4297.5	25647	0.044383
36	6876.7	14619	4299.3	25647	0.044350
38	6875.3	14618	4301.2	25649	0.044297
40	6895.2	14602	4319.0	25652	0.044305
42	6895.2	14601	4319.4	25646	0.044332
44	6895.3	14601	4319.7	25640	0.044357
46	6895.3	14600	4320.1	25635	0.044378
48	6895.3	14599	4320.3	25631	0.044396
50	6895.3	14599	4320.6	25627	0.044412
55	6895.3	14598	4321.0	25620	0.044441
60	6895.3	14597	4321.4	25616	0.044462
65	6895.3	14597	4321.6	25612	0.044475
70	6895.4	14596	4321.7	25610	0.044485
75	6895.4	14596	4321.8	25609	0.044492
80	6895.4	14596	4321.9	25608	0.044497
85	6895.4	14596	4321.9	25607	0.044500
90	6895.4	14596	4322.0	25607	0.044503
95	6895.8	14596	4321.9	25606	0.044513
100	6896.2	14596	4322.1	25605	0.044525

Note: See table A7.2.

Table A8.5
Dynamic paths of selected variables: NRST Plan 1 (Progressive NRST)
(billions of units)

YEAR	GDP	F	L	KL1	RSPA
1	7944.5	14651	4402.1	25847	0.046943
2	7944.9	14658	4398.3	25904	0.046672
3	7945.2	14664	4394.9	25955	0.046430
4	7945.5	14669	4392.0	26000	0.046212
5	7945.8	14673	4389.4	26041	0.046017
6	7946.1	14677	4387.2	26077	0.045842
7	7946.3	14680	4385.3	26110	0.045685
8	7946.5	14683	4383.7	26139	0.045544
9	7946.6	14686	4382.3	26165	0.045418
10	7946.7	14688	4381.1	26189	0.045303
11	7946.8	14690	4380.1	26209	0.045200
12	7946.8	14692	4379.3	26228	0.045108
13	7946.8	14694	4378.7	26245	0.045024
14	7946.8	14695	4378.2	26260	0.044946
15	7946.7	14696	4377.8	26273	0.044876
16	7946.5	14697	4377.6	26285	0.044812
17	7946.3	14698	4377.4	26296	0.044754
18	7946.0	14698	4377.4	26305	0.044699
19	7945.7	14699	4377.5	26314	0.044648
20	7945.3	14699	4377.6	26322	0.044600
21	7944.7	14700	4378.1	26336	0.044509
23	7943.4	14700	4378.5	26342	0.044465
24	7942.5	14700	4379.0	26347	0.044422
25	7941.5	14700	4379.5	26352	0.044378
26	7940.4	14700	4380.1	26357	0.044333
28	7937.5	14700	4381.5	26367	0.044236
30	7956.3	14686	4393.4	26376	0.044113
32	7955.4	14684	4395.3	26366	0.044133
34	7954.2	14682	4397.0	26358	0.044139
36	7952.5	14681	4398.7	26353	0.044130
38	7950.3	14679	4400.4	26349	0.044103
40	7969.9	14665	4412.3	26348	0.044043
42	7970.0	14662	4414.0	26329	0.044123
44	7970.2	14660	4415.3	26313	0.044192
46	7970.3	14659	4416.4	26300	0.044249
48	7970.5	14657	4417.3	26289	0.044295

Table A8.5 (continued)

YEAR	GDP	F	L	KL1	RSPA
50	7970.6	14656	4418.1	26280	0.044334
55	7970.7	14654	4419.4	26265	0.044398
60	7970.8	14653	4420.2	26256	0.044439
65	7970.9	14652	4420.7	26250	0.044464
70	7970.9	14651	4421.0	26246	0.044479
75	7970.9	14651	4421.2	26244	0.044488
80	7970.9	14651	4421.3	26243	0.044493
85	7971.0	14651	4421.3	26242	0.044498
90	7970.9	14651	4421.4	26241	0.044502
95	7971.1	14651	4421.4	26241	0.044503
100	7970.3	14651	4421.2	26241	0.044493

Note: See table A7.2.

Table A8.6
Dynamic paths of selected variables: NRST Plan 2 (Flat NRST) (billions of units)

YEAR	GDP	F	L	KL1	RSPA
1	8088.8	14617	4517.1	25847	0.049791
2	8088.3	14632	4508.0	25965	0.049230
3	8088.0	14645	4499.9	26070	0.048729
4	8087.6	14656	4492.7	26166	0.048279
5	8087.3	14666	4486.3	26251	0.047876
6	8087.0	14675	4480.6	26328	0.047515
7	8086.7	14683	4475.5	26397	0.047191
8	8086.4	14690	4471.1	26459	0.046900
9	8086.2	14697	4467.1	26514	0.046639
10	8085.9	14702	4463.7	26564	0.046403
11	8085.7	14707	4460.6	26609	0.046193
12	8085.3	14712	4457.9	26649	0.046003
13	8085.0	14716	4455.6	26686	0.045830
14	8084.7	14719	4453.6	26718	0.045673
15	8084.4	14722	4451.8	26747	0.045532
16	8083.9	14725	4450.3	26773	0.045403
17	8083.5	14727	4449.0	26797	0.045286
18	8082.9	14729	4448.0	26818	0.045179
19	8082.3	14731	4447.1	26837	0.045080

Table A8.6 (continued)

YEAR	GDP	F	L	KL1	RSPA
20	8081.7	14733	4446.4	26854	0.044989
21	8080.9	14734	4445.9	26869	0.044903
22	8080.1	14735	4445.5	26883	0.044823
23	8079.1	14736	4445.3	26896	0.044747
24	8078.0	14737	4445.1	26908	0.044673
25	8076.7	14737	4445.2	26918	0.044602
26	8075.3	14738	4445.3	26928	0.044531
28	8071.8	14739	4445.9	26946	0.044389
30	8091.0	14726	4457.3	26962	0.044254
32	8090.0	14725	4458.5	26958	0.044247
34	8088.6	14724	4459.8	26955	0.044229
36	8086.7	14722	4461.2	26953	0.044198
38	8084.1	14721	4462.6	26953	0.044151
40	8104.4	14708	4474.4	26954	0.044100
42	8104.6	14705	4475.9	26937	0.044173
44	8104.9	14704	4477.1	26924	0.044233
46	8105.1	14702	4478.0	26913	0.044282
48	8105.3	14701	4478.8	26903	0.044322
50	8105.5	14700	4479.5	26896	0.044354
55	8105.8	14698	4480.6	26883	0.044412
60	8105.9	14697	4481.3	26875	0.044448
65	8106.1	14696	4481.8	26870	0.044469
70	8106.1	14696	4482.0	26867	0.044483
75	8106.2	14696	4482.2	26865	0.044492
80	8106.4	14696	4482.2	26864	0.044500
85	8106.2	14696	4482.4	26863	0.044499
90	8106.1	14696	4482.4	26863	0.044502
95	8106.3	14695	4482.4	26863	0.044503
100	8106.0	14695	4482.3	26862	0.044498

Note: See table A7.2.

Table A8.7
Dynamic paths of full consumption (billions of units)

YEAR	Base Case	Hall-Rabushka	Armey-Shelby	NRST Plan 1	NRST Plan 2
1	14740	14670	14682	14651	14617
2	14727	14670	14678	14658	14632
3	14715	14670	14675	14664	14645
4	14704	14670	14672	14669	14656
5	14694	14670	14669	14673	14666
6	14685	14670	14667	14677	14675
7	14676	14670	14664	14680	14683
8	14669	14669	14662	14683	14690
9	14661	14669	14660	14686	14697
10	14655	14669	14658	14688	14702
11	14649	14668	14656	14690	14707
12	14644	14668	14654	14692	14712
13	14639	14668	14653	14694	14716
14	14634	14667	14651	14695	14719
15	14630	14667	14650	14696	14722
16	14626	14666	14649	14697	14725
17	14623	14666	14647	14698	14727
18	14620	14665	14646	14698	14729
19	14617	14665	14645	14699	14731
20	14614	14665	14644	14699	14733
21	14612	14664	14643	14700	14734
22	14610	14664	14642	14700	14735
23	14608	14663	14642	14700	14736
24	14606	14663	14641	14700	14737
25	14604	14662	14640	14700	14737
26	14603	14662	14639	14700	14738
28	14600	14661	14638	14700	14739
30	14584	14646	14622	14686	14726
32	14581	14645	14621	14684	14725
34	14578	14644	14620	14682	14724
36	14576	14643	14619	14681	14722
38	14574	14642	14618	14679	14721
40	14559	14626	14602	14665	14708
42	14557	14625	14601	14662	14705
44	14554	14624	14601	14660	14704
46	14553	14624	14600	14659	14702

Table A8.7 (continued)

YEAR	Base Case	Hall-Rabushka	Armey-Shelby	NRST Plan 1	NRST Plan 2
48	14551	14623	14599	14657	14701
50	14550	14623	14599	14656	14700
55	14548	14622	14598	14654	14698
60	14546	14621	14597	14653	14697
65	14545	14620	14597	14652	14696
70	14545	14620	14596	14651	14696
75	14545	14620	14596	14651	14696
80	14544	14620	14596	14651	14696
85	14544	14620	14596	14651	14696
90	14544	14620	14596	14651	14696
95	14544	14620	14596	14651	14695
100	14544	14620	14596	14651	14695

Note: For magnitude of relevant price indexes, see table 13 and text.

Table A8.8
Dynamic paths of labor supply (billions of units)

YEAR	Base Case	Hall-Rabushka	Armey-Shelby	NRST Plan 1	NRST Plan 2
1	4175.1	4283.8	4228.5	4402.1	4517.1
2	4183.9	4283.9	4230.7	4398.3	4508.0
3	4191.9	4284.1	4232.9	4394.9	4499.9
4	4199.3	4284.4	4235.0	4392.0	4492.7
5	4206.1	4284.8	4237.1	4389.4	4486.3
6	4212.4	4285.3	4239.1	4387.2	4480.6
7	4218.1	4285.9	4241.0	4385.3	4475.5
8	4223.4	4286.5	4242.9	4383.7	4471.1
9	4228.3	4287.2	4244.8	4382.3	4467.1
10	4232.7	4288.0	4246.6	4381.1	4463.7
11	4236.9	4288.8	4248.4	4380.1	4460.6
12	4240.7	4289.7	4250.2	4379.3	4457.9
13	4244.2	4290.6	4251.8	4378.7	4455.6
14	4247.4	4291.4	4253.4	4378.2	4453.6
15	4250.4	4292.4	4255.1	4377.8	4451.8
16	4253.2	4293.3	4256.6	4377.6	4450.3
17	4255.8	4294.3	4258.2	4377.4	4449.0

Table A8.8 (continued)

YEAR	Base Case	Hall-Rabushka	Armey-Shelby	NRST Plan 1	NRST Plan 2
18	4258.2	4295.4	4259.8	4377.4	4448.0
19	4260.4	4296.4	4261.3	4377.5	4447.1
20	4262.5	4297.5	4262.8	4377.6	4446.4
21	4264.5	4298.6	4264.3	4377.8	4445.9
22	4266.3	4299.7	4265.8	4378.1	4445.5
23	4268.1	4300.8	4267.3	4378.5	4445.3
24	4269.8	4302.0	4268.8	4379.0	4445.1
25	4271.4	4303.2	4270.3	4379.5	4445.2
26	4272.9	4304.5	4271.8	4380.1	4445.3
28	4275.8	4307.2	4274.9	4381.5	4445.9
30	4290.1	4325.1	4294.0	4393.4	4457.3
32	4292.7	4326.7	4295.8	4395.3	4458.5
34	4295.0	4328.3	4297.5	4397.0	4459.8
36	4297.2	4329.9	4299.3	4398.7	4461.2
38	4299.2	4331.7	4301.2	4400.4	4462.6
40	4312.5	4348.6	4319.0	4412.3	4474.4
42	4314.2	4349.1	4319.4	4414.0	4475.9
44	4315.6	4349.6	4319.7	4415.3	4477.1
46	4316.7	4349.9	4320.1	4416.4	4478.0
48	4317.7	4350.3	4320.3	4417.3	4478.8
50	4318.5	4350.5	4320.6	4418.1	4479.5
55	4319.9	4351.1	4321.0	4419.4	4480.6
60	4320.8	4351.4	4321.4	4420.2	4481.3
65	4321.4	4351.6	4321.6	4420.7	4481.8
70	4321.7	4351.8	4321.7	4421.0	4482.0
75	4321.9	4351.9	4321.8	4421.2	4482.2
80	4322.0	4352.0	4321.9	4421.3	4482.2
85	4322.1	4352.0	4321.9	4421.3	4482.4
90	4322.2	4352.0	4322.0	4421.4	4482.4
95	4322.2	4352.0	4321.9	4421.4	4482.4
100	4322.3	4352.2	4322.1	4421.2	4482.3

Table A8.9
Dynamic paths of total capital stock (billions of units)

YEAR	Base Case	Hall-Rabushka	Armey-Shelby	NRST Plan 1	NRST Plan 2
1	25847	25847	25847	25847	25847
2	25751	25855	25826	25904	25965
3	25663	25861	25807	25955	26070
4	25584	25867	25790	26000	26166
5	25512	25872	25773	26041	26251
6	25447	25875	25758	26077	26328
7	25388	25879	25744	26110	26397
8	25334	25881	25731	26139	26459
9	25286	25884	25719	26165	26514
10	25242	25885	25708	26189	26564
11	25203	25887	25698	26209	26609
12	25167	25888	25689	26228	26649
13	25134	25890	25681	26245	26686
14	25105	25891	25674	26260	26718
15	25079	25892	25668	26273	26747
16	25056	25893	25662	26285	26773
17	25035	25894	25657	26296	26797
18	25016	25896	25653	26305	26818
19	25000	25897	25650	26314	26837
20	24985	25898	25647	26322	26854
21	24972	25900	25645	26329	26869
22	24960	25902	25643	26336	26883
23	24951	25904	25642	26342	26896
24	24942	25906	25642	26347	26908
25	24935	25909	25642	26352	26918
26	24929	25912	25643	26357	26928
28	24920	25919	25646	26367	26946
30	24915	25927	25652	26376	26962
32	24897	25925	25649	26366	26958
34	24883	25925	25647	26358	26955
36	24872	25925	25647	26353	26953
38	24865	25927	25649	26349	26953
40	24861	25931	25652	26348	26954
42	24842	25924	25646	26329	26937
44	24826	25918	25640	26313	26924
46	24813	25912	25635	26300	26913

Table A8.9 (continued)

YEAR	Base Case	Hall-Rabushka	Armey-Shelby	NRST Plan 1	NRST Plan 2
48	24802	25908	25631	26289	26903
50	24794	25904	25627	26280	26896
55	24778	25897	25620	26265	26883
60	24768	25892	25616	26256	26875
65	24762	25889	25612	26250	26870
70	24758	25886	25610	26246	26867
75	24756	25885	25609	26244	26865
80	24754	25884	25608	26243	26864
85	24753	25883	25607	26242	26863
90	24753	25883	25607	26241	26863
95	24753	25883	25606	26241	26863
100	24753	25882	25605	26241	26862

Table A8.10
Dynamic paths of real private rate of return, all assets

YEAR	Base Case	Hall-Rabushka	Armey-Shelby	NRST Plan 1	NRST Plan 2
1	0.039762	0.044902	0.043621	0.046943	0.049791
2	0.040148	0.044865	0.043707	0.046672	0.049230
3	0.040503	0.044835	0.043788	0.046430	0.048729
4	0.040827	0.044810	0.043864	0.046212	0.048279
5	0.041125	0.044790	0.043936	0.046017	0.047876
6	0.041398	0.044773	0.044004	0.045842	0.047515
7	0.041647	0.044760	0.044067	0.045685	0.047191
8	0.041875	0.044750	0.044126	0.045544	0.046900
9	0.042084	0.044741	0.044181	0.045418	0.046639
10	0.042274	0.044734	0.044232	0.045303	0.046403
11	0.042447	0.044729	0.044277	0.045200	0.046193
12	0.042605	0.044724	0.044319	0.045108	0.046003
13	0.042749	0.044718	0.044357	0.045024	0.045830
14	0.042879	0.044714	0.044391	0.044946	0.045673
15	0.042997	0.044709	0.044422	0.044876	0.045532
16	0.043103	0.044703	0.044449	0.044812	0.045403
17	0.043199	0.044697	0.044471	0.044754	0.045286

Table A8.10 (continued)

YEAR	Base Case	Hall-Rabushka	Armey-Shelby	NRST Plan 1	NRST Plan 2
18	0.043285	0.044689	0.044490	0.044699	0.045179
19	0.043361	0.044679	0.044505	0.044648	0.045080
20	0.043429	0.044667	0.044515	0.044600	0.044989
21	0.043489	0.044653	0.044521	0.044554	0.044903
22	0.043540	0.044637	0.044522	0.044509	0.044823
23	0.043585	0.044617	0.044518	0.044465	0.044747
24	0.043621	0.044593	0.044509	0.044422	0.044673
25	0.043651	0.044565	0.044495	0.044378	0.044602
26	0.043674	0.044532	0.044474	0.044333	0.044531
28	0.043698	0.044449	0.044411	0.044236	0.044389
30	0.043760	0.044418	0.044402	0.044113	0.044254
32	0.043841	0.044407	0.044398	0.044133	0.044247
34	0.043898	0.044386	0.044383	0.044139	0.044229
36	0.043934	0.044348	0.044350	0.044130	0.044198
38	0.043948	0.044290	0.044297	0.044103	0.044151
40	0.044009	0.044290	0.044305	0.044043	0.044100
42	0.044095	0.044321	0.044332	0.044123	0.044173
44	0.044166	0.044348	0.044357	0.044192	0.044233
46	0.044224	0.044371	0.044378	0.044249	0.044282
48	0.044273	0.044391	0.044396	0.044295	0.044322
50	0.044313	0.044408	0.044412	0.044334	0.044354
55	0.044385	0.044440	0.044441	0.044398	0.044412
60	0.044429	0.044462	0.044462	0.044439	0.044448
65	0.044458	0.044475	0.044475	0.044464	0.044469
70	0.044475	0.044485	0.044485	0.044479	0.044483
75	0.044485	0.044492	0.044492	0.044488	0.044492
80	0.044491	0.044496	0.044497	0.044493	0.044500
85	0.044494	0.044500	0.044500	0.044498	0.044499
90	0.044496	0.044504	0.044503	0.044502	0.044502
95	0.044496	0.044509	0.044513	0.044503	0.044503
100	0.044493	0.044518	0.044525	0.044493	0.044498

Notes

1. For a detailed composition of capital stock in 1996, See table A3.17 or figures A3.1 and A3.2 in Chapter 3.
2. For distributional effects of fundamental tax reform, see Hall (1996, 1997), Fullerton and Rogers (1996), Feenberg, Mitrusi, and Poterba (1997), Gravelle (1995), and Gentry and Hubbard (1997). On transition and other issues, see McLure (1993), Sakar and Zodrow (1993), Poddar and English (1997), Fullerton and Rogers (1997), Engen and Gale (1997), Fox and Murray (1997), Hellerstein (1997), and Bradford (2000).
3. The ST proposal was first introduced in the 104-th Congress of 1996 and again in the 105-th Congress in 1997. See Schaefer (1997).
4. The refund is equal to the tax-inclusive tax rate times the lesser of the poverty level and the wage and salary income of the family unit.
5. See also discussions in Aaron, Gale, and Sly (1999).
6. On tax evasion of consumption tax, see Murray (1997) and Mikesell (1997). To deal with the compliance problem Zodrow (1999) proposes withholding at the manufacturing and wholesale level, bringing the NRST closer to a VAT. To reduce the administrative burden and insure the deduction of investment spending, he proposes a "business tax rebate" for inputs that can be used for both business and personal purposes. The purchaser of such an input would pay the tax at the time of the purchase, but business purchasers would be eligible for a tax rebate.
7. Suppose there are H taxable units indexed by h, $h = 1, \ldots, H$. Let W_k and A_k be the labor income and personal exemptions of taxable unit h. Then the average tax rate at the federal level, t_L^{af}, and the corresponding average marginal tax rate, t_L^{mf}, are defined as

$$t_L^{af} = \frac{\sum\limits_{W_h - A_h > 0} (W_h - A_h) t_F^f}{\sum\limits_{j=1}^{H} W_h}, \quad t_L^{mf} = \frac{\sum\limits_{W_h - A_h > 0} W_h \cdot t_F^f}{\sum\limits_{h=1}^{H} W_h}$$

where t_F^f is the statutory federal flat tax rate applicable to labor. We assume that married couples file jointly. We are indebted to. M.S. Ho for these calculations. For more details, see Ho and Stiroh (1998).
8. Note that t_{P96}^{af} is estimated from a sample of tax returns in the Statistics of Income and t_L^{af} is based on the data from the Current Population Survey for 1996. We estimate that $t_{P96}^{a} = 0.1411$ and $t_{P96}^{af} = 0.1445$, based on the U.S. National Income and Product Accounts. This procedure adjusts the average tax rate of labor income for less than perfect tax compliance and administration. For more details, see chapter 7.
9. A high flat tax rate implies a heavy lump sum tax on "old" capital, offsetting the distorting effects of the tax on labor.
10. Tables A8.3 and A8.4 in the appendix to this chapter present the transition paths of gross domestic product, full consumption, labor supply, capital stock, and the average private rate of rate of return to all assets under the HR and AS proposals. Tables A8.7–A8.10 and figures A8.1–8.4 compare them with those under the base case and Plans 1 and 2 of NRST. Tables A8.1 and A8.2 compare steady-state tax parameters and the steady-state values of selected variables.
11. Revenue shortfalls occur in Plan 7 with $t_l = 0$, and Plan 8 with either $t_l = 0.058$ or $TI = 0$.
12. For example, see Aaron and Gale (1996) and Gale (1999).

13. In 1993, the corporate income taxes were $138.3 billion for the Federal Government and $26.9 billion for the state and local governments. In the same year, the Federal Government collected $508.1 billion of income tax from individuals and the state and local governments collected $124.2 billion. For marginal effective tax rates of investment in the private sector, refer to tables 4.2 through 4.6.
14. Starting from a GDP of $6,374 billion, they estimated that the business tax base was $1,903 billion and the wage tax base, $1,395 billion dollars. See Hall and Rabushka (1995), p. 57.
15. Tables A8.5 and A8.6 in the appendix to this chapter present the transition paths of gross domestic product, full consumption, labor supply, capital stock, and the average private rate of return to all assets for Plans 1 and 2 of the NRST. Tables A8.7–A8.10 and figures A8.1–A8.4 compare them with those under the base case and the HR and AS Flat Tax proposals. Tables A8.1 and A8.2 compare steady-state tax parameters and the steady-state values of selected variables.
16. Allocation of investment between the two adjacent statutory recovery classes that bracket the average recovery period for each of the 51 asset categories under ACRS (1981–1986) and MACRS (1987–) are shown in tables A3.14 and A3.15, respectively.
17. If an investment was made in 1980 in an asset with a recovery period of 17 years, it would be fully depreciated by the end of 1997 (under half-year conventions). Table 8.5a shows that in 1980, the last year of the ADR system, investment in depreciable assets with recovery periods of 17 years or more ($76.0 billions) accounted for 28.3% of the total corporate investment in depreciable assets ($616.6 billions). However $76.0 billions is only 12.3% of total corporate investment in depreciable assets in 1996, and the 1996 depreciation base for investments made in 1980 would be a much smaller fraction of the 1996 corporate investment in depreciable assets. The depreciation base in 1996 for investment made in 1970 must be an even smaller fraction. Table 8.5b tells a similar story for the noncorporate sector.
18. The distinction between consumption and investment goods is not essential for the present purposes.
19. The notion that government bears tax burden is used only to reflect the fact that, in our model, government pays the tax inclusive prices for goods and labor.
20. For other studies and comparison of the models used, see Joint Committee on Taxation (November 1997), Aaron and Gale (1996), Boskin (1996), and Gravelle and Smetters (1997).
21. Rogers (1997), pp. 55–57 and Fullerton and Rogers (1993).
22. In the A-K model, the elasticities are 0.8 for intratemporal substitution and 0.25 for intertemporal substitution. In the Jorgenson-Yun model, intertemporal elasticity of substitution is 0.39. Intratemporal elasticities of substitution are 0.41 between consumption goods and leisure, 0.27 between consumption goods and capital services, 0.17 between leisure and capital services, and 0.34 between the short-lived and long-lived household capital services, where all the elasticities are estimated at the sample average values of the relevant variables, 1970–1996. In production, AAKSW's elasticity of substitution between labor and capital is 1.0. In our model the elasticities of substitution are 0.50 between corporate capital services and labor, 0.70 between noncorporate capital services and labor, 0.47 between corporate and noncorporate capital services, 1.33 between capital services from short- and long-lived corporate assets, and 0.32 between capital services from short- and long-lived noncorporate assets (see tables 6.11 and 6.12).
23. Property taxes increase the social rate of return point for point under the NRST. For business assets under H-R, property tax increases the social rate of return and by $\frac{(1-t_F \cdot D)t^P}{1-t_F}$ where t^P and t_F are the property tax rate and the flat tax rate, respectively, and D equals 1 if property tax is deductible and 0, otherwise. The social rates of return under the NRST are not equalized across the sectors due to sectoral differences in debt/asset ratios and property tax rates.

9 Marginal Cost of Public Spending

The marginal cost of public spending (*MCS*) is the social cost of raising one dollar of tax revenue to finance government spending on goods and services. Previous studies have focused on the tax instruments used to raise funds and the types of benefits generated by government spending as determinants of the *MCS*.[1] However, when the additional tax revenues are used for purposes other than transfer payments, the specific forms of government purchases also affect the cost of public spending.

In this chapter we analyze the cost of public expenditure under the condition that additional tax revenues are precisely equal to the incremental spending, so that the government budget is balanced at the margin. We consider the sources of the tax revenues, the allocation of these revenues among different categories of spending, and the type of benefits resulting from the spending programs. We show that the *MCS* depends on the allocation of public expenditures as well as the revenue sources and the type of benefits.

We define the *MCS* as the ratio of a money measure of the welfare impact of a dollar of additional spending to the impact of an additional dollar of tax revenue.[2] Employing the dynamic general equilibrium model of the U.S. economy we have presented in chapter 5, we estimate the *MCS* for combinations of sources of the tax revenues, categories of public spending, and types of benefits resulting from government programs. These estimates of the *MCS* differ substantially. For example, we find that the *MCS* for public spending on labor services supplied by the household sector is substantially higher than for spending on consumption goods.

Our results suggest that the common assumption that the government sector spends its marginal tax revenues on goods and services may lead to underestimation of the *MCS*. During the period 1970–1996 the government sector spent almost 49 percent of its budget on the labor services of government employees and less than 36 percent on goods and services provided by private businesses, so that the understatement could be considerable. The degree of underestimation depends on the specific spending program.

While there is nothing novel about the notion that *MCS* depends on the type of public spending, it is important to recognize this in the estimation and application of the *MCS*. To estimate the social cost of a public program, it is necessary to calculate a weighted sum of the *MCS* for different categories of spending, where the *MCS* of each category is weighted by the proportion of expenditures in that category. An efficient allocation of public funds requires that the ratio between the marginal social benefit of the spending and the *MCS* must be equalized across all categories of spending.

To illustrate the application of the *MCS* we consider the welfare impact of the end of the Cold War. The end of communism in Eastern Europe, the dissolution of the Warsaw Pact, and the disintegration of the former Soviet Union have had permanent effects on U.S. defense policy, defense spending, and the growth of the U.S. economy. We can define the peace dividend as the saving in defense spending made possible by the end of the military threat posed by the Soviet Union and the Warsaw Pact. We find, roughly speaking, that the welfare gain from the end of the Cold War is the equivalent of one year of the U.S. gross domestic product, a magnitude that dwarfs the impact of the tax reforms considered in chapter 8.

Welfare gains from a cut in defense spending are not adequately measured by the reduction in the dollar value of defense spending. The marginal cost of defense is the sum of the expenditure and the excess burden associated with raising the tax revenues and making the purchases of goods and services required for military purposes. This depends on the required revenues and the specific form of military expenditures. Any measure of the peace dividend must include both the reduction in defense spending and elimination of the excess burden.

Finally, we compare our estimates of the marginal cost of public spending with previous studies. These studies have emphasized the dependence of the *MCS* on the source of tax revenues and the type of benefits of public spending. We have emphasized the allocation of public expenditure as an additional determinant of the *MCS*. Nonetheless, we have been able to find points of comparison with previous studies. Our estimates are substantially lower than earlier estimates.

This is due, primarily, to improved estimates of the parameters describing technology and preferences in our model of the U.S. economy.

9.1 Determinants of the MCS

We first consider the welfare impact of an increment to a public spending program. This is welfare-improving if

$$\Delta V(q,G,M)=\frac{\partial V}{\partial q}\Delta q+\frac{\partial V}{\partial G}\Delta G+\frac{\partial V}{\partial M}\Delta M>0\,, \tag{9.1}$$

where V is the indirect utility function of the representative consumer, q is the vector of consumer prices, G is the vector of government outputs, provided to the public free of charge, and M is exogenous income, which includes transfer payments, T. For simplicity, we assume that exogenous income and transfer payments are identical, so that $M=T$.

The purchasers' price is the sum of the producers' price and the tax rate, that is:

$$q=p+t\,, \tag{9.2}$$

so that equation (9.1) may be rewritten as

$$\Delta V(q,G,T)=\frac{\partial V}{\partial q}\Delta p+\frac{\partial V}{\partial q}\Delta t+\frac{\partial V}{\partial G}\Delta G+\frac{\partial V}{\partial T}\Delta T>0\,, \tag{9.1'}$$

where p is the vector of producer prices and t is the vector of tax rates on private consumption goods. The first term on the right-hand side of (9.1′) represents the welfare effect of endogenous changes in the producer prices. The remaining terms reflect the welfare effects of changes in the tax rates, the provision of public goods, and transfer payments, respectively.

In a cost-benefit framework the first two terms of the right-hand side of equation (9.1′) are counted as costs and the remaining two terms as benefits. We adopt this convention in measuring the MCS, so that we can write the MCS as

$$MCS=\frac{MC}{\Delta R} \tag{9.3}$$

where MC is the money measure of the welfare cost of additional public spending and ΔR is the change in tax revenue.

In our notation, the welfare cost of public spending MC is:

$$MC = -\frac{\dfrac{\partial V}{\partial q}\Delta p + \dfrac{\partial V}{\partial q}\Delta t}{\dfrac{\partial V}{\partial T}} . \tag{9.4}$$

Assuming that government collects taxes from household transactions only, we write ΔR as

$$\Delta R = X(q,G,T)\Delta t + t\Delta X(q,G,T), \tag{9.5}$$

where $X(q,G,T)$ is the vector of demands by the household sector.

Factor supplies are represented by negative entries in the vector of household demands $X(q,G,T)$. Equations (9.3)–(9.5) imply that the marginal cost of spending depends on dp, dt, dG, and dT, where dt represents the sources of the tax revenues and dG and dT distinguish different types of the benefits from public spending. The *MCS* depends on the source of the tax revenues as well as the type of benefits.

Next, we consider the equilibrium of the economy. Government demand may be expressed as $Z = Z(p,G,T,S)$, where Z includes government demand for products of the business sector and factors of production supplied by the household sector and S stands for the budgetary policy that affects Z. The dependence of government demand on prices, the benefits of government spending, and budgetary policy S can be rationalized by a policy of minimizing the budget outlays required for a given set of government programs, subject to the technology for producing public goods.

In addition, we assume that the structure of marginal tax policy Δt is predetermined up to a scale factor, say α

$$\Delta t = \alpha\tau , \tag{9.6}$$

where τ is the unit tax rate chosen to raise public funds at the margin. The net supply of the business sector may be expressed as $Y = Y(p)$, where demands for inputs are represented by negative entries. Since the government's purchase price is equal to the price received by the producer, no taxes are collected on government purchases from the business sector.

Market equilibrium requires

$$\Delta X(q,G,T)+\Delta Z(p,G,T,S)=\Delta Y(p)\ , \tag{9.7}$$

and a balanced budget at the margin implies

$$X\Delta t+t\Delta X=Z\Delta p+p\Delta Z\ . \tag{9.8}$$

Once τ, ΔG, ΔT, and S are determined by the decisions on the sources of additional tax revenues, the benefits of the public spending programs, and the allocation of the government budget among different categories of spending, equations (9.2) and (9.6)–(9.8) determine α and Δp. The choice of Δp and α is affected by budgetary policy, so that the MCS depends on the use of the public funds.

9.2 Dynamic General Equilibrium Model

In order to measure the marginal cost of public spending in the United States, we employ the dynamic general equilibrium model of the U.S. economy we have presented in chapter 5. The model consists of four sectors—households, producers, governments, and the rest of the world. The consumption of publicly provided goods affects the level of consumer welfare. However, it is difficult to measure the contribution of public consumption to welfare, since there are no reliable estimates of the rate of substitution between public and private consumption.

Public services such as law enforcement, fire protection, health care, education, highways, water and sewer services, and national defense, may affect the efficiency of private production. However, currently available evidence on the relationship between public services and the efficiency of private production is very limited.[3] For simplicity we assume that the social welfare function is additively separable in private and public consumption. This is equivalent to assuming, at least at the margin, that public spending does not affect the efficiency of private production.

Government revenues are used to purchase consumption goods, investment goods, and labor services. Revenues are also used to pay interest on government debt and make transfer payments to the household sector and the rest of the world. We assume that the total government expenditure, net of interest payments on government debt, is a constant fraction of gross domestic product (GDP). Under this assumption total government spending, net of interest payments, is allocated in fixed proportions among consumption goods, investment goods, labor services, and transfer payments.

In modeling the U.S. tax system, we distinguish between average and marginal tax rates for labor and capital incomes. In the case of capital income, the effective marginal tax rates are derived from cost of capital formulas. For sales taxes, property taxes, and wealth tax, the average and marginal tax rates are identical. Non-tax payments are assumed to be proportional to labor income. The output of public enterprises is a constant fraction of the total production of consumption goods by the private sector. Labor input of public enterprises is a constant fraction of total labor supplied by the household sector.

The economy is in equilibrium when lifetime wealth is allocated optimally to full consumption in each period and full consumption is allocated optimally among its components—leisure time and consumption of goods and services. We hold fixed the time paths of real government spending, other than interest payments, government debt, and the claims on the rest of the world. We set the relative sizes of government expenditure and the net exports of consumption goods and investment goods in the steady state at sustainable values. Along the transition path toward the steady state, the time paths of government debt and claims on the rest of the world reach their steady-state levels in thirty-nine years and then remain constant.

In our base case government spending is determined by the government budget constraint and the size of government sector deficit implicit in the time path of government debt. Since we assume that the government allocates total spending, net of interest payments, in fixed proportions, we can aggregate the five categories of government spending by means of a linear logarithmic price function. Similarly, the balance of payments deficit is determined by the exogenous time path of claims on the rest of the world. In order to meet the balance of payments constraint, net exports of consumption and investment goods are adjusted in the same proportion.

In each time period, the level of full consumption, capital stock, government debt, and the claims on the rest of the world are predetermined and the four markets clear simultaneously. In the consumption goods market, the demands of household, government, and the rest of the world are balanced with the total supply from the business sector and government enterprises. In the investment goods market, the demands from households, the government, and the rest of the world are met by the supply of the business sector. In the labor market, households are the only suppliers; the employers are business, government, government enterprises, and the rest of the world. Finally, we assume that the capital stock at the beginning of each period is balanced with demands of the households and corporate and noncorporate producers.

9.3 Estimation of the MCS

Given the detailed model of the U.S. tax system we have presented in chapter 5, we can consider many alternative methods for raising tax revenues. We present results for ten sets of tax instruments. These are the following: (1) the corporate income tax, (2) capital income taxes at the individual level, (3) property taxes, (4) all capital taxes, (5) the labor income tax, (6) all income taxes [(1) + (2) + (5) = (4) + (5)], (7) individual income taxes (capital and labor), (8) sales taxes, (9) all taxes, except property taxes, (10) all taxes.

Our dynamic general equilibrium model allows us to distinguish among five categories of public spending: purchases of consumption goods, investment goods, and labor services, transfer payments to households, and transfer payments to the rest of the world. Given our simplified representation of transactions with the rest of the world, we do not estimate the *MCS* for transfer payments to foreigners. However, we estimate the *MCS* for the remaining four categories of public spending and for a proportional expansion of government spending on all five categories.

Given the difficulties of measuring the benefits of public spending, we consider two polar cases, which we label type A and type B benefits. We assume that benefits of type A are additively separable from private consumption in the social welfare function and benefits of type B are perfect substitutes for private consumption. The national security that results from defense spending is an illustration of type A benefits, while the additional private spending resulting from transfer payments to individuals is an example of type B benefits. We do not explicitly model type A benefits, but we model type B benefits as an addition to the lifetime wealth of the consumer.

Although our model is capable of handling public spending programs with a mixture of type A and type B benefits, we assume that public spending on consumption goods, investment goods, and labor services can produce benefits of either type. Whenever a public program involves spending in these three categories, we consider the two polar cases in which the benefits are either type A or type B. For transfer payments, we estimate the *MCS* only for type B benefits. When we consider spending on consumption goods, investment goods, and labor services that produce benefits of type A, a proportional expansion of public spending would produce a mixture of type A and type B benefits, since only benefits of type B are generated by transfer payments.

In order to measure the *MCS*, we first establish a base case by solving the model under the reference tax and spending policies. We then increase the path of a selected category of government spending by five percent and adjust the relevant tax rates proportionally so that the balanced budget condition holds at the margin in each period. When marginal and average tax rates are different, they are adjusted in the same proportion. In the alternative case simulations, we control government debt and the claims on the rest of the world so that they follow the same time paths as in the base case.

The welfare levels of the representative consumer under the reference and the alternative policies are summarized by the inter-temporal welfare index V. As a first step for estimating *MCS*, we need to estimate the welfare cost of the additional spending. If all the benefits are type A, the welfare cost is measured by the change in the welfare index. However, if the marginal spending generates benefits of type B, then the change in the welfare index includes the benefits from the spending program. In order to separate the cost of public spending from the benefits, we subtract the value of type B benefits from the value of the welfare change.

In order to convert the change in the welfare index into a money measure, we employ the inter-temporal expenditure function introduced in chapter 7. The cost of additional spending in the case of type A benefits is estimated as

$$MC = W(PF_0, D_0, V_0) - W(PF_0, D_0, V_1), \tag{9.9a}$$

where the subscripts 0 and 1 indicate the base case and the alternative case, respectively. If part or all of the benefits are type B, the cost of the marginal spending is estimated as

$$MC = W(PF_0, D_0, V_0) - [W(PF_0, D_0, V_1) - \Delta T], \tag{9.9b}$$

where ΔT is the present value of type B benefits.

In computing the present values of type B benefits (ΔT) and the changes in tax revenues (ΔR), we use the representative consumer's marginal rate of inter-temporal substitution as the discount rate. For this purpose we utilize the methodology introduced in chapter 7. Making use of equations (9.9a) or (9.9b) and the change in tax revenues ΔR, we compute MCS according to equation (9.3).

$$MCS = \frac{MC}{\Delta R} .$$

9.4 MCS under the 1996 Tax Law

We first estimate the MCS for U.S. tax policy in 1996. Since the MCS depends on the ten sources of public funds, the five uses of these funds, and the two types of benefits (except for transfer payments), we obtain 90 estimates of the MCS. These are generated by ten combinations of tax programs, combined with four categories of public spending, plus proportional expansion, and two types of benefits. To estimate the MCS, we increase the relevant components of government spending by five percent and adjust the relevant tax rates to balance the budget. Table 9.1 summarizes the results and figure 9.1 shows the MCS for all taxes.

We find that estimates of the MCS in table 9.1 vary widely across tax programs. The most expensive method of financing additional public spending is to increase taxes on labor income at the individual level. The least expensive method is to increase property taxes. Sales taxes are more expensive than property taxes, but substantially cheaper than capital or labor income taxes. We find that the labor income tax is more expensive than the corporate and individual capital income taxes, and that individual capital income tax is more expensive than corporate income tax. The high cost of the labor income tax is at least partly due to the high marginal rate of taxation, since we adjust average and marginal rates of taxation on labor income in the same proportion.

The MCS in each column of table 9.1 corresponds to the same category of public spending with the same type of benefits. Variations in the MCS among the different tax programs indicate potential gains from revenue neutral tax reforms like those we have considered in chapters 7 and 8. For example, a transfer of the tax burden from labor to capital income taxes would generate gains in economic efficiency. A similar transfer from income taxes to sales and property taxes would also generate efficiency gains.

The MCS also varies widely across the different categories of public

Table 9.1
Marginal cost of public spending (1996 tax law)

Revenue Sources	Marginal Public Spending on								
	Consumption Goods		Investment Goods		Labor Services		Transfer Payment	Proportional Expansion	
	A	B	A	B	A	B	B	A	B
1. *Corporate Income Tax*	0.858	0.924	1.165	1.231	1.131	1.198	1.278	1.128	1.184
2. *Individual Capital Income Tax*	0.844	0.910	1.146	1.213	1.111	1.178	1.259	1.108	1.164
3. *Property Tax*	0.752	0.819	1.025	1.092	0.984	1.052	1.133	0.979	1.037
4. *Taxes on Capital Income* (1 + 2)	0.850	0.916	1.154	1.220	1.119	1.186	1.267	1.114	1.171
5. *Labor Income Tax*	0.952	1.017	1.286	1.350	1.241	1.305	1.414	1.225	1.279
6. *Capital and Labor Income Taxes* (1 + 2 + 5 = 4 + 5)	0.901	0.966	1.219	1.284	1.176	1.242	1.339	1.161	1.217
7. *Individual Income Tax*	0.914	0.978	1.235	1.300	1.191	1.257	1.358	1.175	1.231
8. *Sales Tax*	0.779	0.846	1.059	1.126	1.022	1.090	1.171	1.012	1.069
9. *All Taxes Except for Property Tax*	0.871	0.938	1.180	1.246	1.138	1.205	1.299	1.124	1.180
10. *All Taxes*	0.851	0.917	1.154	1.220	1.113	1.179	1.270	1.100	1.156

Notes:
1. Columns A are for type A benefits and columns B are for type B benefits. In Columns B, the value (to consumer) of benefits from public spending is assumed to be equal to the amount of spending.
2. Government spending are increased by 5% and the relevant tax rates are adjusted to keep government budget balanced at the margin.
3. Proportional expansion of public spending includes a proportional increase in transfer payment to households and foreigners. Thus Column A under proportional expansion reflects the effects of type B benefits generated by the transfer component in the spending. Transfer payment to foreigners accounts for 0.85% of total government spending, net of interest payments.
4. Inflation is fixed at 4% per year.

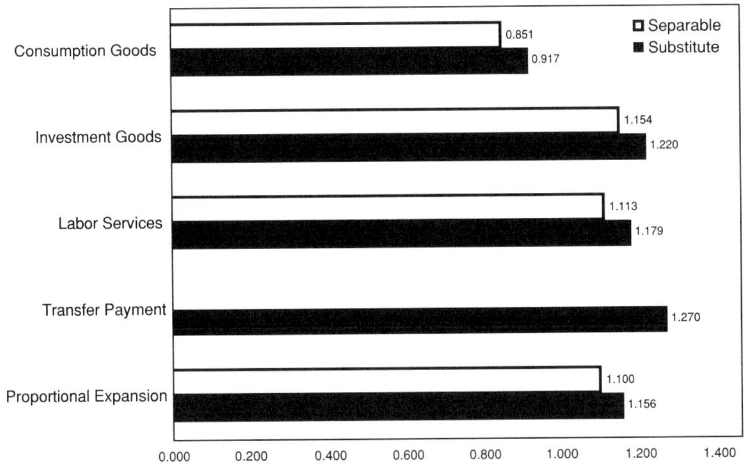

Figure 9.1
Marginal cost of public spending (1996 laws): All taxes.

spending. Transfer payments have the highest *MCS*, while purchases of consumption goods and services have the lowest. Purchases of investment goods are almost as costly as transfer payments, while purchases of labor services are the next most costly. The *MCS* is higher for benefits of Type B, which are perfect substitutes for private consumption, than for benefits of Type A, which are separable from private consumption.[4] A comparison between the two types of benefits gives an indication of the income effect of government spending, since benefits of Type B have an income effect associated with the increase in lifetime income of the representative consumer, while those of Type A do not.

Conceptually, the *MCS* for transfer payments are the same as one plus the marginal excess burden (MEB) of chapter 7. However, the estimates in table 9.1 are slightly different from those in the first column of table 7.10 in that chapter. There are two reasons for this. First, the directions of policy change are different. In this chapter we increase the relevant component of government spending and adjust tax rates to preserve a balanced budget at the margin. In chapter 7 we reduce revenue from the relevant tax program and increase revenue from a hypothetical lump sum tax by the same amount. Second, the size of policy changes are different. In table 9.1, transfer payments are increased by 5% and tax rates are adjusted to balance government budget while, in the first column of table 7.10, chapter 7, tax rates are reduced by 5% and lump sum tax is increased to make up for the lost revenue.

We can compare the ratios of marginal benefits to ratios of the *MCS* to identify potential savings in public spending from reallocations across spending categories. However, if the marginal benefits are equal across all categories of spending, as we assume in the case of type B benefits, variations in the *MCS* across the spending categories indicate potential savings. These could be achieved by reallocating spending from categories with a high *MCS* to categories with a low *MCS*, for example, from transfer payments to consumption goods.

We have already pointed out that table 9.1 shows that the *MCS* of spending with type B benefits is greater than that of the same category with type A benefits. This difference is due to the income effect of type B benefits. These benefits encourage household expenditures on consumption and discourage household supplies of capital and labor services. In our model the income effect raises the level of full consumption. This, in turn, increases private purchases of consumption and investment goods and household demands for leisure.

We have seen that the *MCS* varies widely across the spending categories. Since this aspect of the *MCS* has been ignored in earlier studies, we next examine the sources of the variation in more detail. For this purpose we compare the steady-state resource allocation for each of the five categories of public spending in table 9.1. Although the *MCS* depends on the transition path as well as the steady state of the economy, comparing steady-state allocations is useful for understanding the mechanisms that generate differences in the *MCS* among different categories of public spending.

It is useful to remember some basic patterns. First, a high *MEC* for the marginal source of tax revenue implies a high *MCS*, which may easily be confirmed by comparing the first column of table 7.10 with any column in 9.1. Second, taxes on the goods and services purchased by the spending program tend to lower the *MCS* of the program if the increased demand from the government is met with increased supply. Third, more generally, *MCS* tends to be lower if the spending program induces reallocation of resources so that total tax revenue is increased. The *MCS* is lowered as the burden of government treasury is reduced by the induced increase in tax revenue.

For example, given the source of marginal tax revenue, we may expect that the *MCS* of a government spending program would be low if the spending is concentrated on heavily taxed goods and services with elastic supply. For similar reasons, *MCS* may be high if the marginal spending causes a large reduction in labor supply, which worsens the allocation of time and reduces the tax revenue from labor income. *MCS* may also be high if total capital stock is substantially reduced or capital stock is reallocated from business to household sector or from corporate to noncorporate sector. The interactions between labor and capital allocation also need to be considered. Reduction in labor supply to the business sector tends to inhibit demand for capital services, and vice versa. Increased demand for leisure driven by a larger transfer payment reduces labor supply and increase household demand for capital services.

Table 9.2 gives the steady-state values of selected variables under five alternative public spending programs. Public spending is increased by five percent in each of the spending categories—consumption goods, investment goods, labor services, and transfer payments. In addition, we consider proportional increases in all categories and all except for transfer payments, Proportional Expansion-1 and Proportional Expansion-2 in table 9.2. Each of the spending increases is accompanied by a corresponding tax increase with all taxes increased in the same proportion, as in the last line of table 9.1.

Table 9.2
Resource allocation in the steady states (1996 tax law)

		Marginal Public Spending on					
	Base Case	Cons. Goods	Invest. Goods	Labor	Transfer Payment	Prop. Expansion-1	Prop. Expansion-2
1. *Household Behavior*							
F	14544	14533	14525	14498	14540	14463	14455
C	3539	3531	3529	3510	3532	3485	3484
LJ	13365	13361	13356	13346	13368	13337	13328
HD	1104	1104	1102	1101	1104	1098	1097
L	4322	4326	4331	4341	4319	4350	4358
2. *Business Production*							
LD	3531	3534	3537	3512	3527	3519	3521
QD	1012	1013	1006	1002	1010	995	995
MD	500	500	496	494	498	489	489
CS	3647	3651	3637	3618	3640	3605	3606
IS	1707	1709	1713	1699	1706	1704	1706

Table 9.2 (continued)

	Marginal Public Spending on						
	Base Case	Cons. Goods	Invest. Goods	Labor	Transfer Payment	Prop. Expansion-1	Prop. Expansion-2
3. *Government Spending*							
CG	256	268	256	254	255	266	268
IG	242	242	253	242	242	254	256
LG	705	705	707	741	705	744	750
EL	204	204	203	204	214	214	204
ER	12.0	12.0	12.0	12.0	12.0	12.6	12.7
GS	1418	1419	1419	1421	1419	1425	1425
PGS	0.9923	0.9937	0.9890	0.9929	0.9925	0.9908	0.9903
DGOV	0.00	12.2	12.9	34.4	7756	7827	7685
4. *Capital Allocation*							
VKL	23800	23806	23284	23607	23756	23449	23441
VQL	7851	7856	7800	7756	7827	7685	7685
VML	5363	5367	5320	5295	5345	5239	5238
VHL	10587	10582	10564	10556	10585	10525	10518

Notes: Except for the last column (Prop. Expansion-2), public spending is increased by 5% of the relevant spending categories. In the last columuns, total public spending is increased by 5% with all categories of spending, except for transfer payment, increasing by the same proportion. Marginal funds are raised by increasing all tax rates by the same proportion. The steady states are scaled to the total time endowment of $17, 571 billion units. Inflation is fixed at 4% per year.

Notations:

Proportional Expansion-1: All categories of government spending is increased by 5%.

Proportional Expansion-2: All categories of government spending, except transfer payments to households are increased by 5%.

F: Full consumption

C: Nondurable goods and services

LJ: Leisure

HD: Household capital services

L: Labor supply

LD: Labor used in the business sector

QD: Corporate capital services

MD: Noncorporate capital services

CS: Production of consumption goods

IS: Production of investment goods

CG: Government demand, consumption goods

IG: Government demand, investment goods

LG: Government demand, labor

EL: Transfer to households

ER: Transfer to the rest of the world

GS: Real government spending

PGS: Price index of GS

DGOV: Value of marginal spending

VKL: Lagged value of private capital stock (VQL + VML + VHL)

VQL: Lagged value of corporate capital stock

VML: Lagged value of noncorporate capital stock

VHL: Lagged value of household capital stock

We have seen that the general pattern of the *MCS* is not very sensitive to the type of benefits. We consider only type A benefits for government spending on consumption goods, investment goods, and labor. We find that spending on transfer payments results in an increase in consumption of leisure, relative to the base case, and a corresponding reduction in the supply of labor services. The business sector contracts slightly, while the government sector remains the same, except for the increase in transfer payments.

Public spending on labor services reduces leisure substantially and increases labor supply accordingly. However, the increased supply of labor is more than offset by increased government demand. Consequently, labor services in the business sector are the lowest of all the cases in table 9.2, including the base case. The reduction in labor services in the business sector is associated with a decline in capital services as well. The household sector experiences simultaneous reductions in the consumption of leisure time, purchases of goods and services, and services of housing and consumers' durables.

Government purchases of investment goods reduce the input of capital services in the business sector and the consumption of housing and consumers' durables, relative to the base case. The reduction in capital services is due mainly to the reduced availability and higher price of investment goods. This, in turn, results from the increased government demand. The supply of labor and the level of labor services in the business sector are higher than in the base case. Less capital is allocated to both the business and household sectors. The household sector undergoes reductions in leisure, goods and services, and capital services.

Additional public spending on consumption goods increases total labor supply and the supply of labor services to the business sector. The business sector produces more investment goods, as well as more consumption goods, relative to the base case. More interesting is that, unlike in all the other cases, total capital stock is greater than in the base case, while capital is relocated from the household to the business sector. This aspect of resource allocation explains the relatively low *MCS* for spending on consumption goods. Finally, proportional increases in government spending result in an increase in labor supply, a contraction of the business sector, and lower levels of consumption. Excluding transfer payments from the increase in spending results in slightly less leisure and a slightly greater supply of labor.

9.5 MCS under Fundamental Tax Reform

The tax reform proposals considered in chapter 8 may have large impacts on the *MCS*. We now shift the reference tax policy from the 1996 tax law to the proposals for fundamental tax reform. We consider six proposals for tax reform—two flat tax proposals (Hall-Rabushka and Armey-Shelby) and four national retail sales tax proposals (Plans 1, 2, 4 and 5). All the tax reform proposals are required to be revenue neutral so that the claims on the government and government spending follow the same paths as in the base case. Each reform proposal is represented by a set of tax rates shown in tables 8.3 and 8.4.

To measure *MCS* for the tax reform proposals, we increase government spending in a selected category by 5% and adjust the chosen set of tax rates to keep government budget in balance at the margin. As before, we consider four categories of government spending and a combination of them. The benefits from the marginal spending may be either additively separable from or perfectly substitutable with private consumption. For the flat tax proposals, we consider property tax, flat tax, sales taxes on consumption and investment goods, a combination of flat tax and sales taxes, and all taxes as the set of tax rates to be adjusted for government budget balance. For the NRST proposals, we consider property tax, labor income tax, sales taxes, a combination of labor and sales taxes, and all taxes.

Tables 9.3 and 9.4 show the *MCS* for the Hall-Rabushka and Armey-Shelby flat tax proposals. As in table 9.1, *MCS* varies with government spending category, type of benefits, and the tax rates increased to finance the marginal spending program. We first consider marginal spending on consumption goods, investment goods, labor services, and proportional expansion of government spending. The Hall-Rabushka proposal has higher *MCS* than the Armey-Shelby proposal if the revenue sources are property tax and sales tax; the Armey-Shelby proposal has higher *MCS* if the revenue sources are flat tax, combination of flat tax and sales tax, and all taxes. For transfer payments to the household, Hall-Rabushka proposal has lower *MCS* for all revenue sources. Figures 9.2 and 9.3 compare *MCS* of the Hall-Rabushka and Armey-Shelby flat tax proposals for marginal spending programs financed with a proportional increase in all taxes.

A detailed comparison of tables 9.3 and 9.4 with table 9.1 is not particularly instructive. However, we note that the flat tax proposals lower the *MCS* for proportional expansion of government spending

Table 9.3
Marginal cost of public spending under tax reform proposals—Hall-Rabushka with flat tax adjustment

Revenue Sources	Consumption Goods A	Consumption Goods B	Investment Goods A	Investment Goods B	Labor Services A	Labor Services B	Transfer Payment B	Proportional Expansion A	Proportional Expansion B
1. *Property Tax*	0.777	0.842	0.970	1.034	0.943	1.008	1.109	0.951	1.006
2. *Flat Tax*	0.855	0.918	1.085	1.149	1.033	1.097	1.217	1.038	1.092
3. *Sales Tax*	0.800	0.864	1.001	1.065	0.973	1.038	1.141	0.977	1.032
4. *Flat Tax and Sales Taxes (All Taxes, Except for Property Tax)*	0.841	0.904	1.063	1.127	1.018	1.082	1.198	1.022	1.076
5. *All Taxes*	0.825	0.889	1.041	1.104	1.000	1.064	1.177	1.004	1.058

Column heading: Marginal Public Spending on

Notes: See table 9.1.

Table 9.4
Marginal cost of public spending under tax reform proposals—Armey-Shelby with flat tax adjustment

Revenue Sources	Consumption Goods A	Consumption Goods B	Investment Goods A	Investment Goods B	Labor Services A	Labor Services B	Transfer Payment B	Proportional Expansion A	Proportional Expansion B
1. *Property Tax*	0.766	0.830	0.966	1.030	0.934	0.999	1.121	0.946	1.000
2. *Flat Tax*	0.873	0.937	1.132	1.195	1.064	1.127	1.271	1.075	1.128
3. *Sales Tax*	0.788	0.852	0.996	1.061	0.963	1.027	1.151	0.971	1.025
4. *Flat Tax and Sales Taxes (All Taxes, Except for Property Tax)*	0.852	0.915	1.097	1.161	1.038	1.101	1.240	1.047	1.101
5. *All Taxes*	0.831	0.894	1.065	1.127	1.012	1.076	1.211	1.021	1.075

Column heading: Marginal Public Spending on

Note: See table 9.1.

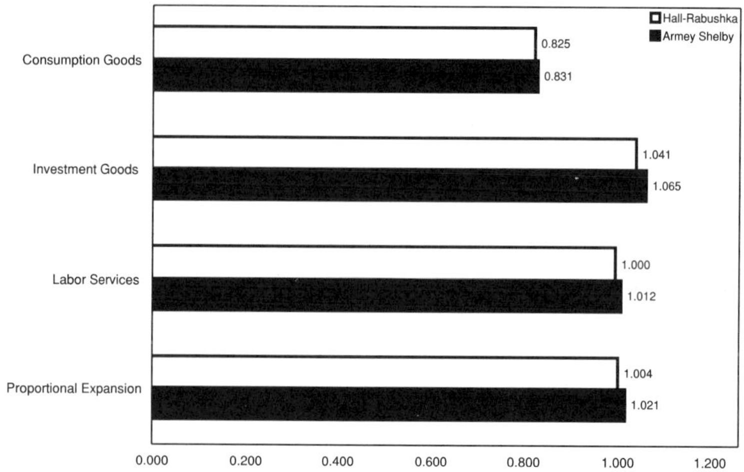

Figure 9.2
Marginal cost of public spending for Flat Tax proposals: All taxes, additively separable benefits.

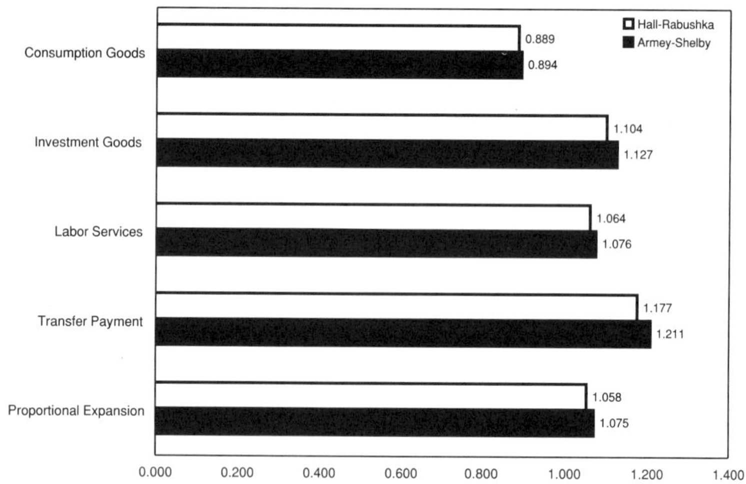

Figure 9.3
Marginal costs of public spending for Flat Tax proposals: All taxes, perfect substitutes.

financed with proportional increases in all tax rates. The Hall-Rabushka proposal lowers the *MCS* from 1.10 to 1.00 for benefits additively separable from private consumption, and from 1.16 to 1.06 for benefits perfectly substitutable with private consumption. The corresponding changes for the Armey-Shelby flat tax proposal are from 1.10 to 1.02 and from 1.16 to 1.08, respectively. A lower *MCS* implies that a public spending program is cheaper to finance. However, it does not follow that the corresponding public spending program is more efficient. As *MCS* varies with the use of public funds, the efficiency of a public spending program depends upon both the marginal cost and the marginal benefit of the spending program.

In tables 9.5a–9.5d, we present the *MCS*s for Plans 1, 2, 4, and 5 of NRST. A number of interesting patterns emerge from the tables. First, financing of public spending on consumption goods is still the cheapest. Second, for Plans 1 and 2 where investment goods and labor services are not taxed, the *MCS* for investment goods and labor services increase substantially relative to the *MCS* of consumption goods and transfer payments. The main reason is that marginal spending on investment goods and labor services do not bring in new tax revenue while spending on consumption goods and transfer payments do. For a similar reason, under Plans 4 and 5, the *MCS* for investment goods is relatively higher than those of labor services and transfer payment.

Third, under the flat sales tax of Plan 2 and the flat sales and labor income taxes of Plan 4, *MCS* is not sensitive to the source of revenue, which reflects the efficiency of tax system as shown in tables 8.10b and 8.10c by the convergence of the *MEC* for various subsets of the tax system. Finally, the sensitivity of *MCS* to the use of tax revenue is substantially reduced by the elimination of tax rate progressivity, allowing the *MCS* to cluster closer to 1.0 under Plans 2 and 4 than under Plans 1 and 5. Figures 9.4a and 9.4b compare *MCS* of the four alternative NRST Plans.

9.6 Welfare Impact of the End of the Cold War

Estimates of the peace dividend resulting from the end of the Cold War have focused on short-term issues, such as the effect on the federal deficit, opportunities for increasing non-defense spending, and potential tax reductions. However, the end of the Cold War is a permanent feature of the world order and the peace dividend must

Table 9.5a
Marginal cost of public spending under tax reform proposals—Plan 1, NRST: Progressive Sales Tax and no Labor Income Tax with sales tax adjustment

Revenue Sources	Marginal Public Spending on								
	Consumption Goods		Investment Goods		Labor Services		Transfer Payment	Proportional Expansion	
	A	B	A	B	A	B	B	A	B
1. *Property Tax*	0.815	0.880	1.278	1.342	1.247	1.311	1.098	1.164	1.218
2. *Labor Income Taxes*	N.A.								
3. *Sales Tax*	0.839	0.903	1.315	1.379	1.286	1.351	1.133	1.198	1.252
4. *Labor and Sales Taxes (All Taxes, Except for Property Tax)*	N.A.								
5. *Sales and Property Taxes (All Taxes}*	0.835	0.898	1.307	1.370	1.277	1.341	1.126	1.190	1.244

Note: See table 9.1.

Table 9.5b
Marginal cost of public spending under tax reform proposals—Plan 2, NRST: Flat Sales Tax and No Labor Income Tax with sales tax adjustment

Revenue Sources	Marginal Public Spending on								
	Consumption Goods		Investment Goods		Labor Services		Transfer Payment	Proportional Expansion	
	A	B	A	B	A	B	B	A	B
1. *Property Tax*	0.847	0.912	1.224	1.289	1.189	1.254	1.069	1.126	1.181
2. *Labor Income Taxes*	N.A.								
3. *Sales Tax*	0.847	0.911	1.223	1.288	1.188	1.253	1.070	1.123	1.178
4. *Labor and Sales Taxes (All Taxes, Except for Property Tax)*	N.A.								
5. *Sales and Property Taxes (All Taxes}*	0.847	0.912	1.224	1.288	1.188	1.254	1.070	1.123	1.178

Note: See table 9.1.

Table 9.5c
Marginal cost of public spending under tax reform proposals—Plan 4, NRST: Flat Sales Tax and Flat Labor Income Tax with sales tax and labor income tax adjustment

Revenue Sources	Consumption Goods A	Consumption Goods B	Investment Goods A	Investment Goods B	Labor Services A	Labor Services B	Transfer Payment B	Proportional Expansion A	Proportional Expansion B
1. *Property Tax*	0.835	0.900	1.092	1.156	1.055	1.120	1.066	1.033	1.087
2. *Labor Income Taxes*	0.840	0.904	1.092	1.157	1.051	1.116	1.071	1.022	1.078
3. *Sales Tax*	0.839	0.903	1.094	1.159	1.058	1.123	1.069	1.033	1.088
4. *Labor and Sales Taxes (All Taxes, Except for Property Tax)*	0.839	0.904	1.093	1.159	1.055	1.120	1.070	1.028	1.083
5. *Labor, Sales and Property Taxes (All Taxes}*	0.839	0.903	1.093	1.158	1.055	1.120	1.070	1.029	1.084

Note: See table 9.1.

Table 9.5d
Marginal cost of public spending under tax reform proposals—Plan 5, NRST: Progressive Sales Tax and Flat Labor Income Tax with sales tax and labor income tax adjustment

Revenue Sources	Consumption Goods A	Consumption Goods B	Investment Goods A	Investment Goods B	Labor Services A	Labor Services B	Transfer Payment B	Proportional Expansion A	Proportional Expansion B
1. *Property Tax*	0.816	0.880	1.117	1.182	1.082	1.147	1.081	1.050	1.105
2.*Labor Income Taxes*	0.821	0.886	1.120	1.185	1.080	1.145	1.089	1.042	1.097
3. *Sales Tax*	0.843	0.907	1.156	1.220	1.122	1.186	1.120	1.086	1.140
4. *Labor and Sales Taxes (All Taxes, Except for Property Tax)*	0.833	0.898	1.140	1.203	1.102	1.167	1.106	1.065	1.120
5. *Labor, Sales and Property Taxes (All Taxes}*	0.830	0.894	1.135	1.198	1.098	1.162	1.101	1.062	1.116

Note: See table 9.1.

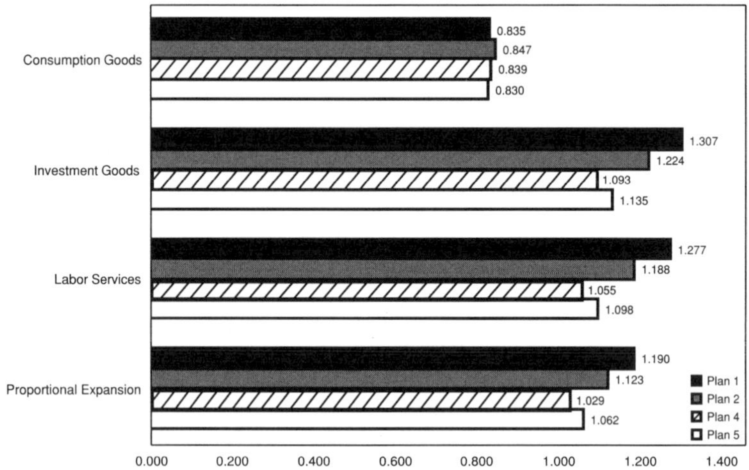

Figure 9.4a
Marginal costs of public spending for national retail sales tax: All taxes, additively separable benefits.

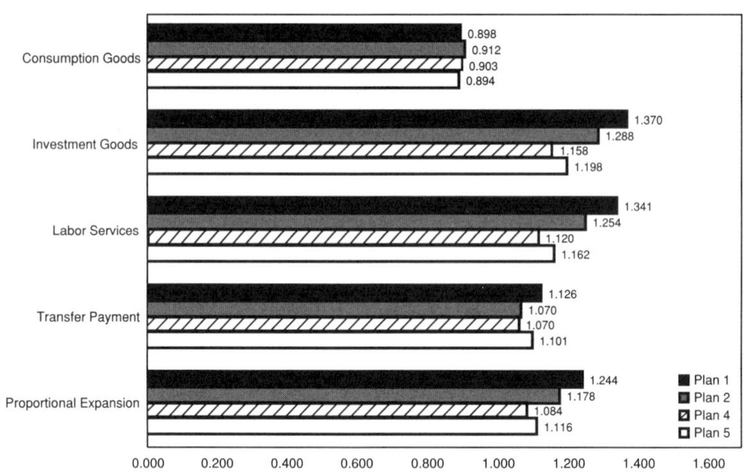

Figure 9.4b
Marginal costs of public spending for national retail sales tax: All taxes, perfect substitutes.

also be examined from a long term perspective. We employ the marginal cost of public spending (*MCS*) to analyze the impact of the end of the Cold War on the future growth of the U.S. economy.

The first step in quantifying the peace dividend is to estimate the time path that U.S. defense spending would have followed if the Cold War had continued. Ideally, the second step would be to identify a time path of U.S. defense spending for maintaining the same level of national security in the new international environment. Since it is impossible to evaluate the benefits of a given expenditure on national security, we consider instead the gains in economic welfare from balanced budget reductions in defense spending and the associated tax revenues.[5]

Defense spending refers to purchases of goods and services for the national defense. We consider a broader definition of defense spending that includes veterans benefits, an important form of transfer payments. In the short run a reduction in defense purchases is unlikely to reduce transfer payments to veterans; in fact, these payments may increase as more military personnel are forced to retire. However, a permanent reduction in defense spending on personnel will ultimately result in a reduction in veterans benefits.

In keeping with the commodity classification of the dynamic general equilibrium model of the U.S. economy presented in chapter 5, we distinguish among four types of defense spending—consumption goods, investment goods, employee compensation, and veterans benefits. We take the tax policy regime of 1996 as a starting point for consideration of the tax changes. The important tax parameters describing this regime include the tax rates, depreciation schedules, and provisions for other deductions summarized in chapter 6.

Consumption goods purchased for defense purposes include expenditures on nondurable goods and services, other than compensation of defense personnel and consumption of government capital used for defense. This includes petroleum products, ammunition, and other nondurable goods, as well as services such as contractual research and development, installation support, weapons support, personnel support, transportation of military materiel, travel of military personnel, and other services.

Purchases of investment goods include expenditures on military equipment and structures. This includes aircraft, missiles, ships, vehicles, electronic equipment, other durable goods, including structures. Defense outlays on labor services are the compensation of military and civilian employees in the defense sector, excluding force-account construction, which is classified as investment in structures. Veterans' benefits are treated as a transfer payment. We exclude the consumption of fixed capital from defense spending, departing from the convention employed in the U.S. National Income and Product Accounts.

There are many alternative ways of offsetting a reduction in defense spending by lowering taxes. We consider adjustments of income tax rates: (1) corporate income tax rates, (2) individual capital income tax rates, and (3) both corporate and individual capital income tax rates. We also consider adjustment of (4) labor income tax rates, (5) all capital and labor income tax rates [(1) + (2) + (4) = (3) + (4)], and (6) individual capital and labor income tax rates. Of these six sets of tax rates, (5) has the broadest tax base followed by (6), (4), and (3).

Our model allows us to distinguish five categories of public spending: purchases of consumption goods, investment goods, and labor services and transfer payments to households and the rest of the world. In order to measure the welfare impact of a cut in defense spending we first establish a base case by solving the model under the reference tax and spending policies. This produces a time path of future growth of the U.S. economy with no cuts in defense spending.

The second step in our analysis is to adjust government spending to incorporate the peace dividend. At the same time we adjust the selected set of tax rates proportionally to meet the balanced budget condition at the margin. When marginal and average tax rates are different, they are adjusted in the same proportion. In all of the alternative case simulations, we hold government debt and the claims on the rest of the world at the same time path as in the base case.

The welfare of the representative consumer in our model is summarized by the inter-temporal welfare index of chapter 7. Since this welfare index does not incorporate the impact of defense expenditures on consumer welfare, the change in the welfare index is a measure of the social cost of the defense spending which is eliminated. If defense spending, including veterans benefits, is cut, the change in the welfare index includes the income effect of reduced transfer payments as well as the cost of the defense spending eliminated by the cut.

In order to convert the change in the welfare index into a money measure, we employ the inter-temporal expenditure function presented in chapter 7. Using this expenditure function, we can compute the money metric welfare change from defense cut, say, ΔW, as

$$\Delta W = W(PF_0, D_0, V_1) - W(PF_0, D_0, V_0) \tag{9.10}$$

where the subscripts 0 and 1 indicate the base case and the alternative case, respectively.

If a defense cut involves purchases only, the money metric welfare change is equal to the social cost of the spending that has been eliminated. However, if defense cut includes veterans benefits, the welfare change ΔW includes the effect of the reduced transfer payments. The change in cost, say ΔC, is obtained by subtracting the value of the transfer payments from the change in welfare ΔW:

$$\Delta C = [W(PF_0, D_0, V_1) - \Delta T] - W(PF_0, D_0, V_0) \tag{9.11}$$

where ΔT is the present value of the change in transfer payments.

To calculate the present value of the change in transfer payments ΔT we first divide by the price of full consumption, converting the reduction into units of full consumption. We then add the change in transfer payments to the path of full consumption in the base case. Finally, we compute the present value of the reduction in transfer payments as the difference between base case welfare and the welfare that can be attained with the reduction in defense spending. We follow the same procedure to compute the present value of the tax cut associated with the reduction in spending ΔR.

In order to measure the peace dividend resulting from the end of the Cold War, we assume that, had the Cold War continued, the share of defense spending in the *GDP* would have remained at the level of 1990. We interpret the decrease in the share from the 1990 level as a reduction due to the ending of the Cold War. Table 9.6 and figure 9.5 give the share of defense spending *SDS* in *GDP* for the period 1970–1997. By 1998, the share of defense spending in *GDP* had decreased from 5.93% of 1990 to 3.63%. Our projections of the future course of the U.S. defense spending, given below, show that the share will continue to decline.

The composition of defense spending by purchases of consumption goods, investment goods, employee compensation, and veterans benefits is given for the period 1970–1997 in table 9.6. In order to capture the reduction of U.S. defense spending, we use the composition of defense spending in 1997 and long-term projections by the Congressional Budget Office (CBO) and Data Resources, Inc. (DRI) given

Table 9.6
Defense spending and the U.S. economy (billions of dollars)

Year	GDP	VDS	SDS	SCGD	SIGD	SLGD	SELD
1970	1035.6	84.4	0.0815	0.2429	0.2322	0.4336	0.0912
1971	1125.4	83.1	0.0738	0.2503	0.1841	0.4597	0.1059
1972	1237.3	87.3	0.0706	0.2337	0.1913	0.4639	0.1111
1973	1382.6	88.1	0.0637	0.2270	0.1850	0.4699	0.1180
1974	1496.9	94.9	0.0634	0.2371	0.1739	0.4647	0.1243
1975	1630.6	105.0	0.0644	0.2105	0.1952	0.4562	0.1381
1976	1819.0	108.8	0.0598	0.2160	0.1903	0.4614	0.1324
1977	2026.9	116.6	0.0575	0.2153	0.2067	0.4597	0.1184
1978	2291.4	124.6	0.0544	0.2127	0.2143	0.4615	0.1116
1979	2557.5	138.9	0.0543	0.2210	0.2311	0.4442	0.1037
1980	2784.2	160.2	0.0575	0.2534	0.2253	0.4276	0.0936
1981	3115.9	186.9	0.0600	0.2579	0.2343	0.4216	0.0861
1982	3242.1	213.7	0.0659	0.2686	0.2457	0.4090	0.0767
1983	3514.5	235.6	0.0670	0.2606	0.2767	0.3922	0.0705
1984	3902.4	263.3	0.0675	0.2510	0.2784	0.4083	0.0623
1985	4180.7	290.4	0.0695	0.2562	0.2893	0.3970	0.0575
1986	4422.2	307.5	0.0695	0.2618	0.2979	0.3860	0.0543
1987	4692.3	323.6	0.0690	0.2664	0.2979	0.3844	0.0513
1988	5049.6	325.6	0.0645	0.2838	0.2761	0.3882	0.0519
1989	5438.7	330.7	0.0608	0.2821	0.2682	0.3973	0.0523
1990	5743.8	340.7	0.0593	0.2809	0.2712	0.3957	0.0522
1991	5916.7	349.0	0.0590	0.2765	0.2633	0.4077	0.0524
1992	6244.4	340.8	0.0546	0.2705	0.2529	0.4199	0.0566
1993	6558.1	325.1	0.0496	0.2756	0.2353	0.4269	0.0621
1994	6947.0	312.6	0.0450	0.2815	0.2258	0.4280	0.0646
1995	7265.4	308.0	0.0424	0.2877	0.2179	0.4269	0.0675
1996	7661.6	315.7	0.0412	0.2924	0.2154	0.4238	0.0684
1997	8110.9	312.1	0.0385	0.3076	0.1935	0.4271	0.0718

Source:
U.S. Department of Commerce, *Survey of Current Business*, various issues.
Notations:
GDP: Gross domestic product
VDS: Defense spending broadly defined to include veterans benefits
SDS: VDS as a share of GDP (VDS/GDP)
SCGD: Share of consumption goods and services in defense spending
SIGD: Share of investment in defense spending
SLGD: Share of employee compensation in defense spending
SELD: Share of veterans benefits in defense spending

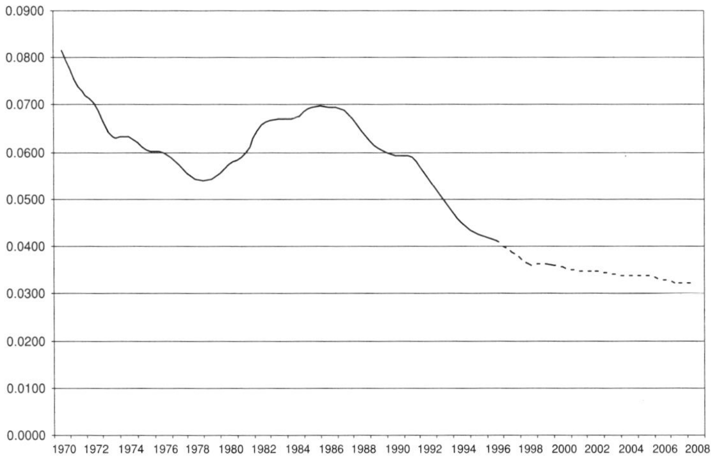

Figure 9.5
The share of defense spending in *GDP* (*SDS*).

in table 9.7. We construct a projection of the defense spending, its share in *GDP*, and its composition for 1998–2008.

The *CBO* estimate of defense purchases of consumption goods and services, *CBO*2 in table 9.7, includes employee compensation as well as purchases of consumers durables, nondurables, and other services. Using the *DRI* projection of the employee compensation, *DRI*2 in table 9.7 and other consumption expenditures for defense, *DRI*4 in table 9.7, we first estimate the employee compensation, *VLGD*, for defense:

$$VLGD = CBO2 \cdot \frac{DRI2}{DRI2 + DRI4}$$

Using the actual 1997 composition of defense expenditures given in table 9.6 we estimate the expenditure on durable consumption goods for defense. The remainder of *CBO*2 is defense spending on consumption goods and services, *VCGD*

$$VCGD = CBO2 \cdot \frac{DRI4}{DRI2 + DRI4} \cdot \frac{NDUR_{97} + OS_{97}}{DUR_{97} + NDUR_{97} + OS_{97}},$$

where DUR_{97} is defense spending on durable consumption goods, $NDUR_{97}$ is defense spending on nondurable consumption goods, and OS_{97} is other services in 1997 from the U.S. National Income and

Table 9.7
Inputs for projection of defense spending

	CBO		DRI		
Year	CBO1	CBO2	DRI1	DRI2	DRI4
1997	8111	252	306.2	133.6	116.2
1998	8487	247	301.0	132.5	113.5
1999	8839	256	309.1	135.5	120.0
2000	9204	264	306.4	137.3	116.4
2001	9572	267	307.5	139.9	115.4
2002	10008	278	311.6	142.5	117.3
2003	10475	287	317.8	146.6	119.4
2004	10955	296	327.3	152.1	123.3
2005	11446	309	340.7	158.2	130.2
2006	11950	316	354.8	164.7	137.3
2007	12473	323	369.5	171.5	144.3
2008	13015	337	385.0	178.6	151.7
2009	—	—	401.4	186.0	159.4

Sources:
Standard and Poors DRI, *Review of the U.S. Economy: Ten Year Projections*, November 1998, p. 116, table 5.1.
Congressional Budget Office, *The Economic and Budget Outlook: An Update*, August 1998, tables 1.2 and 2.8.
Notes:
CBO projections
CBO1: Nominal GDP, CBO table 1.2, p. 16.
CBO2: Purchases of consumption goods and services for defense, CBO table 2.8, p.46.
DRI projections
DRI1: Government consumption for defense (net of "investment"), DRI table 5.1, p.116.
DRI2: Employee compensation for defense
DRI4: Other, defense (include durables, nondurables, other services)

Product Accounts (NIPA), *Survey of Current Business* (October 1998, June 1999), table 3.7.

Since the *CBO* and *DRI* projections do not include defense spending on structures and equipment, we estimate this from the ratio of investment and consumption expenditures for national defense in 1997. We define defense spending on investment goods as the sum of defense spending on durable consumption goods and investment in equipment and structures:

$$VIGD = CBO2 - VCGD - VLGD + CBO2 \cdot \frac{DINV_{97}}{CEXP_{97} - DDEP_{97}},$$

where $DINV_{97}$ is gross investment in equipment and structures for defense, $CEXP_{97}$ is consumption expenditures for defense including consumption of general government fixed capital, $DDEP_{97}$.

Similarly, we estimate veterans benefits, $VELD$, from the share of veterans benefits in total defense spending in 1997, SVB_{97}

$$VELD = (VCGD + VIGD + VLGD) \cdot \frac{SVB_{97}}{1 - SVB_{97}} .$$

Finally, defense purchases, VDP, defense spending, VDS, and the GDP share of defense spending, SDS, are calculated as

$$VDP = VCGD + VIGD + VLGD$$

$$VDS = VDP + VELD$$

$$SDS = \frac{VDS}{GDP} .$$

The projection of SDS is shown in table 9.8 and figure 9.5 and the projection of composition of defense spending is shown in Table 9.8 and figure 9.6.

We calculate the reduction in the defense spending due to the end of the Cold War from the decline in the projected ratios of defense spending to the GDP, relative to the 1990 level. We use the historical averages for 1980–1997 for the composition of defense spending under the scenario of continuation of the Cold War. Table 9.9 gives the welfare effects of the cuts in defense spending for six different subsets of taxes, which are adjusted in the same proportion in order to meet the condition that the government budget must be balanced at the margin. Table 9.9 also gives the present value of the tax reductions.

Since the growth of the U.S. economy is relatively insensitive to the choice of the tax rates to be adjusted, we focus on the case with the adjustment of all income tax rates. Table 9.9 summarizes the welfare impact for the six combinations of defense cuts and tax rates. The welfare gain from defense cuts (ΔW) and the reduction in the social cost of defense spending (ΔC) are very large.

We first consider the case of adjustment of both capital and labor incomes. The welfare gain is \$6.79 trillions (in 1991 dollars), which is greater that the GDP of \$5.92 trillions in 1991, while the reduction in the social cost of defense spending is \$7.18 trillions. Second, the welfare gain and the cost of the defense spending eliminated depends on the tax rates that are adjusted in order to meet the balanced budget

Table 9.8
Projected defense spending and its composition

		Composition of Defense Spending			
Year	SDS	SCGD	SIGD	SLGD	SELD
1998	0.0363	0.3040	0.1928	0.4314	0.0718
1999	0.0362	0.3095	0.1939	0.4248	0.0718
2000	0.0358	0.3023	0.1924	0.4335	0.0718
2001	0.0348	0.2979	0.1914	0.4389	0.0718
2002	0.0347	0.2975	0.1914	0.4394	0.0718
2003	0.0342	0.2958	0.1910	0.4415	0.0718
2004	0.0337	0.2950	0.1908	0.4424	0.0718
2005	0.0337	0.2975	0.1913	0.4394	0.0718
2006	0.0330	0.2996	0.1918	0.4369	0.0718
2007	0.0323	0.3011	0.1921	0.4350	0.0718
2008	0.0323	0.3026	0.1925	0.4331	0.0718

Note: See table 9.6.

Table 9.9
Welfare effects of the reduction in defense spending (billions of 1991 dollars)

Adjusted Taxes	ΔC	ΔW	ΔR	ΔC/ΔR	ΔW/ΔR
1.Corporate Income Tax	6931.2	6532.0	6227.6	1.1130	1.0489
2. Individual Capital Income Tax	6822.8	6423.6	6227.0	1.0957	1.0316
3. Capital Income Tax (Corp. and Ind.)	6844.7	6445.5	6227.3	1.0992	1.0350
4. Labor Income Tax	7769.4	7378.5	6097.3	1.2742	1.2101
5. Capital and Labor Income Tax	7182.4	6787.5	6159.8	1.1660	1.1019
6. Individual Income Tax	7315.1	6921.4	6140.9	1.1912	1.1271

Note: Inflation is fixed at 4% per year.
ΔC: Reduction in the social cost of defense spending
ΔW: Welfare gain from reduction in defense spending
ΔR: Present value of tax reduction

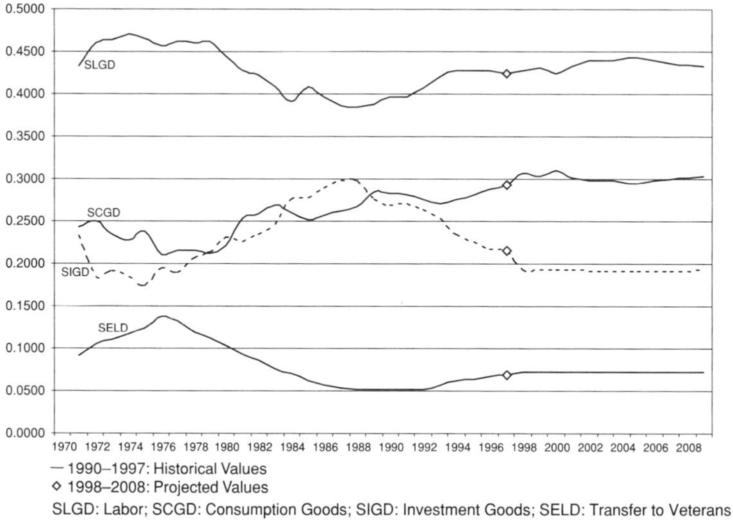

Figure 9.6
Composition of defense spending.

condition. The largest gain arises when the tax rates on individual labor income taxes are reduced; the smallest occurs when the individual capital income tax rate is lowered in response to the defense cut.

Third, the ratio of the welfare impact to the present value of the tax revenue change ($\Delta W/\Delta R$) are largest when taxes on labor income are reduced. Similarly, the ratio of the social cost to the present value of the tax revenue change ($\Delta C/\Delta R$), is highest for labor income tax reductions. For example, the welfare ratio $\Delta W/\Delta R$ is 1.21 for the labor income tax adjustment, 1.03 for the adjustment of individual capital income taxes, and 1.04 for all capital income taxes. Most of the welfare $\Delta W/\Delta R$ and social cost $\Delta C/\Delta R$ ratios are substantially greater than one. The present value of a cut in defense spending underestimates both the welfare gain from the defense cut and the social cost of the defense spending eliminated.

In table 9.9 the social cost ratio $\Delta C/\Delta R$ is larger than the welfare ratio $\Delta W/\Delta R$ because the change in consumer welfare includes the income effect of the reduced transfer payments. These constitute benefits, rather than costs, of the transfer programs. In order to isolate the welfare cost of defense spending, we can subtract the change in transfer payments from the welfare change. As a consequence, the social cost ratio $\Delta C/\Delta R$ is greater than the welfare ratio $\Delta W/\Delta R$.

9.7 Alternative Approaches

Since the seminal paper by Browning (1976), measurement of the marginal cost of public spending has attracted considerable interest. As a consequence, the economic analysis of taxation has been brought closer to the analysis of public spending. However, earlier estimates of the *MCS* were based on different definitions of the welfare cost of tax increases. In addition, the estimates were based on different models with a wide range of parameter values. Not surprisingly, the estimated values of the *MCS* have varied substantially. Table 9.10 compares our results with four other studies.

Employing a partial equilibrium model with labor tax, Browning (1987) has revised his earlier estimates and reported that the *MCS* is 1.318 if income and substitution effects of tax increase cancel out and the benefits of the additional spending does not affect labor supply. The *MCS* is 1.469 if the income effect of tax increase and that of the benefits from additional public spending cancel and the substitution effect of tax increase increases labor supply. In the former case, labor supply is unaffected by the additional spending while, in the latter case, labor supply changes along the compensated labor supply curve.

Stuart (1984) uses a static general equilibrium model with a labor income tax and reports substantially lower estimates. He reports that the *MCS* is 1.072 if the benefits of public spending are separable from private consumption and 1.207 if the benefits are perfect substitutes for private consumption. In a similar model, but with taxes on both capital and labor, Hansson and Stuart (1985) estimate the *MCS* for Sweden and report substantially higher values, 1.69 and 2.29, respectively. These larger values are attributable to high marginal tax rates in Sweden.

Ballard, Shoven, and Whalley (BSW: 1985a) use a dynamic general equilibrium model with nineteen production sectors, twelve consumer groups, and a detailed description of the U.S. tax system. They consider benefits that are separable from private consumption and report that the *MCS* is 1.332 if all taxes are used to raise the additional funds, and 1.230 if labor taxes at industry level are used. Fullerton and Henderson (1989a) employ a model that is similar to BSW but with a much more detailed representation of capital income taxes based on the cost of capital approach. They report that the *MCS* is 1.169 for additional funds from a labor tax at the industry level.[6]

Table 9.10
Comparison with other studies

Author(s)	Key Features	MCS Type A Benefits	MCS Transfer Payment
Browning (1987)[1)]	Partial equilibrium model, tax on labor (U.S.)	1.318	1.469
Stuart (1984)	Static general equilibrium model, tax on labor (U.S)	1.072	1.207
Hansson and Stuart (1985)[2)]	Static general equilibrium model, taxes on capital and labor (Sweden)	1.69 (0.98)	2.29 (1.24)
Ballard, Shoven and Whalley (1985a)[3)]	Dynamic general equilibrium model, U.S. tax system (1973)	1.332 (1.170–1.332)	n.a.
Jorgenson and Yun[4)]	Dynamic general equilibrium model, U.S. tax system (1996):		
	Labor income tax	1.187	1.414
	Capital and labor income tax	1.128	1.339
	All taxes, except for property tax	1.092	1.299

Notes:
1): Welfare cost includes substitution effects only, but changes in tax revenue are based on actual labor supply. For spending with type A benefits, income and substitution effects are assumed to cancel out, leaving labor supply unchanged. For transfer payment, income effects of taxation and public spending are assumed to cancel out, resulting in a change in labor supply that is equal to the compensated change.
2): Marginal funds are raised with historical tax mix at the marginal labor tax rate of 0.7. In the parentheses are the figures for marginal funds raised with constant tax progressivity.
3): The ranges in the parentheses include the MCS for four combinations of savings and labor supply elasticities, with the elasticities of 0.0 and 0.4 for savings and 0.0, 0.15 for labor supply.
4): For spending with type A benefits, all public spendings, except for transfer payments, are increased by the same proportion.

Fullerton (1991) attempts to reconcile these diverse estimates of the *MCS*. He shows that the differences can be traced to differences in the definition. In particular, he emphasizes the difference between Browning's measure of the welfare cost of the tax increase and those of Stuart and BSW. Browning, who uses a compensated labor supply curve, captures the substitution effects but ignores the income effects, while Stuart and BSW capture both the income and the substitution effects.[7]

Wildasin (1984), Stuart (1984), Hansson and Stuart (1985), and BSW (1985a) have made clear the conceptual differences between their measures of the cost of public spending and that of Browning (1976, 1987). Ballard (1990) points out that Browning's results could be used for the analysis of differential tax incidence and a balanced budget expansion of public spending, provided that the benefits from spending are perfect substitutes for private consumption. Under this assumption the benefits must be equal to the additional tax revenue, so that the income effect of the increased revenue is offset by the income effect of the benefits from the public spending.

As we have already mentioned, earlier studies have emphasized the dependence of the *MCS* on the source of tax revenues and the type of benefits, but have ignored the effects of the category of public spending. As a result, the scope of comparisons between our estimates of the *MCS* and those of other studies are limited. The differences in the representation of the tax system further limits the scope of comparison. However, the studies of BSW (1985a) and Fullerton and Henderson (1989a) are based on dynamic general equilibrium models with detailed representations of the U.S. economy and the U.S. tax system. In table 9.11 we compare the central results of BSW, Fullerton and Henderson, and our estimates of the *MCS* for various sources of tax revenues. Since BSW and Fullerton and Henderson consider a proportional expansion of government spending programs that are additively separable from private consumption, we report the *MCS* of a proportional expansion, excluding transfer payments, in table 9.11.

BSW's capital taxes at industry level include corporate income taxes, the corporate franchise tax, and property taxes, while our capital income taxes include corporate and individual capital income taxes. Individual capital income includes dividends, interest, and capital gains on private assets such as capital in the corporate, noncorporate, and household sectors and government debt. Thus BSW's capital tax is close to our corporate income tax. BSW's labor income taxes

Table 9.11
Detailed comparison with BSW and Fullerton and Henderson

Authors	Taxes	MCS
Ballard, Shoven and Whalley (1985a)[1)]	1. All taxes	1.332 (1.170-1.332)
	2. Capital taxes at industry level	1.463 (1.181–1.463)
	3. Labor taxes at industry level	1.230 (1.112–1.234)
	4. Consumer sales taxes	1.388 (1.251–1.388)
	5. Sales taxes on commodities other than alcohol, tobacco, and gasoline	1.115 (1.026–1.119)
	6. Income taxes	1.314 (1.163–1.314)
	7. Output taxes	1.279 (1.147–1.279)
Fullerton and Henderson (1989a)[2)]	1. Corporate income tax	1.310
	2. Corporate and noncorporate income taxes	1.252
	3. Labor tax at industry level	1.169
	4. Personal income tax	1.247
Jorgenson and Yun (1996 law)[3)]	1. Corporate income tax	1.098
	2. Individual capital income taxes	1.078
	3. Property taxes	0.951
	4. Capital income taxes, corporate and individual (1 + 2)	1.084
	5. Labor income tax	1.187
	6. Capital and labor income tax (1 + 2 + 5 = 4 + 5)	1.128
	7. Individual income tax (2 + 5)	1.141
	8. Sales taxes	0.983
	9. All taxes, except for property tax (1 + 2 + 5 + 8)	1.092
	10. All taxes (1 + 2 + 3 + 5 + 8)	1.068

Notes:
1): The central results are obtained with uncompensated savings elasticity of 0.4 and uncompensated labor supply elasticity of 0.15. The ranges in the parentheses include the MCS for four combinations of savings and labor supply elasticities, with the elasticities of 0.0 and 0.4 for savings and 0.0, 0.15 for labor supply.
2): The central results are obtained with uncompensated savings elasticity of 0.4, uncompensated labor supply elasticity of 0.15, and asset substitution elasticity of 1.0 within and between the corporate and noncorporate sectors.
3): The MCS are for proportional expansion of government spending other than transfer payment to household. All benefits are separable from private consumption.

include social security taxes and contributions to unemployment insurance and workmen's compensation, while our labor income taxes represent only the portion of the individual income attributable to labor income. Their labor taxes at the industry level are not comparable to our labor income tax.

We can compare our estimates of the *MCS* for all taxes with BSW's estimates for all taxes. Similarly, we can compare our estimates for the corporate income tax with BSW's estimates of capital taxes at the industry level and our estimates for the individual income tax with BSW's estimates for income taxes. Finally, we can compare our estimates for sales taxes with BSW's estimates for sales taxes on commodities other than alcohol, tobacco, and gasoline.

Keeping in mind that BSW's composition of spending may be different from ours, we find that our estimates of the *MCS* are less than those of BSW. BSW's estimate of the *MCS* for all taxes, capital taxes at the industry level and sales taxes are substantially higher than our estimate of the *MCS* for all taxes, corporate income tax and sales taxes, respectively. Finally, BSW's estimate of the *MCS* for consumer sales taxes is very large compared to our estimate for sales taxes

Fullerton and Henderson's central results in table 9.11 are generally lower than the corresponding figures of BSW. Due to the differences in the definition of the taxes, Fullerton and Henderson's *MCS* for corporate and noncorporate income taxes and for labor taxes at industry level are not comparable with our estimates of the *MCS* for capital income taxes and labor income taxes. For the individual income tax and the corporate income tax the comparison may be more meaningful and we find that their results are substantially higher.

An important motivation for estimating the *MCS* is to provide information for the cost-benefit analysis of public spending programs. Our approach is particularly well suited for cost-benefit analysis, since we estimate the *MCS* for every combination of the sources of funds, the uses of funds, and the types of benefits. Given the cost of a government spending program, a cost-benefit analysis would require only an estimate of the social value of type A benefits, which are separable from private consumption, together with our estimates of the *MCS*.

Previous studies on the *MCS* have recognized that the cost depends on the source of funds and the type of benefits. However, little attention has been paid to the use of the funds. We interpret public spending program as a production process by which inputs are transformed into outputs. In this setting, general equilibrium considerations lead to the conclusion that the *MCS* depends on the use of the additional funds as well. Using a dynamic general equilibrium model of the U.S. economy, we have demonstrated that estimates of the *MCS* differ substantially among alternative categories of public spending.

To the extent that we can compare our study with BSW (1985a) and Fullerton and Henderson (1989a), we find that there are substantial differences among the estimated values of the *MCS*. This indicates that use of a dynamic general equilibrium model with detailed description of the tax system is not sufficient to guarantee a narrow range of estimates. In order to reconcile the differences among the estimated values of the *MCS*, we need definitions that are precisely comparable. In addition, there are obvious benefits from more realistic modeling of the economy and better estimates of the parameters describing technology and preferences.

Notes

1. The effect of benefits from public spending is the same as the "expenditure effect" of Hansson and Stuart (1985).
2. In the literature, the terms "marginal cost of public funds (*MCF*)", "marginal excess burden taxation (*MEB*)", and "marginal welfare cost of taxation (*MWC*)" are used for our concept of the marginal cost of public spending (*MCS*). Our concept of the *MCS* is the same as the *MWC* or one plus the *MEB*. However, we prefer a terminology that emphasizes the fact that the cost depends on the allocation of government expenditures. Wildasin (1984) uses the term "marginal social cost of public expenditure," which is in line with this view.
3. See Barro (1990), Aschauer (1989), Berndt and Hansson (1991), Holtz-Eakin (1991, 1992), Hulten and Schwab (1984, 1991), Munnell (1990), and Fernald (1999).
4. BSW (1985a) and Fullerton and Henderson (1989a) report the *MCS* for a number of other tax instruments used to raise the additional funds. Here, we mention only those that are comparable to the results of other studies. For a more detailed description of their results, see table 9.11 below.
5. For a recent review and evaluation of defense cut after the end of the cold war, see Michael O'Hanlon (1999).
6. BSW (1985a) and Fullerton and Henderson (1989a) report the *MCS* for a number of other taxes used to raise marginal funds. In table 9.11, we present the results that may be compared with ours.
7. Stuart uses Hicks' compensating surplus, while BSW employ the equivalent variation. Fullerton suggests that this difference is unimportant. Comparison of Mayshar's (1991) results with Stuart's (1984) supports this view.

References

Aaron, Henry J., and William B. Gale (eds.). 1996. *Economic Effects of Fundamental Tax Reform*. Washington, DC: Brookings Institution.

Aaron, Henry J., William B. Gale, and James Sly. 1999. The Rocky Road to Tax Reform. In *Setting National Priorities—The 2000 Election and Beyond*, eds. Henry J. Aaron and Robert D. Reischauer, 211–266. Washington, DC: Brookings Institution.

Altig, David, Alan J. Auerbach, Lawrence J. Kotlikoff, Kent A. Smetters, and Jan Walliser. 1999. Simulating Fundamental Tax Reform in the U.S., Mimeo.

———. 1997. *Simulating U.S. Tax Reform*. Technical Paper Series, Macroeconomic Analysis and Tax Analysis Division, Congressional Budget Office, September.

Amemiya, Takeshi. 1977. The Maximum Likelihood Estimator and the Nonlinear Three-Stage Least-Squares Estimator in the General Nonlinear Simultaneous Equation Model. *Econometrica* 45, no. 4 (May): 955–968.

Americans for Fair Tax. The Fair Tax: Good for Taxpayers, Good for Business, Good for the Economy. *http:/www.fairtax.org/issues/aft1.htm*

Armey, Dick, and Richard Shelby. Freedom and Fairness Restoration Act of 1995, H.R. 2060 and S.1050, Bill Summary and Status for the 104th Congress.

Arrow, Kenneth J. 1964. Optimal Capital Policy, the Cost of Capital, and Myopic Decision Rules. *Annals of the Institute of Statistical Mathematics* 16, nos. 1/2: 21–30.

———. 1968. Optimal Capital Policy with Irreversible Investments. In *Value, Capital, and Growth*, ed. James N. Wolfe, 1–19, Papers in Honor of Sir John Hicks. Chicago, IL: Aldine Publishing Company.

Aschauer, David A. 1989. Is Public Expenditure Productive? *Journal of Monetary Economics* 23, no. 2 (March): 177–200.

Atkinson, Anthony B., and Joseph E. Stiglitz, 1980. *Lectures on Public Economics*. Cambridge, MA: MIT Press.

Auerbach, Alan J. 1979. Wealth Maximization and the Cost of Capital. *Quarterly Journal of Economics* 93, no. 3 (August): 433–446.

———. 1983a. Corporate Taxation in the U.S. *Brookings Papers on Economic Activity*, no. 2: 451–505.

———. 1983b. Taxation, Corporate Financial Policy, and the Cost of Capital. *Journal of Economic Literature* 21, no. 3 (September): 905–940.

———. 1984. Taxes, Firm Financial Policy, and the Cost of Capital: An Empirical Analysis. *Journal of Public Economics* 23, nos. 1/2 (February/March): 27–57.

———. 1985. The Theory of Excess Burden and Optimal Taxation. In *Handbook of Public Economics*, vol. 1, eds. Alan J. Auerbach and Martin S. Feldstein, 61–127. Amsterdam: North-Holland.

———. 1987. The Tax Reform Act of 1986 and the Cost of Capital. *Journal of Economic Perspectives* 1 (Summer): 73–86.

———. 1989a. The Deadweight Loss from "Non-Neutral" Capital Income Taxation. *Journal of Public Economics* 40, no. 1 (October): 1–36.

———. 1989b. Tax Reform and Adjustment Costs: The Impact on Investment and Market Value. *International Economic Review* 30, no. 4 (November): 1–36.

———. 1996. Tax Reform, Capital Allocation, Efficiency and Growth, Burch Working Paper No. B96–19. Berkeley, CA: University of California.

———. 1997. The Future of Fundamental Tax Reform. *American Economic Review* 87, no. 2 (May): 143–146.

Auerbach, Alan J., and Dale W. Jorgenson. 1980. Inflation-Proof Depreciation of Assets. *Harvard Business Review* 58, no. 5 (September-October): 113–118.

Auerbach, Alan J., and Lawrence J. Kotlikoff. 1987. *Dynamic Fiscal Policy*. Cambridge: Cambridge University Press.

Auerbach, Alan J., Lawrence J. Kotlikoff, Kent Smetters, and Jan Walliser. 1997. Fundamental Tax Reform and Macroeconomic Performance. In Joint Committee on Taxation, *Joint Committee on Taxation Tax Modeling Project and 1997 Tax Symposium Paper*. Washington, DC: U.S. Government Printing Office (November): 83–100.

Auerbach, Alan J., and Joel Slemrod. 1997. The Economic Effects of the Tax Reform Act of 1986. *Journal of Economic Literature* 35, no. 2 (June): 589–632.

Bailey, Martin J. 1969. "Capital Gains and Income Taxation." In *The Taxation of Income from Capital*, eds. Arnold C. Harberger and Martin J. Bailey, 11–49. Washington: Brookings Institution.

———. 1981. Productivity and the Services of Capital and Labor. *Brookings Papers on Economic Activity* 1: 1–50.

Ballard, Charles L. 1990. Marginal Welfare Cost Calculations: Differential Analysis vs. Balanced Budget Analysis. *Journal of Public Economics* 41, no. 2 (March): 263–276.

Ballard, Charles L., Don Fullerton, John B. Shoven, and John Whalley. 1985. *A General Equilibrium Model for Tax Policy Evaluation.* Chicago, IL: University of Chicago Press.

Ballard, Charles L., John B. Shoven, and John Whalley. 1985a. General Equilibrium Computations of the Marginal Welfare Costs of Taxes in the United States. *American Economic Review* 75, no. 1 (March): 128–138.

———. 1985b. The Total Welfare Cost of the United States Tax System: A General Equilibrium Approach. *National Tax Journal* 38, no. 2 (June): 125–140.

Ballentine, J. Gregory. 1987. Comment. In *The Effects of Taxation on Capital Accumulatiobn*, ed. Martin S. Feldstein, 437–443. Chicago, IL: University of Chicago Press.

Barro, Robert J. 1974. Are Government Bonds Net Wealth? *Journal of Political Economy* 82, no. 6 (November–December): 1095–1117.

———. 1990. Government Spending in a Simple Model of Endogenous Growth. *Journal of Political Economy* 98, no. 5, part 2 (October): S103–S125.

Barro, Robert J., and Chaipat Sahasakul. 1983. Measuring the Average Marginal Tax Rate from the Individual Income Tax. *Journal of Business* 56, no. 4 (November-December): 419–452.

———. 1986. Average and Marginal Tax Rates from Social Security and the Individual Income Tax. *Journal of Business* 59, no. 4 (November-December): 555–566.

Beidleman, Carl R. 1976. Economic Depreciation in a Capital Goods Industry. *National Tax Journal* 29, no. 4 (December): 379–390.

Berkovec, James, and Don Fullerton. 1992. A General Equilibrium Model of Housing, Taxes, and Portfolio Choice. *Journal of Political Economy* 100, no. 2 (April): 390–429.

Berndt, Ernst R., and Bengt Hansson. 1991. Measuring the Contribution of Public Infrastructure Capital in Sweden, Paper presented at the Industrial Institute for Economic and Social Research Seminar Capital, Its Value, Its Rate of Return and its Productivity. Saltsjobaden, Sweden.

Biorn, Erik. 1989. *Taxation, Technology and the User Cost of Capital.* Amsterdam: North-Holland.

———. 1998. Survival and Efficiency Curves for Capital and the Time-Age-Profile of Vintage Prices. *Empirical Economics* 23, no. 4: 611–633.

Birnbaum, Jeffrey H., and Alan S. Murray. 1987. *Showdown at Gucci Gulch.* New York: Random House.

Boadway, Robin, Neil Bruce, and Jack M. Mintz. 1984. Taxation, Inflation, and the Effective Marginal Tax Rate on Capital in Canada. *Canadian Journal of Economics* 17, no. 1 (February): 62–79.

Boskin. Michael J. 1996. *Frontiers of Tax Reform*. Stanford, CA: Hoover Institution Press.

Bradford, David F. 1981. The Incidence and Allocation Effect of a Tax on Corporate Distribution. *Journal of Public Economics* 15, no. 1 (January): 1–22.

———. 1986. *Untangling the Income Tax*. Cambridge, MA: Harvard University Press.

———. 1996. Consumption Taxes: Some Fundamental Transition Issues. In *Frontiers of Tax Reform*, ed. Michael J. Boskin, 123–150. Stanford, CA: Hoover Institution Press.

———. 2000. *Taxation, Wealth, and Saving*. Cambridge, MA: MIT Press.

Bradford, David F. and Don Fullerton. 1981. Pitfalls in the Construction and Use of Effective Tax Rates. In *Depreciation, Inflation, and the Taxation of Income from Capital*, ed. Charles R. Hulten, 251–278. Washington, DC: Urban Institute Press.

Brazell, D.W., L. Dworin, and M. Walsh. 1989. A History of Federal Depreciation Policy. Washington, DC: Office of Tax Analysis, U.S. Department of Treasury.

Browning, E.K. 1976. The Marginal Cost of Public Funds. *Journal of Political Economy* 84, no. 2 (April): 283–298.

———. 1987. The Marginal Cost of Taxation. *American Economic Review* 77, no. 1 (March): 11–23.

Bureau of Economic Analysis. 1977. *The National Income and Product Accounts of the United States, 1929–1974: Statistical Tables, A Supplement to the Survey of Current Business*. Washington, DC: U.S. Department of Commerce.

———. 1986. *The National Income and Product Accounts of the United States, 1929–1982: Statistical Tables*. Washington: U.S. Department of Commerce.

———. 1987. *Fixed Reproducible Tangible Wealth in the United States, 1925–1985*. Washington, DC: U.S. Government Printing Office.

Chamley, Christophe. 1981. The Welfare Cost of Capital Income Taxation in a Growing Economy. *Journal of Political Economy* 89, no. 3 (June): 468–496.

Chirinko, Robert S., and Robert Eisner. 1983. Tax Policy and Investment in Major U.S. Macroeconometric Models. *Journal of Public Economics* 20, no. 2 (March): 139–166.

Chow, Gregory C. 1967. Technological Change and the Demand for Computers. *American Economic Review*. 57, no. 5 (December): 1117–1130.

Christensen, Laurits R., and Dale W. Jorgenson. 1973a. Measuring Economic Performance in the Private Sector. In *The Measurement of Economic and Social Performance*, ed. Milton Moss, 233–251. New York, NY: Columbia University Press.

———. 1973b. U.S. Income, Saving and Wealth, 1929–1969. *Review of Income and Wealth*, ser. 19, no. 4 (December): 329–362.

Christensen, Laurits R., Dale W. Jorgenson, and Lawrence J. Lau. 1971. Conjugate Duality and the Transcendental Logarithmic Production Function. *Econometrica* 39, no. 4 (July): 255–256.

———. 1973. Transcendental Logarithmic Production Frontiers. *The Review of Economics and Statistics* 55, no. 1 (February): 28–45.

———. 1975. Transcendental Logarithmic Utility Functions. *American Economic Review* 65, no. 3 (June): 367–383.

Coen, Robert. 1975. Investment Behavior, the Measurement of Depreciation, and Tax Policy. *American Economic Review* 65, no. 1 (March): 59–74.

———. 1980. Depreciation, Profits, and Rates of Return in Manufacturing Industries. In *The Measurement of Capital*, ed. Dan. Usher, 121–152. Chicago, IL: University of Chicago Press.

Cole, Rosanne, Y.C. Chen, Joan A. Barquin-Stolleman, Ellen Dulberger, Nurhan Helvacian, and James H. Hodge. 1986. Quality-Adjusted Price Indexes for Computer Processors and Selected Peripheral Equipment. *Survey of Current Business* 66, no. 1 (January): 41–50.

Congressional Budget Office. 1997. The Economic Effects of Comprehensive Tax Reform, Congress of the United States, July.

Court, Andrew T. 1939. Hedonic Price Indexes with Automotive Examples. In *The Dynamics of Automobile Demand*, 99–17. New York: General Motors Corporation.

Diamond, Peter A., and Daniel L. McFadden. 1974. Some Uses of the Expenditure Function in Public Finance. *Journal of Public Economics* 3, no. 1 (February): 3–21.

Diamond, Peter A., and J.A. Mirrlees. 1971a. Optimal Taxation and Public Production I: Production Efficiency. *American Economic Review* 61, no. 1 (March): 8–27.

———. 1971b. Optimal Taxation and Public Production II: Tax Rules. *American Economic Review* 61, no. 3 (September): 261–278.

Diewert, W. Erwin. 1980. Aggregation Problems in the Measurement of Capital. In *The Measurement of Capital*, ed. Dan Usher, 433–528. Chicago, IL: University of Chicago Press.

Doms, Mark E. 1996. Estimating Capital Efficiency Schedules within Production Functions. *Economic Inquiry* 34, no. 1 (January): 78–92.

Dulberger, Ellen. 1989. The Application of a Hedonic Model to a Quality-Adjusted Price Index for Computer Processors. In *Technology and Capital Formation*, eds. Dale W. Jorgenson and Ralph Landau, 37–76. Cambridge, MA: MIT Press.

Eisner, Robert. 1972. Components of Capital Expenditures: Replacement and Modernization. *Review of Economics and Statistics* 54, no. 3 (August): 297–305.

Eissa, Nada. 1996. Tax Reforms and Labor Supply. In *Tax Policy and the Economy*, ed. James M. Poterba, vol. 10, 119–151. Cambridge, MA: MIT Press.

Engen, Eric, and William Gale. 1997. Macroeconomic Effects of Fundamental Tax Reform: Simulations with a Stochastic Life-Cycle, Overlapping Generations, General Equilibrium Model. In Joint Committee on Taxation, *Joint Committee on Taxation Tax Modeling Project and 1997 Tax Symposium Paper*, Washington, DC: U.S. Government Printing Office (November): 101–129.

Engen, Eric, Jane Gravelle, and Kent Smetters. 1997. Dynamic Tax Models: Why They Do the Things They Do. *National Tax Journal*, vol. 50, no. 3 (September): 657–682.

Fair, Ray C., and John B. Taylor. 1983. Solution and Maximum Likelihood Estimation of Dynamic Nonlinear Rational Expectations Model. *Econometrica* 51, no. 4 (July): 1169–1185.

Feenberg, Daniel R., Andrew W. Mitrusi, and James M. Poterba. 1997. Distributional Effects of Adopting a National Retail Sales Tax. In *Tax Policy and the Economy*, vol. 11, 49–89, ed. James M. Poterba. Cambridge, MA: MIT Press.

Feldstein, Martin S. 1974. Social Security, Induced Retirement, and Aggregate Capital Accumulation. *Journal of Political Economy* 82, no. 5 (September/October): 905–926.

———. 1978. The Welfare Cost of Capital Income Taxation. *Journal of Political Economy* 80, no. 2, part 2 (April): S29–S51.

———. 1983. Inflation, Tax Rules and Capital Formation. Chicago, IL: University of Chicago Press.

——— (ed.). 1987. *The Effects of Taxation and Capital Accumulation*. Chicago, IL: University of Chicago Press.

———. 1995a. The Effect of Marginal Tax Rates on Taxable Income: A Panel Study of the 1986 Tax Reform Act. *Journal of Political Economy* 103, no. 3 (June): 551–573.

———. 1995b. Behavioral Responses to Tax Rates: Evidence from TRA86. *American Economic Review* 85, no. 2 (May): 170–174.

Feldstein, Martin S., and Daniel Feenberg. 1996. The Effect of Increased Tax Rates on Taxable Income and Economic Efficiency: A Preliminary Analysis of the 1993 Tax Rate Increases. In *Tax Policy and the Economy*, ed. James M. Poterba, vol. 10, 89–118. Cambridge, MA: MIT Press.

Feldstein, Martin S., and David K. Foot. 1974. The Other Half of Gross Investment: Replacement and Modernization Expenditures. *Review of Economics and Statistics* 56, no. 1 (February): 49–58.

Feldstein, Martin S., and Joosung Jun. 1987. The Effects of Tax Rules on Nonresidential Fixed Investment: Some Preliminary Evidence from the 1980s. In *The Effects of Taxation on Capital Accumulation*, ed. Martin S. Feldstein, 101–156. Chicago, IL: University of Chicago Press.

Feldstein, Martin S., and Lawrence H. Summers. 1979. Inflation and the Taxation of Capital Income in the Corporate Sector. *National Tax Journal* 32, no. 4 (December): 445–470.

Feldstein, Martin S., James Poterba, and Louis Dicks-Mireaux. 1983. The Effective Tax Rate and the Pretax Rate of Return. *Journal of Public Economics* 21, no 2 (July): 49–58.

Fernald, John. 1999. Roads to Prosperity? Assessing the Link Between Public Capital and Productivity. *American Economic Review* 88, no. 3 (June): 619–638.

Fisher, Irving. 1961. *The Theory of Interest*. New York: A.M. Kelley.

Fox, William F., and Matthew N. Murray. 1997. The Sales Tax and Electronic Commerce: So What's New? *National Tax Journal*, vol. 50, no. 3 (September): 573–592.

Fraumeni, Barbara M. 1997. The Measurement of Depreciation in the U.S. National Income and Product Accounts. *Survey of Current Business* 77, no. 7 (July): 7–23.

Fullerton, Don. 1984. Which Effective Tax Rate? *National Tax Journal* 37, no. 1 (March): 23–41.

———. 1987. The Indexation of Interest, Depreciation, and Capital Gains and Tax Reform in the United States. *Journal of Public Economics* 32, no. 1 (February): 25–52.

———. 1991. Reconciling Recent Estimates of the Marginal Cost of Taxation. *American Economic Review* 81, no. 1 (March): 302–308.

Fullerton, Don, Robert Gillette, and James Mackie. 1987. Investment Incentives under the Tax Reform Act of 1986. In Office of Tax Analysis, *Compendium of Tax Research 1987*, 131–171. Washington, DC: U.S. Government Printing Office.

Fullerton, Don, and Yolanda K. Henderson. 1989a. The Marginal Excess Burden of Different Capital Tax Instrument. *The Review of Economics and Statistics* 71, no. 3 (August): 435–442.

———. 1989b. A Disaggregate Equilibrium Model of the Tax Distortions Among Assets, Sectors, and Industries. *International Economic Review* 30, no. 2 (May): 391–413.

Fullerton, Don, Yolanda K. Henderson, and James Mackie. 1987. Investment Allocation and Growth under the Tax Reform Act of 1986. In Office of Tax Analysis, *Compendium of Tax Research 1987,* 173–201. Washington, DC: U.S. Government Pringing Office.

Fullerton, Don, and Diane Lim Rogers. 1993. *Who Bears the Lifetime Tax Burden?* Washington, DC: Brookings Institution.

———. 1996. Lifetime Effects of Fundamental Tax Reform. In *Economic Effects of Fundamental Tax Reform,* eds. Henry Aaron and William B. Gale, 321–352. Washington, DC: Brooking Institution.

———. 1997. Neglected Effects on the Uses Side: Even a Uniform Tax Would Change Relative Goods Prices. *American Economic Review* 87, no. 2 (May): 120–125.

Fuss, Melvyn, Daniel L. McFadden, and Yair Mundlak. 1978. A Survey of Functional Forms in the Economic Analysis of Production. *Production Economics,* vol. 1, eds. Melvyn Fuss and Daniel L. McFadden, 219–268, Amsterdam: North-Holland.

Gale, William G. 1999. The Required Tax Rate in a National Retail Sales Tax. *National Tax Journal,* 52, no. 3 (September): 443–457.

Gale, William G., and John Karl Scholz. 1994. Intergenerational Transfers and the Accumulation of Wealth. *Journal of Economic Perspectives* 8, no. 4 (Fall): 145–160.

Gentry, William M., and R. Glenn Hubbard. 1997. Distributional Implications of Introducing a Broad–Based Consumption Tax. In *Tax Policy and the Economy,* ed. James M. Poterba, vol. 11, 1–47, Cambridge, MA: MIT Press.

Gordon, Robert J. 1989. The Post War Evolution of Computer Prices. In *Technology and Capital Formation,* eds. Dale Jorgenson and Ralph Landau, 77–126, Cambridge, MA: MIT Press

———. 1990. *The Measurement of Durable Goods Prices.* Chicago, IL: University of Chicago Press.

Gordon, Roger J., and Dale W. Jorgenson. 1976. The Investment Tax Credit and Counter-Cyclical Policy. In *Parameters and Policies in the U.S. Economy,* ed. Otto Eckstein, 275–314. Amsterdam: North-Holland.

Gordon, Roger H., and Soren Bo Nielsen. 1997. Tax Evasion in an Open Economy: Value-Added vs. Income Taxation. *Journal of Public Economics* 66, vo. 2 (November): 173–197.

Gravelle, Jane G. 1981. The Social Cost of Nonneutral Taxation: Estimates for Nonresidential Capital. In *Depreciation, Inflation, and the Taxation of Income from Capital*, ed. Charles R. Hulten, 239–250. Washington, DC: Urban Institute Press.

———. 1984. Comparative Analysis of Five Tax Proposals: Effects of Business Income Tax Provisions. Washington, DC: Congressional Research Service, Report 84–832E.

———. 1994. *The Economic Effects of Taxing Capital Income*. Cabridge, MA: MIT Press.

———. 1995. The Flat Tax and Other Proposals: Who Will Bear the Tax Burden? CRS Report for Congress, Congressional Research Service, November.

Griliches, Zvi. 1961. Hedonic Price Indexes for Automobiles: An Econometric Analysis of Quality Change. In *The Price Statistics of the Federal Government*, 137–196. New York: National Bureau of Economic Research.

Haavelmo, Trygve. 1960. *A Study in the Theory of Investment*. Chicago, IL: University of Chicago Press.

Hall, Robert E. 1968. Technical Change and Capital from the Point of View of the Dual. *Review of Economic Studies* 35(1), no. 101 (January): 35–46.

———. 1971. The Measurement of Quality Changes from Vintage Price Data. In *Price Indexes and Quality Change*, ed. Zvi Griliches, 240–271. Cambridge, MA: Harvard University Press.

———. 1981. Tax Treatment of Depreciation, Capital Gains, and Interest in an Inflationary Economy. In *Depreciation, Inflation, and the Taxation of Income from Capital*, ed. Charles R. Hulten, 149–166. Washington, DC: Urban Institute Press.

———. 1996. The Effects of Tax Reform on Prices and Assets. In *Tax Policy and the Economy*, ed. James M. Poterba, vol. 10, 71–88, Cambridge, MA: MIT Press.

———. 1997. Potential Disruption from the Move to a Consumption Tax. *American Economic Review* 87, no. 2 (May): 147–150.

Hall, Robert E., and Dale W. Jorgenson. 1967. Tax Policy and Investment Behavior. *The American Economic Review* 57, no. 3 (June): 391–414.

———. 1969. Tax Policy and Investment Behavior: Reply and Further Results. *The American Economic Review* 59, no. 3 (June): 388–401.

———. 1971. Application of the Theory of Optimal Capital Accumulation. In *Tax Incentives and Capital Spending*, ed. Gary Fromm, 9–60. Washington, DC: Brookings Institution.

Hall, Robert E., and Alvin Rabushka. 1983. *Low Tax, Simple Tax, Fair Tax*, McGraw Hill.

———. 1995. *The Flat Tax*, 2nd ed.. Stanford, CA: Hoover Institution Press.

Hansson, I., and C. Stuart. 1985. Tax Revenue and the Marginal Cost of Public Funds in Sweden. *Journal of Public Economics* 27, no. 3 (August): 331–353.

Harberger, Arnold C. 1962. The Incidence of the Corporation Tax. *Journal of Political Economy* 70, no. 3 (June): 215–240.

———. 1966. Efficiency Effects of Taxes on Income from Capital. In *Effects of the Corporation Income Tax*, ed. Marian Krzyzaniak, 107–117. Detroit, MI: Wayne State University Press.

Harberger, Arnold C., and Martin J. Bailey, eds. 1969. *The Taxation of Income from Capital*. Washington, DC: Brookings Institution.

Hausman, Jerry A. 1981. Labor Supply. In *How Taxes Affect Economic Behavior*, eds. Henry J. Aaron and J.A. Pechman, 27–72. Washington, DC: Brookings Institution.

———. 1985. Taxes and Labor Supply. In *Handbook of Public Economics*, vol. 1, eds. Alan J. Auerbach and Martin S. Feldstein, 213–263. Amsterdam: North-Holland.

Hellerstein, Walter. 1997. Transaction Taxes and Electronic Commerce: Designing State Taxes that Works in an Interstate Environment? *National Tax Journal* 50, no. 3 (September): 593–606.

Henderson, Yolanda K. 1991. Applications of General Equilibrium Models to the 1986 Tax Reform Act in the United States. *de Economist* 139, no. 2 (Spring): 147–168.

Hirshleifer, Jack. 1970. *Investment, Interest and Capital*. Englewood Cliffs, NJ: Prentice-Hall.

Ho, Mun S., and Kevin J. Stiroh. 1998. Revenue, Progressivity, and the Flat Tax. *Contemporary Economic Policy* 45, no. 1 (January): 85–97.

Holtz-Eakin, Douglas. 1991. Solow and the States: Capital Accumulation, Productivity and Economic Growth. Working Paper: Syracuse University.

———. 1992. Public Sector Capital and the Productivity Puzzle. *Review of Economics and Statistics* 76, no. 1 (February): 12–21.

Hotelling, Harold S. 1925. A General Mathematical Theory of Depreciation. *Journal of the American Statistical Association* 20, no. 151 (September): 340–353.

Howitt, Peter, and Hans-Werner Sinn. 1989. Gradual Reform of Capital Income Taxation. *American Economic Review* 79, no. 1 (March): 106–124.

Hubbard, G. Glenn. 1997. How Different Are Income and Consumption Taxes? *American Economic Review* 87, no. 2 (May): 138–142.

Hulten, Charles R. (ed.). 1981. *Depreciation, Inflation, and the Taxation of Income from Capital*. Washington, DC: Urban Institute Press.

———. 1990. The Measurement of Capital. In *Fifty Years of Economic Measurement*, eds. Erwin R. Berndt and John E. Triplett, 119–152. Chicago, IL: The University of Chicago Press.

Hulten, Charles R., and James W. Robertson. 1984. The Taxation of High Technology Industries. *National Tax Journal* 37, no. 3 (September): 327–345.

Hulten, Charles R., James W. Robertson, and Frank C. Wykoff. 1989. Energy, Obsolescence, and the Productivity Slowdown. In *Technology and Capital Formation*, eds. Dale W. Jorgenson and Ralph Landau, 225–258. Cambridge, MA: MIT Press.

Hulten, Charles R., and Robert M. Schwab. 1984. Regional Productivity Growth in U.S. Manufacturing: 1951–1978. *American Economic Review* 74, no. 1 (March): 152–162.

———. 1991. Public Capital Formation and the Growth of Regional Manufacturing Industries. *National Tax Journal* 44, no. 4 (December): 121–134.

Hulten, Charles R., and Frank C. Wykoff. 1980. Economic Depreciation and the Taxation of Structures in U.S. Manufacturing Industries Empirical Analysis. In *Measurement of Capital*, ed. D. Usher, 83–109. Chicago, IL: University of Chicago Press.

———. 1981a. Economic Depreciation and Accelerated Depreciation: An Evaluation of the Conable-Jones 10–5–3 Proposal. *National Tax Journal* 37, no. 3 (September): 327–345.

———. 1981b. The Estimation of Economic Depreciation Using Vintage Asset Prices: An Application of the Box-Cox Power Transformation. *Journal of Econometrics* 15, no. 3 (April): 367–396.

———. 1981c. The Measurement of Economic Depreciation. *Depreciation, Inflation, and the Taxation of Income from Capital*, ed. Charles R. Hulten, 81–125. Washington, DC: Urban Institute Press.

Joint Committee on Taxation. 1987. General Explanation of the Tax Reform Act of 1986. Washington, DC: Government Printing Office, 1987.

———. 1997. *Joint Committee on Taxation Tax Modeling Project and 1997 Tax Symposium Papers*. Washington, DC: Government Printing Office, November.

Jorgenson, Dale W. 1963. Capital Theory and Investment Behavior. *American Economic Review* 53, no. 2 (May): 347–259.

———. 1965. Anticipations and Investment Behavior. In *The Brookings Quarterly Model of the United States*, eds. James S. Duesenberry, Gary Fromm, Lawrence R. Klein, and Edwin Kuh. Chicago: Rand-McNally.

———. 1966. The Embodiment Hypothesis. *Journal of Political Economy* 74, no. 1 (February): 1–17.

———. 1967a. Seasonal Adjustment of Data for Econometric Analysis. *Journal of the American Statistical Association* 62, no. 317 (March): 137–140.

———. 1967b. The Theory of Investment Behavior. In *The Determinants of Investment Behavior*, ed. Robert Ferber, Conference of the Universities—National Bureau of Economic Research, 129–156. New York, NY: Columbia University Press.

———. 1971a. Econometric Studies of Investment Behavior: A Review. *Journal of Economic Literature* 9, 4 (December): 1111–1147.

———. 1971b. The Economic Impact of Investment Incentives. In Joint Economic Committee, *Long-Term Implications of Current Tax and Spending Proposals*. Washington: Ninety-Second Congress, First Session, 176–92.

———. 1973. The Economic Theory of Replacement and Depreciation. In *Econometrics and Economic Theory*, ed. W. Sellekaerts, 189–221. New York, NY: Macmillan.

———. 1986. Econometric Methods for Modeling Producer Behavior. In *Handbook of Econometrics*, eds. Zvi Griliches and Michael D. Intriligator, vol. 3, 1841–1915. Amsterdam: North-Holland.

———. 1989. Capital as a Factor of Production. In *Technology and Capital Formation*, eds. Dale W. Jorgenson and Ralph Landau, 1–36. Cambridge, MA: MIT Press.

———. 1993. Introduction and Summary. In *Tax Reform and the Cost of Capital: An International Comparison*, eds. Dale W. Jorgenson and Ralph Landau, 1–56. Washington, DC: Brookings Institution.

———. 1996. *Tax Policy and the Cost of Capital*. Cambridge, MA: MIT Press.

Jorgenson, Dale, W., and Barbara M. Fraumeni, 1981. Relative Prices and Technical Change. In *Modeling and Measuring Natural Resource Substitution*, eds. Ernst R. Berndt and Barry C. Field, 17–47. Cambridge, MA: MIT Press.

Jorgenson, Dale W., Frank M. Gollop, and Barbara M. Fraumeni. 1987. *Productivity and U.S. Economic Growth*. Cambridge, MA: Harvard University Press.

Jorgenson, Dale W., and Jean-Jacques Laffont. 1974. Efficient Estimation of Nonlinear Simultaneous Equations with Additive Disturbances. *Annals of Social and Economic Measurement* 3, no. 1 (October): 615–640.

Jorgenson, Dale W., and Ralph Landau (eds.). 1989. *Technology and Capital Formation*. Cambridge, MA: MIT Press.

Jorgenson, Dale W., and Lawrence J. Lau. 1975. The Structure of Consumer Preferences. *Annals of Social and Economic Measurement* 4, no. 1 (January): 49–101.

Jorgenson, Dale W., and Calvin D. Siebert. 1968a. A Comparison of Alternative Theories of Corporate Investment Behavior. *American Economic Review* 58, no. 4 (September): 681–712.

———. 1968b. Optimal Capital Accumulation and Corporate Investment Behavior. *Journal of Political Economy* 76, no. 6 (November/December): 1123–1151.

Jorgenson, Dale W., and Martin A. Sullivan. 1981. Inflation and Corporate Capital Recovery. In *Depreciation, Inflation, and Taxation of Income from Capital*, ed. Charles R. Hulten, 171–237, 311–313. Washington, DC: Urban Institute Press.

Jorgenson, Dale W., and Peter J. Wilcoxen. 1997. The Effects of Fundamental Tax Reform and the Feasibility of Dynamic Revenue Estimation. In Joint Committee on Taxation, *Joint Committee on Taxation Tax Modeling Project and 1997 Tax Symposium Paper*. Washington, DC: U.S. Government Printing Office (November): 131–151.

Jorgenson, Dale W., and Kun-Young Yun. 1986a. The Efficiency of Capital Allocation. *Scandinavian Journal of Economics* 88, no. 1: 85–107.

———. 1986b. Tax Policy and Capital Allocation. *Scandinavian Journal of Economics* 88, no. 2: 355–377.

———. 1990. Tax Reform and U.S. Economic Growth. *Journal of Political Economy* 98, no. 5, part 2 (October): S151–S193.

———. 1991a. The Excess Burden of U.S. Taxation. *Journal of Accounting, Auditing, and Finance* 6, no. 4 (Fall): 487–509.

———. 1991b. *Tax Reform and the Cost of Capital.* Oxford: Oxford University Press.

Judd, Kenneth L. 1987. The Welfare Cost of Factor Taxation in a Perfect Foresight Model. *Journal of Political Economy* 95, no. 4 (August): 675–709.

Kay, J.A. 1980. The Deadweight Loss from a Tax System. *Journal of Public Economics* 13, no. 1 (February): 111–119.

King, Mervin A. 1977. *Public Policy and the Corporation*. London: Chapman and Hall.

King, Mervin A., and Don Fullerton (eds.). 1984. *The Taxation of Income from Capital: A Comparative Study of the U.S., U.K., Sweden, and West Germany.* Chicago: University of Chicago Press.

Kotlikoff, Lawrence J. 1988. Intergenerational Transfers and Saving. *Journal of Economic Perspectives* 2, no. 2 (Spring): 41–58.

———. 1998. The A-K Model—Its Past, Present, and Future, National Bureau of Economic Research Working Paper no. 6684, August.

Kotlikoff , Lawrence J., and Lawrence H. Summers. 1981. The Role of Intergenerational Transfers in Aggregate Capital Accumulation. *Journal of Political Economy* 89, no. 4 (August): 706–732.

Lipton, David, James Poterba, Jeffrey Sachs, and Lawrence H. Summers. 1982. Multiple Shooting in Rational Expectations Models. *Econometrica* 51, no. 4 (May): 1329–1333.

Lodin, Sven-Olaf. 1976. Progressive Expenditure Tax—An Alternative? Stockholm: LiberFolag.

Lucas, Robert E., Jr. 1967. Adjustment Costs and the Theory of Supply. *Journal of Political Economy* 75, no. 4, part 1 (August): 321–334.

———. 1976. Econometric Policy Evaluation: A Critique. In *The Phillips Curve and Labour Markets*, 19–46, eds. Karl Brunner and Allan H. Meltzer. Amsterdam: North-Holland.

———. 1990. Supply Side Economics: An Analytical Review. *Oxford Economic Papers 42*, no. 3 (August): 293–316.

Malpezzi, Steven, Lawrence J. Ozanne, and Thomas G. Thibodeaux. 1987. Microeconomic Estimates of Housing Depreciation. *Land Economics* 63, no. 4 (November): 372–385.

Mayshar, J. 1990. On Measures of Excess Burden and Their Applications. *Journal of Public Economics* 43, no. 3 (December): 263–289.

———. 1991. On Measuring the Marginal Cost of Funds Analytically. *American Economic Review* 85, no. 5: 1329–1335.

McFadden, Daniel L. 1963. Further Results on CES Production Functions. *Review of Economic Studies* 30(2), no. 83 (June): 73–83.

McLure, Charles E., Jr. 1979. *Must Corporate Income Be Taxed Twice?* Washington, DC: Brookings Institution

———. 1993. Economic, Administrative, and Political Factors in Choosing a General Consumption Tax. *National Tax Journal* 46, no. 3 (September): 345–358.

McLure, Charles E. Jr., and George R. Zodrow. 1987. Tresury I and the Tax Reform Act of 1986: The Economics and Politics of Tax Reform. *Journal of Economic Perspectives* 1 (Summer): 37–58.

Meade, James Edward. 1978. *The Structure and Reform of Direct Taxation*: Report of a Committee Chaired by Professor James Edward Meade. London: Allen and Unwin.

Meyer, John, and Edwin Kuh. 1957. *The Investment Decision*. Cambridge, MA: Harvard University Press.

Mikesell, John L. 1997. The American Retail Sales Tax: Considerations on their Structure, Operations and Potential as a Foundation for a Federal Sales Tax. *National Tax Journal* 50, no. 1 (March): 149–165.

Modigliani, Franco. 1988. The Role of Intergenerational Transfers and Life Cycle Saving in the Accumulation of Wealth. *Journal of Economic Perspectives* 2, no. 2 (Spring): 15–40.

Munnell, Alicia H. 1990. How Does Public Infrastructure Affect Regional Economic Performance. In *Is There a Shortfall in Public Capital Investment?*, ed. Alicia H. Munnell, 69–103. Boston, MA: Federal Reserve Bank of Boston.

Murray, Matthew N. 1997. Would Tax Evasion and Tax Avoidance Undermine a National Sales Tax? *National Tax Journal* 50, no. 1 (March): 167–182.

Office of Industrial Economics. 1975. *Building Statistics*. Washington, DC: U.S. Department of the Treasury.

Office of Tax Analysis. 1990. Depreciation of Scientific Instruments, March. Washington, DC: U.S. Department of the Treasury.

———. 1991a. Depreciation of Business-Use Passenger Cars, April. Washington, DC: U.S. Department of the Treasury.

———. 1991b. Depreciation of Business-Use Light Trucks, September. Washington, DC: U.S. Department of the Treasury.

O'Hanlon, Michael. 1999. Defense and Foreign Policy: Time to End the Budget Cuts. In *Setting National Priorities—The 2000 Election and Beyond*, eds. Henry J. Aaron and Robert D. Reischauer, 37–72. Washington, DC: Brooking Institution.

Oliner, Stephen D. 1993. Constant Quality Price Change, Depreciation, and Retirement of Mainframe Computers. In *Price Measurements and Their Uses*, eds. M.F. Foss, M.E. Manser, and A.H. Young, 19–61. Chicago, IL: University of Chicago Press.

———. 1994. Estimates of Depreciation and Retirement for Computer Peripheral Equipment, Board of Governors of the Federal Reserve System, May.

———. 1996. New Evidence on the Retirement and Depreciation of Machine Tools. *Economic Inquiry* 34, no. 1 (January): 57–77.

Pakes, A., and Zvi Griliches. 1984. Estimating Distributed Lags in Short Panels with an Application to the Specification of Depreciation Patterns and Capital Stock Constructs. *Review of Economic Studies* 51(2), no. 165 (April): 243–262.

Pechman, Joseph A. 1987. *Federal Tax Policy*, 5th ed. Washington, DC: Brookings Institution.

Poddar, Satya and Morley English. 1997. Taxation of Financial Service Under a Value-Added Tax: Applying the Cash-Flow Approach. *National Tax Journal* 50, no. 1 (March): 89–111.

Poterba, James M., and Lawrence H. Summers. 1983. Dividend Taxes, Corporate Investment, and *Q*. *Journal of Public Economics* 22, no. 2 (November): 135–167.

———. 1985. The Economic Effects of Dividend Taxation. In *Recent Advances in Corporate Finance*, eds. Edward I. Altman and Marti G. Subrahmanyam, 227–284. Homewood, IL: Richard D. Irwin.

Rogers, Diane Lim. 1997. Assessing the Effects of Fundamental Tax Reform with the Fullerton-Rogers General Equilibrium Model. In Joint Committee on Taxation, *Joint Committee on Taxation Tax Modeling Project and 1997 Tax Symposium Paper*. Washington, DC: U.S. Government Printing Office (November): 49–82.

Rosenberg, Leonard G. 1969. Taxation of Income from Capital by Industry Group. In *The Taxation of Income from Capital*, eds. Arnold C. Harberger and Martin J. Bailey, 123–184. Washington, DC: Brookings Institution.

Sakar, Shounak, and George R. Zodrow. 1993. Transitional Issues in Moving to a Direct Consumption Tax. *National Tax Journal* 46, no. 3 (September): 359–376.

Schaefer, Dan *et al.* 1997. National Retail Sales Tax Act of 1996, H.R.3039 introduced in the 104th Congress, March 6, 1996. Also National Retail Sales Tax Act of 1997, H.R.2001 Introduced in the 105th Congress, June 19, 1997.

Scott, Maurice F.G. 1987. Note on King and Fullerton's Formulae to Estimate the Taxation of Income from Capital. *Journal of Public Economics* 34, no. 2 (November): 253–264.

Shoven, J.B. 1976. The Incidence and Efficiency Effect of Taxes on Income from Capital. *Journal of Political Economy* 84, no. 6 (December): 1261–1284.

Sinn, Hans-Werner. 1987. *Capital Income Taxation and Resource Allocation*. Amsterdam, North-Holland.

———. 1991. Taxation and the Cost of Capital, The "Old" View, the "New" View, and Another View. In *Tax Policy and the Economy*, vol. 5, ed. David Bradford, 25–54. Cambridge, MA: MIT Press.

Skinner, Jonathan. 1996. The Dynamic Efficiency Cost of Not Taxing Housing. *Journal of Public Economics* 59, no. 3 (February): 397–417.

Slemrod, Joel (ed.). 1990. *Do Taxes Matter? The Impact of the Tax Reform Act of 1986*. Cambridge, MA: MIT Press.

———. 1997. Deconstructing the Income Tax. *American Economic Review*. 87, no. 2 (May): 151–155.

Stiglitz, Joseph E. 1973. Taxation, Corporate Financial Policy, and the Cost of Capital. *Journal of Public Economics* 2, no. 1 (February): 1–34.

Stiglitz, Joseph E., and P.S. Dasgupta. 1971. Differential Taxation and Economic Efficiency. *Review of Economic Studies*, 38(2), no. 114 (April): 151–1174.

Strong, John S. 1989. The Market Valuation of Credit Market Debt. In *Technology and Capital Formation*, eds. Dale W. Jorgenson and Ralph Landau, 373–408. Cambridge, MA: MIT Press.

Stuart, C. 1984. Welfare Costs per Dollar of Additional Tax Revenue in the United States. *American Economic Review* 74, no. 3 (June): 452–462.

Summers, Lawrence H. 1981. Capital Taxation and Accumulation in a Life-Cycle Growth Model. *American Economic Review* 71, no. 4 (September): 533–544.

———. 1983. The Non-adjustment of Nominal Interest Rates: A Study of the Fisher Effect. In *Macroeconomics, Prices and Quantities: Essays in Memory of Arthur M. Okun*, 204–241, ed. James Tobin. Washington: Brookings Institution.

———. 1987. Investment Incentives and the Discounting of Depreciation Allowances. In *The Effect of Taxation on Capital Accumulation*, ed. Martin S. Feldstein, 295–304. Chicago, IL: Chicago University Press.

Taubman, Paul, and Robert Rasche. 1969. Economic and Tax Depreciation of Office Buildings. *National Tax Journal* 22, no. 3 (September): 334–346.

Terborgh, George. 1954. *Realistic Depreciation Policy*. Washington, DC: Machinery and Allied Products Institute.

Triest, R.K. 1990. The Relationship between the Marginal Cost of Public Funds and Marginal Excess Burden. *American Economic Review* 80, no. 3 (June): 557–566.

Triplett, Jack E. 1975. The Measurement of Inflation: A Survey of Research on the Accuracy of Price Indexes. In *Analysis of Inflation*, ed. Paul H. Earl: 19–82. Lexington, MA: Heath.

———. 1986. The Economic Interpretation of Hedonic Methods. *Survey of Current Business* 66, no. 1 (January): 36–40.

———. 1987. Hedonic Functions and Hedonic Indexes. In *The New Palgrave*, eds. J. Eatwell, M. Milgate, and P. Newman, vol. 2, 630–634. New York, NY: Stockton.

———. 1989. Price and Technological Change in a Capital Good: A Survey of Research on Computers. In *Technology and Capital Formation*, eds. Dale W. Jorgenson and Ralph Landau, 127–213. Cambridge, MA: MIT Press.

———. 1990. Hedonic Methods in Statistical Agency Environments: An Intellectual Biopsy. In *Fifty Years of Economic Measurement*, eds. Ernst Berndt and Jack E. Triplett, 207–238. Chicago, IL: University of Chicago Press.

U.S. Department of the Treasury. 1977. *Blueprints for Basic Tax Reform*. Washington, DC: Office of Tax Analysis.

———. 1987. *Compendium of Tax Research 1987*. Washington, DC: Office of Tax Analysis.

———. 1984. *Tax Reform for Simplicity, Fairness, and Economic Growth*, 3 vols., Washington, DC: U.S. Government Printing Office.

———. 1987. Tax Reform Act of 1986.

Uzawa, Hirofumi. 1962. Production Functions with Constant Elasticities of Substitution. *Review of Economic Studies* 29(3), no. 81 (October): 291–299.

Walras, Leon. 1954. *Elements of Pure Economics*. Translated by W. Jaffe (1874). Reprint, Homewood, NJ: Irwin.

Waugh, Frederick V. 1929. *Quality as a Determinant of Vegetable Prices*. New York, NY: Colombia University Press.

Wildasin, D.E. 1984. On Public Good Provision with Distortionary Taxation. *Economic Inquiry* 22, no. 2 (April): 227–243.

Winfrey, Robley. 1935. *Statistical Analyses of Industrial Property Retirements*. Bulletin 125. Ames, IOWA: Iowa State College of Agricultural and Mechanical Arts.

Wykoff, Frank C. 1989. Economic Depreciation and the User Cost of Business-Leased Automobiles. In *Technology and Capital Formation*, eds. Dale W. Jorgenson and Ralph Landau, 259–292. Cambridge, MA: MIT Press.

Zodrow, George R. 1995. Taxation, Uncertainty, and the Choice of a Consumption Tax Base. *Journal of Public Economic* 58, no. 2 (October): 257–265.

———. 1999. The Sales Tax, the VAT, and Taxes in Between—Or, is the Only Good NRST a VAT in Drag? *National Tax Journal* 52, no. 3 (September): 429–442.

Index